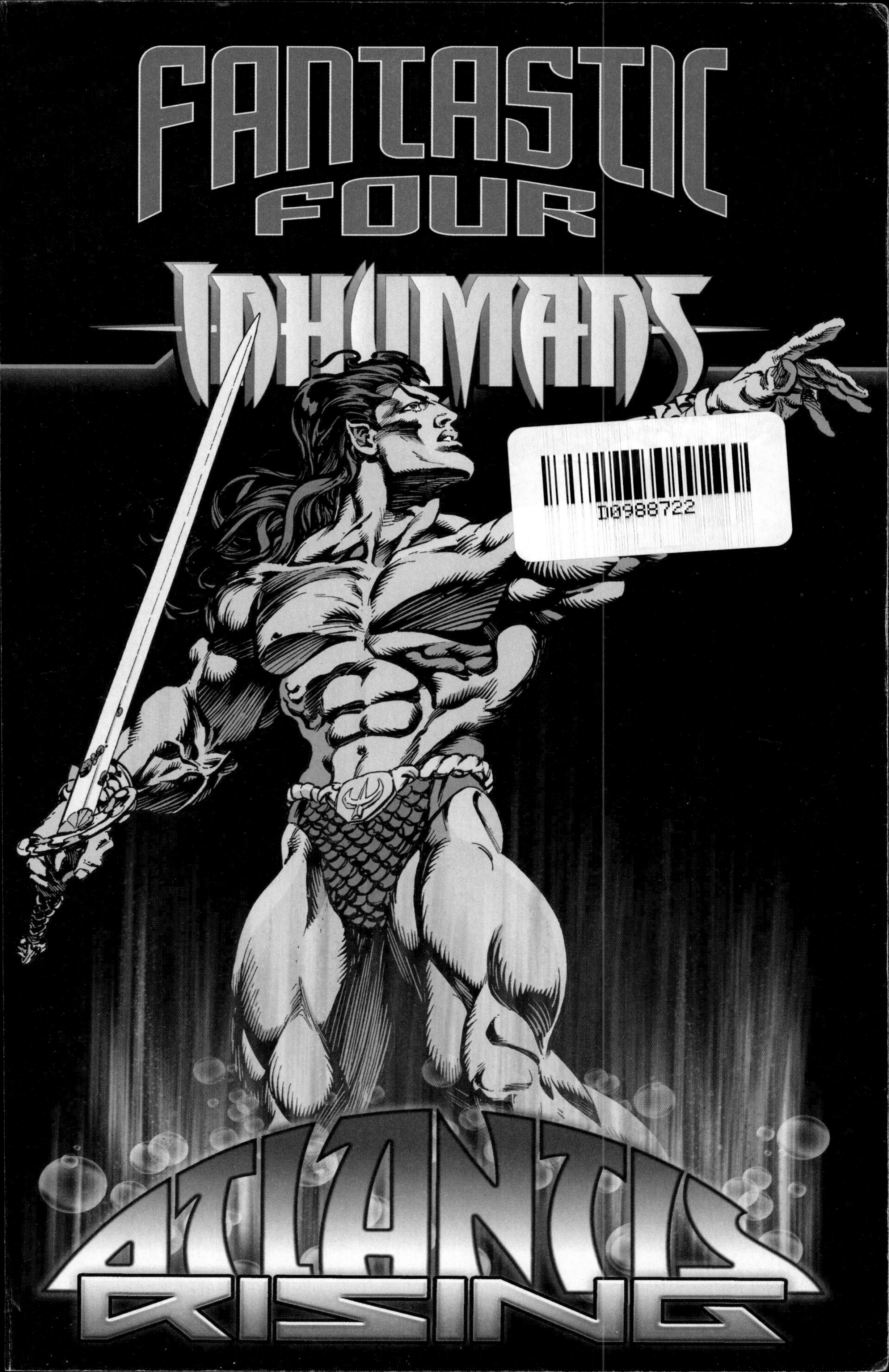
FANTASTIC FOUR
INHUMANS
ATLANTIS RISING

FANTASTIC FOUR

RESEARCH: **KEVIN GARCIA**   LAYOUT: **JEPH YORK**
PRODUCTION: **COLORTEK & RYAN DEVALL**

COLLECTION EDITOR: **NELSON RIBEIRO**
ASSISTANT EDITOR: **ALEX STARBUCK**
EDITORS, SPECIAL PROJECTS: **MARK D. BEAZLEY & JENNIFER GRÜNWALD**
SENIOR EDITOR, SPECIAL PROJECTS: **JEFF YOUNGQUIST**
SVP OF PRINT & DIGITAL PUBLISHING SALES: **DAVID GABRIEL**

EDITOR IN CHIEF: **AXEL ALONSO**
CHIEF CREATIVE OFFICER: **JOE QUESADA**
PUBLISHER: **DAN BUCKLEY**
EXECUTIVE PRODUCER: **ALAN FINE**

SPECIAL THANKS TO
JERAMY BONNELLE

FANTASTIC FOUR/INHUMANS: ATLANTIS RISING. Contains material originally published in magazine form as NAMOR THE SUB-MARINER #60-62, FANTASTIC FOUR: ATLANTIS RISING #1-2, FANTASTIC FORCE #8-9,
FANTASTIC FOUR #401-402 and FANTASTIC FOUR UNLIMITED #11. First printing 2014. ISBN# 978-0-7851-8548-2. Published by MARVEL WORLDWIDE, INC., a subsidiary of MARVEL ENTERTAINMENT, LLC. OFFICE OF
PUBLICATION: 135 West 50th Street, New York, NY 10020. Copyright © 1995 and 2014 Marvel Characters, Inc. All rights reserved. All characters featured in this issue and the distinctive names and likenesses thereof,
and all related indicia are trademarks of Marvel Characters, Inc. No similarity between any of the names, characters, persons, and/or institutions in this magazine with those of any living or dead person or institution is
intended, and any such similarity which may exist is purely coincidental. **Printed in the U.S.A.** ALAN FINE, EVP - Office of the President, Marvel Worldwide, Inc. and EVP & CMO Marvel Characters B.V.; DAN BUCKLEY,
Publisher & President - Print, Animation & Digital Divisions; JOE QUESADA, Chief Creative Officer; TOM BREVOORT, SVP of Publishing; DAVID BOGART, SVP of Operations & Procurement, Publishing; C.B. CEBULSKI, SVP
of Creator & Content Development; DAVID GABRIEL, SVP of Print & Digital Publishing Sales; JIM O'KEEFE, VP of Operations & Logistics; DAN CARR, Executive Director of Publishing Technology; SUSAN CRESPI, Editorial
Operations Manager; ALEX MORALES, Publishing Operations Manager; STAN LEE, Chairman Emeritus. For information regarding advertising in Marvel Comics or on Marvel.com, please contact Niza Disla, Director of
Marvel Partnerships, at ndisla@marvel.com. For Marvel subscription inquiries, please call 800-217-9158. **Manufactured between 11/15/2013 and 12/23/2013 by R.R. DONNELLEY, INC., SALEM, VA, USA.**

10 9 8 7 6 5 4 3 2 1

INHUMANS

WRITERS

GLENN HERDLING, TOM DEFALCO, TOM BREVOORT, MIKE KANTEROVICH & ROY THOMAS WITH PAUL RYAN

PENCILERS

GEOF ISHERWOOD, M.C. WYMAN, DANTE BASTIANONI, PAUL RYAN, DOUG BRAITHWAITE & HERB TRIMPE

INKERS

GEOF ISHERWOOD, REY GARCIA, DON HUDSON, RALPH CABRERA, DAN BULANADI, ROBIN RIGGS & HERB TRIMPE WITH KEVIN YATES, SAM DE LA ROSA & SANDU FLOREA

COLORISTS

GLYNIS OLIVER, MIKE ROCKWITZ, JOHN KALISZ & JOE ANDREANI

LETTERERS

MICHAEL HIGGINS, CHRIS ELIOPOULOS, JOHN WORKMAN, JIM NOVAK & JOHN COSTANZA

ASSISTANT EDITORS

JOE ANDREANI & MIKE MARTS

EDITORS

MIKE ROCKWITZ, RALPH MACCHIO & NEL YOMTOV

FRONT COVER ARTISTS

MC WYMAN, REY GARCIA & CHRIS SOTOMAYOR

BACK COVER ARTISTS

CLAUDIO CASTELLINI & THOMAS MASON

ATLANTIS RISING

PREVIOUSLY...

MONTHS AGO, THE HUMAN TORCH'S WIFE ALICIA MASTERS WAS REVEALED AS A SKRULL SPY NAMED LYJA. THOUGH THIS BETRAYAL ROCKED THE TORCH, LYJA TRULY LOVED HIM; SHE AIDED THE FANTASTIC FOUR ON SEVERAL OCCASIONS, BECOMING THEIR GRUDGING ALLY. SOON AFTERWARD, MR. FANTASTIC'S FATHER, THE TIME-TRAVELING SCIENTIST NATHANIEL RICHARDS, ABDUCTED HIS YOUNG GRANDSON FRANKLIN RICHARDS, CLAIMING THAT FRANKLIN'S UNSTABLE PSI-POWERS WERE A THREAT. BRINGING HIM TO ELSEWHEN, A DIMENSION RULED BY THE TIME GUARDIAN WARLORD KARGUL, NATHANIEL RAISED FRANKLIN TO ADULTHOOD AND TRAINED HIM ALONGSIDE NATHANIEL'S DAUGHTER HUNTARA, WHILE KARGUL CREATED ARMOR TO CONTROL FRANKLIN'S POWERS.

NATHANIEL CONVINCED THE ADULT FRANKLIN, NOW CALLED PSI-LORD, TO RETURN WITH HIM TO THEIR HOME DIMENSION; THE TWO ARRIVED MOMENTS AFTER YOUNG FRANKLIN HAD BEEN TAKEN. THOUGH THE FF REACTED POORLY TO PSI-LORD, HE AND NATHANIEL ALLIED UNEASILY WITH THE TEAM UNTIL A BATTLE AGAINST THE ALIEN HUNGER SEEMINGLY KILLED MR. FANTASTIC AND DR. DOOM. HUNTARA, OPENLY DISTRUSTFUL OF NATHANIEL'S MANIPULATIVE WAYS, TRAVELED TO EARTH AND SOON ALLIED WITH PSI-LORD, THE INHUMAN DEVLOR AND THE WAKANDAN VIBRAXAS TO FORM A TEAM CALLED FANTASTIC FORCE. LYJA ALSO AIDED THE FORCE, WHILE SECRETLY ROMANCING THE HUMAN TORCH AGAIN AS "LAURA GREEN."

MEANWHILE, THE FF MOURNED MR. FANTASTIC. THE THING'S FACE, RECENTLY SCARRED BY WOLVERINE, SLOWLY HEALED, WHILE THE INVISIBLE WOMAN HIRED SCOTT LANG, THE SECOND ANT-MAN, TO AID THE TEAM. NATHANIEL TOOK OVER DR. DOOM'S LATVERIAN CASTLE AND FOUND KRISTOFF VERNARD, A YOUNG BOY WHOSE MIND HAD BEEN OVERPRINTED WITH DOOM'S MEMORIES. KRISTOFF BECAME AN ALLY TO THE FF, AIDED BY HIS MANSERVANT BORIS, WHO HID A SECRET AGENDA. RECENTLY, VIBRAXAS ACCIDENTALLY KILLED A GANG MEMBER IN SELF-DEFENSE, AND HUNTARA SWORE TO KARGUL THAT SHE WOULD EXECUTE FRANKLIN IF HIS POWERS FLARED OUT OF CONTROL.

ELSEWHERE, NAMOR THE SUB-MARINER, KING OF ATLANTIS, DEALT WITH RECENT SHAKEUPS. YEARS AGO, NAMOR'S WIFE MARRINA BECAME THE EVIL LEVIATHAN, AND NAMOR WAS FORCED TO KILL HER USING HIS ALLY THE BLACK KNIGHT'S CURSED EBONY BLADE. LATER, THE BLADE TRANSFORMED SEAN DOLAN INTO THE TORTURED BLOODWRAITH. NAMOR'S OLD FOE LLYRA RECENTLY REVEALED HER SON LLYRON, CLAIMING HIM TO BE NAMOR'S SON AND HEIR TO THE THRONE OF ATLANTIS. LLYRON INGRATIATED HIMSELF WITH ATLANTIS' RULING COUNCIL; HE SOON FRAMED NAMOR FOR AN ATTACK ON THE UNITED NATIONS. NAMOR WAS BANISHED FROM ATLANTIS, BUT ALLIED WITH ANDROMEDA, A FELLOW ATLANTEAN WHO HAD ONCE DIED AND BEEN MAGICALLY REBORN IN THE BODY OF HUMAN GENEVIEVE CROSS.

ELSEWHERE, THE SECRETIVE RACE KNOWN AS THE INHUMANS DWELLED IN THE MOON'S MYSTERIOUS BLUE AREA, AFTER HAVING MOVED THEIR SECRET CITY ATTILAN SEVERAL TIMES FROM ITS ORIGINAL LOCATION NEAR NOW-SUNKEN ATLANTIS. WHEN BLACK BOLT, THE INHUMANS' KING, DISCOVERED THAT THEIR GENETICS COUNCIL WAS CORRUPT, HE AND THE ROYAL FAMILY REJECTED THE INHUMANS AND MOVED TO EARTH; A NEW COUNCIL WAS SOON ELECTED TO GOVERN IN THE ROYALS' PLACE. THE AQUATIC INHUMAN TRITON WAS SUMMONED BY STINGRAY, HEAD OF THE UNDERSEA COMPLEX HYDROPOLIS, TO AID NAMOR, BUT TRITON WAS LOST WHEN A NUCLEAR BOMB DETONATED.

MEANWHILE, TWO SCIENTISTS INVESTIGATE STRANGE OCEANIC PHENOMENA IN THE AZORES ISLANDS...

MATERIAL FROM *NAMOR THE SUB-MARINER* #58-59

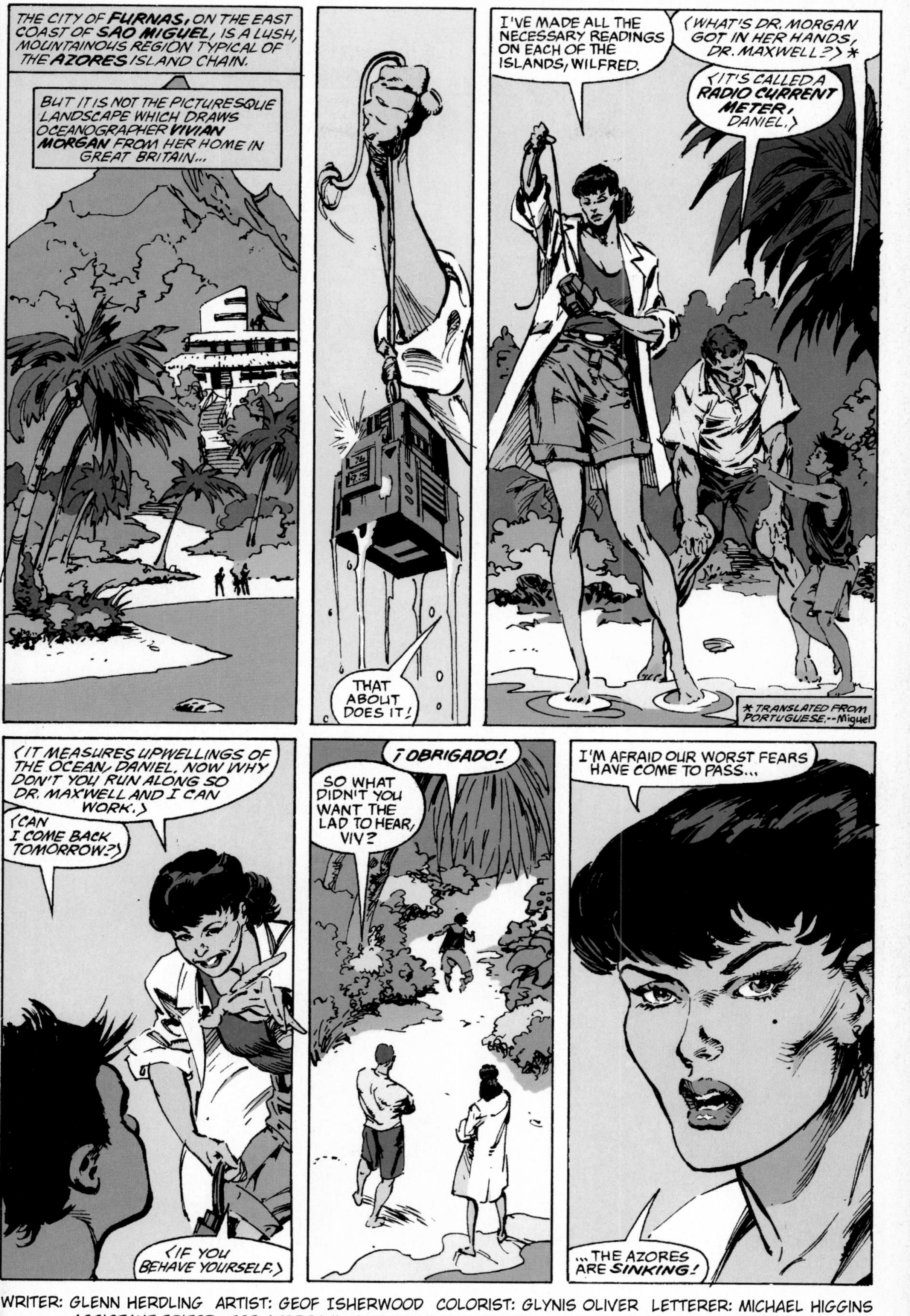
THE CITY OF FURNAS, ON THE EAST COAST OF SAO MIGUEL, IS A LUSH, MOUNTAINOUS REGION TYPICAL OF THE AZORES ISLAND CHAIN.
BUT IT IS NOT THE PICTURESQUE LANDSCAPE WHICH DRAWS OCEANOGRAPHER VIVIAN MORGAN FROM HER HOME IN GREAT BRITAIN...
THAT ABOUT DOES IT!
I'VE MADE ALL THE NECESSARY READINGS ON EACH OF THE ISLANDS, WILFRED.
‹WHAT'S DR. MORGAN GOT IN HER HANDS, DR. MAXWELL?› *
‹IT'S CALLED A RADIO CURRENT METER, DANIEL.›
* TRANSLATED FROM PORTUGUESE. --Miguel
‹IT MEASURES UPWELLINGS OF THE OCEAN, DANIEL. NOW WHY DON'T YOU RUN ALONG SO DR. MAXWELL AND I CAN WORK.›
‹CAN I COME BACK TOMORROW?›
‹IF YOU BEHAVE YOURSELF.›
¡OBRIGADO!
SO WHAT DIDN'T YOU WANT THE LAD TO HEAR, VIV?
I'M AFRAID OUR WORST FEARS HAVE COME TO PASS...
...THE AZORES ARE SINKING!

WRITER: GLENN HERDLING ARTIST: GEOF ISHERWOOD COLORIST: GLYNIS OLIVER LETTERER: MICHAEL HIGGINS
ASSISTANT EDITOR: JOE ANDREANI EDITOR: MIKE ROCKWITZ GROUP EDITOR: RALPH MACCHIO

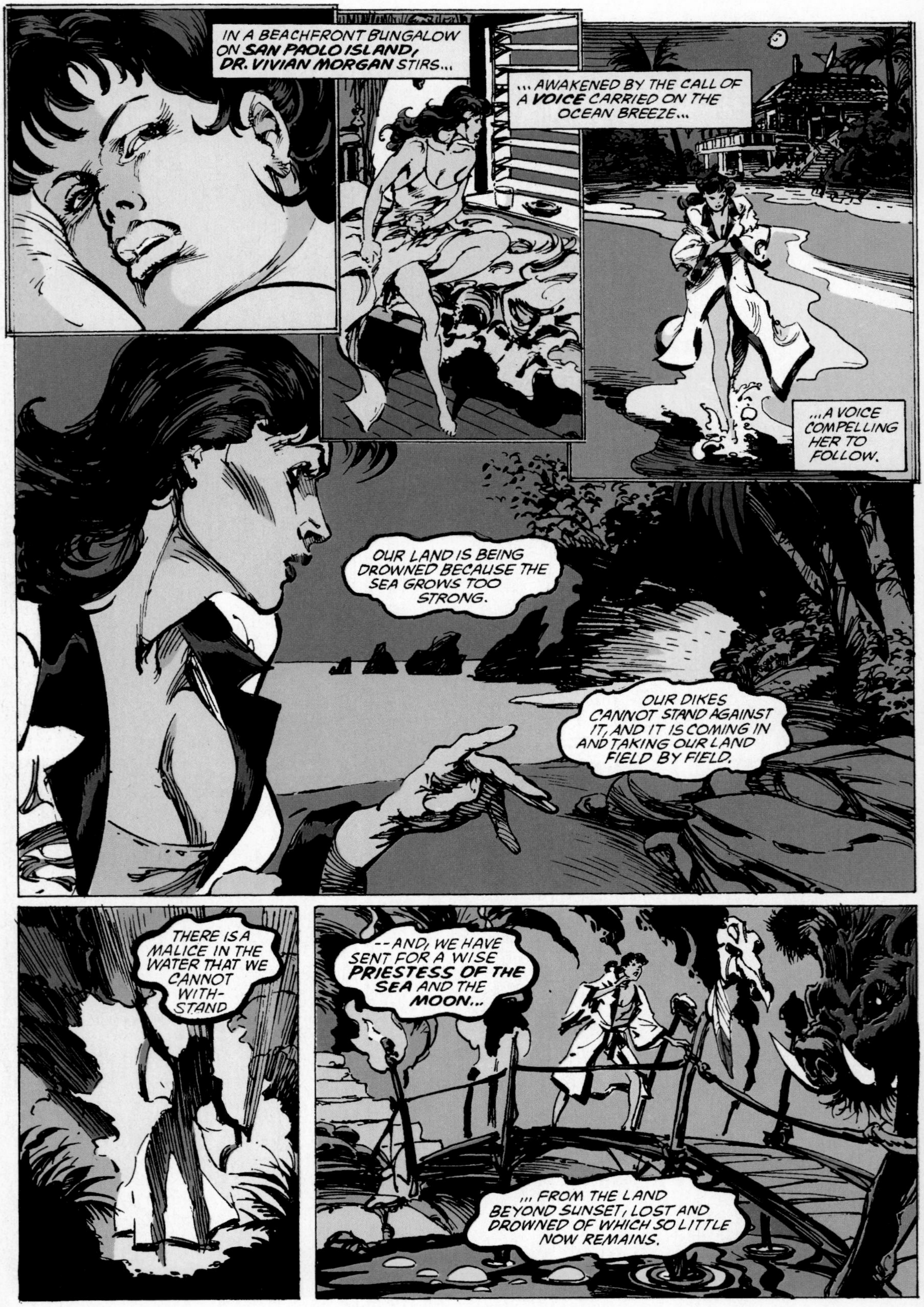
IN A BEACHFRONT BUNGALOW ON SAN PAOLO ISLAND, DR. VIVIAN MORGAN STIRS...
...AWAKENED BY THE CALL OF A VOICE CARRIED ON THE OCEAN BREEZE...
...A VOICE COMPELLING HER TO FOLLOW.
OUR LAND IS BEING DROWNED BECAUSE THE SEA GROWS TOO STRONG.
OUR DIKES CANNOT STAND AGAINST IT, AND IT IS COMING IN AND TAKING OUR LAND FIELD BY FIELD.
THERE IS A MALICE IN THE WATER THAT WE CANNOT WITH-STAND
--AND, WE HAVE SENT FOR A WISE PRIESTESS OF THE SEA AND THE MOON...
...FROM THE LAND BEYOND SUNSET, LOST AND DROWNED OF WHICH SO LITTLE NOW REMAINS.

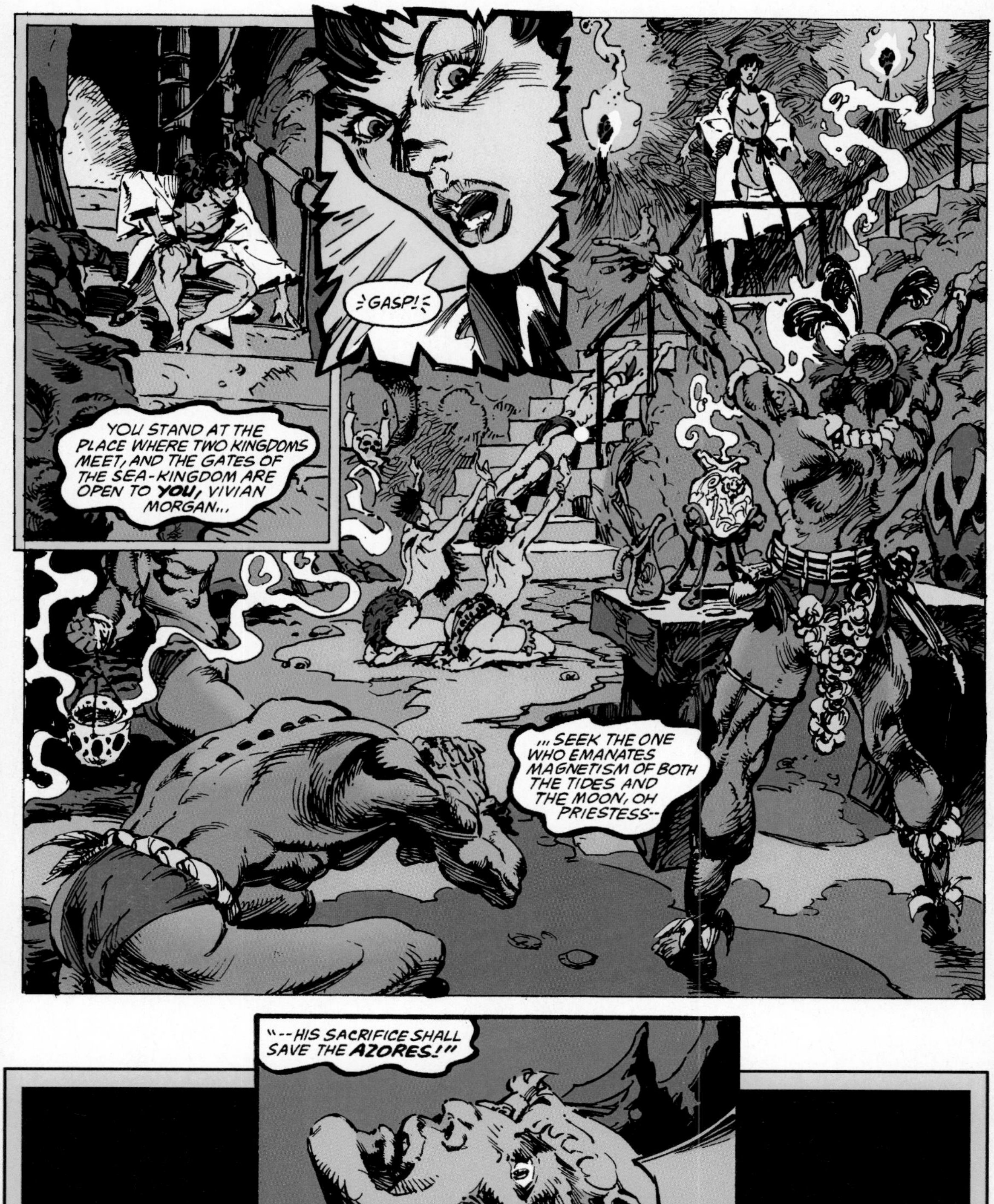
GASP!
YOU STAND AT THE PLACE WHERE TWO KINGDOMS MEET, AND THE GATES OF THE SEA-KINGDOM ARE OPEN TO YOU, VIVIAN MORGAN...
...SEEK THE ONE WHO EMANATES MAGNETISM OF BOTH THE TIDES AND THE MOON, OH PRIESTESS--

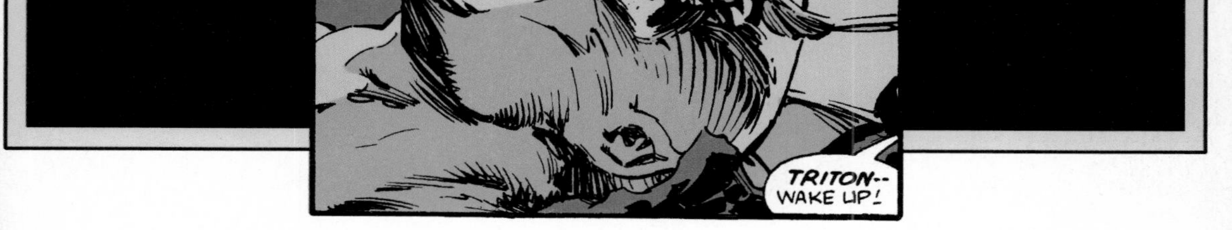
"--HIS SACRIFICE SHALL SAVE THE AZORES!"
TRITON-- WAKE UP!

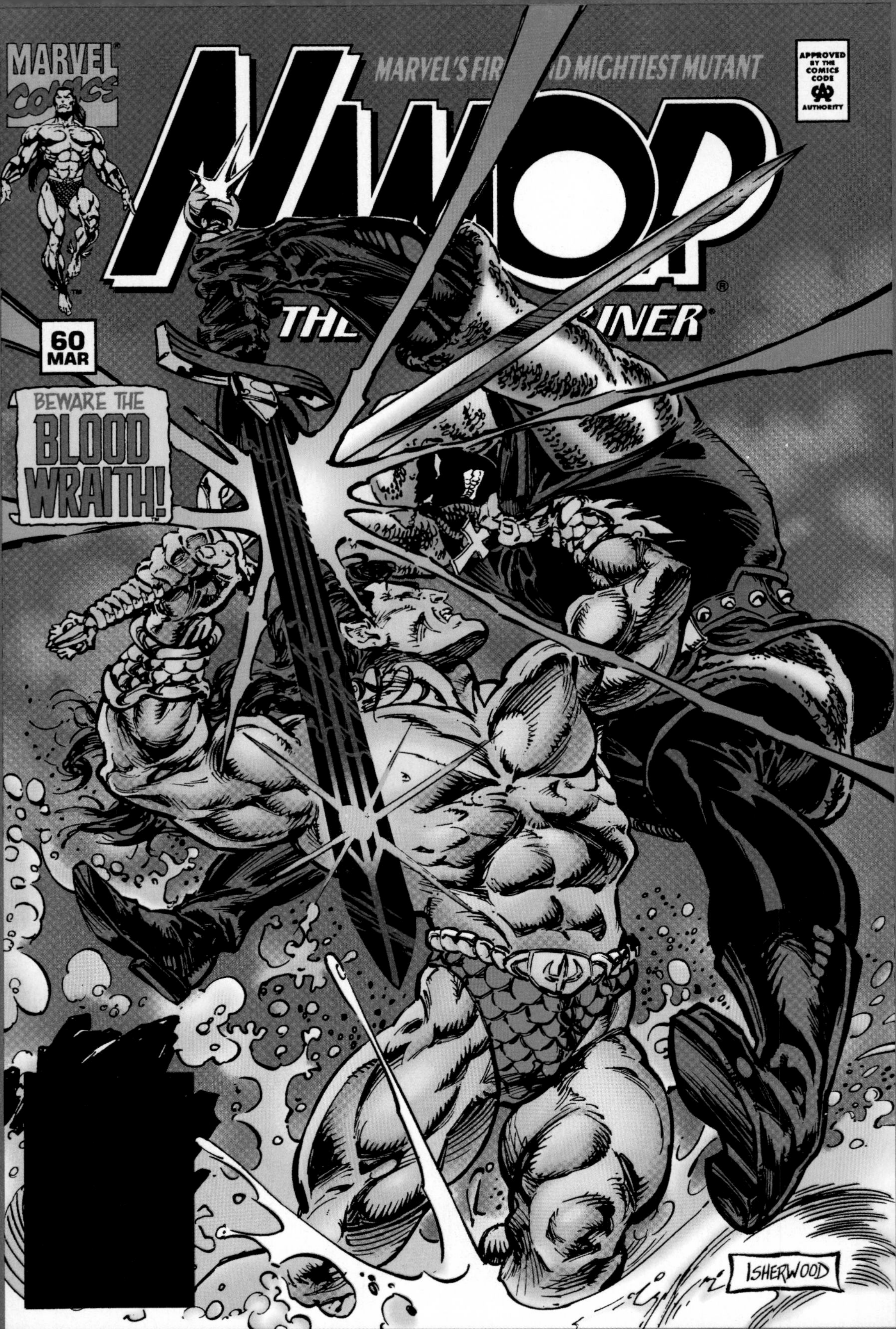
MARVEL COMICS
MIGHTIEST MUTANT
APPROVED BY THE COMICS CODE AUTHORITY
60
MAR
BEWARE THE BLOOD WRAITH!
ISHERWOOD

SCION OF AN AIR-BREATHING FATHER AND A WATER-BREATHING MOTHER, GIFTED WITH SUPERHUMAN STRENGTH AND THE POWER OF FLIGHT, THE AVENGING SON OF ATLANTIS HAS BATTLED FOR AND AGAINST HUMANITY SINCE WORLD WAR II! NOW, THE WEALTH OF THE ETERNAL SEAS AT HIS COMMAND, HE HAS SET UP A NEW CAMPAIGN OF CONQUEST. . .AGAINST THE ENEMIES OF THE ENVIRONMENT ITSELF! STAN LEE PRESENTS . . .

NAMOR, THE SUB-MARINER!

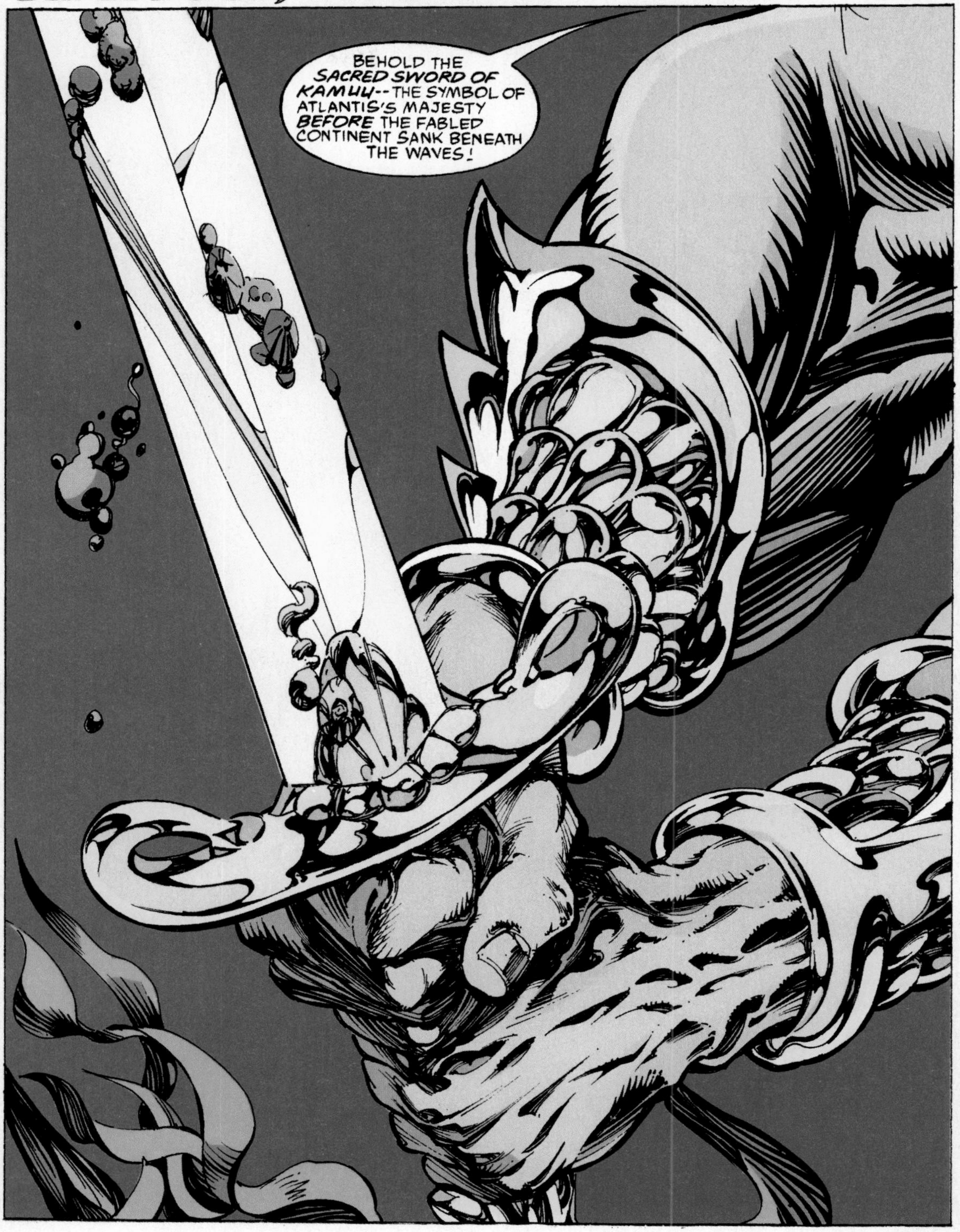
BEHOLD THE SACRED SWORD OF KAMUU-- THE SYMBOL OF ATLANTIS'S MAJESTY BEFORE THE FABLED CONTINENT SANK BENEATH THE WAVES!

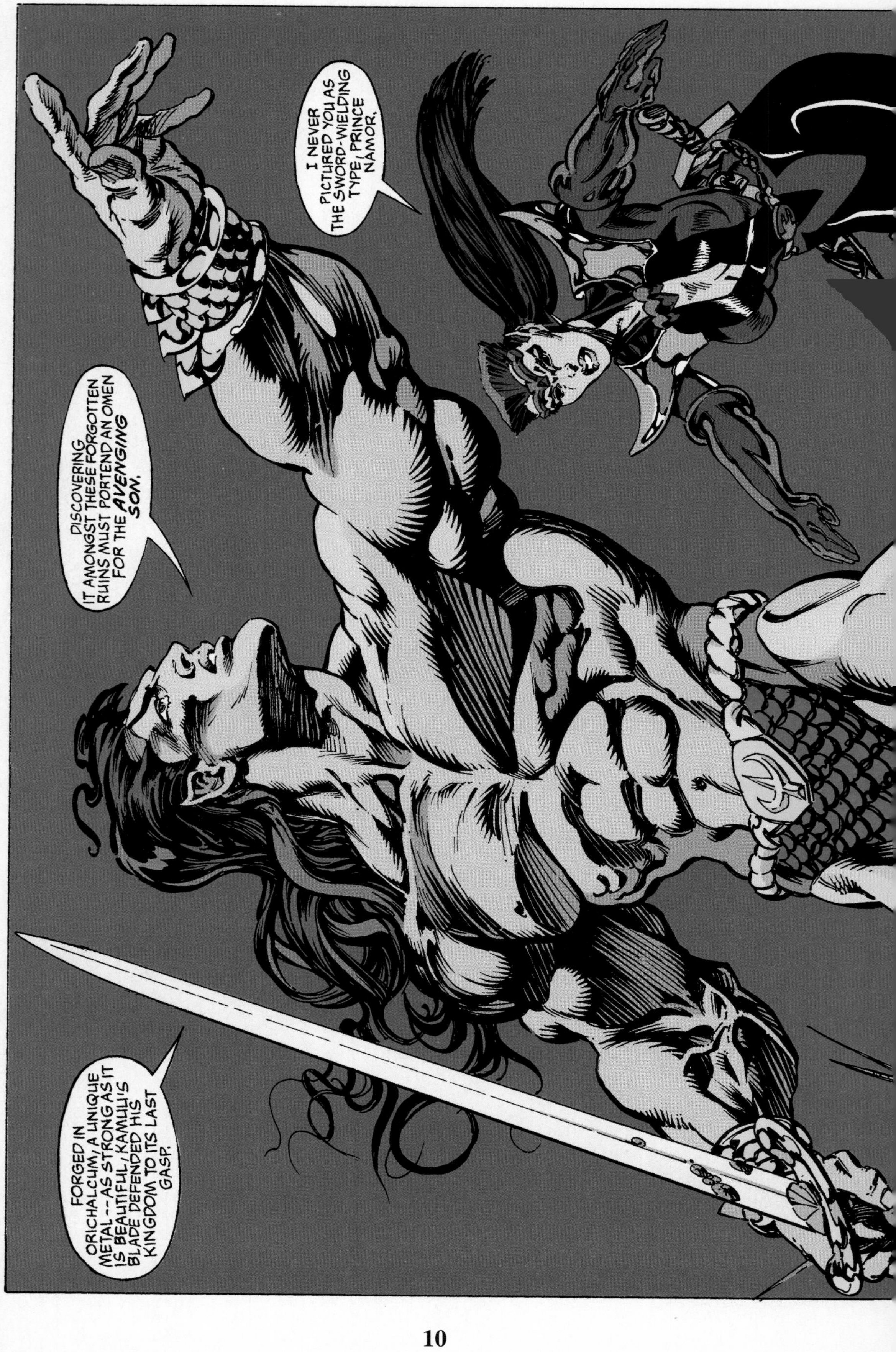
FORGED IN ORICHALCUM, A UNIQUE METAL -- AS STRONG AS IT IS BEAUTIFUL, KAMUU'S BLADE DEFENDED HIS KINGDOM TO ITS LAST GASP.
DISCOVERING IT AMONGST THESE FORGOTTEN RUINS MUST PORTEND AN OMEN FOR THE AVENGING SON.
I NEVER PICTURED YOU AS THE SWORD-WIELDING TYPE, PRINCE NAMOR.

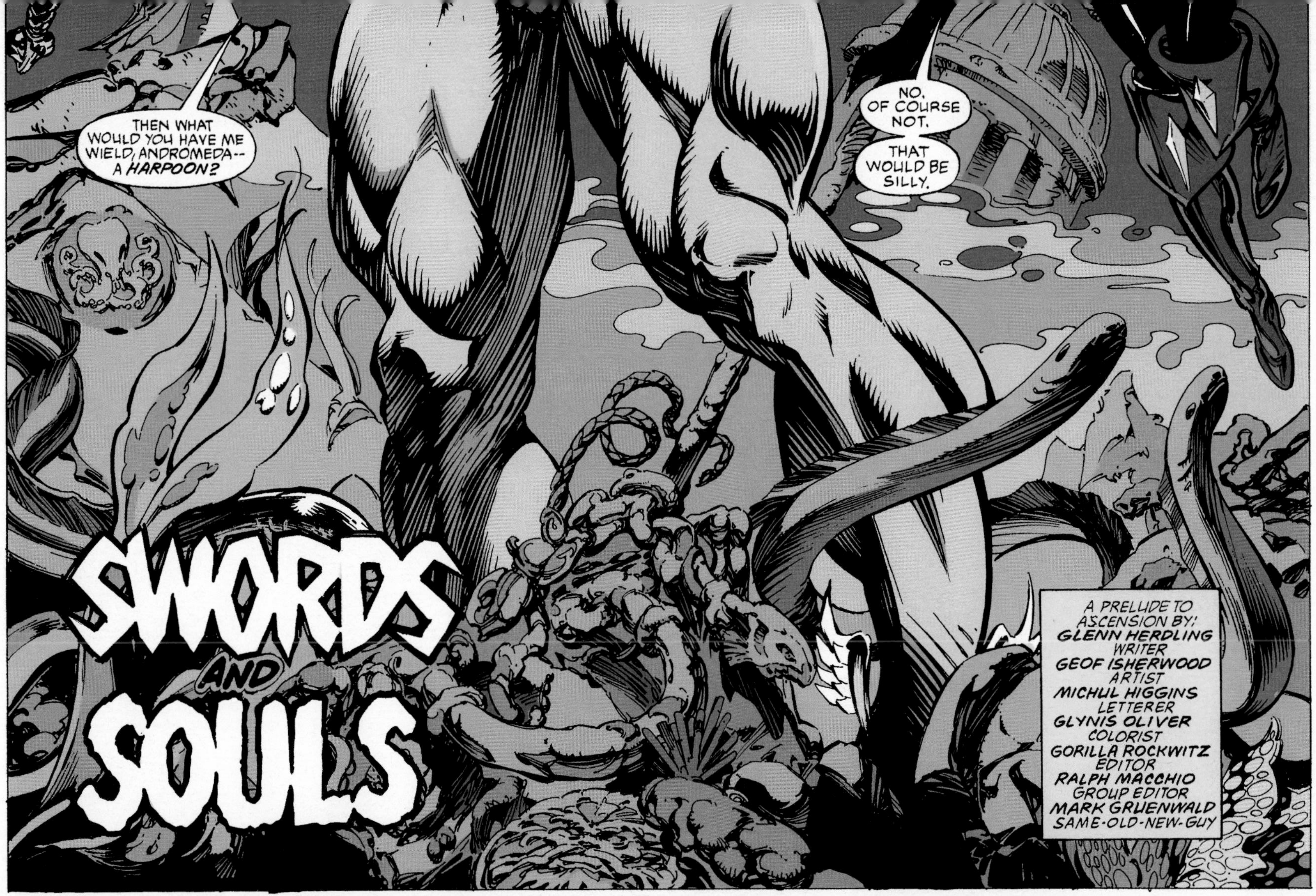
THEN WHAT WOULD YOU HAVE ME WIELD, ANDROMEDA-- A HARPOON?
NO, OF COURSE NOT.
THAT WOULD BE SILLY.
SWORDS AND SOULS
A PRELUDE TO ASCENSION BY:
GLENN HERDLING WRITER
GEOF ISHERWOOD ARTIST
MICHUL HIGGINS LETTERER
GLYNIS OLIVER COLORIST
GORILLA ROCKWITZ EDITOR
RALPH MACCHIO GROUP EDITOR
MARK GRUENWALD SAME-OLD-NEW-GUY

ATLANTIS RISING

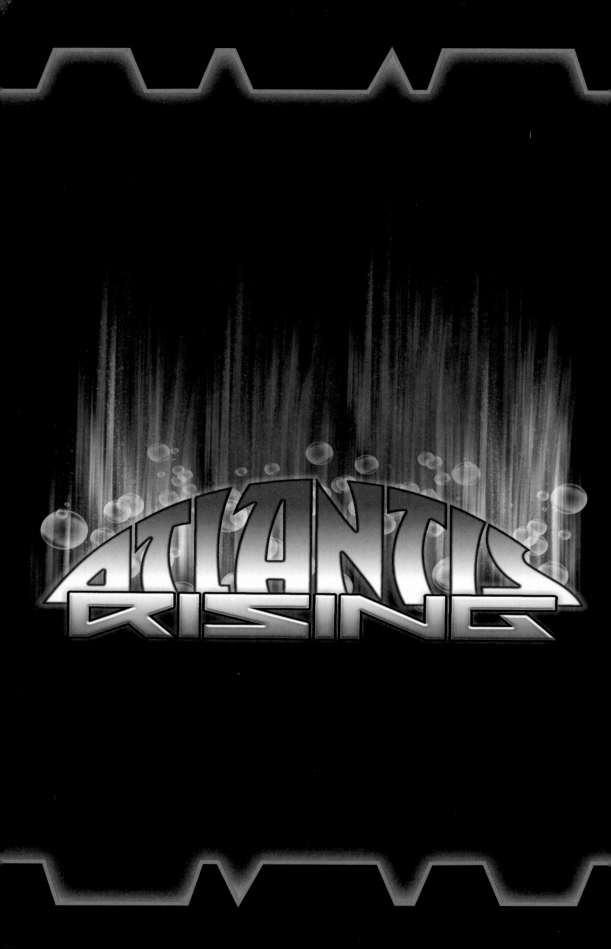

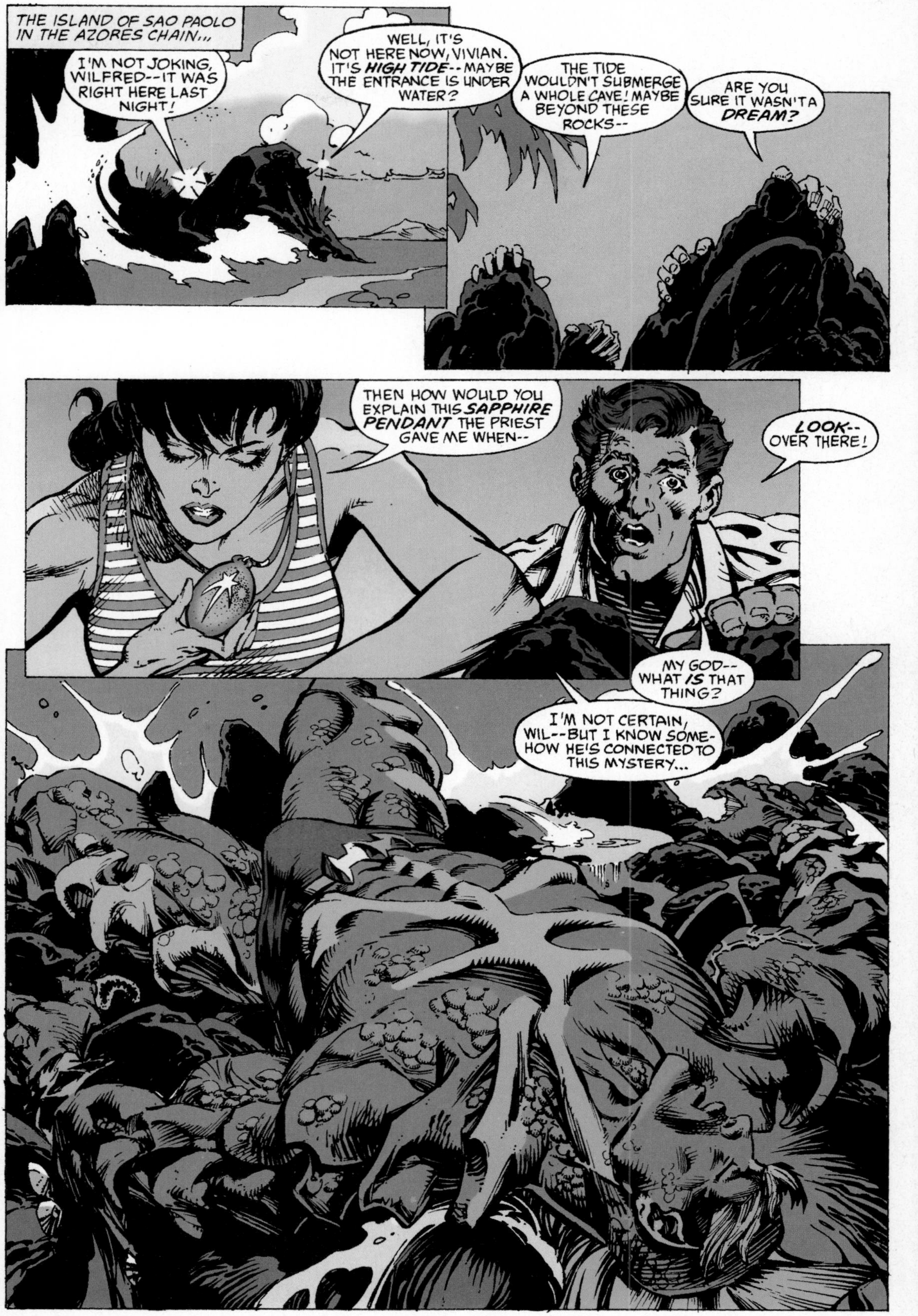
THE ISLAND OF SAO PAOLO IN THE AZORES CHAIN...
I'M NOT JOKING, WILFRED--IT WAS RIGHT HERE LAST NIGHT!
WELL, IT'S NOT HERE NOW, VIVIAN. IT'S HIGH TIDE--MAYBE THE ENTRANCE IS UNDER WATER?
THE TIDE WOULDN'T SUBMERGE A WHOLE CAVE! MAYBE BEYOND THESE ROCKS--
ARE YOU SURE IT WASN'T A DREAM?
THEN HOW WOULD YOU EXPLAIN THIS SAPPHIRE PENDANT THE PRIEST GAVE ME WHEN--
LOOK--OVER THERE!
MY GOD--WHAT IS THAT THING?
I'M NOT CERTAIN, WIL--BUT I KNOW SOMEHOW HE'S CONNECTED TO THIS MYSTERY...

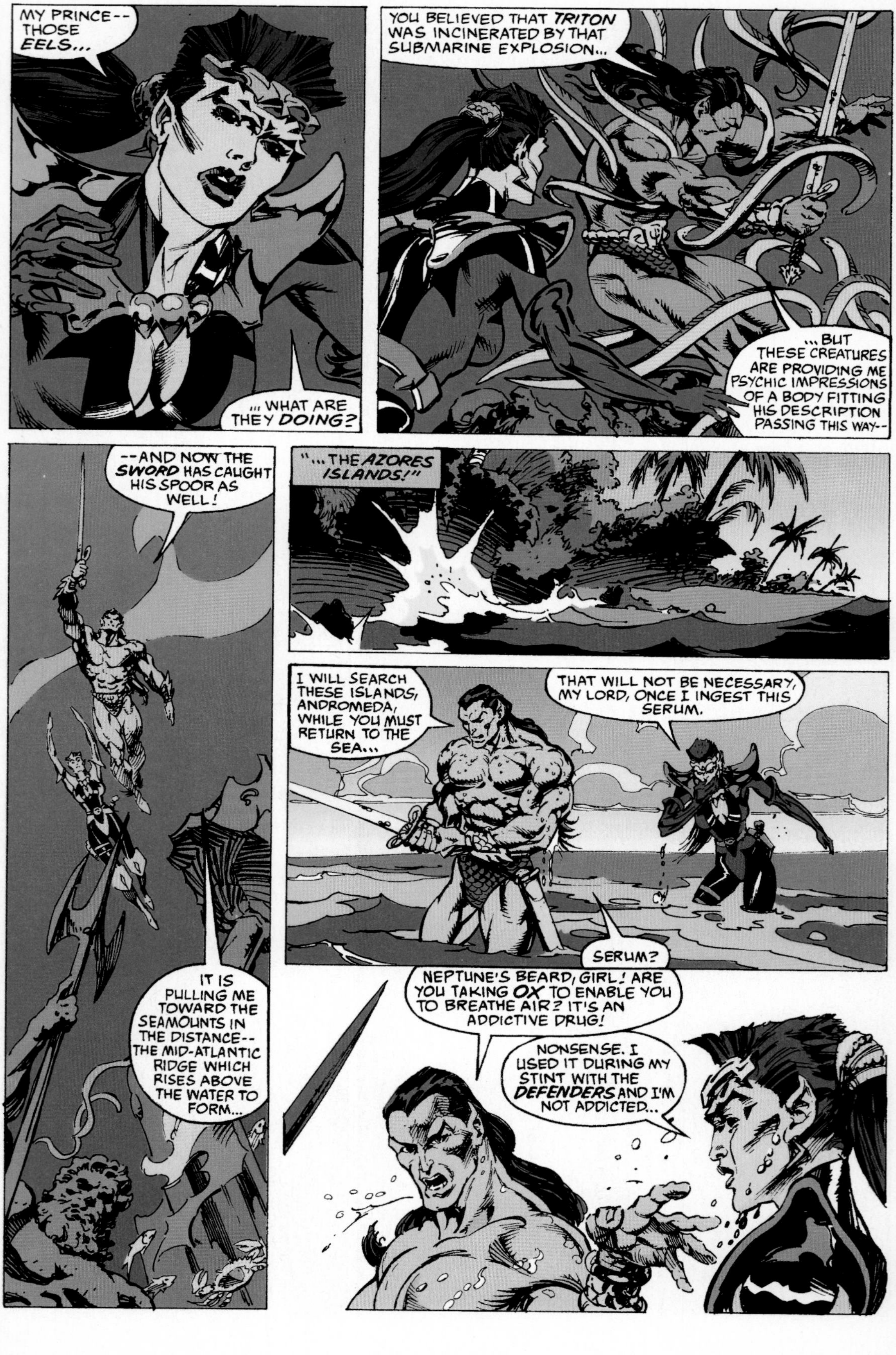
MY PRINCE-- THOSE EELS...
...WHAT ARE THEY DOING?
YOU BELIEVED THAT TRITON WAS INCINERATED BY THAT SUBMARINE EXPLOSION...
...BUT THESE CREATURES ARE PROVIDING ME PSYCHIC IMPRESSIONS OF A BODY FITTING HIS DESCRIPTION PASSING THIS WAY--
--AND NOW THE SWORD HAS CAUGHT HIS SPOOR AS WELL!
IT IS PULLING ME TOWARD THE SEAMOUNTS IN THE DISTANCE-- THE MID-ATLANTIC RIDGE WHICH RISES ABOVE THE WATER TO FORM...
"...THE AZORES ISLANDS!"
I WILL SEARCH THESE ISLANDS, ANDROMEDA, WHILE YOU MUST RETURN TO THE SEA...
THAT WILL NOT BE NECESSARY, MY LORD, ONCE I INGEST THIS SERUM.
SERUM?
NEPTUNE'S BEARD, GIRL! ARE YOU TAKING OX TO ENABLE YOU TO BREATHE AIR? IT'S AN ADDICTIVE DRUG!
NONSENSE. I USED IT DURING MY STINT WITH THE DEFENDERS AND I'M NOT ADDICTED...

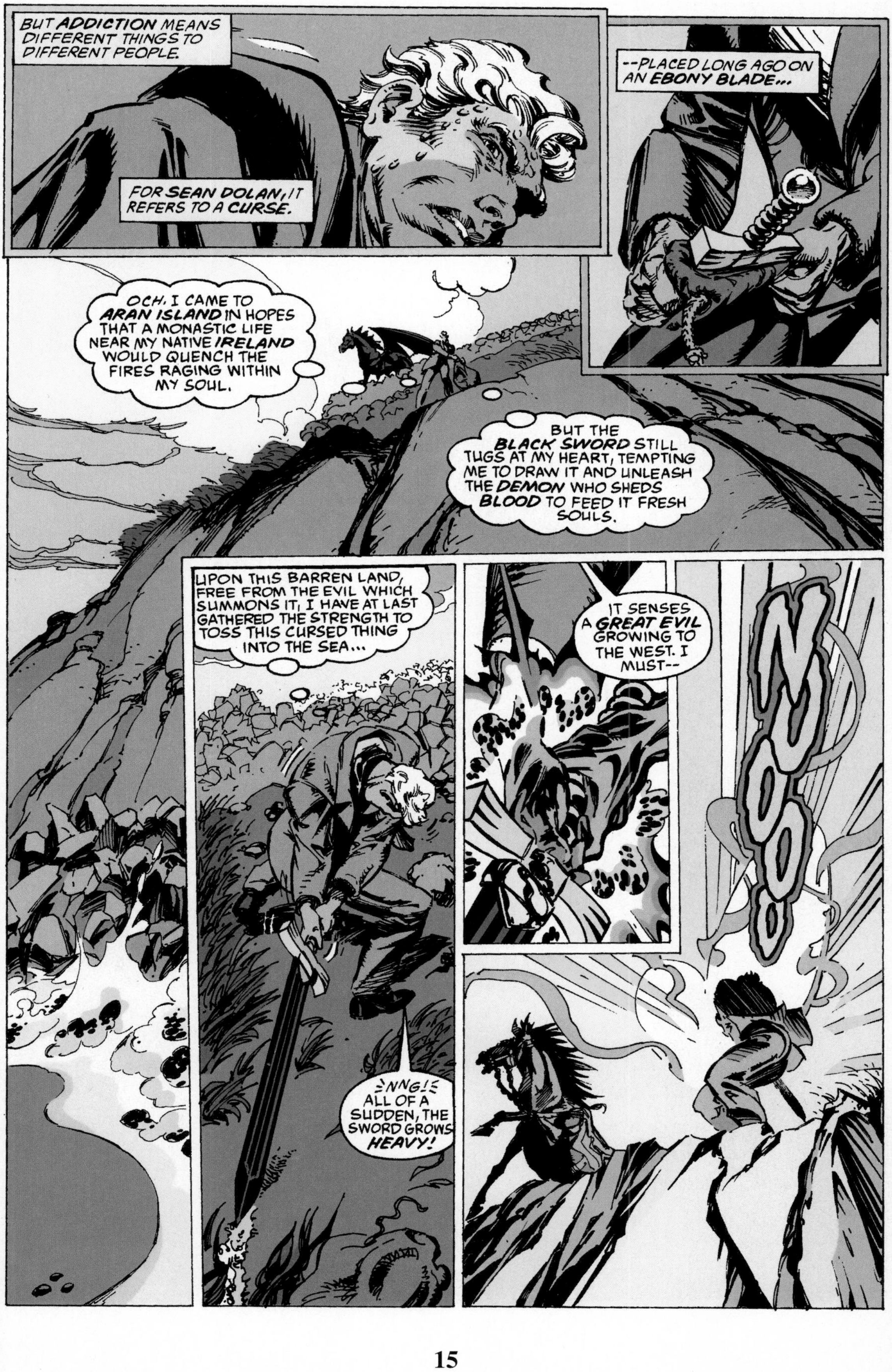
BUT ADDICTION MEANS DIFFERENT THINGS TO DIFFERENT PEOPLE.
FOR SEAN DOLAN, IT REFERS TO A CURSE.
--PLACED LONG AGO ON AN EBONY BLADE...
OCH. I CAME TO ARAN ISLAND IN HOPES THAT A MONASTIC LIFE NEAR MY NATIVE IRELAND WOULD QUENCH THE FIRES RAGING WITHIN MY SOUL.
BUT THE BLACK SWORD STILL TUGS AT MY HEART, TEMPTING ME TO DRAW IT AND UNLEASH THE DEMON WHO SHEDS BLOOD TO FEED IT FRESH SOULS.
UPON THIS BARREN LAND, FREE FROM THE EVIL WHICH SUMMONS IT, I HAVE AT LAST GATHERED THE STRENGTH TO TOSS THIS CURSED THING INTO THE SEA...
NNG! ALL OF A SUDDEN, THE SWORD GROWS HEAVY!
IT SENSES A GREAT EVIL GROWING TO THE WEST. I MUST--
NOOOO

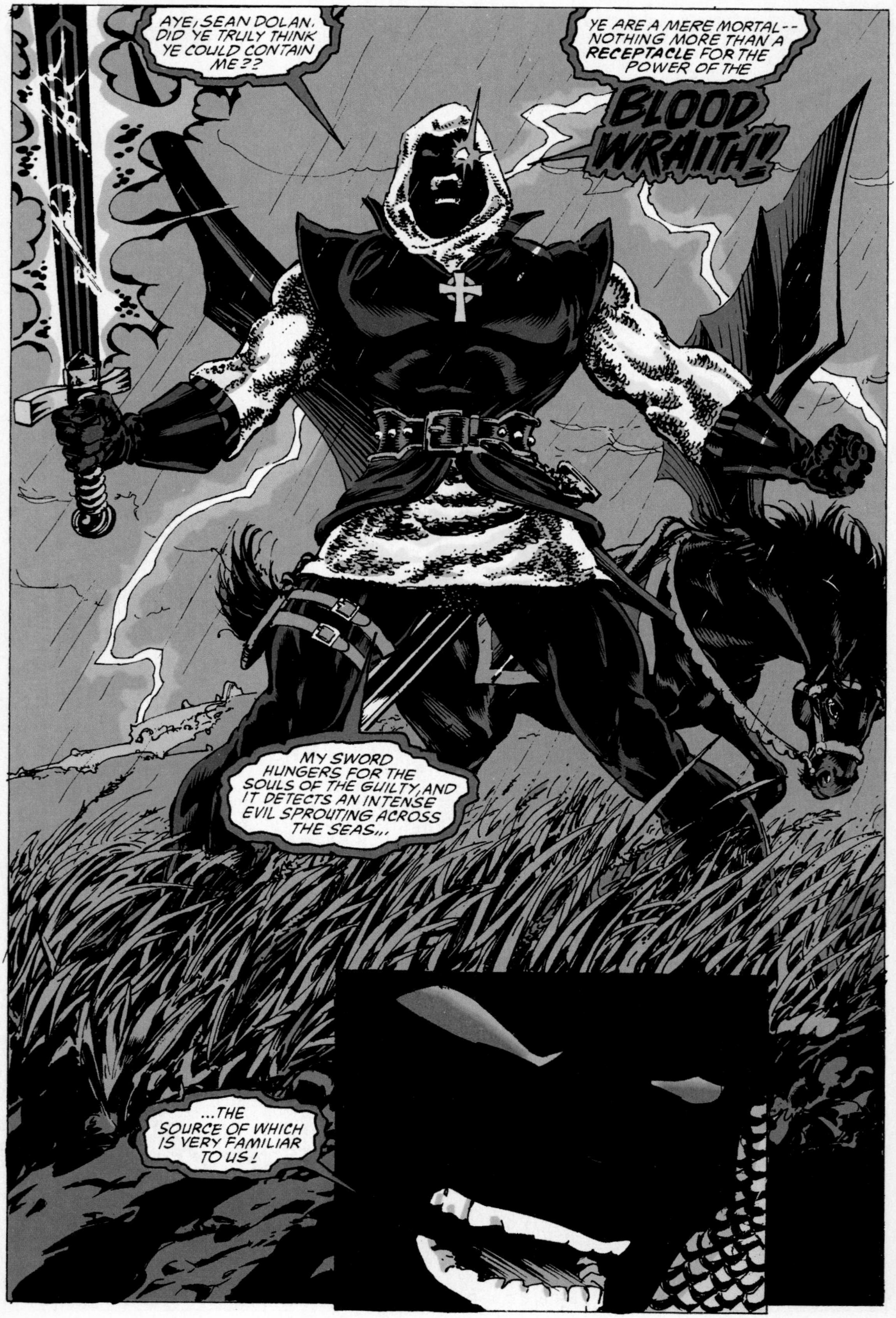
AYE, SEAN DOLAN. DID YE TRULY THINK YE COULD CONTAIN ME??
YE ARE A MERE MORTAL-- NOTHING MORE THAN A RECEPTACLE FOR THE POWER OF THE
BLOOD WRAITH!
MY SWORD HUNGERS FOR THE SOULS OF THE GUILTY, AND IT DETECTS AN INTENSE EVIL SPROUTING ACROSS THE SEAS...
...THE SOURCE OF WHICH IS VERY FAMILIAR TO US!

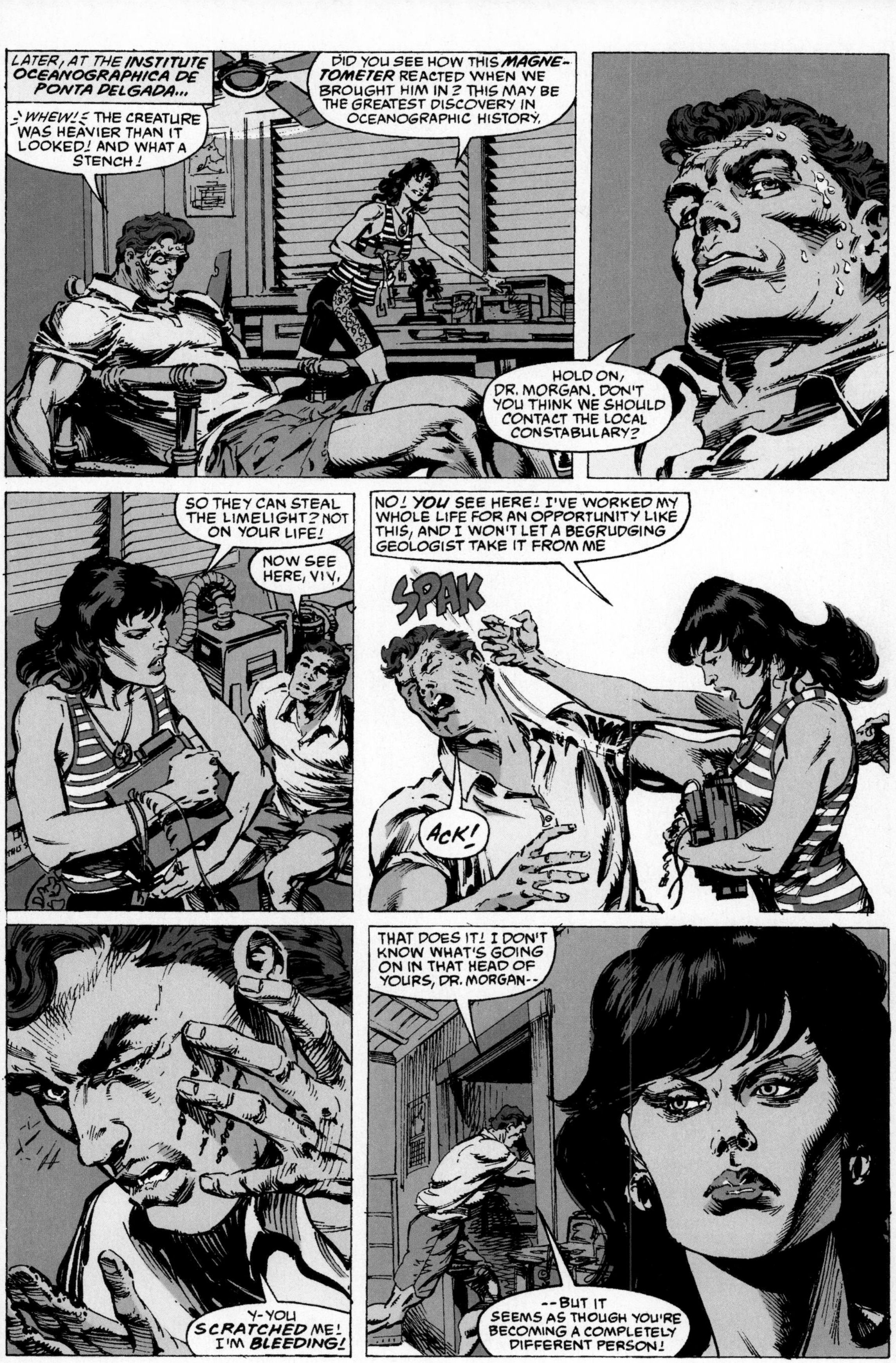

LATER, AT THE INSTITUTE OCEANOGRAPHICA DE PONTA DELGADA...
WHEW! THE CREATURE WAS HEAVIER THAN IT LOOKED! AND WHAT A STENCH!
DID YOU SEE HOW THIS MAGNETOMETER REACTED WHEN WE BROUGHT HIM IN? THIS MAY BE THE GREATEST DISCOVERY IN OCEANOGRAPHIC HISTORY.
HOLD ON, DR. MORGAN. DON'T YOU THINK WE SHOULD CONTACT THE LOCAL CONSTABULARY?
SO THEY CAN STEAL THE LIMELIGHT? NOT ON YOUR LIFE!
NOW SEE HERE, VIV,
NO! YOU SEE HERE! I'VE WORKED MY WHOLE LIFE FOR AN OPPORTUNITY LIKE THIS, AND I WON'T LET A BEGRUDGING GEOLOGIST TAKE IT FROM ME
SPAK
ACK!
Y-YOU SCRATCHED ME! I'M BLEEDING!
THAT DOES IT! I DON'T KNOW WHAT'S GOING ON IN THAT HEAD OF YOURS, DR. MORGAN--
--BUT IT SEEMS AS THOUGH YOU'RE BECOMING A COMPLETELY DIFFERENT PERSON!

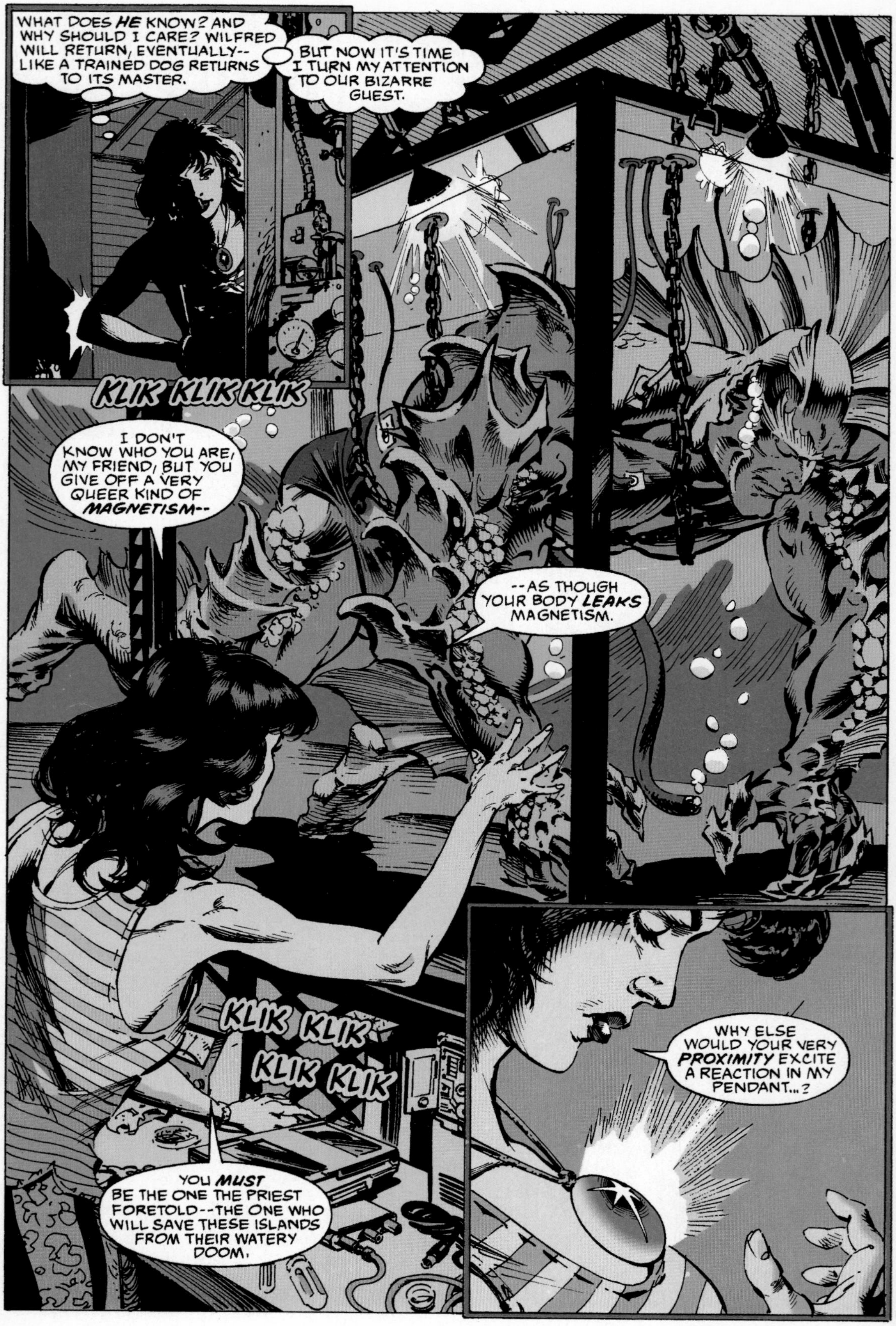

WHAT DOES *HE* KNOW? AND WHY SHOULD I CARE? WILFRED WILL RETURN, EVENTUALLY-- LIKE A TRAINED DOG RETURNS TO ITS MASTER.
BUT NOW IT'S TIME I TURN MY ATTENTION TO OUR BIZARRE GUEST.
KLIK KLIK KLIK
I DON'T KNOW WHO YOU ARE, MY FRIEND, BUT YOU GIVE OFF A VERY QUEER KIND OF *MAGNETISM*--
--AS THOUGH YOUR BODY *LEAKS* MAGNETISM.
KLIK KLIK
KLIK KLIK
YOU *MUST* BE THE ONE THE PRIEST FORETOLD--THE ONE WHO WILL SAVE THESE ISLANDS FROM THEIR WATERY DOOM.
WHY ELSE WOULD YOUR VERY *PROXIMITY* EXCITE A REACTION IN MY PENDANT...?

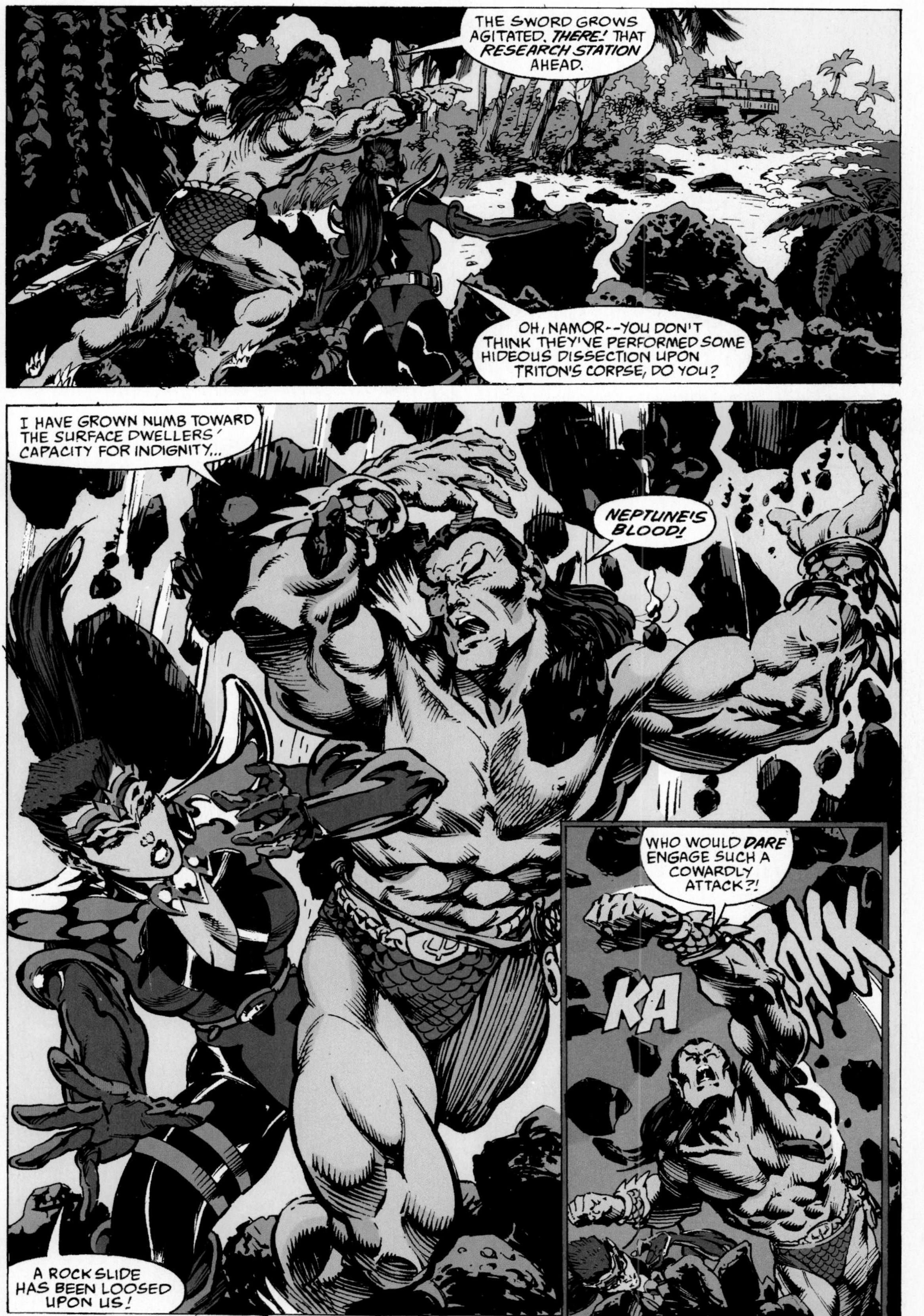
THE SWORD GROWS AGITATED. THERE! THAT RESEARCH STATION AHEAD.
OH, NAMOR--YOU DON'T THINK THEY'VE PERFORMED SOME HIDEOUS DISSECTION UPON TRITON'S CORPSE, DO YOU?
I HAVE GROWN NUMB TOWARD THE SURFACE DWELLERS' CAPACITY FOR INDIGNITY...
NEPTUNE'S BLOOD!
A ROCK SLIDE HAS BEEN LOOSED UPON US!
KA
WHO WOULD DARE ENGAGE SUCH A COWARDLY ATTACK?!

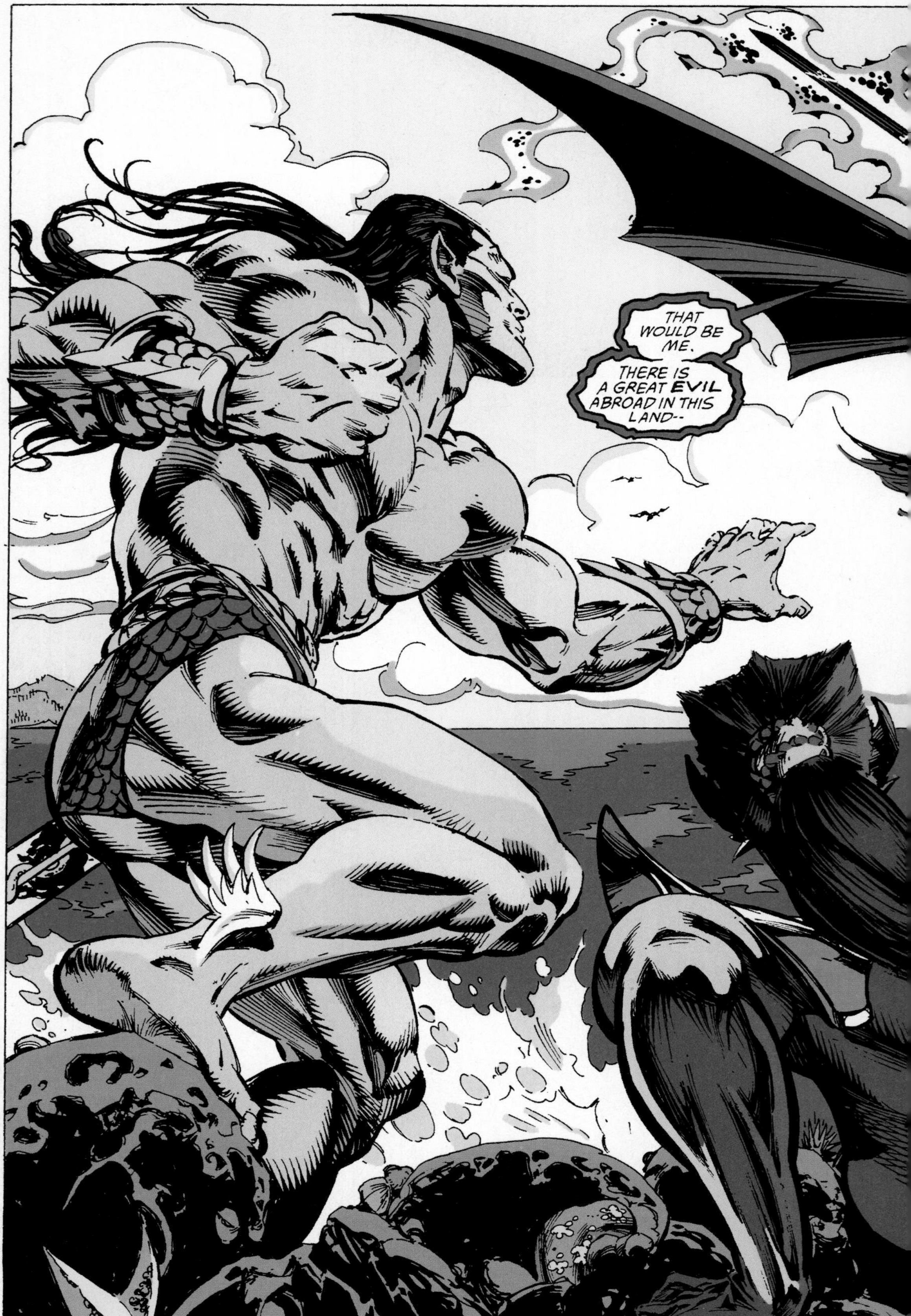
THAT WOULD BE ME.
THERE IS A GREAT EVIL ABROAD IN THIS LAND--

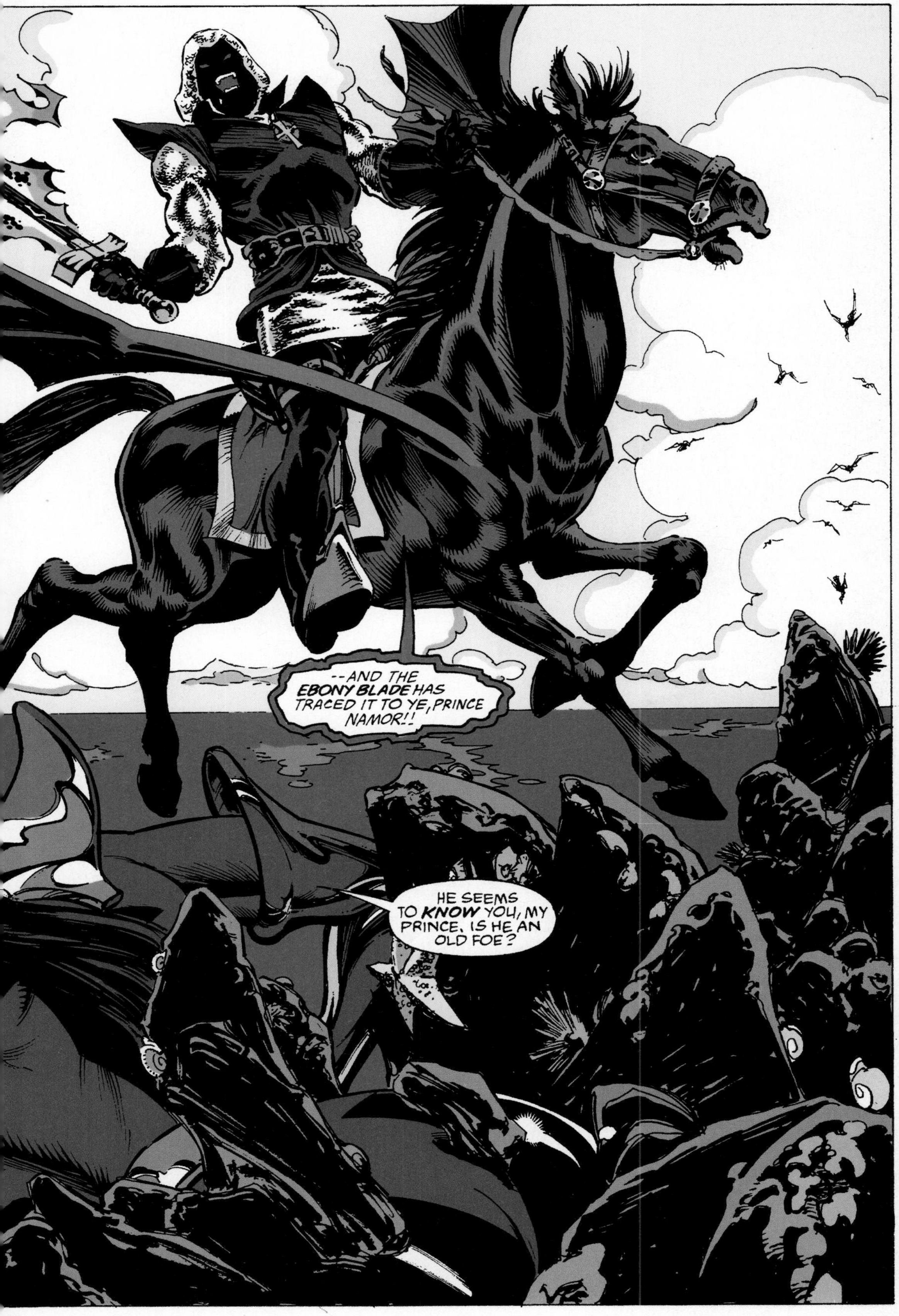
--AND THE EBONY BLADE HAS TRACED IT TO YE, PRINCE NAMOR!!
HE SEEMS TO KNOW YOU, MY PRINCE. IS HE AN OLD FOE?

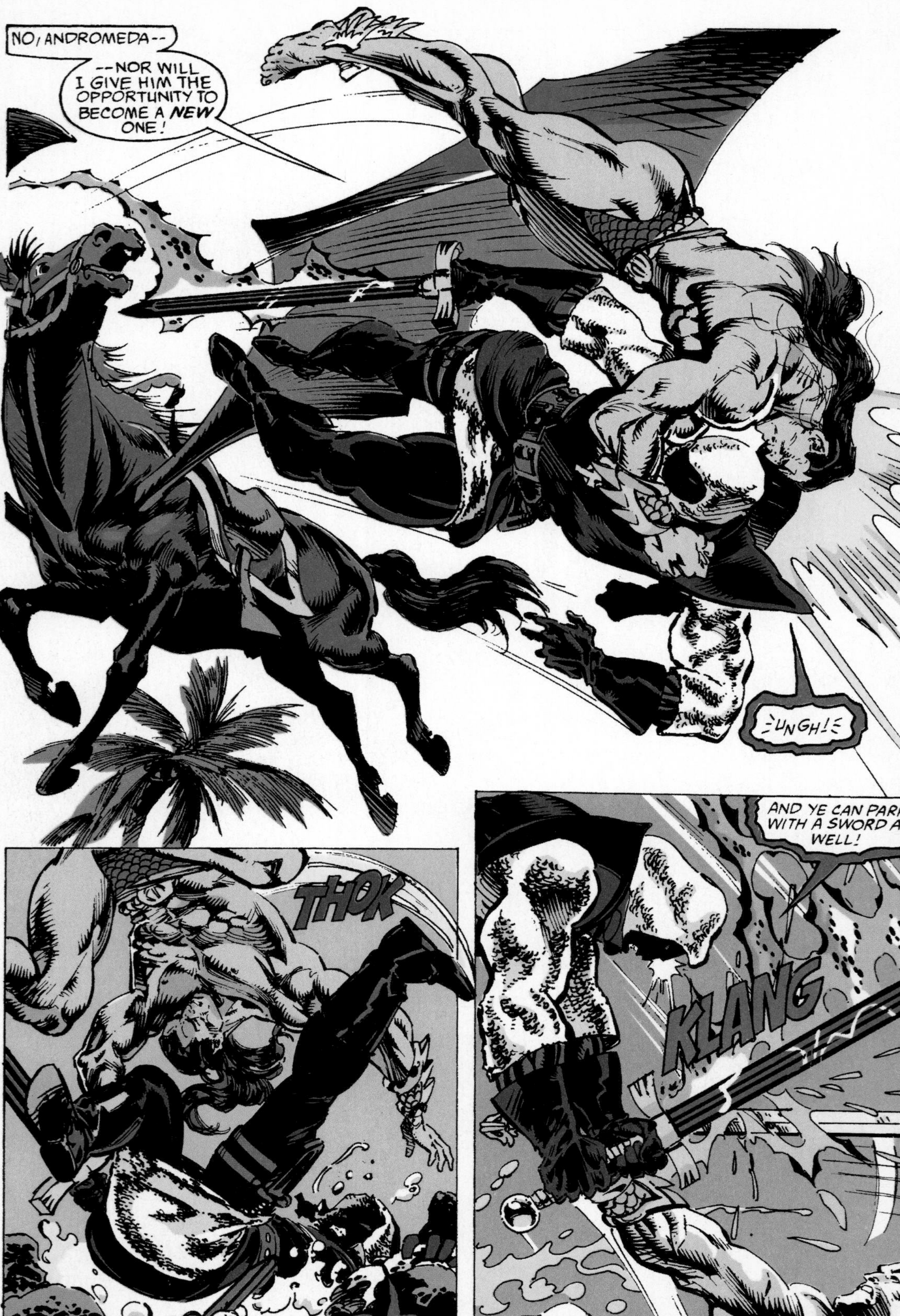
NO, ANDROMEDA--
--NOR WILL I GIVE HIM THE OPPORTUNITY TO BECOME A NEW ONE!
UNGH!
THOK
GOOD-- YE BRING THE BATTLE TO ME!
AND YE CAN PARRY WITH A SWORD AS WELL!
KLANG

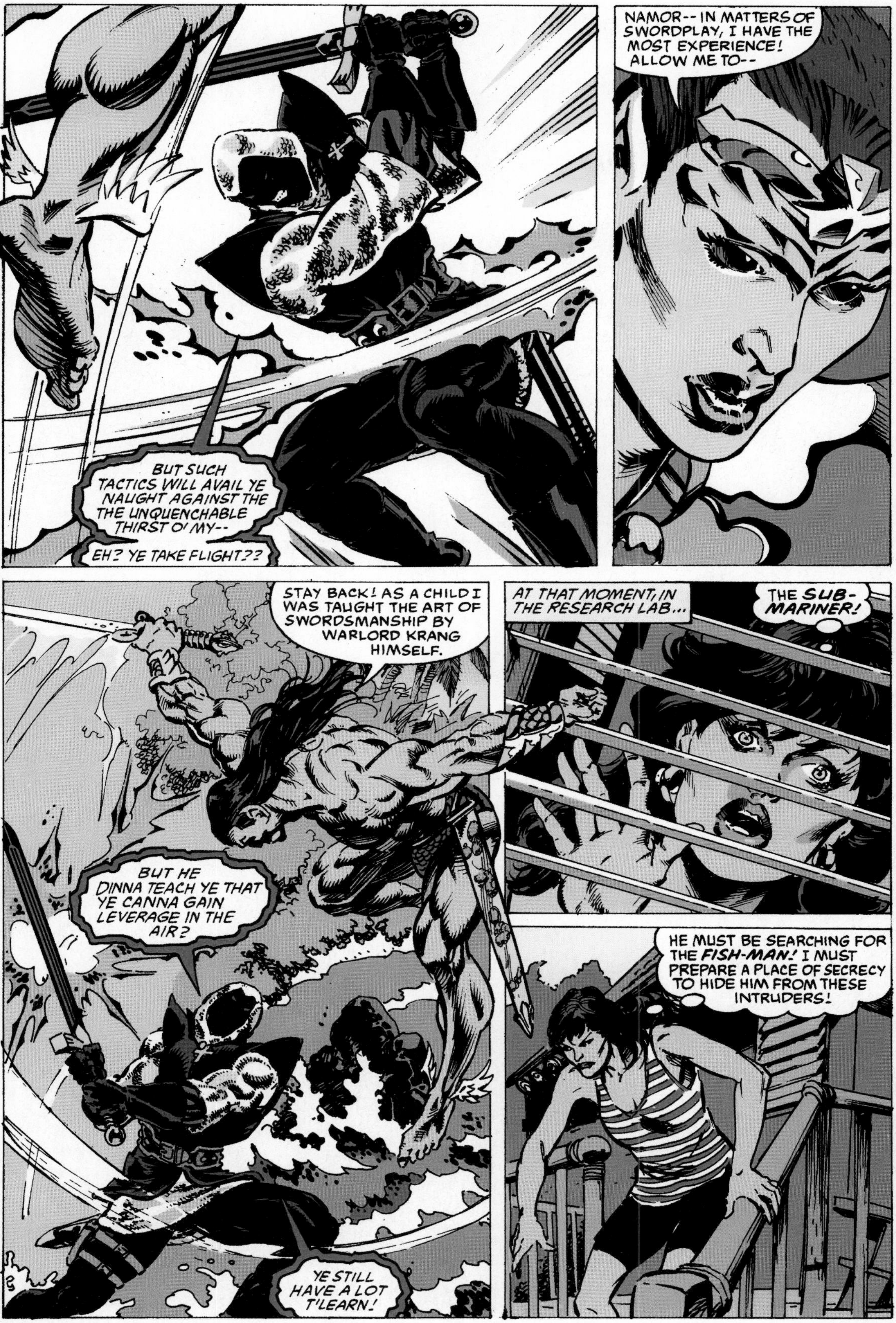
BUT SUCH TACTICS WILL AVAIL YE NAUGHT AGAINST THE THE UNQUENCHABLE THIRST O' MY--
EH? YE TAKE FLIGHT??
NAMOR-- IN MATTERS OF SWORDPLAY, I HAVE THE MOST EXPERIENCE! ALLOW ME TO--
STAY BACK! AS A CHILD I WAS TAUGHT THE ART OF SWORDSMANSHIP BY WARLORD KRANG HIMSELF.
BUT HE DINNA TEACH YE THAT YE CANNA GAIN LEVERAGE IN THE AIR?
YE STILL HAVE A LOT T'LEARN!
AT THAT MOMENT, IN THE RESEARCH LAB...
THE SUB-MARINER!
HE MUST BE SEARCHING FOR THE FISH-MAN! I MUST PREPARE A PLACE OF SECRECY TO HIDE HIM FROM THESE INTRUDERS!

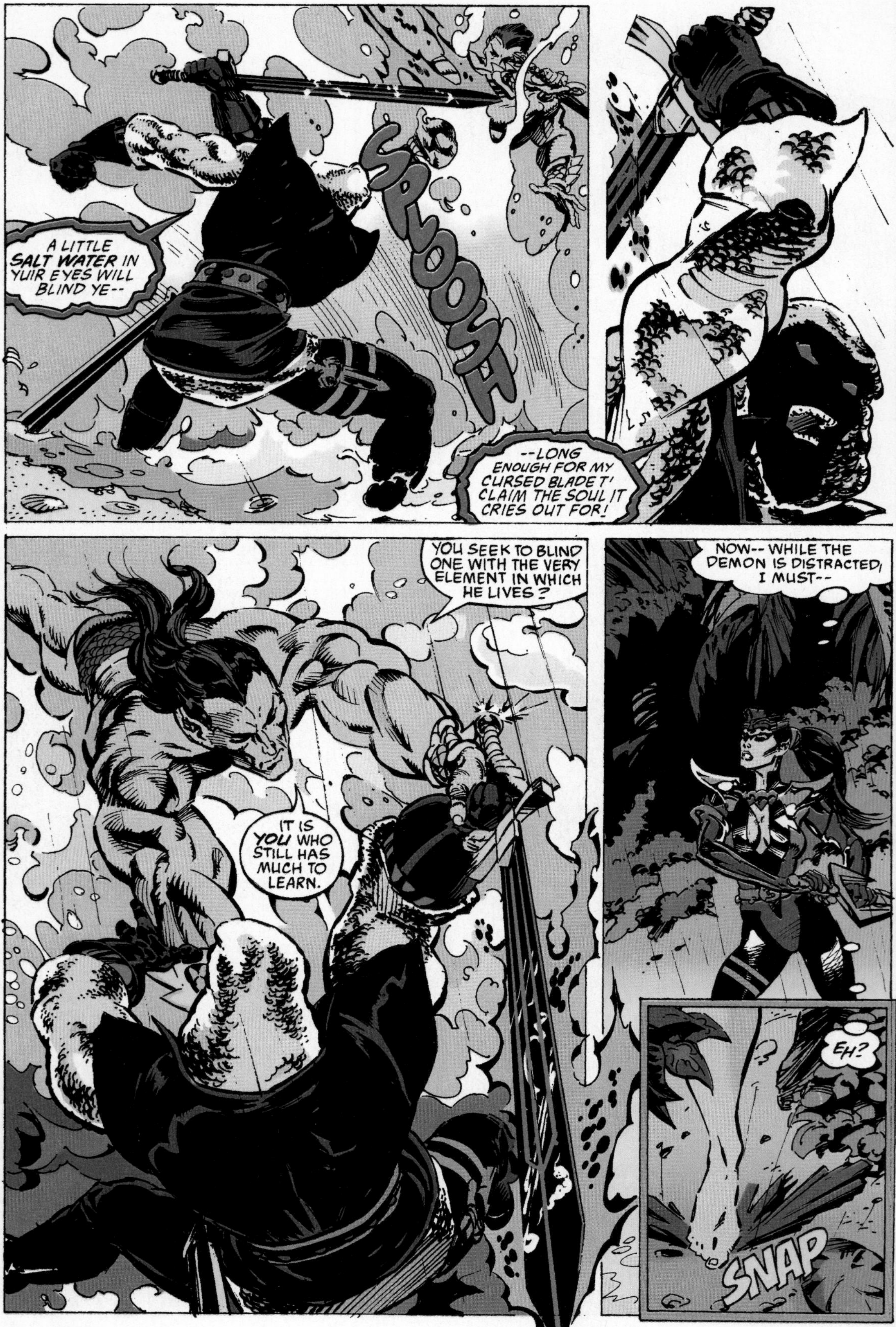
A LITTLE SALT WATER IN YUIR EYES WILL BLIND YE--
SPLOOSH
--LONG ENOUGH FOR MY CURSED BLADE T' CLAIM THE SOUL IT CRIES OUT FOR!
YOU SEEK TO BLIND ONE WITH THE VERY ELEMENT IN WHICH HE LIVES?
IT IS YOU WHO STILL HAS MUCH TO LEARN.
NOW-- WHILE THE DEMON IS DISTRACTED, I MUST--
EH?
SNAP

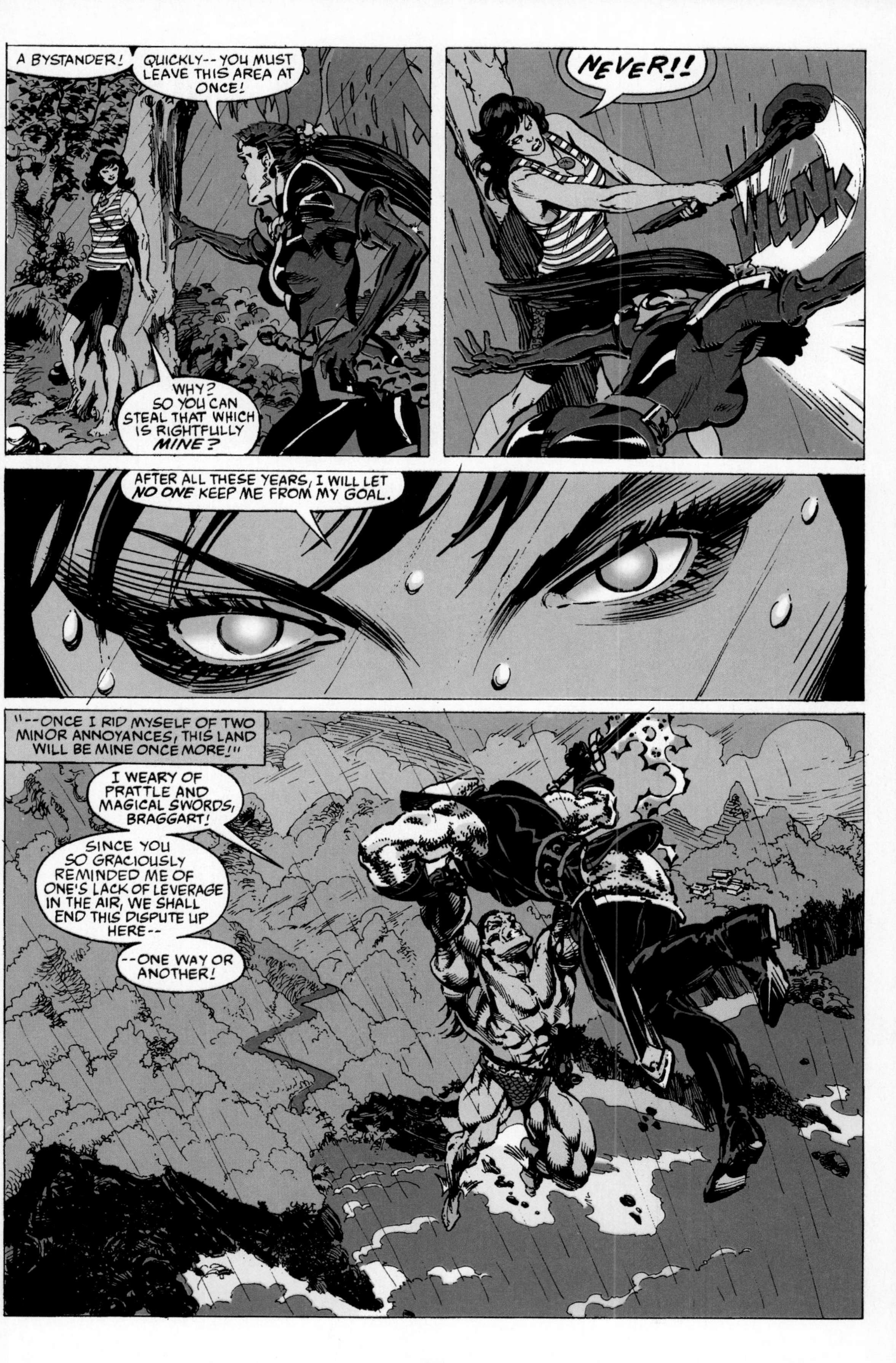
A BYSTANDER!
QUICKLY--YOU MUST LEAVE THIS AREA AT ONCE!
WHY? SO YOU CAN STEAL THAT WHICH IS RIGHTFULLY MINE?
NEVER!!
WUNK
AFTER ALL THESE YEARS, I WILL LET NO ONE KEEP ME FROM MY GOAL.
"--ONCE I RID MYSELF OF TWO MINOR ANNOYANCES, THIS LAND WILL BE MINE ONCE MORE!"
I WEARY OF PRATTLE AND MAGICAL SWORDS, BRAGGART!
SINCE YOU SO GRACIOUSLY REMINDED ME OF ONE'S LACK OF LEVERAGE IN THE AIR, WE SHALL END THIS DISPUTE UP HERE--
--ONE WAY OR ANOTHER!

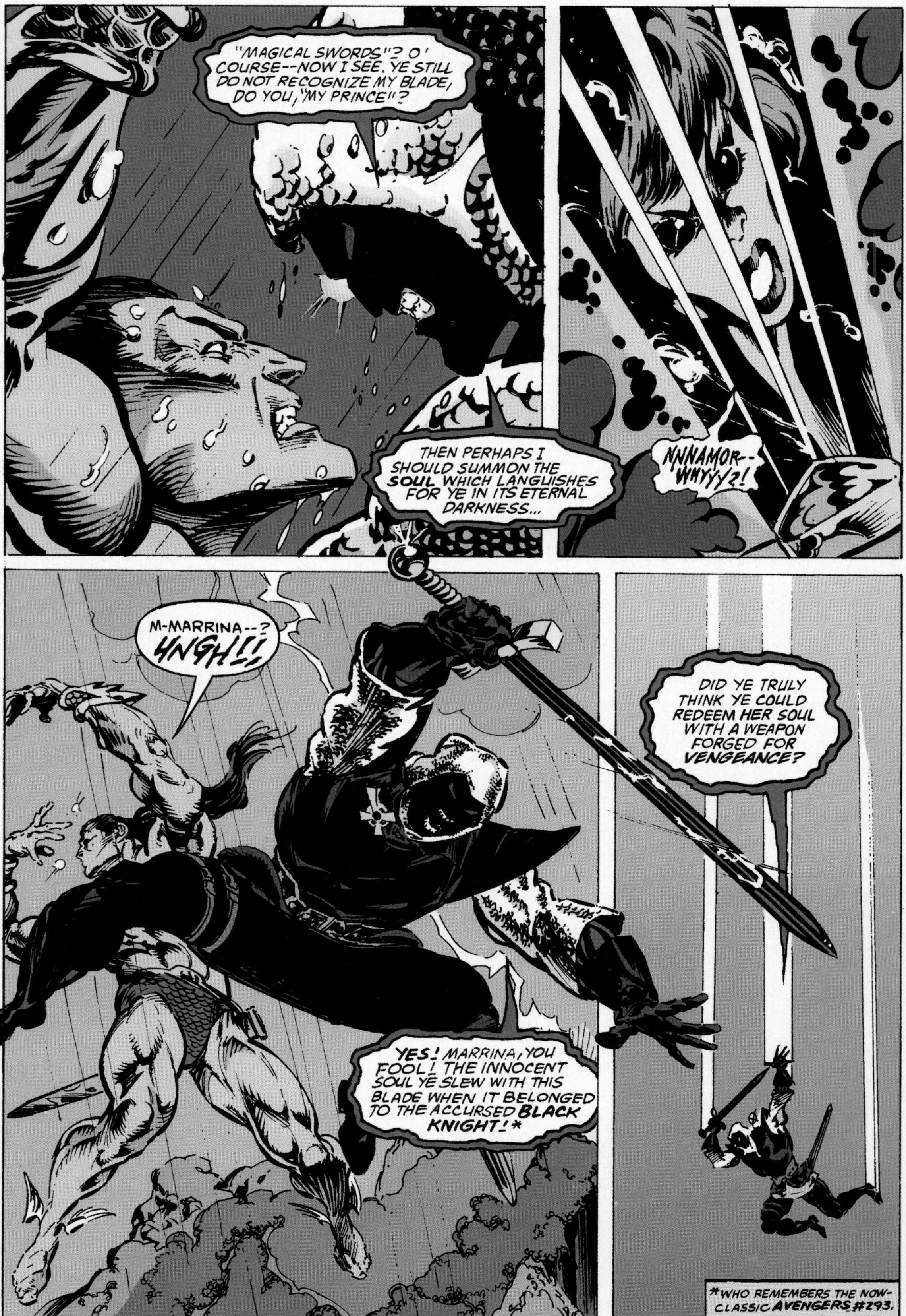
"MAGICAL SWORDS"? O' COURSE--NOW I SEE. YE STILL DO NOT RECOGNIZE MY BLADE, DO YOU, "MY PRINCE"?
THEN PERHAPS I SHOULD SUMMON THE SOUL WHICH LANGUISHES FOR YE IN ITS ETERNAL DARKNESS...
NNNAMOR-- WHYYY?!
M-MARRINA--? UNGH!!
DID YE TRULY THINK YE COULD REDEEM HER SOUL WITH A WEAPON FORGED FOR VENGEANCE?
YES! MARRINA, YOU FOOL! THE INNOCENT SOUL YE SLEW WITH THIS BLADE WHEN IT BELONGED TO THE ACCURSED BLACK KNIGHT!*
*WHO REMEMBERS THE NOW-CLASSIC AVENGERS #293.
--Mnemonic Mike

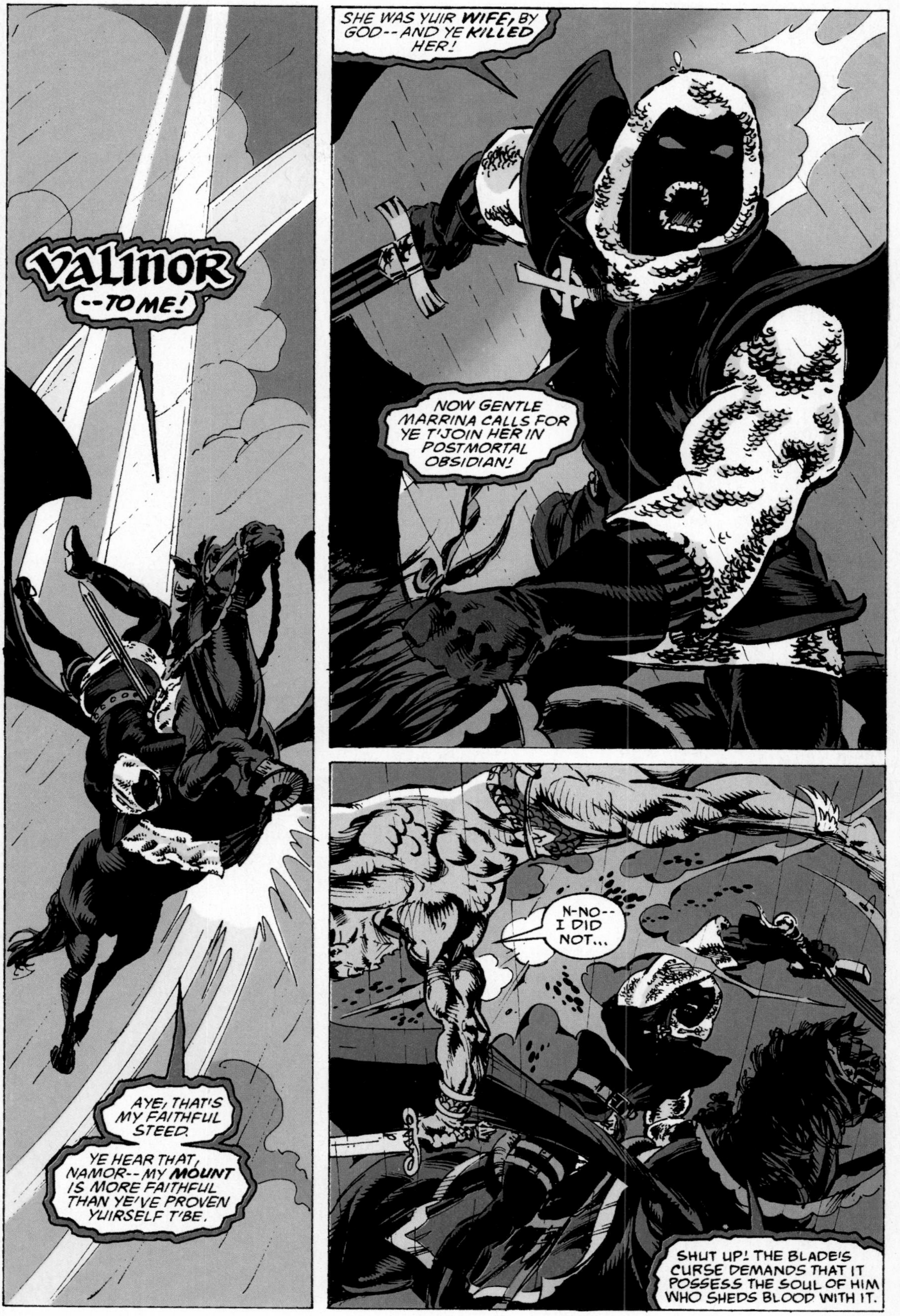

VALINOR
--TO ME!
SHE WAS YUIR WIFE, BY GOD--AND YE KILLED HER!
NOW GENTLE MARRINA CALLS FOR YE T'JOIN HER IN POSTMORTAL OBSIDIAN!
AYE, THAT'S MY FAITHFUL STEED.
YE HEAR THAT, NAMOR--MY MOUNT IS MORE FAITHFUL THAN YE'VE PROVEN YUIRSELF T'BE.
N-NO--I DID NOT...
SHUT UP! THE BLADE'S CURSE DEMANDS THAT IT POSSESS THE SOUL OF HIM WHO SHEDS BLOOD WITH IT.

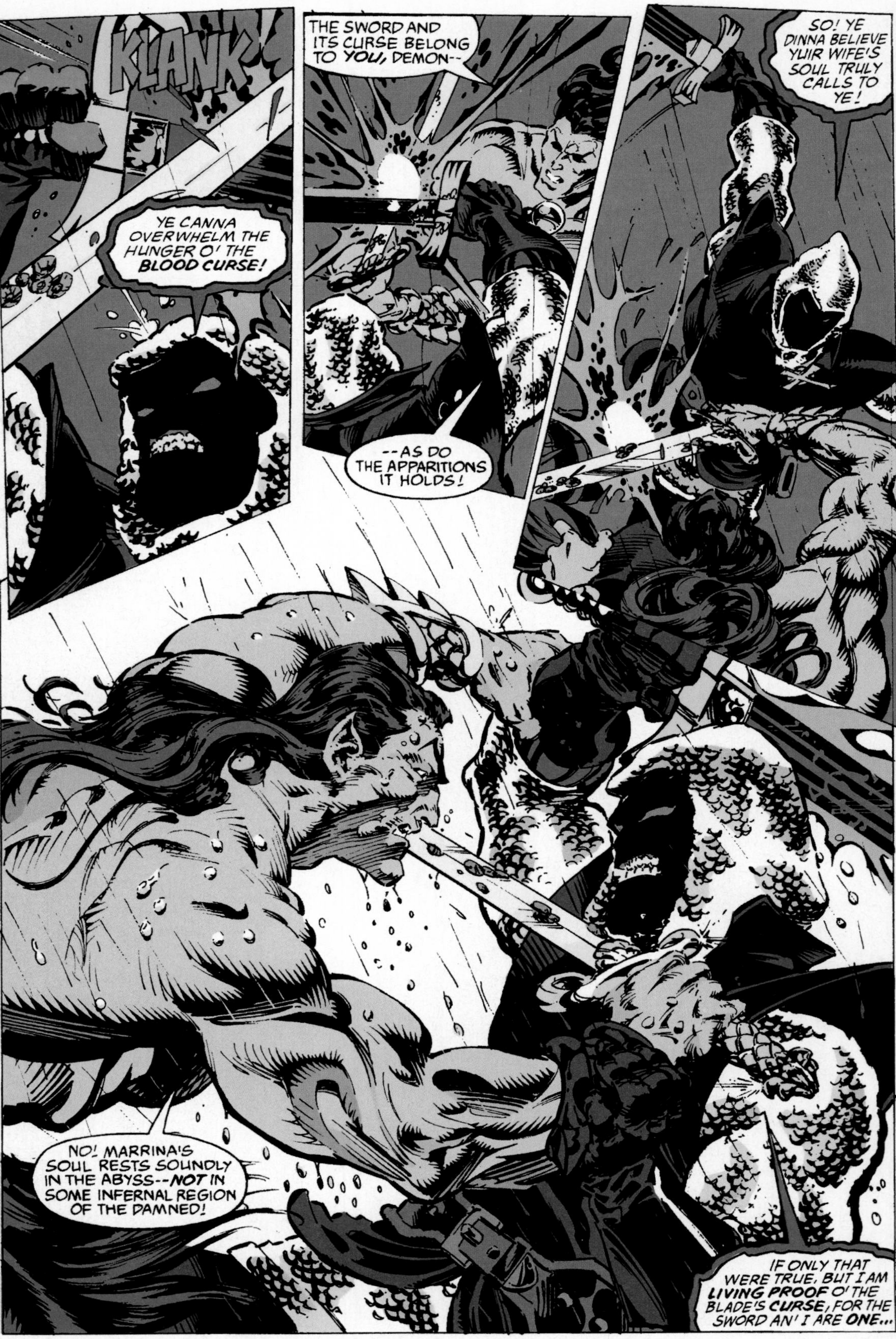
KLANK!
YE CANNA OVERWHELM THE HUNGER O' THE BLOOD CURSE!
THE SWORD AND ITS CURSE BELONG TO YOU, DEMON--
--AS DO THE APPARITIONS IT HOLDS!
SO! YE DINNA BELIEVE YUIR WIFE'S SOUL TRULY CALLS TO YE!
NO! MARRINA'S SOUL RESTS SOUNDLY IN THE ABYSS--NOT IN SOME INFERNAL REGION OF THE DAMNED!
IF ONLY THAT WERE TRUE, BUT I AM LIVING PROOF O' THE BLADE'S CURSE, FOR THE SWORD AN' I ARE ONE...

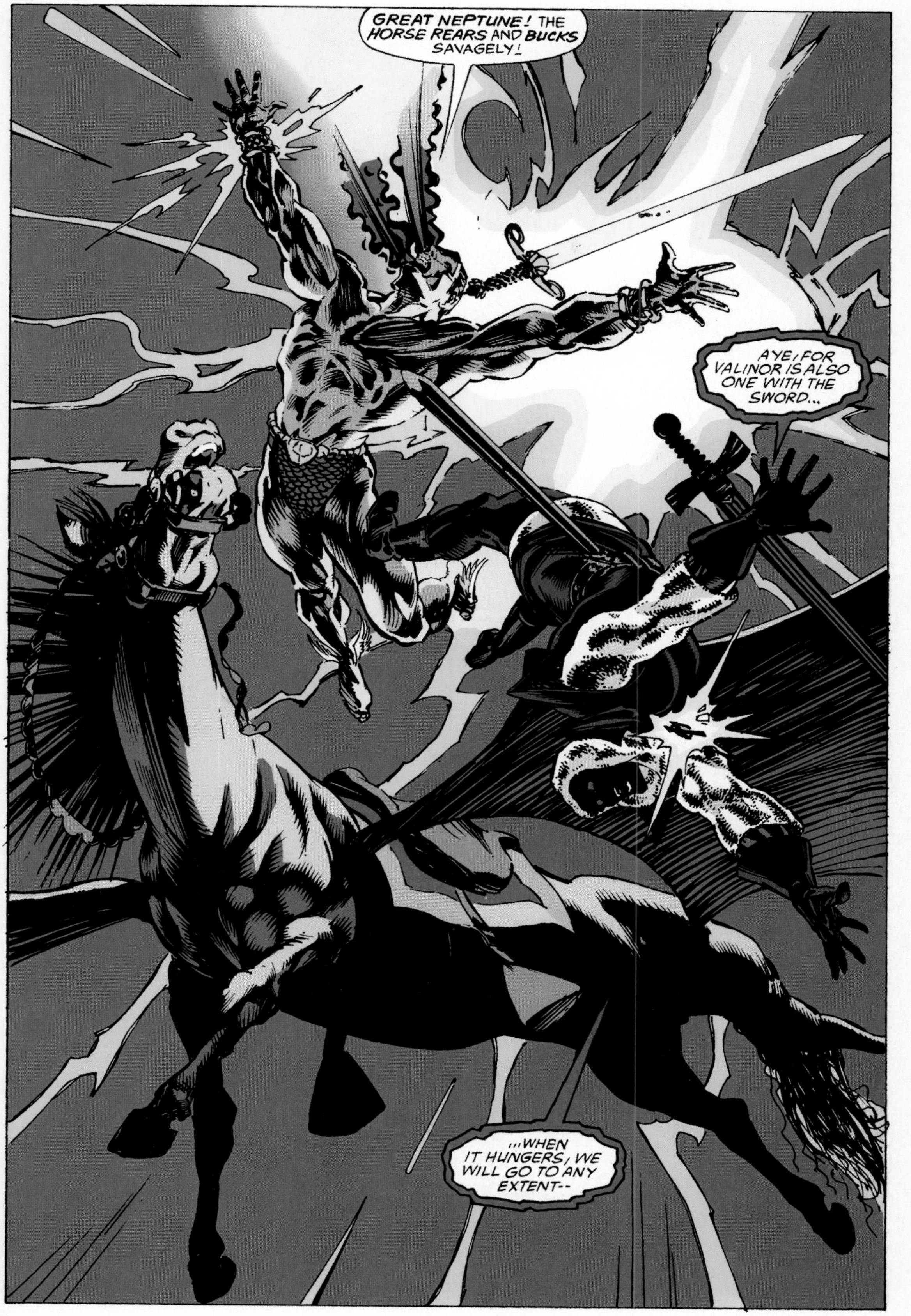
GREAT NEPTUNE! THE HORSE REARS AND BUCKS SAVAGELY!
AYE, FOR VALINOR IS ALSO ONE WITH THE SWORD...
...WHEN IT HUNGERS, WE WILL GO TO ANY EXTENT--

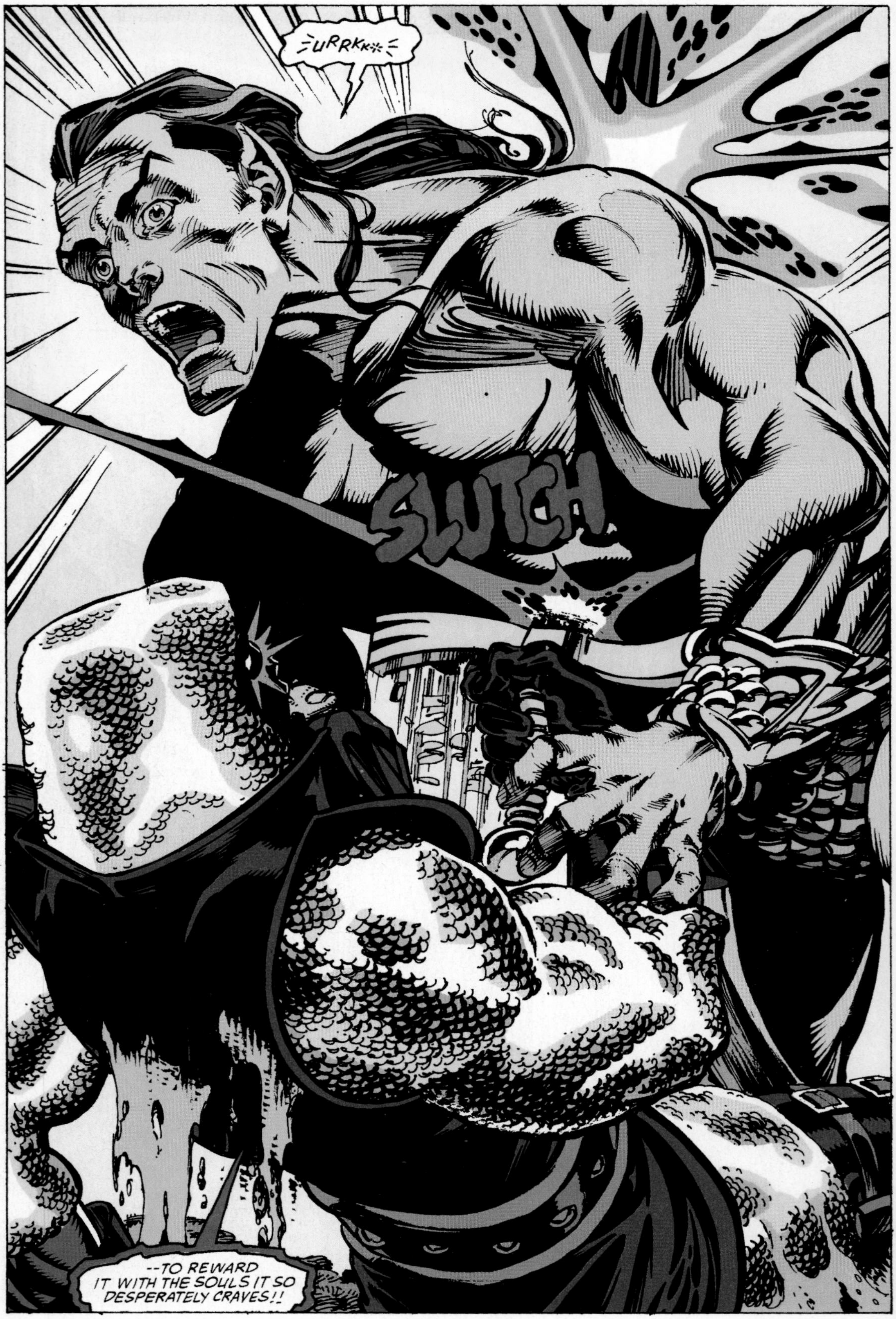
URRKK
SLUTCH
--TO REWARD IT WITH THE SOULS IT SO DESPERATELY CRAVES!!

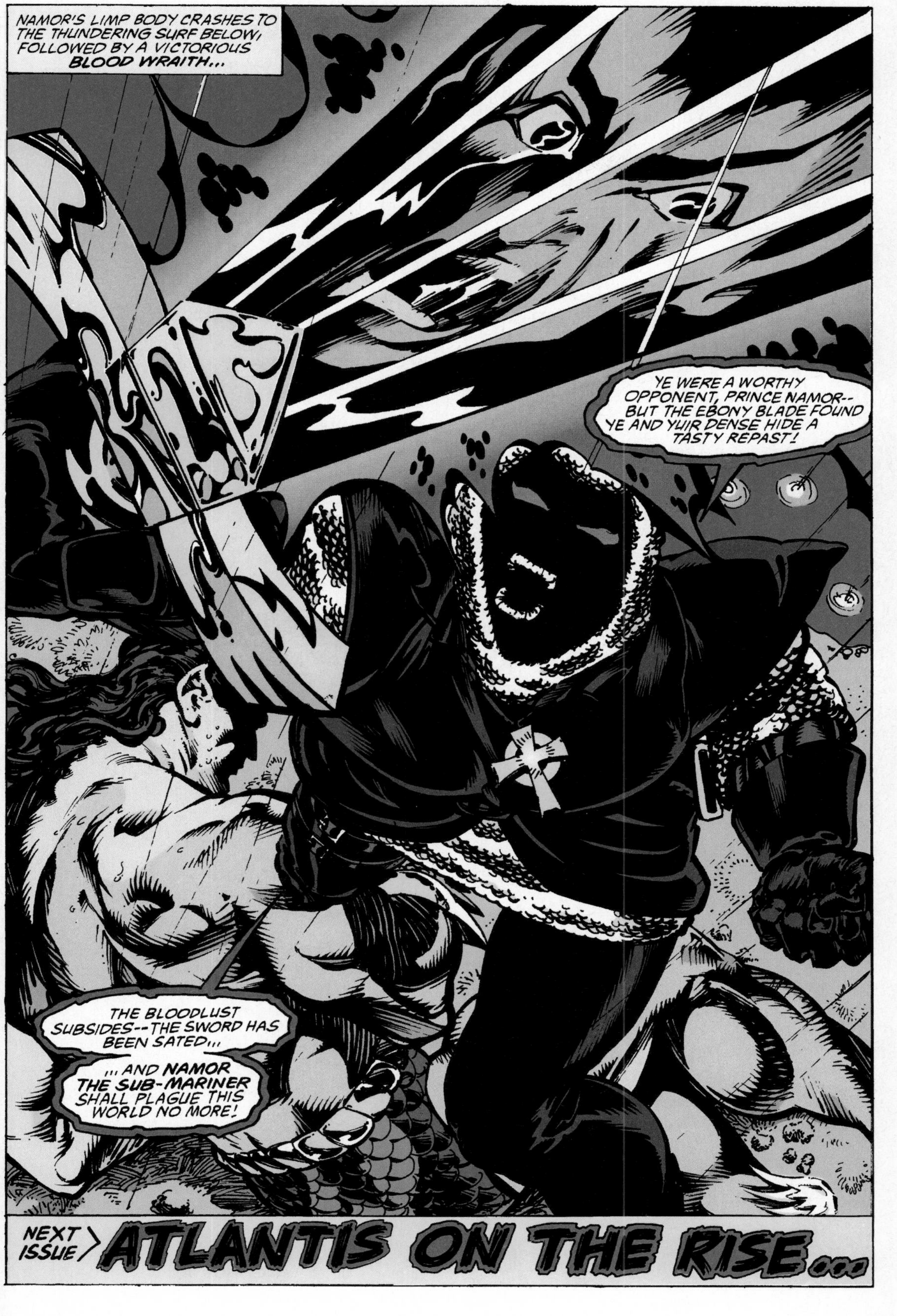
NAMOR'S LIMP BODY CRASHES TO THE THUNDERING SURF BELOW, FOLLOWED BY A VICTORIOUS BLOOD WRAITH...
YE WERE A WORTHY OPPONENT, PRINCE NAMOR-- BUT THE EBONY BLADE FOUND YE AND YUIR DENSE HIDE A TASTY REPAST!
THE BLOODLUST SUBSIDES--THE SWORD HAS BEEN SATED...
...AND NAMOR THE SUB-MARINER SHALL PLAGUE THIS WORLD NO MORE!
NEXT ISSUE ATLANTIS ON THE RISE...

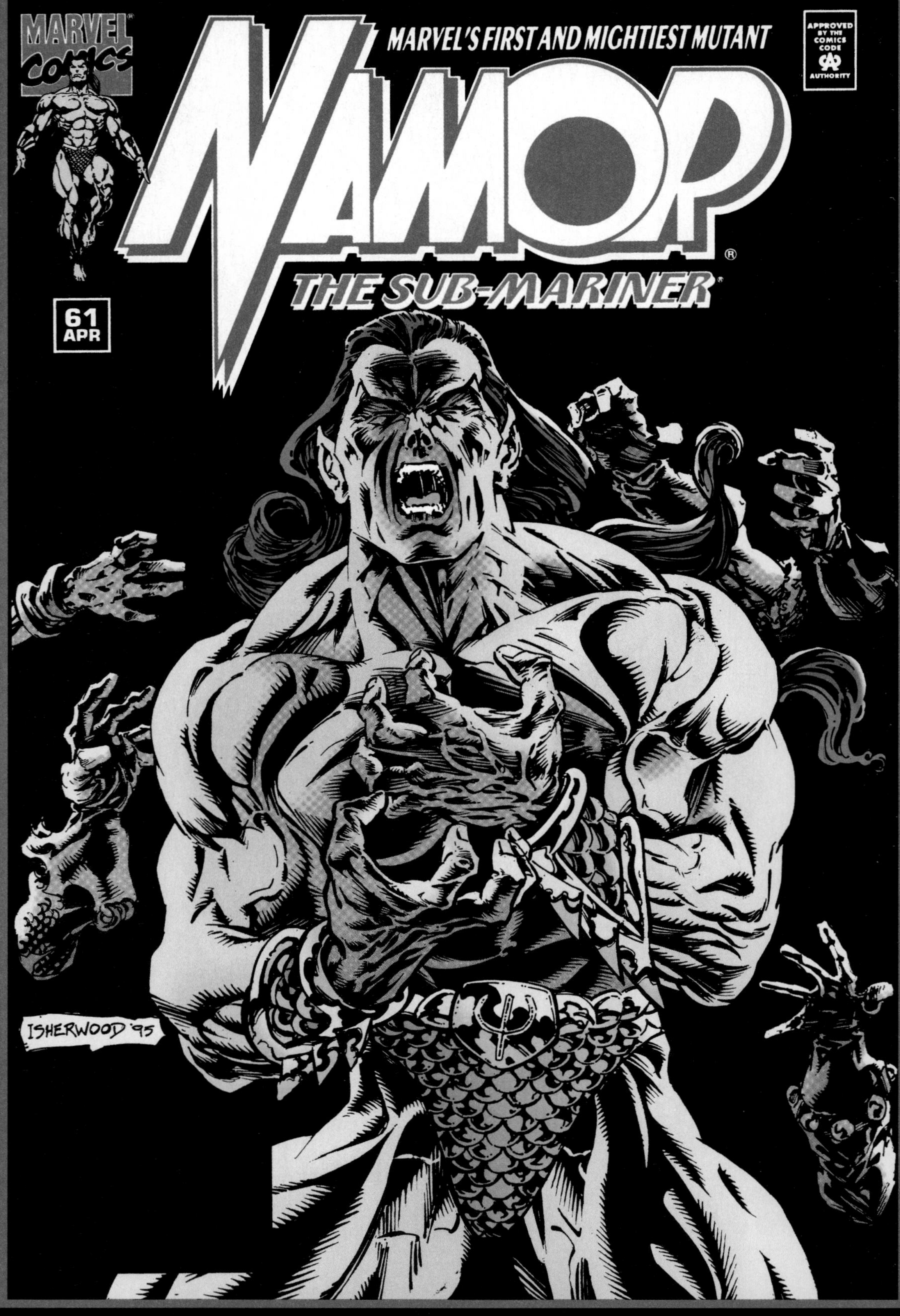
MARVEL COMICS
MARVEL'S FIRST AND MIGHTIEST MUTANT
APPROVED BY THE COMICS CODE AUTHORITY
NAMOR
THE SUB-MARINER
61
APR
ISHERWOOD '95

SCION OF AN AIR-BREATHING FATHER AND A WATER-BREATHING MOTHER, GIFTED WITH SUPERHUMAN STRENGTH AND THE POWER OF FLIGHT, THE AVENGING SON OF ATLANTIS HAS BATTLED FOR AND AGAINST HUMANITY SINCE WORLD WAR II! NOW, THE WEALTH OF THE ETERNAL SEAS AT HIS COMMAND, HE HAS SET UP A NEW CAMPAIGN OF CONQUEST. . .AGAINST THE ENEMIES OF THE ENVIRONMENT ITSELF! STAN LEE PRESENTS . . .

NAMOR, THE SUB-MARINER!

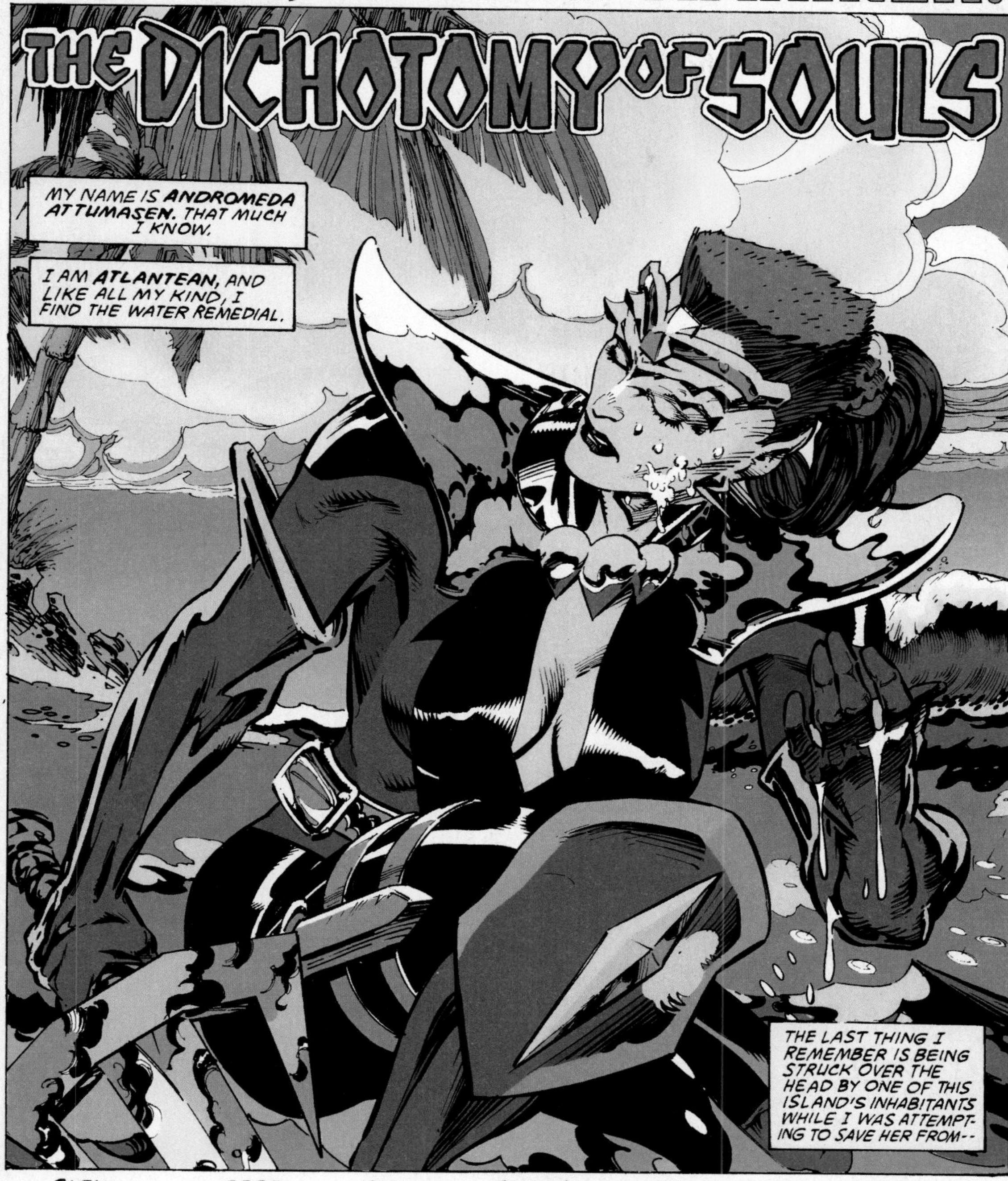
THE DICHOTOMY OF SOULS
MY NAME IS ANDROMEDA ATTUMASEN. THAT MUCH I KNOW.
I AM ATLANTEAN, AND LIKE ALL MY KIND, I FIND THE WATER REMEDIAL.
THE LAST THING I REMEMBER IS BEING STRUCK OVER THE HEAD BY ONE OF THIS ISLAND'S INHABITANTS WHILE I WAS ATTEMPTING TO SAVE HER FROM--

GLENN HERDLING WRITER · GEOF ISHERWOOD ARTIST · MICHUL HIGGINS LETTERER · GLYNIS OLIVER COLORIST · MIKE ROCKWITZ & RALPH MACCHIO EDITORS · MARK GRUENWALD NEPTUNE

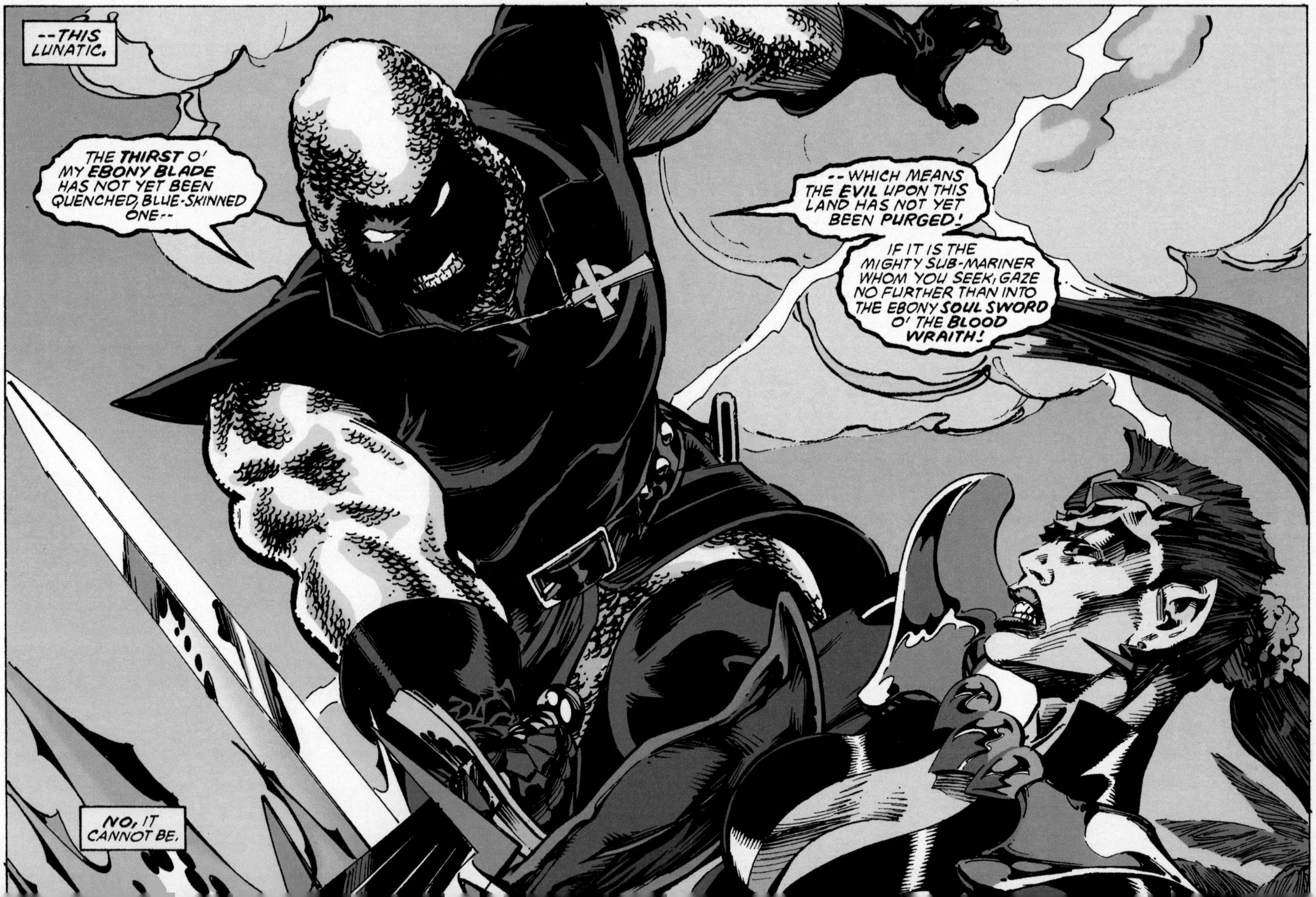
--THIS LUNATIC.
THE THIRST O' MY EBONY BLADE HAS NOT YET BEEN QUENCHED, BLUE-SKINNED ONE--
--WHICH MEANS THE EVIL UPON THIS LAND HAS NOT YET BEEN PURGED!
IF IT IS THE MIGHTY SUB-MARINER WHOM YOU SEEK, GAZE NO FURTHER THAN INTO THE EBONY SOUL SWORD O' THE BLOOD WRAITH!
NO, IT CANNOT BE.

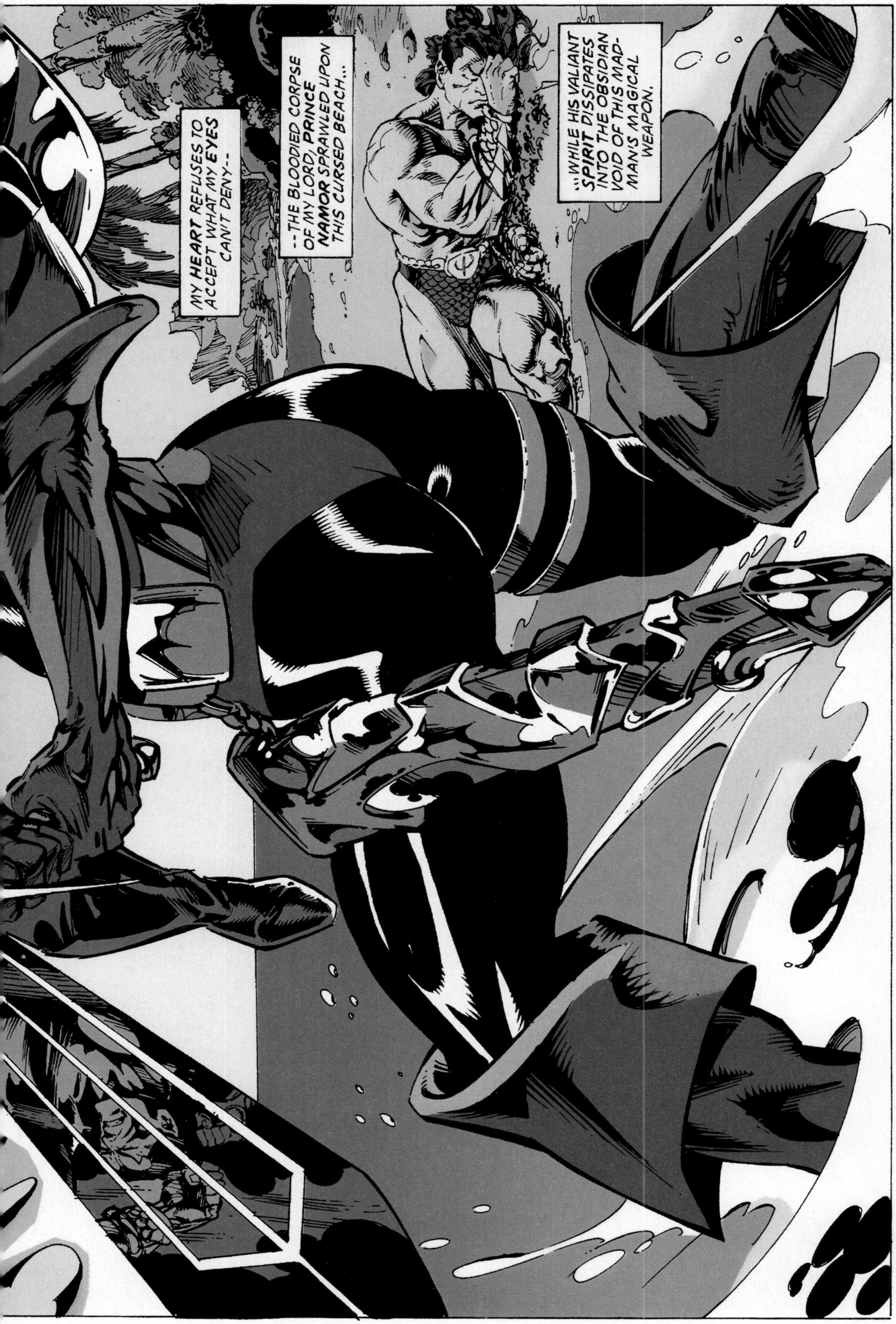
MY HEART REFUSES TO ACCEPT WHAT MY EYES CAN'T DENY--
--THE BLOODIED CORPSE OF MY LORD, PRINCE NAMOR SPRAWLED UPON THIS CURSED BEACH...
...WHILE HIS VALIANT SPIRIT DISSIPATES INTO THE OBSIDIAN VOID OF THIS MAGICAL MAN'S MAGICAL WEAPON.

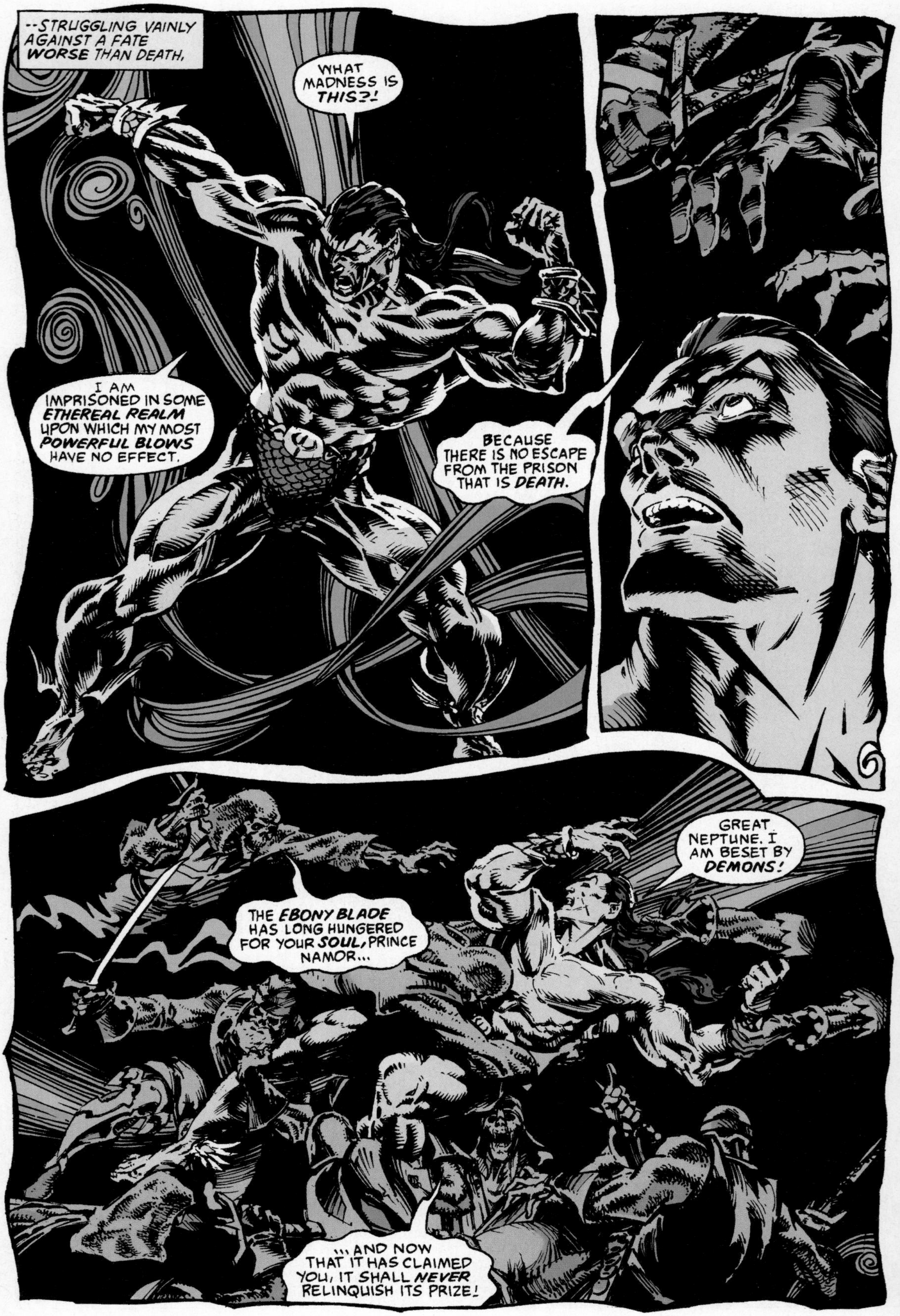
--STRUGGLING VAINLY AGAINST A FATE WORSE THAN DEATH.
WHAT MADNESS IS THIS?!
I AM IMPRISONED IN SOME ETHEREAL REALM UPON WHICH MY MOST POWERFUL BLOWS HAVE NO EFFECT.
BECAUSE THERE IS NO ESCAPE FROM THE PRISON THAT IS DEATH.
GREAT NEPTUNE. I AM BESET BY DEMONS!
THE EBONY BLADE HAS LONG HUNGERED FOR YOUR SOUL, PRINCE NAMOR...
...AND NOW THAT IT HAS CLAIMED YOU, IT SHALL NEVER RELINQUISH ITS PRIZE!

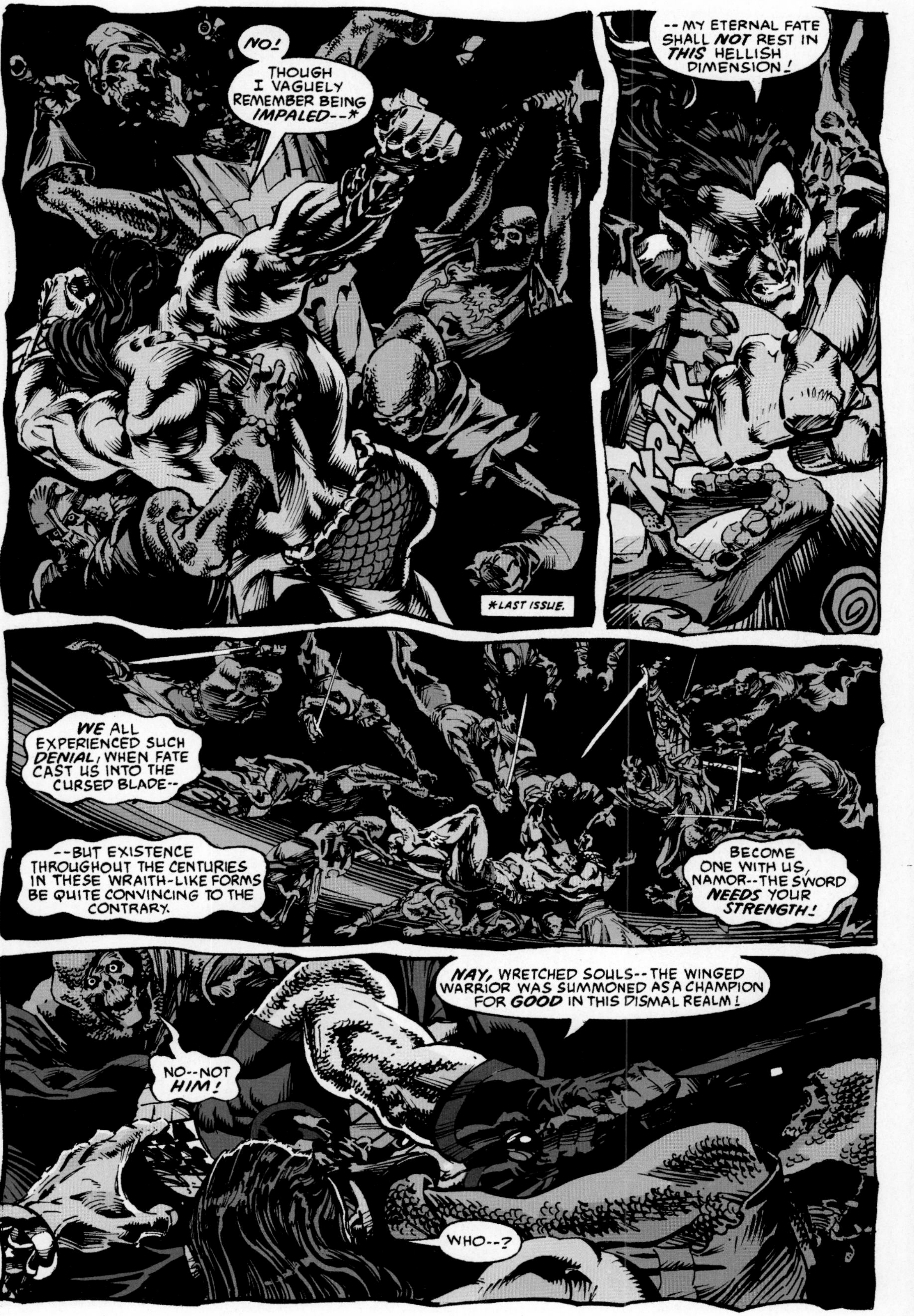
NO! THOUGH I VAGUELY REMEMBER BEING IMPALED--*
*LAST ISSUE.
--MY ETERNAL FATE SHALL NOT REST IN THIS HELLISH DIMENSION!
KRAK
WE ALL EXPERIENCED SUCH DENIAL, WHEN FATE CAST US INTO THE CURSED BLADE--
--BUT EXISTENCE THROUGHOUT THE CENTURIES IN THESE WRAITH-LIKE FORMS BE QUITE CONVINCING TO THE CONTRARY.
BECOME ONE WITH US, NAMOR--THE SWORD NEEDS YOUR STRENGTH!
NAY, WRETCHED SOULS--THE WINGED WARRIOR WAS SUMMONED AS A CHAMPION FOR GOOD IN THIS DISMAL REALM!
NO--NOT HIM!
WHO--?

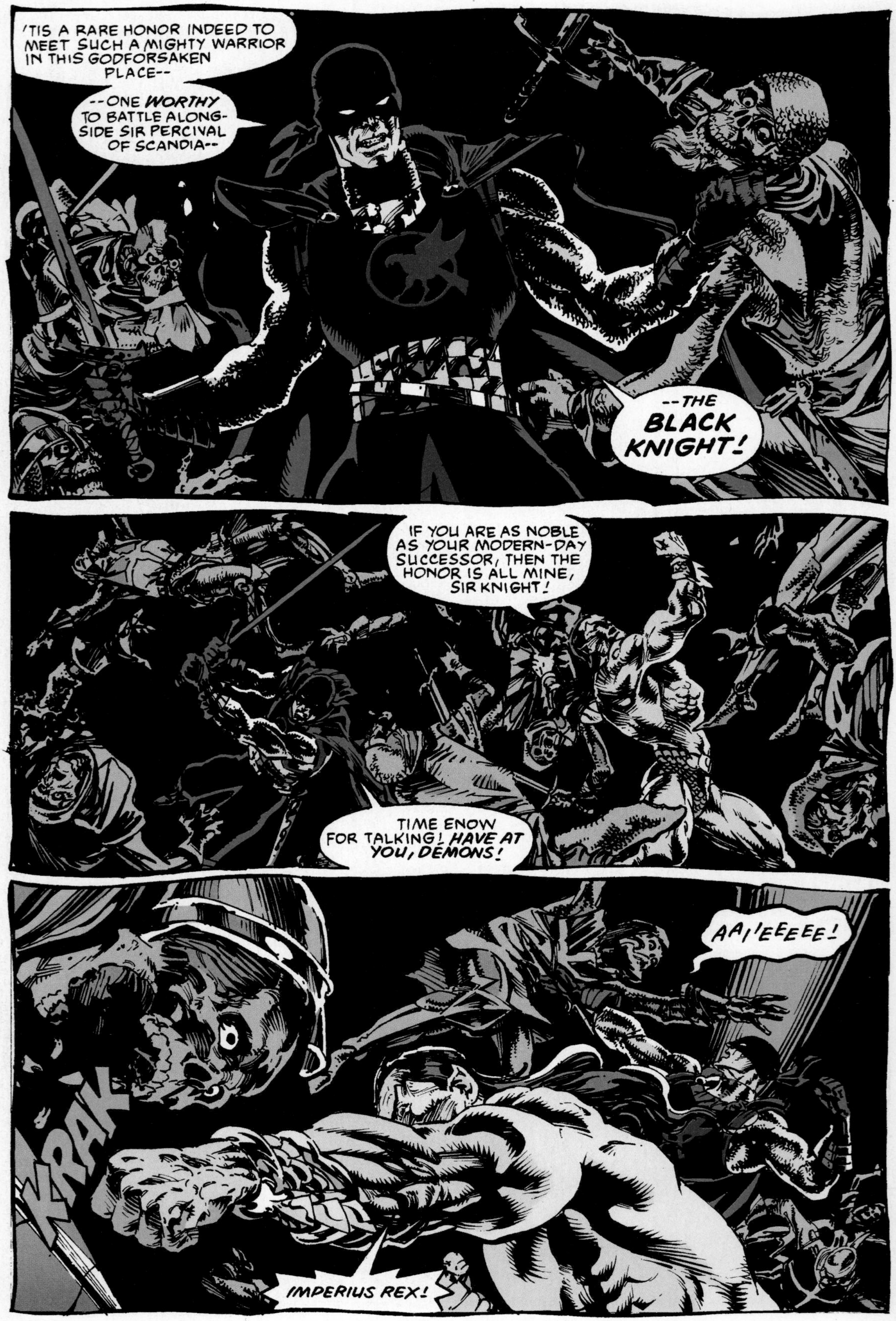

'TIS A RARE HONOR INDEED TO MEET SUCH A MIGHTY WARRIOR IN THIS GODFORSAKEN PLACE--
--ONE WORTHY TO BATTLE ALONGSIDE SIR PERCIVAL OF SCANDIA--
--THE BLACK KNIGHT!
IF YOU ARE AS NOBLE AS YOUR MODERN-DAY SUCCESSOR, THEN THE HONOR IS ALL MINE, SIR KNIGHT!
TIME ENOW FOR TALKING! HAVE AT YOU, DEMONS!
AAIIEEEEE!
KRAK
IMPERIUS REX!

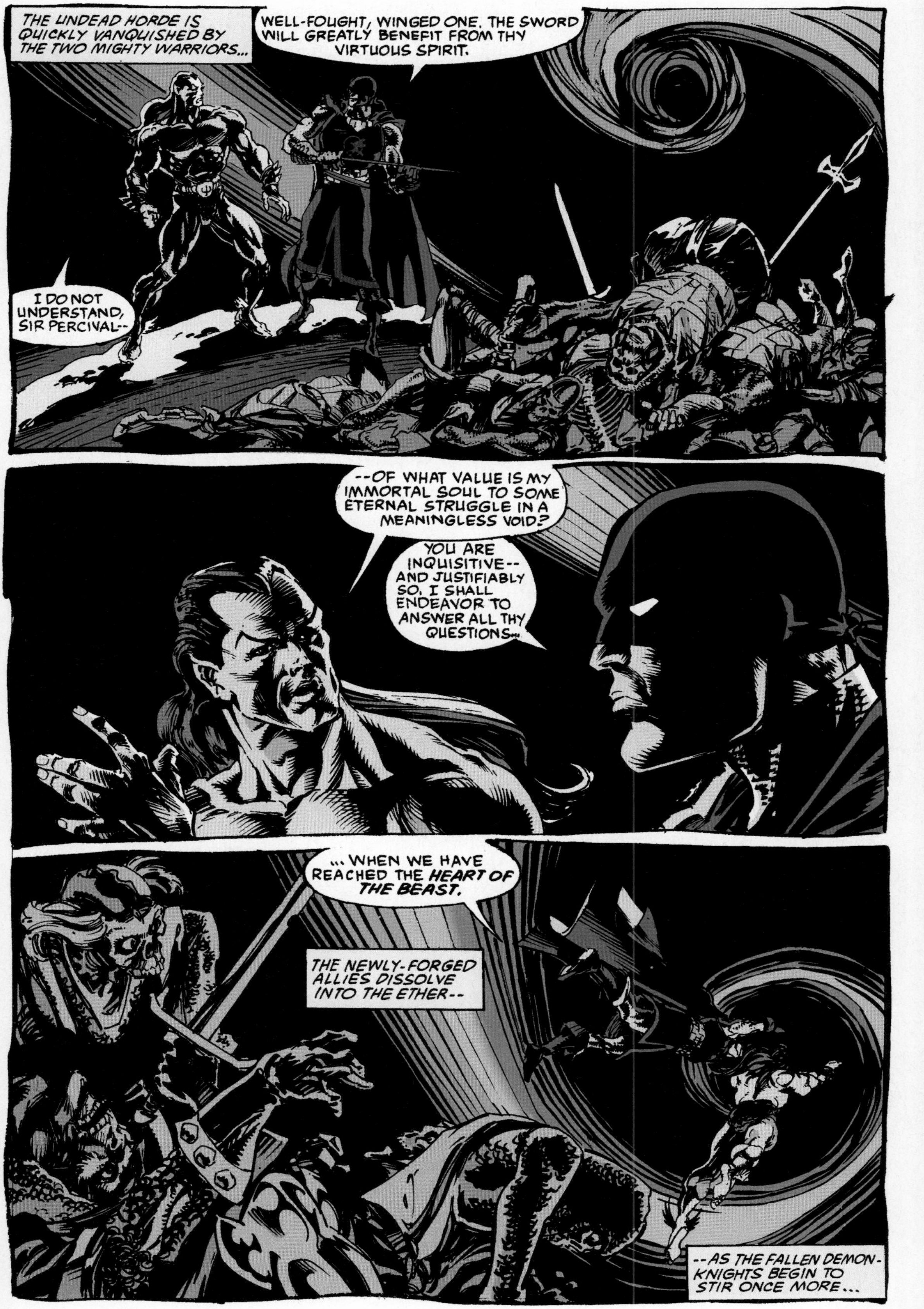
THE UNDEAD HORDE IS QUICKLY VANQUISHED BY THE TWO MIGHTY WARRIORS...
WELL-FOUGHT, WINGED ONE. THE SWORD WILL GREATLY BENEFIT FROM THY VIRTUOUS SPIRIT.
I DO NOT UNDERSTAND, SIR PERCIVAL--
--OF WHAT VALUE IS MY IMMORTAL SOUL TO SOME ETERNAL STRUGGLE IN A MEANINGLESS VOID?
YOU ARE INQUISITIVE-- AND JUSTIFIABLY SO. I SHALL ENDEAVOR TO ANSWER ALL THY QUESTIONS...
...WHEN WE HAVE REACHED THE HEART OF THE BEAST.
THE NEWLY-FORGED ALLIES DISSOLVE INTO THE ETHER--
--AS THE FALLEN DEMON-KNIGHTS BEGIN TO STIR ONCE MORE...

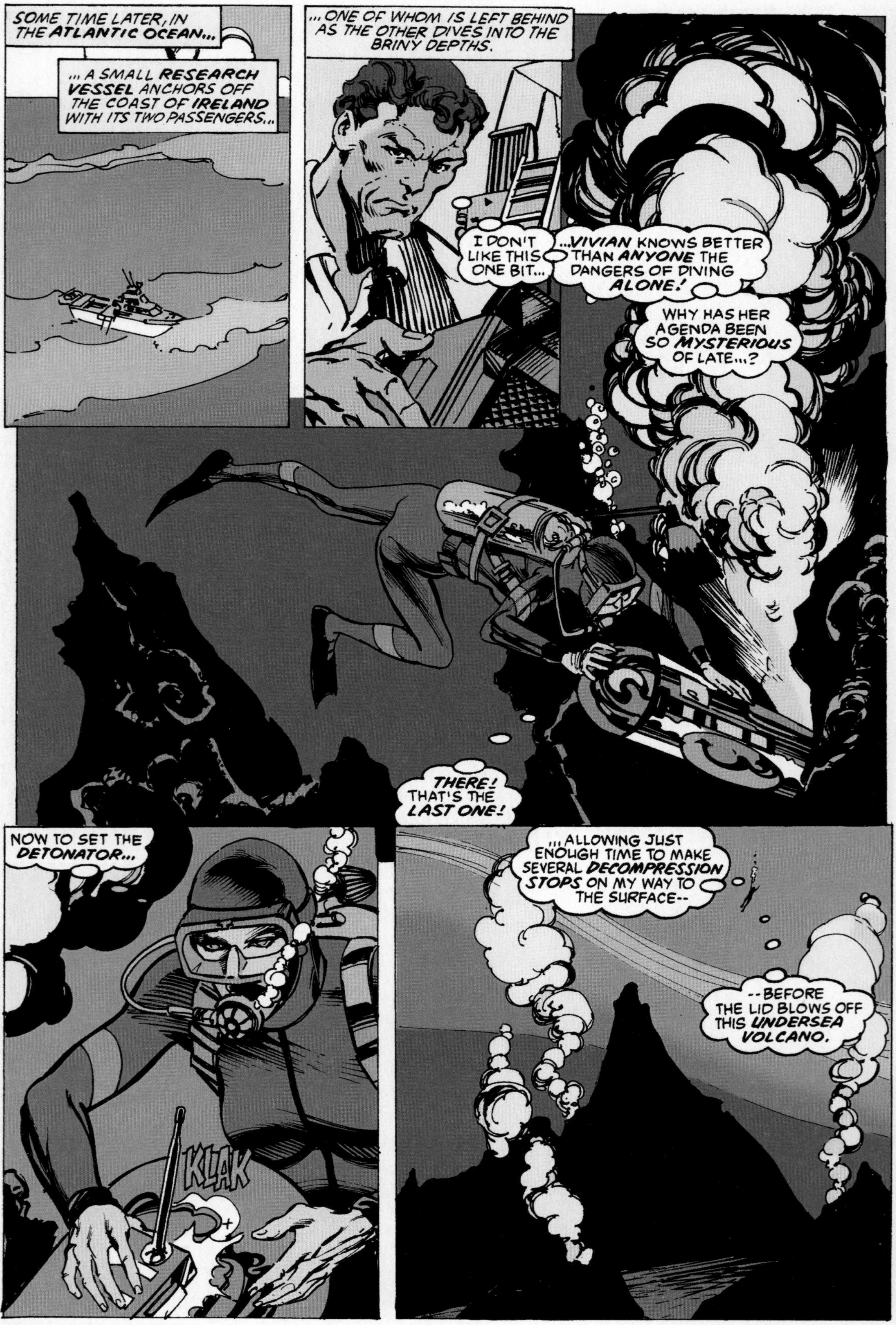

SOME TIME LATER, IN THE ATLANTIC OCEAN...
...A SMALL RESEARCH VESSEL ANCHORS OFF THE COAST OF IRELAND WITH ITS TWO PASSENGERS...
...ONE OF WHOM IS LEFT BEHIND AS THE OTHER DIVES INTO THE BRINY DEPTHS.
I DON'T LIKE THIS ONE BIT...
...VIVIAN KNOWS BETTER THAN ANYONE THE DANGERS OF DIVING ALONE!
WHY HAS HER AGENDA BEEN SO MYSTERIOUS OF LATE...?
THERE! THAT'S THE LAST ONE!
NOW TO SET THE DETONATOR...
KLAK
...ALLOWING JUST ENOUGH TIME TO MAKE SEVERAL DECOMPRESSION STOPS ON MY WAY TO THE SURFACE--
--BEFORE THE LID BLOWS OFF THIS UNDERSEA VOLCANO.

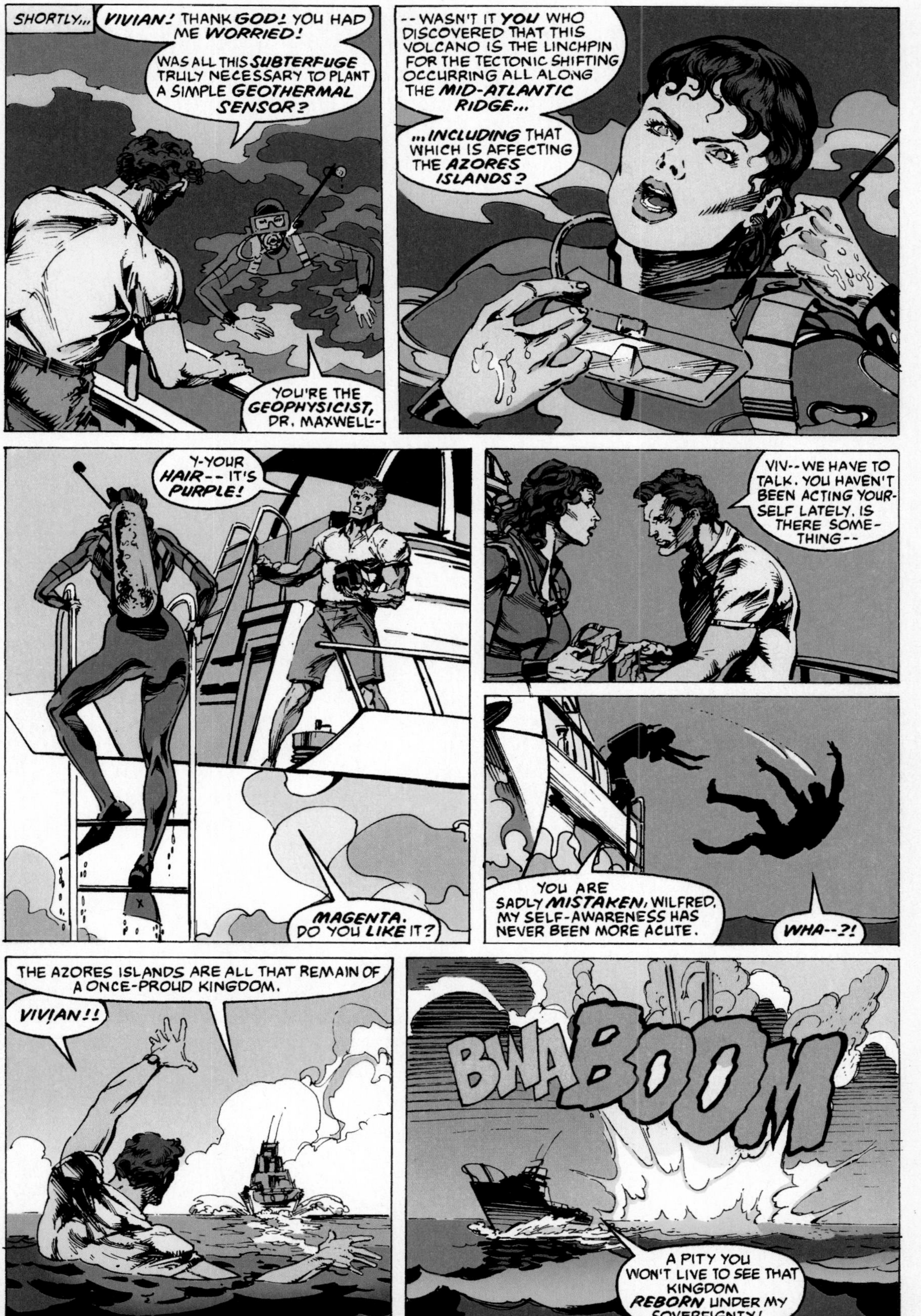
SHORTLY...
VIVIAN! THANK GOD! YOU HAD ME WORRIED!
WAS ALL THIS SUBTERFUGE TRULY NECESSARY TO PLANT A SIMPLE GEOTHERMAL SENSOR?
YOU'RE THE GEOPHYSICIST, DR. MAXWELL-
--WASN'T IT YOU WHO DISCOVERED THAT THIS VOLCANO IS THE LINCHPIN FOR THE TECTONIC SHIFTING OCCURRING ALL ALONG THE MID-ATLANTIC RIDGE...
...INCLUDING THAT WHICH IS AFFECTING THE AZORES ISLANDS?
Y-YOUR HAIR-- IT'S PURPLE!
MAGENTA. DO YOU LIKE IT?
VIV--WE HAVE TO TALK. YOU HAVEN'T BEEN ACTING YOURSELF LATELY. IS THERE SOMETHING--
YOU ARE SADLY MISTAKEN, WILFRED. MY SELF-AWARENESS HAS NEVER BEEN MORE ACUTE.
WHA--?!
THE AZORES ISLANDS ARE ALL THAT REMAIN OF A ONCE-PROUD KINGDOM.
VIVIAN!!
BWABOOM
A PITY YOU WON'T LIVE TO SEE THAT KINGDOM REBORN UNDER MY SOVEREIGNTY!

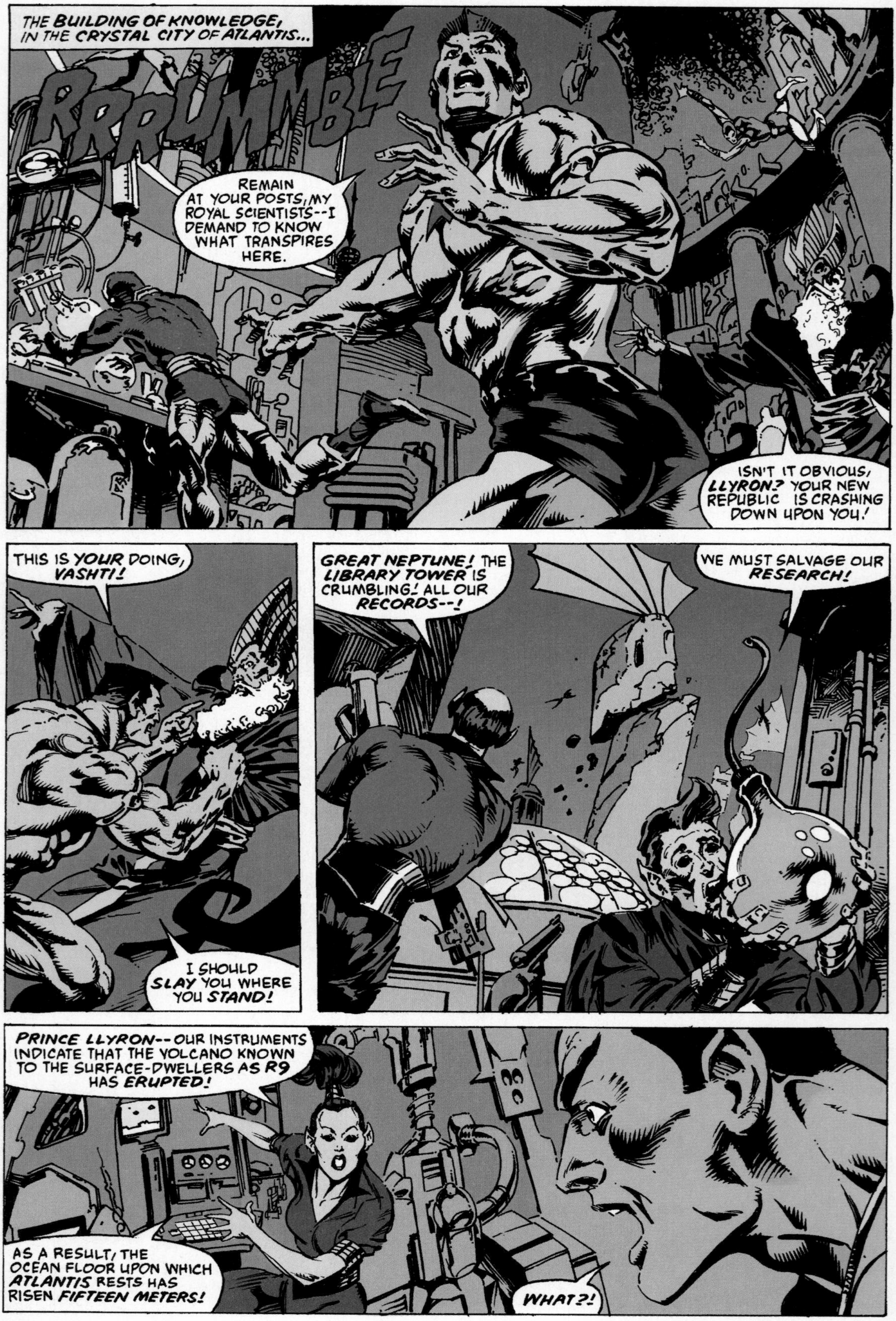
THE BUILDING OF KNOWLEDGE, IN THE CRYSTAL CITY OF ATLANTIS...
RRRUMMBLE
REMAIN AT YOUR POSTS, MY ROYAL SCIENTISTS--I DEMAND TO KNOW WHAT TRANSPIRES HERE.
ISN'T IT OBVIOUS, LLYRON? YOUR NEW REPUBLIC IS CRASHING DOWN UPON YOU!
THIS IS YOUR DOING, VASHTI!
I SHOULD SLAY YOU WHERE YOU STAND!
GREAT NEPTUNE! THE LIBRARY TOWER IS CRUMBLING! ALL OUR RECORDS--!
WE MUST SALVAGE OUR RESEARCH!
PRINCE LLYRON--OUR INSTRUMENTS INDICATE THAT THE VOLCANO KNOWN TO THE SURFACE-DWELLERS AS R9 HAS ERUPTED!
AS A RESULT, THE OCEAN FLOOR UPON WHICH ATLANTIS RESTS HAS RISEN FIFTEEN METERS!
WHAT?!

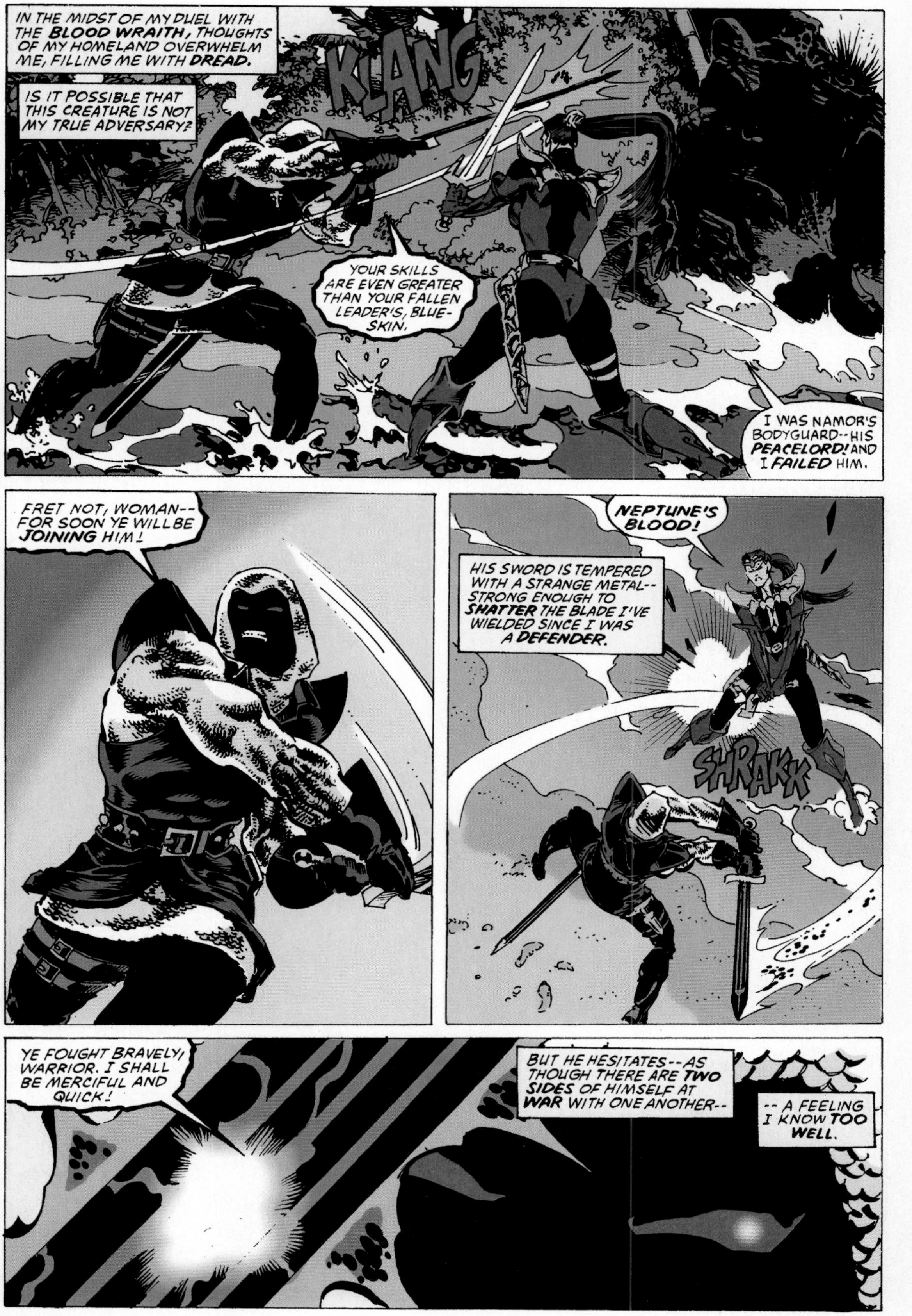

IN THE MIDST OF MY DUEL WITH THE BLOOD WRAITH, THOUGHTS OF MY HOMELAND OVERWHELM ME, FILLING ME WITH DREAD.
KLANG
IS IT POSSIBLE THAT THIS CREATURE IS NOT MY TRUE ADVERSARY?
YOUR SKILLS ARE EVEN GREATER THAN YOUR FALLEN LEADER'S, BLUE-SKIN.
I WAS NAMOR'S BODYGUARD--HIS PEACELORD! AND I FAILED HIM.
FRET NOT, WOMAN--FOR SOON YE WILL BE JOINING HIM!
NEPTUNE'S BLOOD!
HIS SWORD IS TEMPERED WITH A STRANGE METAL--STRONG ENOUGH TO SHATTER THE BLADE I'VE WIELDED SINCE I WAS A DEFENDER.
SHRAKK
YE FOUGHT BRAVELY, WARRIOR. I SHALL BE MERCIFUL AND QUICK!
BUT HE HESITATES--AS THOUGH THERE ARE TWO SIDES OF HIMSELF AT WAR WITH ONE ANOTHER--
--A FEELING I KNOW TOO WELL.

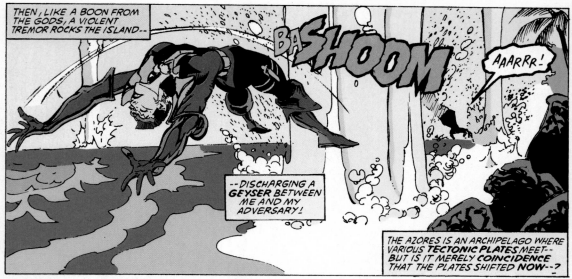

THEN, LIKE A BOON FROM THE GODS, A VIOLENT TREMOR ROCKS THE ISLAND--

BaSHOOM

AAARRR!

--DISCHARGING A GEYSER BETWEEN ME AND MY ADVERSARY!

THE AZORES IS AN ARCHIPELAGO WHERE VARIOUS TECTONIC PLATES MEET-- BUT IS IT MERELY COINCIDENCE THAT THE PLATES SHIFTED NOW--?

NAMOR.

OH, MY HANDSOME PRINCE-- THERE IS SO MUCH I NEVER TOLD YOU ABOUT MYSELF...

...ABOUT MY FEELINGS FOR YOU.

...SO MUCH THAT WILL NEVER BE SAID, BE- CAUSE THE WARRIOR INSIDE ME BELIEVED SHE HAD TO JUSTIFY HER EXISTENCE.

NOW THAT WARRIOR INSTINCT CALLS TO ME AGAIN-- NAMOR'S ORICHALCUM SWORD.

KLANK

CURSE YOUR LUCK, WOMAN!

BLOOD WRAITH'S BACK--

44

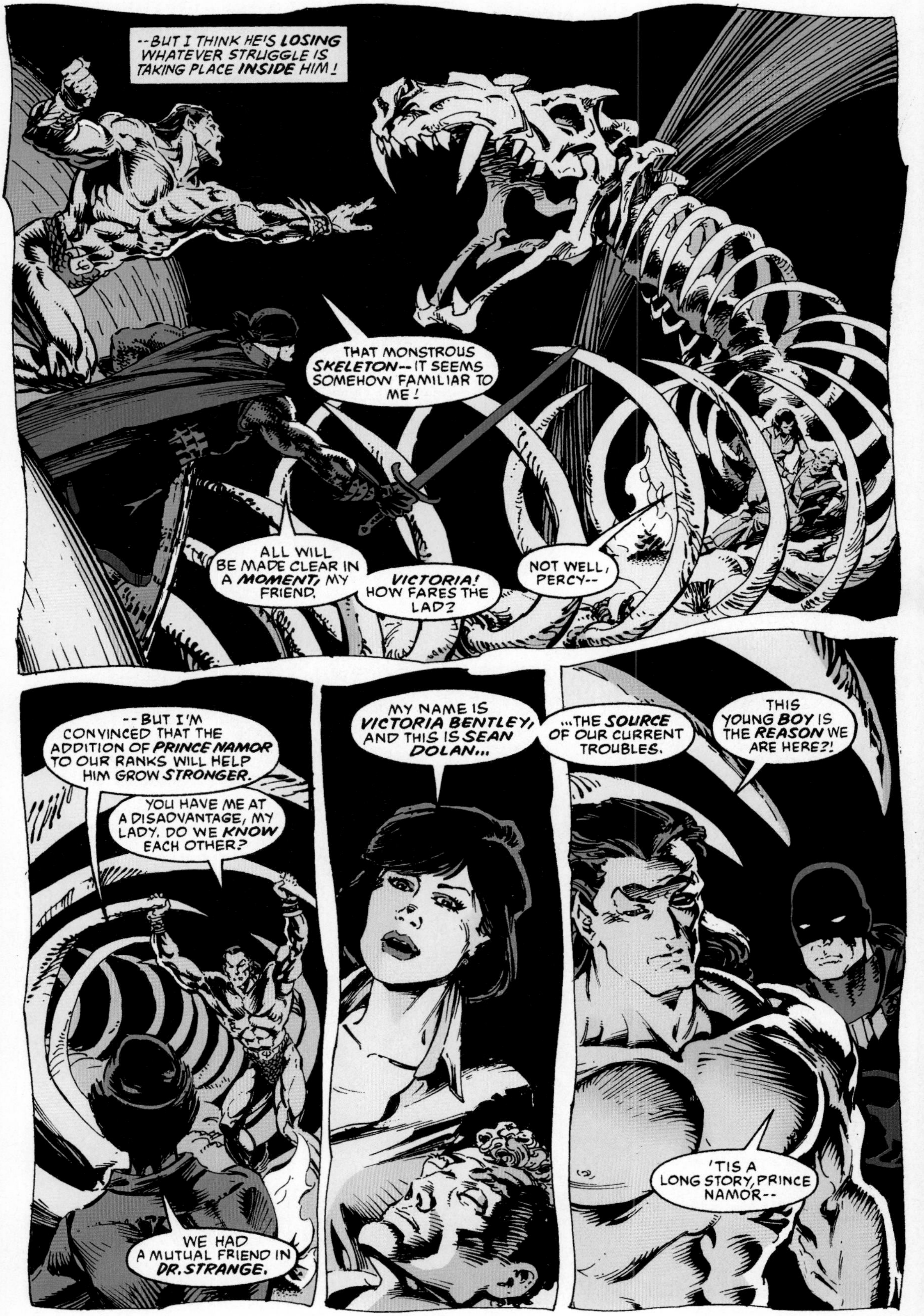
--BUT I THINK HE'S LOSING WHATEVER STRUGGLE IS TAKING PLACE INSIDE HIM!
THAT MONSTROUS SKELETON--IT SEEMS SOMEHOW FAMILIAR TO ME!
ALL WILL BE MADE CLEAR IN A MOMENT, MY FRIEND.
VICTORIA! HOW FARES THE LAD?
NOT WELL, PERCY--
--BUT I'M CONVINCED THAT THE ADDITION OF PRINCE NAMOR TO OUR RANKS WILL HELP HIM GROW STRONGER.
YOU HAVE ME AT A DISADVANTAGE, MY LADY. DO WE KNOW EACH OTHER?
WE HAD A MUTUAL FRIEND IN DR. STRANGE.
MY NAME IS VICTORIA BENTLEY, AND THIS IS SEAN DOLAN...
...THE SOURCE OF OUR CURRENT TROUBLES.
THIS YOUNG BOY IS THE REASON WE ARE HERE?!
'TIS A LONG STORY, PRINCE NAMOR--

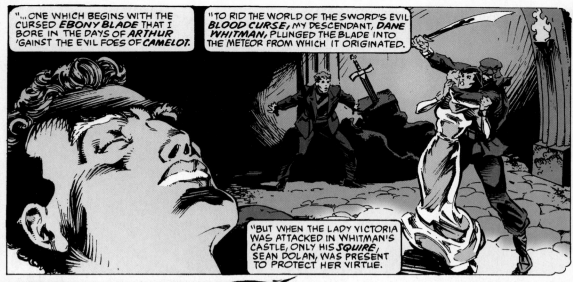

"...ONE WHICH BEGINS WITH THE CURSED *EBONY BLADE* THAT I BORE IN THE DAYS OF *ARTHUR* 'GAINST THE EVIL FOES OF *CAMELOT.*

"TO RID THE WORLD OF THE SWORD'S EVIL *BLOOD CURSE,* MY DESCENDANT, *DANE WHITMAN,* PLUNGED THE BLADE INTO THE METEOR FROM WHICH IT ORIGINATED.

"BUT WHEN THE LADY VICTORIA WAS ATTACKED IN WHITMAN'S CASTLE, ONLY HIS *SQUIRE,* SEAN DOLAN, WAS PRESENT TO PROTECT HER VIRTUE.

"WITHOUT THINKING, THE LAD HEAVED THE *SWORD* FROM THE STONE--

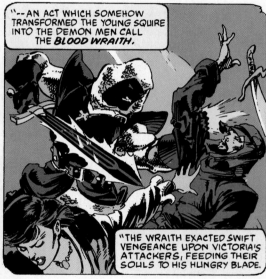

"--AN ACT WHICH SOMEHOW TRANSFORMED THE YOUNG SQUIRE INTO THE DEMON MEN CALL THE *BLOOD WRAITH.*

"THE WRAITH EXACTED SWIFT VENGEANCE UPON VICTORIA'S ATTACKERS, FEEDING THEIR SOULS TO HIS HUNGRY BLADE.

"SCANT WEEKS LATER, SEAN FOUND HIMSELF IN A *THREE-WAY DUEL* OPPOSITE DANE WHITMAN AND A GARISH JESTER.

"THE BLOOD WRAITH BESTED HIS FORMER MASTER AND WOULD HAVE SLAIN HIM--

"--HAD IT NOT BEEN FOR LADY VICTORIA'S SELF-SACRIFICING INTERVENTION."*

* THE PRECEDING FLASHBACK COURTESY OF *AVENGERS ANNUAL #22* AND *AVENGERS #366.*

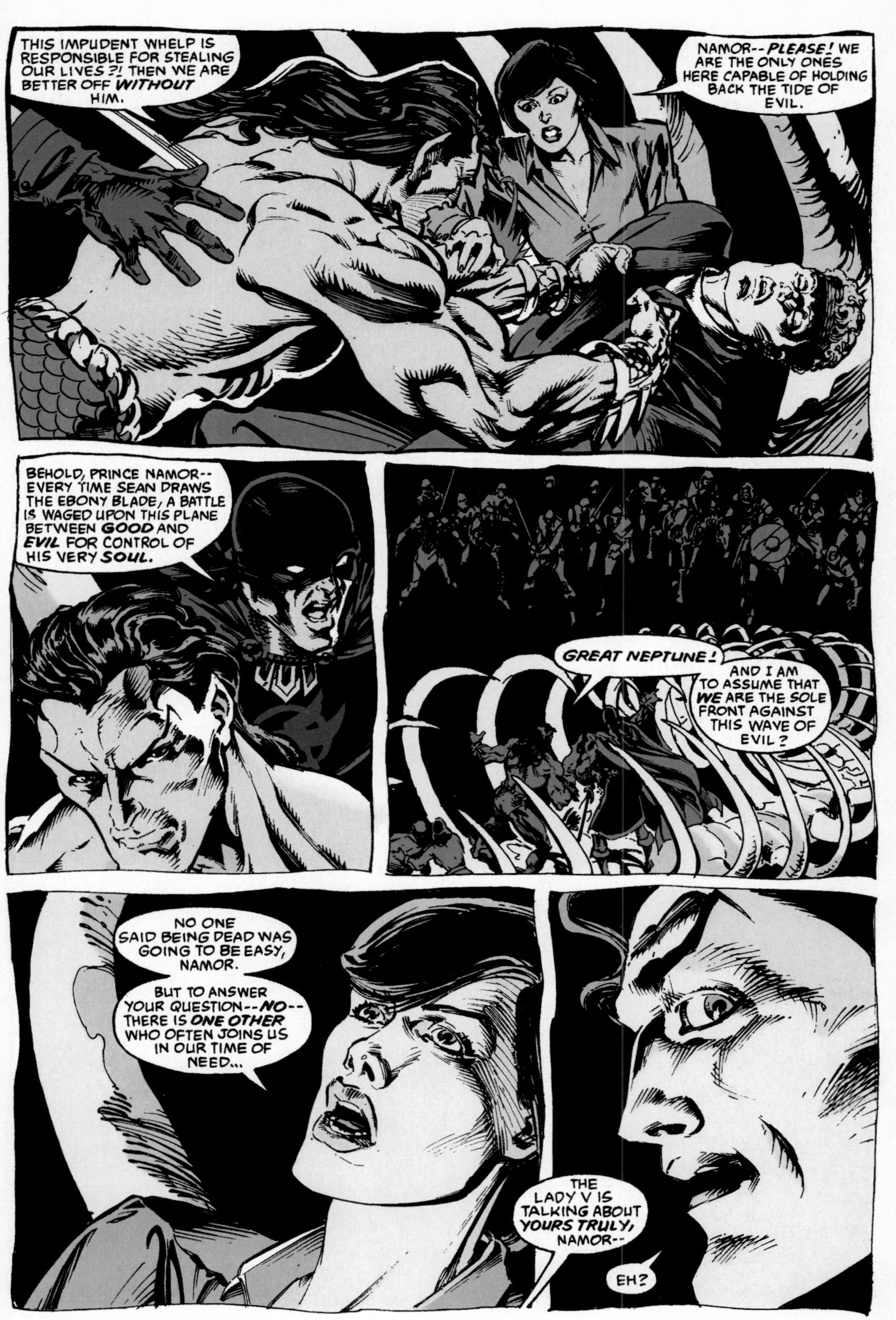

THIS IMPUDENT WHELP IS RESPONSIBLE FOR STEALING OUR LIVES ?! THEN WE ARE BETTER OFF **WITHOUT** HIM.
NAMOR-- **PLEASE!** WE ARE THE ONLY ONES HERE CAPABLE OF HOLDING BACK THE TIDE OF EVIL.
BEHOLD, PRINCE NAMOR-- EVERY TIME SEAN DRAWS THE EBONY BLADE, A BATTLE IS WAGED UPON THIS PLANE BETWEEN **GOOD** AND **EVIL** FOR CONTROL OF HIS VERY **SOUL.**
GREAT NEPTUNE!
AND I AM TO ASSUME THAT **WE** ARE THE SOLE FRONT AGAINST THIS WAVE OF EVIL?
NO ONE SAID BEING DEAD WAS GOING TO BE EASY, NAMOR.
BUT TO ANSWER YOUR QUESTION-- **NO**-- THERE IS **ONE OTHER** WHO OFTEN JOINS US IN OUR TIME OF NEED...
THE LADY V IS TALKING ABOUT **YOURS TRULY,** NAMOR--
EH?

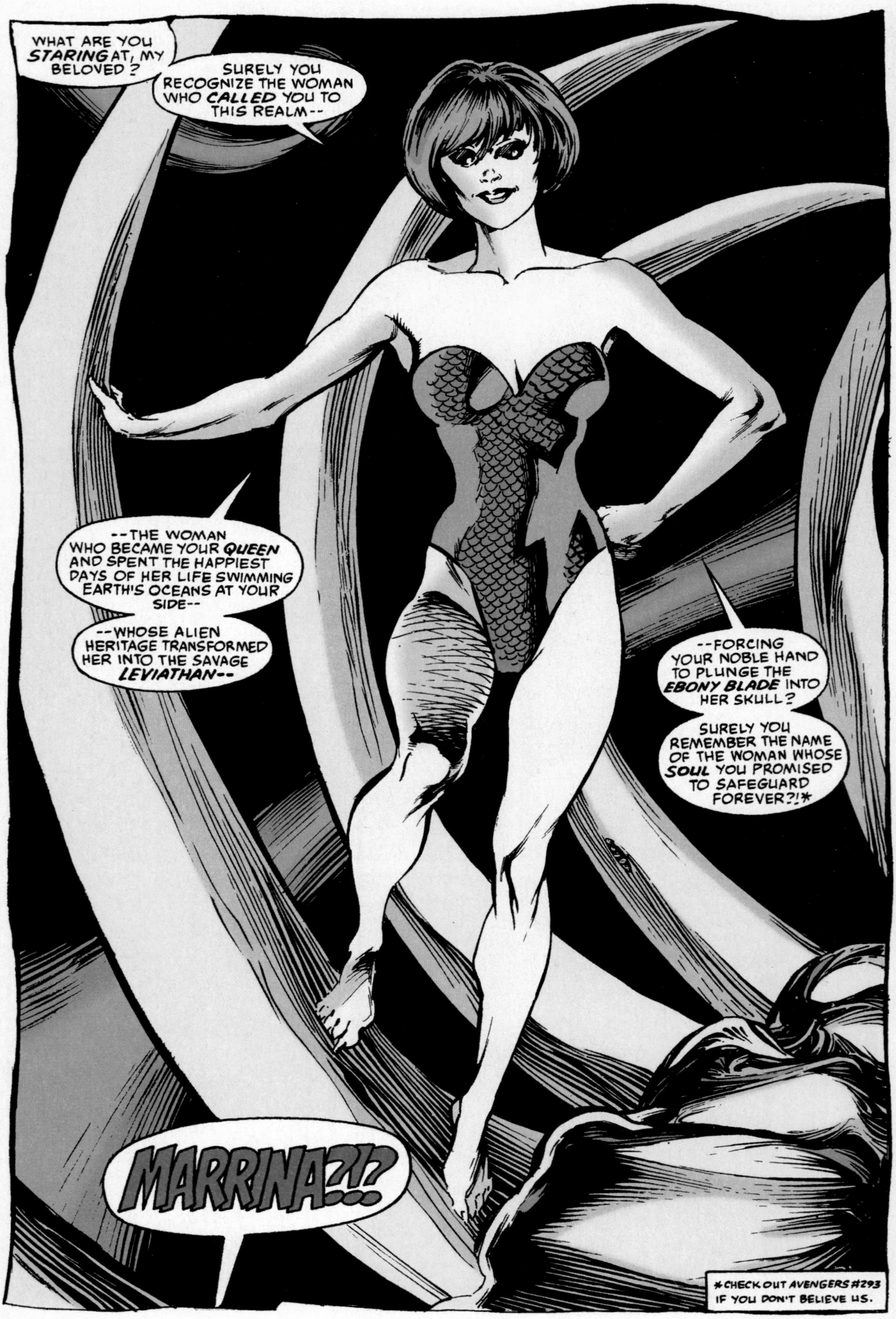
WHAT ARE YOU STARING AT, MY BELOVED?
SURELY YOU RECOGNIZE THE WOMAN WHO CALLED YOU TO THIS REALM--
--THE WOMAN WHO BECAME YOUR QUEEN AND SPENT THE HAPPIEST DAYS OF HER LIFE SWIMMING EARTH'S OCEANS AT YOUR SIDE--
--WHOSE ALIEN HERITAGE TRANSFORMED HER INTO THE SAVAGE LEVIATHAN--
--FORCING YOUR NOBLE HAND TO PLUNGE THE EBONY BLADE INTO HER SKULL?
SURELY YOU REMEMBER THE NAME OF THE WOMAN WHOSE SOUL YOU PROMISED TO SAFEGUARD FOREVER?!*
MARRINA?!?
*CHECK OUT AVENGERS #293 IF YOU DON'T BELIEVE US.

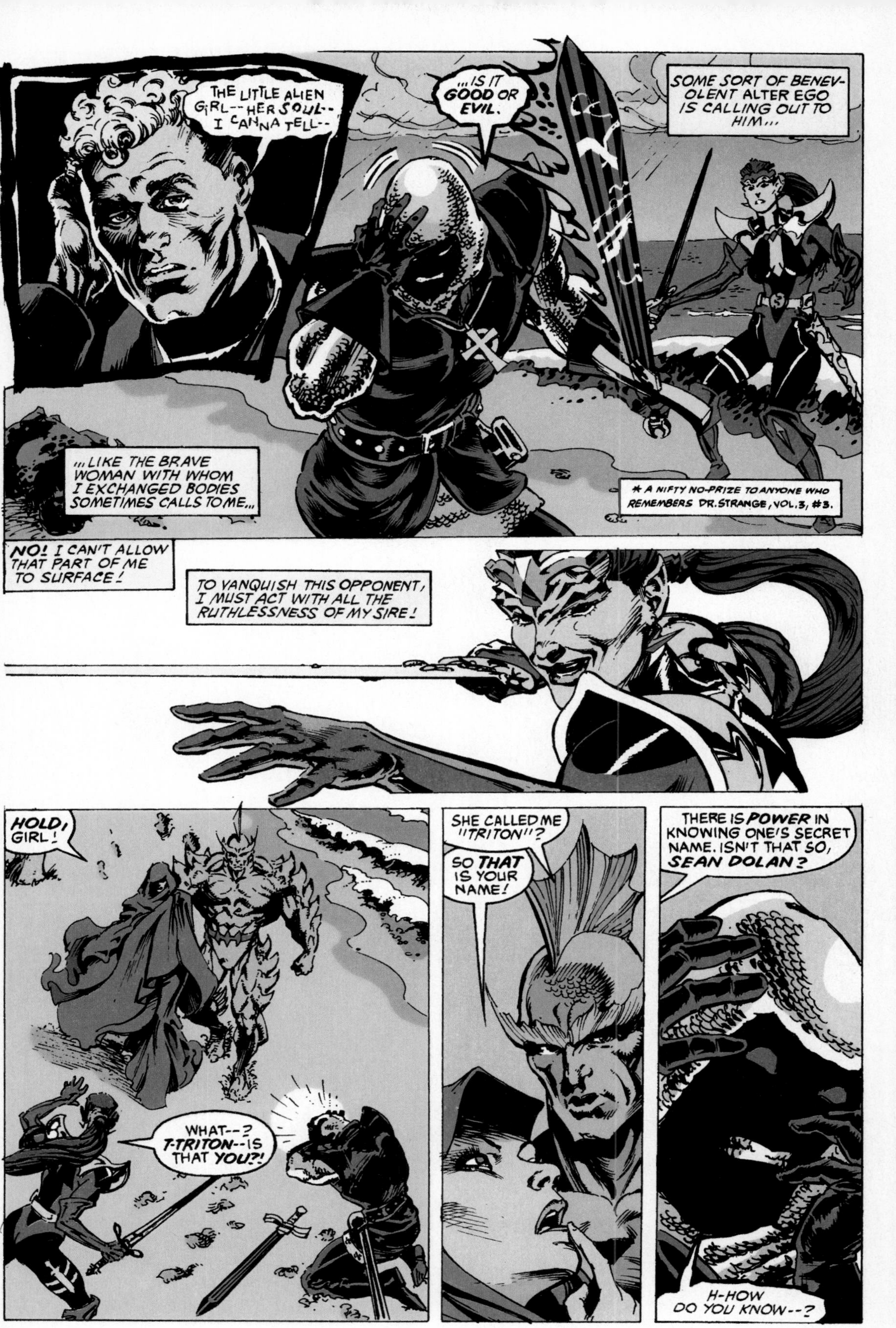
THE LITTLE ALIEN GIRL-- HER SOUL-- I CANNA TELL--
...IS IT GOOD OR EVIL.
SOME SORT OF BENEVOLENT ALTER EGO IS CALLING OUT TO HIM...
...LIKE THE BRAVE WOMAN WITH WHOM I EXCHANGED BODIES SOMETIMES CALLS TO ME...
* A NIFTY NO-PRIZE TO ANYONE WHO REMEMBERS DR. STRANGE, VOL.3, #3.
NO! I CAN'T ALLOW THAT PART OF ME TO SURFACE!
TO VANQUISH THIS OPPONENT, I MUST ACT WITH ALL THE RUTHLESSNESS OF MY SIRE!
HOLD, GIRL!
WHAT--? T-TRITON--IS THAT YOU?!
SHE CALLED ME "TRITON"?
SO THAT IS YOUR NAME!
THERE IS POWER IN KNOWING ONE'S SECRET NAME. ISN'T THAT SO, SEAN DOLAN?
H-HOW DO YOU KNOW--?

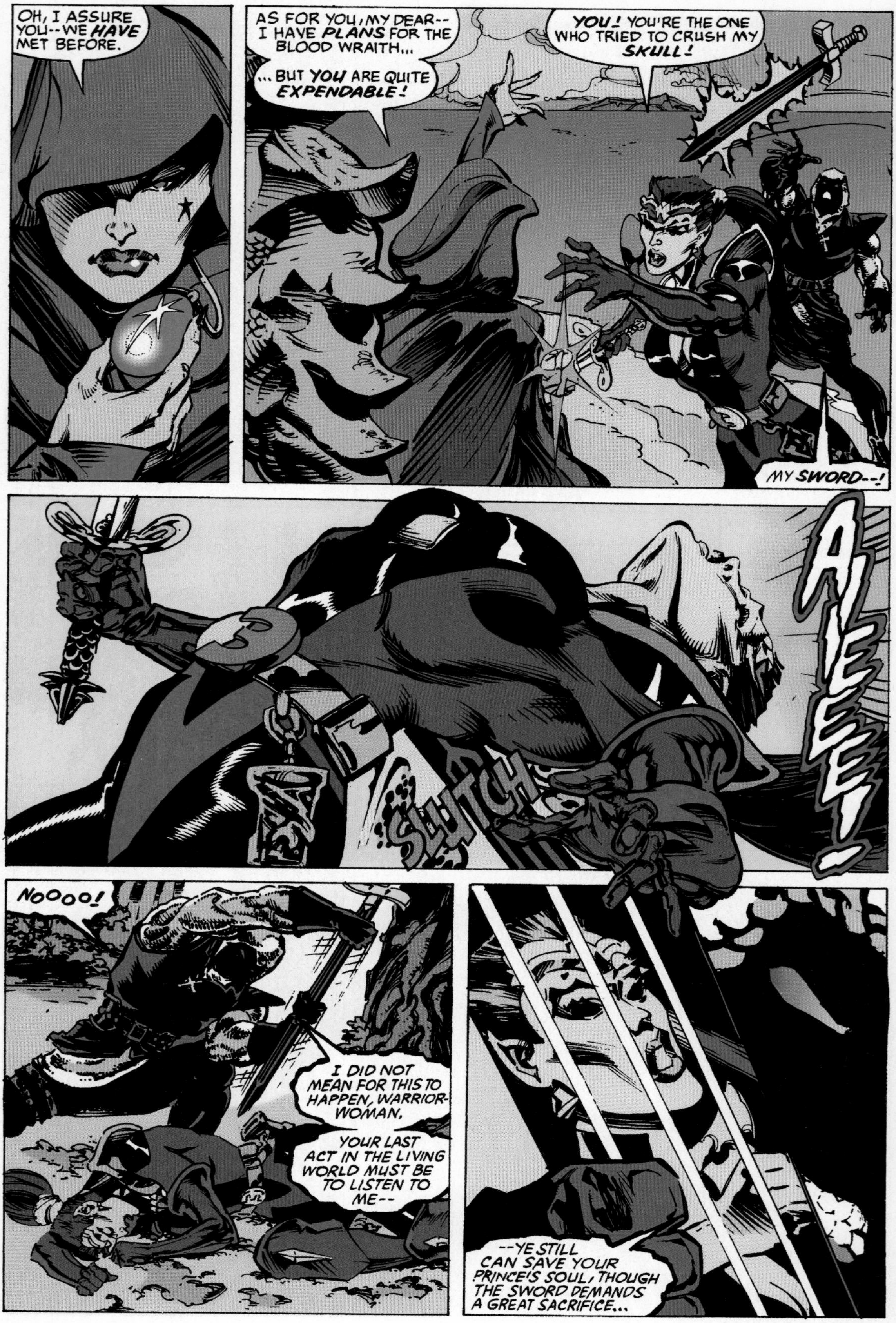
OH, I ASSURE YOU--WE HAVE MET BEFORE.
AS FOR YOU, MY DEAR-- I HAVE PLANS FOR THE BLOOD WRAITH...
...BUT YOU ARE QUITE EXPENDABLE!
YOU! YOU'RE THE ONE WHO TRIED TO CRUSH MY SKULL!
MY SWORD--!
AIEEEE!
SLUTCH
NOOOO!
I DID NOT MEAN FOR THIS TO HAPPEN, WARRIOR-WOMAN.
YOUR LAST ACT IN THE LIVING WORLD MUST BE TO LISTEN TO ME--
--YE STILL CAN SAVE YOUR PRINCE'S SOUL, THOUGH THE SWORD DEMANDS A GREAT SACRIFICE...

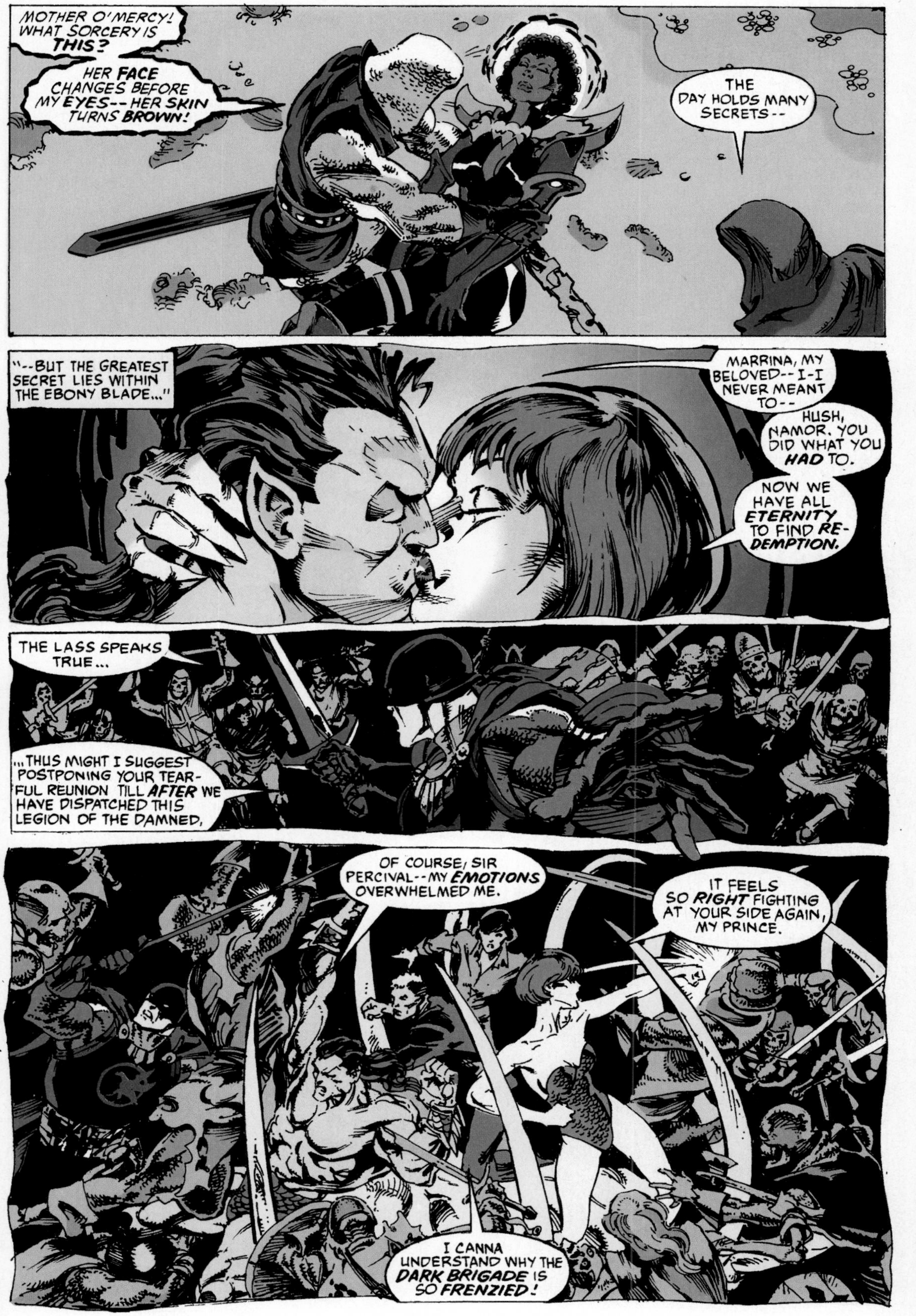
MOTHER O'MERCY! WHAT SORCERY IS THIS?
HER FACE CHANGES BEFORE MY EYES-- HER SKIN TURNS BROWN!
THE DAY HOLDS MANY SECRETS --
"--BUT THE GREATEST SECRET LIES WITHIN THE EBONY BLADE..."
MARRINA, MY BELOVED-- I-I NEVER MEANT TO--
HUSH, NAMOR. YOU DID WHAT YOU HAD TO.
NOW WE HAVE ALL ETERNITY TO FIND REDEMPTION.
THE LASS SPEAKS TRUE...
...THUS MIGHT I SUGGEST POSTPONING YOUR TEARFUL REUNION TILL AFTER WE HAVE DISPATCHED THIS LEGION OF THE DAMNED.
OF COURSE, SIR PERCIVAL--MY EMOTIONS OVERWHELMED ME.
IT FEELS SO RIGHT FIGHTING AT YOUR SIDE AGAIN, MY PRINCE.
I CANNA UNDERSTAND WHY THE DARK BRIGADE IS SO FRENZIED!

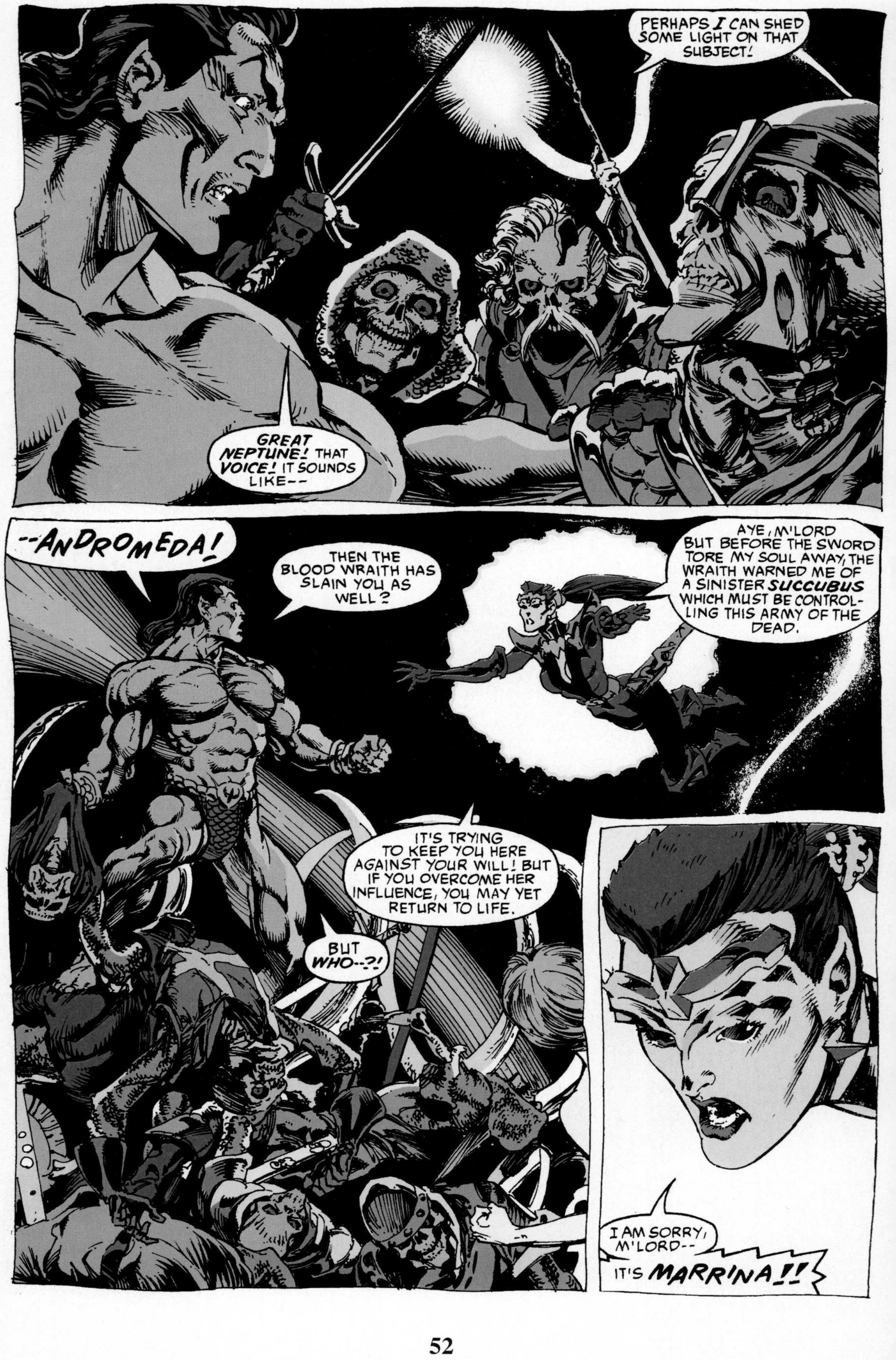
PERHAPS I CAN SHED SOME LIGHT ON THAT SUBJECT!
GREAT NEPTUNE! THAT VOICE! IT SOUNDS LIKE--
--ANDROMEDA!
THEN THE BLOOD WRAITH HAS SLAIN YOU AS WELL?
AYE, M'LORD BUT BEFORE THE SWORD TORE MY SOUL AWAY, THE WRAITH WARNED ME OF A SINISTER SUCCUBUS WHICH MUST BE CONTROLLING THIS ARMY OF THE DEAD.
IT'S TRYING TO KEEP YOU HERE AGAINST YOUR WILL! BUT IF YOU OVERCOME HER INFLUENCE, YOU MAY YET RETURN TO LIFE.
BUT WHO--?!
I AM SORRY, M'LORD--
IT'S MARRINA!!

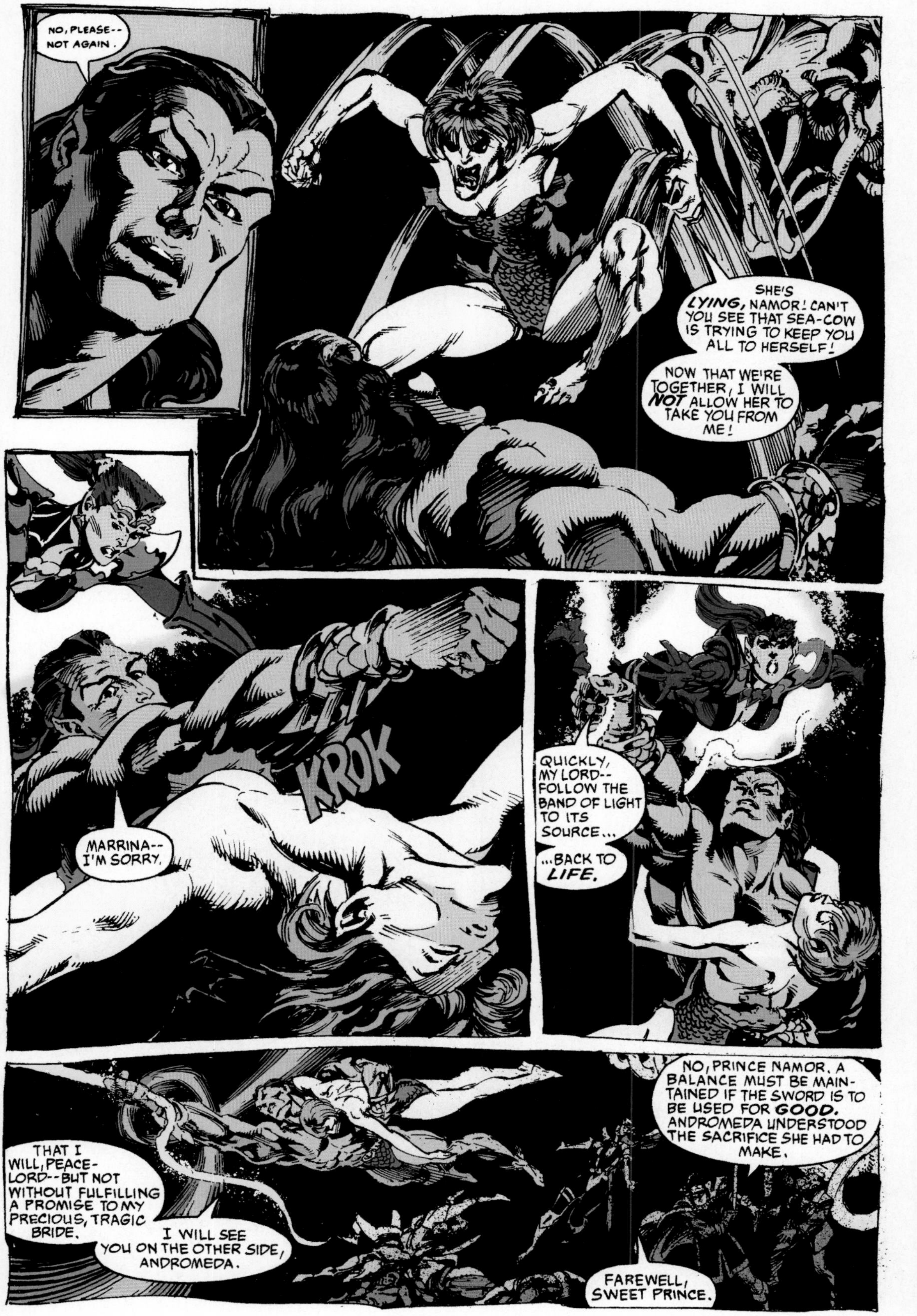

NO, PLEASE-- NOT AGAIN.
SHE'S LYING, NAMOR! CAN'T YOU SEE THAT SEA-COW IS TRYING TO KEEP YOU ALL TO HERSELF!
NOW THAT WE'RE TOGETHER, I WILL NOT ALLOW HER TO TAKE YOU FROM ME!
KROK
MARRINA-- I'M SORRY.
QUICKLY, MY LORD-- FOLLOW THE BAND OF LIGHT TO ITS SOURCE...
...BACK TO LIFE.
NO, PRINCE NAMOR. A BALANCE MUST BE MAINTAINED IF THE SWORD IS TO BE USED FOR GOOD. ANDROMEDA UNDERSTOOD THE SACRIFICE SHE HAD TO MAKE.
THAT I WILL, PEACE-LORD--BUT NOT WITHOUT FULFILLING A PROMISE TO MY PRECIOUS, TRAGIC BRIDE.
I WILL SEE YOU ON THE OTHER SIDE, ANDROMEDA.
FAREWELL, SWEET PRINCE.

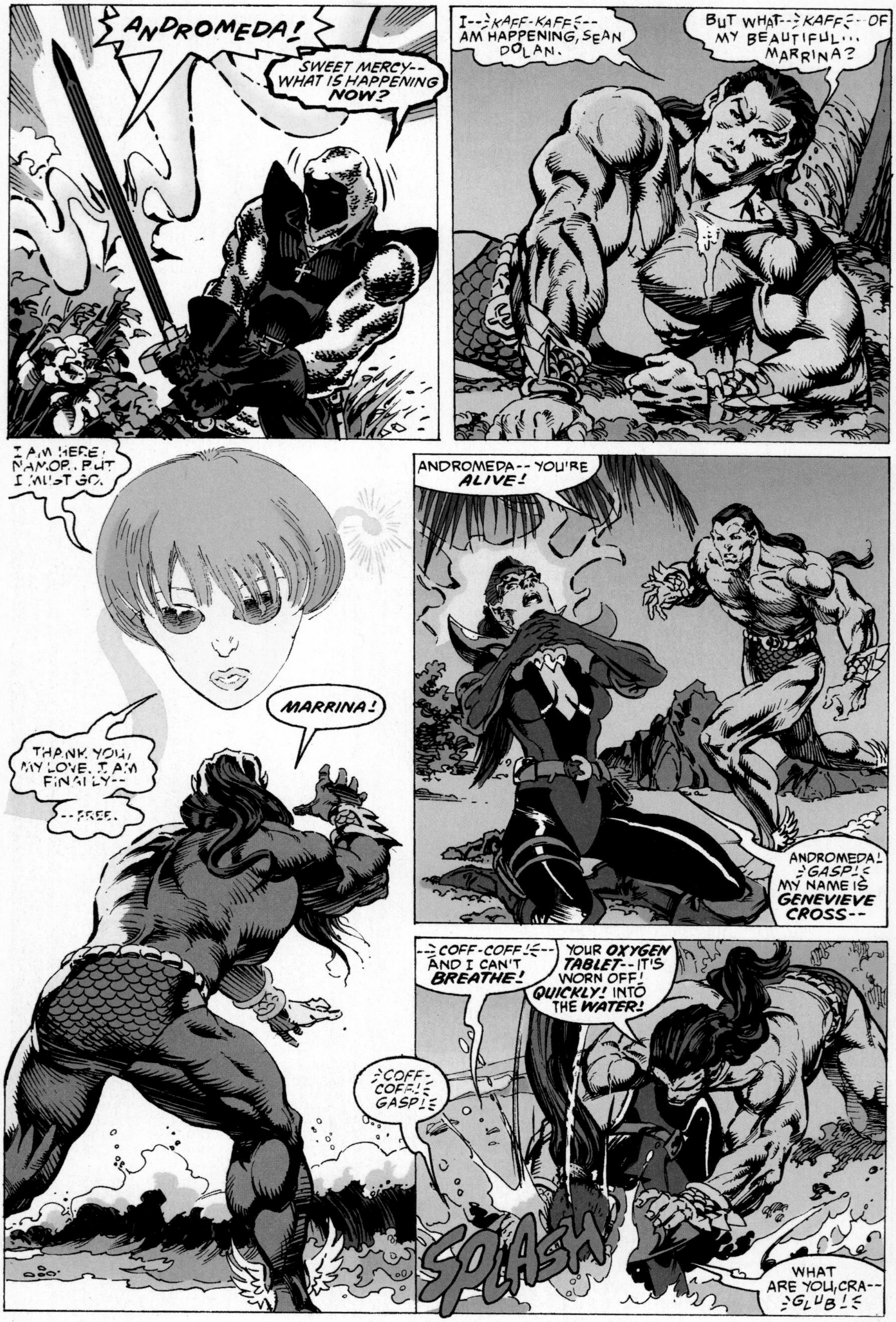

ANDROMEDA!
SWEET MERCY-- WHAT IS HAPPENING NOW?
I--KAFF-KAFF--- AM HAPPENING, SEAN DOLAN.
BUT WHAT--KAFF--OF MY BEAUTIFUL... MARRINA?
I AM HERE, NAMOR. BUT I MUST GO.
ANDROMEDA-- YOU'RE ALIVE!
MARRINA!
THANK YOU, MY LOVE. I AM FINALLY--
--FREE.
ANDROMEDA! GASP! MY NAME IS GENEVIEVE CROSS--
--COFF-COFF!-- AND I CAN'T BREATHE!
YOUR OXYGEN TABLET--IT'S WORN OFF! QUICKLY! INTO THE WATER!
COFF-COFF! GASP!
SPLASH
WHAT ARE YOU, CRA-- GLUB!

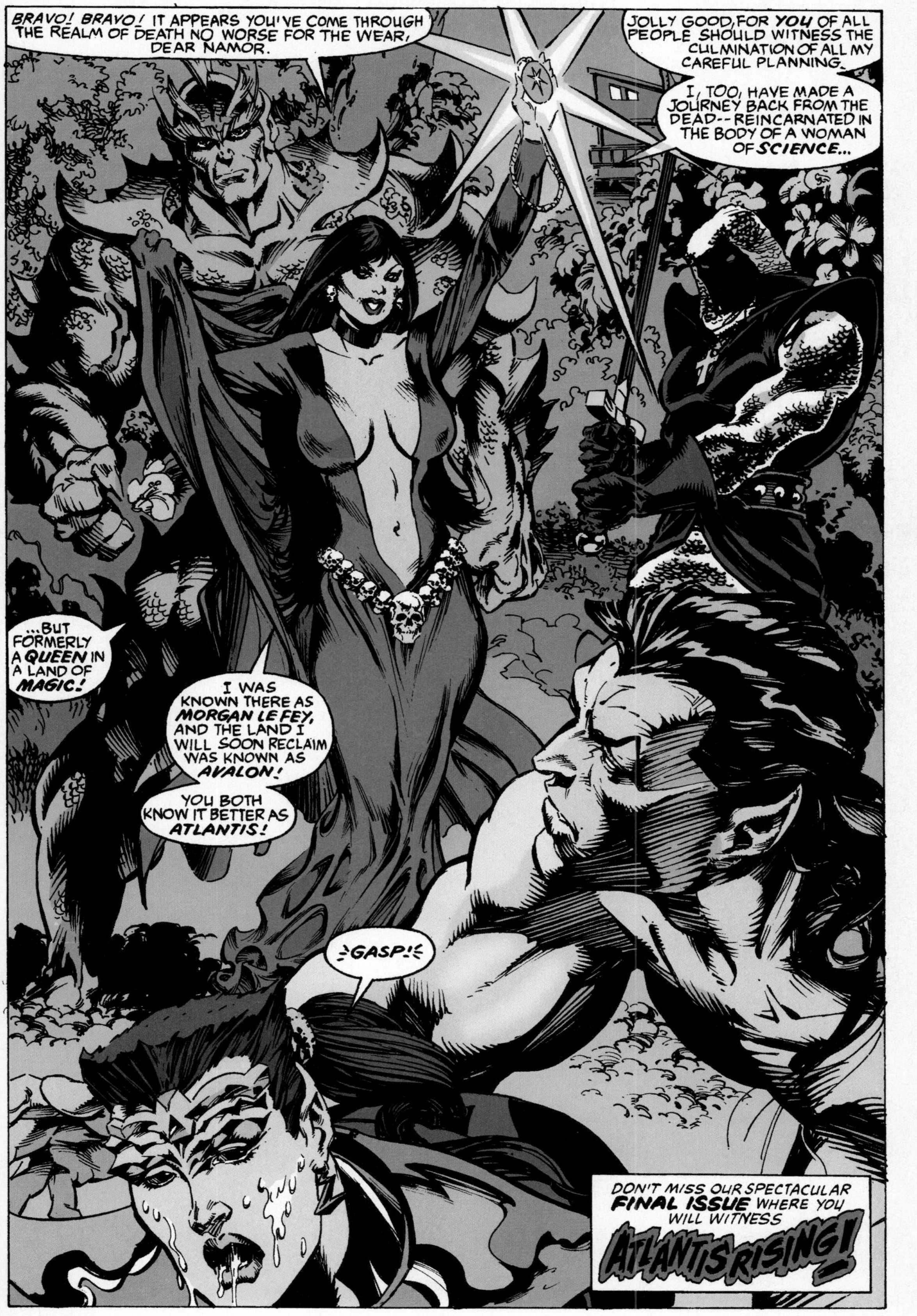
BRAVO! BRAVO! IT APPEARS YOU'VE COME THROUGH THE REALM OF DEATH NO WORSE FOR THE WEAR, DEAR NAMOR.
JOLLY GOOD, FOR YOU OF ALL PEOPLE SHOULD WITNESS THE CULMINATION OF ALL MY CAREFUL PLANNING.
I, TOO, HAVE MADE A JOURNEY BACK FROM THE DEAD--REINCARNATED IN THE BODY OF A WOMAN OF SCIENCE...
...BUT FORMERLY A QUEEN IN A LAND OF MAGIC!
I WAS KNOWN THERE AS MORGAN LE FEY, AND THE LAND I WILL SOON RECLAIM WAS KNOWN AS AVALON!
YOU BOTH KNOW IT BETTER AS ATLANTIS!
GASP!
DON'T MISS OUR SPECTACULAR FINAL ISSUE WHERE YOU WILL WITNESS
ATLANTIS RISING!

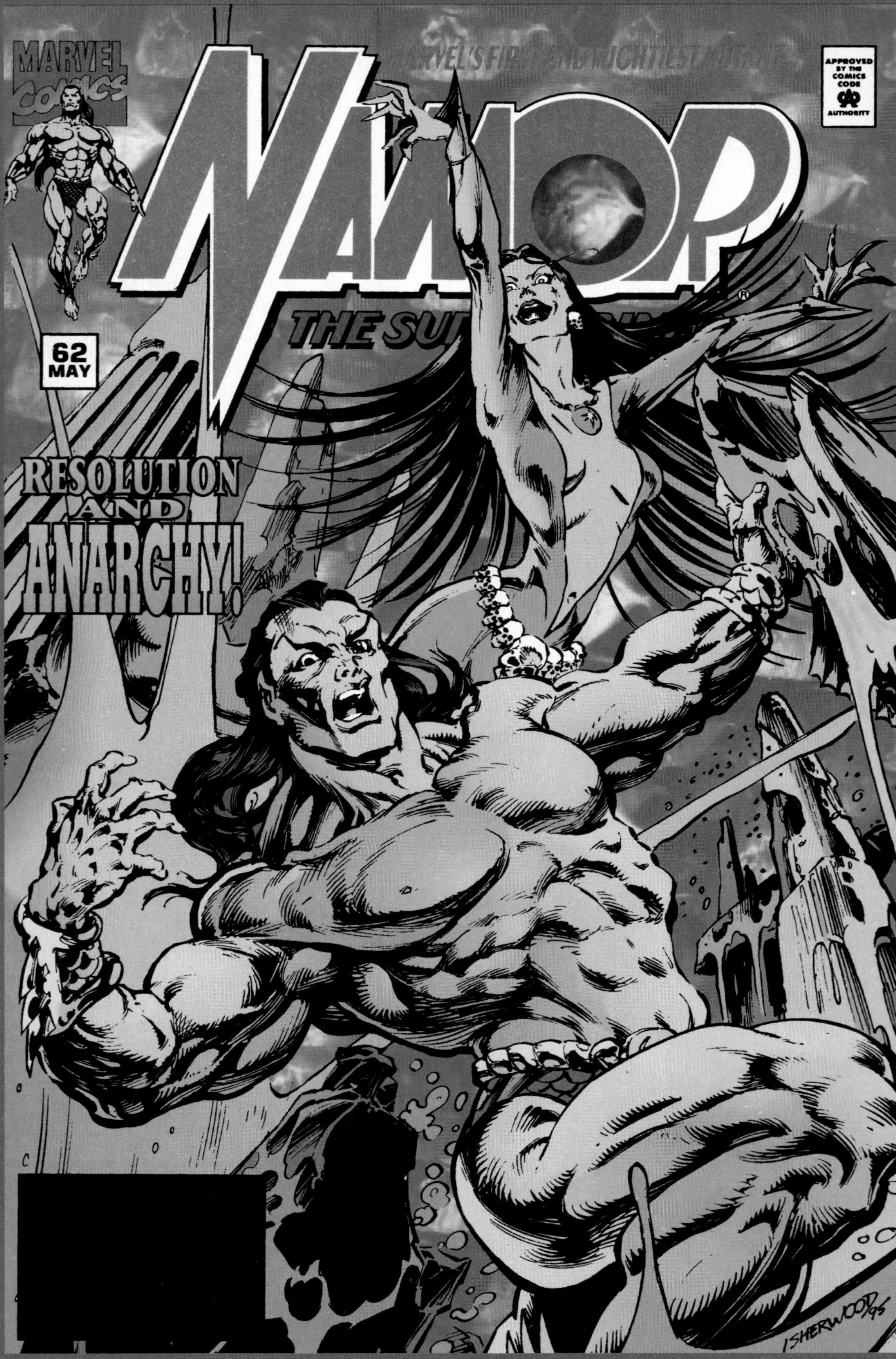

MARVEL COMICS
MARVEL'S FIRST AND MIGHTIEST MUTANT
APPROVED BY THE COMICS CODE AUTHORITY
NAMOR
THE SU
62
MAY
RESOLUTION AND ANARCHY!
ISHERWOOD '95

SCION OF AN AIR-BREATHING FATHER AND A WATER-BREATHING MOTHER, GIFTED WITH SUPERHUMAN STRENGTH AND THE POWER OF FLIGHT, THE AVENGING SON OF ATLANTIS HAS BATTLED FOR AND AGAINST HUMANITY SINCE WORLD WAR II! NOW, THE WEALTH OF THE ETERNAL SEAS AT HIS COMMAND, HE HAS SET UP A NEW CAMPAIGN OF CONQUEST. . .AGAINST THE ENEMIES OF THE ENVIRONMENT ITSELF! STAN LEE PRESENTS. . .*NAMOR, THE SUB-MARINER!*

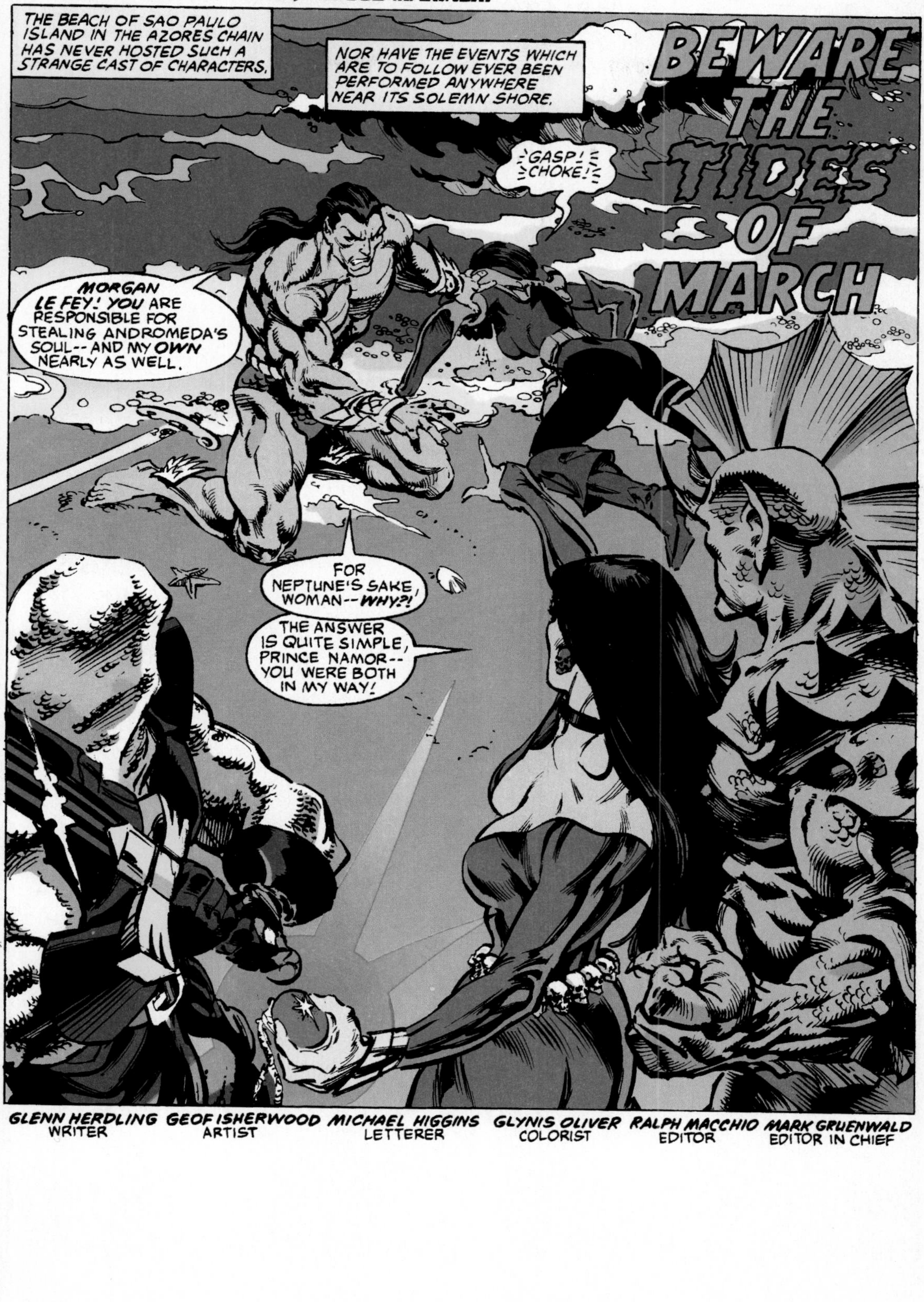

THE BEACH OF SAO PAULO ISLAND IN THE AZORES CHAIN HAS NEVER HOSTED SUCH A STRANGE CAST OF CHARACTERS.
NOR HAVE THE EVENTS WHICH ARE TO FOLLOW EVER BEEN PERFORMED ANYWHERE NEAR ITS SOLEMN SHORE.
BEWARE THE TIDES OF MARCH
GASP! CHOKE!
MORGAN LE FEY! YOU ARE RESPONSIBLE FOR STEALING ANDROMEDA'S SOUL--AND MY OWN NEARLY AS WELL.
FOR NEPTUNE'S SAKE WOMAN--WHY?!
THE ANSWER IS QUITE SIMPLE, PRINCE NAMOR--YOU WERE BOTH IN MY WAY!

GLENN HERDLING WRITER · **GEOF ISHERWOOD** ARTIST · **MICHAEL HIGGINS** LETTERER · **GLYNIS OLIVER** COLORIST · **RALPH MACCHIO** EDITOR · **MARK GRUENWALD** EDITOR IN CHIEF

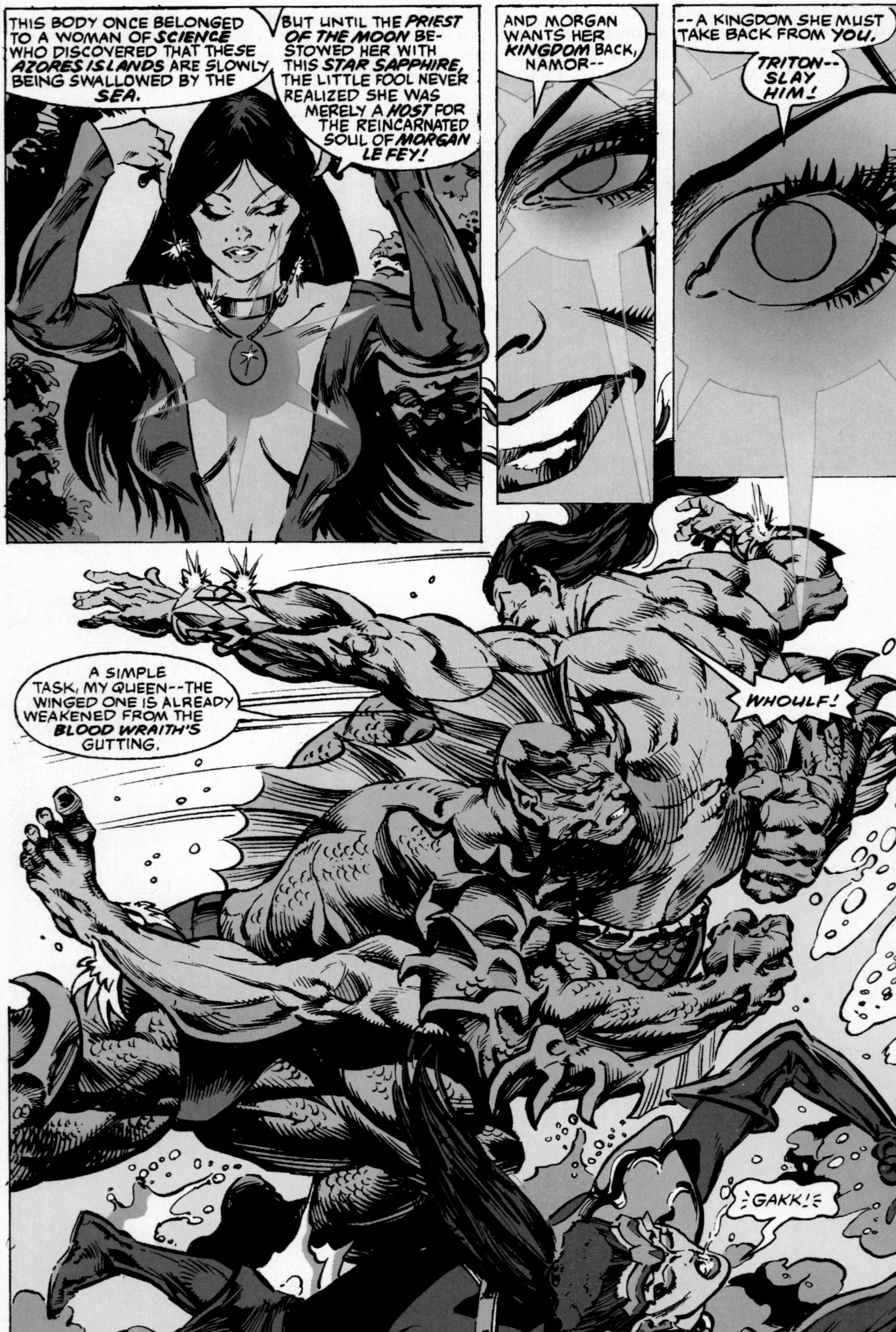

THIS BODY ONCE BELONGED TO A WOMAN OF SCIENCE WHO DISCOVERED THAT THESE AZORES ISLANDS ARE SLOWLY BEING SWALLOWED BY THE SEA.
BUT UNTIL THE PRIEST OF THE MOON BESTOWED HER WITH THIS STAR SAPPHIRE, THE LITTLE FOOL NEVER REALIZED SHE WAS MERELY A HOST FOR THE REINCARNATED SOUL OF MORGAN LE FEY!
AND MORGAN WANTS HER KINGDOM BACK, NAMOR--
--A KINGDOM SHE MUST TAKE BACK FROM YOU.
TRITON-- SLAY HIM!
A SIMPLE TASK, MY QUEEN--THE WINGED ONE IS ALREADY WEAKENED FROM THE BLOOD WRAITH'S GUTTING.
WHOULF!
GAKK!

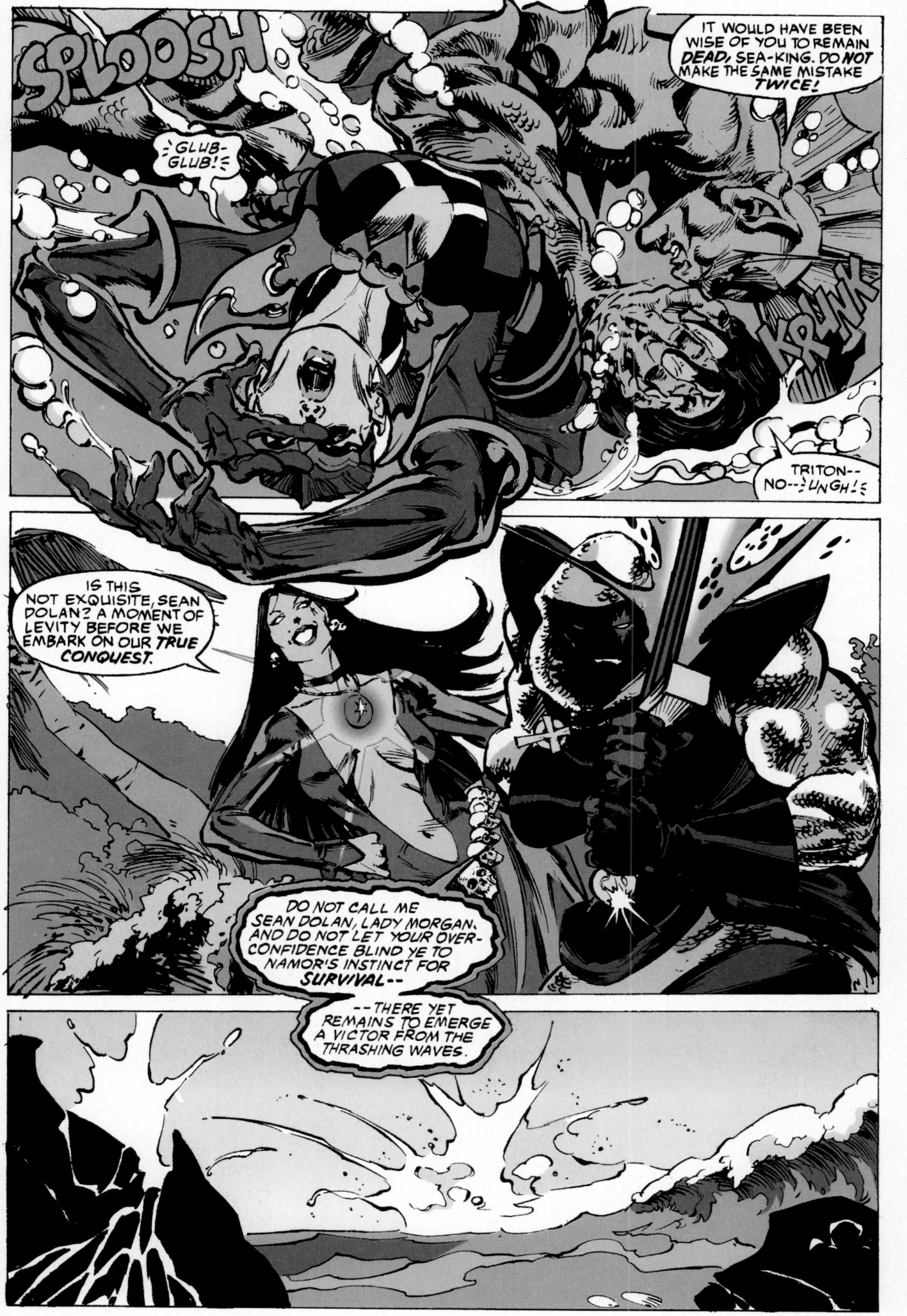
SPLOOSH
IT WOULD HAVE BEEN WISE OF YOU TO REMAIN DEAD, SEA-KING. DO NOT MAKE THE SAME MISTAKE TWICE!
GLUB-GLUB!
KRUNK
TRITON-- NO--UNGH!
IS THIS NOT EXQUISITE, SEAN DOLAN? A MOMENT OF LEVITY BEFORE WE EMBARK ON OUR TRUE CONQUEST.
DO NOT CALL ME SEAN DOLAN, LADY MORGAN. AND DO NOT LET YOUR OVER-CONFIDENCE BLIND YE TO NAMOR'S INSTINCT FOR SURVIVAL--
--THERE YET REMAINS TO EMERGE A VICTOR FROM THE THRASHING WAVES.

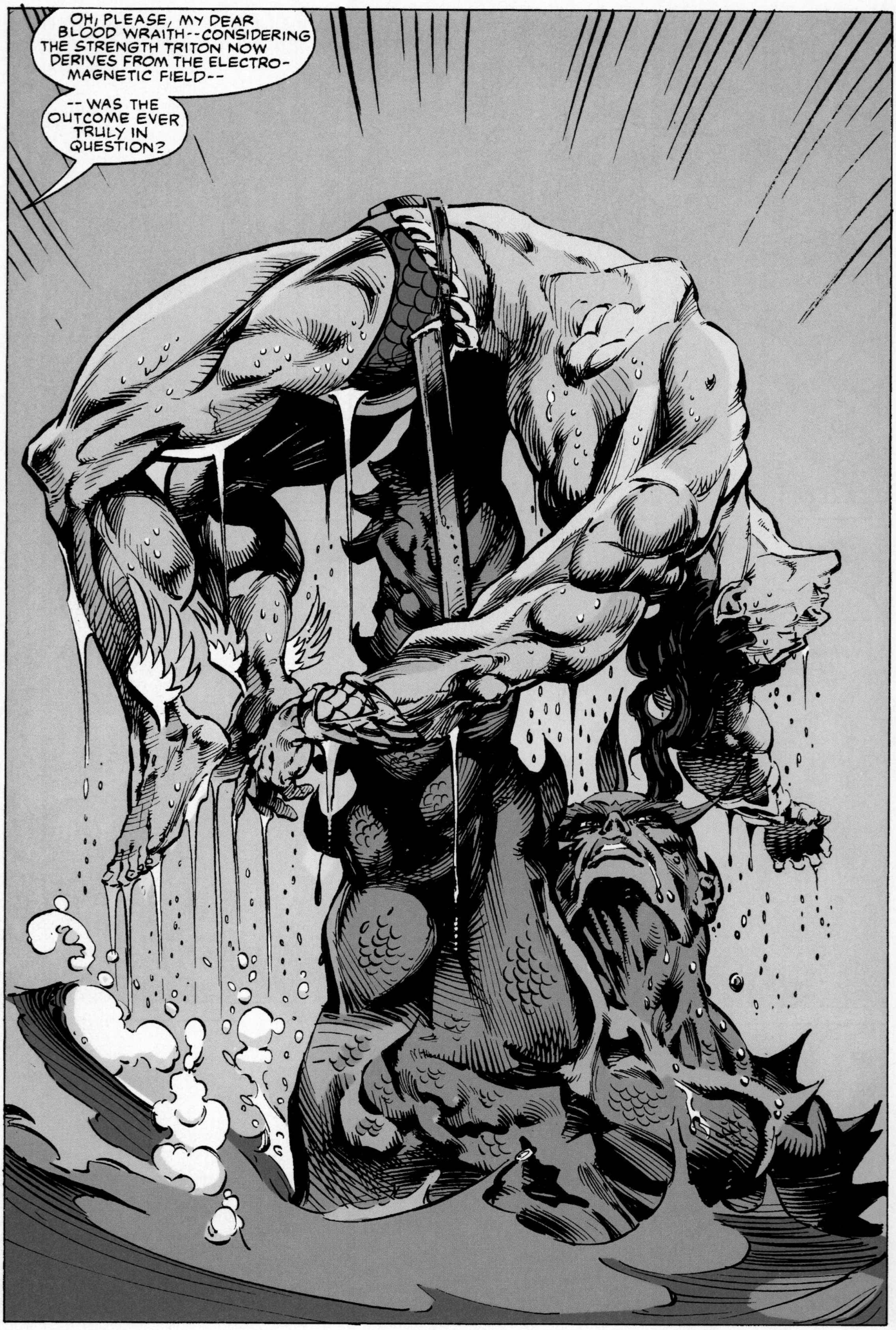
OH, PLEASE, MY DEAR BLOOD WRAITH--CONSIDERING THE STRENGTH TRITON NOW DERIVES FROM THE ELECTRO-MAGNETIC FIELD--
-- WAS THE OUTCOME EVER TRULY IN QUESTION?

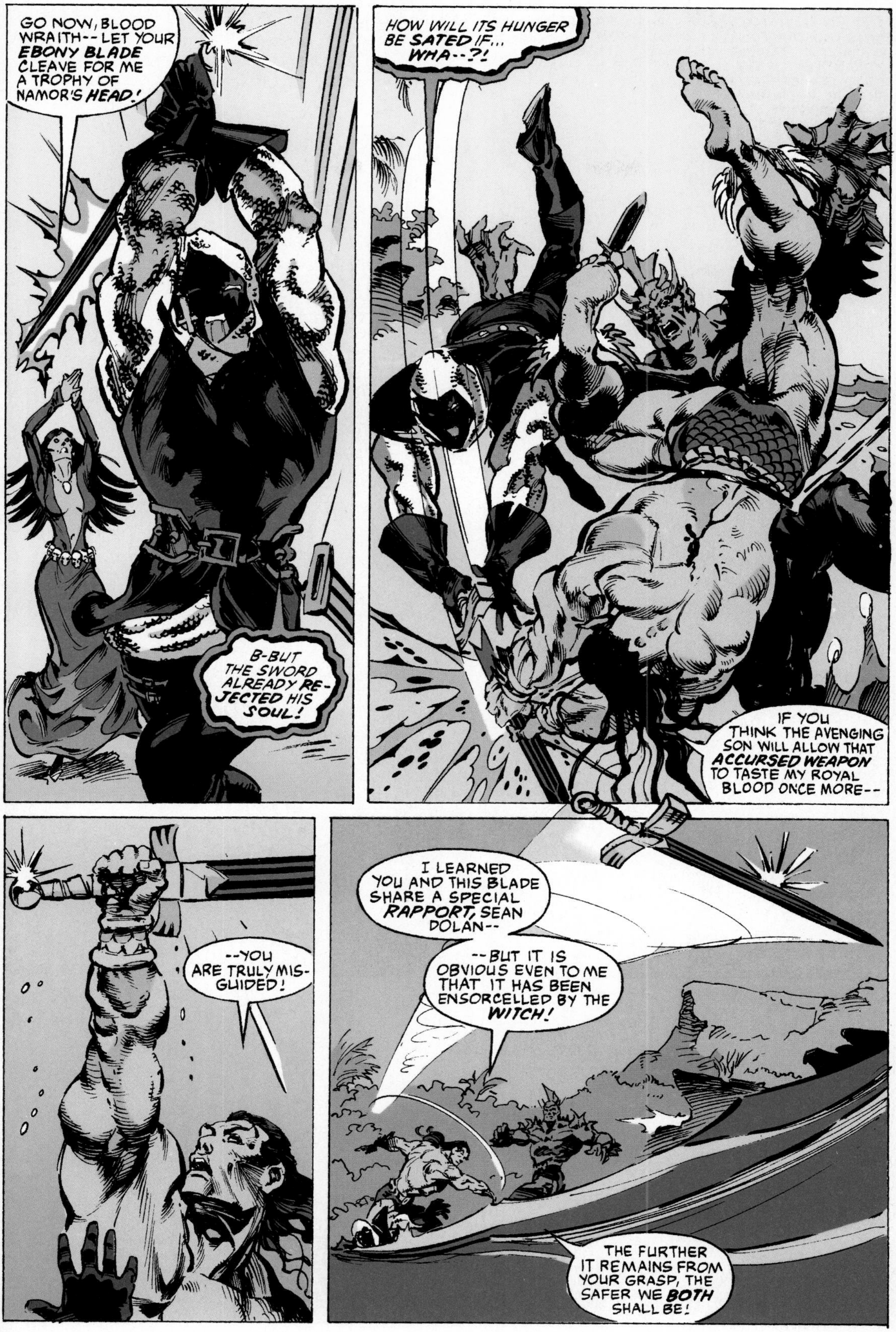
GO NOW, BLOOD WRAITH--LET YOUR EBONY BLADE CLEAVE FOR ME A TROPHY OF NAMOR'S HEAD!
B-BUT THE SWORD ALREADY RE-JECTED HIS SOUL!
HOW WILL ITS HUNGER BE SATED IF... WHA--?!
IF YOU THINK THE AVENGING SON WILL ALLOW THAT ACCURSED WEAPON TO TASTE MY ROYAL BLOOD ONCE MORE--
--YOU ARE TRULY MIS-GUIDED!
I LEARNED YOU AND THIS BLADE SHARE A SPECIAL RAPPORT, SEAN DOLAN--
--BUT IT IS OBVIOUS EVEN TO ME THAT IT HAS BEEN ENSORCELLED BY THE WITCH!
THE FURTHER IT REMAINS FROM YOUR GRASP, THE SAFER WE BOTH SHALL BE!

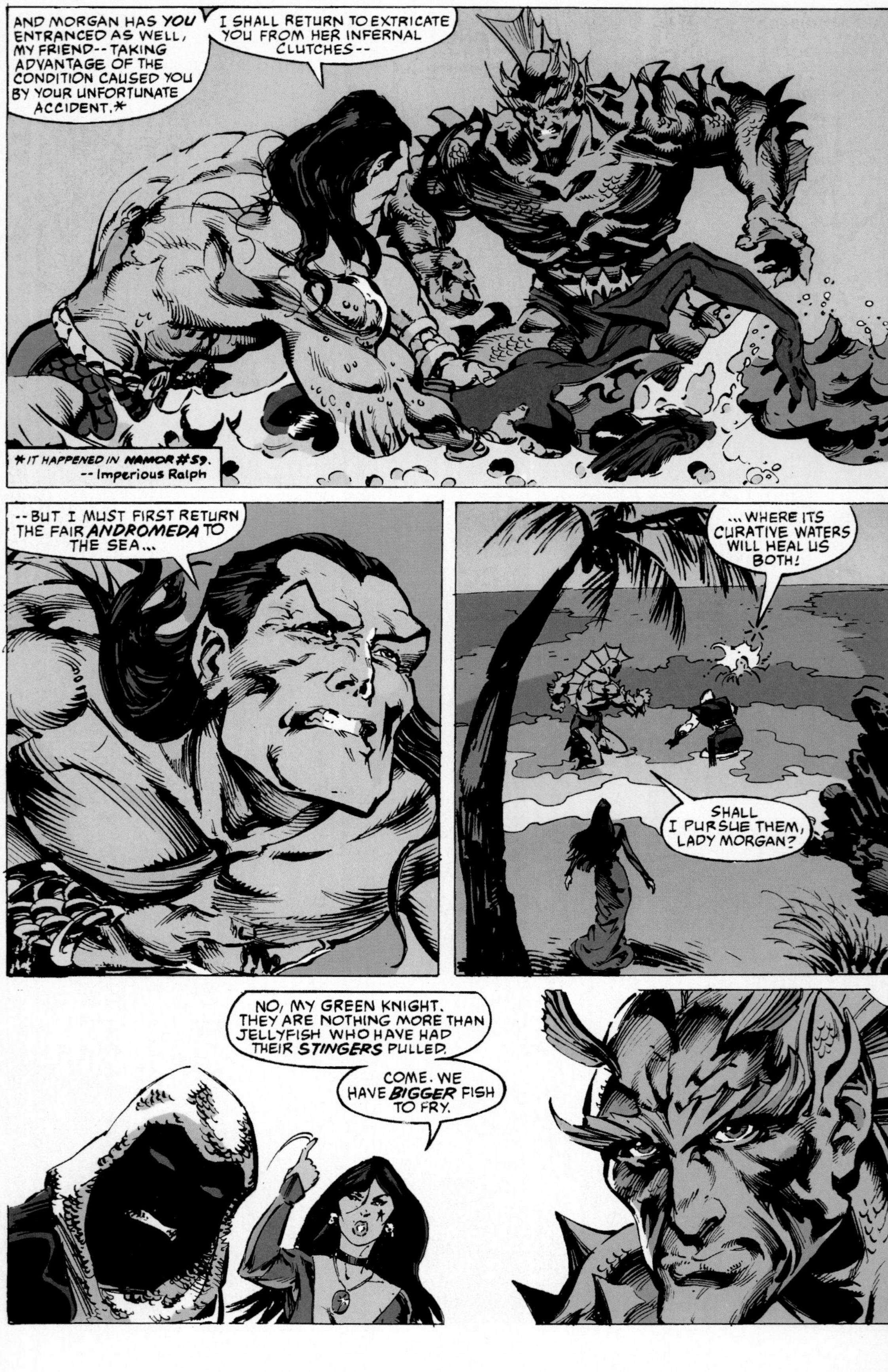
AND MORGAN HAS YOU ENTRANCED AS WELL, MY FRIEND-- TAKING ADVANTAGE OF THE CONDITION CAUSED YOU BY YOUR UNFORTUNATE ACCIDENT.*
I SHALL RETURN TO EXTRICATE YOU FROM HER INFERNAL CLUTCHES--
*IT HAPPENED IN NAMOR #59. --Imperious Ralph
--BUT I MUST FIRST RETURN THE FAIR ANDROMEDA TO THE SEA...
...WHERE ITS CURATIVE WATERS WILL HEAL US BOTH!
SHALL I PURSUE THEM, LADY MORGAN?
NO, MY GREEN KNIGHT. THEY ARE NOTHING MORE THAN JELLYFISH WHO HAVE HAD THEIR STINGERS PULLED.
COME. WE HAVE BIGGER FISH TO FRY.

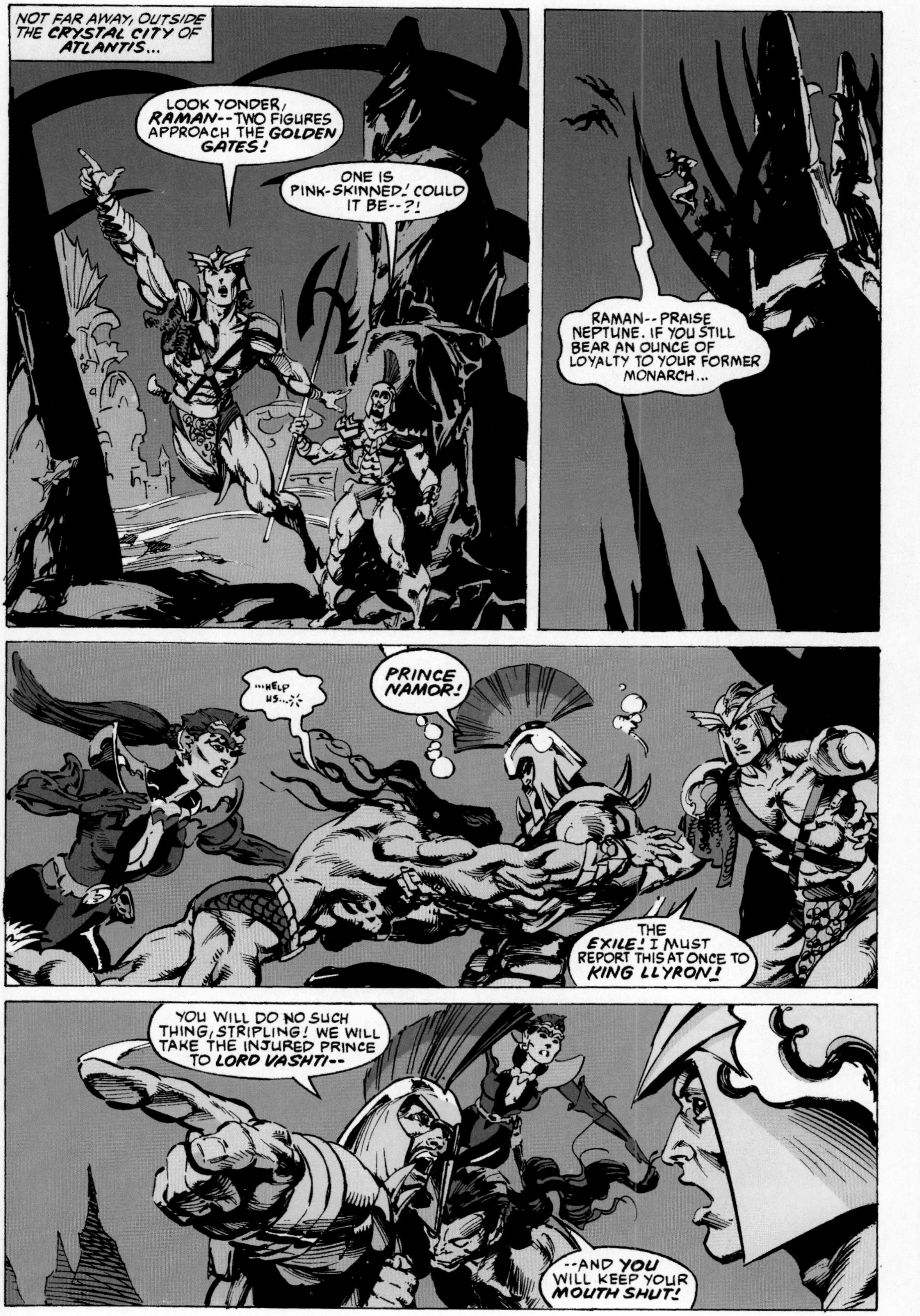
NOT FAR AWAY, OUTSIDE THE CRYSTAL CITY OF ATLANTIS...
LOOK YONDER, RAMAN--TWO FIGURES APPROACH THE GOLDEN GATES!
ONE IS PINK-SKINNED! COULD IT BE--?!
RAMAN--PRAISE NEPTUNE. IF YOU STILL BEAR AN OUNCE OF LOYALTY TO YOUR FORMER MONARCH...
...HELP US...
PRINCE NAMOR!
THE EXILE! I MUST REPORT THIS AT ONCE TO KING LLYRON!
YOU WILL DO NO SUCH THING, STRIPLING! WE WILL TAKE THE INJURED PRINCE TO LORD VASHTI--
--AND YOU WILL KEEP YOUR MOUTH SHUT!

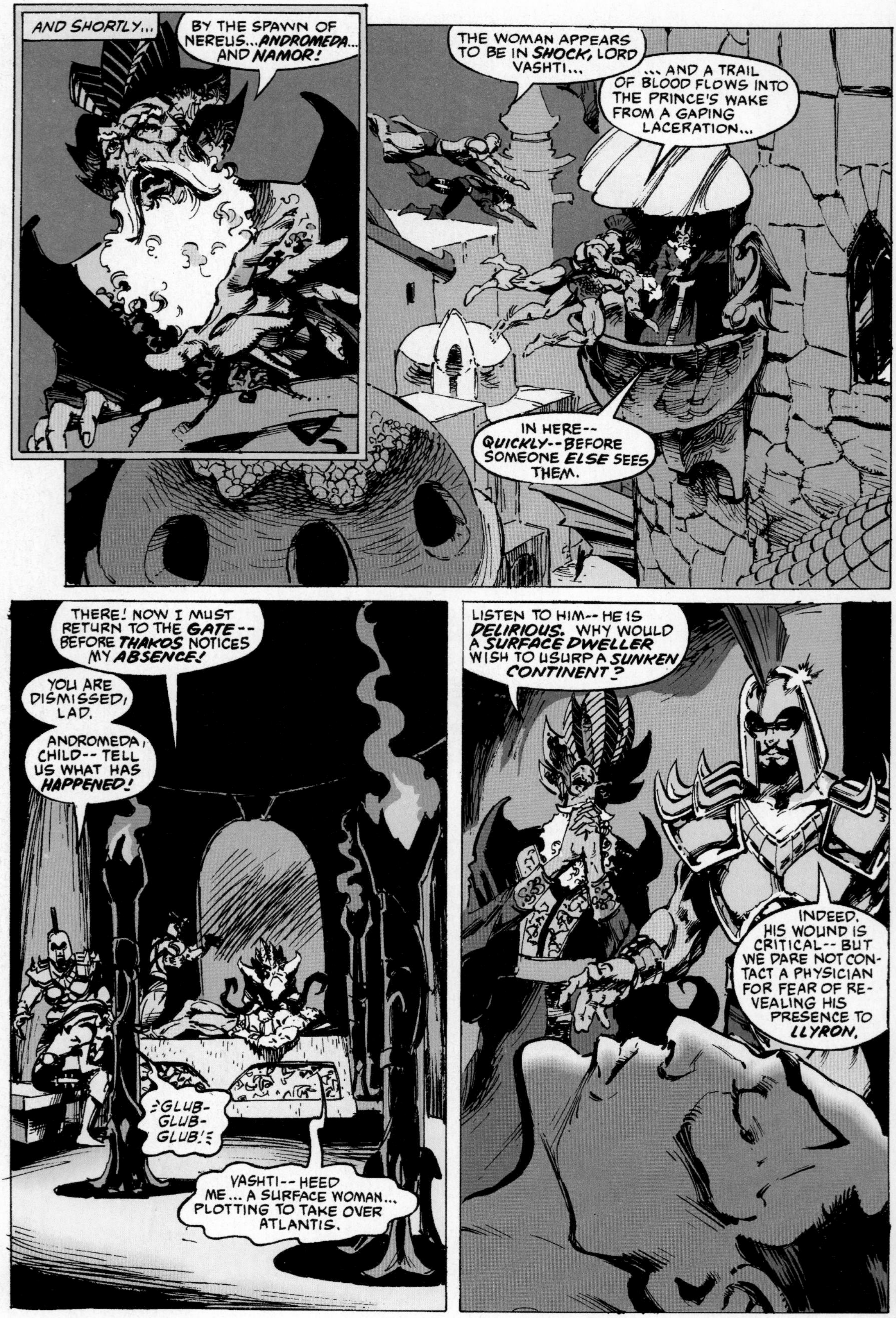

AND SHORTLY...
BY THE SPAWN OF NEREUS...ANDROMEDA... AND NAMOR!
THE WOMAN APPEARS TO BE IN SHOCK, LORD VASHTI...
...AND A TRAIL OF BLOOD FLOWS INTO THE PRINCE'S WAKE FROM A GAPING LACERATION...
IN HERE-- QUICKLY--BEFORE SOMEONE ELSE SEES THEM.
THERE! NOW I MUST RETURN TO THE GATE-- BEFORE THAKOS NOTICES MY ABSENCE!
YOU ARE DISMISSED, LAD.
ANDROMEDA, CHILD--TELL US WHAT HAS HAPPENED!
GLUB-GLUB-GLUB!
VASHTI--HEED ME... A SURFACE WOMAN... PLOTTING TO TAKE OVER ATLANTIS.
LISTEN TO HIM--HE IS DELIRIOUS. WHY WOULD A SURFACE DWELLER WISH TO USURP A SUNKEN CONTINENT?
INDEED. HIS WOUND IS CRITICAL--BUT WE DARE NOT CONTACT A PHYSICIAN FOR FEAR OF REVEALING HIS PRESENCE TO LLYRON.

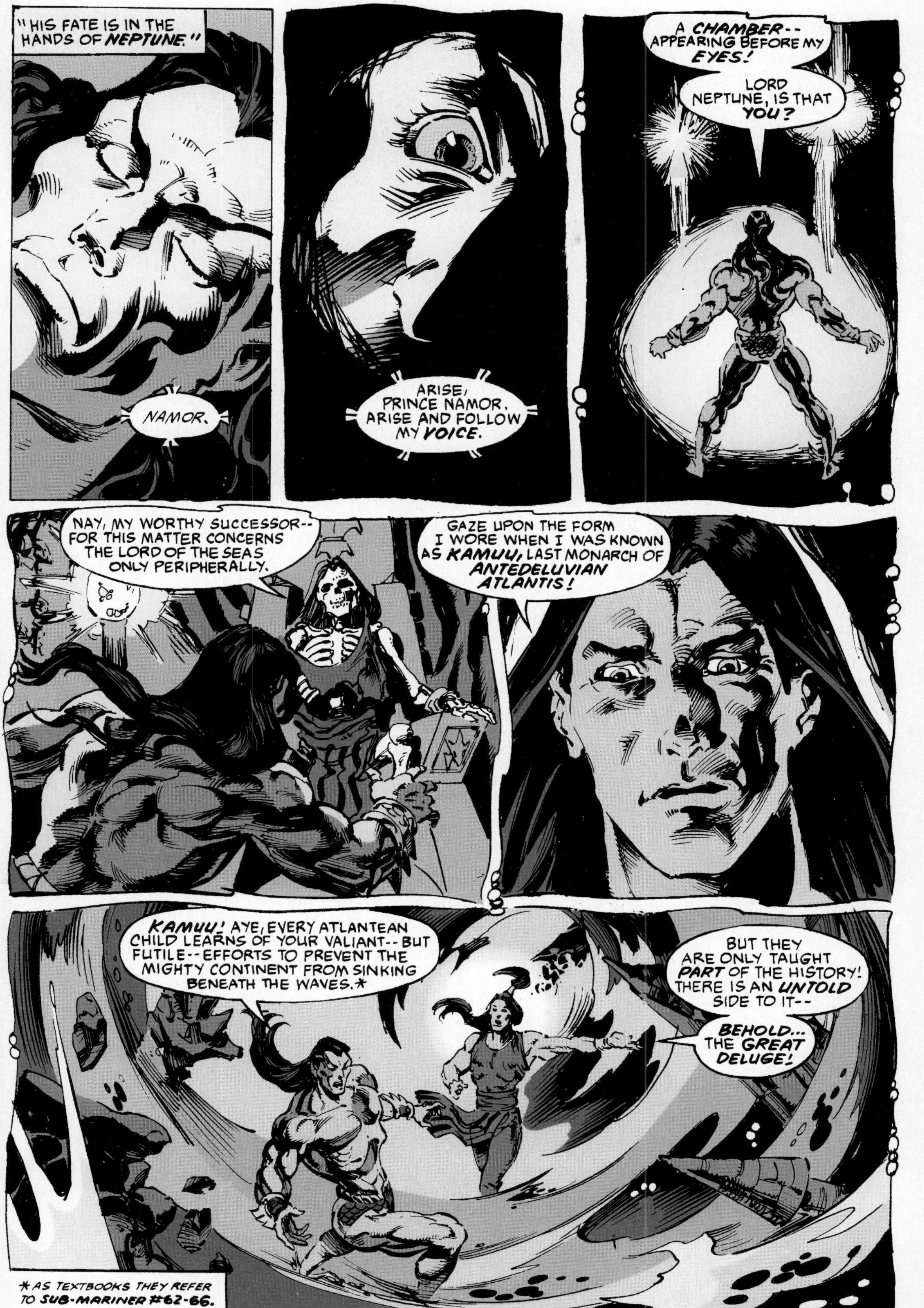
"HIS FATE IS IN THE HANDS OF NEPTUNE."
NAMOR.
ARISE, PRINCE NAMOR. ARISE AND FOLLOW MY VOICE.
A CHAMBER-- APPEARING BEFORE MY EYES!
LORD NEPTUNE, IS THAT YOU?
NAY, MY WORTHY SUCCESSOR-- FOR THIS MATTER CONCERNS THE LORD OF THE SEAS ONLY PERIPHERALLY.
GAZE UPON THE FORM I WORE WHEN I WAS KNOWN AS KAMUU, LAST MONARCH OF ANTEDELUVIAN ATLANTIS!
KAMUU! AYE, EVERY ATLANTEAN CHILD LEARNS OF YOUR VALIANT-- BUT FUTILE-- EFFORTS TO PREVENT THE MIGHTY CONTINENT FROM SINKING BENEATH THE WAVES.*
BUT THEY ARE ONLY TAUGHT PART OF THE HISTORY! THERE IS AN UNTOLD SIDE TO IT--
BEHOLD... THE GREAT DELUGE!
*AS TEXTBOOKS THEY REFER TO SUB-MARINER #62-66. --Professor Macchio

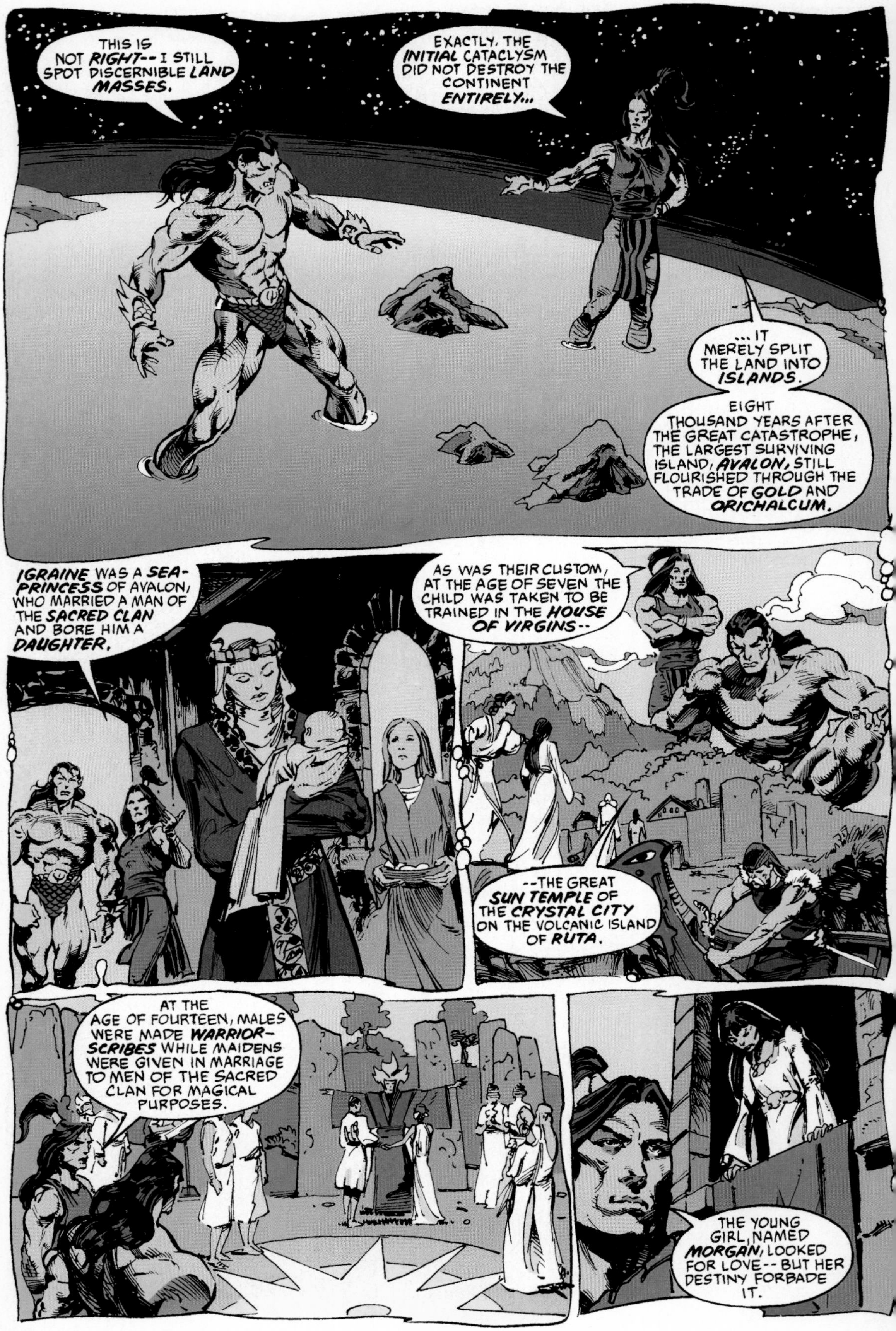
THIS IS NOT RIGHT-- I STILL SPOT DISCERNIBLE LAND MASSES.
EXACTLY, THE INITIAL CATACLYSM DID NOT DESTROY THE CONTINENT ENTIRELY...
... IT MERELY SPLIT THE LAND INTO ISLANDS.
EIGHT THOUSAND YEARS AFTER THE GREAT CATASTROPHE, THE LARGEST SURVIVING ISLAND, AVALON, STILL FLOURISHED THROUGH THE TRADE OF GOLD AND ORICHALCUM.
IGRAINE WAS A SEA-PRINCESS OF AVALON, WHO MARRIED A MAN OF THE SACRED CLAN AND BORE HIM A DAUGHTER.
AS WAS THEIR CUSTOM, AT THE AGE OF SEVEN THE CHILD WAS TAKEN TO BE TRAINED IN THE HOUSE OF VIRGINS--
--THE GREAT SUN TEMPLE OF THE CRYSTAL CITY ON THE VOLCANIC ISLAND OF RUTA.
AT THE AGE OF FOURTEEN, MALES WERE MADE WARRIOR-SCRIBES WHILE MAIDENS WERE GIVEN IN MARRIAGE TO MEN OF THE SACRED CLAN FOR MAGICAL PURPOSES.
THE YOUNG GIRL, NAMED MORGAN, LOOKED FOR LOVE-- BUT HER DESTINY FORBADE IT.

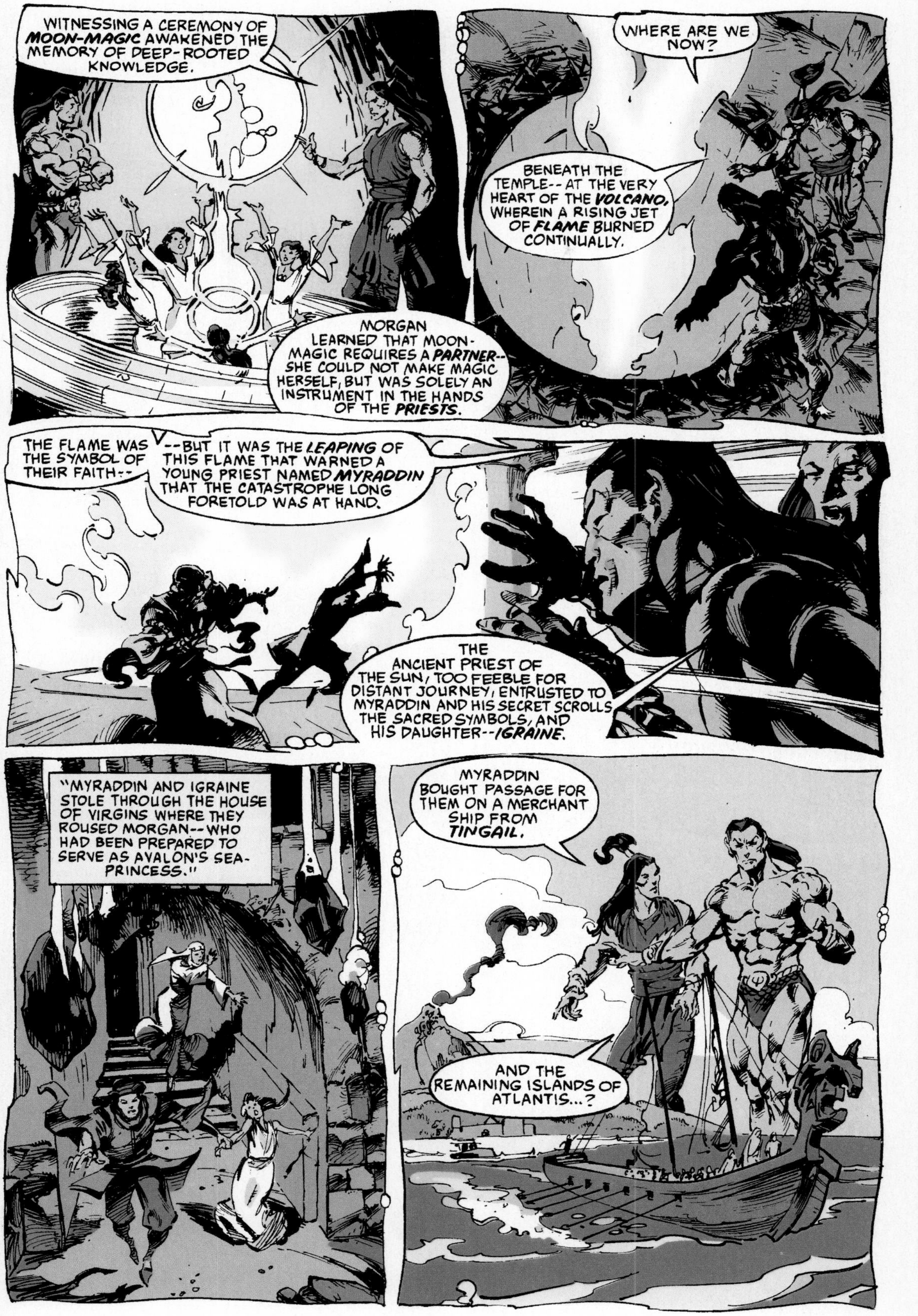
WITNESSING A CEREMONY OF MOON-MAGIC AWAKENED THE MEMORY OF DEEP-ROOTED KNOWLEDGE.
MORGAN LEARNED THAT MOON-MAGIC REQUIRES A PARTNER-- SHE COULD NOT MAKE MAGIC HERSELF, BUT WAS SOLELY AN INSTRUMENT IN THE HANDS OF THE PRIESTS.
WHERE ARE WE NOW?
BENEATH THE TEMPLE-- AT THE VERY HEART OF THE VOLCANO, WHEREIN A RISING JET OF FLAME BURNED CONTINUALLY.
THE FLAME WAS THE SYMBOL OF THEIR FAITH--
--BUT IT WAS THE LEAPING OF THIS FLAME THAT WARNED A YOUNG PRIEST NAMED MYRADDIN THAT THE CATASTROPHE LONG FORETOLD WAS AT HAND.
THE ANCIENT PRIEST OF THE SUN, TOO FEEBLE FOR DISTANT JOURNEY, ENTRUSTED TO MYRADDIN AND HIS SECRET SCROLLS THE SACRED SYMBOLS, AND HIS DAUGHTER--IGRAINE.
"MYRADDIN AND IGRAINE STOLE THROUGH THE HOUSE OF VIRGINS WHERE THEY ROUSED MORGAN--WHO HAD BEEN PREPARED TO SERVE AS AVALON'S SEA-PRINCESS."
MYRADDIN BOUGHT PASSAGE FOR THEM ON A MERCHANT SHIP FROM TINGAIL.
AND THE REMAINING ISLANDS OF ATLANTIS...?

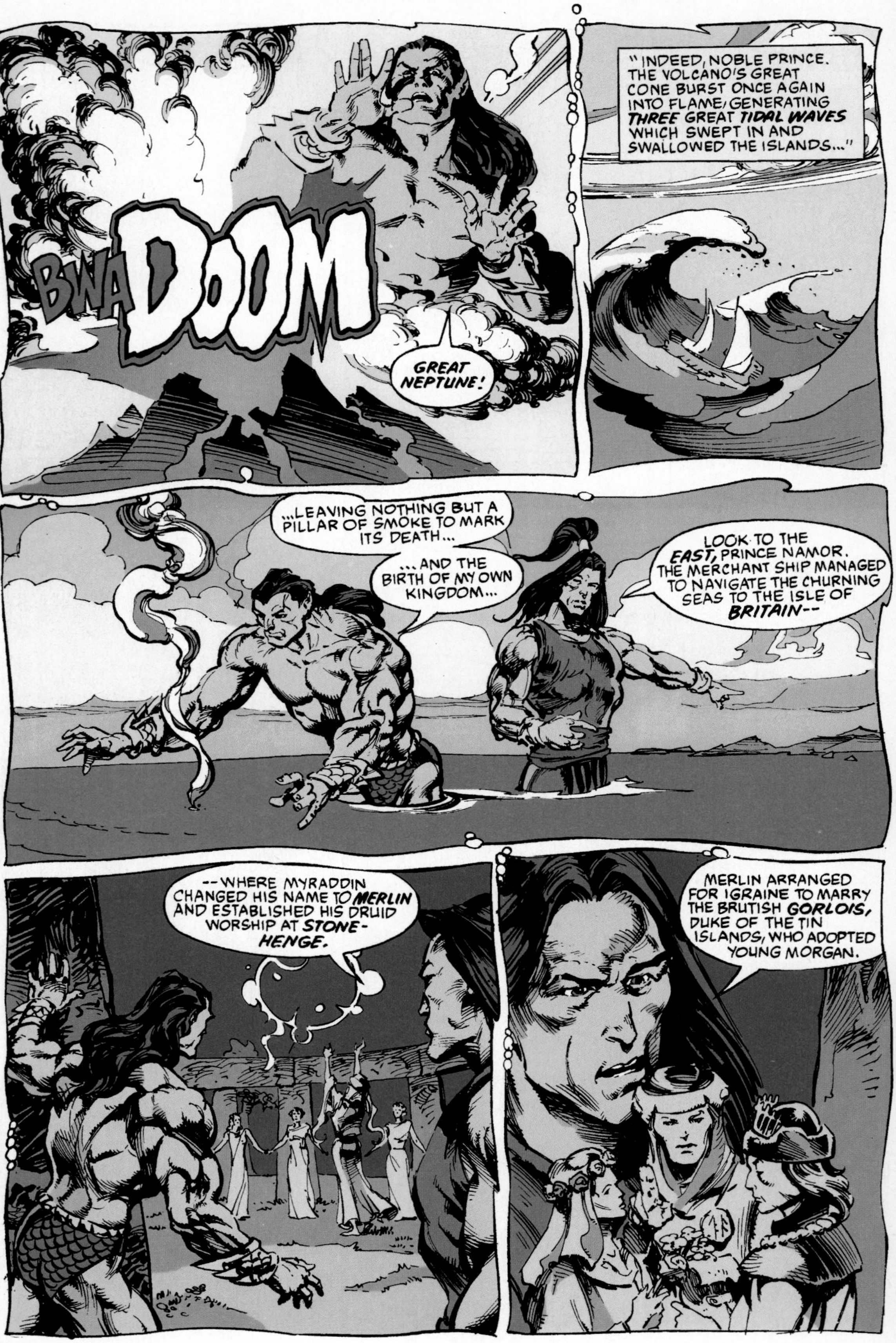
BWADOOM
GREAT NEPTUNE!
"INDEED, NOBLE PRINCE. THE VOLCANO'S GREAT CONE BURST ONCE AGAIN INTO FLAME, GENERATING THREE GREAT TIDAL WAVES WHICH SWEPT IN AND SWALLOWED THE ISLANDS..."
...LEAVING NOTHING BUT A PILLAR OF SMOKE TO MARK ITS DEATH...
...AND THE BIRTH OF MY OWN KINGDOM...
LOOK TO THE EAST, PRINCE NAMOR. THE MERCHANT SHIP MANAGED TO NAVIGATE THE CHURNING SEAS TO THE ISLE OF BRITAIN--
--WHERE MYRADDIN CHANGED HIS NAME TO MERLIN AND ESTABLISHED HIS DRUID WORSHIP AT STONE-HENGE.
MERLIN ARRANGED FOR IGRAINE TO MARRY THE BRUTISH GORLOIS, DUKE OF THE TIN ISLANDS, WHO ADOPTED YOUNG MORGAN.

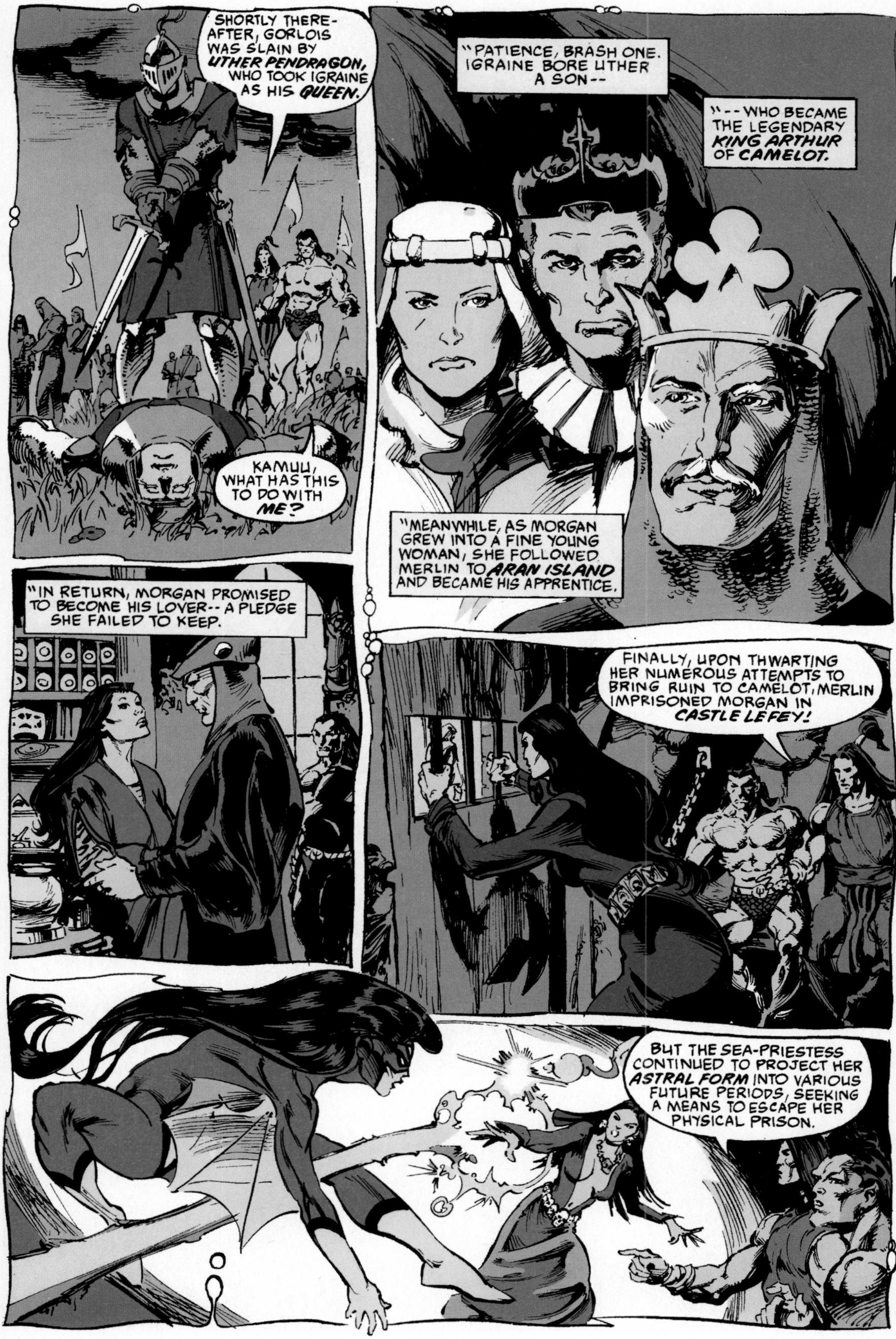
SHORTLY THERE-AFTER, GORLOIS WAS SLAIN BY UTHER PENDRAGON, WHO TOOK IGRAINE AS HIS QUEEN.
KAMUU, WHAT HAS THIS TO DO WITH ME?
"PATIENCE, BRASH ONE. IGRAINE BORE UTHER A SON--
"--WHO BECAME THE LEGENDARY KING ARTHUR OF CAMELOT.
"MEANWHILE, AS MORGAN GREW INTO A FINE YOUNG WOMAN, SHE FOLLOWED MERLIN TO ARAN ISLAND AND BECAME HIS APPRENTICE.
"IN RETURN, MORGAN PROMISED TO BECOME HIS LOVER-- A PLEDGE SHE FAILED TO KEEP.
FINALLY, UPON THWARTING HER NUMEROUS ATTEMPTS TO BRING RUIN TO CAMELOT, MERLIN IMPRISONED MORGAN IN CASTLE LEFEY!
BUT THE SEA-PRIESTESS CONTINUED TO PROJECT HER ASTRAL FORM INTO VARIOUS FUTURE PERIODS, SEEKING A MEANS TO ESCAPE HER PHYSICAL PRISON.

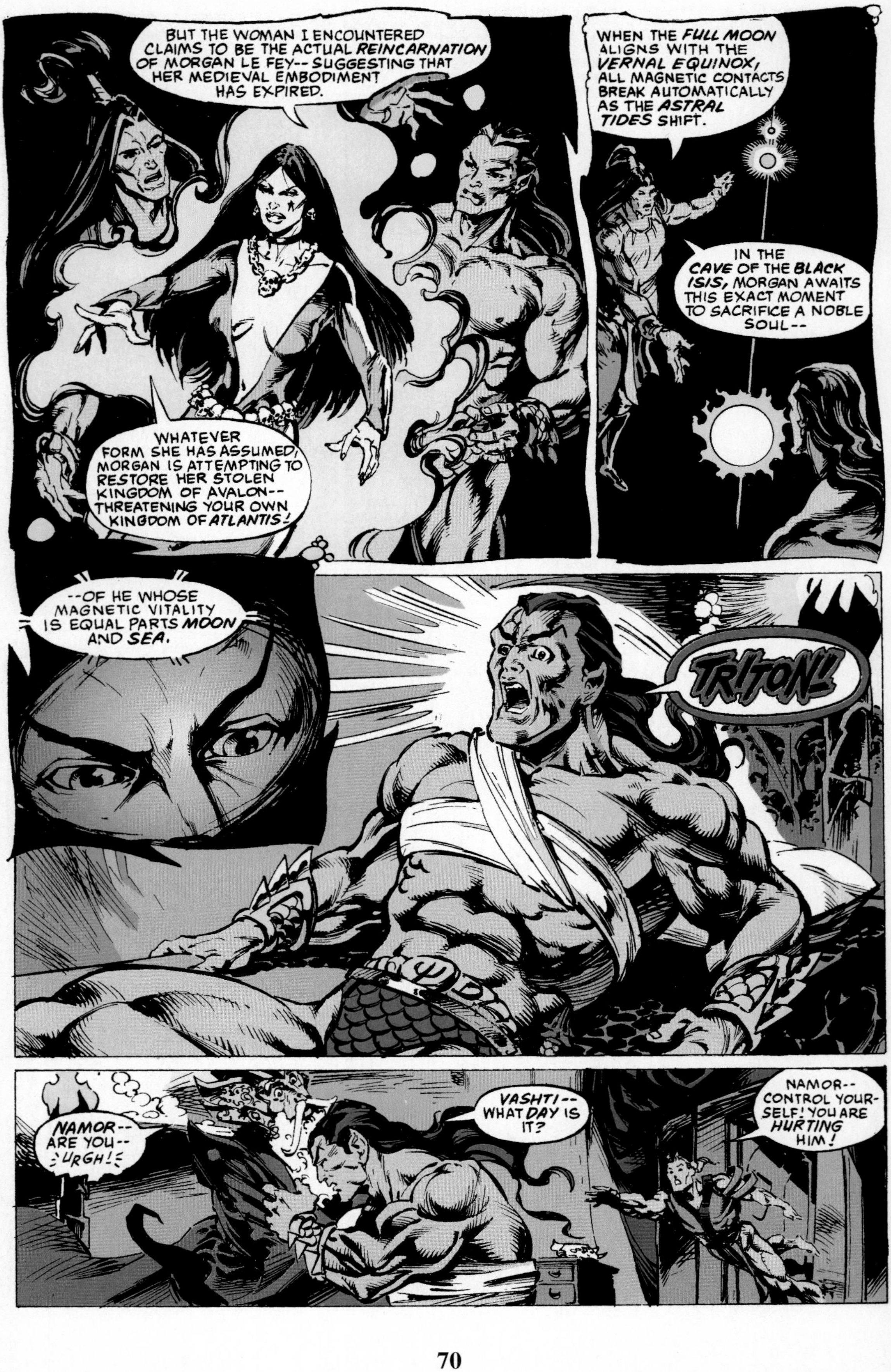
BUT THE WOMAN I ENCOUNTERED CLAIMS TO BE THE ACTUAL REINCARNATION OF MORGAN LE FEY-- SUGGESTING THAT HER MEDIEVAL EMBODIMENT HAS EXPIRED.
WHATEVER FORM SHE HAS ASSUMED, MORGAN IS ATTEMPTING TO RESTORE HER STOLEN KINGDOM OF AVALON-- THREATENING YOUR OWN KINGDOM OF ATLANTIS!
WHEN THE FULL MOON ALIGNS WITH THE VERNAL EQUINOX, ALL MAGNETIC CONTACTS BREAK AUTOMATICALLY AS THE ASTRAL TIDES SHIFT.
IN THE CAVE OF THE BLACK ISIS, MORGAN AWAITS THIS EXACT MOMENT TO SACRIFICE A NOBLE SOUL--
--OF HE WHOSE MAGNETIC VITALITY IS EQUAL PARTS MOON AND SEA.
TRITON!!
NAMOR-- ARE YOU-- URGH!
VASHTI-- WHAT DAY IS IT?
NAMOR-- CONTROL YOURSELF! YOU ARE HURTING HIM!

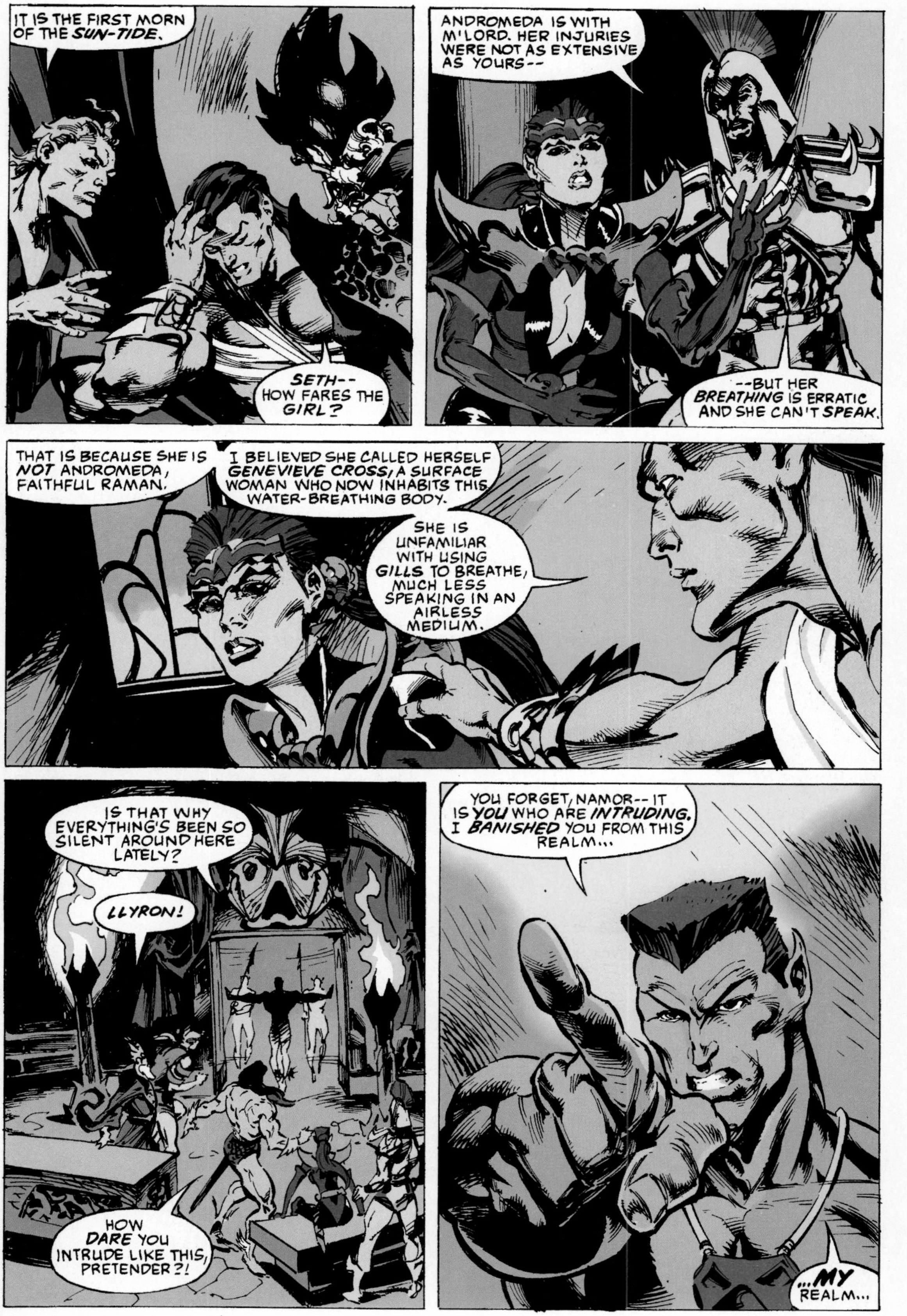
IT IS THE FIRST MORN OF THE SUN-TIDE.
SETH-- HOW FARES THE GIRL?
ANDROMEDA IS WITH M'LORD. HER INJURIES WERE NOT AS EXTENSIVE AS YOURS--
--BUT HER BREATHING IS ERRATIC AND SHE CAN'T SPEAK.
THAT IS BECAUSE SHE IS NOT ANDROMEDA, FAITHFUL RAMAN.
I BELIEVED SHE CALLED HERSELF GENEVIEVE CROSS, A SURFACE WOMAN WHO NOW INHABITS THIS WATER-BREATHING BODY.
SHE IS UNFAMILIAR WITH USING GILLS TO BREATHE, MUCH LESS SPEAKING IN AN AIRLESS MEDIUM.
IS THAT WHY EVERYTHING'S BEEN SO SILENT AROUND HERE LATELY?
LLYRON!
HOW DARE YOU INTRUDE LIKE THIS, PRETENDER?!
YOU FORGET, NAMOR-- IT IS YOU WHO ARE INTRUDING. I BANISHED YOU FROM THIS REALM...
...MY REALM...

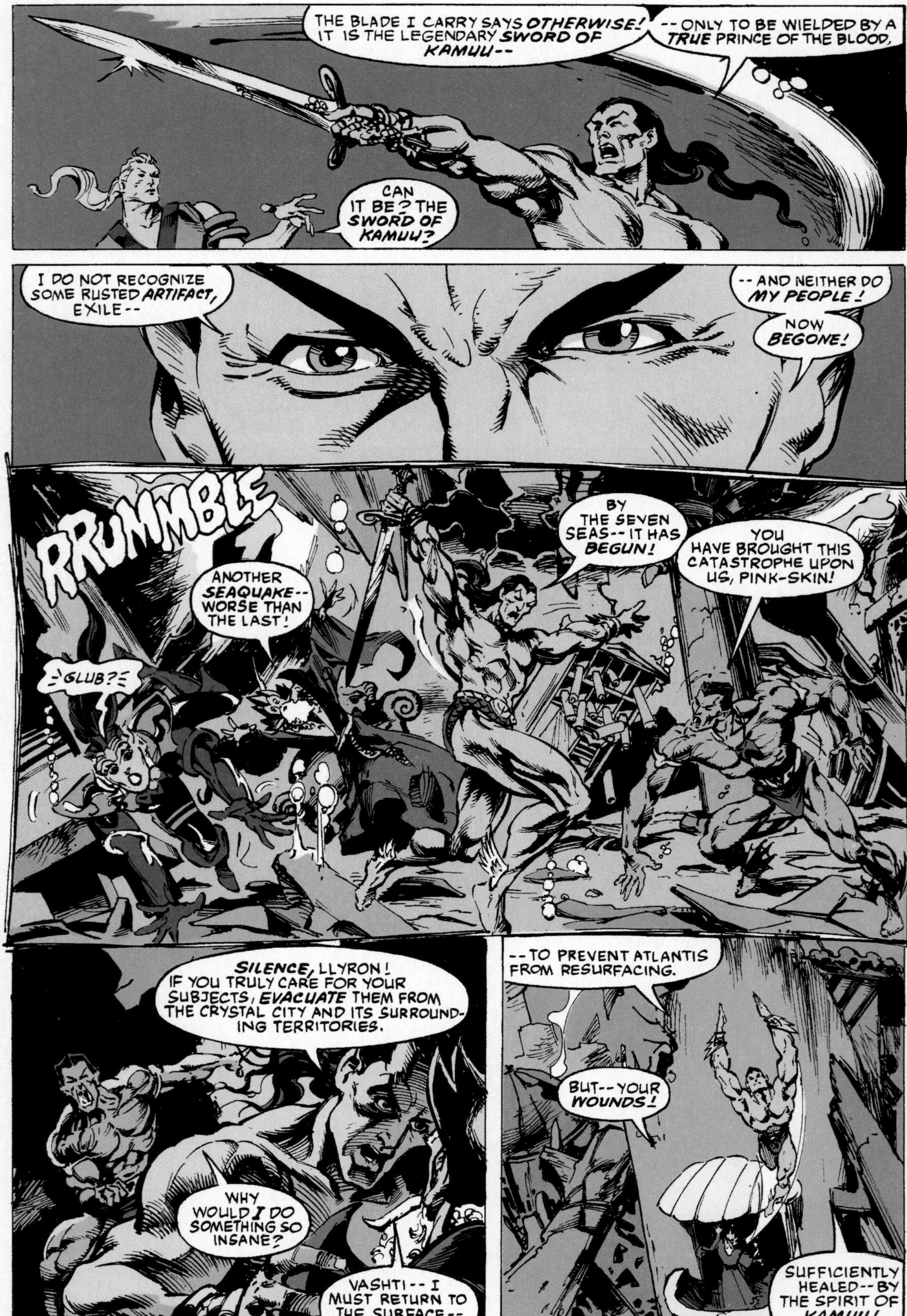

THE BLADE I CARRY SAYS OTHERWISE! IT IS THE LEGENDARY SWORD OF KAMUU--
--ONLY TO BE WIELDED BY A TRUE PRINCE OF THE BLOOD,
CAN IT BE? THE SWORD OF KAMUU?
I DO NOT RECOGNIZE SOME RUSTED ARTIFACT, EXILE--
--AND NEITHER DO MY PEOPLE!
NOW BEGONE!
RRUMMBLE
ANOTHER SEAQUAKE-- WORSE THAN THE LAST!
BY THE SEVEN SEAS-- IT HAS BEGUN!
YOU HAVE BROUGHT THIS CATASTROPHE UPON US, PINK-SKIN!
GLUB?
SILENCE, LLYRON! IF YOU TRULY CARE FOR YOUR SUBJECTS, EVACUATE THEM FROM THE CRYSTAL CITY AND ITS SURROUNDING TERRITORIES.
WHY WOULD I DO SOMETHING SO INSANE?
VASHTI-- I MUST RETURN TO THE SURFACE--
--TO PREVENT ATLANTIS FROM RESURFACING.
BUT--YOUR WOUNDS!
SUFFICIENTLY HEALED--BY THE SPIRIT OF KAMUU!

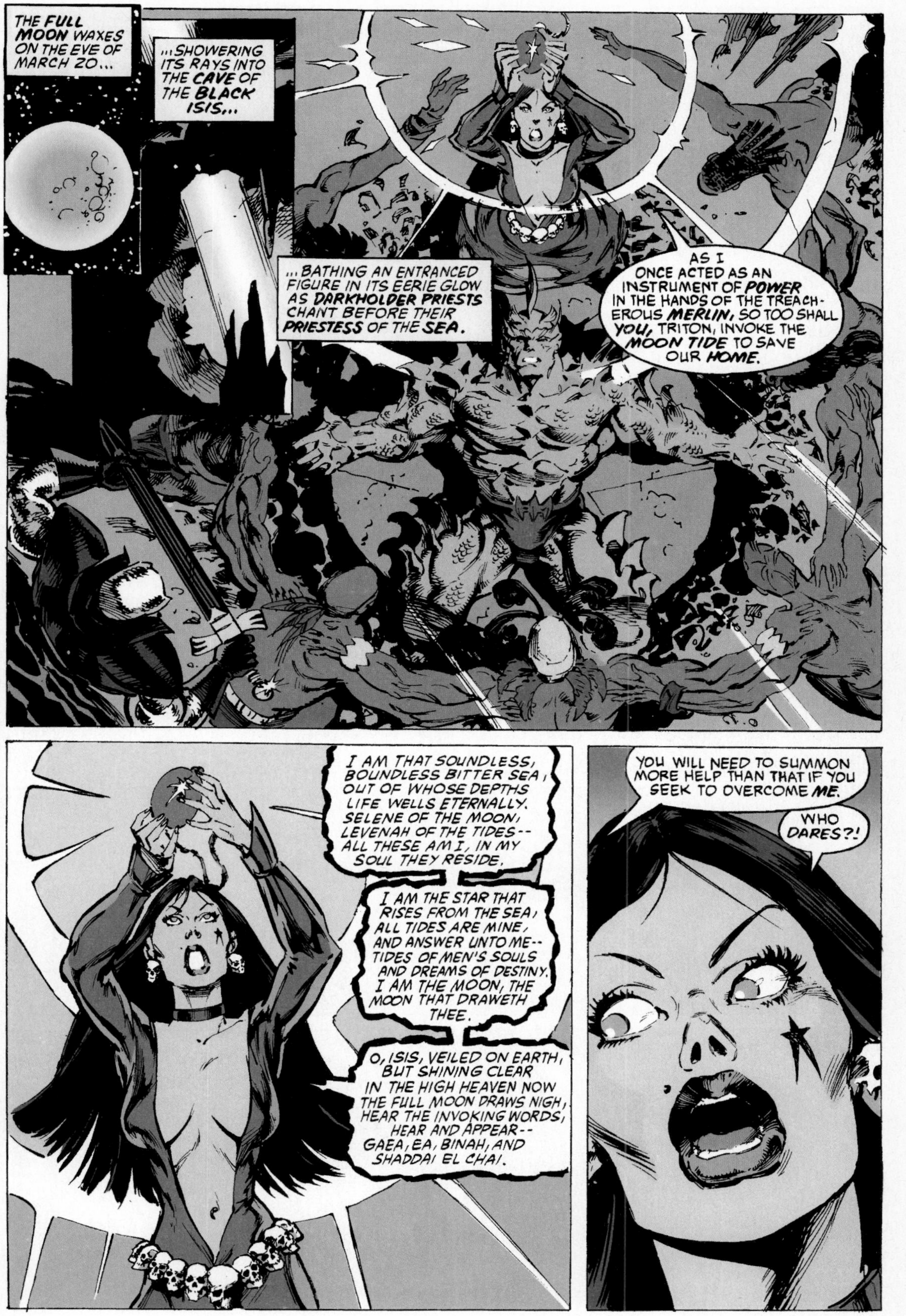
THE FULL MOON WAXES ON THE EVE OF MARCH 20...
...SHOWERING ITS RAYS INTO THE CAVE OF THE BLACK ISIS...
...BATHING AN ENTRANCED FIGURE IN ITS EERIE GLOW AS DARKHOLDER PRIESTS CHANT BEFORE THEIR PRIESTESS OF THE SEA.
AS I ONCE ACTED AS AN INSTRUMENT OF POWER IN THE HANDS OF THE TREACHEROUS MERLIN, SO TOO SHALL YOU, TRITON, INVOKE THE MOON TIDE TO SAVE OUR HOME.
I AM THAT SOUNDLESS, BOUNDLESS BITTER SEA, OUT OF WHOSE DEPTHS LIFE WELLS ETERNALLY. SELENE OF THE MOON, LEVENAH OF THE TIDES-- ALL THESE AM I, IN MY SOUL THEY RESIDE.
I AM THE STAR THAT RISES FROM THE SEA, ALL TIDES ARE MINE, AND ANSWER UNTO ME-- TIDES OF MEN'S SOULS AND DREAMS OF DESTINY. I AM THE MOON, THE MOON THAT DRAWETH THEE.
O, ISIS, VEILED ON EARTH, BUT SHINING CLEAR IN THE HIGH HEAVEN NOW THE FULL MOON DRAWS NIGH, HEAR THE INVOKING WORDS, HEAR AND APPEAR-- GAEA, EA, BINAH, AND SHADDAI EL CHAI.
YOU WILL NEED TO SUMMON MORE HELP THAN THAT IF YOU SEEK TO OVERCOME ME.
WHO DARES?!

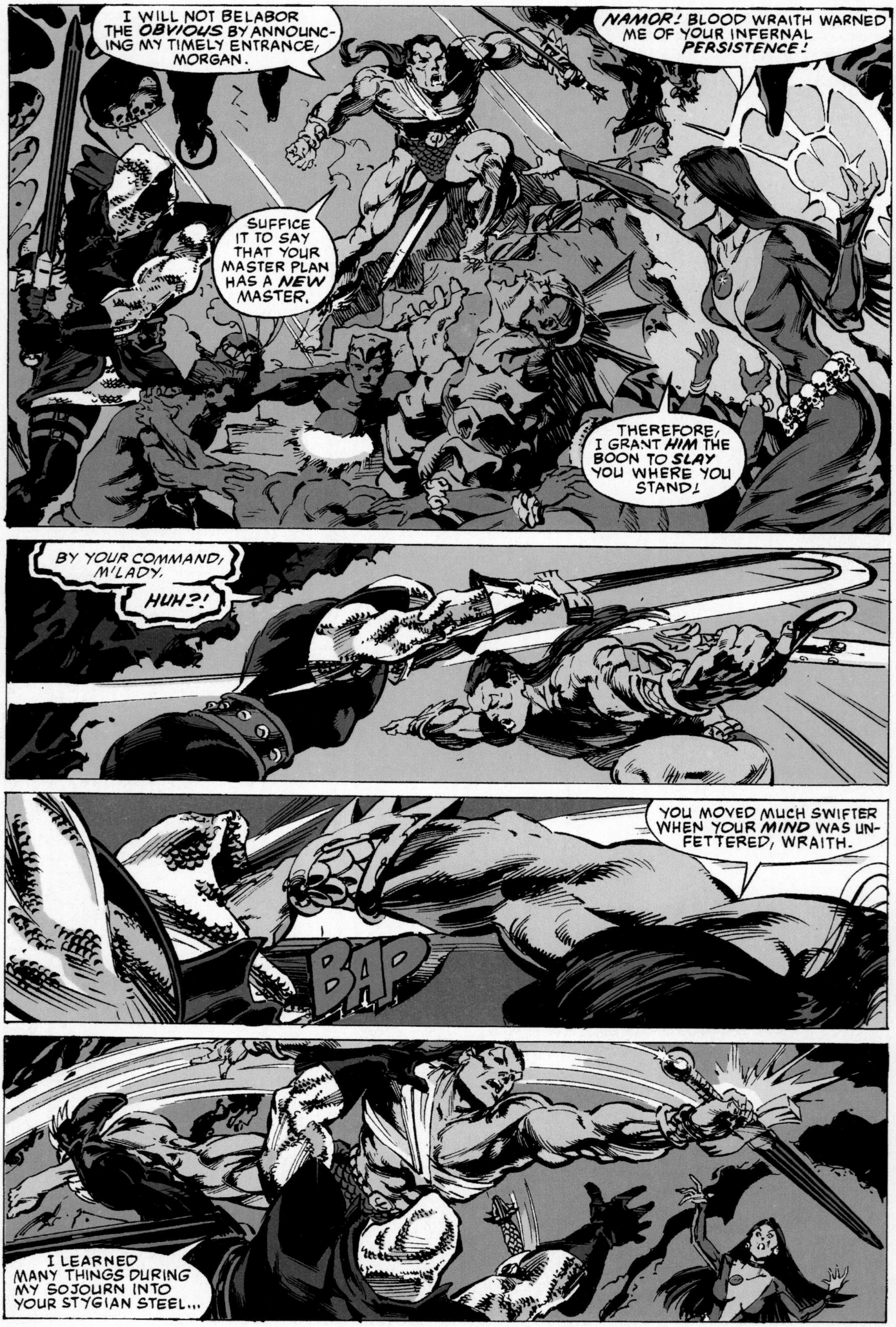
I WILL NOT BELABOR THE *OBVIOUS* BY ANNOUNCING MY TIMELY ENTRANCE, MORGAN.
SUFFICE IT TO SAY THAT YOUR MASTER PLAN HAS A *NEW* MASTER.
NAMOR! BLOOD WRAITH WARNED ME OF YOUR INFERNAL *PERSISTENCE!*
THEREFORE, I GRANT *HIM* THE BOON TO *SLAY* YOU WHERE YOU STAND!
BY YOUR COMMAND, M'LADY.
HUH?!
YOU MOVED MUCH SWIFTER WHEN YOUR *MIND* WAS UNFETTERED, WRAITH.
BAP
I LEARNED MANY THINGS DURING MY SOJOURN INTO YOUR STYGIAN STEEL...

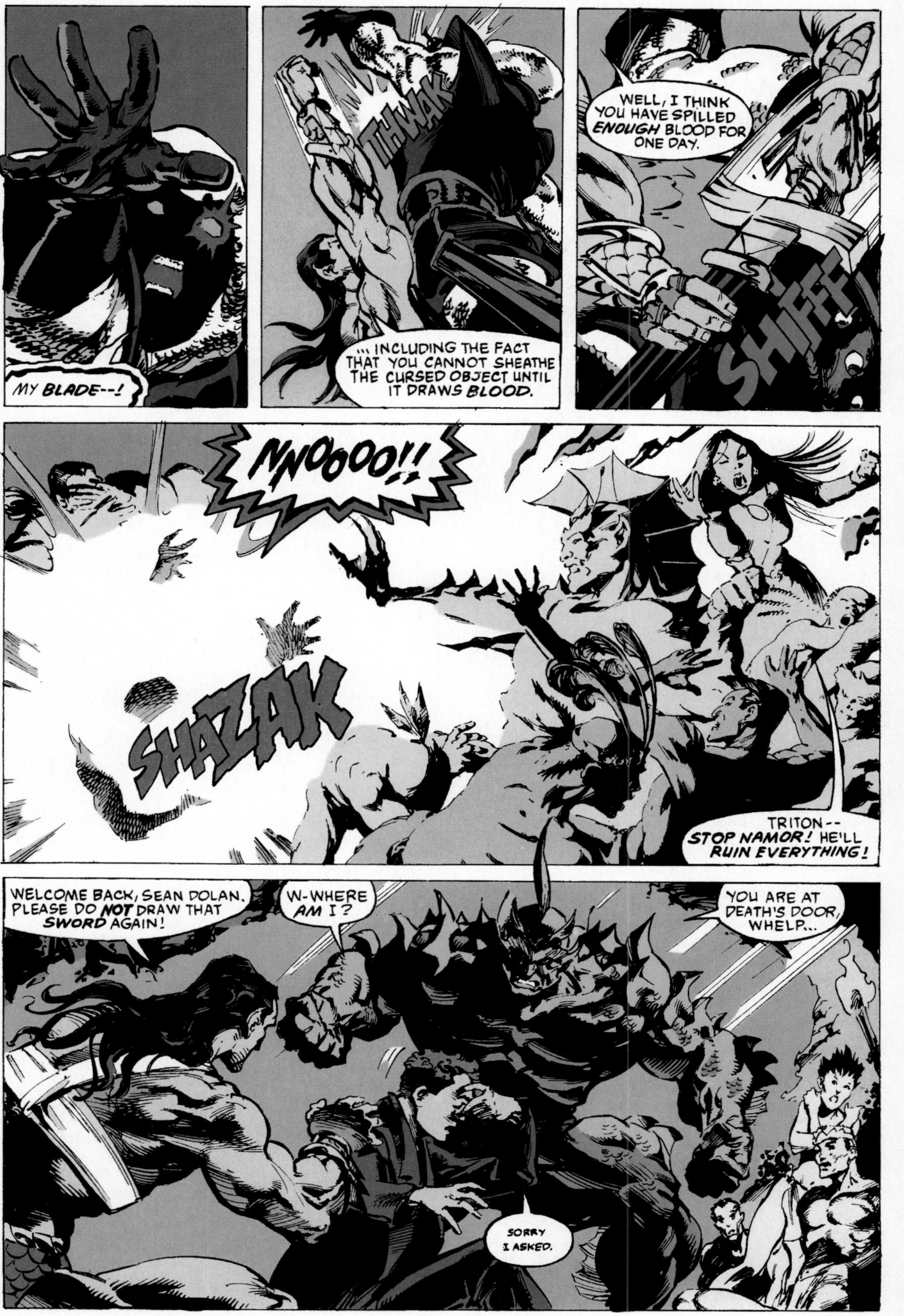
MY BLADE--!
THWAK
...INCLUDING THE FACT THAT YOU CANNOT SHEATHE THE CURSED OBJECT UNTIL IT DRAWS BLOOD.
WELL, I THINK YOU HAVE SPILLED ENOUGH BLOOD FOR ONE DAY.
SHIFF
NNOOOO!!
SHAZAK
TRITON -- STOP NAMOR! HE'LL RUIN EVERYTHING!
WELCOME BACK, SEAN DOLAN. PLEASE DO NOT DRAW THAT SWORD AGAIN!
W-WHERE AM I?
YOU ARE AT DEATH'S DOOR, WHELP...
SORRY I ASKED.

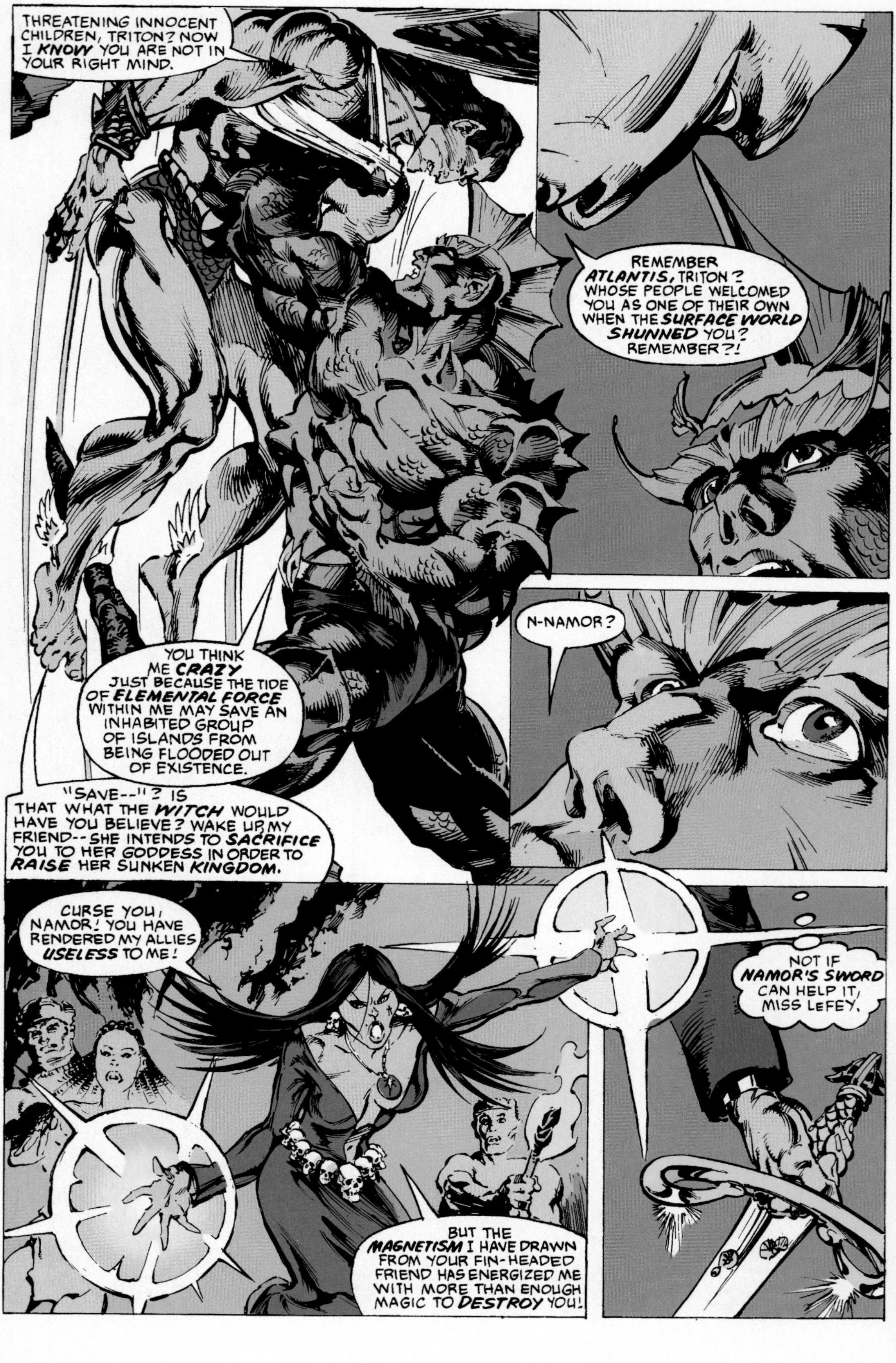
THREATENING INNOCENT CHILDREN, TRITON? NOW I KNOW YOU ARE NOT IN YOUR RIGHT MIND.
REMEMBER ATLANTIS, TRITON? WHOSE PEOPLE WELCOMED YOU AS ONE OF THEIR OWN WHEN THE SURFACE WORLD SHUNNED YOU? REMEMBER?!
YOU THINK ME CRAZY JUST BECAUSE THE TIDE OF ELEMENTAL FORCE WITHIN ME MAY SAVE AN INHABITED GROUP OF ISLANDS FROM BEING FLOODED OUT OF EXISTENCE.
"SAVE--"? IS THAT WHAT THE WITCH WOULD HAVE YOU BELIEVE? WAKE UP, MY FRIEND--SHE INTENDS TO SACRIFICE YOU TO HER GODDESS IN ORDER TO RAISE HER SUNKEN KINGDOM.
N-NAMOR?
CURSE YOU, NAMOR! YOU HAVE RENDERED MY ALLIES USELESS TO ME!
BUT THE MAGNETISM I HAVE DRAWN FROM YOUR FIN-HEADED FRIEND HAS ENERGIZED ME WITH MORE THAN ENOUGH MAGIC TO DESTROY YOU!
NOT IF NAMOR'S SWORD CAN HELP IT, MISS LEFEY.

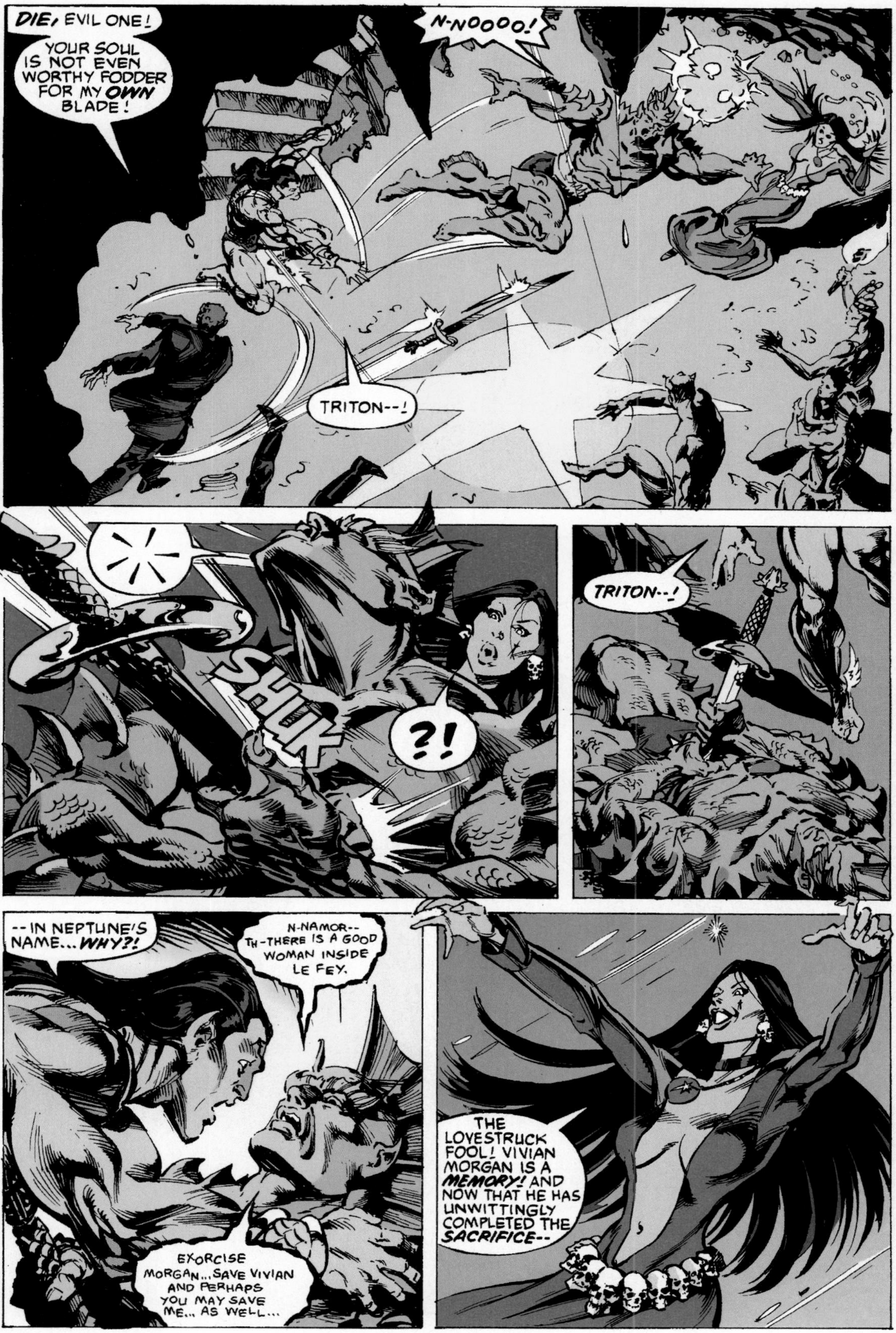

DIE, EVIL ONE!
YOUR SOUL IS NOT EVEN WORTHY FODDER FOR MY OWN BLADE!
N-NOOOO!
TRITON--!
SHUK
?!
TRITON--!
--IN NEPTUNE'S NAME... WHY?!
N-NAMOR-- TH-THERE IS A GOOD WOMAN INSIDE LE FEY.
EXORCISE MORGAN... SAVE VIVIAN AND PERHAPS YOU MAY SAVE ME... AS WELL...
THE LOVESTRUCK FOOL! VIVIAN MORGAN IS A MEMORY! AND NOW THAT HE HAS UNWITTINGLY COMPLETED THE SACRIFICE--

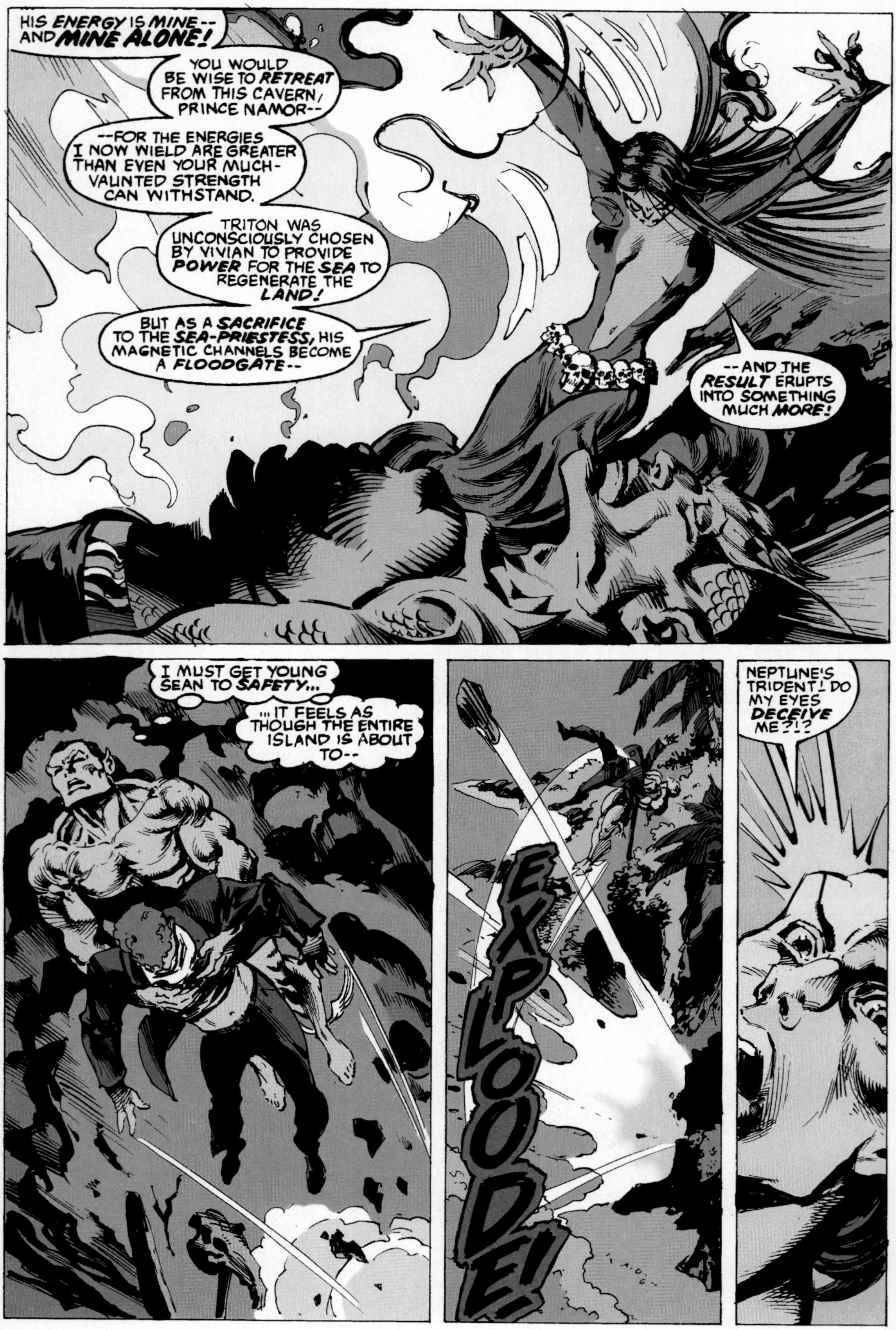
HIS ENERGY IS MINE-- AND MINE ALONE!
YOU WOULD BE WISE TO RETREAT FROM THIS CAVERN, PRINCE NAMOR--
--FOR THE ENERGIES I NOW WIELD ARE GREATER THAN EVEN YOUR MUCH-VAUNTED STRENGTH CAN WITHSTAND.
TRITON WAS UNCONSCIOUSLY CHOSEN BY VIVIAN TO PROVIDE POWER FOR THE SEA TO REGENERATE THE LAND!
BUT AS A SACRIFICE TO THE SEA-PRIESTESS, HIS MAGNETIC CHANNELS BECOME A FLOODGATE--
--AND THE RESULT ERUPTS INTO SOMETHING MUCH MORE!
I MUST GET YOUNG SEAN TO SAFETY...
...IT FEELS AS THOUGH THE ENTIRE ISLAND IS ABOUT TO--
EXPLODE!
NEPTUNE'S TRIDENT! DO MY EYES DECEIVE ME?!?

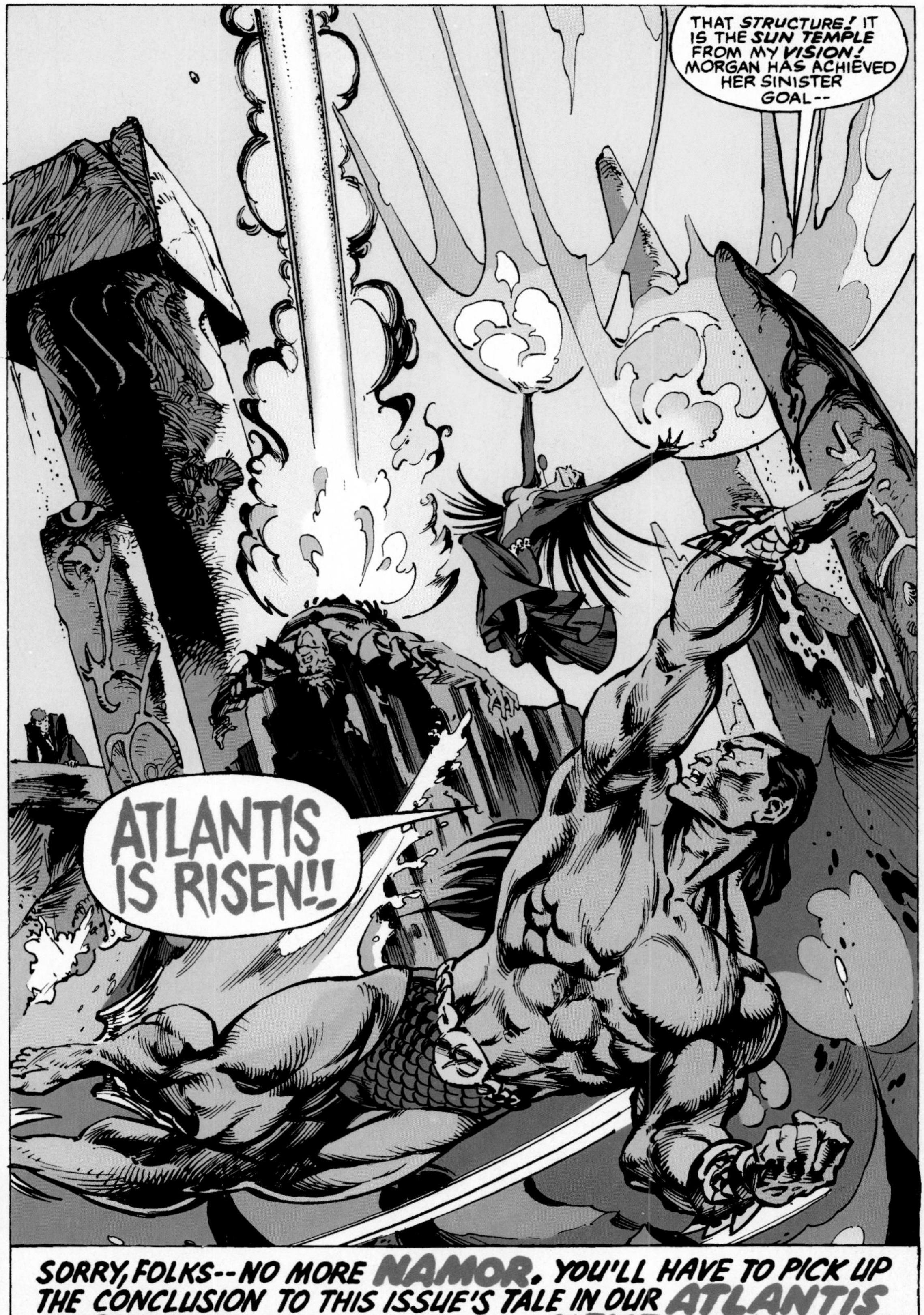
THAT STRUCTURE! IT IS THE SUN TEMPLE FROM MY VISION! MORGAN HAS ACHIEVED HER SINISTER GOAL--
ATLANTIS IS RISEN!!

SORRY, FOLKS--NO MORE NAMOR. YOU'LL HAVE TO PICK UP THE CONCLUSION TO THIS ISSUE'S TALE IN OUR ATLANTIS RISING SPECTACULAR--ON SALE NEXT MONTH!!

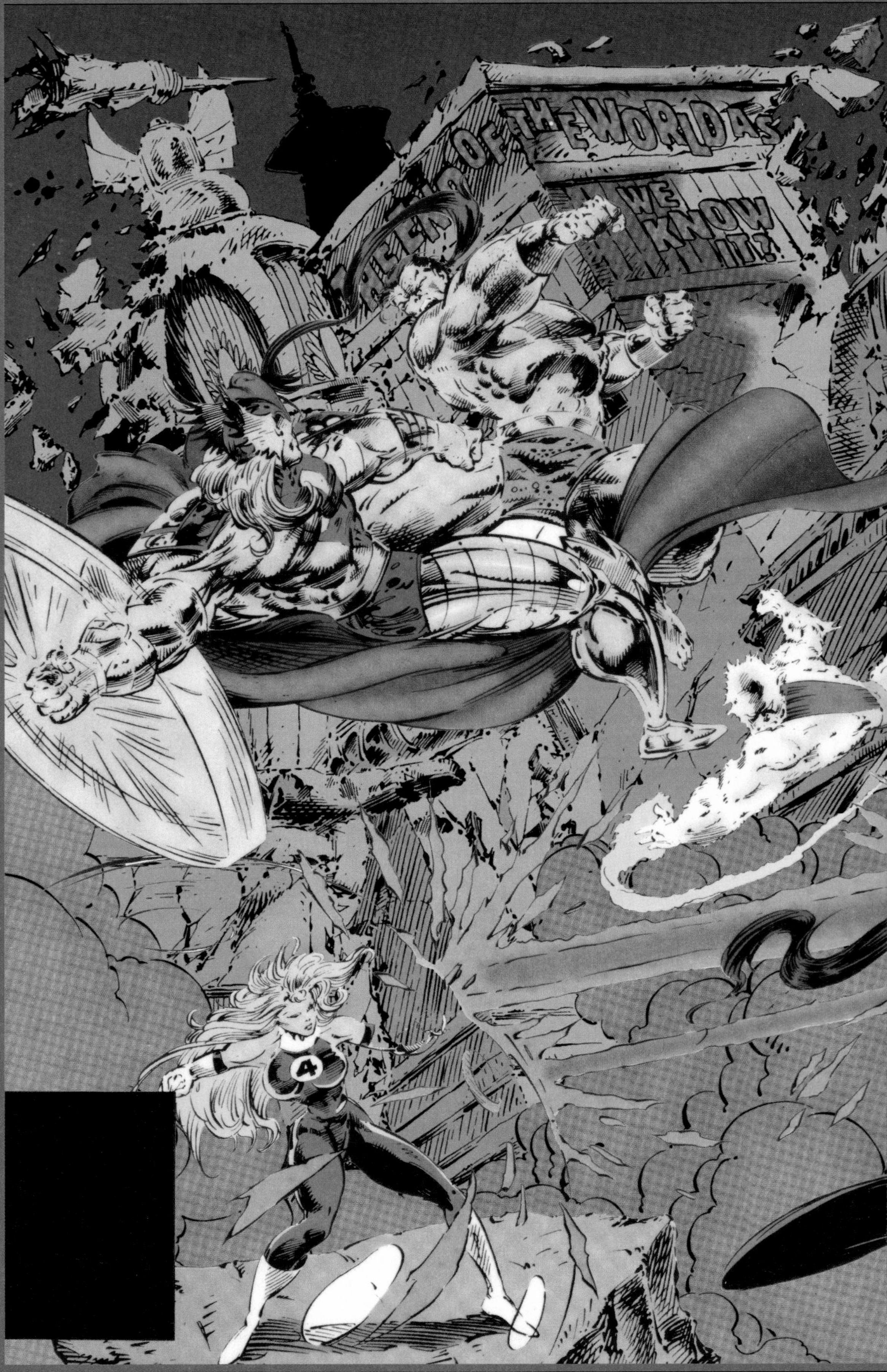
OF THE WORLD AS
WE KNOW IT?

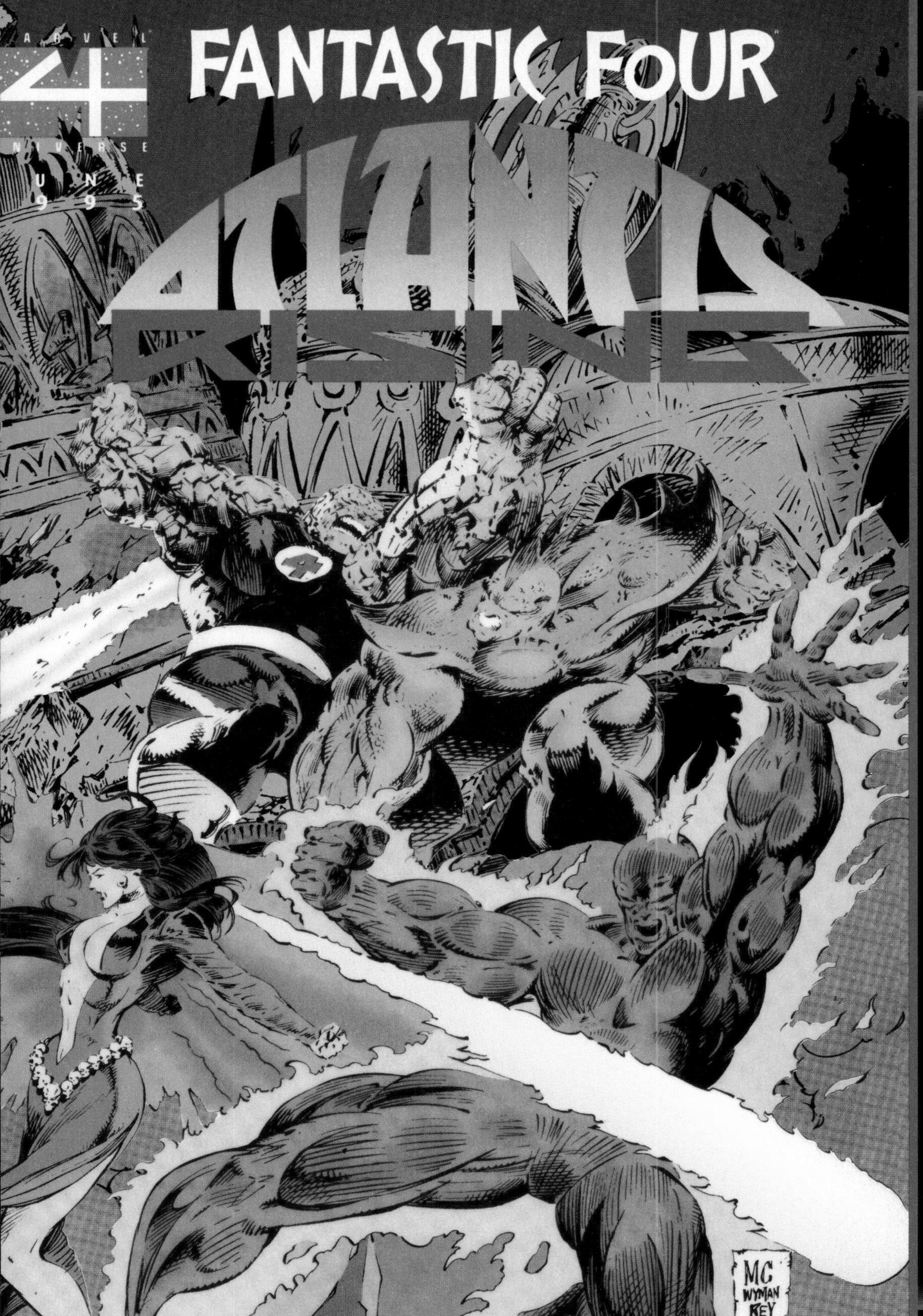
MARVEL UNIVERSE
JUNE 1995
FANTASTIC FOUR
ATLANTIS RISING
MC WYMAN REY GARCIA '95

FANTASTIC FOUR: ATLANTIS RISING #1-2 HAD CLEAR ACETATE OUTER COVERS FEATURING THE ISSUES' CHARACTERS, OVERLAID ON INNER COVERS DEPICTING THE BACKGROUNDS.

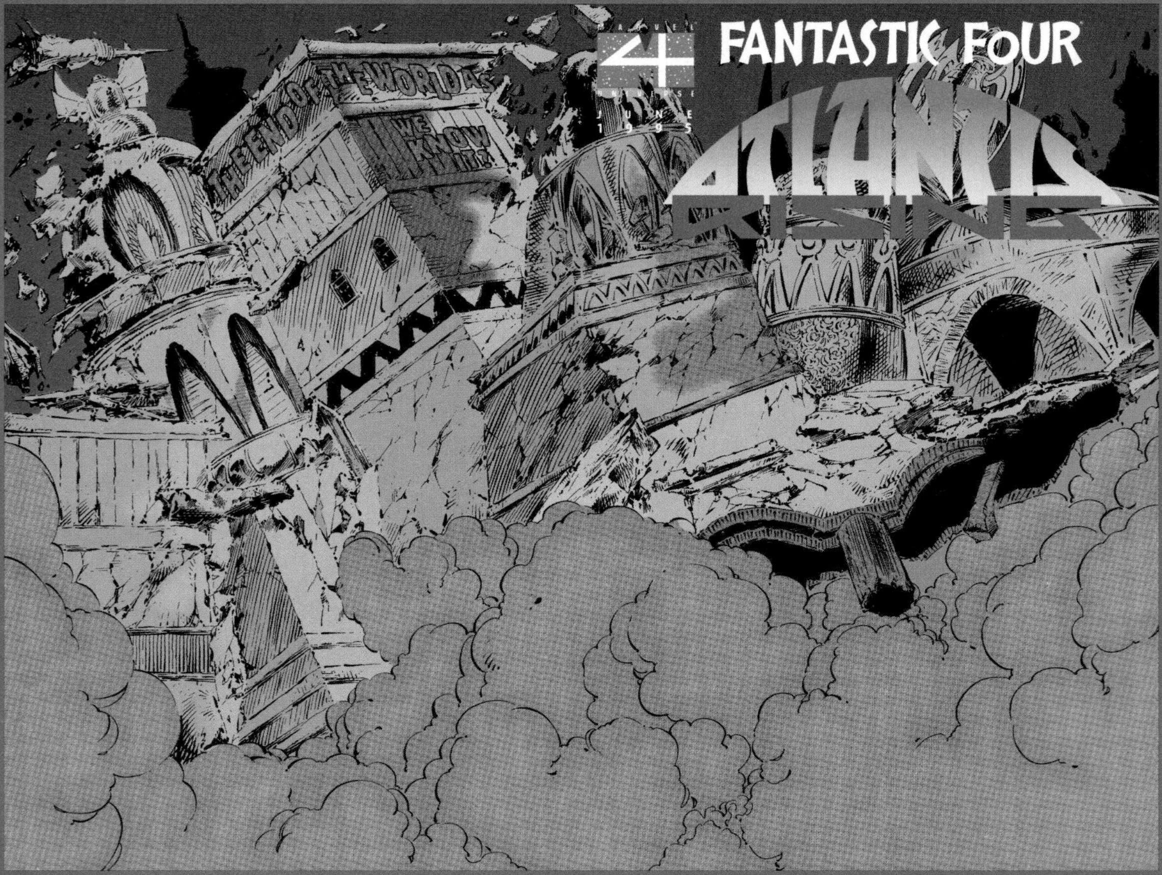
MARVEL
4
UNIVERSE
JUNE 1995
FANTASTIC FOUR
ATLANTIS RISING
THE END OF THE WORLD AS
WE KNOW

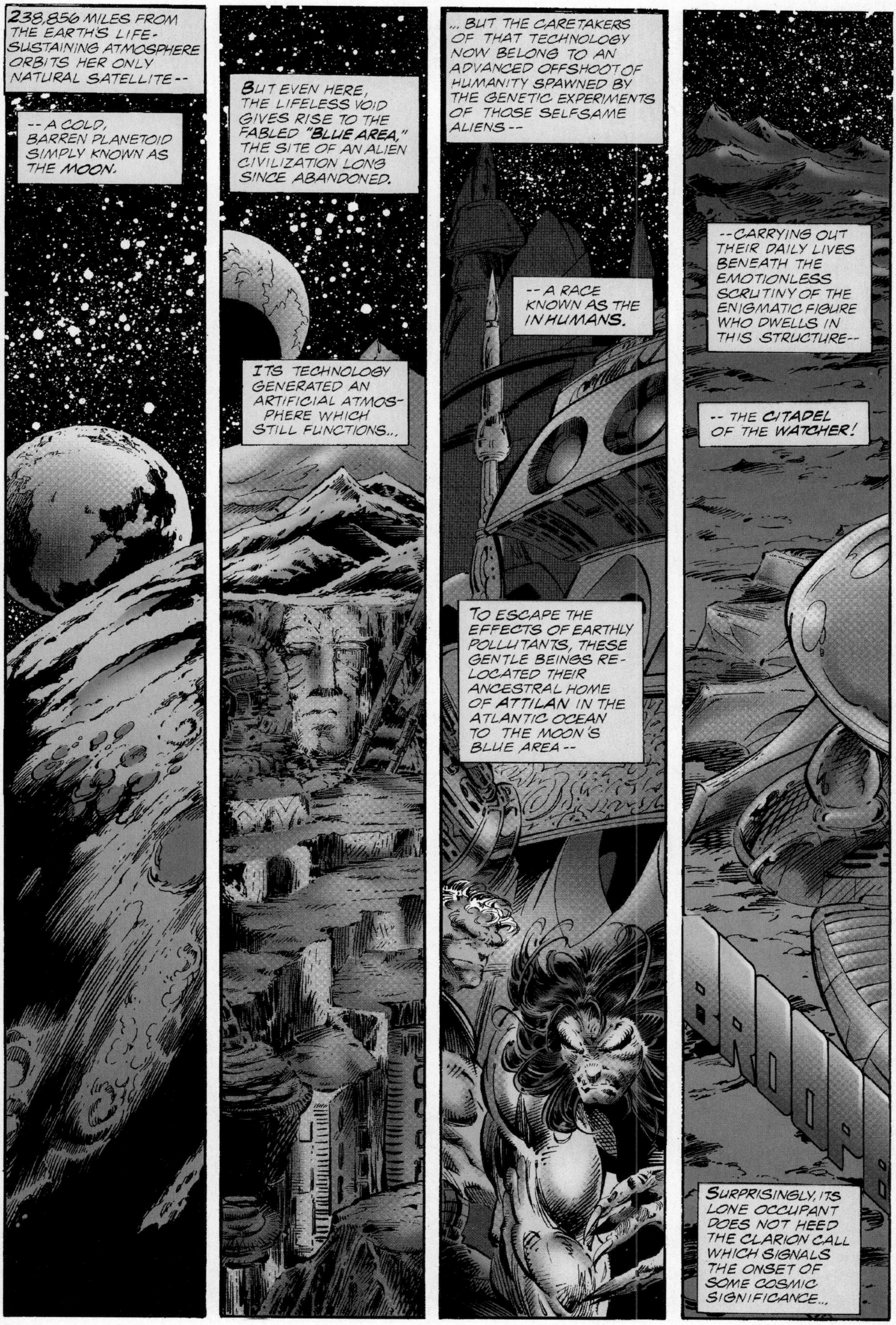
238,856 MILES FROM THE EARTH'S LIFE-SUSTAINING ATMOSPHERE ORBITS HER ONLY NATURAL SATELLITE--
-- A COLD, BARREN PLANETOID SIMPLY KNOWN AS THE MOON.
BUT EVEN HERE, THE LIFELESS VOID GIVES RISE TO THE FABLED "BLUE AREA," THE SITE OF AN ALIEN CIVILIZATION LONG SINCE ABANDONED.
ITS TECHNOLOGY GENERATED AN ARTIFICIAL ATMOSPHERE WHICH STILL FUNCTIONS...
... BUT THE CARETAKERS OF THAT TECHNOLOGY NOW BELONG TO AN ADVANCED OFFSHOOT OF HUMANITY SPAWNED BY THE GENETIC EXPERIMENTS OF THOSE SELFSAME ALIENS --
-- A RACE KNOWN AS THE INHUMANS.
TO ESCAPE THE EFFECTS OF EARTHLY POLLUTANTS, THESE GENTLE BEINGS RELOCATED THEIR ANCESTRAL HOME OF ATTILAN IN THE ATLANTIC OCEAN TO THE MOON'S BLUE AREA --
--CARRYING OUT THEIR DAILY LIVES BENEATH THE EMOTIONLESS SCRUTINY OF THE ENIGMATIC FIGURE WHO DWELLS IN THIS STRUCTURE--
-- THE CITADEL OF THE WATCHER!
SURPRISINGLY, ITS LONE OCCUPANT DOES NOT HEED THE CLARION CALL WHICH SIGNALS THE ONSET OF SOME COSMIC SIGNIFICANCE...

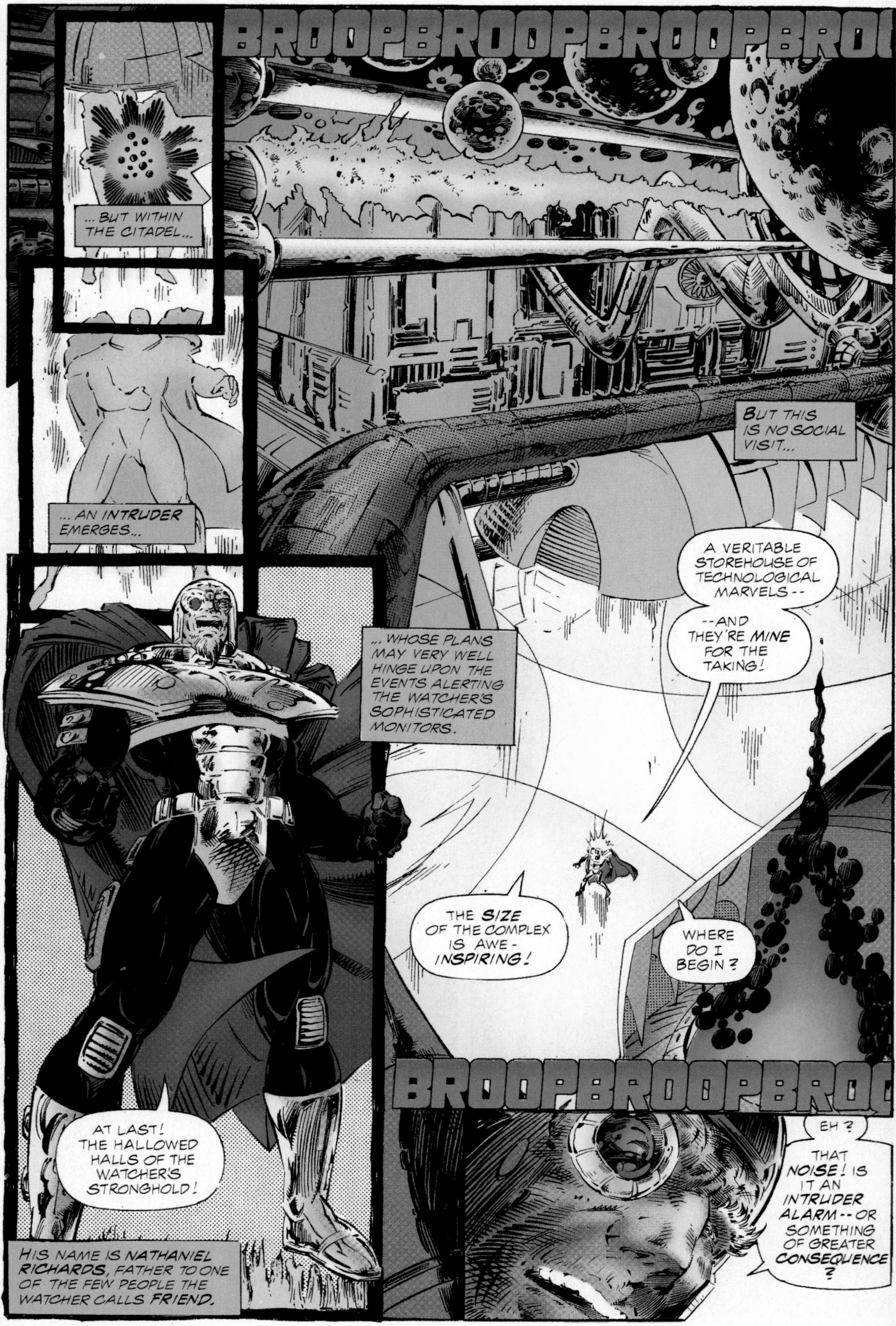
BROOPBROOPBROOPBROO
...BUT WITHIN THE CITADEL...
...AN INTRUDER EMERGES...
BUT THIS IS NO SOCIAL VISIT...
...WHOSE PLANS MAY VERY WELL HINGE UPON THE EVENTS ALERTING THE WATCHER'S SOPHISTICATED MONITORS.
A VERITABLE STOREHOUSE OF TECHNOLOGICAL MARVELS--
--AND THEY'RE MINE FOR THE TAKING!
THE SIZE OF THE COMPLEX IS AWE-INSPIRING!
WHERE DO I BEGIN?
AT LAST! THE HALLOWED HALLS OF THE WATCHER'S STRONGHOLD!
HIS NAME IS NATHANIEL RICHARDS, FATHER TO ONE OF THE FEW PEOPLE THE WATCHER CALLS FRIEND.
BROOPBROOPBROO
EH?
THAT NOISE! IS IT AN INTRUDER ALARM--OR SOMETHING OF GREATER CONSEQUENCE?

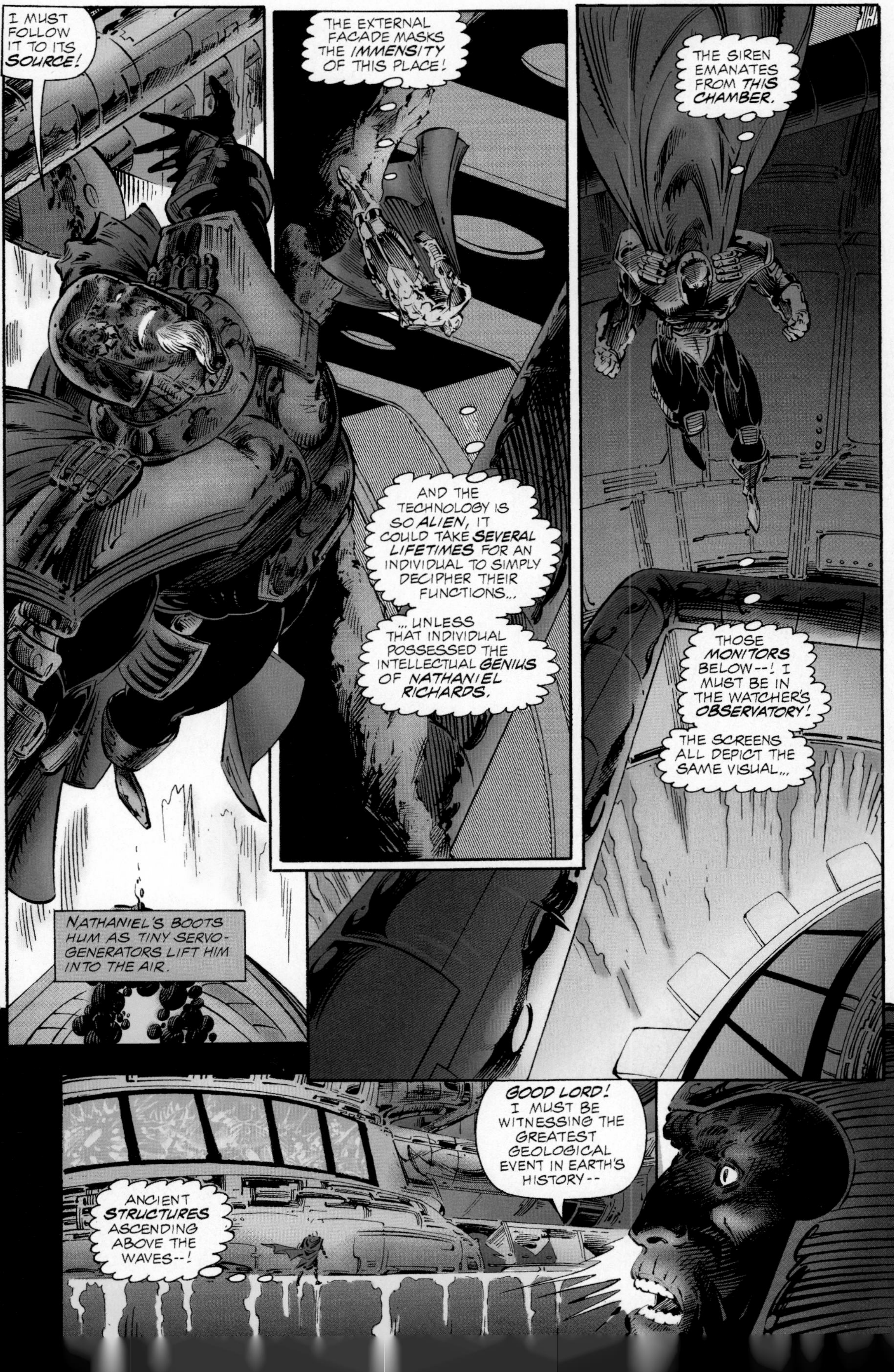
I MUST FOLLOW IT TO ITS SOURCE!
NATHANIEL'S BOOTS HUM AS TINY SERVO-GENERATORS LIFT HIM INTO THE AIR.
THE EXTERNAL FACADE MASKS THE IMMENSITY OF THIS PLACE!
AND THE TECHNOLOGY IS SO ALIEN, IT COULD TAKE SEVERAL LIFETIMES FOR AN INDIVIDUAL TO SIMPLY DECIPHER THEIR FUNCTIONS...
...UNLESS THAT INDIVIDUAL POSSESSED THE INTELLECTUAL GENIUS OF NATHANIEL RICHARDS.
THE SIREN EMANATES FROM THIS CHAMBER.
THOSE MONITORS BELOW--! I MUST BE IN THE WATCHER'S OBSERVATORY!
THE SCREENS ALL DEPICT THE SAME VISUAL...
ANCIENT STRUCTURES ASCENDING ABOVE THE WAVES--!
GOOD LORD! I MUST BE WITNESSING THE GREATEST GEOLOGICAL EVENT IN EARTH'S HISTORY--

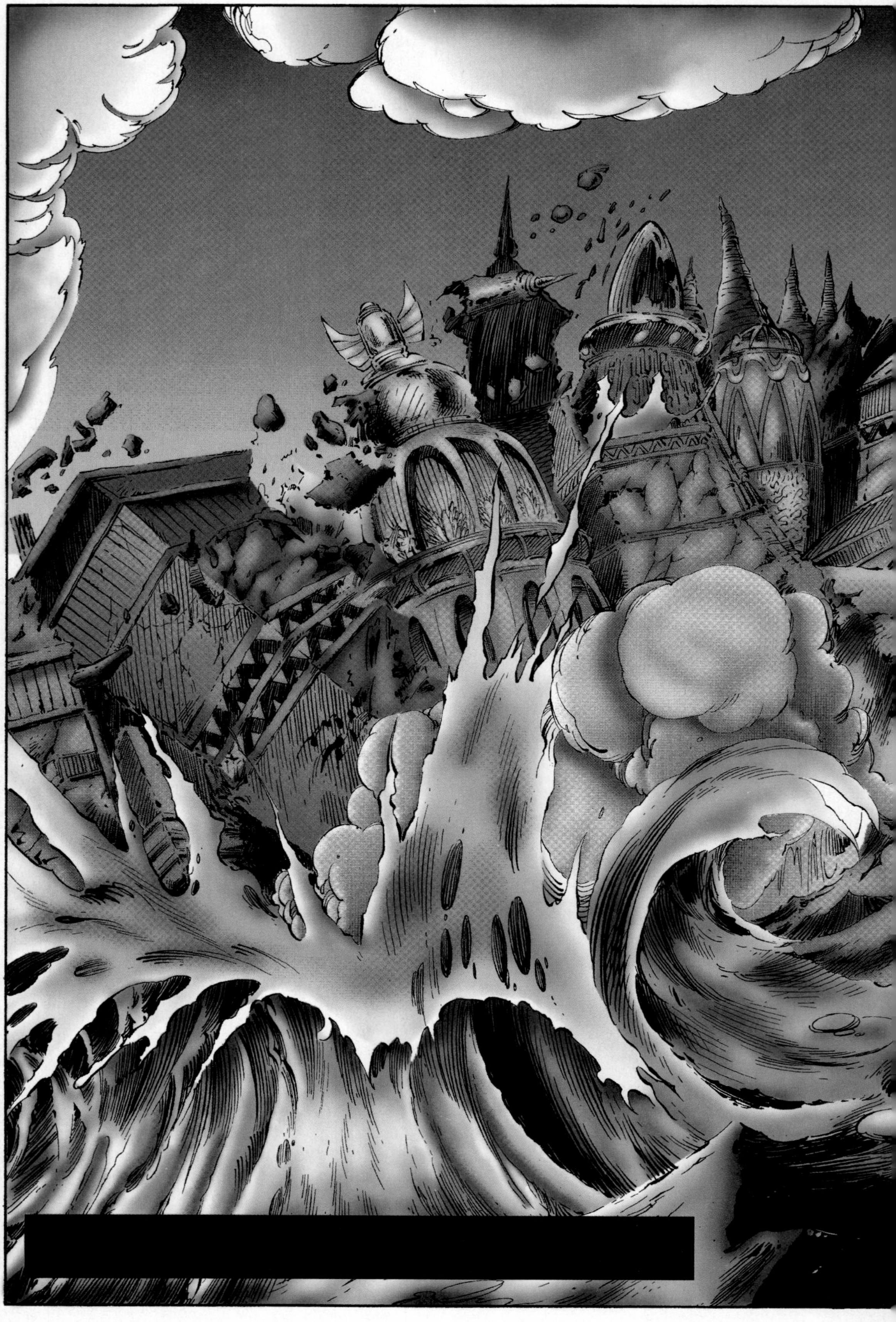
[redacted]

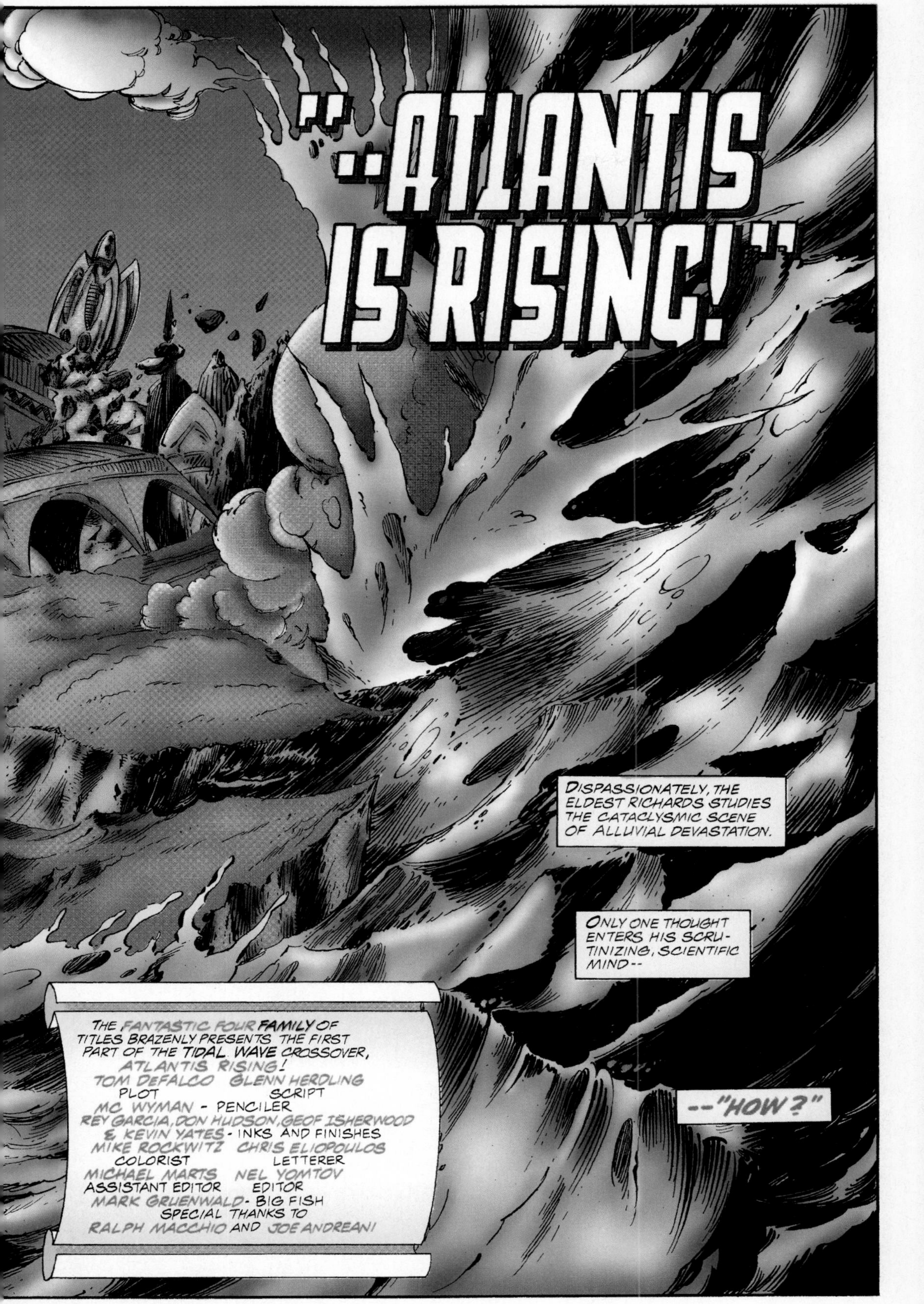
"..ATLANTIS IS RISING!"
DISPASSIONATELY, THE ELDEST RICHARDS STUDIES THE CATACLYSMIC SCENE OF ALLUVIAL DEVASTATION.
ONLY ONE THOUGHT ENTERS HIS SCRUTINIZING, SCIENTIFIC MIND--
--"HOW?"
THE FANTASTIC FOUR FAMILY OF TITLES BRAZENLY PRESENTS THE FIRST PART OF THE TIDAL WAVE CROSSOVER, ATLANTIS RISING!
TOM DEFALCO PLOT GLENN HERDLING SCRIPT
MC WYMAN - PENCILER
REY GARCIA, DON HUDSON, GEOF ISHERWOOD & KEVIN YATES - INKS AND FINISHES
MIKE ROCKWITZ COLORIST CHRIS ELIOPOULOS LETTERER
MICHAEL MARTS ASSISTANT EDITOR NEL YOMTOV EDITOR
MARK GRUENWALD - BIG FISH
SPECIAL THANKS TO RALPH MACCHIO AND JOE ANDREANI

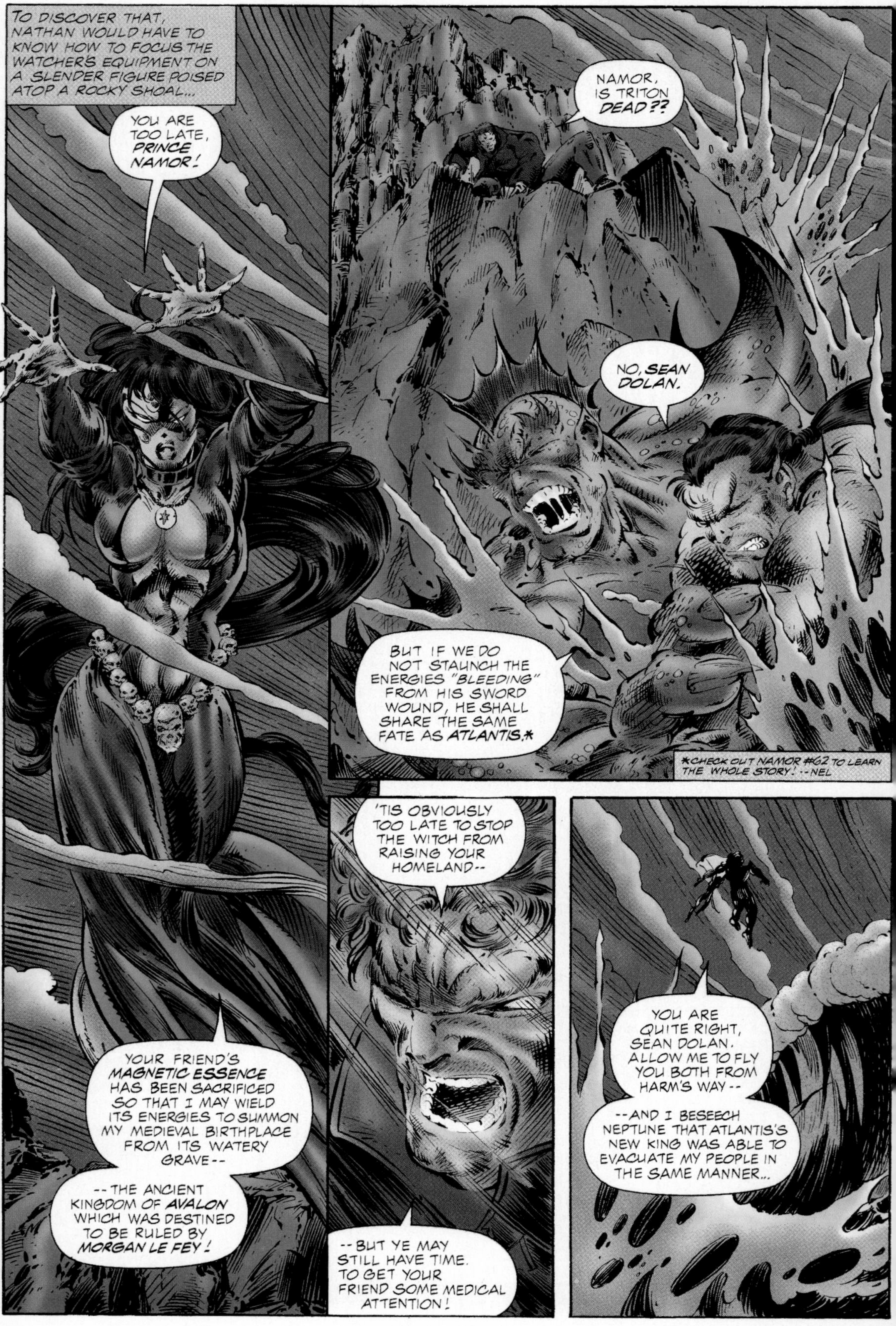
TO DISCOVER THAT, NATHAN WOULD HAVE TO KNOW HOW TO FOCUS THE WATCHER'S EQUIPMENT ON A SLENDER FIGURE POISED ATOP A ROCKY SHOAL...
YOU ARE TOO LATE, PRINCE NAMOR!
NAMOR, IS TRITON DEAD??
NO, SEAN DOLAN.
BUT IF WE DO NOT STAUNCH THE ENERGIES "BLEEDING" FROM HIS SWORD WOUND, HE SHALL SHARE THE SAME FATE AS ATLANTIS.*
*CHECK OUT NAMOR #62 TO LEARN THE WHOLE STORY! --NEL
YOUR FRIEND'S MAGNETIC ESSENCE HAS BEEN SACRIFICED SO THAT I MAY WIELD ITS ENERGIES TO SUMMON MY MEDIEVAL BIRTHPLACE FROM ITS WATERY GRAVE--
--THE ANCIENT KINGDOM OF AVALON WHICH WAS DESTINED TO BE RULED BY MORGAN LE FEY!
'TIS OBVIOUSLY TOO LATE TO STOP THE WITCH FROM RAISING YOUR HOMELAND--
--BUT YE MAY STILL HAVE TIME TO GET YOUR FRIEND SOME MEDICAL ATTENTION!
YOU ARE QUITE RIGHT, SEAN DOLAN. ALLOW ME TO FLY YOU BOTH FROM HARM'S WAY--
--AND I BESEECH NEPTUNE THAT ATLANTIS'S NEW KING WAS ABLE TO EVACUATE MY PEOPLE IN THE SAME MANNER...

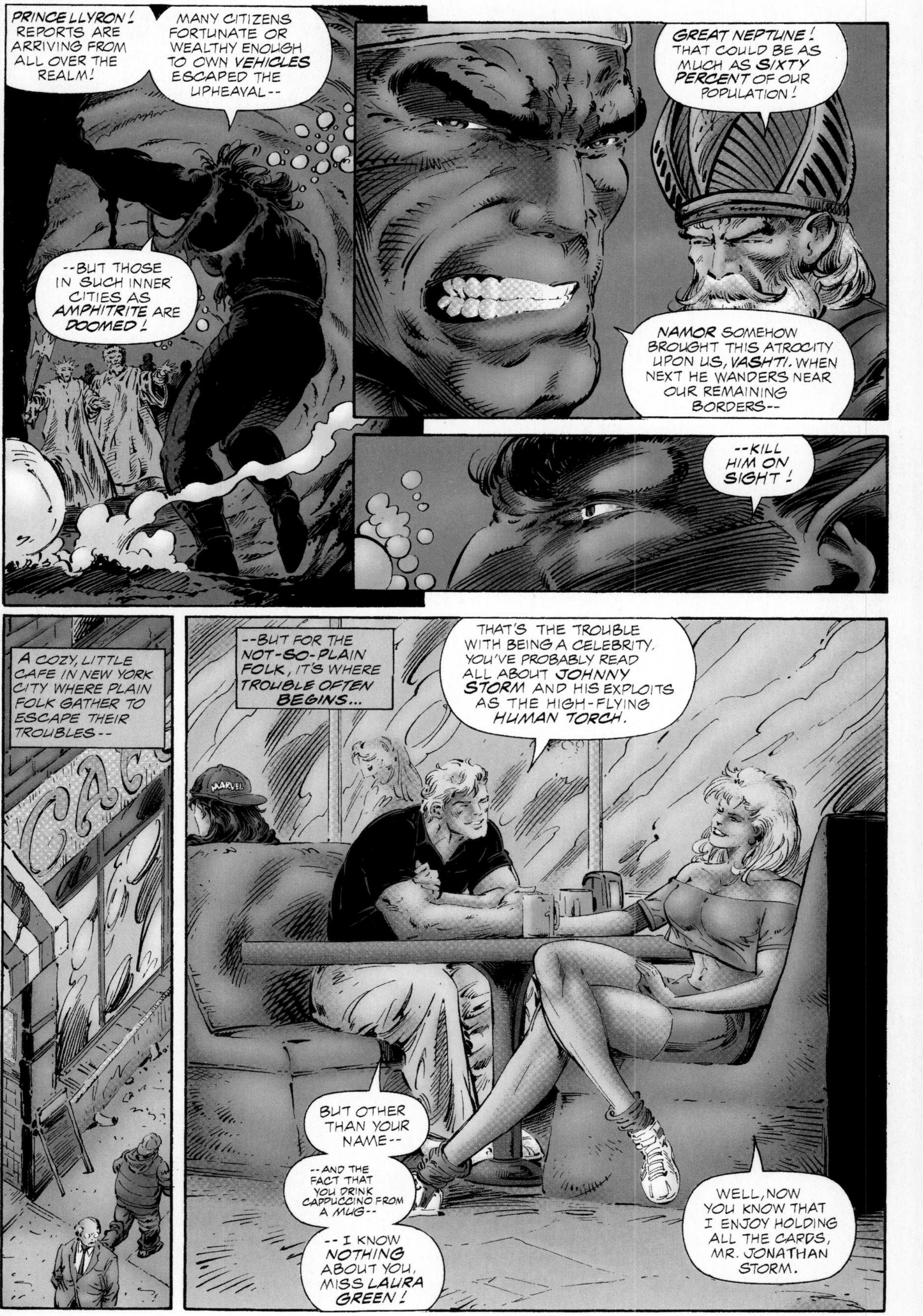
PRINCE LLYRON! REPORTS ARE ARRIVING FROM ALL OVER THE REALM!
MANY CITIZENS FORTUNATE OR WEALTHY ENOUGH TO OWN VEHICLES ESCAPED THE UPHEAVAL--
--BUT THOSE IN SUCH INNER CITIES AS AMPHITRITE ARE DOOMED!
GREAT NEPTUNE! THAT COULD BE AS MUCH AS SIXTY PERCENT OF OUR POPULATION!
NAMOR SOMEHOW BROUGHT THIS ATROCITY UPON US, VASHTI. WHEN NEXT HE WANDERS NEAR OUR REMAINING BORDERS--
--KILL HIM ON SIGHT!
A COZY, LITTLE CAFE IN NEW YORK CITY WHERE PLAIN FOLK GATHER TO ESCAPE THEIR TROUBLES--
--BUT FOR THE NOT-SO-PLAIN FOLK, IT'S WHERE TROUBLE OFTEN BEGINS...
THAT'S THE TROUBLE WITH BEING A CELEBRITY. YOU'VE PROBABLY READ ALL ABOUT JOHNNY STORM AND HIS EXPLOITS AS THE HIGH-FLYING HUMAN TORCH.
MARVEL
BUT OTHER THAN YOUR NAME--
--AND THE FACT THAT YOU DRINK CAPPUCCINO FROM A MUG--
--I KNOW NOTHING ABOUT YOU, MISS LAURA GREEN!
WELL, NOW YOU KNOW THAT I ENJOY HOLDING ALL THE CARDS, MR. JONATHAN STORM.

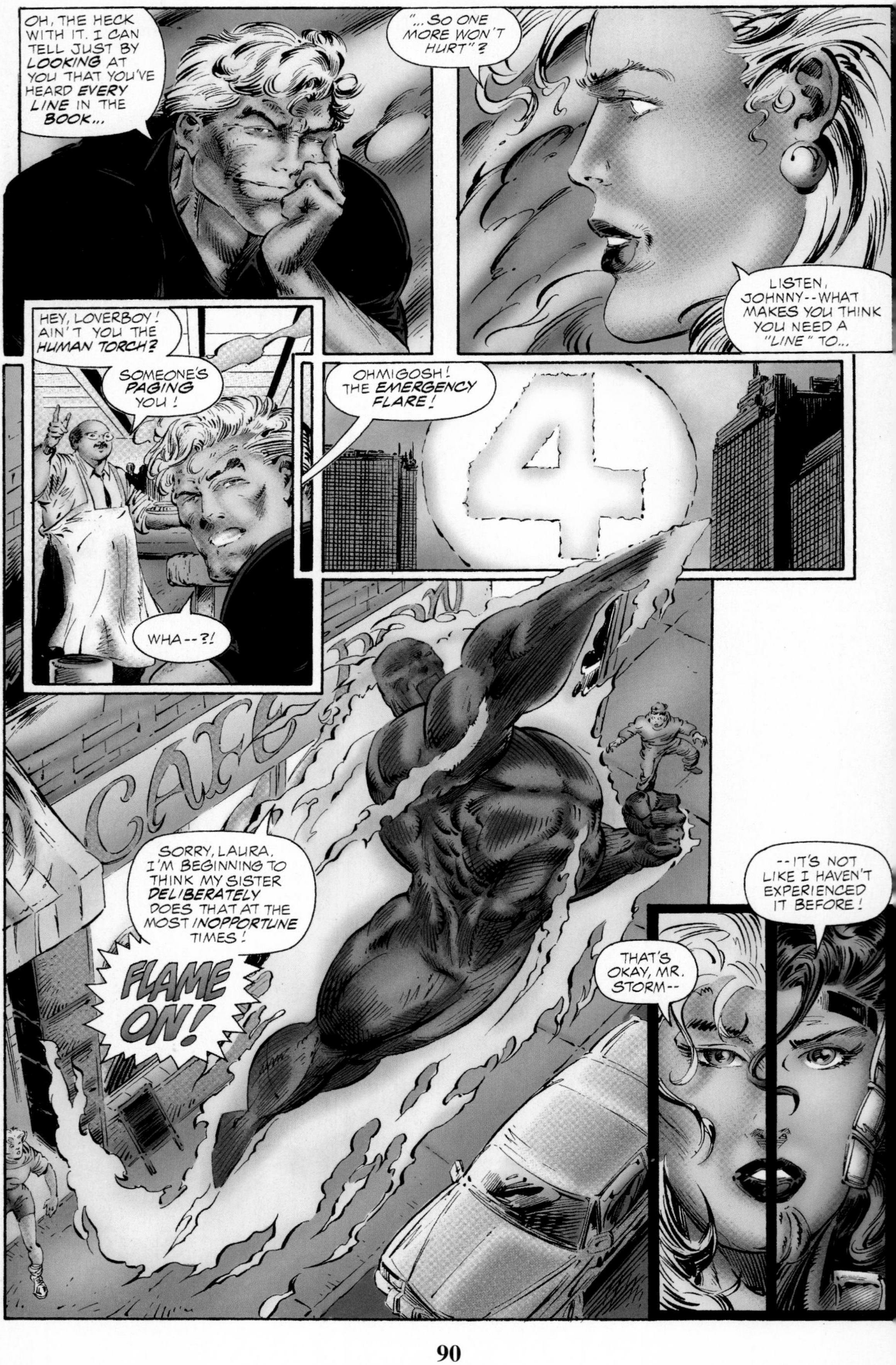
OH, THE HECK WITH IT. I CAN TELL JUST BY LOOKING AT YOU THAT YOU'VE HEARD EVERY LINE IN THE BOOK...
"...SO ONE MORE WON'T HURT"?
LISTEN, JOHNNY--WHAT MAKES YOU THINK YOU NEED A "LINE" TO...
HEY, LOVERBOY! AIN'T YOU THE HUMAN TORCH?
SOMEONE'S PAGING YOU!
WHA--?!
OHMIGOSH! THE EMERGENCY FLARE!
SORRY, LAURA. I'M BEGINNING TO THINK MY SISTER DELIBERATELY DOES THAT AT THE MOST INOPPORTUNE TIMES!
FLAME ON!
THAT'S OKAY, MR. STORM--
--IT'S NOT LIKE I HAVEN'T EXPERIENCED IT BEFORE!

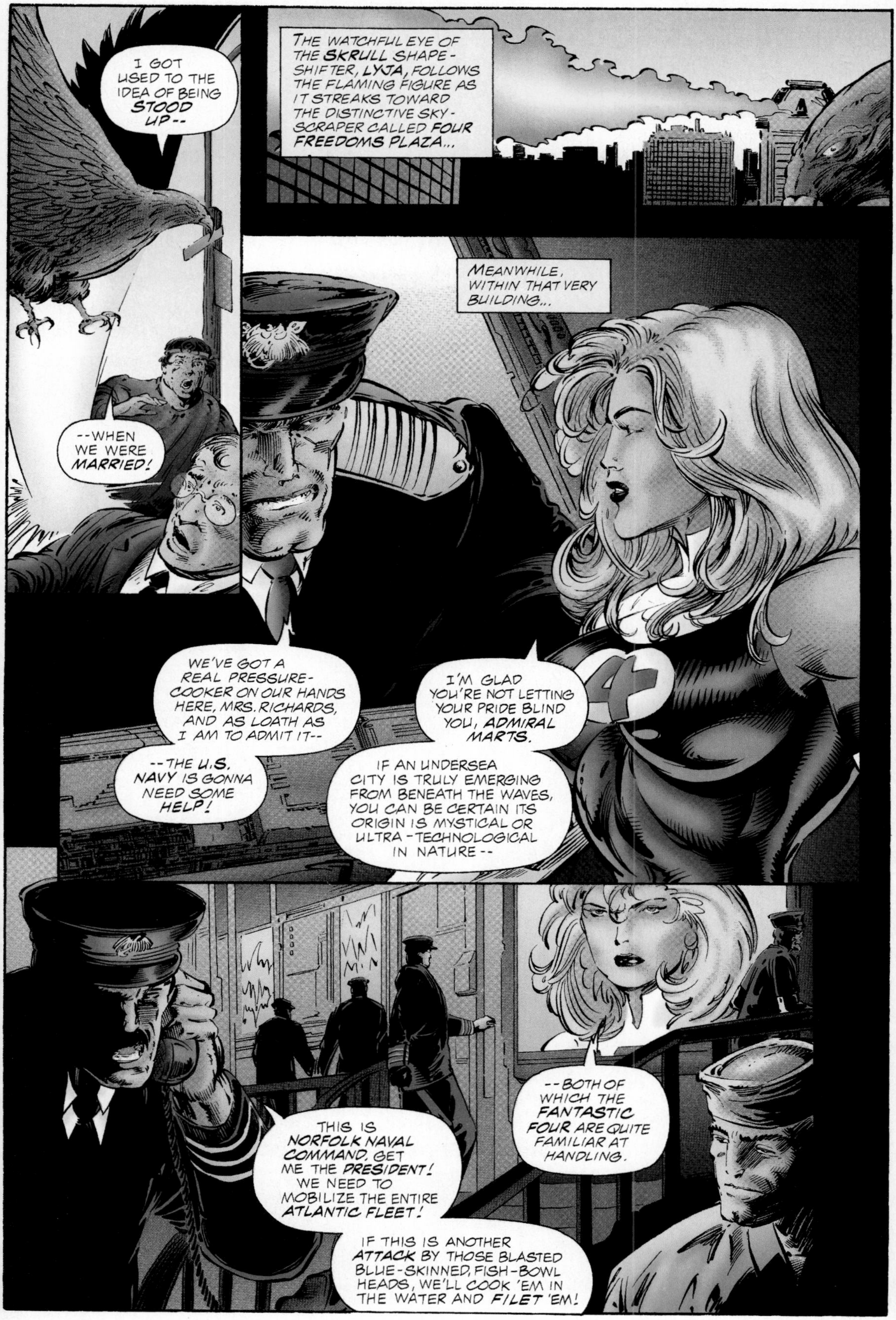
I GOT USED TO THE IDEA OF BEING STOOD UP--
THE WATCHFUL EYE OF THE SKRULL SHAPE-SHIFTER, LYJA, FOLLOWS THE FLAMING FIGURE AS IT STREAKS TOWARD THE DISTINCTIVE SKY-SCRAPER CALLED FOUR FREEDOMS PLAZA...
--WHEN WE WERE MARRIED!
MEANWHILE, WITHIN THAT VERY BUILDING...
WE'VE GOT A REAL PRESSURE-COOKER ON OUR HANDS HERE, MRS. RICHARDS, AND AS LOATH AS I AM TO ADMIT IT--
--THE U.S. NAVY IS GONNA NEED SOME HELP!
I'M GLAD YOU'RE NOT LETTING YOUR PRIDE BLIND YOU, ADMIRAL MARTS.
IF AN UNDERSEA CITY IS TRULY EMERGING FROM BENEATH THE WAVES, YOU CAN BE CERTAIN ITS ORIGIN IS MYSTICAL OR ULTRA-TECHNOLOGICAL IN NATURE--
--BOTH OF WHICH THE FANTASTIC FOUR ARE QUITE FAMILIAR AT HANDLING.
THIS IS NORFOLK NAVAL COMMAND. GET ME THE PRESIDENT! WE NEED TO MOBILIZE THE ENTIRE ATLANTIC FLEET!
IF THIS IS ANOTHER ATTACK BY THOSE BLASTED BLUE-SKINNED, FISH-BOWL HEADS, WE'LL COOK 'EM IN THE WATER AND FILET 'EM!

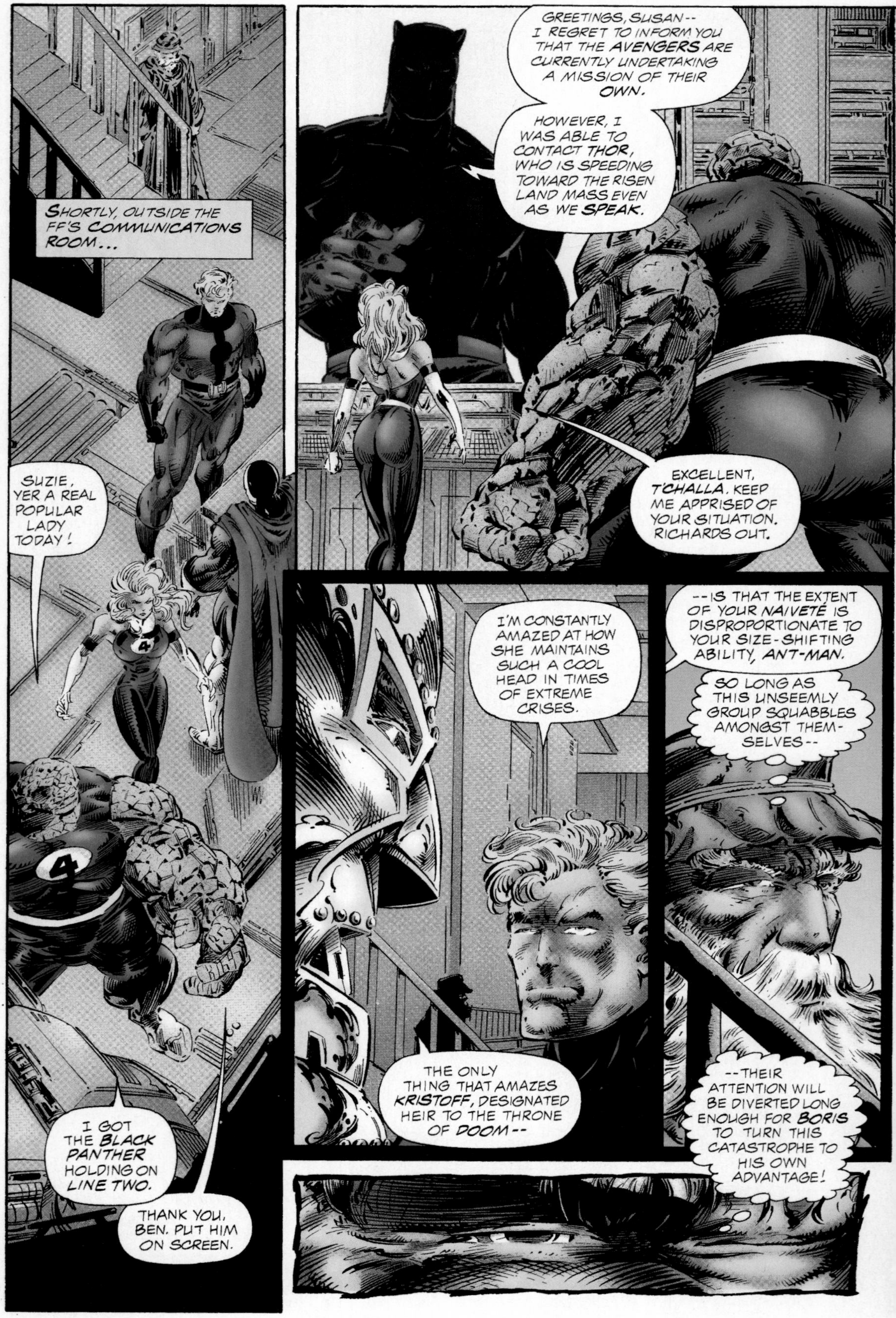
SHORTLY, OUTSIDE THE FF'S COMMUNICATIONS ROOM...
SUZIE, YER A REAL POPULAR LADY TODAY!
I GOT THE BLACK PANTHER HOLDING ON LINE TWO.
THANK YOU, BEN. PUT HIM ON SCREEN.
GREETINGS, SUSAN-- I REGRET TO INFORM YOU THAT THE AVENGERS ARE CURRENTLY UNDERTAKING A MISSION OF THEIR OWN.
HOWEVER, I WAS ABLE TO CONTACT THOR, WHO IS SPEEDING TOWARD THE RISEN LAND MASS EVEN AS WE SPEAK.
EXCELLENT, T'CHALLA. KEEP ME APPRISED OF YOUR SITUATION. RICHARDS OUT.
I'M CONSTANTLY AMAZED AT HOW SHE MAINTAINS SUCH A COOL HEAD IN TIMES OF EXTREME CRISES.
THE ONLY THING THAT AMAZES KRISTOFF, DESIGNATED HEIR TO THE THRONE OF DOOM--
--IS THAT THE EXTENT OF YOUR NAIVETÉ IS DISPROPORTIONATE TO YOUR SIZE-SHIFTING ABILITY, ANT-MAN.
SO LONG AS THIS UNSEEMLY GROUP SQUABBLES AMONGST THEM-SELVES--
--THEIR ATTENTION WILL BE DIVERTED LONG ENOUGH FOR BORIS TO TURN THIS CATASTROPHE TO HIS OWN ADVANTAGE!

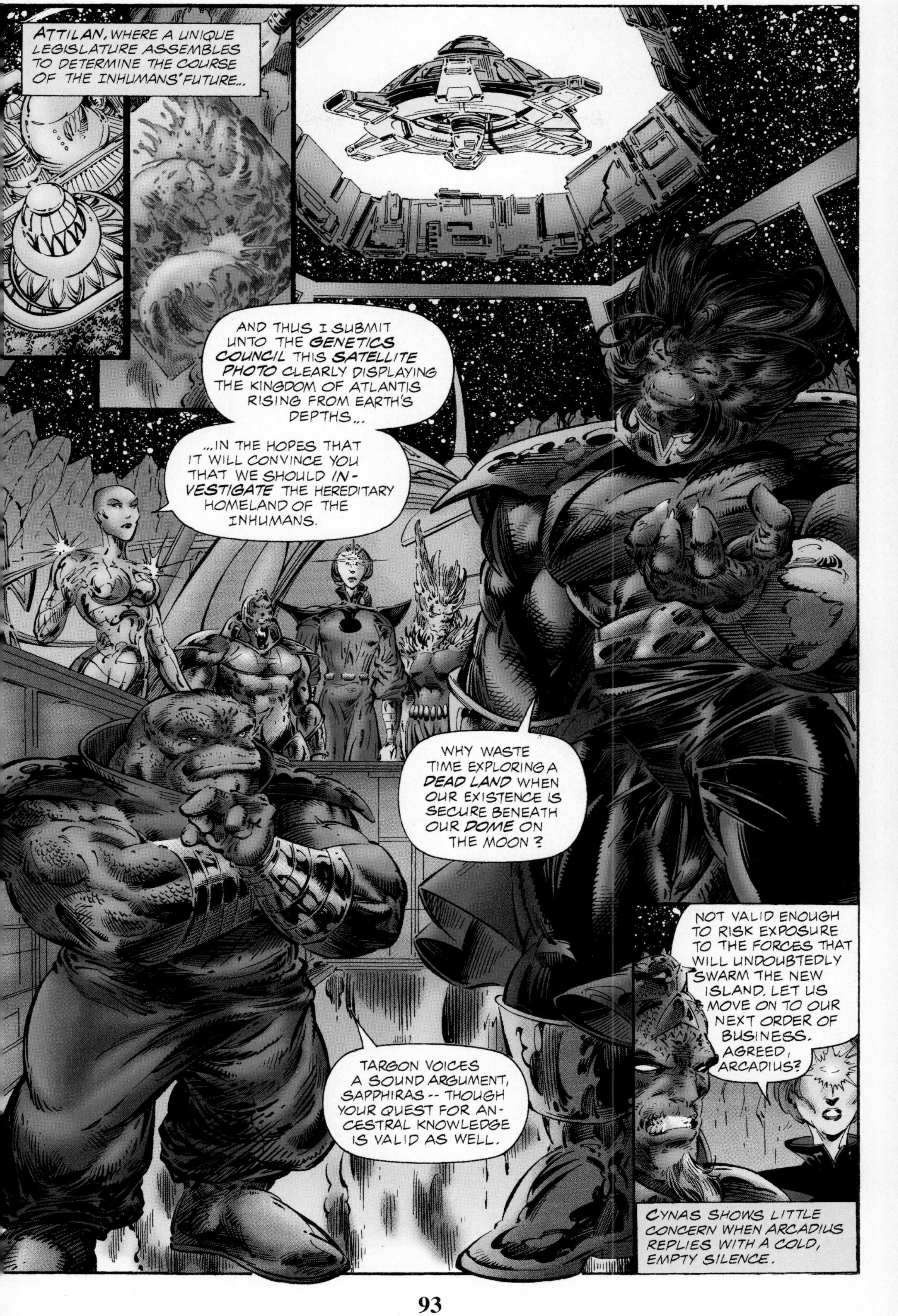
ATTILAN, WHERE A UNIQUE LEGISLATURE ASSEMBLES TO DETERMINE THE COURSE OF THE INHUMANS' FUTURE...
AND THUS I SUBMIT UNTO THE GENETICS COUNCIL THIS SATELLITE PHOTO CLEARLY DISPLAYING THE KINGDOM OF ATLANTIS RISING FROM EARTH'S DEPTHS...
...IN THE HOPES THAT IT WILL CONVINCE YOU THAT WE SHOULD INVESTIGATE THE HEREDITARY HOMELAND OF THE INHUMANS.
WHY WASTE TIME EXPLORING A DEAD LAND WHEN OUR EXISTENCE IS SECURE BENEATH OUR DOME ON THE MOON?
TARGON VOICES A SOUND ARGUMENT, SAPPHIRAS -- THOUGH YOUR QUEST FOR ANCESTRAL KNOWLEDGE IS VALID AS WELL.
NOT VALID ENOUGH TO RISK EXPOSURE TO THE FORCES THAT WILL UNDOUBTEDLY SWARM THE NEW ISLAND. LET US MOVE ON TO OUR NEXT ORDER OF BUSINESS. AGREED, ARCADIUS?
CYNAS SHOWS LITTLE CONCERN WHEN ARCADIUS REPLIES WITH A COLD, EMPTY SILENCE.

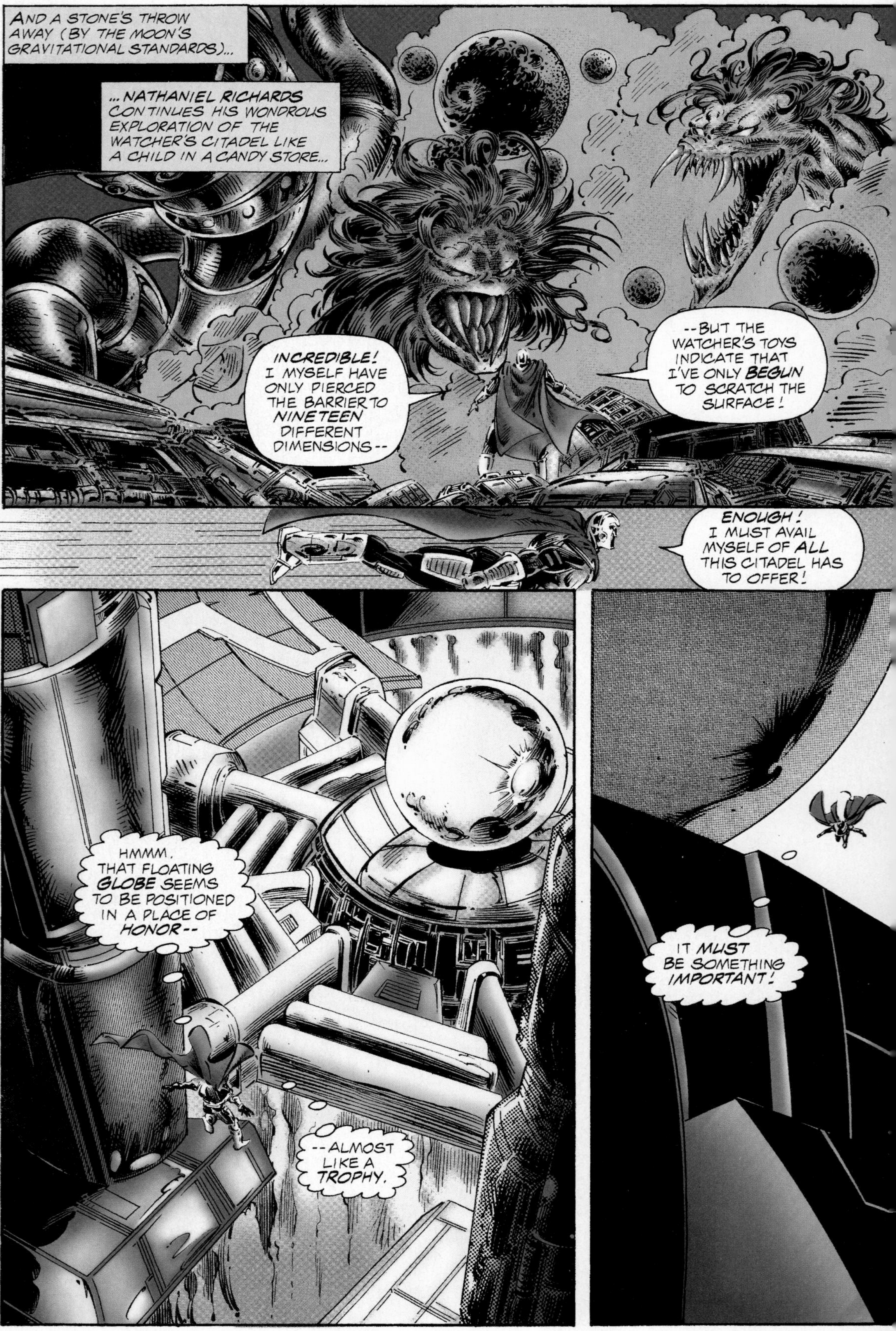
AND A STONE'S THROW AWAY (BY THE MOON'S GRAVITATIONAL STANDARDS)...
...NATHANIEL RICHARDS CONTINUES HIS WONDROUS EXPLORATION OF THE WATCHER'S CITADEL LIKE A CHILD IN A CANDY STORE...
INCREDIBLE! I MYSELF HAVE ONLY PIERCED THE BARRIER TO NINETEEN DIFFERENT DIMENSIONS--
--BUT THE WATCHER'S TOYS INDICATE THAT I'VE ONLY BEGUN TO SCRATCH THE SURFACE!
ENOUGH! I MUST AVAIL MYSELF OF ALL THIS CITADEL HAS TO OFFER!
HMMM. THAT FLOATING GLOBE SEEMS TO BE POSITIONED IN A PLACE OF HONOR--
--ALMOST LIKE A TROPHY.
IT MUST BE SOMETHING IMPORTANT!

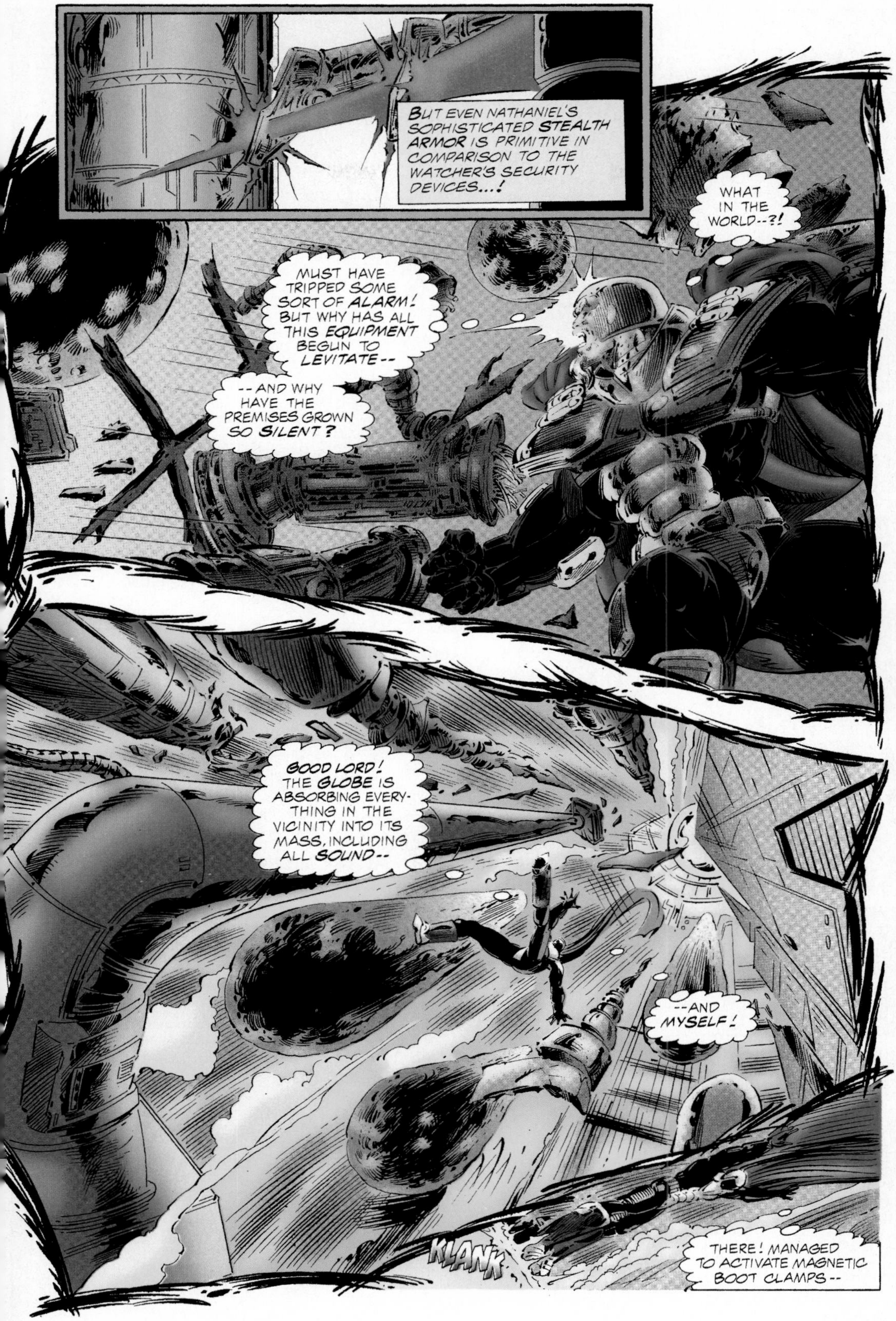
BUT EVEN NATHANIEL'S SOPHISTICATED STEALTH ARMOR IS PRIMITIVE IN COMPARISON TO THE WATCHER'S SECURITY DEVICES...!
WHAT IN THE WORLD--?!
MUST HAVE TRIPPED SOME SORT OF ALARM! BUT WHY HAS ALL THIS EQUIPMENT BEGUN TO LEVITATE--
--AND WHY HAVE THE PREMISES GROWN SO SILENT?
GOOD LORD! THE GLOBE IS ABSORBING EVERY-THING IN THE VICINITY INTO ITS MASS, INCLUDING ALL SOUND--
--AND MYSELF!
KLANK
THERE! MANAGED TO ACTIVATE MAGNETIC BOOT CLAMPS--

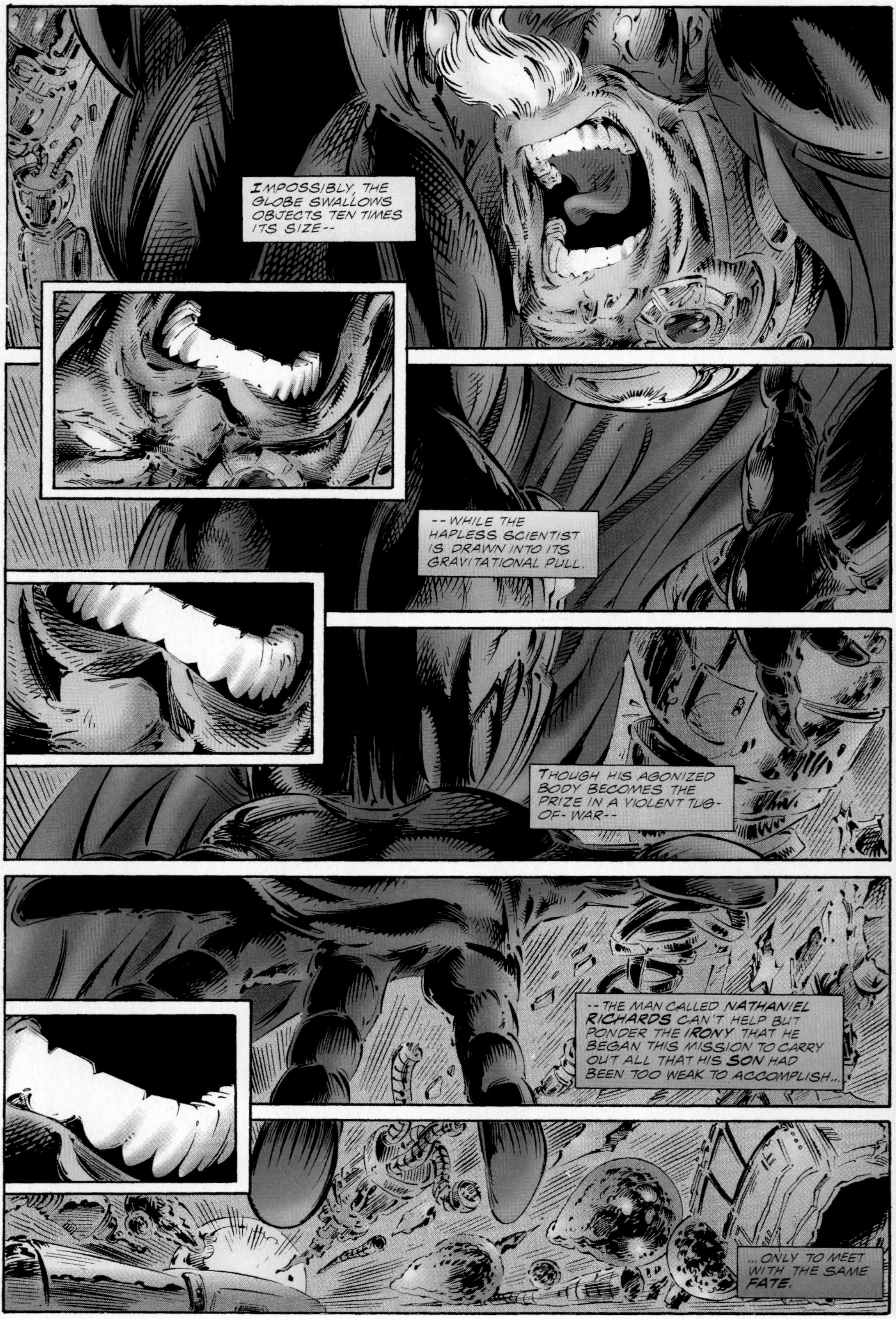
IMPOSSIBLY, THE GLOBE SWALLOWS OBJECTS TEN TIMES ITS SIZE--
--WHILE THE HAPLESS SCIENTIST IS DRAWN INTO ITS GRAVITATIONAL PULL.
THOUGH HIS AGONIZED BODY BECOMES THE PRIZE IN A VIOLENT TUG-OF-WAR--
--THE MAN CALLED NATHANIEL RICHARDS CAN'T HELP BUT PONDER THE IRONY THAT HE BEGAN THIS MISSION TO CARRY OUT ALL THAT HIS SON HAD BEEN TOO WEAK TO ACCOMPLISH...
...ONLY TO MEET WITH THE SAME FATE.

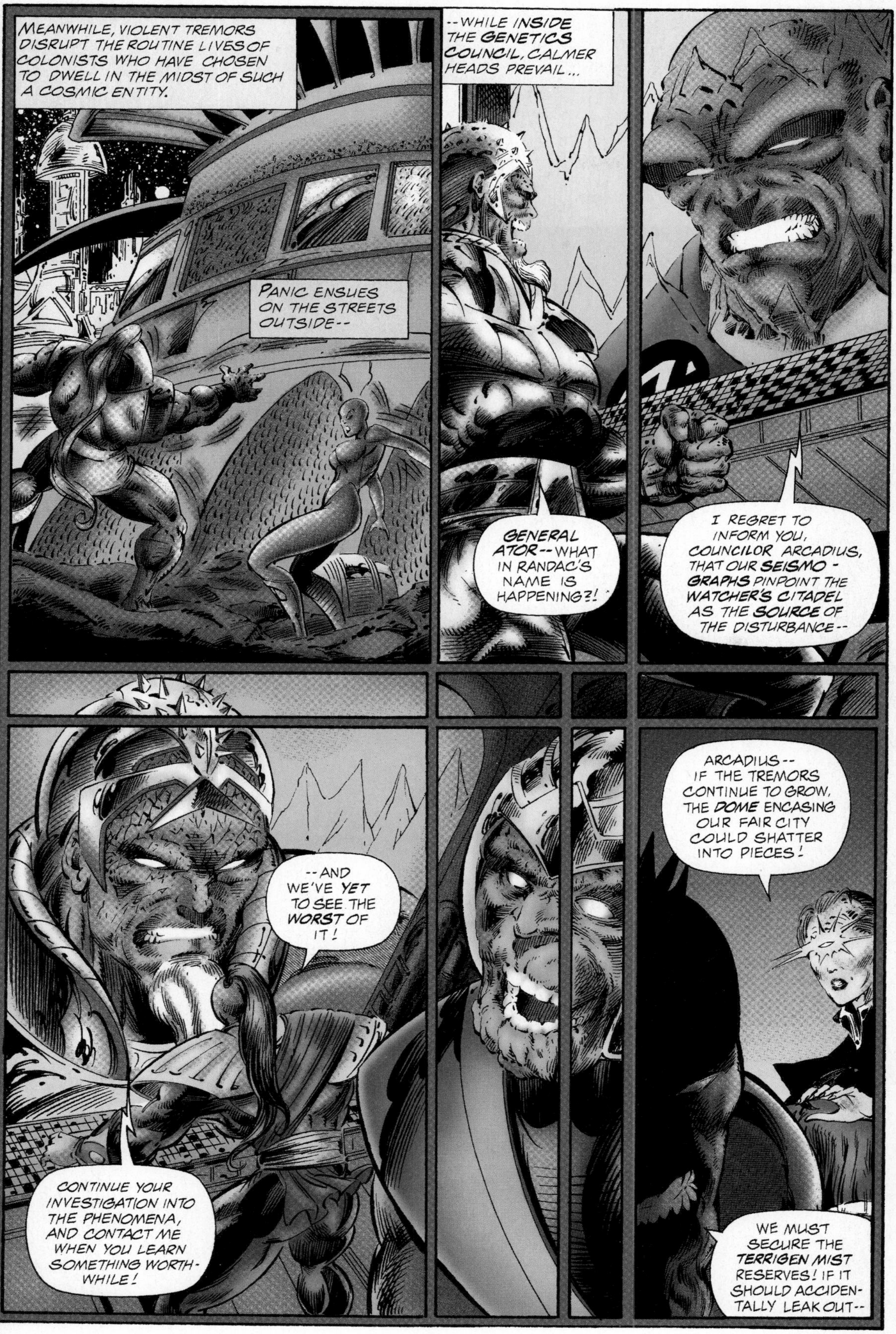
MEANWHILE, VIOLENT TREMORS DISRUPT THE ROUTINE LIVES OF COLONISTS WHO HAVE CHOSEN TO DWELL IN THE MIDST OF SUCH A COSMIC ENTITY.
PANIC ENSUES ON THE STREETS OUTSIDE--
--WHILE INSIDE THE GENETICS COUNCIL, CALMER HEADS PREVAIL...
GENERAL ATOR--WHAT IN RANDAC'S NAME IS HAPPENING?!
I REGRET TO INFORM YOU, COUNCILOR ARCADIUS, THAT OUR SEISMO-GRAPHS PINPOINT THE WATCHER'S CITADEL AS THE SOURCE OF THE DISTURBANCE--
--AND WE'VE YET TO SEE THE WORST OF IT!
CONTINUE YOUR INVESTIGATION INTO THE PHENOMENA, AND CONTACT ME WHEN YOU LEARN SOMETHING WORTH-WHILE!
ARCADIUS--IF THE TREMORS CONTINUE TO GROW, THE DOME ENCASING OUR FAIR CITY COULD SHATTER INTO PIECES!
WE MUST SECURE THE TERRIGEN MIST RESERVES! IF IT SHOULD ACCIDEN-TALLY LEAK OUT--

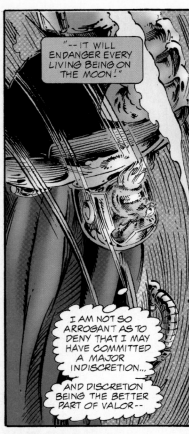

"--IT WILL ENDANGER EVERY LIVING BEING ON THE MOON!"

I AM NOT SO ARROGANT AS TO DENY THAT I MAY HAVE COMMITTED A MAJOR INDISCRETION...

AND DISCRETION BEING THE BETTER PART OF VALOR--

--IT BEHOOVES ME AT THIS TIME TO BEAT A HASTY RETREAT.

BAMF!

A TELEPORTATION MATRIX ENVELOPS THE ELDERLY TECHNOLOGIST--

--LEAVING NOT A SOUL TO WITNESS THE MOST FLAGRANT CONTRADICTION OF SPATIAL GEOMETRY...

...AS THE INVETERATE HOME OF THE WATCHER BEGINS TO QUIVER--

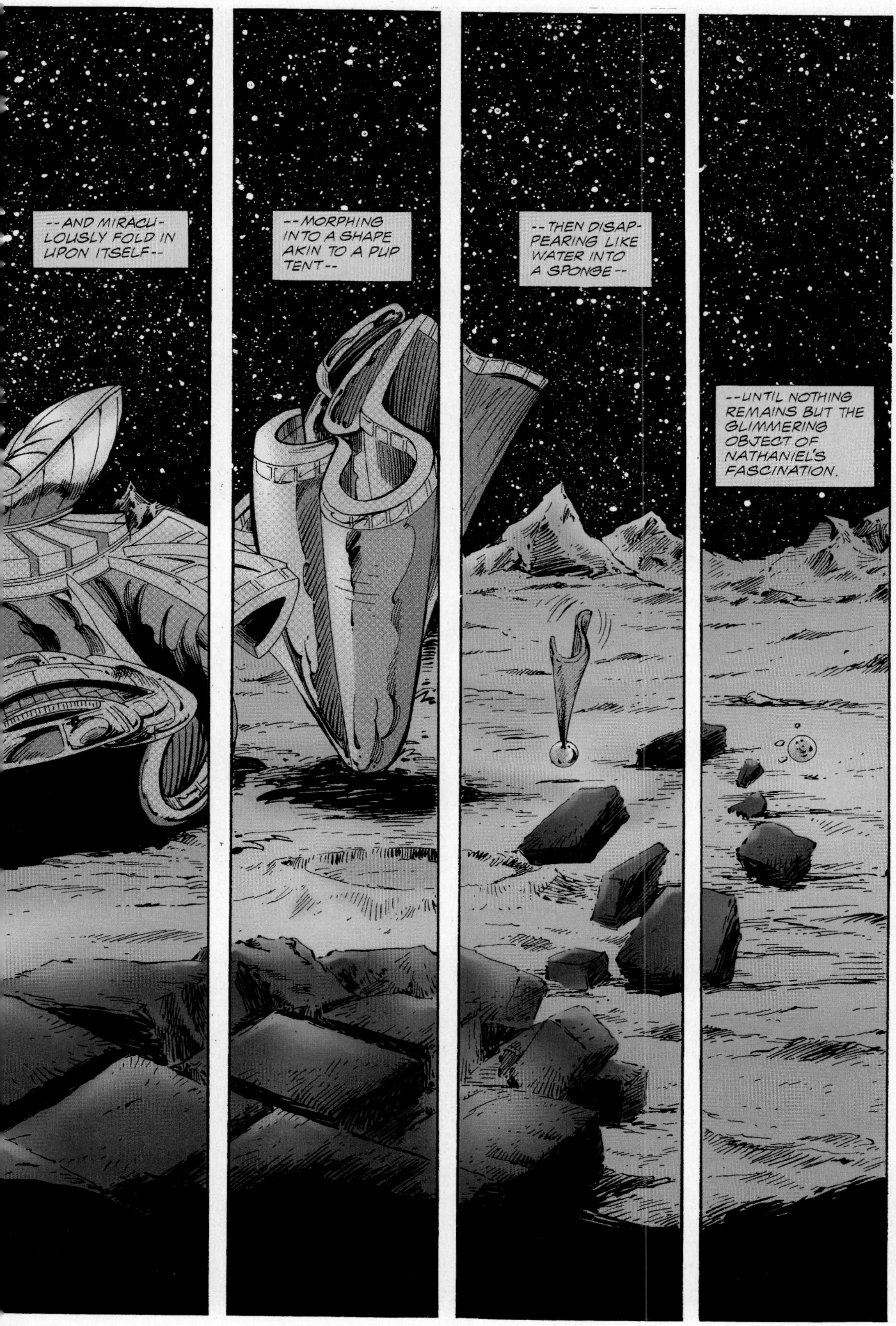
--AND MIRACU-LOUSLY FOLD IN UPON ITSELF--
--MORPHING INTO A SHAPE AKIN TO A PUP TENT--
--THEN DISAP-PEARING LIKE WATER INTO A SPONGE--
--UNTIL NOTHING REMAINS BUT THE GLIMMERING OBJECT OF NATHANIEL'S FASCINATION.

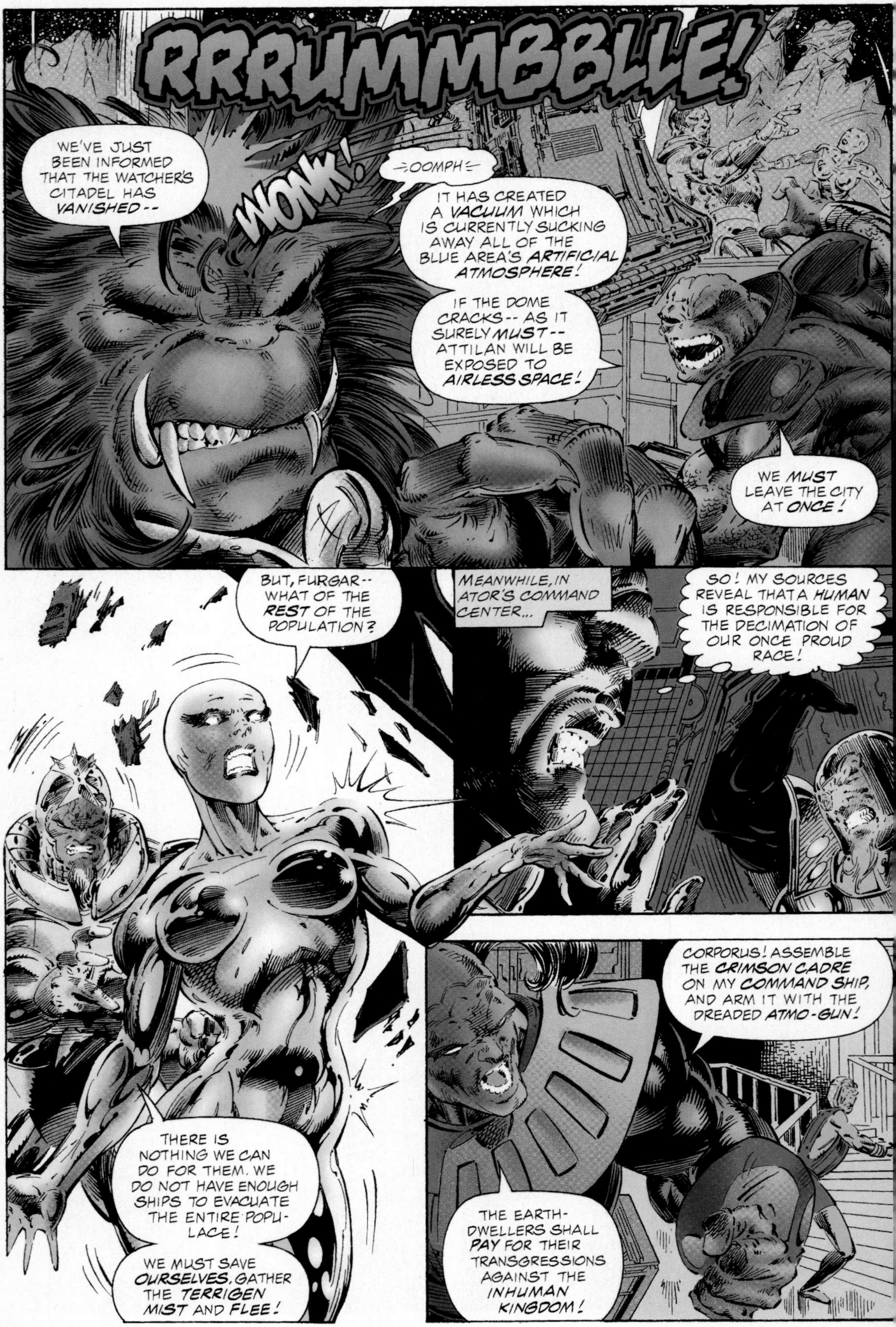
RRRUMMMBBLLE!
WE'VE JUST BEEN INFORMED THAT THE WATCHER'S CITADEL HAS VANISHED--
WONK!
OOMPH
IT HAS CREATED A VACUUM WHICH IS CURRENTLY SUCKING AWAY ALL OF THE BLUE AREA'S ARTIFICIAL ATMOSPHERE!
IF THE DOME CRACKS-- AS IT SURELY MUST-- ATTILAN WILL BE EXPOSED TO AIRLESS SPACE!
WE MUST LEAVE THE CITY AT ONCE!
BUT, FURGAR-- WHAT OF THE REST OF THE POPULATION?
THERE IS NOTHING WE CAN DO FOR THEM. WE DO NOT HAVE ENOUGH SHIPS TO EVACUATE THE ENTIRE POPU-LACE!
WE MUST SAVE OURSELVES. GATHER THE TERRIGEN MIST AND FLEE!
MEANWHILE, IN ATOR'S COMMAND CENTER...
SO! MY SOURCES REVEAL THAT A HUMAN IS RESPONSIBLE FOR THE DECIMATION OF OUR ONCE PROUD RACE!
CORPORUS! ASSEMBLE THE CRIMSON CADRE ON MY COMMAND SHIP, AND ARM IT WITH THE DREADED ATMO-GUN!
THE EARTH-DWELLERS SHALL PAY FOR THEIR TRANSGRESSIONS AGAINST THE INHUMAN KINGDOM!

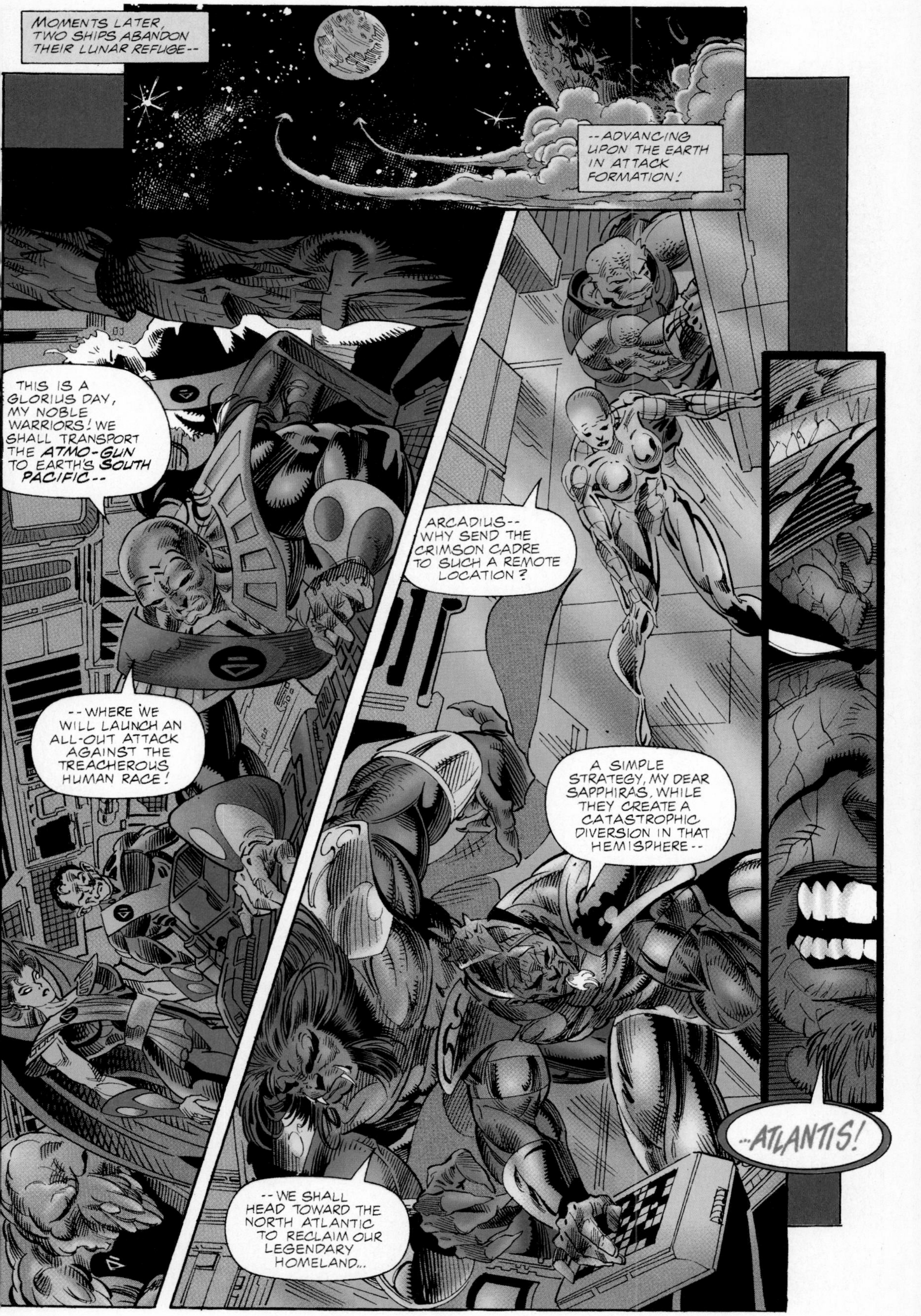
MOMENTS LATER, TWO SHIPS ABANDON THEIR LUNAR REFUGE--
--ADVANCING UPON THE EARTH IN ATTACK FORMATION!
THIS IS A GLORIUS DAY, MY NOBLE WARRIORS! WE SHALL TRANSPORT THE ATMO-GUN TO EARTH'S SOUTH PACIFIC--
--WHERE WE WILL LAUNCH AN ALL-OUT ATTACK AGAINST THE TREACHEROUS HUMAN RACE!
ARCADIUS--WHY SEND THE CRIMSON CADRE TO SUCH A REMOTE LOCATION?
A SIMPLE STRATEGY, MY DEAR SAPPHIRAS. WHILE THEY CREATE A CATASTROPHIC DIVERSION IN THAT HEMISPHERE--
--WE SHALL HEAD TOWARD THE NORTH ATLANTIC TO RECLAIM OUR LEGENDARY HOMELAND...
...ATLANTIS!

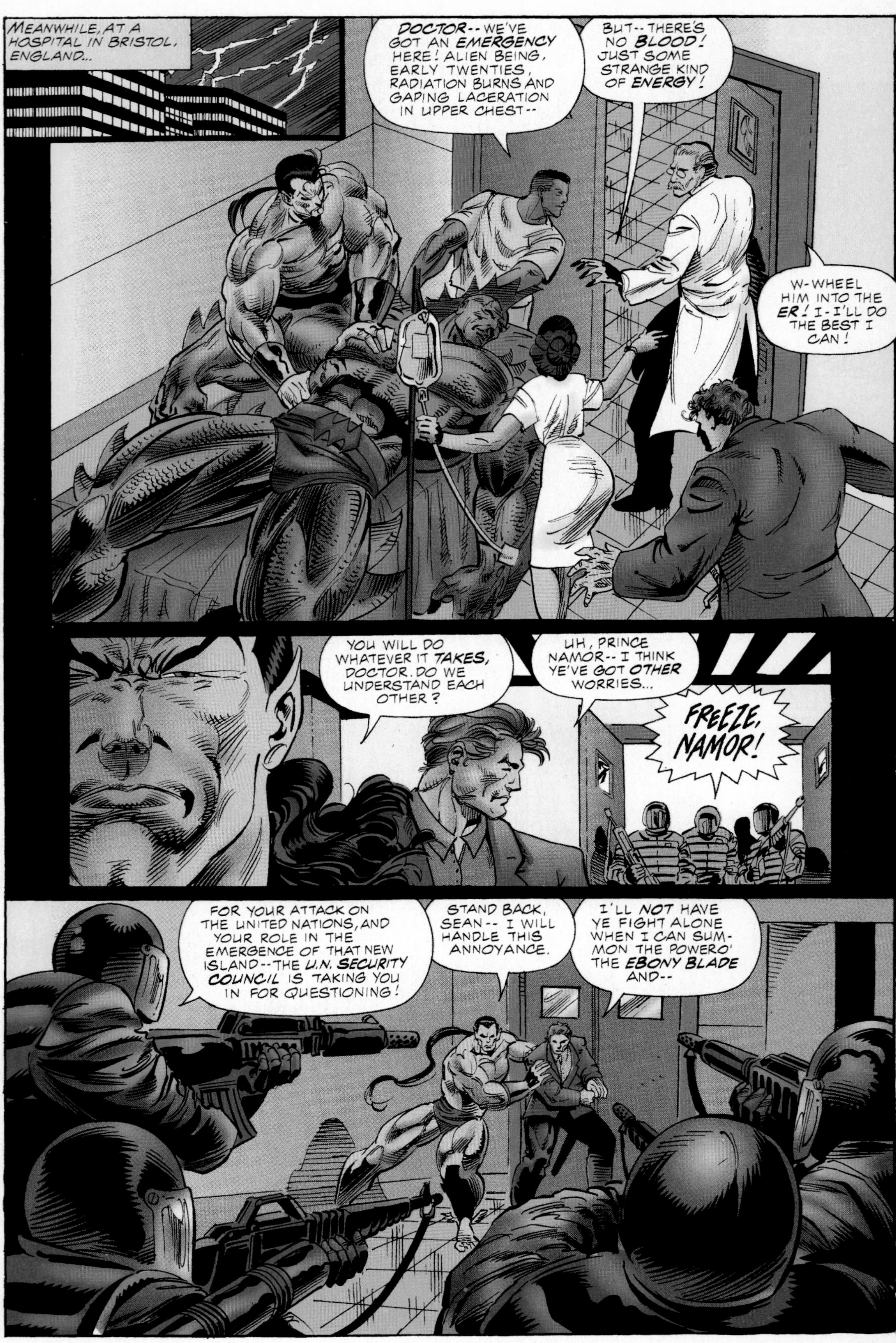
MEANWHILE, AT A HOSPITAL IN BRISTOL, ENGLAND...
DOCTOR-- WE'VE GOT AN EMERGENCY HERE! ALIEN BEING, EARLY TWENTIES, RADIATION BURNS AND GAPING LACERATION IN UPPER CHEST--
BUT-- THERE'S NO BLOOD! JUST SOME STRANGE KIND OF ENERGY!
W-WHEEL HIM INTO THE ER! I-I'LL DO THE BEST I CAN!
YOU WILL DO WHATEVER IT TAKES, DOCTOR. DO WE UNDERSTAND EACH OTHER?
UH, PRINCE NAMOR-- I THINK YE'VE GOT OTHER WORRIES...
FREEZE, NAMOR!
FOR YOUR ATTACK ON THE UNITED NATIONS, AND YOUR ROLE IN THE EMERGENCE OF THAT NEW ISLAND--THE U.N. SECURITY COUNCIL IS TAKING YOU IN FOR QUESTIONING!
STAND BACK, SEAN-- I WILL HANDLE THIS ANNOYANCE.
I'LL NOT HAVE YE FIGHT ALONE WHEN I CAN SUMMON THE POWER O' THE EBONY BLADE AND--

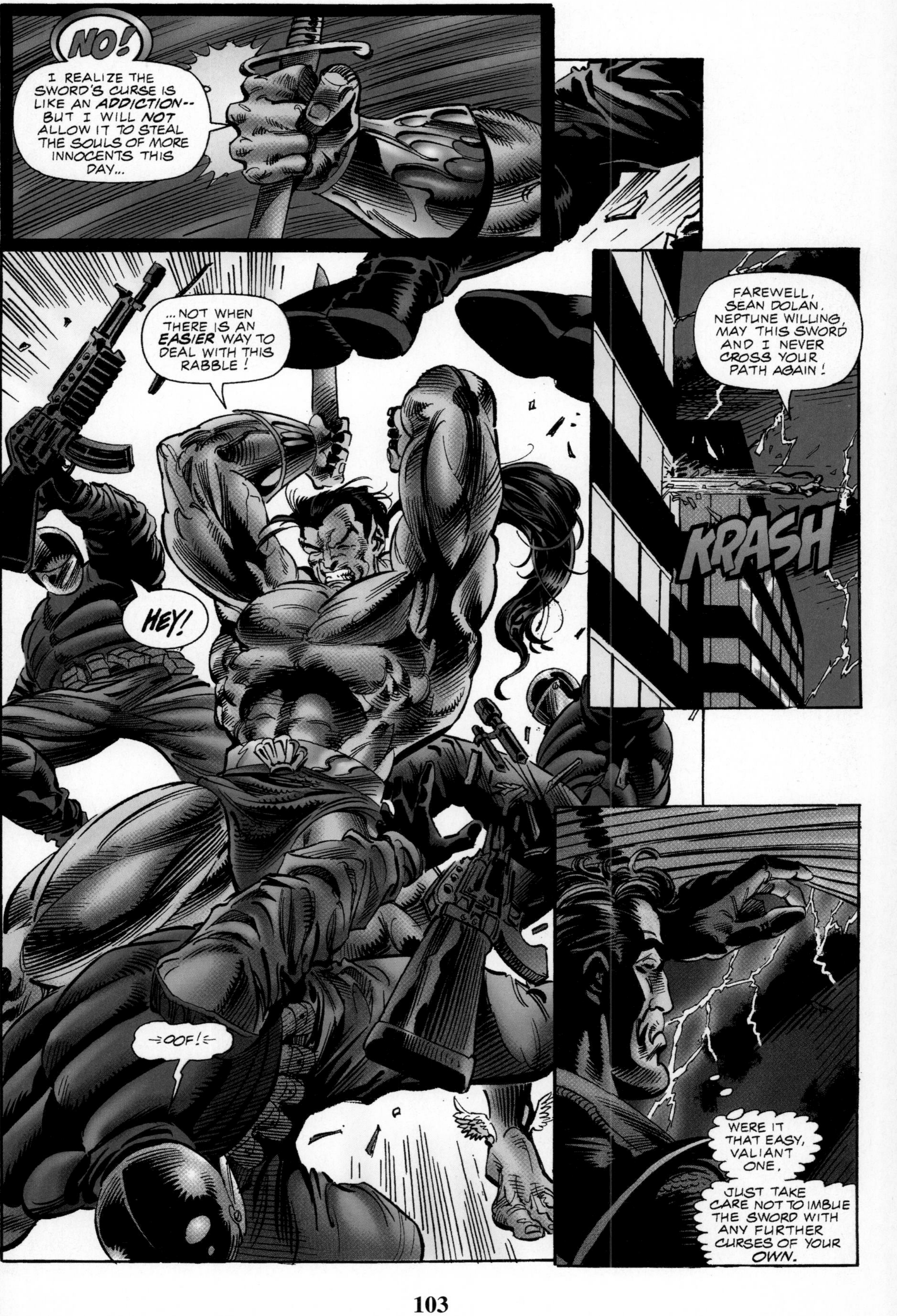
NO!
I REALIZE THE SWORD'S CURSE IS LIKE AN ADDICTION-- BUT I WILL NOT ALLOW IT TO STEAL THE SOULS OF MORE INNOCENTS THIS DAY...
...NOT WHEN THERE IS AN EASIER WAY TO DEAL WITH THIS RABBLE!
HEY!
=OOF!=
FAREWELL, SEAN DOLAN. NEPTUNE WILLING, MAY THIS SWORD AND I NEVER CROSS YOUR PATH AGAIN!
KRASH
WERE IT THAT EASY, VALIANT ONE.
JUST TAKE CARE NOT TO IMBUE THE SWORD WITH ANY FURTHER CURSES OF YOUR OWN.

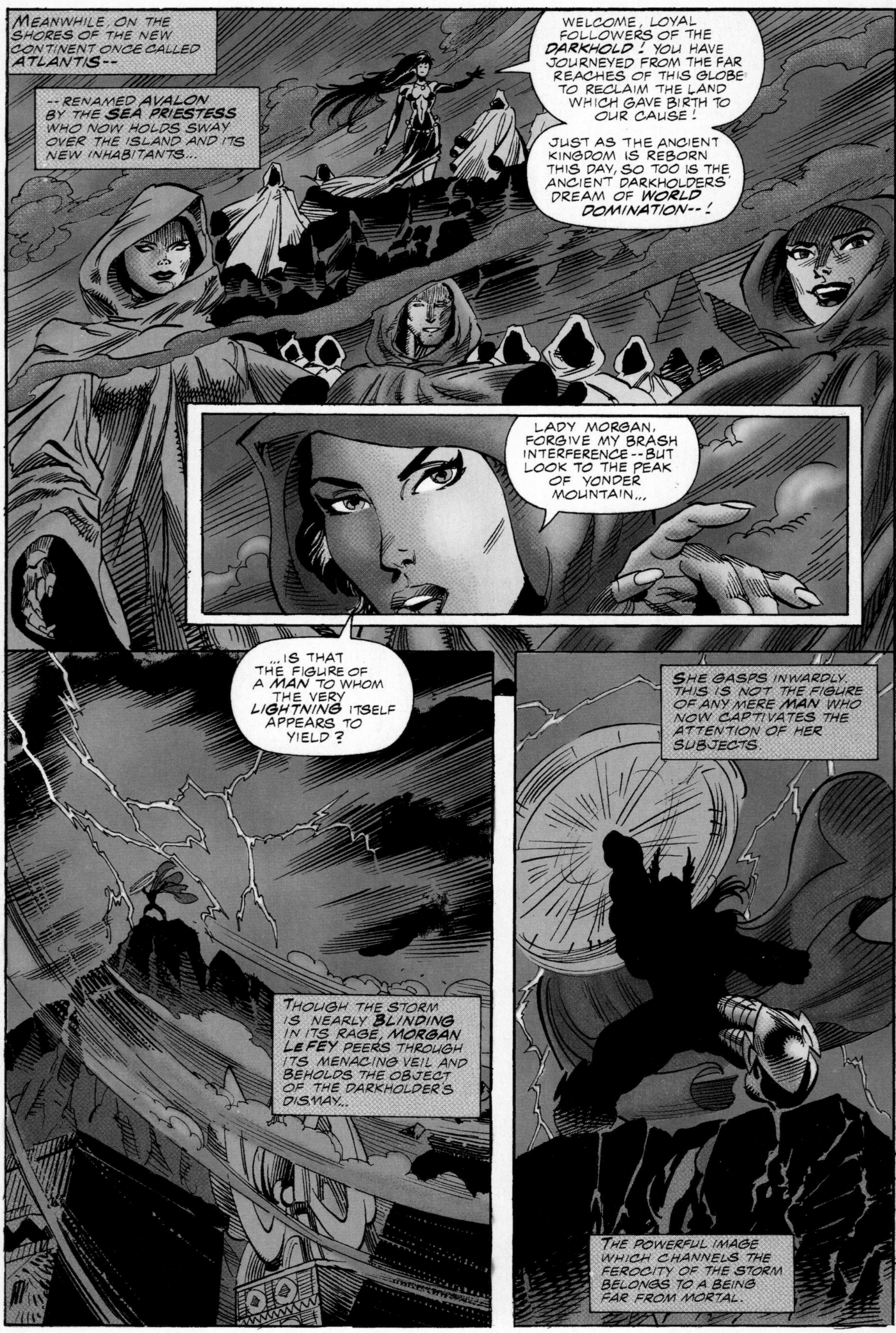

MEANWHILE, ON THE SHORES OF THE NEW CONTINENT ONCE CALLED ATLANTIS--
WELCOME, LOYAL FOLLOWERS OF THE DARKHOLD! YOU HAVE JOURNEYED FROM THE FAR REACHES OF THIS GLOBE TO RECLAIM THE LAND WHICH GAVE BIRTH TO OUR CAUSE!
--RENAMED AVALON BY THE SEA PRIESTESS WHO NOW HOLDS SWAY OVER THE ISLAND AND ITS NEW INHABITANTS...
JUST AS THE ANCIENT KINGDOM IS REBORN THIS DAY, SO TOO IS THE ANCIENT DARKHOLDERS' DREAM OF WORLD DOMINATION--!
LADY MORGAN, FORGIVE MY BRASH INTERFERENCE--BUT LOOK TO THE PEAK OF YONDER MOUNTAIN...
...IS THAT THE FIGURE OF A MAN TO WHOM THE VERY LIGHTNING ITSELF APPEARS TO YIELD?
THOUGH THE STORM IS NEARLY BLINDING IN ITS RAGE, MORGAN LEFEY PEERS THROUGH ITS MENACING VEIL AND BEHOLDS THE OBJECT OF THE DARKHOLDER'S DISMAY...
SHE GASPS INWARDLY. THIS IS NOT THE FIGURE OF ANY MERE MAN WHO NOW CAPTIVATES THE ATTENTION OF HER SUBJECTS.
THE POWERFUL IMAGE WHICH CHANNELS THE FEROCITY OF THE STORM BELONGS TO A BEING FAR FROM MORTAL.

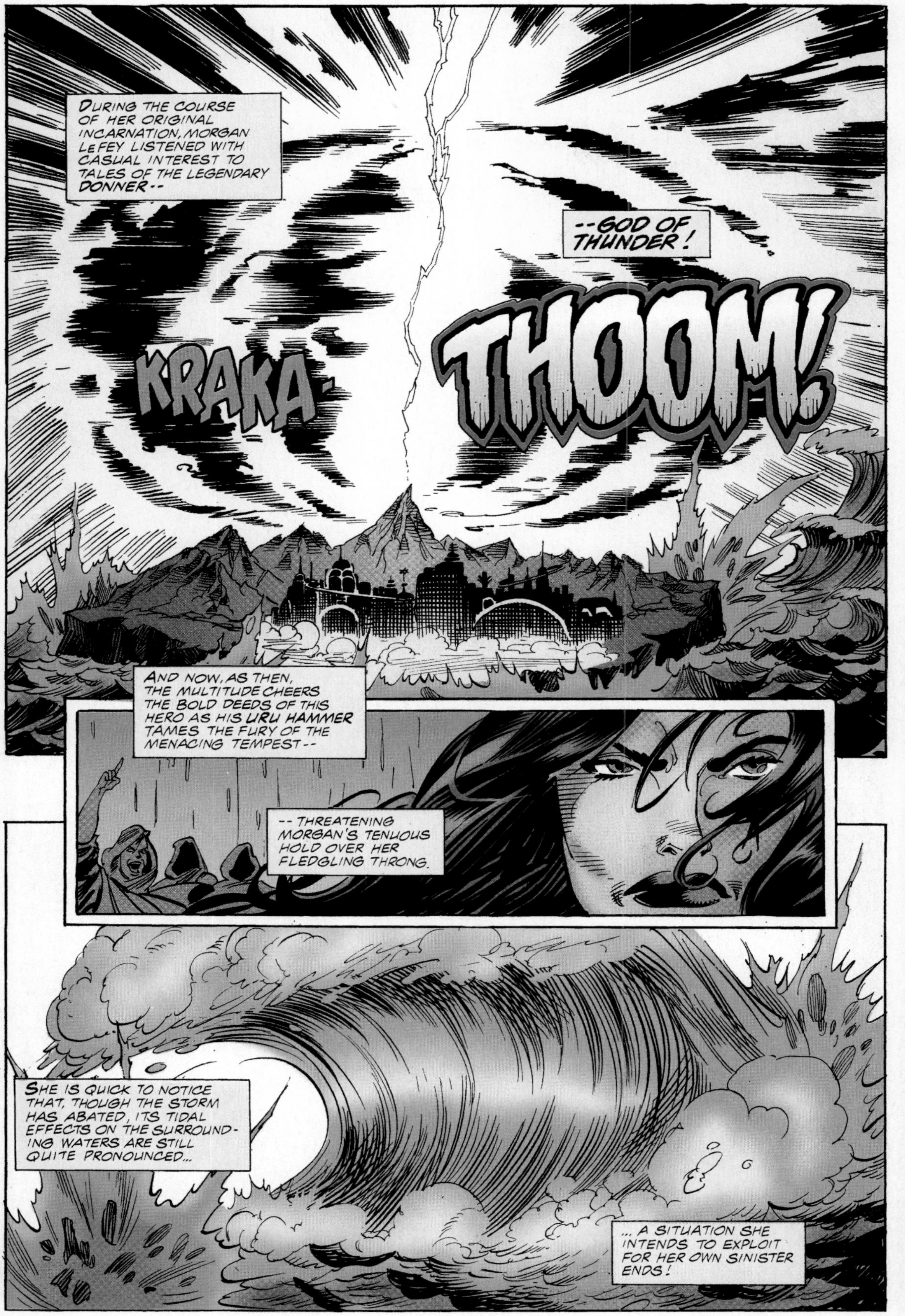

DURING THE COURSE OF HER ORIGINAL INCARNATION, MORGAN LEFEY LISTENED WITH CASUAL INTEREST TO TALES OF THE LEGENDARY DONNER--
--GOD OF THUNDER!
KRAKA-
THOOM!
AND NOW, AS THEN, THE MULTITUDE CHEERS THE BOLD DEEDS OF THIS HERO AS HIS URU HAMMER TAMES THE FURY OF THE MENACING TEMPEST--
--THREATENING MORGAN'S TENUOUS HOLD OVER HER FLEDGLING THRONG.
SHE IS QUICK TO NOTICE THAT, THOUGH THE STORM HAS ABATED, ITS TIDAL EFFECTS ON THE SURROUNDING WATERS ARE STILL QUITE PRONOUNCED...
...A SITUATION SHE INTENDS TO EXPLOIT FOR HER OWN SINISTER ENDS!

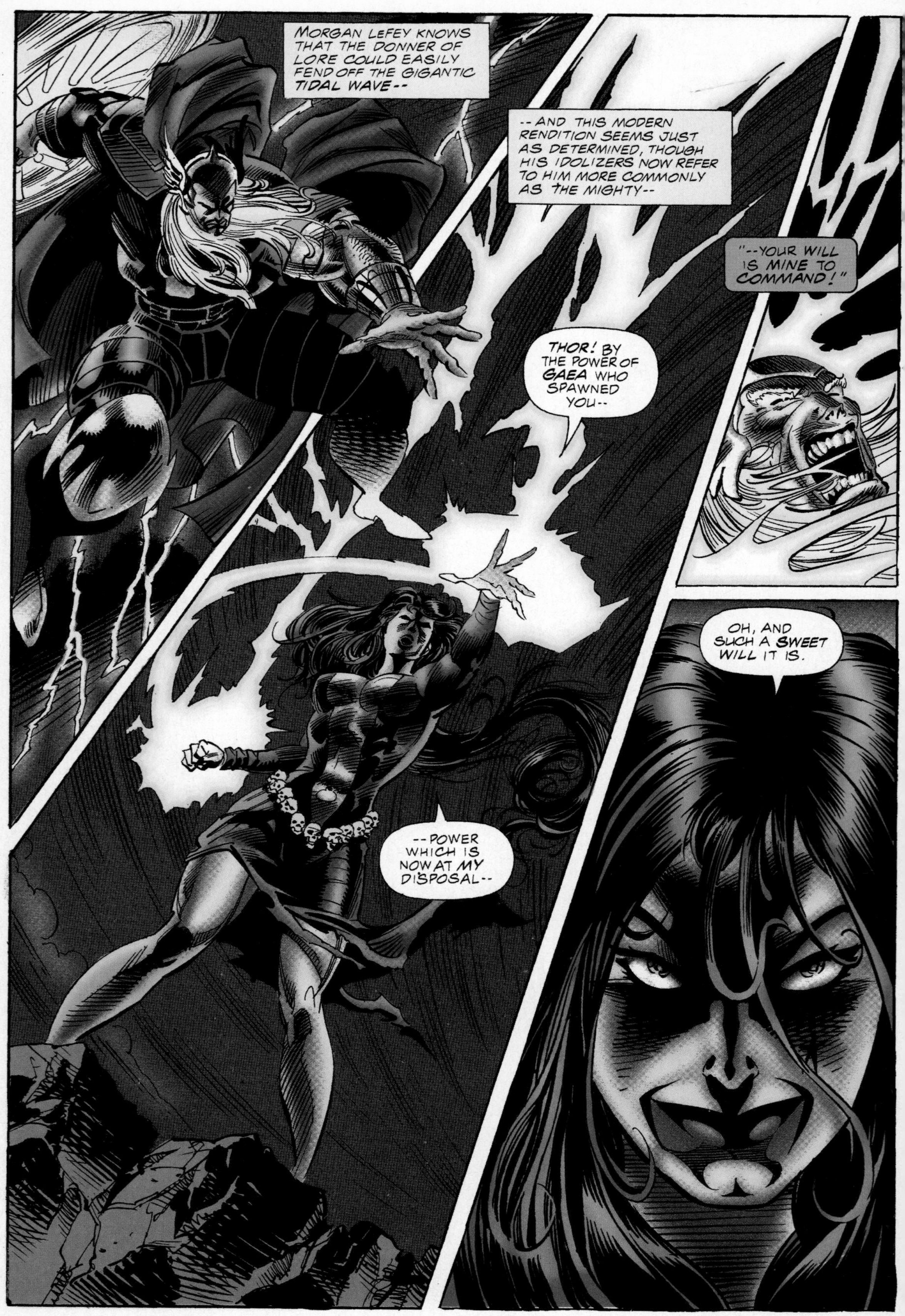
MORGAN LEFEY KNOWS THAT THE DONNER OF LORE COULD EASILY FEND OFF THE GIGANTIC TIDAL WAVE--
--AND THIS MODERN RENDITION SEEMS JUST AS DETERMINED, THOUGH HIS IDOLIZERS NOW REFER TO HIM MORE COMMONLY AS THE MIGHTY--
THOR! BY THE POWER OF GAEA WHO SPAWNED YOU--
--POWER WHICH IS NOW AT MY DISPOSAL--
"--YOUR WILL IS MINE TO COMMAND!"
OH, AND SUCH A SWEET WILL IT IS.

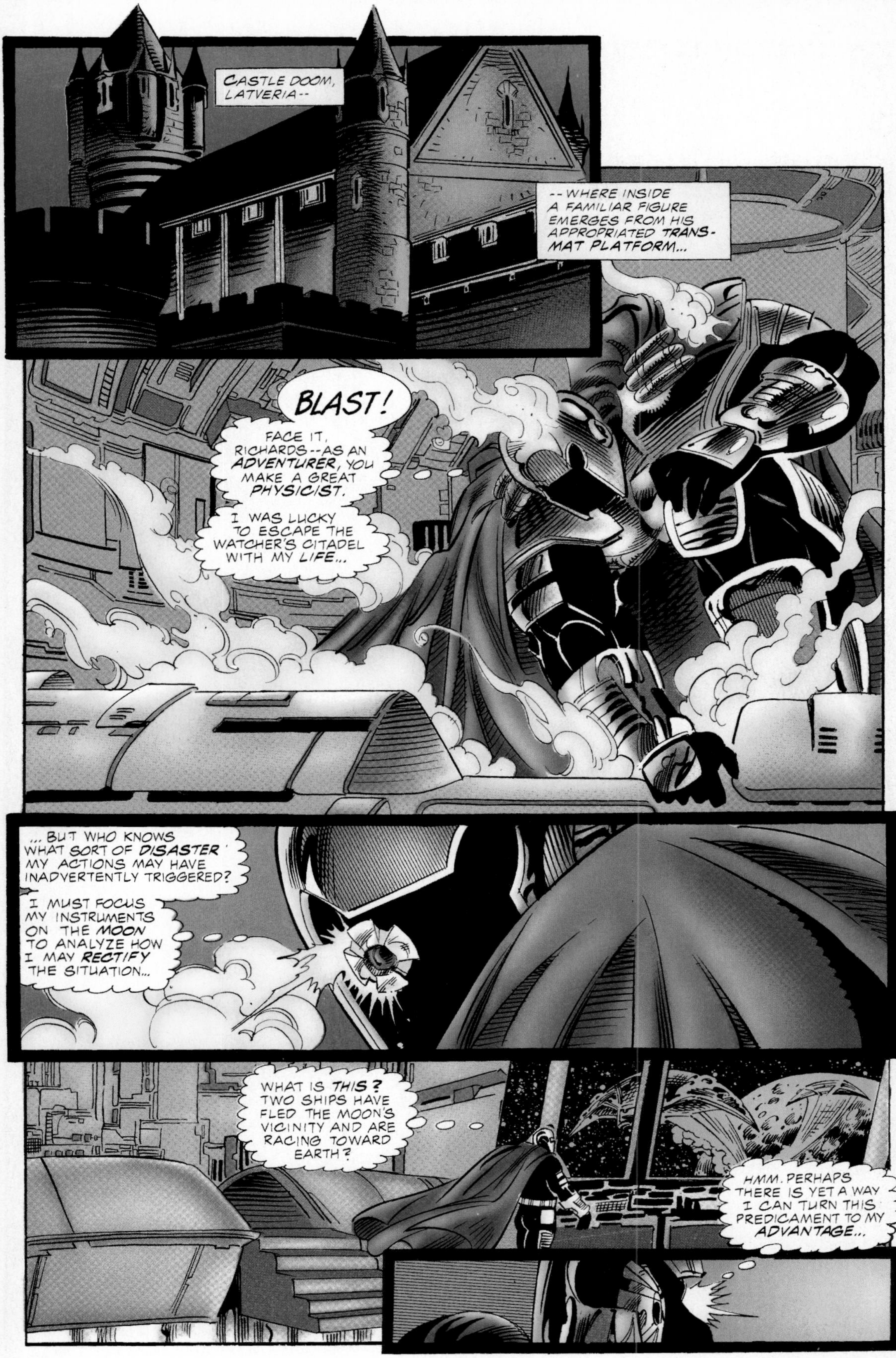
CASTLE DOOM, LATVERIA--
--WHERE INSIDE A FAMILIAR FIGURE EMERGES FROM HIS APPROPRIATED TRANS-MAT PLATFORM...
BLAST!
FACE IT, RICHARDS--AS AN ADVENTURER, YOU MAKE A GREAT PHYSICIST.
I WAS LUCKY TO ESCAPE THE WATCHER'S CITADEL WITH MY LIFE...
... BUT WHO KNOWS WHAT SORT OF DISASTER MY ACTIONS MAY HAVE INADVERTENTLY TRIGGERED?
I MUST FOCUS MY INSTRUMENTS ON THE MOON TO ANALYZE HOW I MAY RECTIFY THE SITUATION...
WHAT IS THIS? TWO SHIPS HAVE FLED THE MOON'S VICINITY AND ARE RACING TOWARD EARTH?
HMM. PERHAPS THERE IS YET A WAY I CAN TURN THIS PREDICAMENT TO MY ADVANTAGE...

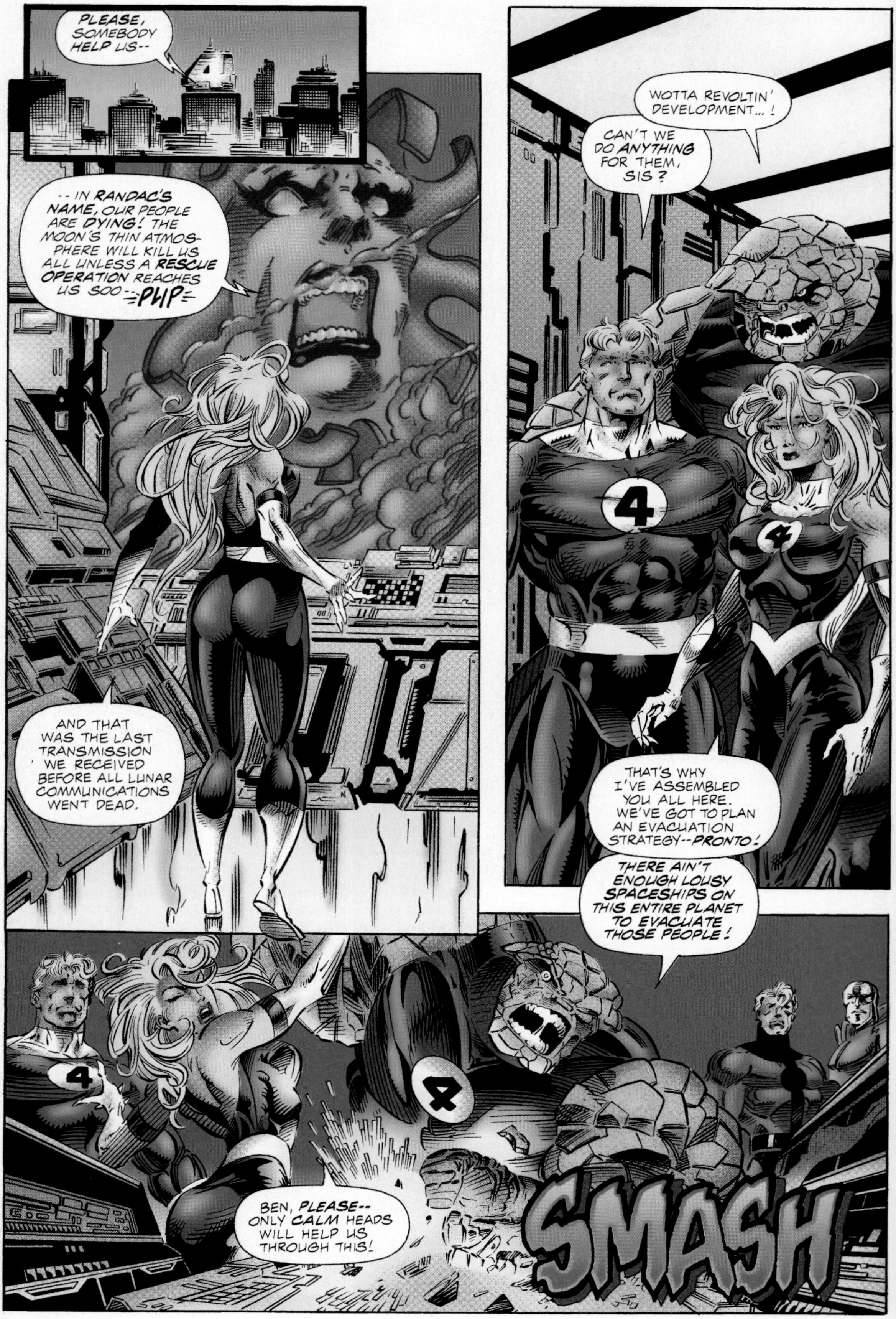

PLEASE, SOMEBODY HELP US--
--IN RANDAC'S NAME, OUR PEOPLE ARE DYING! THE MOON'S THIN ATMOSPHERE WILL KILL US ALL UNLESS A RESCUE OPERATION REACHES US SOO--PLIP
AND THAT WAS THE LAST TRANSMISSION WE RECEIVED BEFORE ALL LUNAR COMMUNICATIONS WENT DEAD.
WOTTA REVOLTIN' DEVELOPMENT...!
CAN'T WE DO ANYTHING FOR THEM, SIS?
THAT'S WHY I'VE ASSEMBLED YOU ALL HERE. WE'VE GOT TO PLAN AN EVACUATION STRATEGY--PRONTO!
THERE AIN'T ENOUGH LOUSY SPACESHIPS ON THIS ENTIRE PLANET TO EVACUATE THOSE PEOPLE!
SMASH
BEN, PLEASE-- ONLY CALM HEADS WILL HELP US THROUGH THIS!

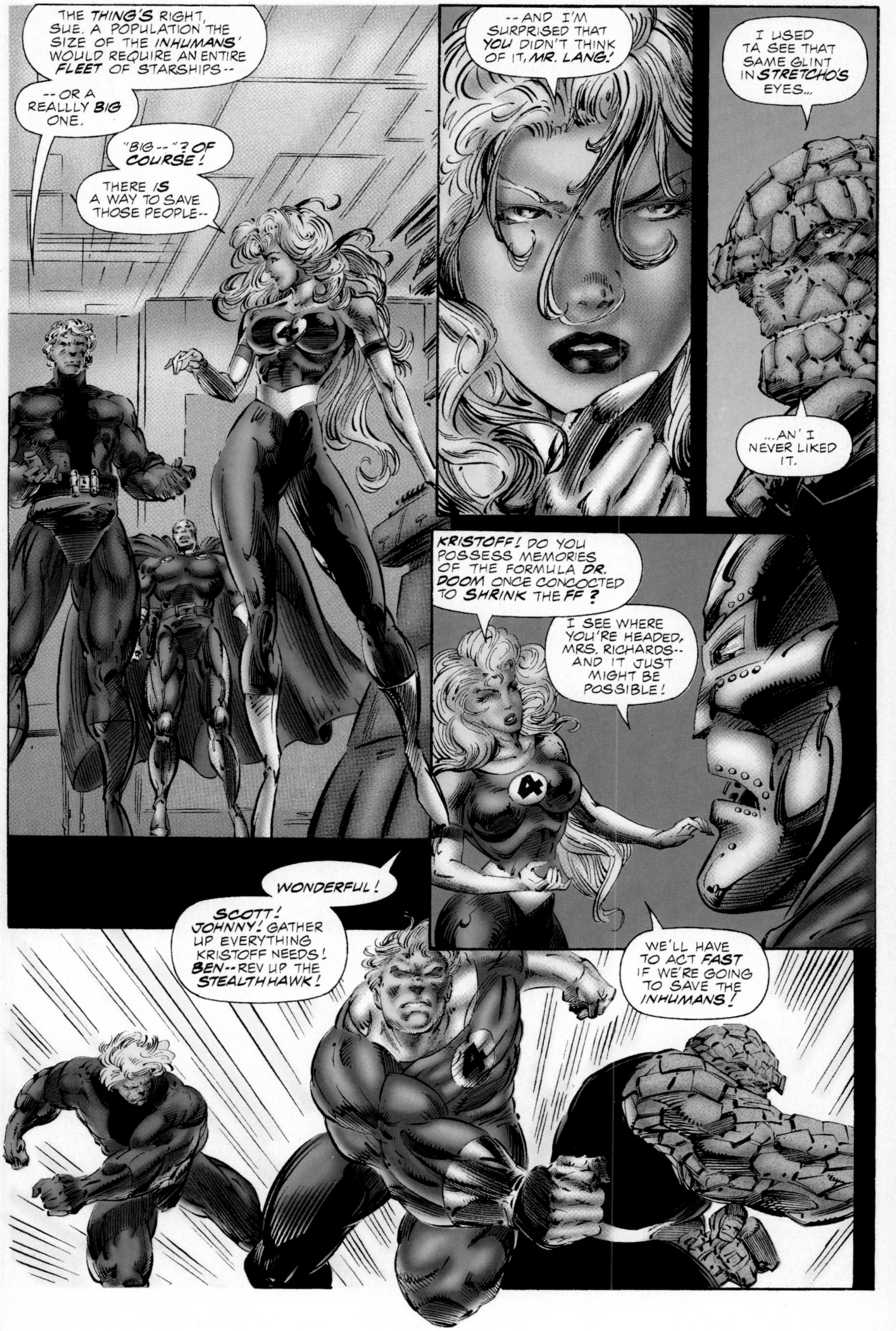
THE THING'S RIGHT, SUE. A POPULATION THE SIZE OF THE INHUMANS' WOULD REQUIRE AN ENTIRE FLEET OF STARSHIPS--
--OR A REALLLY BIG ONE.
"BIG--"? OF COURSE!
THERE IS A WAY TO SAVE THOSE PEOPLE--
--AND I'M SURPRISED THAT YOU DIDN'T THINK OF IT, MR. LANG!
I USED TA SEE THAT SAME GLINT IN STRETCHO'S EYES...
...AN' I NEVER LIKED IT.
KRISTOFF! DO YOU POSSESS MEMORIES OF THE FORMULA DR. DOOM ONCE CONCOCTED TO SHRINK THE FF?
I SEE WHERE YOU'RE HEADED, MRS. RICHARDS-- AND IT JUST MIGHT BE POSSIBLE!
WONDERFUL!
SCOTT! JOHNNY! GATHER UP EVERYTHING KRISTOFF NEEDS! BEN--REV UP THE STEALTHHAWK!
WE'LL HAVE TO ACT FAST IF WE'RE GOING TO SAVE THE INHUMANS!

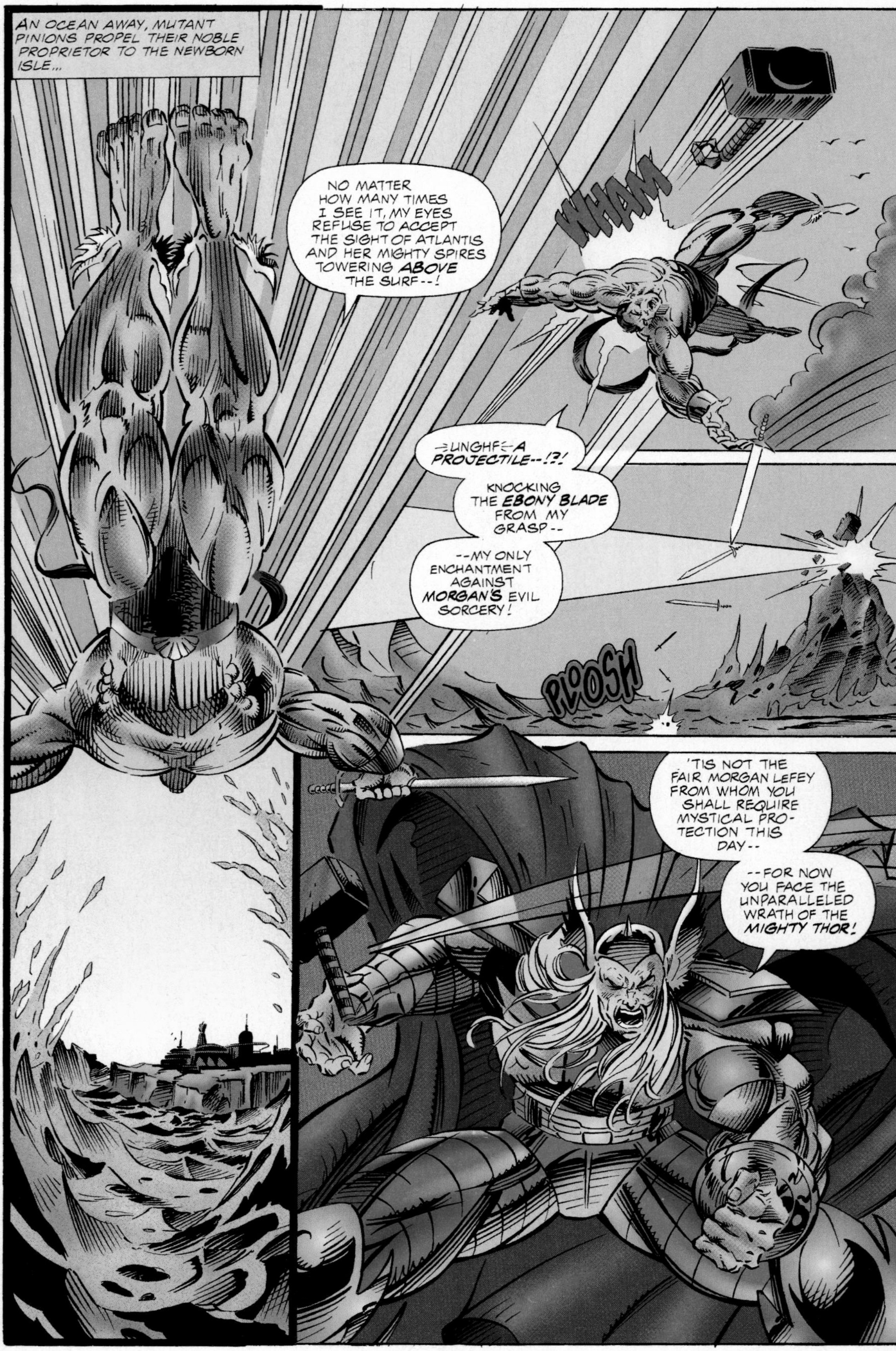

AN OCEAN AWAY, MUTANT PINIONS PROPEL THEIR NOBLE PROPRIETOR TO THE NEWBORN ISLE...
NO MATTER HOW MANY TIMES I SEE IT, MY EYES REFUSE TO ACCEPT THE SIGHT OF ATLANTIS AND HER MIGHTY SPIRES TOWERING ABOVE THE SURF--!
WHAM
UNGHF-- A PROJECTILE--!?!
KNOCKING THE EBONY BLADE FROM MY GRASP--
--MY ONLY ENCHANTMENT AGAINST MORGAN'S EVIL SORCERY!
PLOOSH
'TIS NOT THE FAIR MORGAN LEFEY FROM WHOM YOU SHALL REQUIRE MYSTICAL PROTECTION THIS DAY--
--FOR NOW YOU FACE THE UNPARALLELED WRATH OF THE MIGHTY THOR!

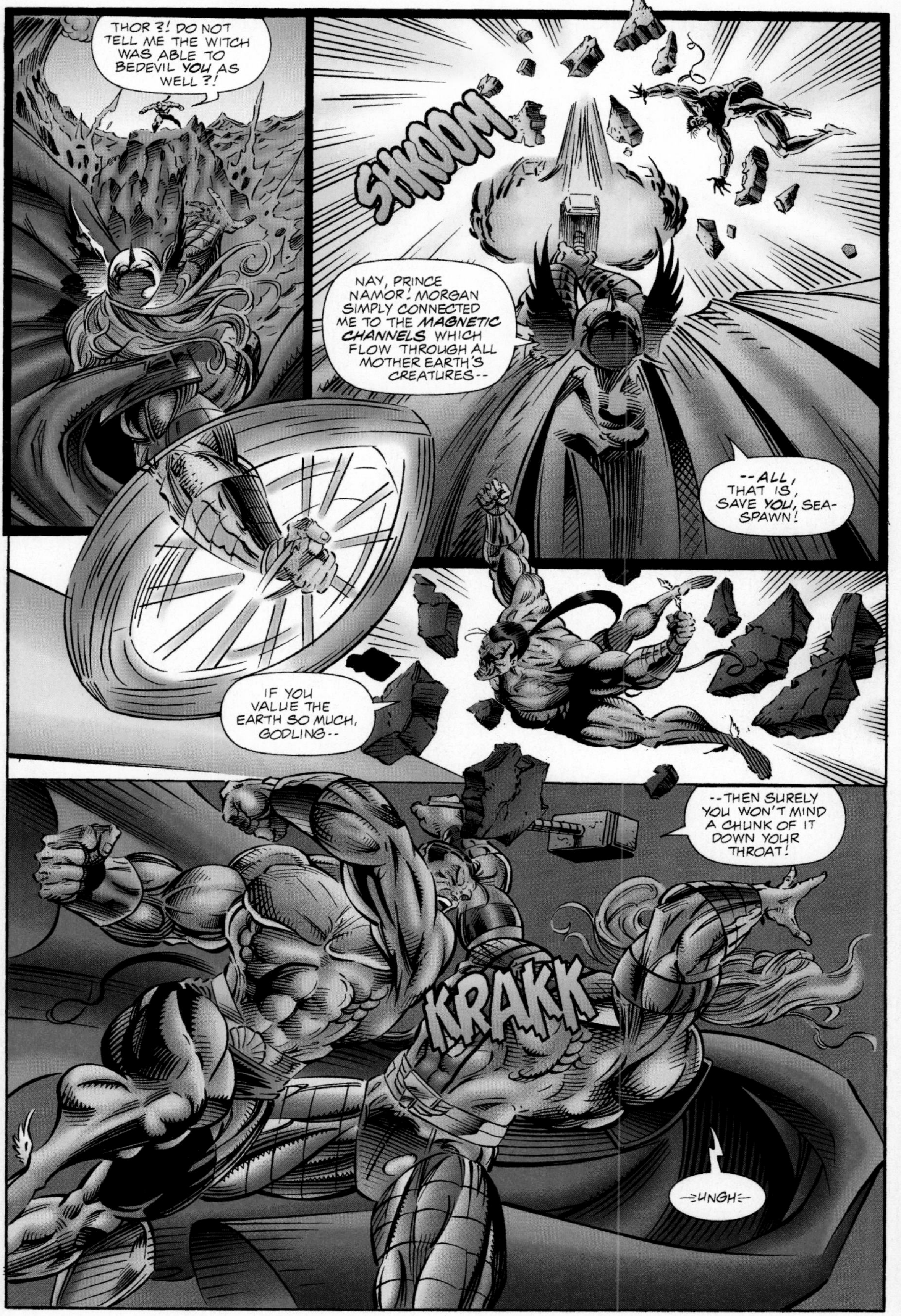
THOR?! DO NOT TELL ME THE WITCH WAS ABLE TO BEDEVIL YOU AS WELL?!
SHOOM
NAY, PRINCE NAMOR! MORGAN SIMPLY CONNECTED ME TO THE MAGNETIC CHANNELS WHICH FLOW THROUGH ALL MOTHER EARTH'S CREATURES--
--ALL, THAT IS, SAVE YOU, SEA-SPAWN!
IF YOU VALUE THE EARTH SO MUCH, GODLING--
--THEN SURELY YOU WON'T MIND A CHUNK OF IT DOWN YOUR THROAT!
KRAKK
UNGH

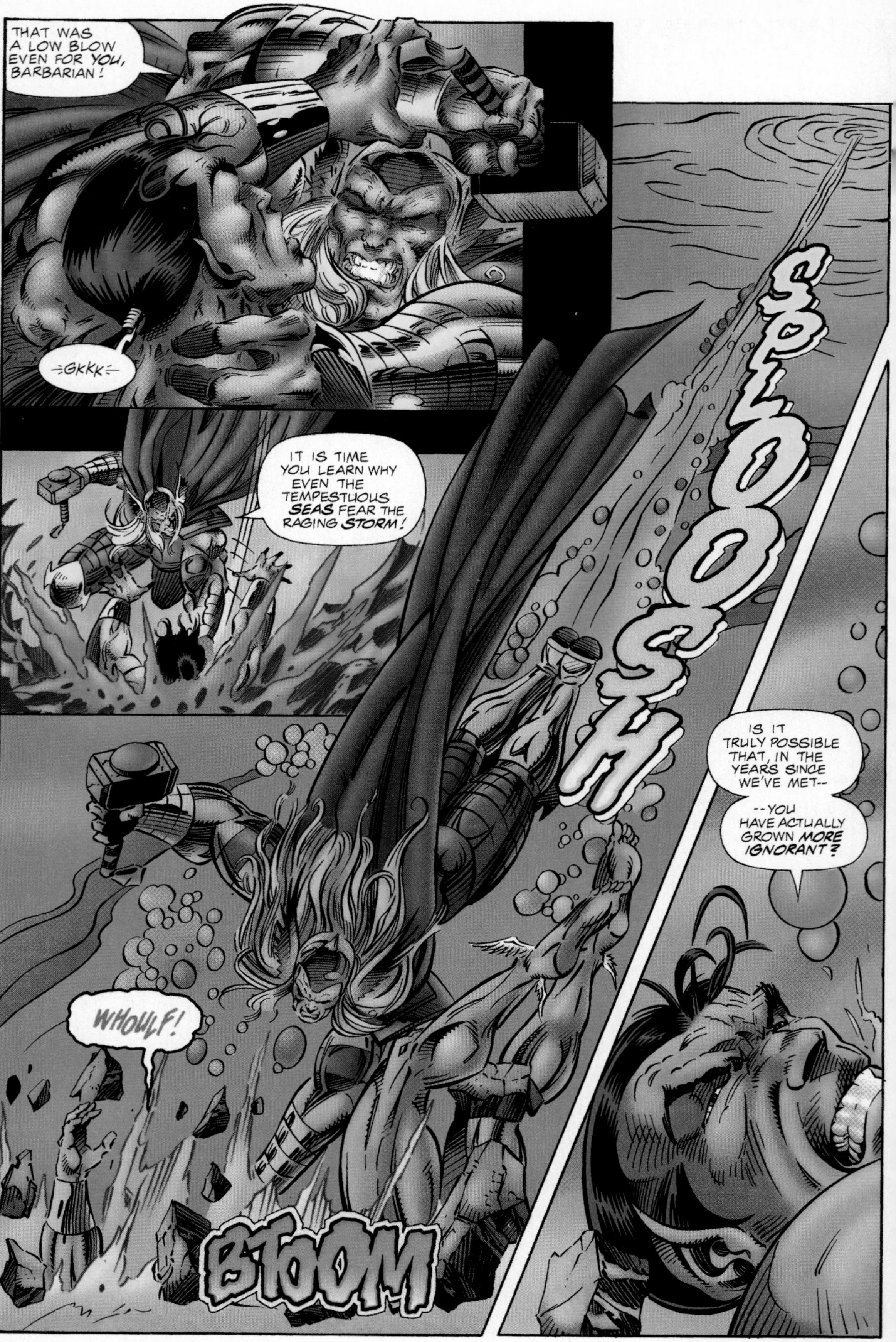
THAT WAS A LOW BLOW EVEN FOR *YOU*, BARBARIAN!
GKKK
IT IS TIME YOU LEARN WHY EVEN THE TEMPESTUOUS *SEAS* FEAR THE RAGING *STORM*!
SPLOOOOSH
IS IT TRULY POSSIBLE THAT, IN THE YEARS SINCE WE'VE MET--
--YOU HAVE ACTUALLY GROWN *MORE IGNORANT*?
WHOULF!
BTOOM

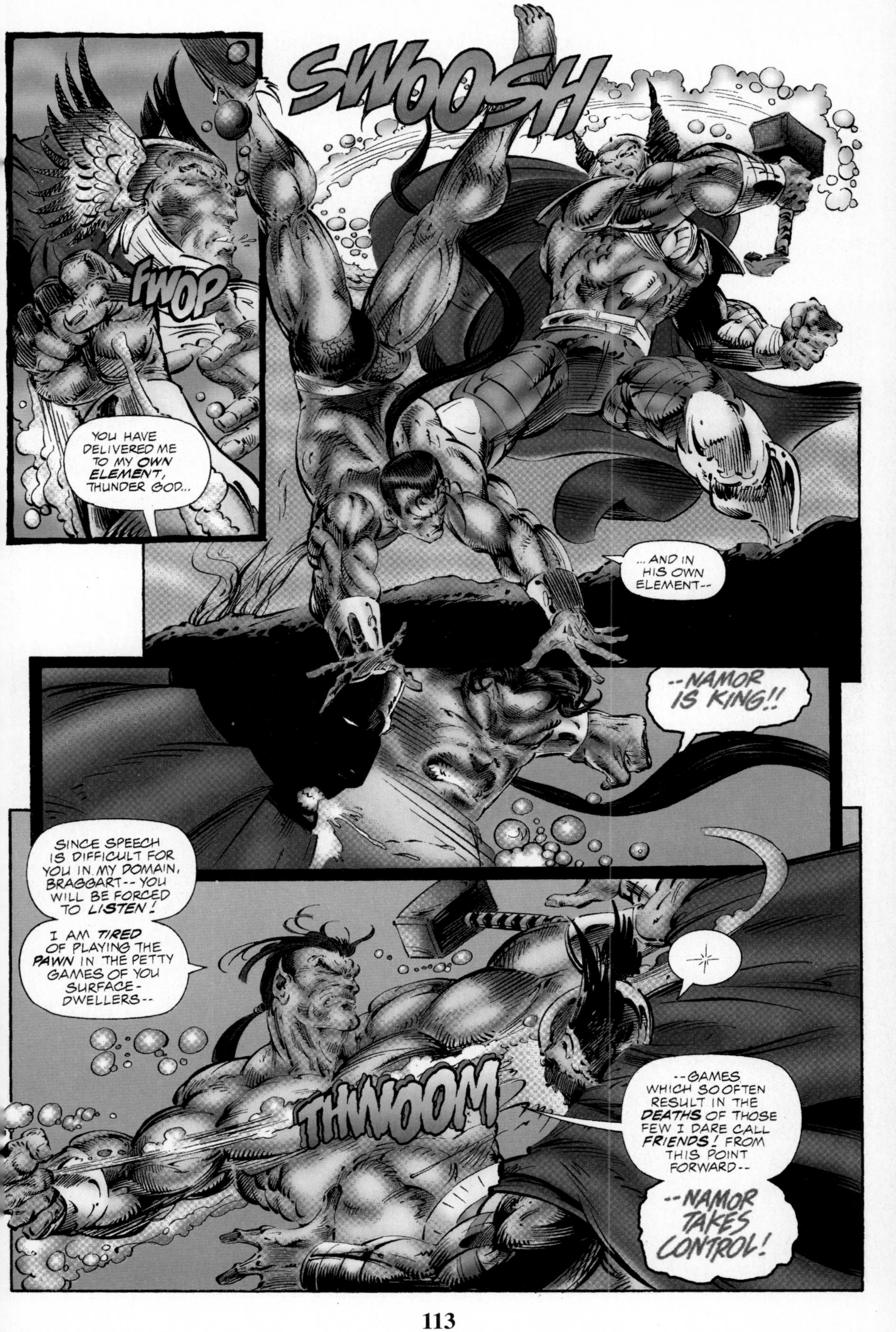
SWOOSH
FWOP
YOU HAVE DELIVERED ME TO MY OWN ELEMENT, THUNDER GOD...
...AND IN HIS OWN ELEMENT--
--NAMOR IS KING!!
SINCE SPEECH IS DIFFICULT FOR YOU IN MY DOMAIN, BRAGGART-- YOU WILL BE FORCED TO LISTEN!
I AM TIRED OF PLAYING THE PAWN IN THE PETTY GAMES OF YOU SURFACE-DWELLERS--
THWOOM
--GAMES WHICH SO OFTEN RESULT IN THE DEATHS OF THOSE FEW I DARE CALL FRIENDS! FROM THIS POINT FORWARD--
--NAMOR TAKES CONTROL!

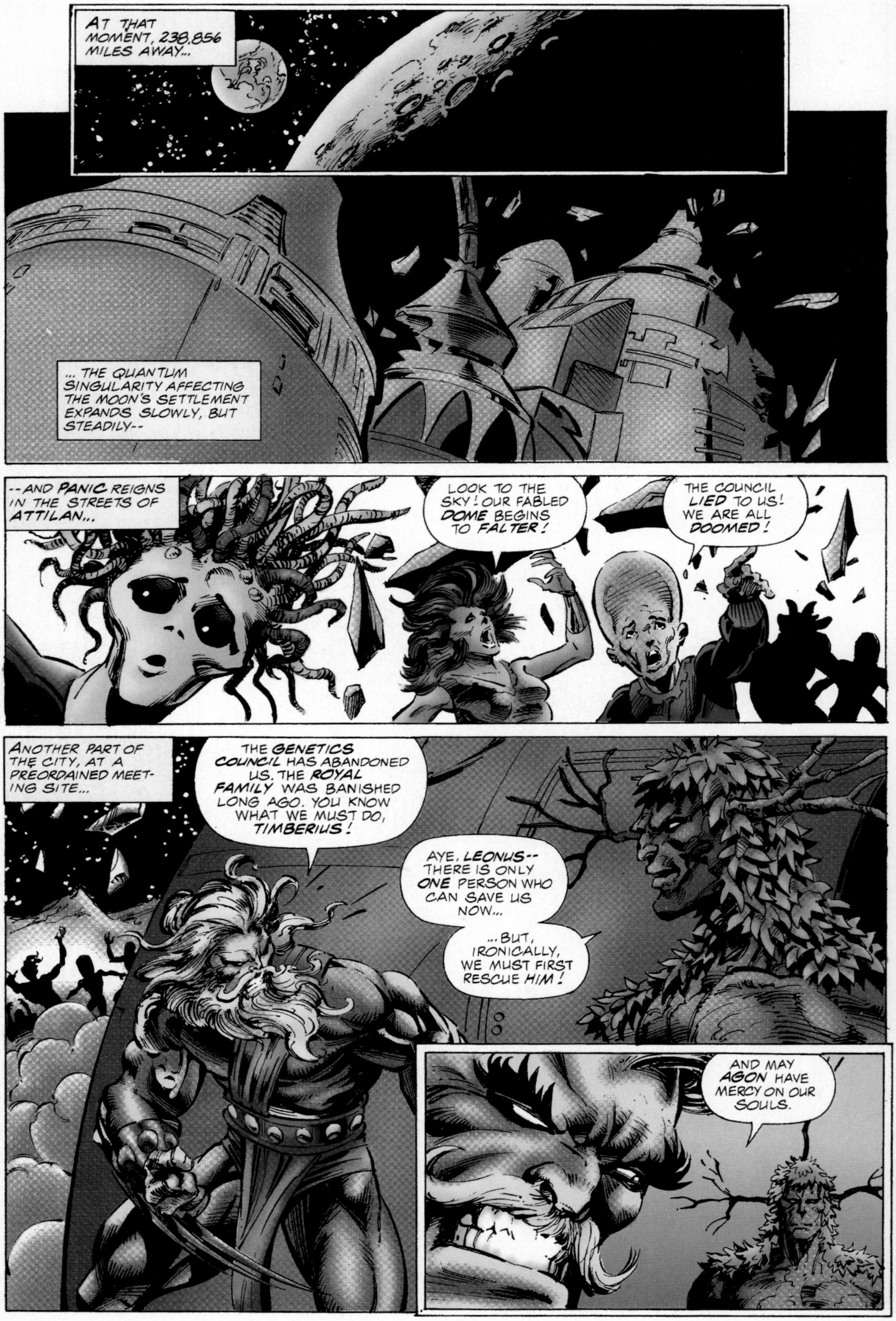
AT THAT MOMENT, 238,856 MILES AWAY...
... THE QUANTUM SINGULARITY AFFECTING THE MOON'S SETTLEMENT EXPANDS SLOWLY, BUT STEADILY--
--AND PANIC REIGNS IN THE STREETS OF ATTILAN...
LOOK TO THE SKY! OUR FABLED DOME BEGINS TO FALTER!
THE COUNCIL LIED TO US! WE ARE ALL DOOMED!
ANOTHER PART OF THE CITY, AT A PREORDAINED MEETING SITE...
THE GENETICS COUNCIL HAS ABANDONED US. THE ROYAL FAMILY WAS BANISHED LONG AGO. YOU KNOW WHAT WE MUST DO, TIMBERIUS!
AYE, LEONUS-- THERE IS ONLY ONE PERSON WHO CAN SAVE US NOW...
...BUT, IRONICALLY, WE MUST FIRST RESCUE HIM!
AND MAY AGON HAVE MERCY ON OUR SOULS.

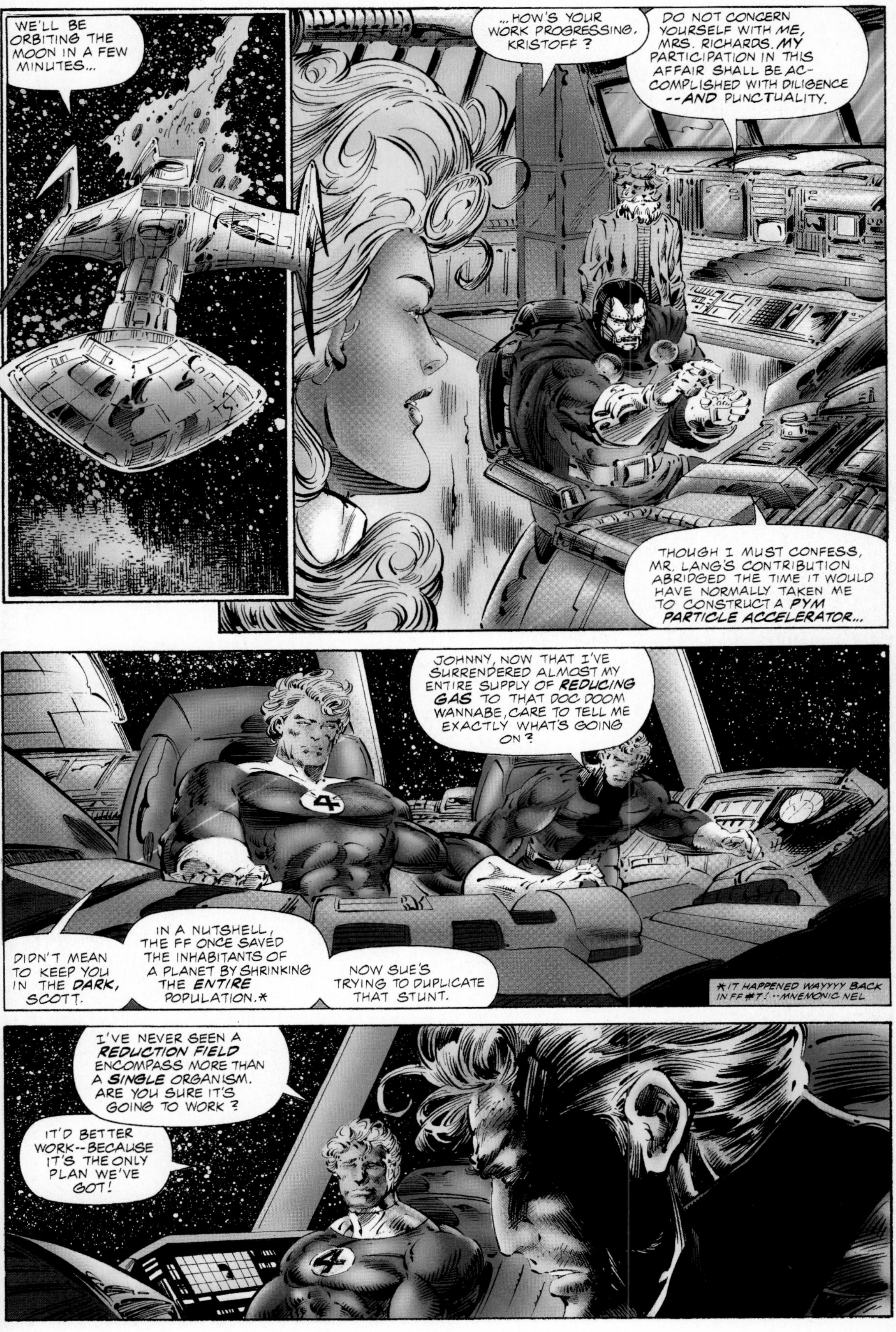
WE'LL BE ORBITING THE MOON IN A FEW MINUTES...
...HOW'S YOUR WORK PROGRESSING, KRISTOFF?
DO NOT CONCERN YOURSELF WITH ME, MRS. RICHARDS. MY PARTICIPATION IN THIS AFFAIR SHALL BE ACCOMPLISHED WITH DILIGENCE --AND PUNCTUALITY.
THOUGH I MUST CONFESS, MR. LANG'S CONTRIBUTION ABRIDGED THE TIME IT WOULD HAVE NORMALLY TAKEN ME TO CONSTRUCT A PYM PARTICLE ACCELERATOR...
JOHNNY, NOW THAT I'VE SURRENDERED ALMOST MY ENTIRE SUPPLY OF REDUCING GAS TO THAT DOC DOOM WANNABE, CARE TO TELL ME EXACTLY WHAT'S GOING ON?
DIDN'T MEAN TO KEEP YOU IN THE DARK, SCOTT.
IN A NUTSHELL, THE FF ONCE SAVED THE INHABITANTS OF A PLANET BY SHRINKING THE ENTIRE POPULATION.*
NOW SUE'S TRYING TO DUPLICATE THAT STUNT.
*IT HAPPENED WAYYYY BACK IN FF #7! --MNEMONIC NEL
I'VE NEVER SEEN A REDUCTION FIELD ENCOMPASS MORE THAN A SINGLE ORGANISM. ARE YOU SURE IT'S GOING TO WORK?
IT'D BETTER WORK--BECAUSE IT'S THE ONLY PLAN WE'VE GOT!

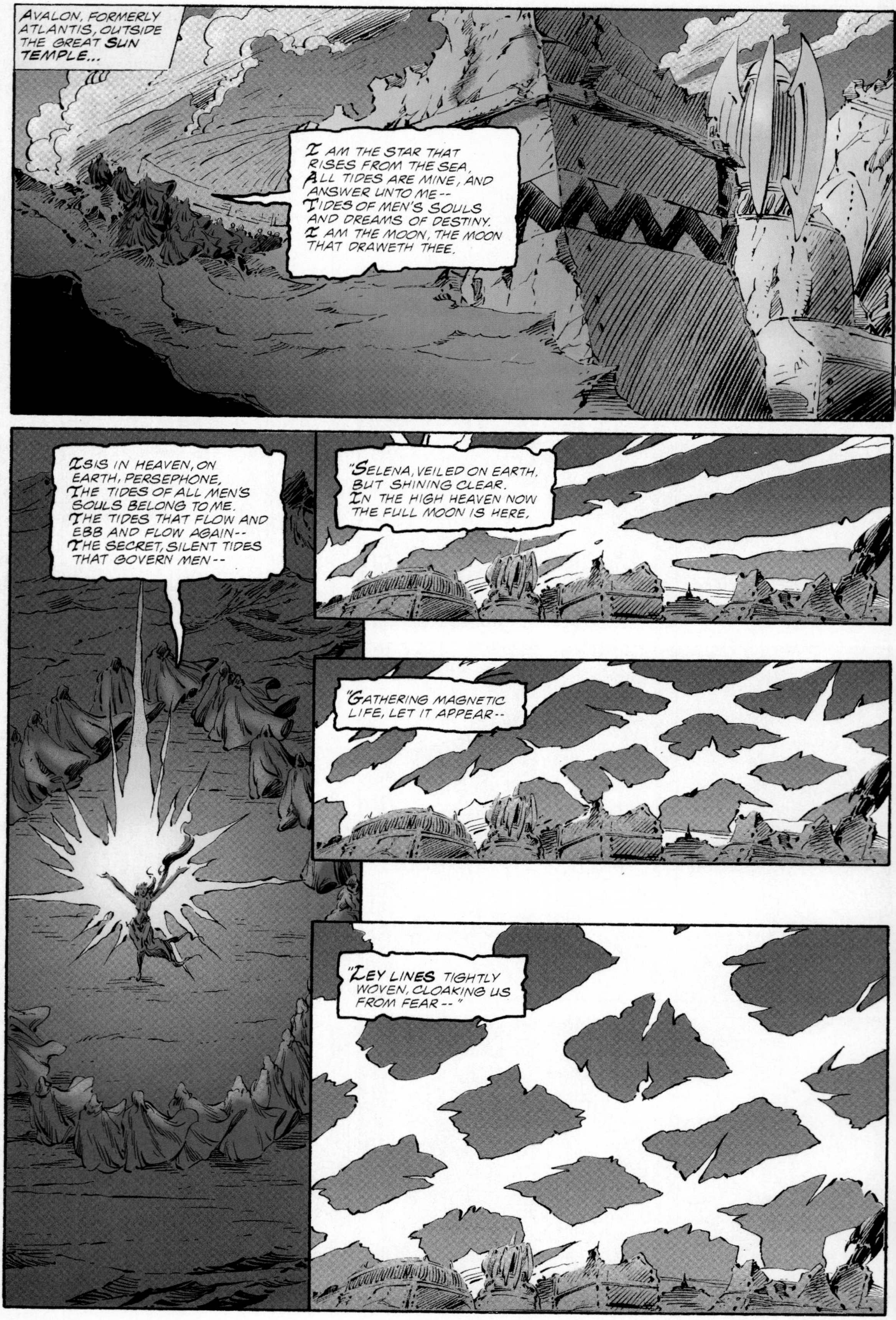
AVALON, FORMERLY ATLANTIS, OUTSIDE THE GREAT SUN TEMPLE...
I AM THE STAR THAT RISES FROM THE SEA, ALL TIDES ARE MINE, AND ANSWER UNTO ME-- TIDES OF MEN'S SOULS AND DREAMS OF DESTINY. I AM THE MOON, THE MOON THAT DRAWETH THEE.
ISIS IN HEAVEN, ON EARTH, PERSEPHONE, THE TIDES OF ALL MEN'S SOULS BELONG TO ME. THE TIDES THAT FLOW AND EBB AND FLOW AGAIN-- THE SECRET, SILENT TIDES THAT GOVERN MEN--
"SELENA, VEILED ON EARTH, BUT SHINING CLEAR. IN THE HIGH HEAVEN NOW THE FULL MOON IS HERE.
"GATHERING MAGNETIC LIFE, LET IT APPEAR--
"LEY LINES TIGHTLY WOVEN, CLOAKING US FROM FEAR--"

AT THAT VERY INSTANT, A SHORT DISTANCE AWAY...

ENOUGH, SUB-MARINER! I SHALL TOLERATE YOUR WOEFUL LAMENTATIONS *NO LONGER!*

PTHOK

IF IT IS *ATLANTIS* YOU TRULY DESIRE--

-- 'TIS *ATLANTIS* YOU WILL SURELY *HAVE!*

UNGH

FZHAK

W-WHAT IS *THIS?!*

SOME SORT OF *ENERGY BARRIER*--

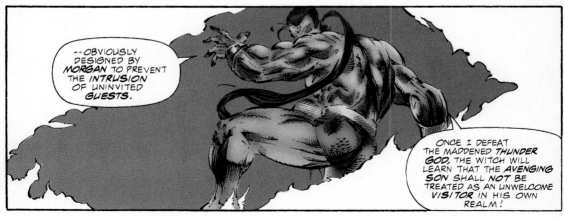

--OBVIOUSLY DESIGNED BY *MORGAN* TO PREVENT THE *INTRUSION* OF UNINVITED *GUESTS.*

ONCE I DEFEAT THE MADDENED *THUNDER GOD,* THE WITCH WILL LEARN THAT THE *AVENGING SON* SHALL *NOT* BE TREATED AS AN UNWELCOME *VISITOR* IN HIS OWN REALM!

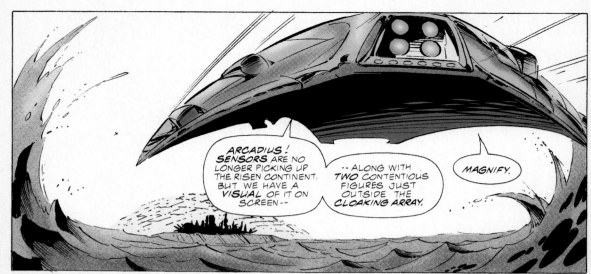

ARCADIUS! SENSORS ARE NO LONGER PICKING UP THE RISEN CONTINENT, BUT WE HAVE A VISUAL OF IT ON SCREEN--

--ALONG WITH TWO CONTENTIOUS FIGURES JUST OUTSIDE THE CLOAKING ARRAY.

MAGNIFY.

IDIOT. HE IS NAMOR, PRINCE OF ATLANTIS -- OR PERHAPS FORMER PRINCE, NOW THAT HIS KINGDOM RESTS ABOVE THE WAVES!

I MUST LEARN WHAT ROLE HE PLAYS IN THIS AFFAIR. SUBDUE HIM!

RANDAC'S GENES! DO YOU REALIZE WHO THAT IS?

THE GOLDEN-HAIRED ONE IS THE LEGENDARY THOR, BUT THE OTHER...

LEONARD NIMOY?

OD'S BLOOD!

FZAPP

MY OPPONENT IS STRUCK A BLOW FROM BEHIND!

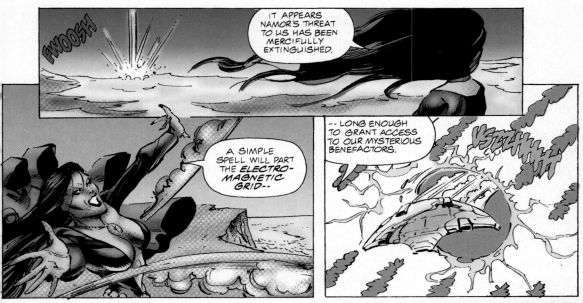

IT APPEARS NAMOR'S THREAT TO US HAS BEEN MERCIFULLY EXTINGUISHED.

A SIMPLE SPELL WILL PART THE *ELECTRO-MAGNETIC GRID*--

-- LONG ENOUGH TO GRANT ACCESS TO OUR MYSTERIOUS BENEFACTORS.

FWOOSH

VSTZHHH

WHETHER THEY COME AS *ALLIES* OR *ENEMIES*, I STAND PREPARED...

GREETINGS, MY FRIENDS! PLEASE ACCEPT MY HOSPITALITY AS AVALON'S FIRST GUESTS.

I AM *MORGAN LE FEY* -- AND *THIS IS MY KINGDOM.*

INCORRECT, WOMAN, THIS IS THE *ANCESTRAL HOME* OF THE *INHUMANS* -- AND *YOU* ARE TRESPASSING.

CYNAS, *PLEASE* -- WHERE ARE YOUR *MANNERS* ?

I'M CERTAIN WE CAN WORK OUT AN *ARRANGEMENT* WITH THE LOVELY MISS LE FEY THAT WILL BE *MUTUALLY SATISFYING*...

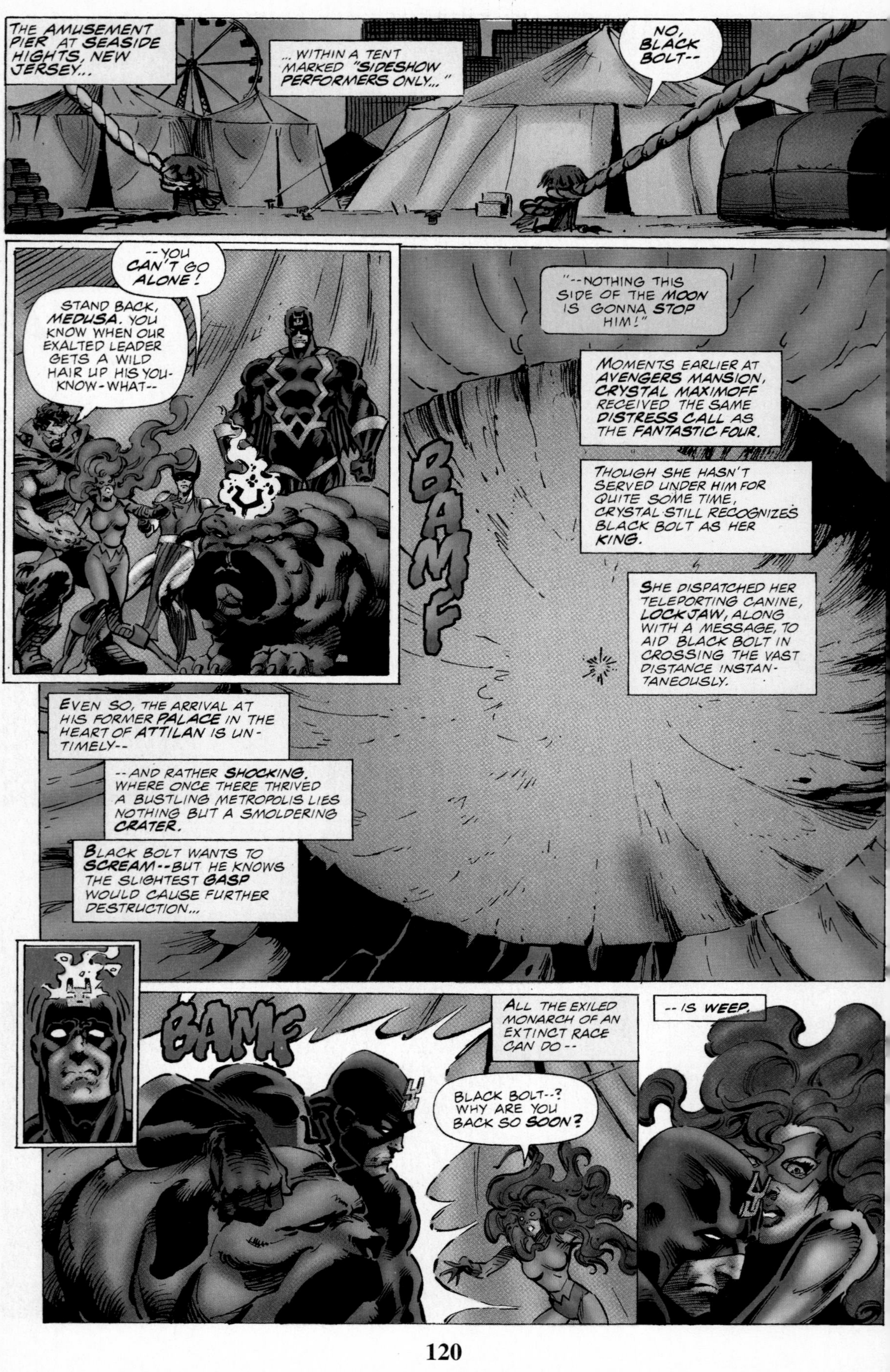
THE AMUSEMENT PIER AT SEASIDE HIGHTS, NEW JERSEY...
...WITHIN A TENT MARKED "SIDESHOW PERFORMERS ONLY..."
NO, BLACK BOLT--
--YOU CAN'T GO ALONE!
STAND BACK, MEDUSA. YOU KNOW WHEN OUR EXALTED LEADER GETS A WILD HAIR UP HIS YOU-KNOW-WHAT--
"--NOTHING THIS SIDE OF THE MOON IS GONNA STOP HIM!"
MOMENTS EARLIER AT AVENGERS MANSION, CRYSTAL MAXIMOFF RECEIVED THE SAME DISTRESS CALL AS THE FANTASTIC FOUR.
THOUGH SHE HASN'T SERVED UNDER HIM FOR QUITE SOME TIME, CRYSTAL STILL RECOGNIZES BLACK BOLT AS HER KING.
SHE DISPATCHED HER TELEPORTING CANINE, LOCKJAW, ALONG WITH A MESSAGE, TO AID BLACK BOLT IN CROSSING THE VAST DISTANCE INSTANTANEOUSLY.
BAMF
EVEN SO, THE ARRIVAL AT HIS FORMER PALACE IN THE HEART OF ATTILAN IS UNTIMELY--
--AND RATHER SHOCKING. WHERE ONCE THERE THRIVED A BUSTLING METROPOLIS LIES NOTHING BUT A SMOLDERING CRATER.
BLACK BOLT WANTS TO SCREAM--BUT HE KNOWS THE SLIGHTEST GASP WOULD CAUSE FURTHER DESTRUCTION...
BAMF
ALL THE EXILED MONARCH OF AN EXTINCT RACE CAN DO--
--IS WEEP.
BLACK BOLT--? WHY ARE YOU BACK SO SOON?

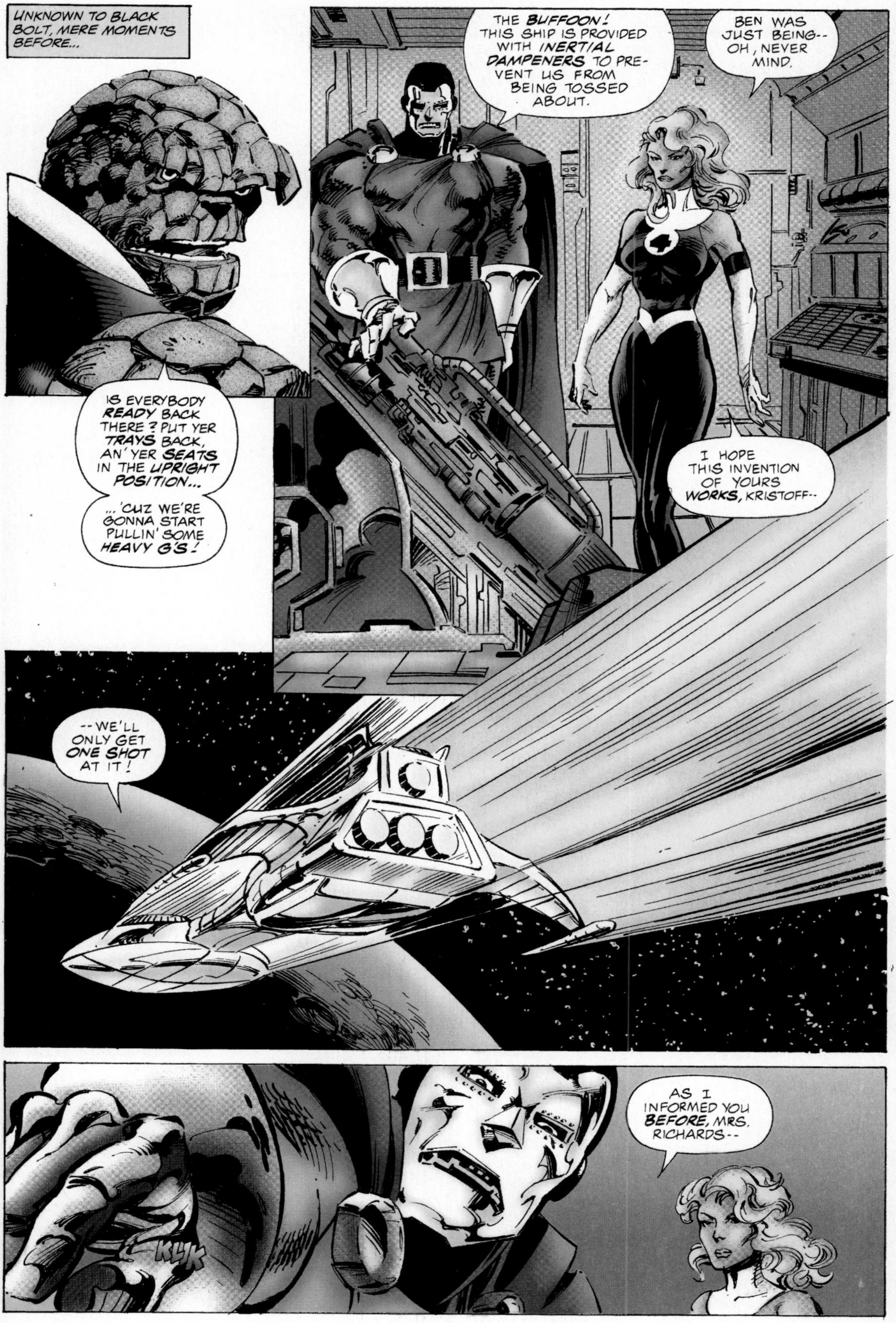
UNKNOWN TO BLACK BOLT, MERE MOMENTS BEFORE...
IS EVERYBODY READY BACK THERE? PUT YER TRAYS BACK, AN' YER SEATS IN THE UPRIGHT POSITION...
...'CUZ WE'RE GONNA START PULLIN' SOME HEAVY G'S!
THE BUFFOON! THIS SHIP IS PROVIDED WITH INERTIAL DAMPENERS TO PREVENT US FROM BEING TOSSED ABOUT.
BEN WAS JUST BEING-- OH, NEVER MIND.
I HOPE THIS INVENTION OF YOURS WORKS, KRISTOFF--
--WE'LL ONLY GET ONE SHOT AT IT!
KLIK
AS I INFORMED YOU BEFORE, MRS. RICHARDS--

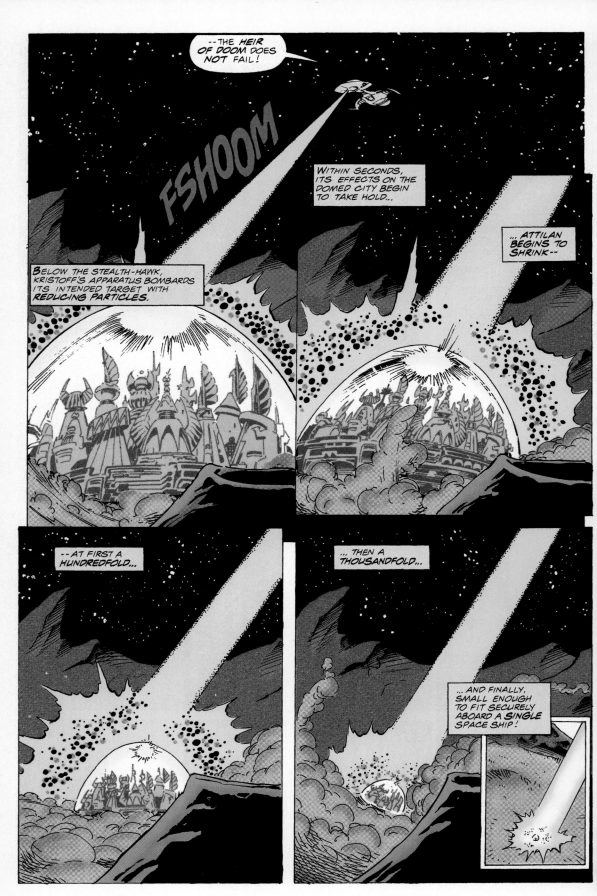

--THE *HEIR OF DOOM* DOES NOT FAIL!

FSHOOM

WITHIN SECONDS, ITS EFFECTS ON THE DOMED CITY BEGIN TO TAKE HOLD...

...ATTILAN BEGINS TO SHRINK--

BELOW THE STEALTH-HAWK, KRISTOFF'S APPARATUS BOMBARDS ITS INTENDED TARGET WITH *REDUCING PARTICLES.*

--AT FIRST A *HUNDREDFOLD*...

... THEN A *THOUSANDFOLD*...

... AND FINALLY, SMALL ENOUGH TO FIT SECURELY ABOARD A *SINGLE* SPACE SHIP!

122

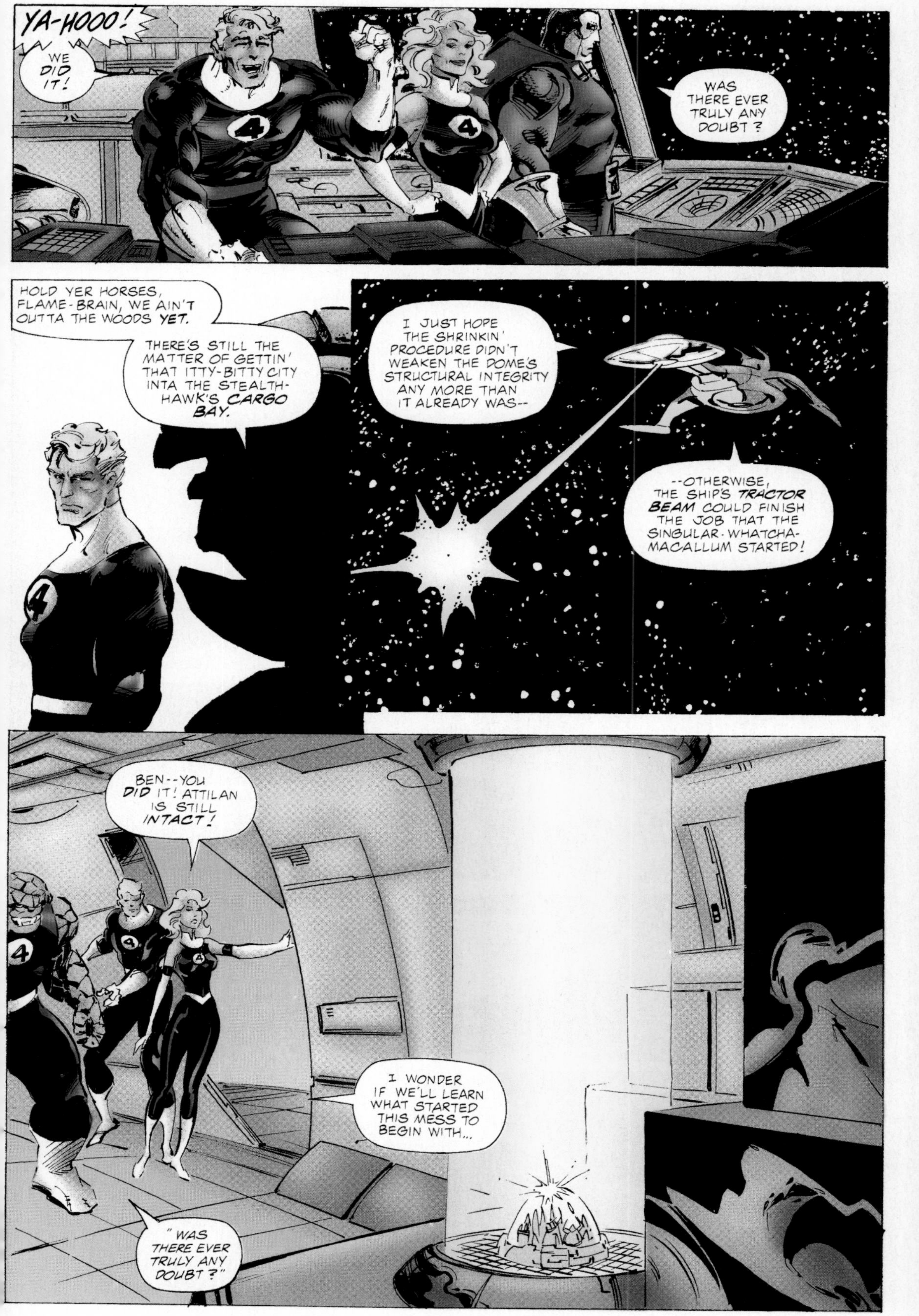
YA-HOOO!
WE DID IT!
WAS THERE EVER TRULY ANY DOUBT?
HOLD YER HORSES, FLAME-BRAIN, WE AIN'T OUTTA THE WOODS YET.
THERE'S STILL THE MATTER OF GETTIN' THAT ITTY-BITTY CITY INTA THE STEALTH-HAWK'S CARGO BAY.
I JUST HOPE THE SHRINKIN' PROCEDURE DIDN'T WEAKEN THE DOME'S STRUCTURAL INTEGRITY ANY MORE THAN IT ALREADY WAS--
--OTHERWISE, THE SHIP'S TRACTOR BEAM COULD FINISH THE JOB THAT THE SINGULAR-WHATCHA-MACALLUM STARTED!
BEN--YOU DID IT! ATTILAN IS STILL INTACT!
I WONDER IF WE'LL LEARN WHAT STARTED THIS MESS TO BEGIN WITH...
"WAS THERE EVER TRULY ANY DOUBT?"

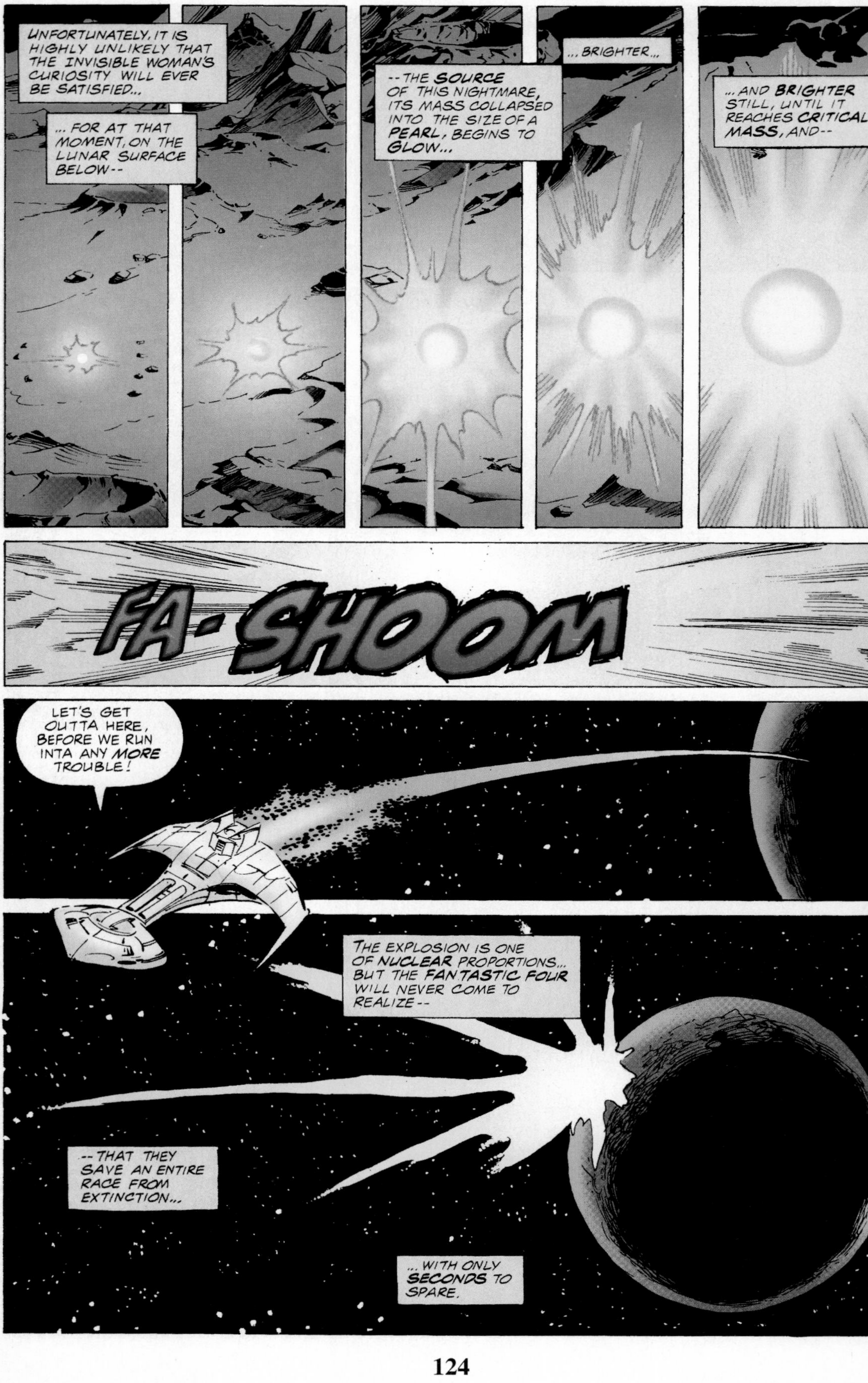
UNFORTUNATELY, IT IS HIGHLY UNLIKELY THAT THE INVISIBLE WOMAN'S CURIOSITY WILL EVER BE SATISFIED...
... FOR AT THAT MOMENT, ON THE LUNAR SURFACE BELOW--
--THE SOURCE OF THIS NIGHTMARE, ITS MASS COLLAPSED INTO THE SIZE OF A PEARL, BEGINS TO GLOW...
... BRIGHTER...
... AND BRIGHTER STILL, UNTIL IT REACHES CRITICAL MASS, AND--
FA-SHOOM
LET'S GET OUTTA HERE, BEFORE WE RUN INTA ANY MORE TROUBLE!
THE EXPLOSION IS ONE OF NUCLEAR PROPORTIONS... BUT THE FANTASTIC FOUR WILL NEVER COME TO REALIZE--
--THAT THEY SAVE AN ENTIRE RACE FROM EXTINCTION...
... WITH ONLY SECONDS TO SPARE.

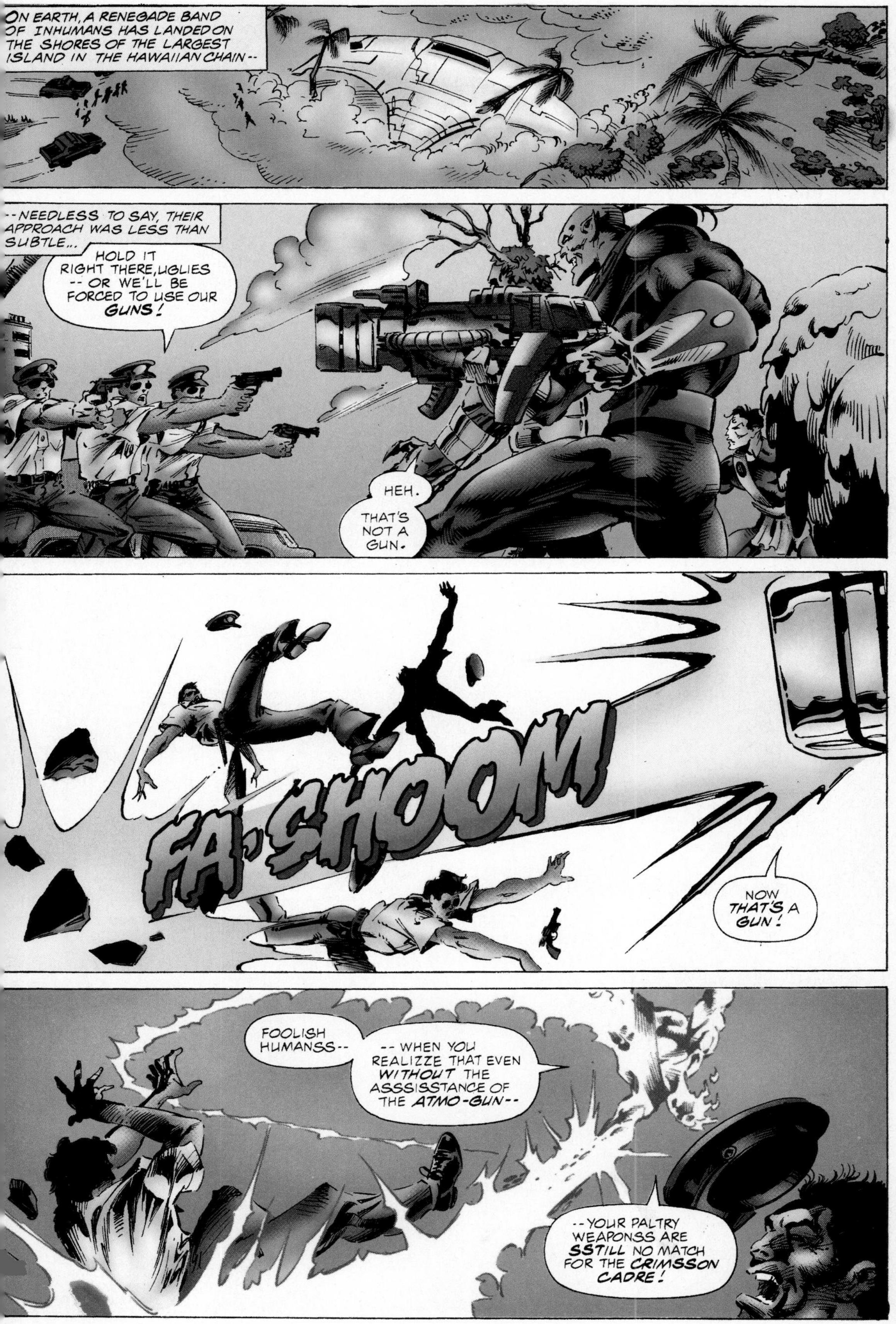
ON EARTH, A RENEGADE BAND OF INHUMANS HAS LANDED ON THE SHORES OF THE LARGEST ISLAND IN THE HAWAIIAN CHAIN--
--NEEDLESS TO SAY, THEIR APPROACH WAS LESS THAN SUBTLE...
HOLD IT RIGHT THERE, UGLIES -- OR WE'LL BE FORCED TO USE OUR GUNS!
HEH.
THAT'S NOT A GUN.
FA-SHOOM
NOW THAT'S A GUN!
FOOLISH HUMANSS--
--WHEN YOU REALIZZE THAT EVEN WITHOUT THE ASSSISSTANCE OF THE ATMO-GUN--
--YOUR PALTRY WEAPONSS ARE SSTILL NO MATCH FOR THE CRIMSSON CADRE!

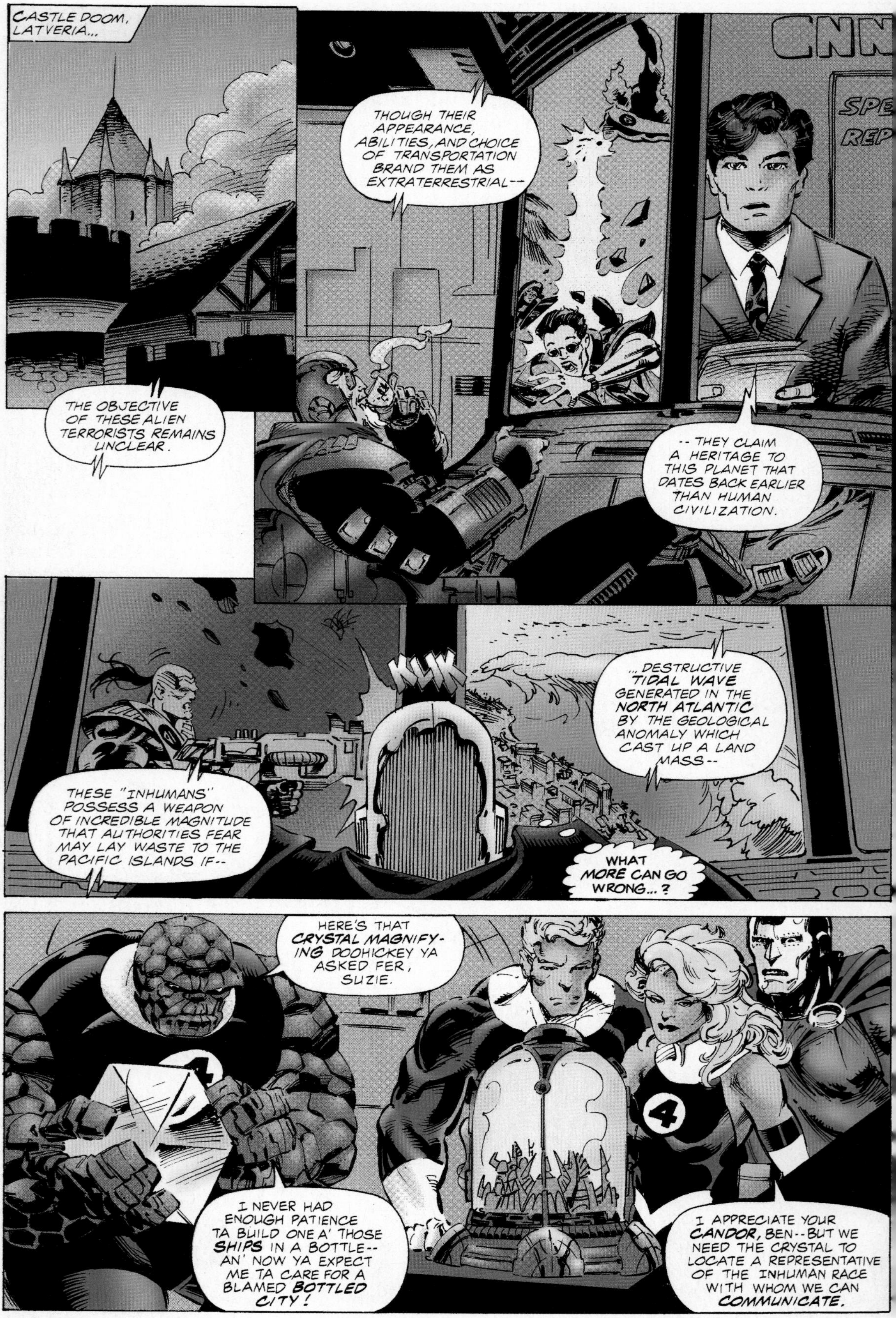
CASTLE DOOM, LATVERIA...
THOUGH THEIR APPEARANCE, ABILITIES, AND CHOICE OF TRANSPORTATION BRAND THEM AS EXTRATERRESTRIAL--
CNN
SPE
REP
THE OBJECTIVE OF THESE ALIEN TERRORISTS REMAINS UNCLEAR.
-- THEY CLAIM A HERITAGE TO THIS PLANET THAT DATES BACK EARLIER THAN HUMAN CIVILIZATION.
KLIK
...DESTRUCTIVE TIDAL WAVE GENERATED IN THE NORTH ATLANTIC BY THE GEOLOGICAL ANOMALY WHICH CAST UP A LAND MASS--
THESE "INHUMANS" POSSESS A WEAPON OF INCREDIBLE MAGNITUDE THAT AUTHORITIES FEAR MAY LAY WASTE TO THE PACIFIC ISLANDS IF--
WHAT MORE CAN GO WRONG...?
HERE'S THAT CRYSTAL MAGNIFYING DOOHICKEY YA ASKED FER, SUZIE.
I NEVER HAD ENOUGH PATIENCE TA BUILD ONE A' THOSE SHIPS IN A BOTTLE-- AN' NOW YA EXPECT ME TA CARE FOR A BLAMED BOTTLED CITY!
I APPRECIATE YOUR CANDOR, BEN--BUT WE NEED THE CRYSTAL TO LOCATE A REPRESENTATIVE OF THE INHUMAN RACE WITH WHOM WE CAN COMMUNICATE.

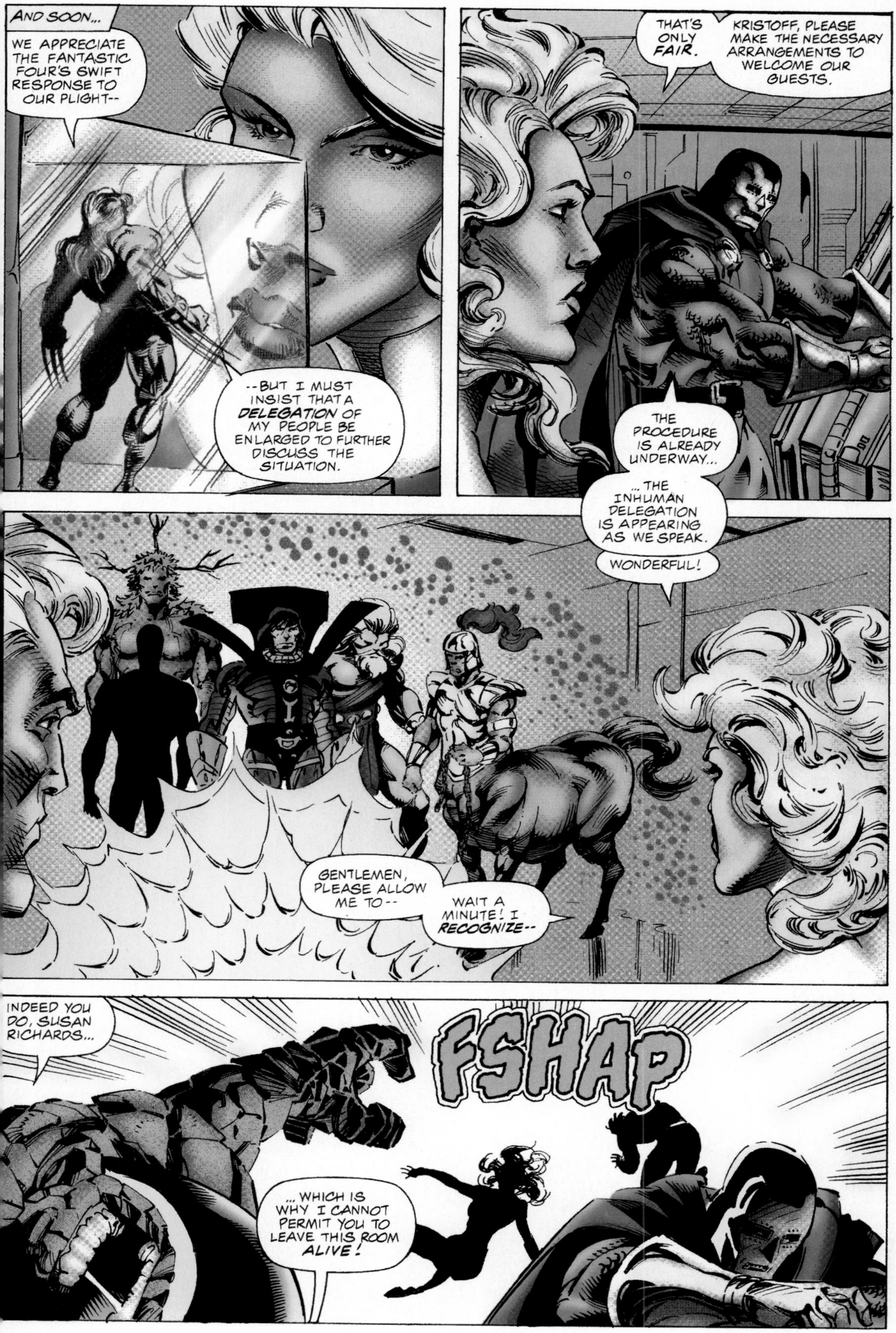
AND SOON...
WE APPRECIATE THE FANTASTIC FOUR'S SWIFT RESPONSE TO OUR PLIGHT--
--BUT I MUST INSIST THAT A DELEGATION OF MY PEOPLE BE ENLARGED TO FURTHER DISCUSS THE SITUATION.
THAT'S ONLY FAIR.
KRISTOFF, PLEASE MAKE THE NECESSARY ARRANGEMENTS TO WELCOME OUR GUESTS.
THE PROCEDURE IS ALREADY UNDERWAY...
...THE INHUMAN DELEGATION IS APPEARING AS WE SPEAK.
WONDERFUL!
GENTLEMEN, PLEASE ALLOW ME TO--
WAIT A MINUTE! I RECOGNIZE--
INDEED YOU DO, SUSAN RICHARDS...
FSHAP
...WHICH IS WHY I CANNOT PERMIT YOU TO LEAVE THIS ROOM ALIVE!

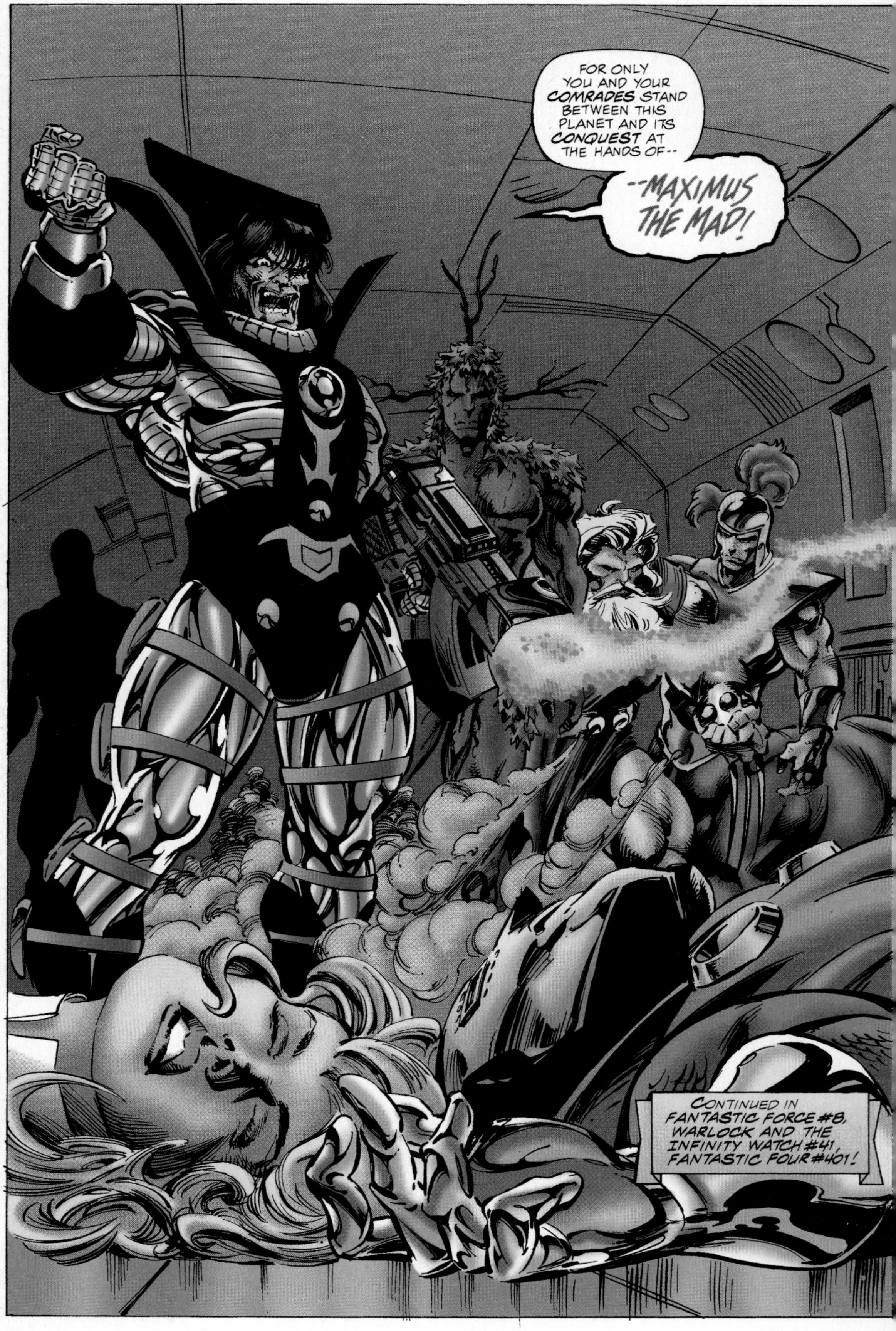
FOR ONLY YOU AND YOUR COMRADES STAND BETWEEN THIS PLANET AND ITS CONQUEST AT THE HANDS OF--
--MAXIMUS THE MAD!
CONTINUED IN FANTASTIC FORCE #8, WARLOCK AND THE INFINITY WATCH #41, FANTASTIC FOUR #401!

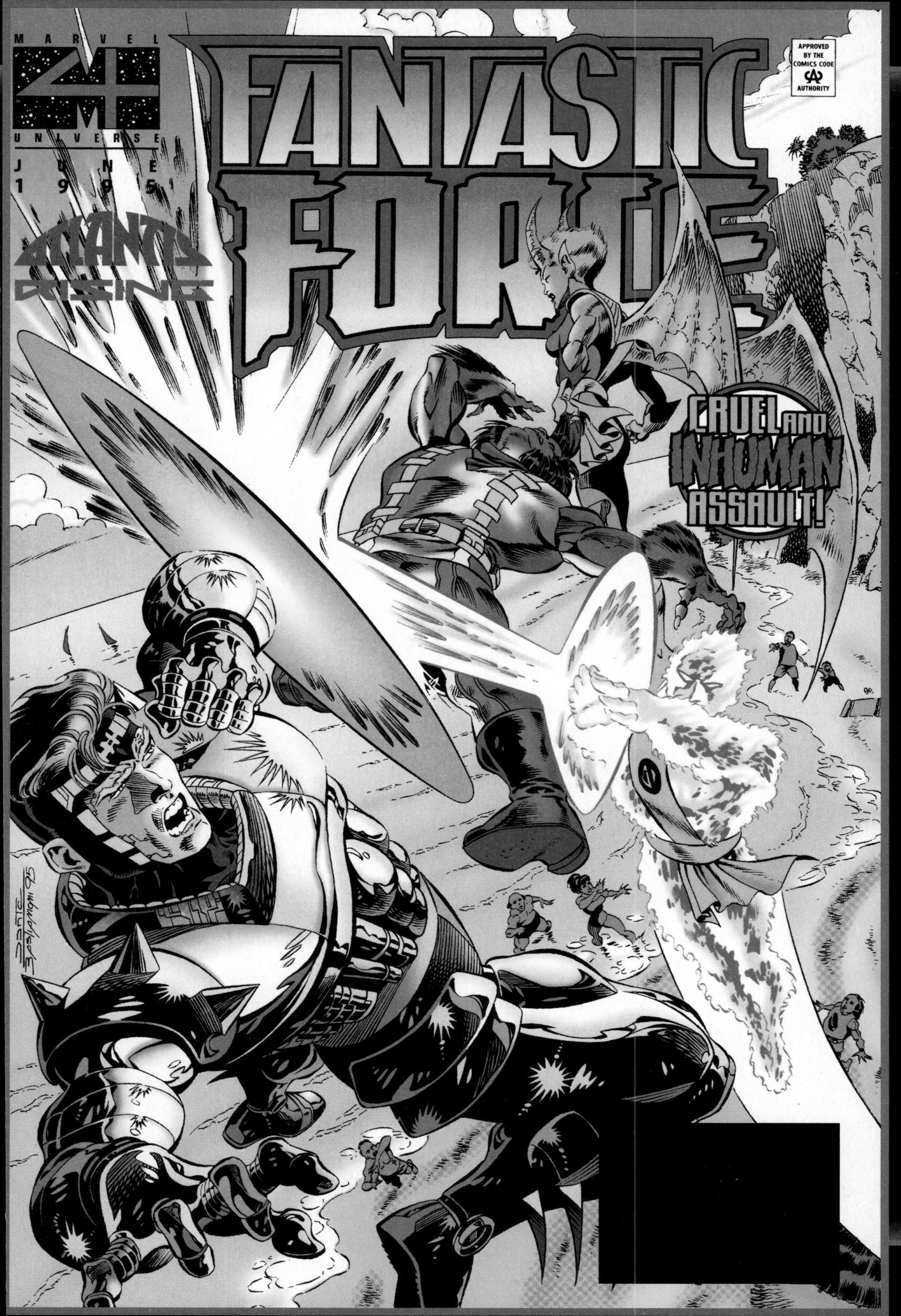
MARVEL
UNIVERSE
JUNE 1995
FANTASTIC FORCE
APPROVED BY THE COMICS CODE AUTHORITY
ATLANTIS RISING
CRUEL AND INHUMAN ASSAULT!

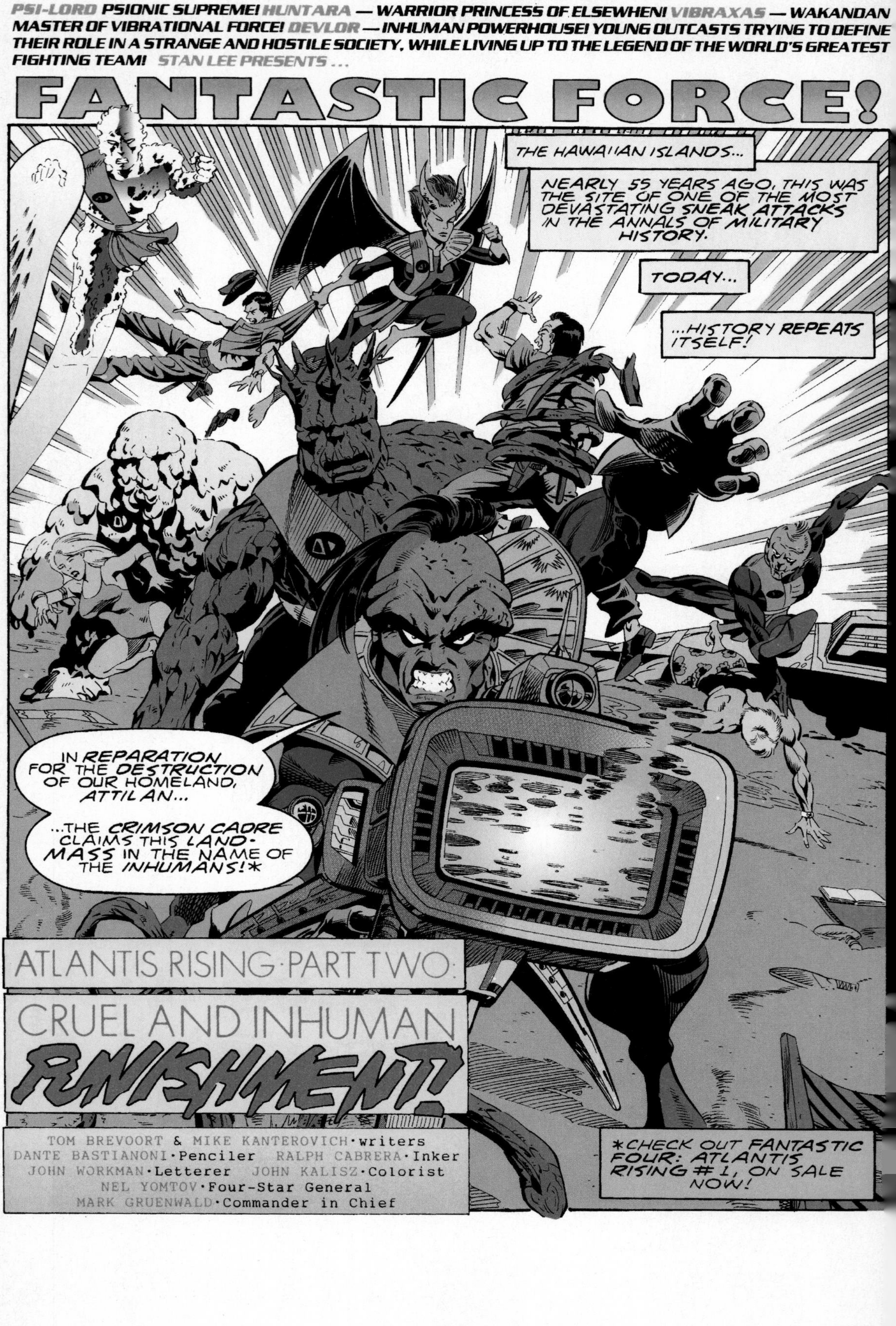
PSI-LORD PSIONIC SUPREME! HUNTARA — WARRIOR PRINCESS OF ELSEWHEN! VIBRAXAS — WAKANDAN MASTER OF VIBRATIONAL FORCE! DEVLOR — INHUMAN POWERHOUSE! YOUNG OUTCASTS TRYING TO DEFINE THEIR ROLE IN A STRANGE AND HOSTILE SOCIETY, WHILE LIVING UP TO THE LEGEND OF THE WORLD'S GREATEST FIGHTING TEAM! STAN LEE PRESENTS ...
FANTASTIC FORCE!
THE HAWAIIAN ISLANDS...
NEARLY 55 YEARS AGO, THIS WAS THE SITE OF ONE OF THE MOST DEVASTATING SNEAK ATTACKS IN THE ANNALS OF MILITARY HISTORY.
TODAY...
...HISTORY REPEATS ITSELF!
IN REPARATION FOR THE DESTRUCTION OF OUR HOMELAND, ATTILAN...
...THE CRIMSON CADRE CLAIMS THIS LAND-MASS IN THE NAME OF THE INHUMANS!*
ATLANTIS RISING·PART TWO:
CRUEL AND INHUMAN
PUNISHMENT!
TOM BREVOORT & MIKE KANTEROVICH·writers
DANTE BASTIANONI·Penciler RALPH CABRERA·Inker
JOHN WORKMAN·Letterer JOHN KALISZ·Colorist
NEL YOMTOV·Four-Star General
MARK GRUENWALD·Commander in Chief
*CHECK OUT FANTASTIC FOUR: ATLANTIS RISING #1, ON SALE NOW!

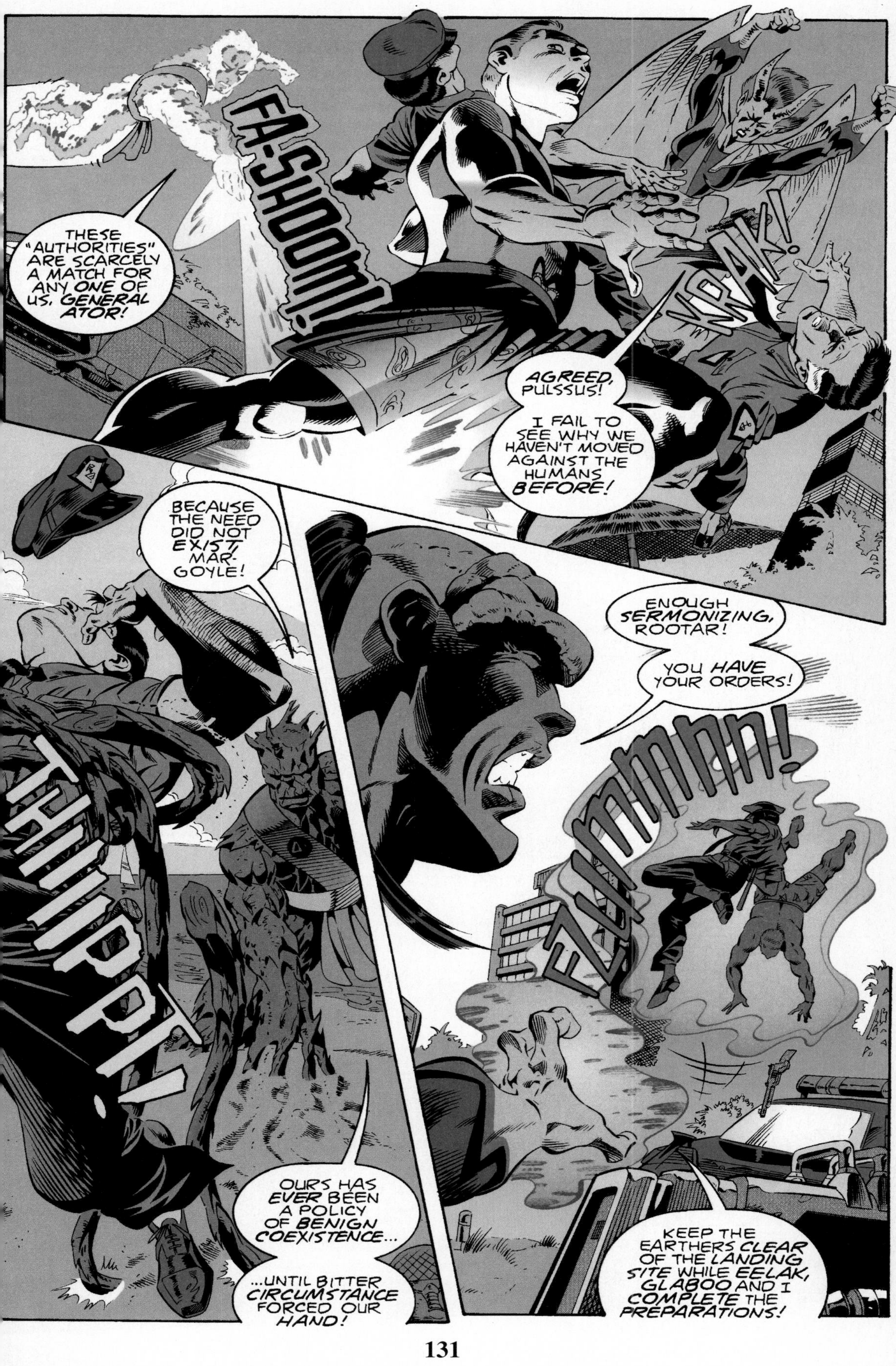
FA-SHOOM!!
THESE "AUTHORITIES" ARE SCARCELY A MATCH FOR ANY ONE OF US, GENERAL ATOR!
YRAK!
AGREED, PULSSUS!
I FAIL TO SEE WHY WE HAVEN'T MOVED AGAINST THE HUMANS BEFORE!
BECAUSE THE NEED DID NOT EXIST, MAR-GOYLE!
THHHPPT!
OURS HAS EVER BEEN A POLICY OF BENIGN COEXISTENCE...
...UNTIL BITTER CIRCUMSTANCE FORCED OUR HAND!
ENOUGH SERMONIZING, ROOTAR!
YOU HAVE YOUR ORDERS!
FZUMMMMNN!
KEEP THE EARTHERS CLEAR OF THE LANDING SITE WHILE EELAK, GLABOO AND I COMPLETE THE PREPARATIONS!

NOW THAT A SUITABLE *BEACHHEAD* HAS BEEN ESTABLISHED...

...WE MUST *SECURE* OUR NEW ACQUISITION!

AND THE *ATMO-GUN* OF MAXIMUS...

KCHUKT!

...SHALL PROVIDE THE *MEANS!*

AT ITS HIGHEST SETTING, THE *ETHEREAL RESONANCE* IT GENERATES, WHILE INOFFENSIVE TO OUR TERRIGEN-AUGMENTED PHYSIOLOGIES...

...WOULD PROVE QUITE *SHATTERING* TO THOSE *LESS FORTUNATE!*

KLIKT! WREEEEEEEE

EEEEEEEEEEEEEEE

"STILL, THERE IS NO CALL FOR *MINDLESS SLAUGHTER!*

"NOT WHEN *MASS EXODUS* WILL SUFFICE!

"ONCE THE HUMAN *INFESTATION* HAS BEEN DRIVEN FROM THESE SHORES, THE ISLE MAY BE REFASHIONED INTO A NEW *GREAT REFUGE!*"

132

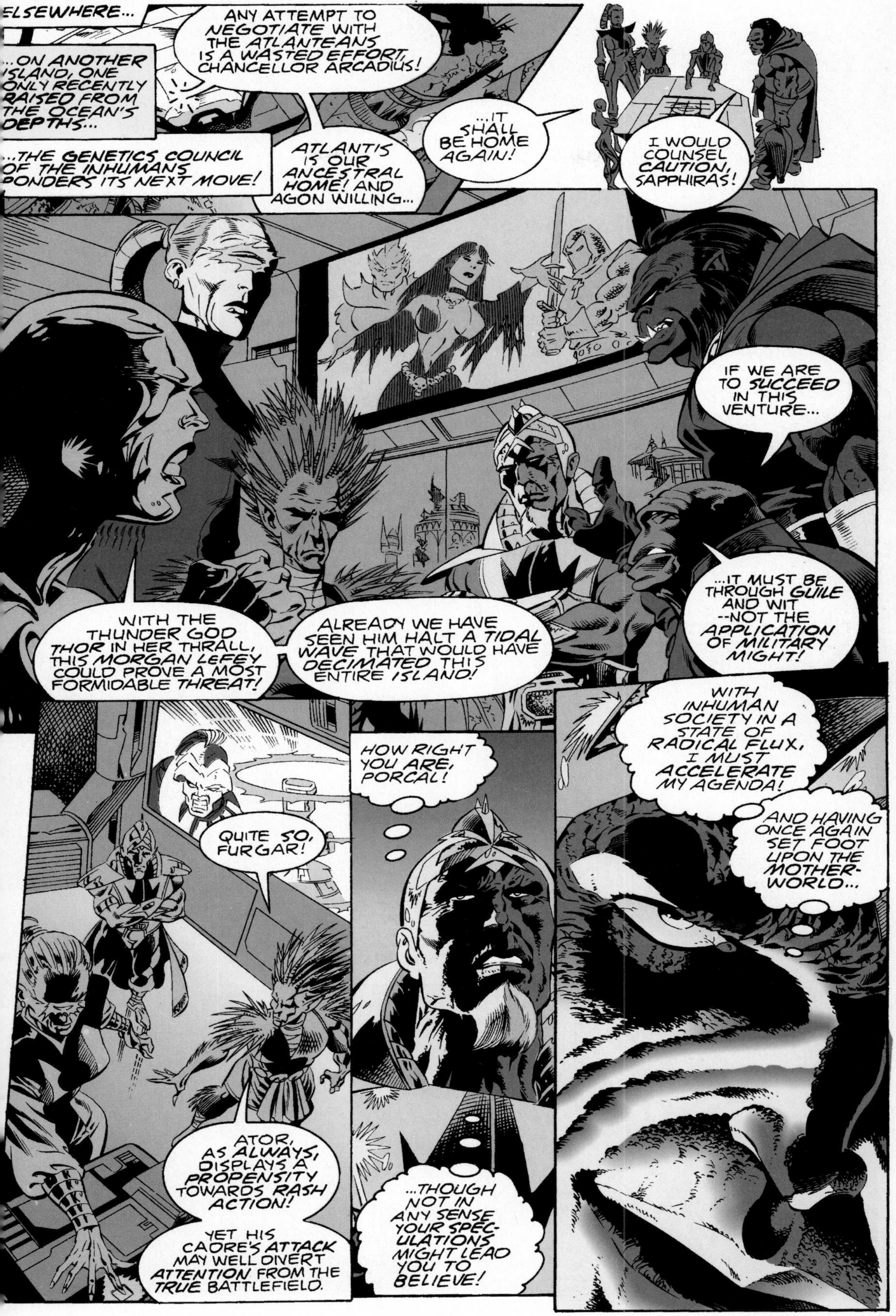
ELSEWHERE...
...ON ANOTHER ISLAND, ONE ONLY RECENTLY RAISED FROM THE OCEAN'S DEPTHS...
...THE GENETICS COUNCIL OF THE INHUMANS PONDERS ITS NEXT MOVE!
ANY ATTEMPT TO NEGOTIATE WITH THE ATLANTEANS IS A WASTED EFFORT, CHANCELLOR ARCADIUS!
ATLANTIS IS OUR ANCESTRAL HOME! AND AGON WILLING...
...IT SHALL BE HOME AGAIN!
I WOULD COUNSEL CAUTION, SAPPHIRAS!
IF WE ARE TO SUCCEED IN THIS VENTURE...
...IT MUST BE THROUGH GUILE AND WIT --NOT THE APPLICATION OF MILITARY MIGHT!
WITH THE THUNDER GOD THOR IN HER THRALL, THIS MORGAN LEFEY COULD PROVE A MOST FORMIDABLE THREAT!
ALREADY WE HAVE SEEN HIM HALT A TIDAL WAVE THAT WOULD HAVE DECIMATED THIS ENTIRE ISLAND!
QUITE SO, FURGAR!
ATOR, AS ALWAYS, DISPLAYS A PROPENSITY TOWARDS RASH ACTION!
YET HIS CADRE'S ATTACK MAY WELL DIVERT ATTENTION FROM THE TRUE BATTLEFIELD.
HOW RIGHT YOU ARE, PORCAL!
...THOUGH NOT IN ANY SENSE YOUR SPECULATIONS MIGHT LEAD YOU TO BELIEVE!
WITH INHUMAN SOCIETY IN A STATE OF RADICAL FLUX, I MUST ACCELERATE MY AGENDA!
AND HAVING ONCE AGAIN SET FOOT UPON THE MOTHER-WORLD...

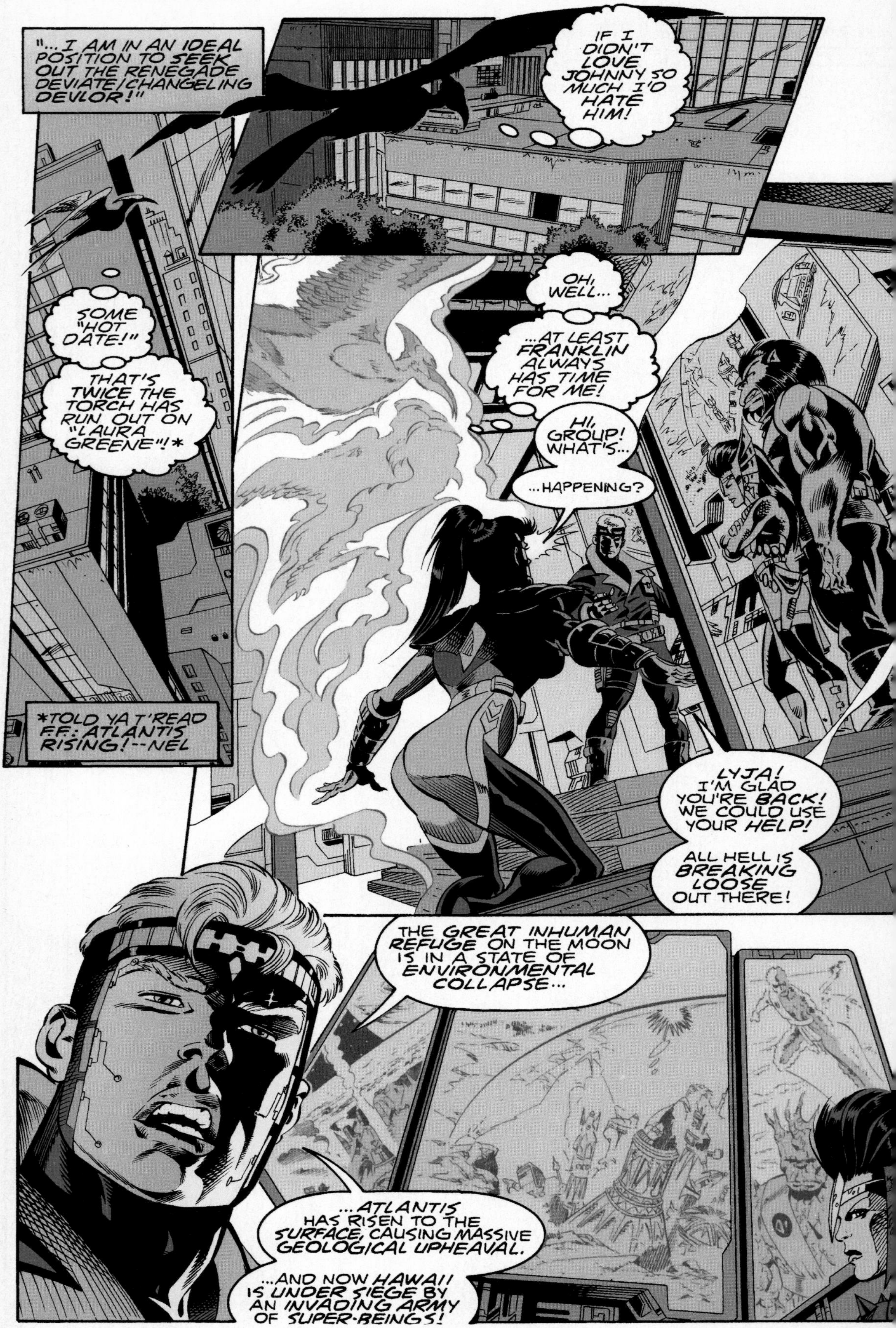
"...I AM IN AN IDEAL POSITION TO SEEK OUT THE RENEGADE DEVIATE/CHANGELING DEVLOR!"
IF I DIDN'T LOVE JOHNNY SO MUCH I'D HATE HIM!
SOME "HOT DATE!"
THAT'S TWICE THE TORCH HAS RUN OUT ON "LAURA GREENE"!*
*TOLD YA T'READ F.F.: ATLANTIS RISING!--NEL
OH, WELL...
...AT LEAST FRANKLIN ALWAYS HAS TIME FOR ME!
HI, GROUP! WHAT'S...
...HAPPENING?
LYJA! I'M GLAD YOU'RE BACK! WE COULD USE YOUR HELP!
ALL HELL IS BREAKING LOOSE OUT THERE!
THE GREAT INHUMAN REFUGE ON THE MOON IS IN A STATE OF ENVIRONMENTAL COLLAPSE...
...ATLANTIS HAS RISEN TO THE SURFACE, CAUSING MASSIVE GEOLOGICAL UPHEAVAL.
...AND NOW HAWAII IS UNDER SIEGE BY AN INVADING ARMY OF SUPER-BEINGS!

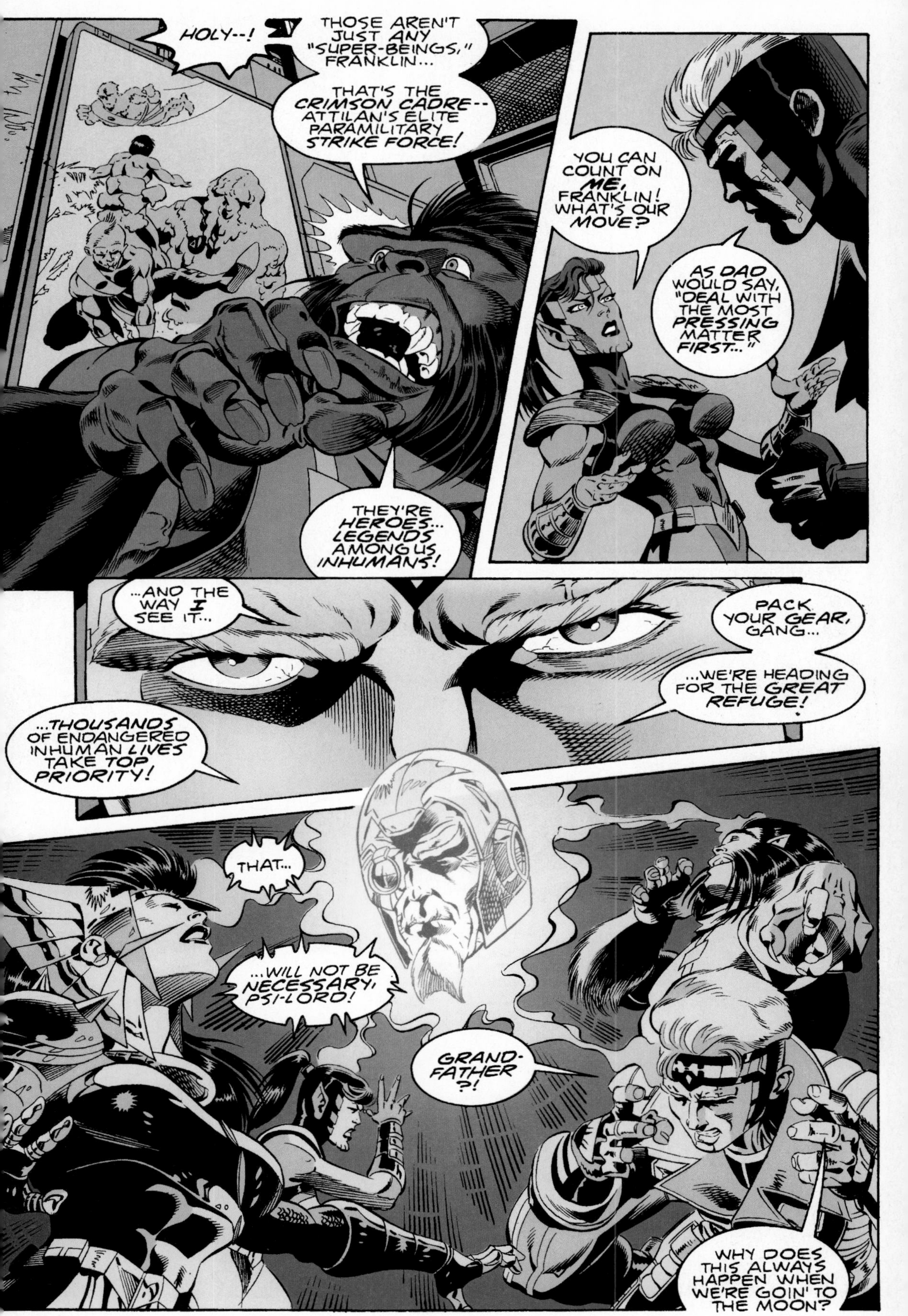
HOLY--!
THOSE AREN'T JUST ANY "SUPER-BEINGS," FRANKLIN...
THAT'S THE CRIMSON CADRE--ATTILAN'S ELITE PARAMILITARY STRIKE FORCE!
THEY'RE HEROES... LEGENDS AMONG US INHUMANS!
YOU CAN COUNT ON ME, FRANKLIN! WHAT'S OUR MOVE?
AS DAD WOULD SAY, "DEAL WITH THE MOST PRESSING MATTER FIRST..."
...AND THE WAY I SEE IT...
...THOUSANDS OF ENDANGERED INHUMAN LIVES TAKE TOP PRIORITY!
PACK YOUR GEAR, GANG...
...WE'RE HEADING FOR THE GREAT REFUGE!
THAT...
...WILL NOT BE NECESSARY, PSI-LORD!
GRAND-FATHER?!
WHY DOES THIS ALWAYS HAPPEN WHEN WE'RE GOIN' TO THE MOON?

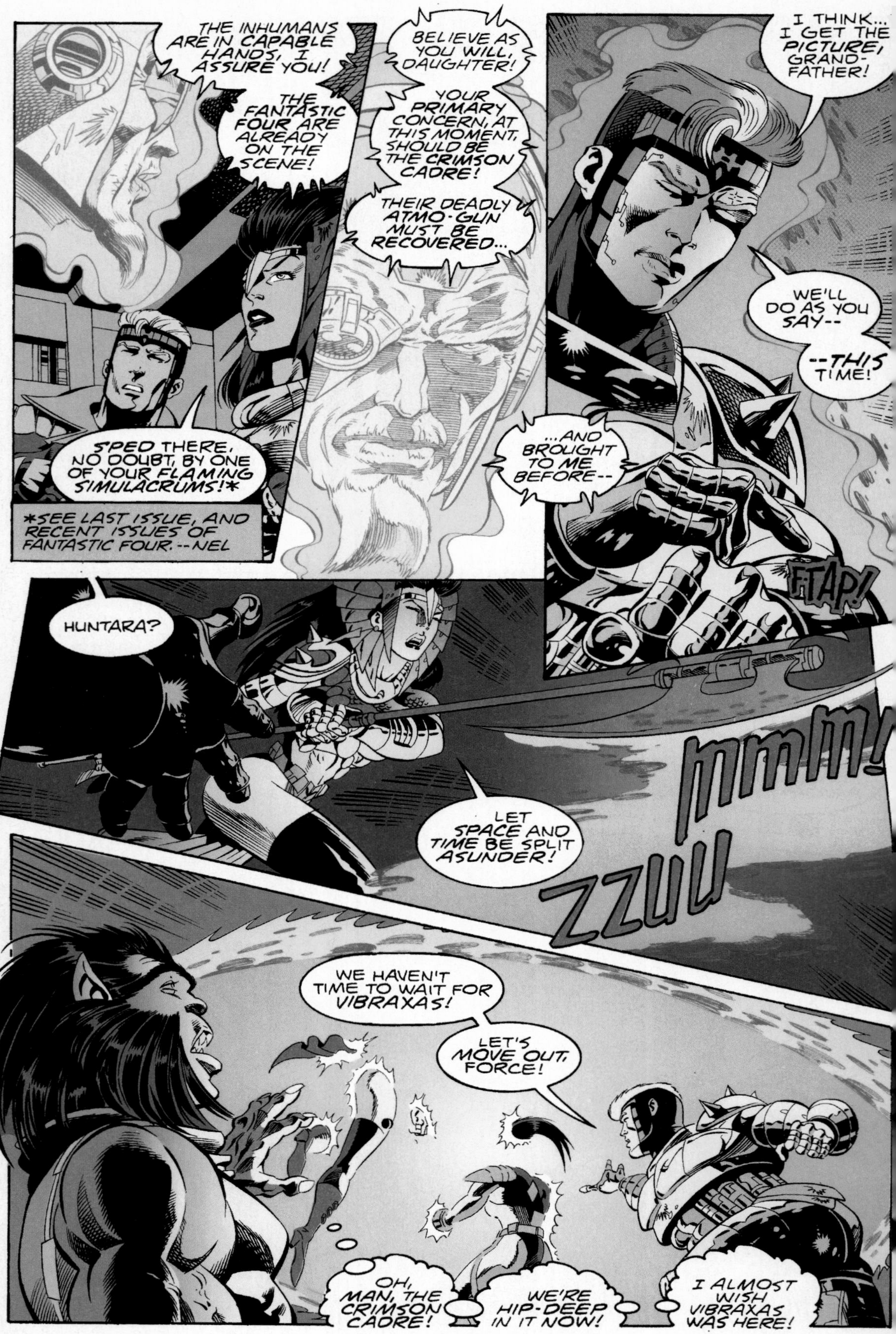
THE INHUMANS ARE IN CAPABLE HANDS, I ASSURE YOU!
THE FANTASTIC FOUR ARE ALREADY ON THE SCENE!
SPED THERE, NO DOUBT, BY ONE OF YOUR FLAMING SIMULACRUMS!*
*SEE LAST ISSUE, AND RECENT ISSUES OF FANTASTIC FOUR. --NEL
BELIEVE AS YOU WILL, DAUGHTER!
YOUR PRIMARY CONCERN, AT THIS MOMENT, SHOULD BE THE CRIMSON CADRE!
THEIR DEADLY ATMO-GUN MUST BE RECOVERED...
...AND BROUGHT TO ME BEFORE--
I THINK... I GET THE PICTURE, GRAND-FATHER!
WE'LL DO AS YOU SAY--
--THIS TIME!
FTAP!
HUNTARA?
LET SPACE AND TIME BE SPLIT ASUNDER!
ZZUUMMMM!
WE HAVEN'T TIME TO WAIT FOR VIBRAXAS!
LET'S MOVE OUT, FORCE!
OH, MAN, THE CRIMSON CADRE!
WE'RE HIP-DEEP IN IT NOW!
I ALMOST WISH VIBRAXAS WAS HERE!

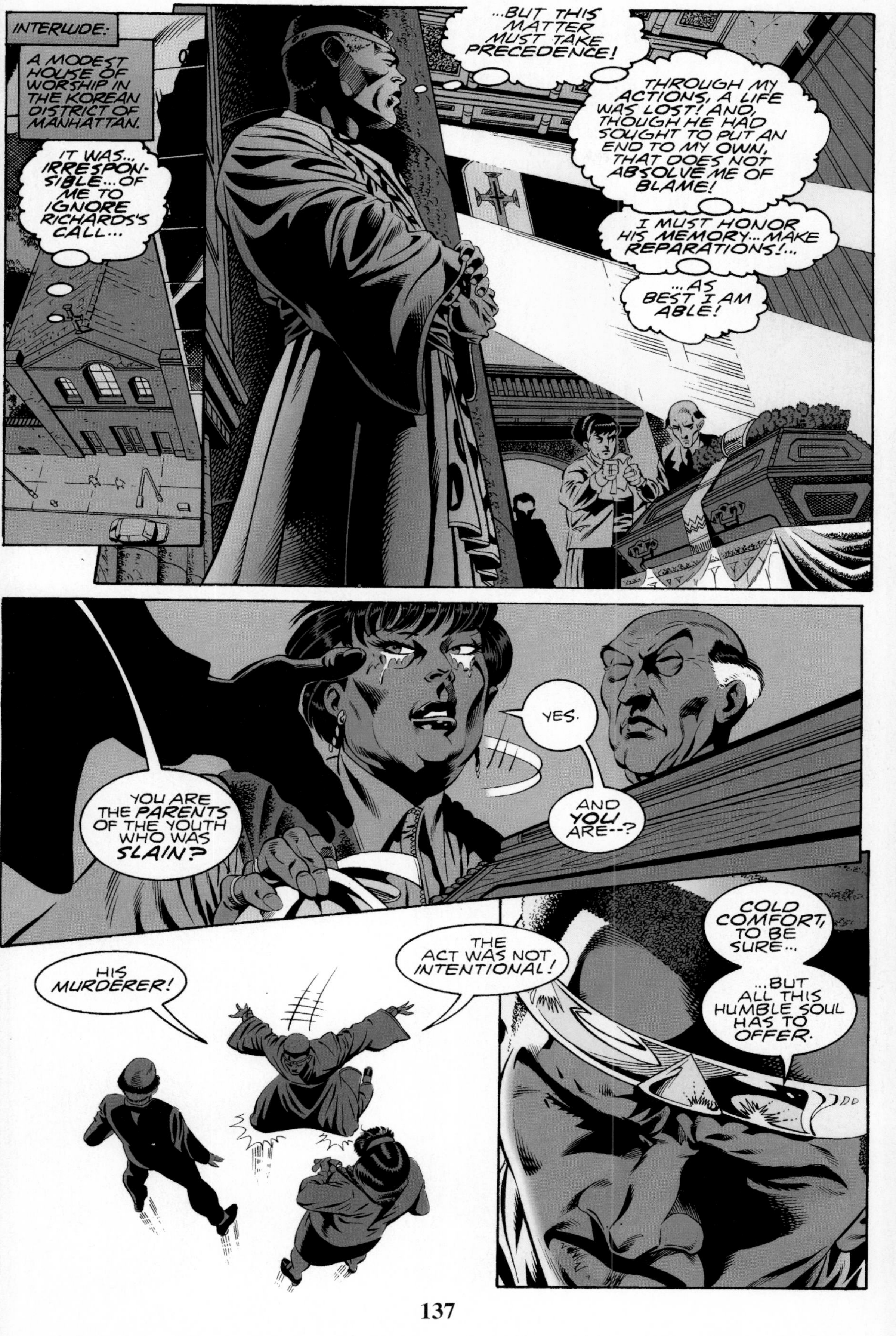

INTERLUDE:
A MODEST HOUSE OF WORSHIP IN THE KOREAN DISTRICT OF MANHATTAN.
IT WAS... IRRESPONSIBLE... OF ME TO IGNORE RICHARDS'S CALL...
...BUT THIS MATTER MUST TAKE PRECEDENCE!
THROUGH MY ACTIONS, A LIFE WAS LOST! AND, THOUGH HE HAD SOUGHT TO PUT AN END TO MY OWN, THAT DOES NOT ABSOLVE ME OF BLAME!
I MUST HONOR HIS MEMORY... MAKE REPARATIONS!...
...AS BEST I AM ABLE!
YOU ARE THE PARENTS OF THE YOUTH WHO WAS SLAIN?
YES.
AND YOU ARE--?
HIS MURDERER!
THE ACT WAS NOT INTENTIONAL!
COLD COMFORT, TO BE SURE...
...BUT ALL THIS HUMBLE SOUL HAS TO OFFER.

COME, MY WIFE! I RECOGNIZE HIM!

MY SON IS DEAD...

...AND THIS ONE'S WORDS CAN CHANGE NOTHING!

YOU MUST EXCUSE MY HUSBAND. HE HAS TAKEN THIS HARD...

YES. OUR OLDEST BOY WAS ALSO SLAIN IN A GANG-RELATED INCIDENT SEVERAL YEARS AGO!

IT WAS WHAT DROVE HIS BROTHER TO THE SONS OF SINANJU!

...EVEN HARDER THAN THE FIRST TIME!

FIRST TIME--?

I KNOW IT SOUNDS HARSH, BUT...

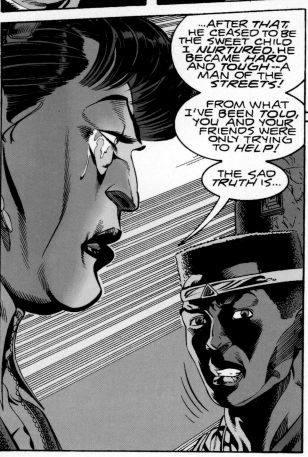

...AFTER THAT, HE CEASED TO BE THE SWEET CHILD I NURTURED. HE BECAME HARD AND TOUGH--A MAN OF THE STREETS!

FROM WHAT I'VE BEEN TOLD, YOU AND YOUR FRIENDS WERE ONLY TRYING TO HELP!

THE SAD TRUTH IS...

...IF YOU HADN'T KILLED HIM...

...SOME-ONE ELSE WOULD HAVE!

138

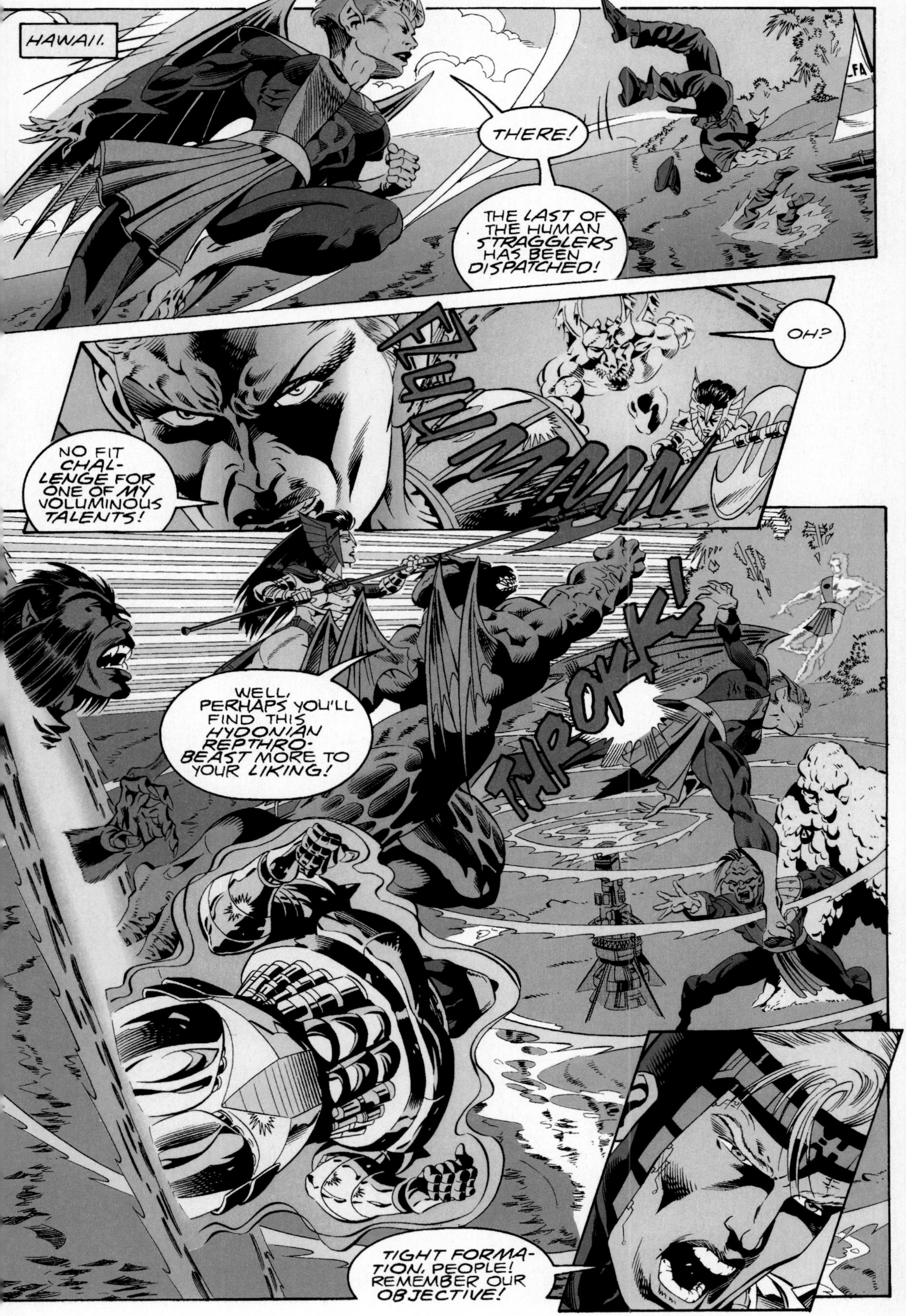
HAWAII.
THERE!
THE LAST OF THE HUMAN STRAGGLERS HAS BEEN DISPATCHED!
FLUMMMMN
OH?
NO FIT CHAL-LENGE FOR ONE OF MY VOLUMINOUS TALENTS!
WELL, PERHAPS YOU'LL FIND THIS HYDONIAN REPTHRO-BEAST MORE TO YOUR LIKING!
THROKK!
TIGHT FORMA-TION, PEOPLE! REMEMBER OUR OBJECTIVE!

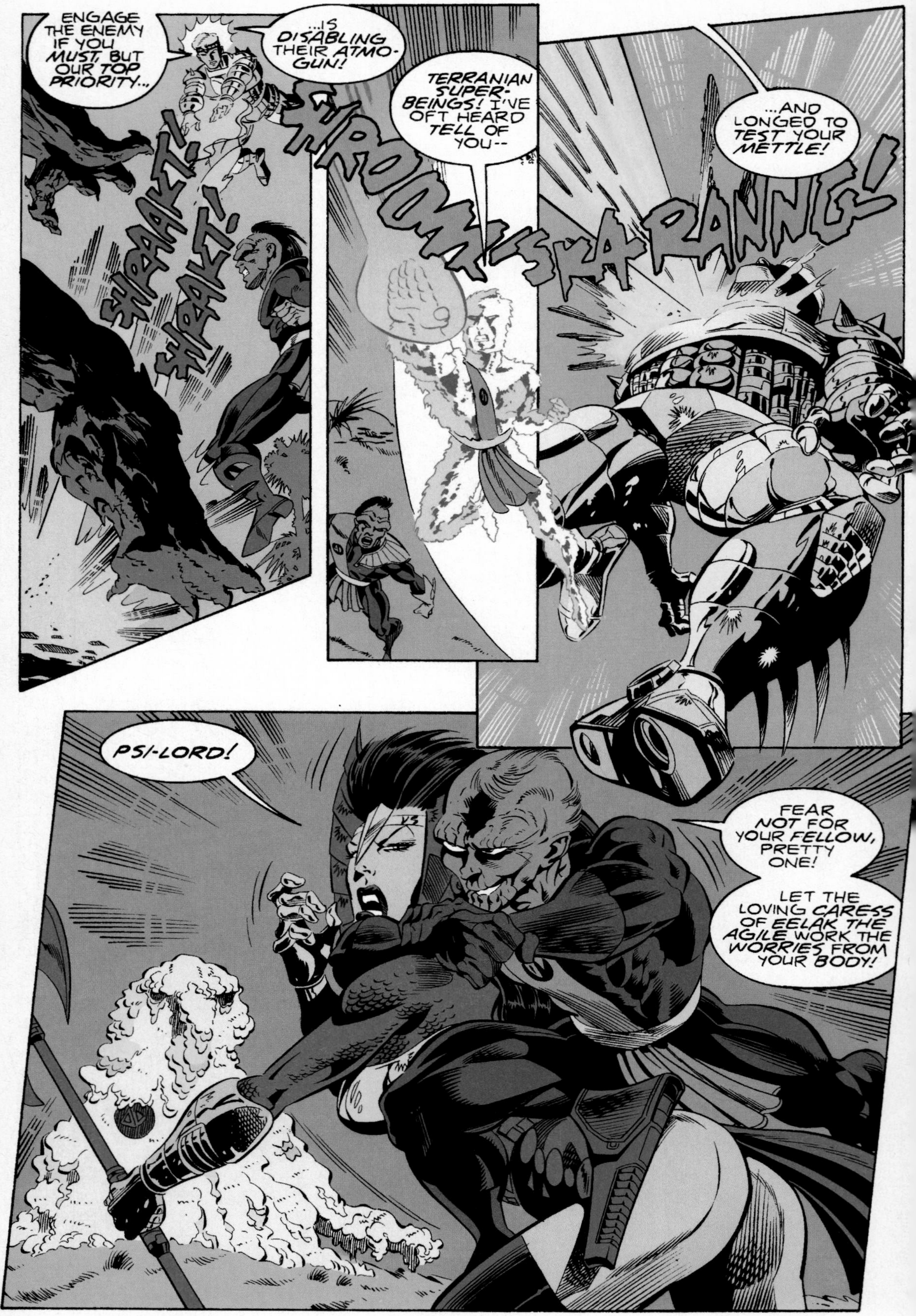
ENGAGE THE ENEMY IF YOU MUST, BUT OUR TOP PRIORITY...
...IS DISABLING THEIR ATMO-GUN!
SHRAAKT! SHRAAKT!
TERRANIAN SUPER-BEINGS! I'VE OFT HEARD TELL OF YOU--
WHROOM!
...AND LONGED TO TEST YOUR METTLE!
SKA-RANNG!
PSI-LORD!
FEAR NOT FOR YOUR FELLOW, PRETTY ONE!
LET THE LOVING CARESS OF EELAK THE AGILE WORK THE WORRIES FROM YOUR BODY!

LET GO, SLIME-DEVIL!

I'D NOT SCRAPE MY BOOT-SOLE WITH THE LIKES OF YOU!

M-MY HEAD!

FRANKLIN'S ARMOR... HUNTARA'S SCYTHE... SHIELDING THEM FROM THE ATMO-EFFECT...

BUT I--

SHOOMP!

I KNOW YOU, BOY!

YOU'RE THE CRIPPLE--THE ONE WHOSE TERRIGEN-ENHANCED FORM WAS UNSTABLE!

NO TRUE INHUMAN ARE YOU!

WHUUMP

THUUK!

AND THUS, NO SUCCOR ARE YOU DUE!

GYAKK!

GLABOO... SMASH!

THUNK

FALL, YOU ABOMINATION!

BY KRONUS--

MY SCYTHE-- HELD FAST BY THE STUFF OF YOUR BODY?

141

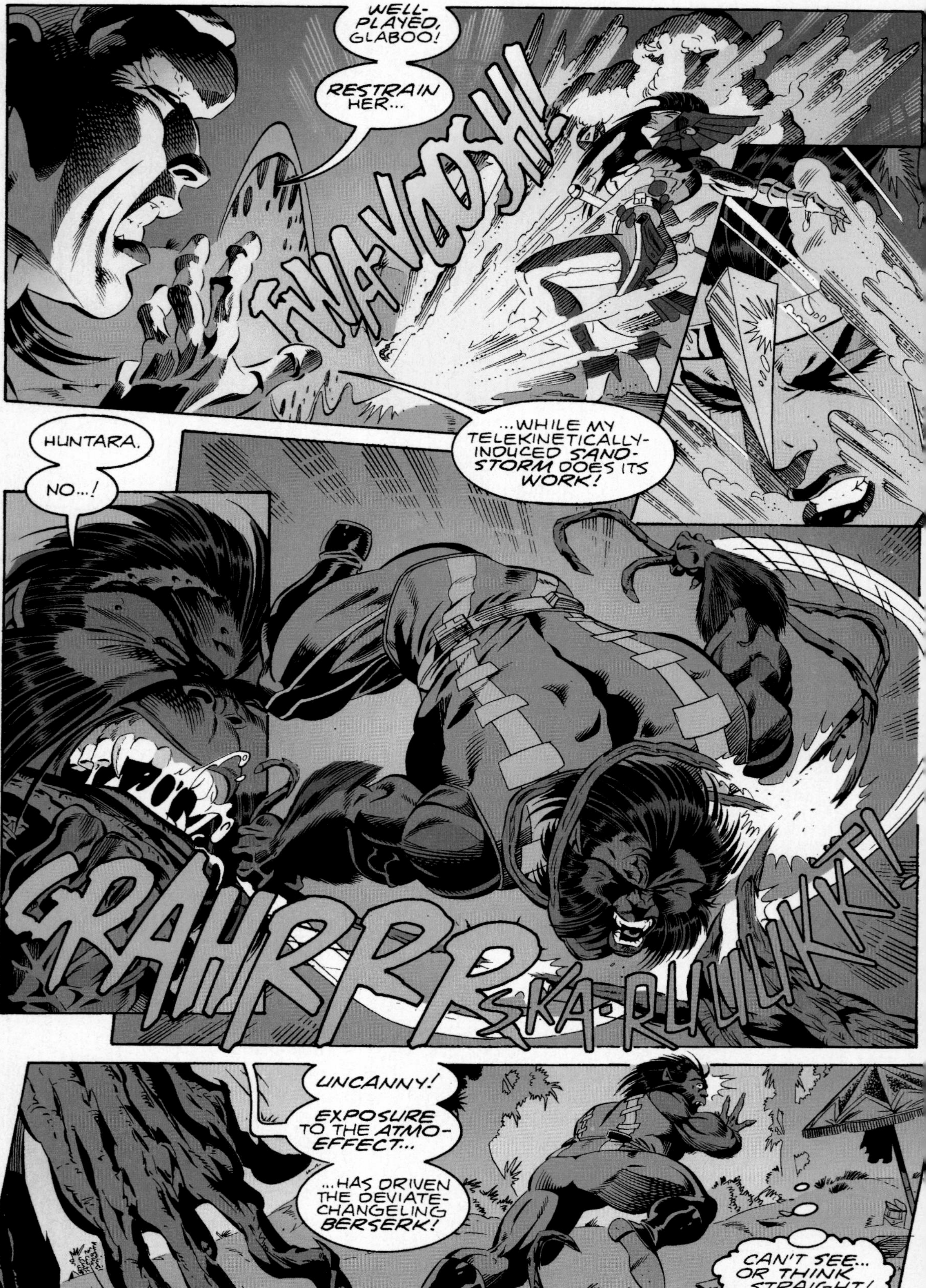
WELL-PLAYED, GLABOO!
RESTRAIN HER...
TWAVOOSH!
...WHILE MY TELEKINETICALLY-INDUCED SANDSTORM DOES ITS WORK!
HUNTARA.
NO...!
GRAHRRR
SKA-RUUUKT!
UNCANNY!
EXPOSURE TO THE ATMO-EFFECT...
...HAS DRIVEN THE DEVIATE-CHANGELING BERSERK!
CAN'T SEE... OR THINK STRAIGHT!
GOTTA ...GET CLEAR!

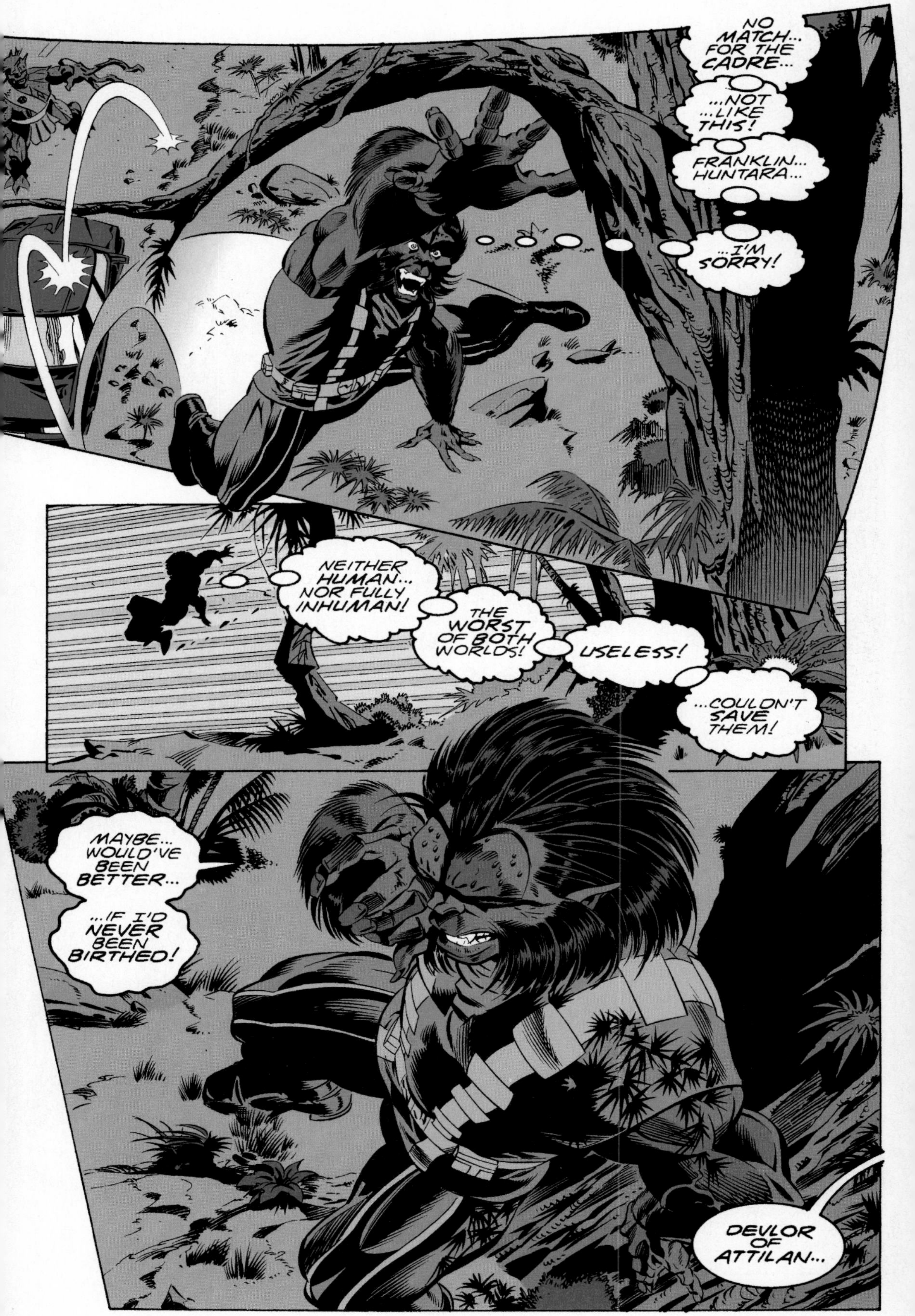
NO MATCH... FOR THE CADRE...
...NOT ...LIKE THIS!
FRANKLIN... HUNTARA...
...I'M SORRY!
NEITHER HUMAN... NOR FULLY INHUMAN!
THE WORST OF BOTH WORLDS!
USELESS!
...COULDN'T SAVE THEM!
MAYBE... WOULD'VE BEEN BETTER...
...IF I'D NEVER BEEN BIRTHED!
DEVLOR OF ATTILAN...

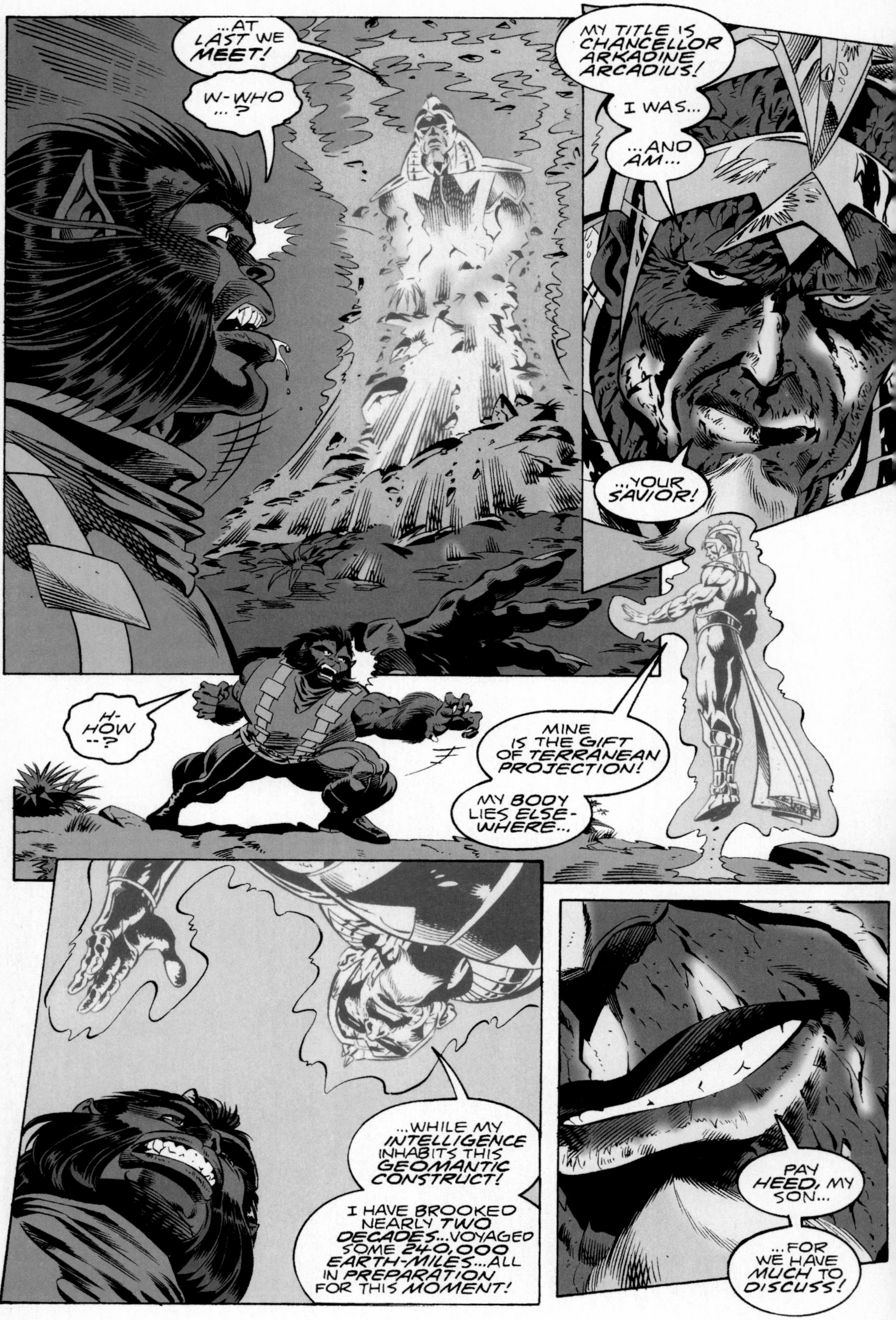
...AT LAST WE MEET!
W-WHO ...?
MY TITLE IS CHANCELLOR ARKADINE ARCADIUS!
I WAS...
...AND AM...
...YOUR SAVIOR!
H-HOW --?
MINE IS THE GIFT OF TERRANEAN PROJECTION!
MY BODY LIES ELSE-WHERE...
...WHILE MY INTELLIGENCE INHABITS THIS GEOMANTIC CONSTRUCT!
I HAVE BROOKED NEARLY TWO DECADES...VOYAGED SOME 240,000 EARTH-MILES...ALL IN PREPARATION FOR THIS MOMENT!
PAY HEED, MY SON...
...FOR WE HAVE MUCH TO DISCUSS!

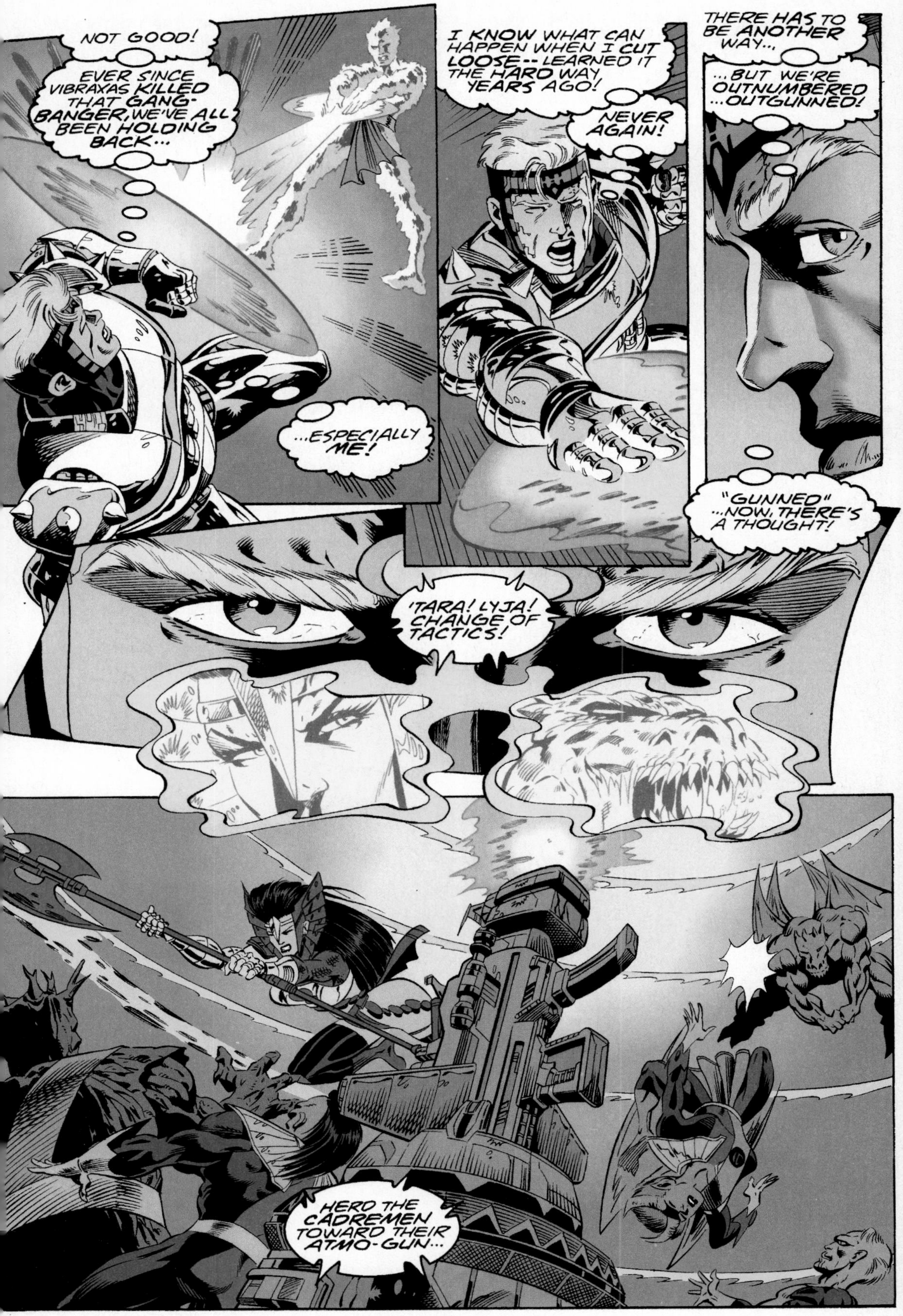
NOT GOOD!
EVER SINCE VIBRAXAS KILLED THAT GANG-BANGER, WE'VE ALL BEEN HOLDING BACK...
...ESPECIALLY ME!
I KNOW WHAT CAN HAPPEN WHEN I CUT LOOSE--LEARNED IT THE HARD WAY YEARS AGO!
NEVER AGAIN!
THERE HAS TO BE ANOTHER WAY...
...BUT WE'RE OUTNUMBERED ...OUTGUNNED!
"GUNNED" ...NOW, THERE'S A THOUGHT!
'TARA! LYJA! CHANGE OF TACTICS!
HERD THE CADREMEN TOWARD THEIR ATMO-GUN...

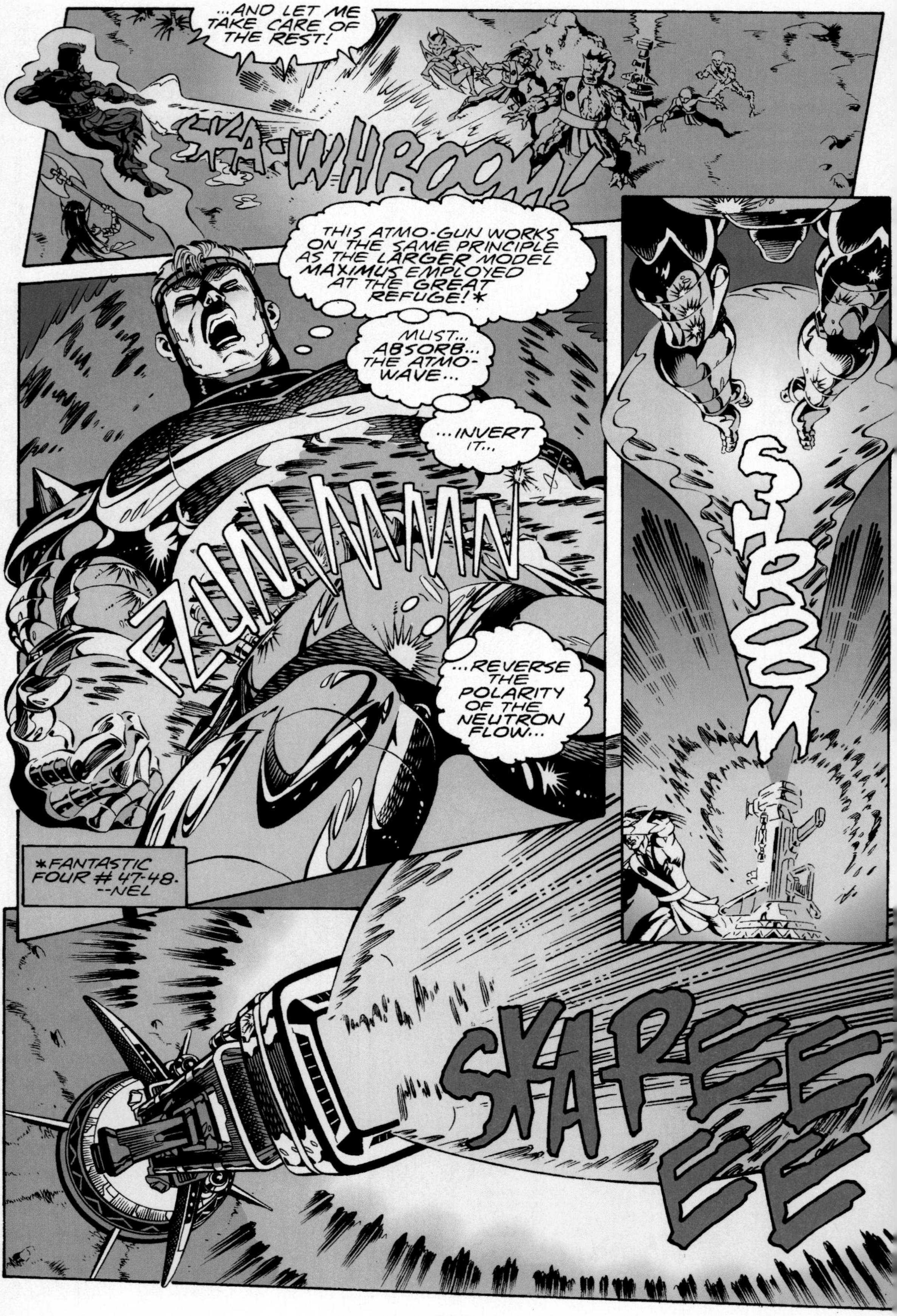
...AND LET ME TAKE CARE OF THE REST!
SKA-WHROOM!
THIS ATMO-GUN WORKS ON THE SAME PRINCIPLE AS THE LARGER MODEL MAXIMUS EMPLOYED AT THE GREAT REFUGE!*
MUST... ABSORB... THE ATMO-WAVE...
...INVERT IT...
FZUMMMMN
...REVERSE THE POLARITY OF THE NEUTRON FLOW...
*FANTASTIC FOUR #47-48. --NEL
SHROOM
SKAREEEEE

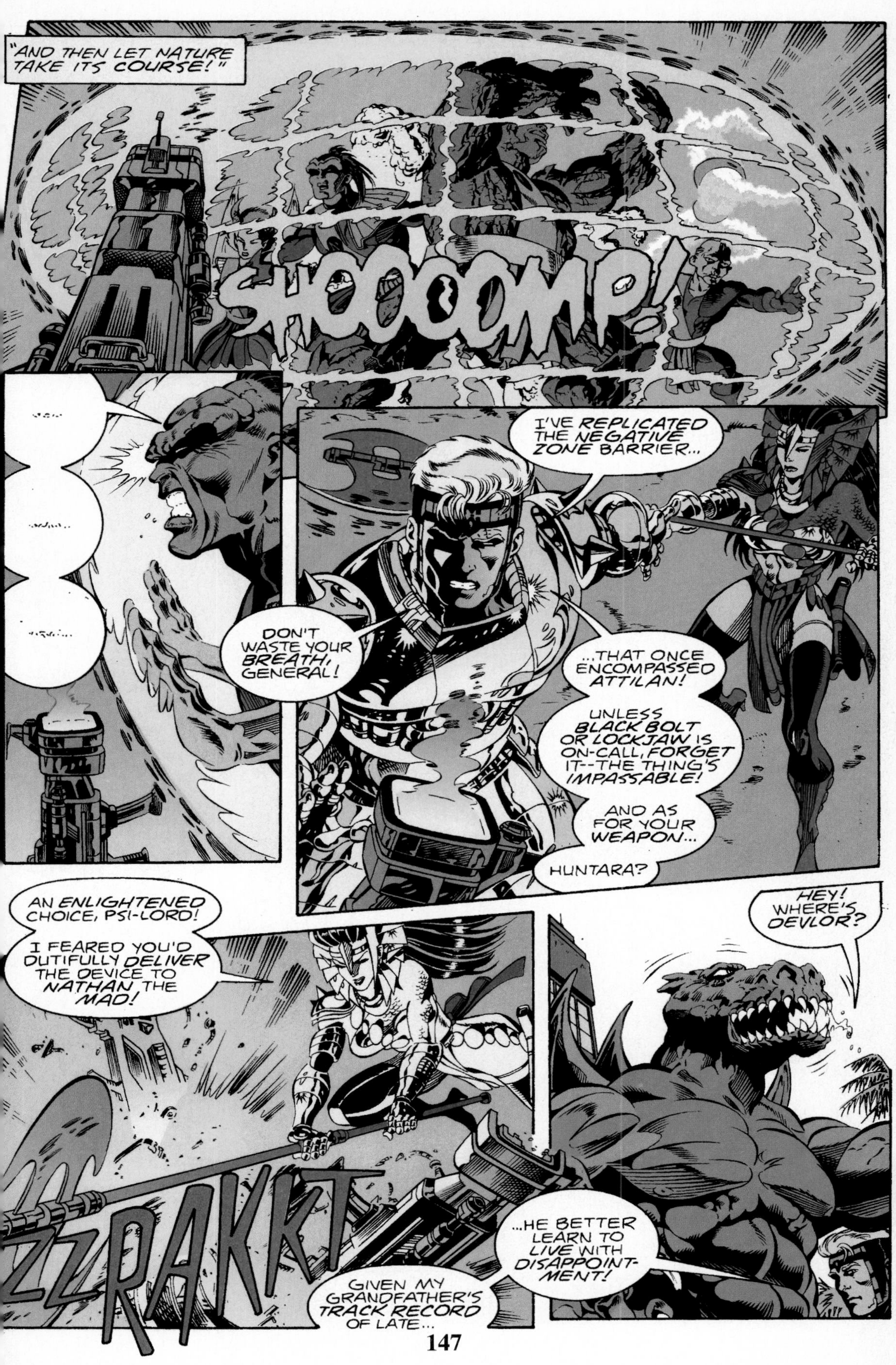
"AND THEN LET NATURE TAKE ITS COURSE!"
SHOOOOMP!
I'VE REPLICATED THE NEGATIVE ZONE BARRIER...
DON'T WASTE YOUR BREATH, GENERAL!
...THAT ONCE ENCOMPASSED ATTILAN!
UNLESS BLACK BOLT OR LOCKJAW IS ON-CALL, FORGET IT--THE THING'S IMPASSABLE!
AND AS FOR YOUR WEAPON...
HUNTARA?
AN ENLIGHTENED CHOICE, PSI-LORD!
I FEARED YOU'D DUTIFULLY DELIVER THE DEVICE TO NATHAN THE MAD!
HEY! WHERE'S DEVLOR?
ZZRAKKT
GIVEN MY GRANDFATHER'S TRACK RECORD OF LATE...
...HE BETTER LEARN TO LIVE WITH DISAPPOINT-MENT!

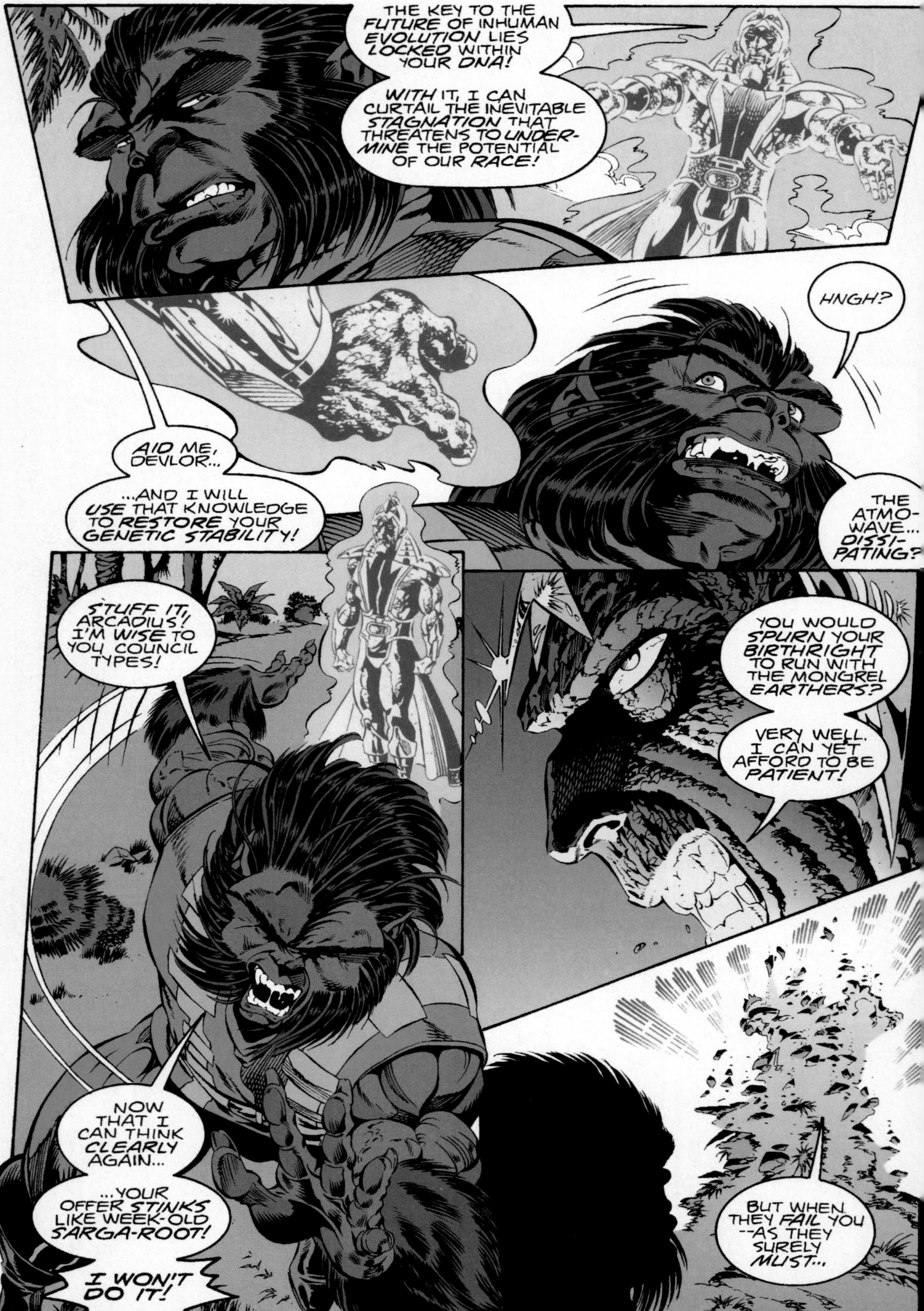
THE KEY TO THE FUTURE OF INHUMAN EVOLUTION LIES LOCKED WITHIN YOUR DNA!
WITH IT, I CAN CURTAIL THE INEVITABLE STAGNATION THAT THREATENS TO UNDERMINE THE POTENTIAL OF OUR RACE!
HNGH?
AID ME, DEVLOR...
...AND I WILL USE THAT KNOWLEDGE TO RESTORE YOUR GENETIC STABILITY!
THE ATMO-WAVE... DISSI-PATING?
STUFF IT, ARCADIUS! I'M WISE TO YOU COUNCIL TYPES!
NOW THAT I CAN THINK CLEARLY AGAIN...
...YOUR OFFER STINKS LIKE WEEK-OLD SARGA-ROOT!
I WON'T DO IT!
YOU WOULD SPURN YOUR BIRTHRIGHT TO RUN WITH THE MONGREL EARTHERS?
VERY WELL. I CAN YET AFFORD TO BE PATIENT!
BUT WHEN THEY FAIL YOU --AS THEY SURELY MUST...

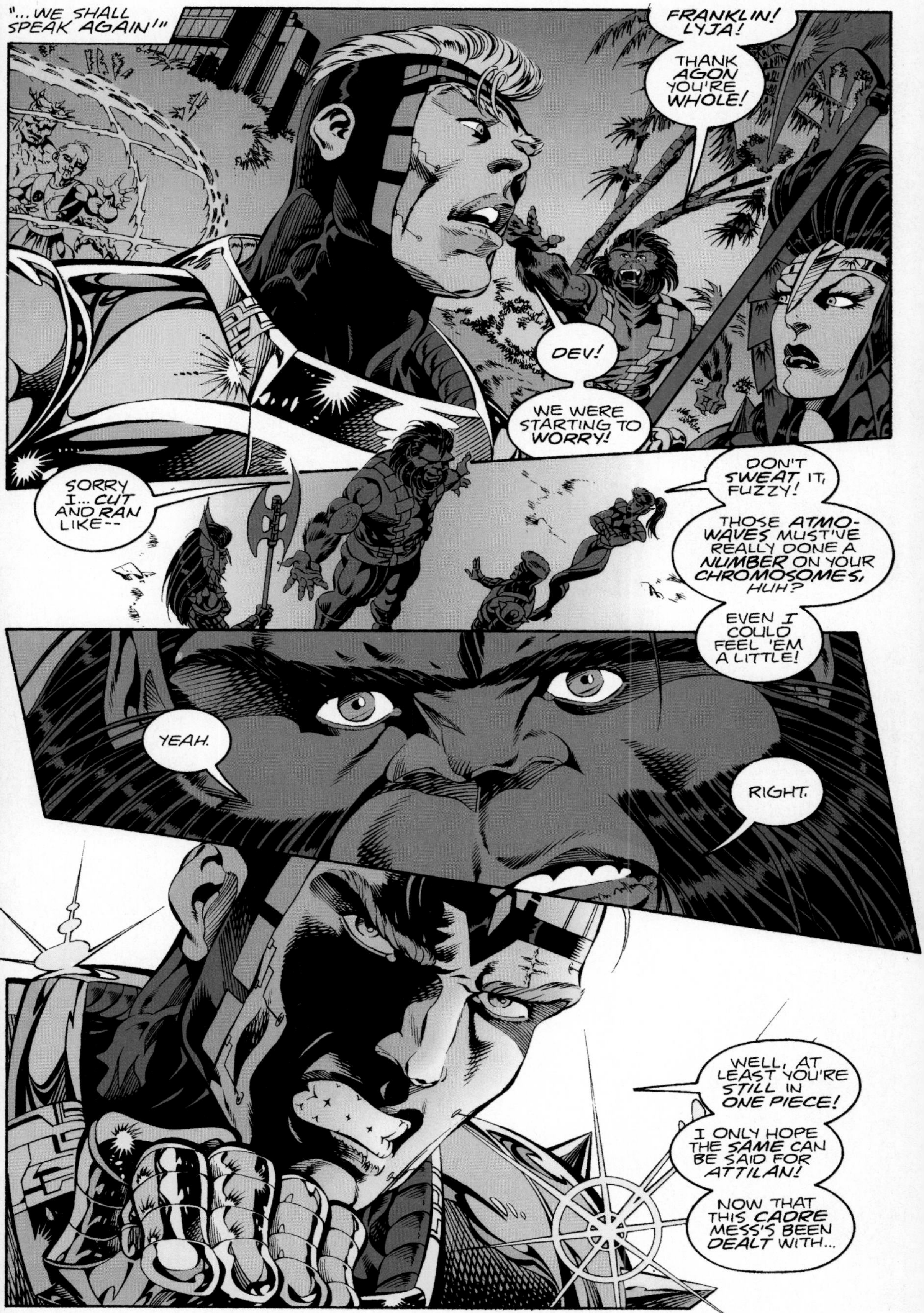
"...WE SHALL SPEAK AGAIN'"
FRANKLIN! LYJA!
THANK AGON YOU'RE WHOLE!
DEV!
WE WERE STARTING TO WORRY!
SORRY I... CUT AND RAN LIKE--
DON'T SWEAT IT, FUZZY!
THOSE ATMO-WAVES MUST'VE REALLY DONE A NUMBER ON YOUR CHROMOSOMES, HUH?
EVEN I COULD FEEL 'EM A LITTLE!
YEAH.
RIGHT.
WELL, AT LEAST YOU'RE STILL IN ONE PIECE!
I ONLY HOPE THE SAME CAN BE SAID FOR ATTILAN!
NOW THAT THIS CADRE MESS'S BEEN DEALT WITH...

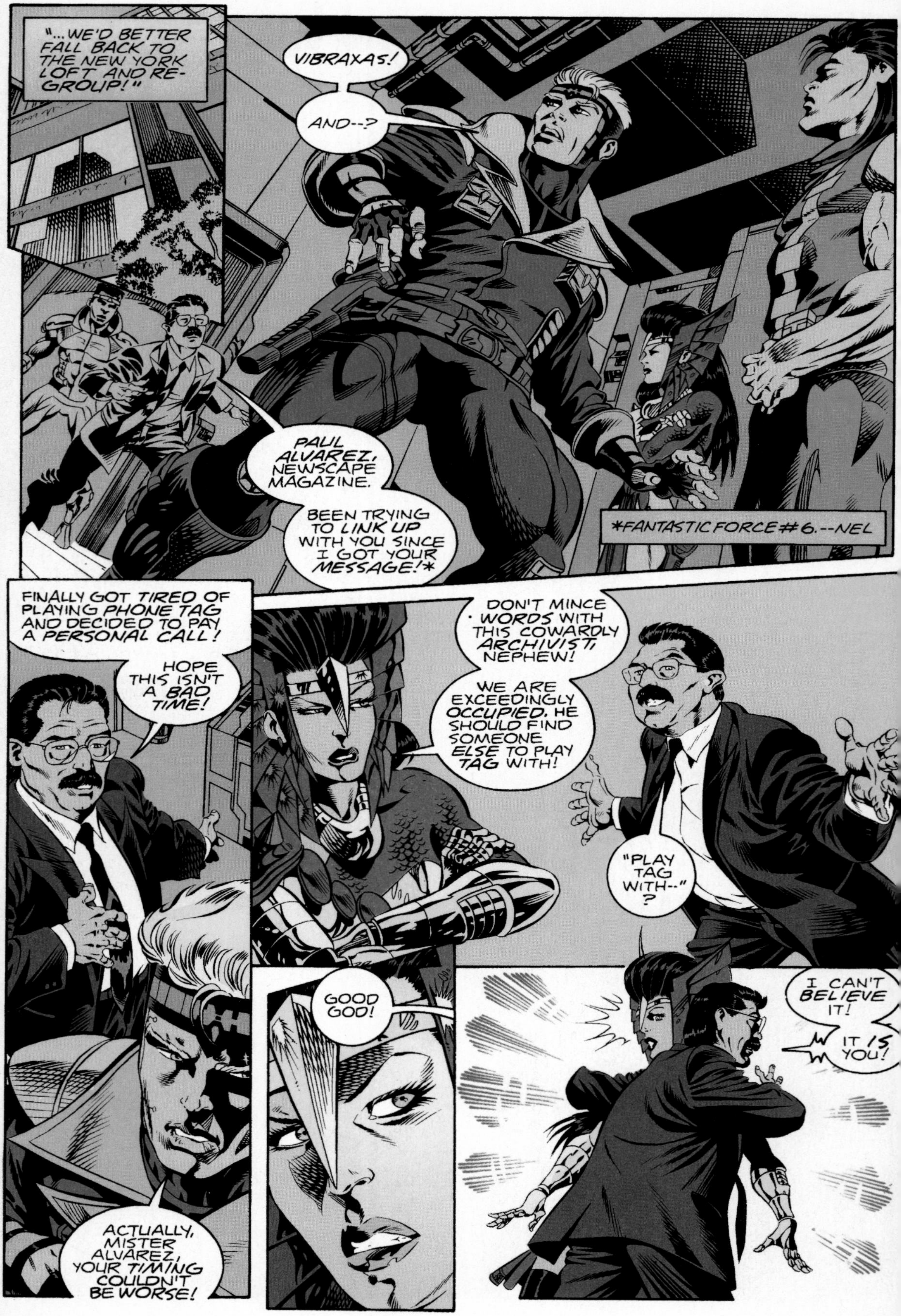
"...WE'D BETTER FALL BACK TO THE NEW YORK LOFT AND RE-GROUP!"
VIBRAXAS!
AND--?
PAUL ALVAREZ, NEWSCAPE MAGAZINE.
BEEN TRYING TO LINK UP WITH YOU SINCE I GOT YOUR MESSAGE!*
*FANTASTIC FORCE #6.--NEL
FINALLY GOT TIRED OF PLAYING PHONE TAG AND DECIDED TO PAY A PERSONAL CALL!
HOPE THIS ISN'T A BAD TIME!
DON'T MINCE WORDS WITH THIS COWARDLY ARCHIVIST, NEPHEW!
WE ARE EXCEEDINGLY OCCUPIED. HE SHOULD FIND SOMEONE ELSE TO PLAY TAG WITH!
"PLAY TAG WITH--" ?
ACTUALLY, MISTER ALVAREZ, YOUR TIMING COULDN'T BE WORSE!
GOOD GOD!
I CAN'T BELIEVE IT!
IT IS YOU!

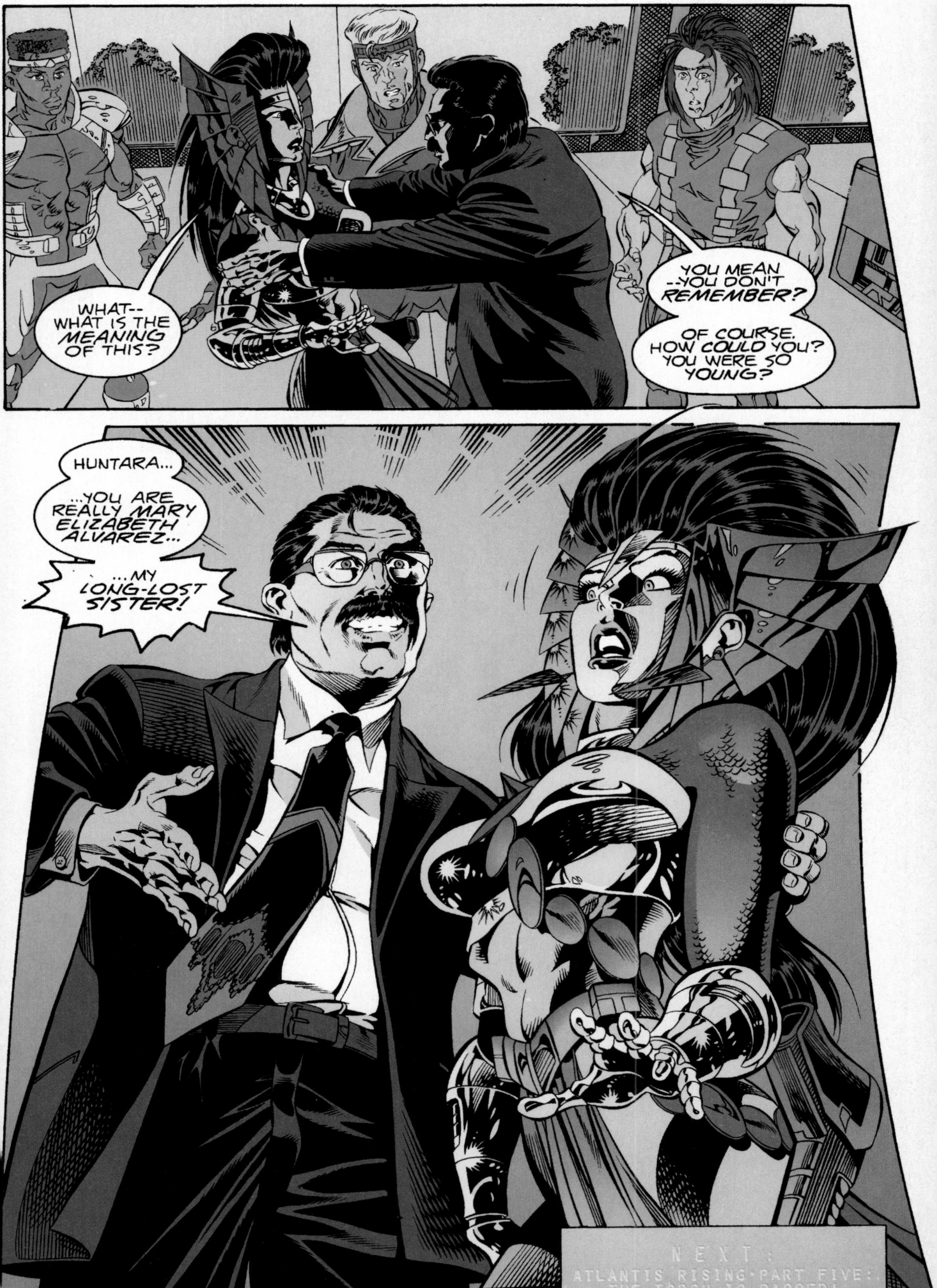
WHAT-- WHAT IS THE MEANING OF THIS?
YOU MEAN --YOU DON'T REMEMBER?
OF COURSE. HOW COULD YOU? YOU WERE SO YOUNG?
HUNTARA...
...YOU ARE REALLY MARY ELIZABETH ALVAREZ...
...MY LONG-LOST SISTER!
NEXT: ATLANTIS RISING PART FIVE: THE TORCH IS PASSED!

MARVEL UNIVERSE
JUNE 1995
THE WORLD'S GREATEST COMIC MAGAZINE!
APPROVED BY THE COMICS CODE AUTHORITY
Fantastic Four®
ATLANTIS RISING
ONLY $1.50 U.S.
AS THE TORCH BURNS SO SHALL THE F.F. PERISH!

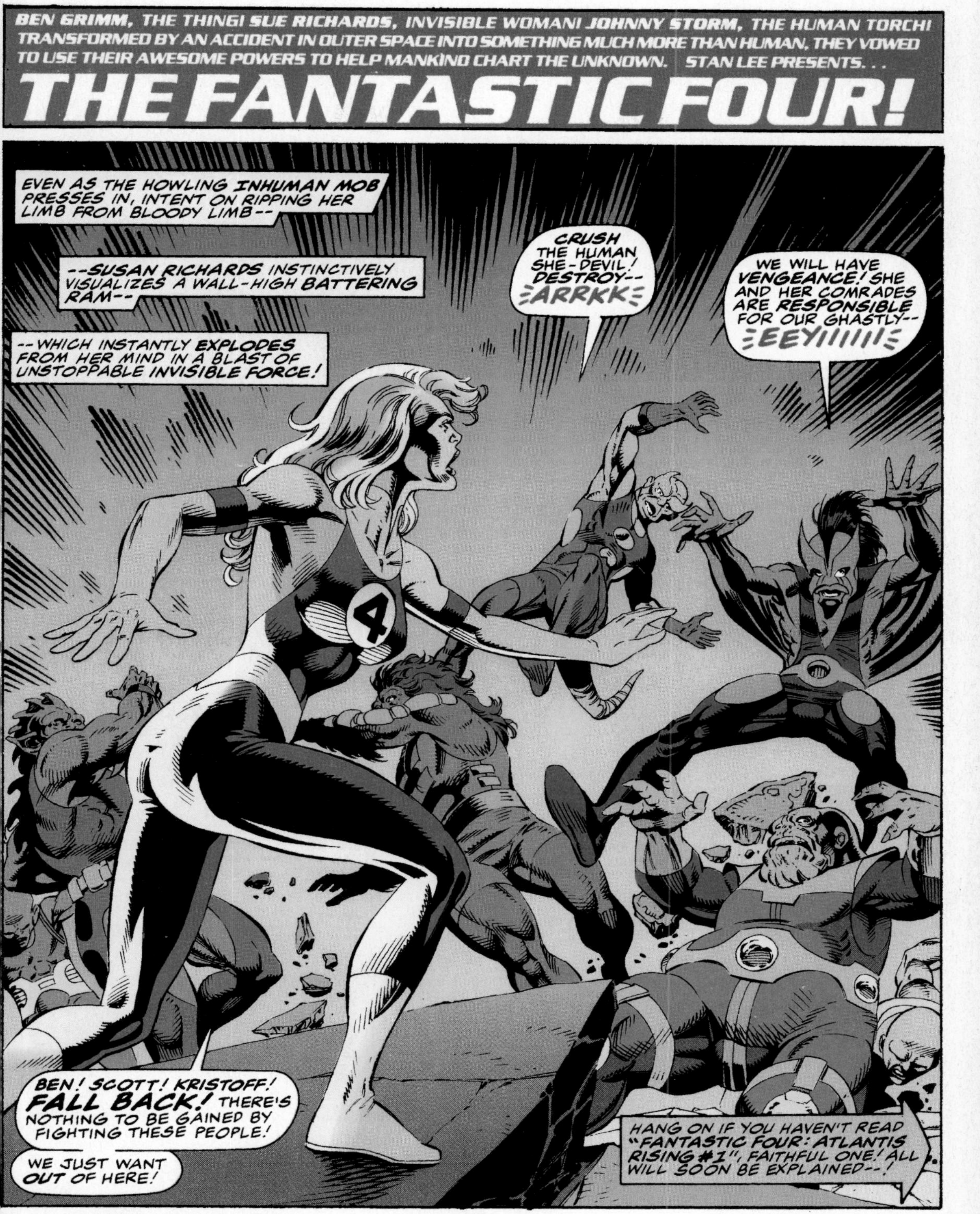
BEN GRIMM, THE THING! SUE RICHARDS, INVISIBLE WOMAN! JOHNNY STORM, THE HUMAN TORCH! TRANSFORMED BY AN ACCIDENT IN OUTER SPACE INTO SOMETHING MUCH MORE THAN HUMAN, THEY VOWED TO USE THEIR AWESOME POWERS TO HELP MANKIND CHART THE UNKNOWN. STAN LEE PRESENTS. . .
THE FANTASTIC FOUR!
EVEN AS THE HOWLING INHUMAN MOB PRESSES IN, INTENT ON RIPPING HER LIMB FROM BLOODY LIMB--
--SUSAN RICHARDS INSTINCTIVELY VISUALIZES A WALL-HIGH BATTERING RAM--
--WHICH INSTANTLY EXPLODES FROM HER MIND IN A BLAST OF UNSTOPPABLE INVISIBLE FORCE!
CRUSH THE HUMAN SHE-DEVIL! DESTROY-- ARRKK
WE WILL HAVE VENGEANCE! SHE AND HER COMRADES ARE RESPONSIBLE FOR OUR GHASTLY-- EEYIIIIII
BEN! SCOTT! KRISTOFF! FALL BACK! THERE'S NOTHING TO BE GAINED BY FIGHTING THESE PEOPLE!
WE JUST WANT OUT OF HERE!
HANG ON IF YOU HAVEN'T READ "FANTASTIC FOUR: ATLANTIS RISING #1", FAITHFUL ONE! ALL WILL SOON BE EXPLAINED--!

TOM DEFALCO & PAUL RYAN
SCRIPT, PLOT & PENCILS

DAN BULANADI - INKS

JOHN KALISZ - COLORS

JIM NOVAK - LETTERING

NEL YOMTOV - EDITOR

MARK GRUENWALD
EDITOR IN CHIEF

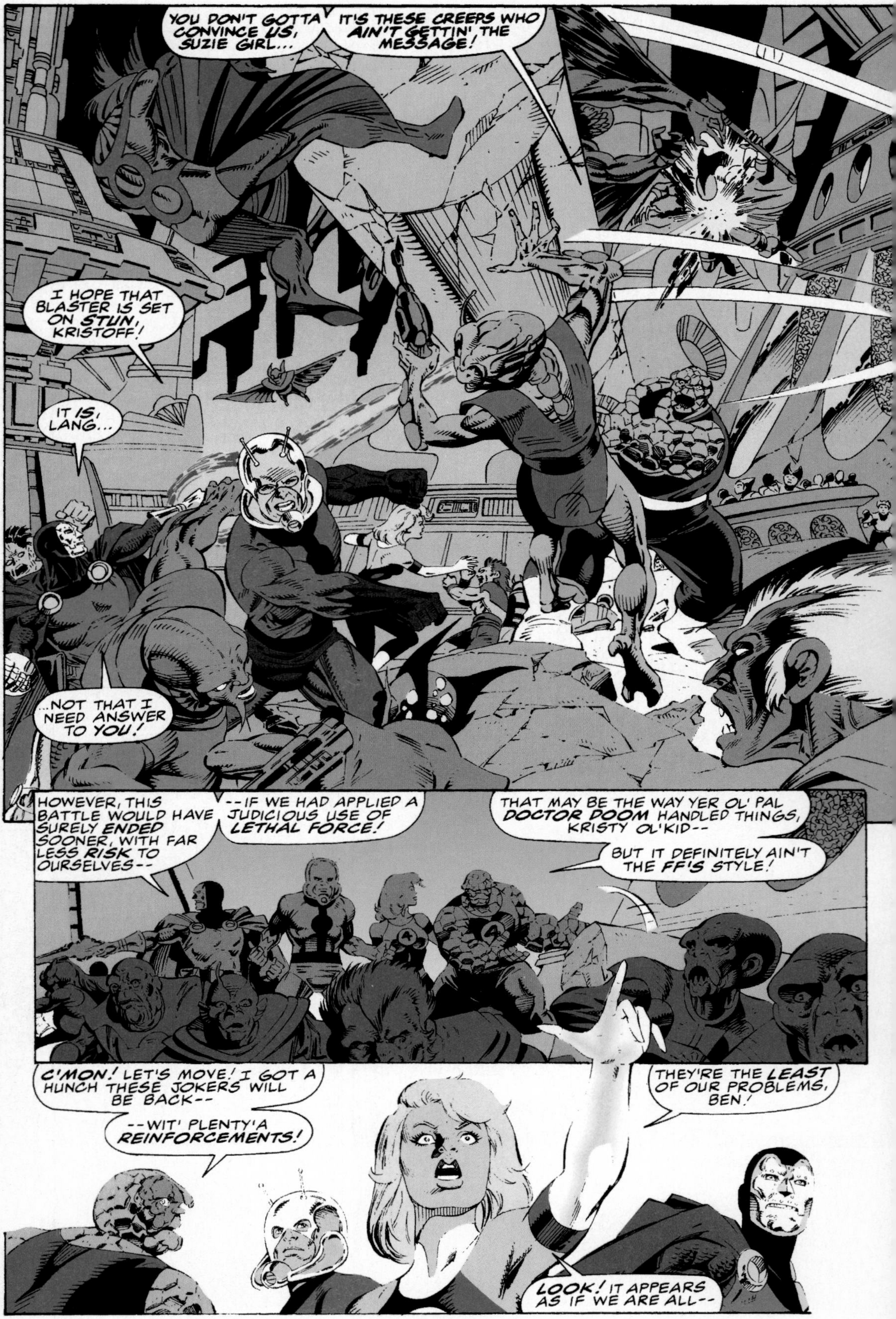
YOU DON'T GOTTA CONVINCE US, SUZIE GIRL...
IT'S THESE CREEPS WHO AIN'T GETTIN' THE MESSAGE!
I HOPE THAT BLASTER IS SET ON STUN, KRISTOFF!
IT IS, LANG...
...NOT THAT I NEED ANSWER TO YOU!
HOWEVER, THIS BATTLE WOULD HAVE SURELY ENDED SOONER, WITH FAR LESS RISK TO OURSELVES--
--IF WE HAD APPLIED A JUDICIOUS USE OF LETHAL FORCE!
THAT MAY BE THE WAY YER OL' PAL DOCTOR DOOM HANDLED THINGS, KRISTY OL' KID--
BUT IT DEFINITELY AIN'T THE FF'S STYLE!
C'MON! LET'S MOVE! I GOT A HUNCH THESE JOKERS WILL BE BACK--
--WIT' PLENTY'A REINFORCEMENTS!
THEY'RE THE LEAST OF OUR PROBLEMS, BEN!
LOOK! IT APPEARS AS IF WE ARE ALL--

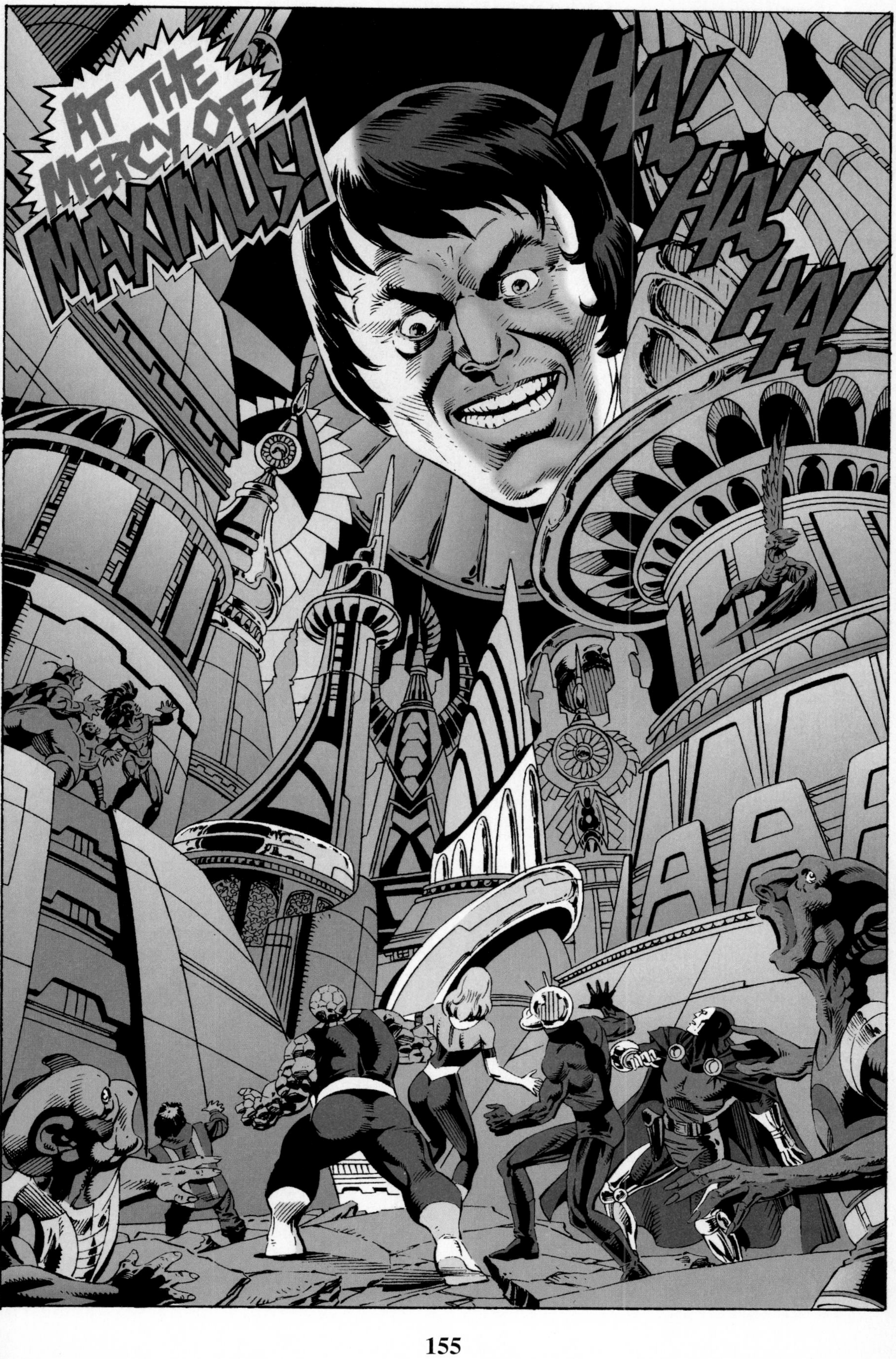
AT THE MERCY OF MAXIMUS!
HA! HA! HA! HA!

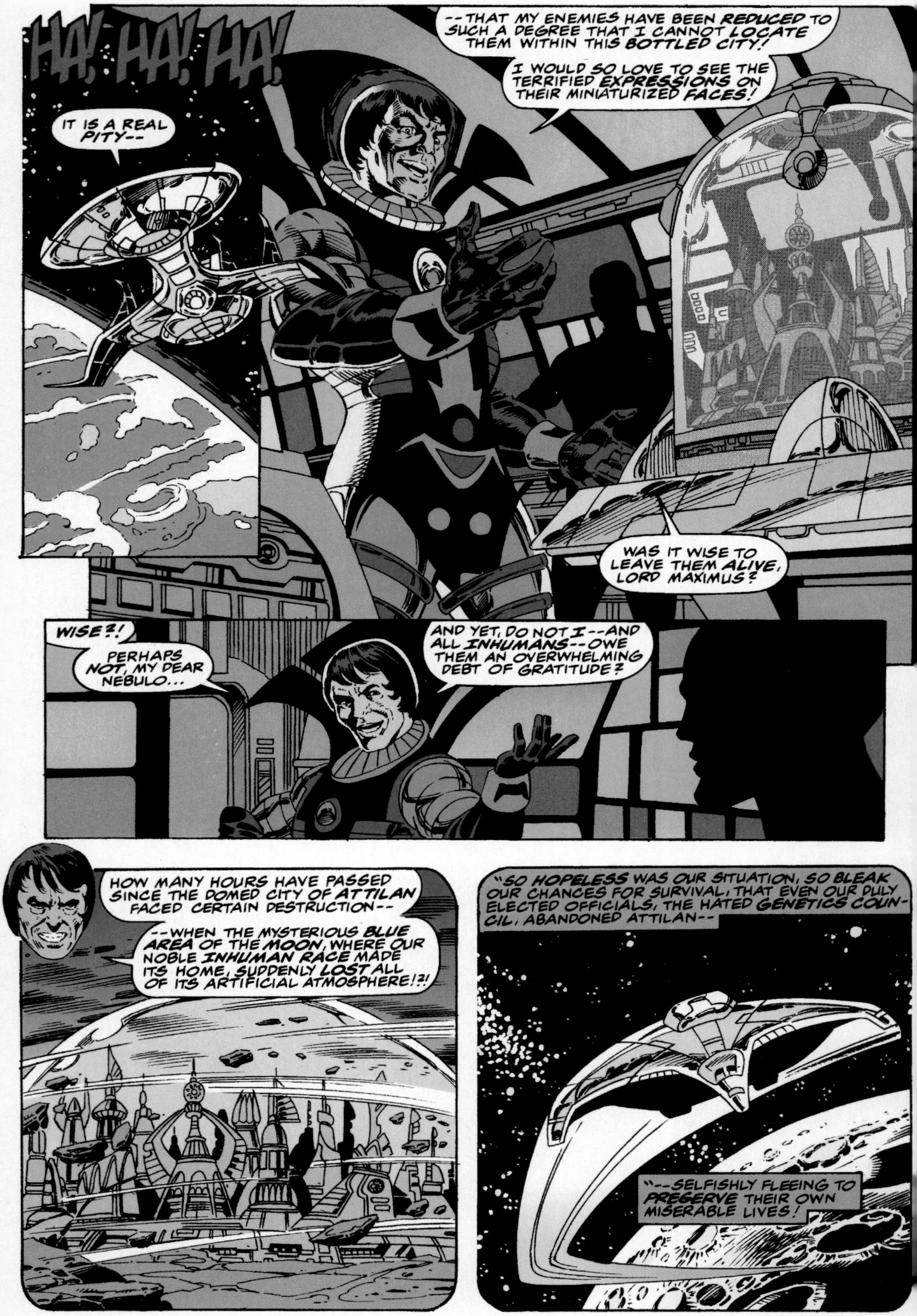
HA! HA! HA!
IT IS A REAL PITY--
--THAT MY ENEMIES HAVE BEEN REDUCED TO SUCH A DEGREE THAT I CANNOT LOCATE THEM WITHIN THIS BOTTLED CITY!
I WOULD SO LOVE TO SEE THE TERRIFIED EXPRESSIONS ON THEIR MINIATURIZED FACES!
WAS IT WISE TO LEAVE THEM ALIVE, LORD MAXIMUS?
WISE?!
PERHAPS NOT, MY DEAR NEBULO...
AND YET, DO NOT I--AND ALL INHUMANS--OWE THEM AN OVERWHELMING DEBT OF GRATITUDE?
HOW MANY HOURS HAVE PASSED SINCE THE DOMED CITY OF ATTILAN FACED CERTAIN DESTRUCTION--
--WHEN THE MYSTERIOUS BLUE AREA OF THE MOON, WHERE OUR NOBLE INHUMAN RACE MADE ITS HOME, SUDDENLY LOST ALL OF ITS ARTIFICIAL ATMOSPHERE!?!
"SO HOPELESS WAS OUR SITUATION, SO BLEAK OUR CHANCES FOR SURVIVAL, THAT EVEN OUR DULY ELECTED OFFICIALS, THE HATED GENETICS COUNCIL, ABANDONED ATTILAN--
"--SELFISHLY FLEEING TO PRESERVE THEIR OWN MISERABLE LIVES!

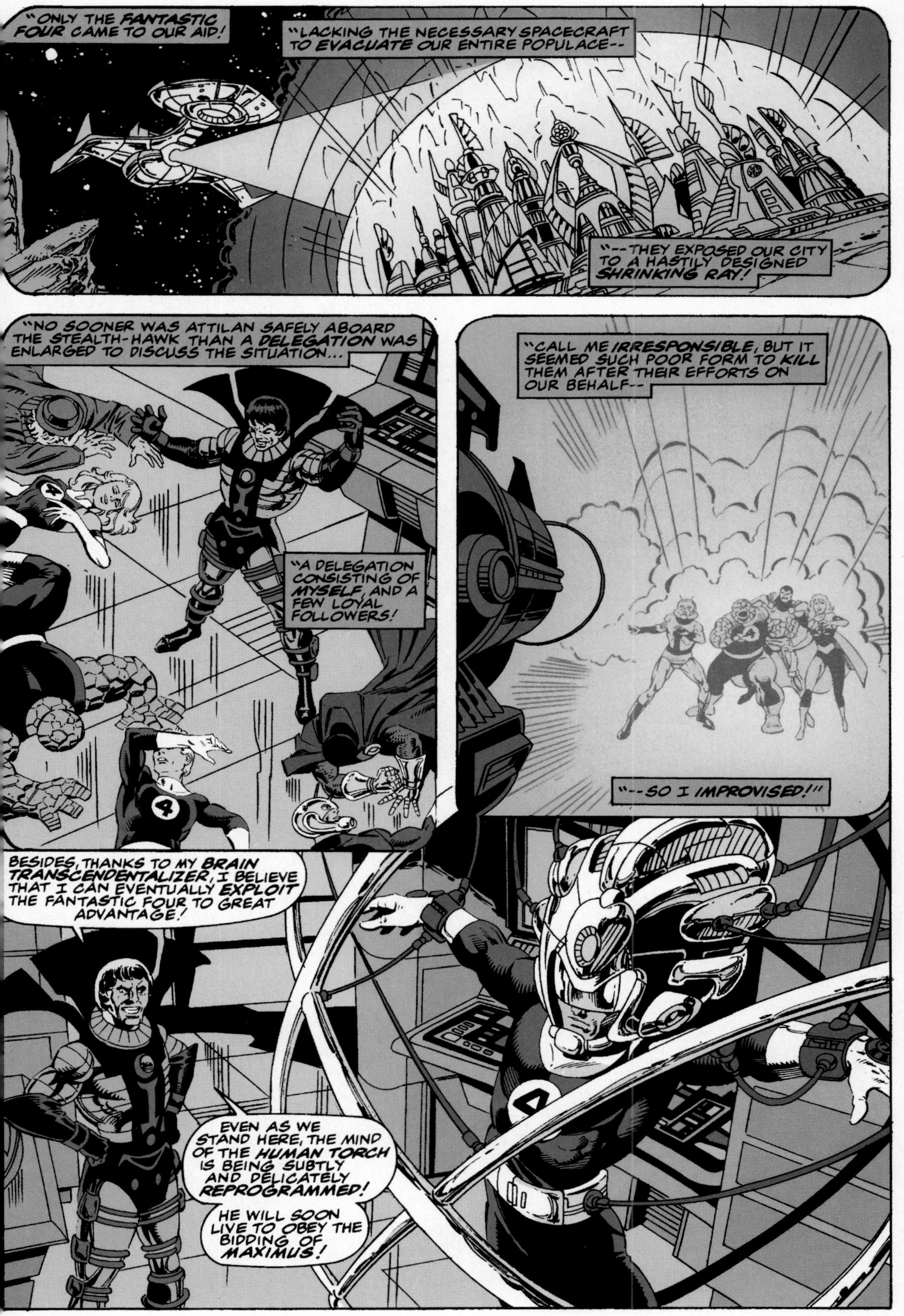
"ONLY THE FANTASTIC FOUR CAME TO OUR AID!
"LACKING THE NECESSARY SPACECRAFT TO EVACUATE OUR ENTIRE POPULACE--
"--THEY EXPOSED OUR CITY TO A HASTILY DESIGNED SHRINKING RAY!
"NO SOONER WAS ATTILAN SAFELY ABOARD THE STEALTH-HAWK THAN A DELEGATION WAS ENLARGED TO DISCUSS THE SITUATION...
"A DELEGATION CONSISTING OF MYSELF, AND A FEW LOYAL FOLLOWERS!
"CALL ME IRRESPONSIBLE, BUT IT SEEMED SUCH POOR FORM TO KILL THEM AFTER THEIR EFFORTS ON OUR BEHALF--
"--SO I IMPROVISED!"
BESIDES, THANKS TO MY BRAIN TRANSCENDENTALIZER, I BELIEVE THAT I CAN EVENTUALLY EXPLOIT THE FANTASTIC FOUR TO GREAT ADVANTAGE!
EVEN AS WE STAND HERE, THE MIND OF THE HUMAN TORCH IS BEING SUBTLY AND DELICATELY REPROGRAMMED!
HE WILL SOON LIVE TO OBEY THE BIDDING OF MAXIMUS!

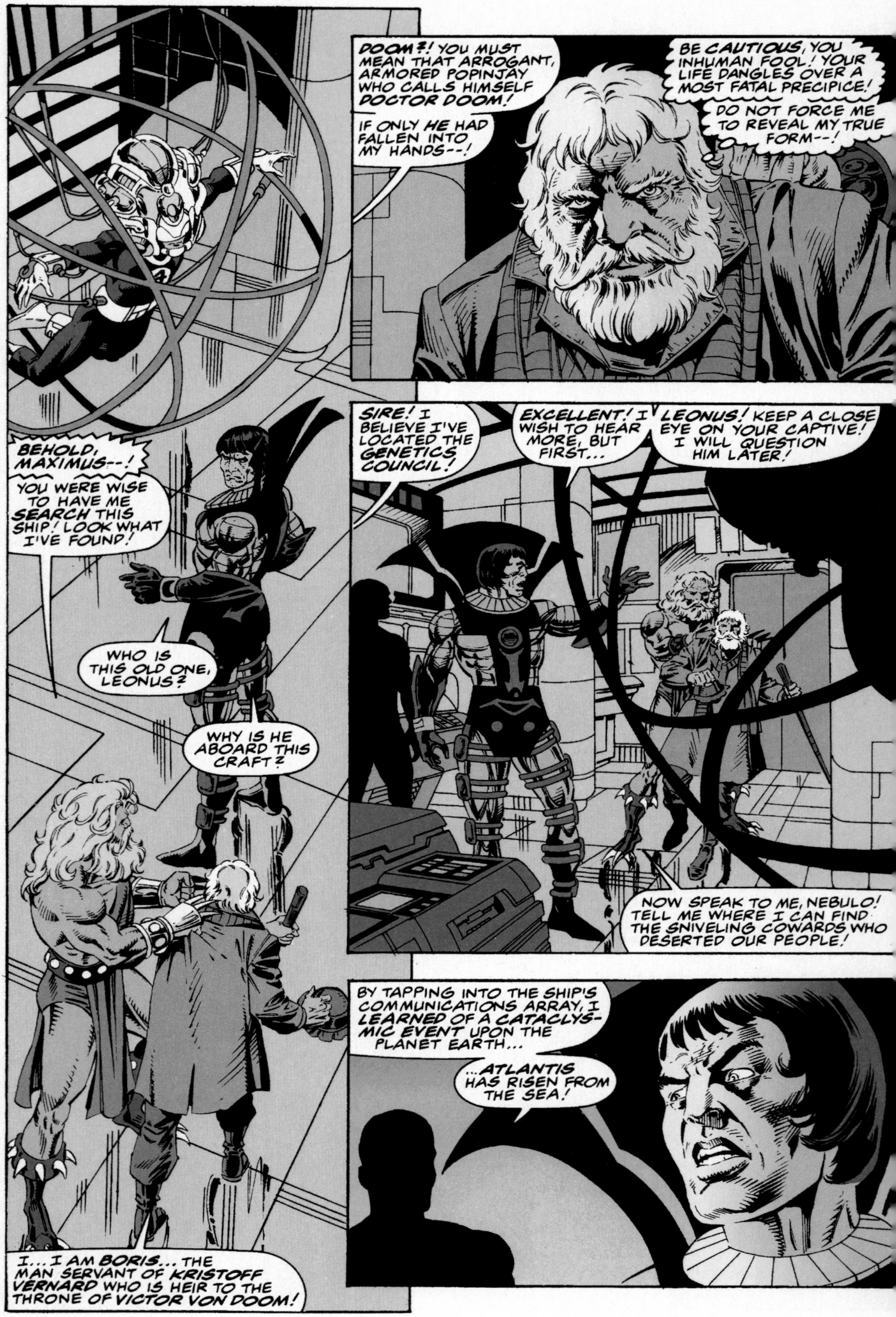
DOOM?! YOU MUST MEAN THAT ARROGANT, ARMORED POPINJAY WHO CALLS HIMSELF DOCTOR DOOM!
IF ONLY HE HAD FALLEN INTO MY HANDS--!
BE CAUTIOUS, YOU INHUMAN FOOL! YOUR LIFE DANGLES OVER A MOST FATAL PRECIPICE!
DO NOT FORCE ME TO REVEAL MY TRUE FORM--!
BEHOLD, MAXIMUS--!
YOU WERE WISE TO HAVE ME SEARCH THIS SHIP! LOOK WHAT I'VE FOUND!
WHO IS THIS OLD ONE, LEONUS?
WHY IS HE ABOARD THIS CRAFT?
I... I AM BORIS... THE MAN SERVANT OF KRISTOFF VERNARD WHO IS HEIR TO THE THRONE OF VICTOR VON DOOM!
SIRE! I BELIEVE I'VE LOCATED THE GENETICS COUNCIL!
EXCELLENT! I WISH TO HEAR MORE, BUT FIRST...
LEONUS! KEEP A CLOSE EYE ON YOUR CAPTIVE! I WILL QUESTION HIM LATER!
NOW SPEAK TO ME, NEBULO! TELL ME WHERE I CAN FIND THE SNIVELING COWARDS WHO DESERTED OUR PEOPLE!
BY TAPPING INTO THE SHIP'S COMMUNICATIONS ARRAY, I LEARNED OF A CATACLYSMIC EVENT UPON THE PLANET EARTH...
...ATLANTIS HAS RISEN FROM THE SEA!

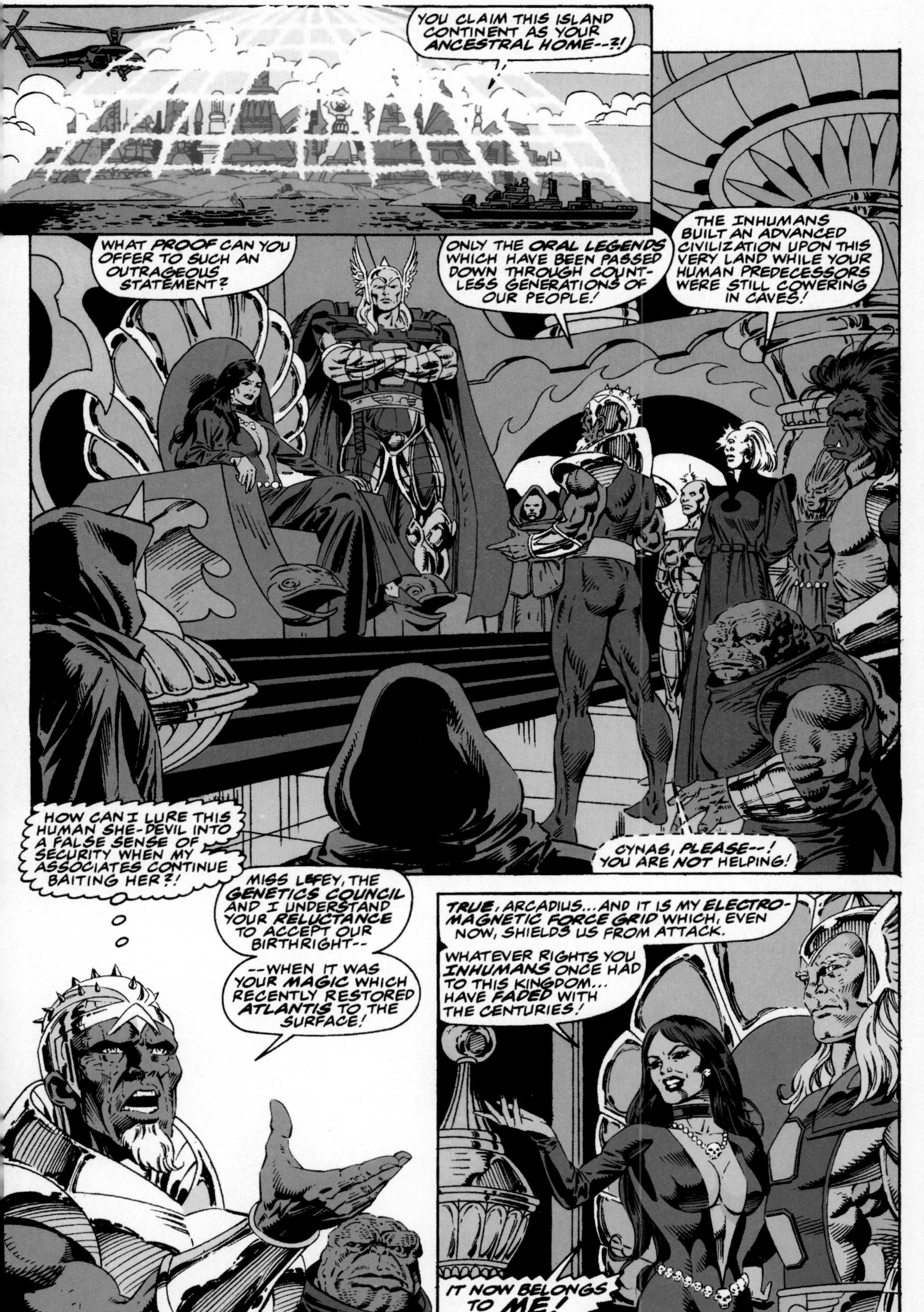
YOU CLAIM THIS ISLAND CONTINENT AS YOUR ANCESTRAL HOME--?!
WHAT PROOF CAN YOU OFFER TO SUCH AN OUTRAGEOUS STATEMENT?
ONLY THE ORAL LEGENDS WHICH HAVE BEEN PASSED DOWN THROUGH COUNTLESS GENERATIONS OF OUR PEOPLE!
THE INHUMANS BUILT AN ADVANCED CIVILIZATION UPON THIS VERY LAND WHILE YOUR HUMAN PREDECESSORS WERE STILL COWERING IN CAVES!
HOW CAN I LURE THIS HUMAN SHE-DEVIL INTO A FALSE SENSE OF SECURITY WHEN MY ASSOCIATES CONTINUE BAITING HER?!
CYNAS, PLEASE--! YOU ARE NOT HELPING!
MISS LEFEY, THE GENETICS COUNCIL AND I UNDERSTAND YOUR RELUCTANCE TO ACCEPT OUR BIRTHRIGHT--
--WHEN IT WAS YOUR MAGIC WHICH RECENTLY RESTORED ATLANTIS TO THE SURFACE!
TRUE, ARCADIUS... AND IT IS MY ELECTRO-MAGNETIC FORCE GRID WHICH, EVEN NOW, SHIELDS US FROM ATTACK.
WHATEVER RIGHTS YOU INHUMANS ONCE HAD TO THIS KINGDOM... HAVE FADED WITH THE CENTURIES!
IT NOW BELONGS TO ME!

BEWARE, WOMAN! NOT EVEN YOU CAN DEFY THE GENETICS COUNCIL OF THE INHUMANS!

CALM DOWN, TARGON! THIS IS NO TIME FOR ONE OF YOUR FOOLISH TEMPER TANTRUMS!

TAKE HEED, BESTIAL ONE!

NONE MAY HARM MORGAN LE FEY WHILE THE THUNDER GOD LIVES!

RELAX, THOR! BY THE POWER OF GAEA WHICH BINDS YOU TO MY WILL... I COMMAND YOU TO LAY DOWN YOUR HAMMER!

THERE IS NO NEED FOR VIOLENCE!

WHILE I WON'T SURRENDER THIS LAND, I WILL SHARE IT!

LET US BE ALLIES, ARCADIUS! THERE IS ROOM ON THIS CONTINENT FOR BOTH OUR RACES!

SO LONG AS ONE IS MASTER... AND THE OTHER SLAVE!

THERE IS WISDOM IN YOUR WORDS, LADY MORGAN...

AND YOUR UNVOICED THOUGHTS!

I WILL EVEN HELP YOU LOCATE YOUR MISSING PEOPLE...

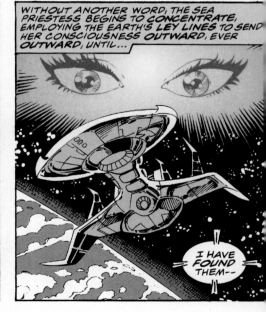

WITHOUT ANOTHER WORD, THE SEA PRIESTESS BEGINS TO CONCENTRATE, EMPLOYING THE EARTH'S LEY LINES TO SEND HER CONSCIOUSNESS OUTWARD, EVER OUTWARD, UNTIL...

I HAVE FOUND THEM—

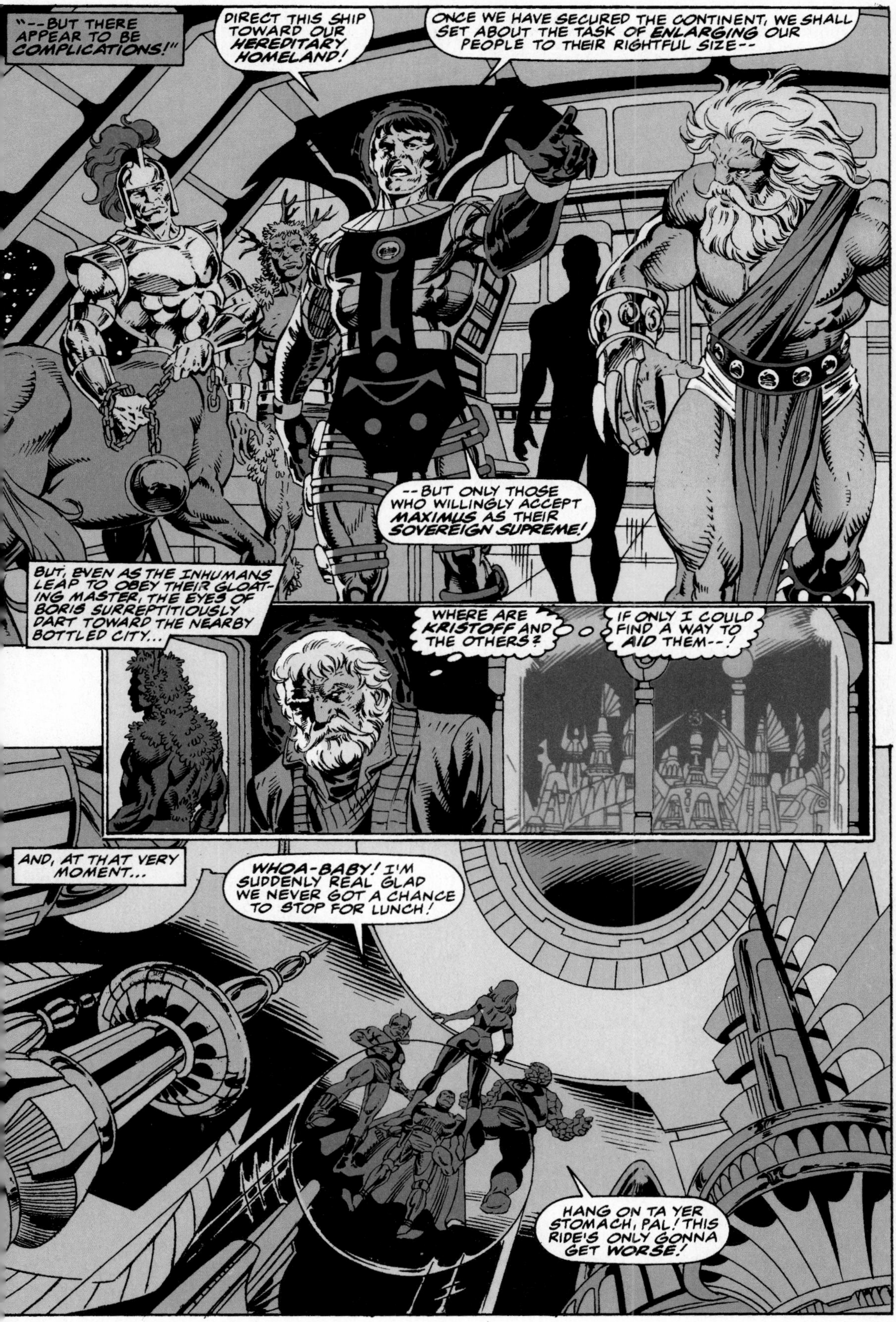
"--BUT THERE APPEAR TO BE COMPLICATIONS!"
DIRECT THIS SHIP TOWARD OUR HEREDITARY HOMELAND!
ONCE WE HAVE SECURED THE CONTINENT, WE SHALL SET ABOUT THE TASK OF ENLARGING OUR PEOPLE TO THEIR RIGHTFUL SIZE--
--BUT ONLY THOSE WHO WILLINGLY ACCEPT MAXIMUS AS THEIR SOVEREIGN SUPREME!
BUT, EVEN AS THE INHUMANS LEAP TO OBEY THEIR GLOATING MASTER, THE EYES OF BORIS SURREPTITIOUSLY DART TOWARD THE NEARBY BOTTLED CITY...
WHERE ARE KRISTOFF AND THE OTHERS?
IF ONLY I COULD FIND A WAY TO AID THEM--!
AND, AT THAT VERY MOMENT...
WHOA-BABY! I'M SUDDENLY REAL GLAD WE NEVER GOT A CHANCE TO STOP FOR LUNCH!
HANG ON TA YER STOMACH, PAL! THIS RIDE'S ONLY GONNA GET WORSE!

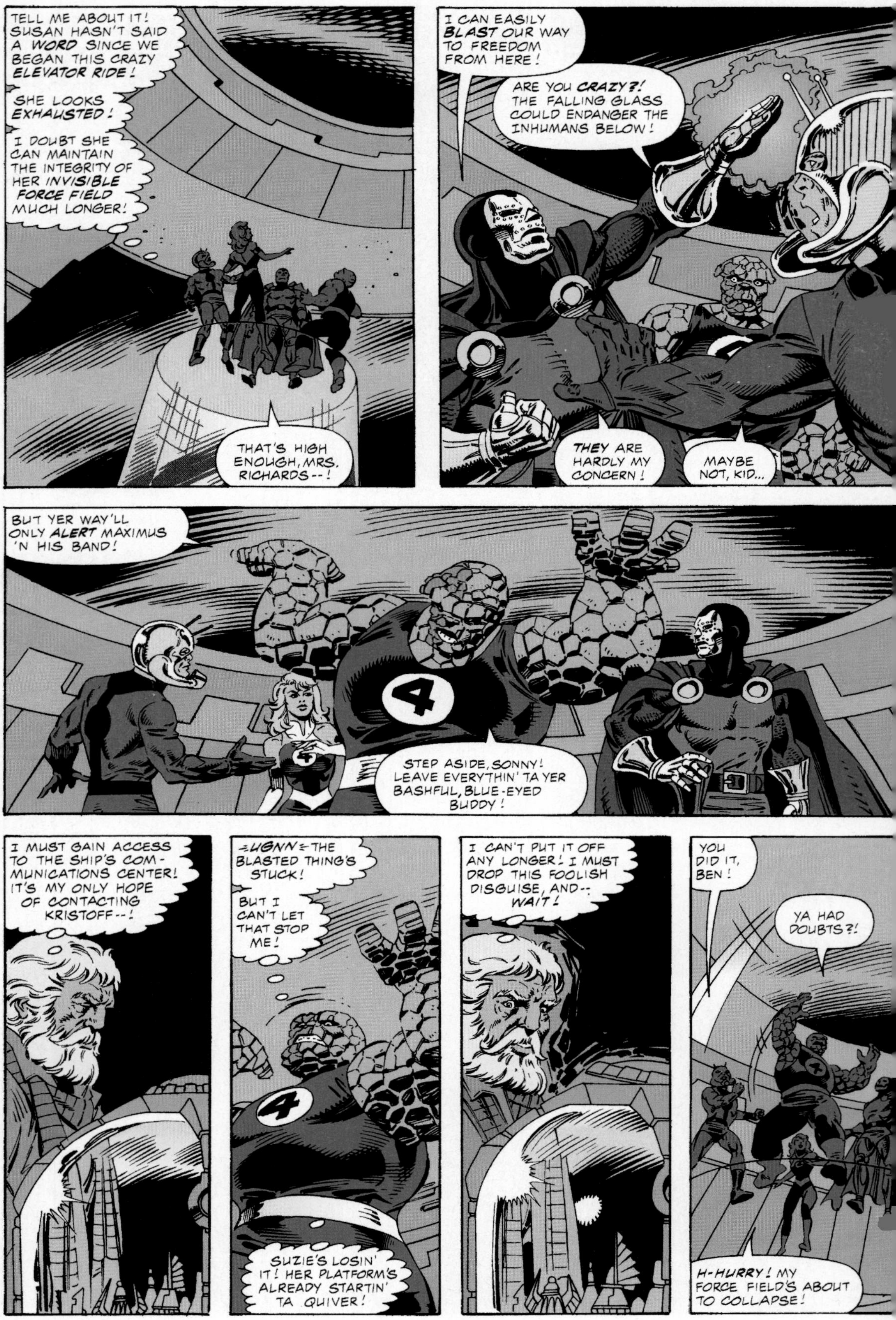

TELL ME ABOUT IT! SUSAN HASN'T SAID A WORD SINCE WE BEGAN THIS CRAZY ELEVATOR RIDE!
SHE LOOKS EXHAUSTED!
I DOUBT SHE CAN MAINTAIN THE INTEGRITY OF HER INVISIBLE FORCE FIELD MUCH LONGER!
THAT'S HIGH ENOUGH, MRS. RICHARDS--!
I CAN EASILY BLAST OUR WAY TO FREEDOM FROM HERE!
ARE YOU CRAZY?! THE FALLING GLASS COULD ENDANGER THE INHUMANS BELOW!
THEY ARE HARDLY MY CONCERN!
MAYBE NOT, KID...
BUT YER WAY'LL ONLY ALERT MAXIMUS 'N HIS BAND!
STEP ASIDE, SONNY! LEAVE EVERYTHIN' TA YER BASHFUL, BLUE-EYED BUDDY!
I MUST GAIN ACCESS TO THE SHIP'S COM-MUNICATIONS CENTER! IT'S MY ONLY HOPE OF CONTACTING KRISTOFF--!
=UGNN= THE BLASTED THING'S STUCK!
BUT I CAN'T LET THAT STOP ME!
SUZIE'S LOSIN' IT! HER PLATFORM'S ALREADY STARTIN' TA QUIVER!
I CAN'T PUT IT OFF ANY LONGER! I MUST DROP THIS FOOLISH DISGUISE, AND-- WAIT!
YOU DID IT, BEN!
YA HAD DOUBTS?!
H-HURRY! MY FORCE FIELD'S ABOUT TO COLLAPSE!

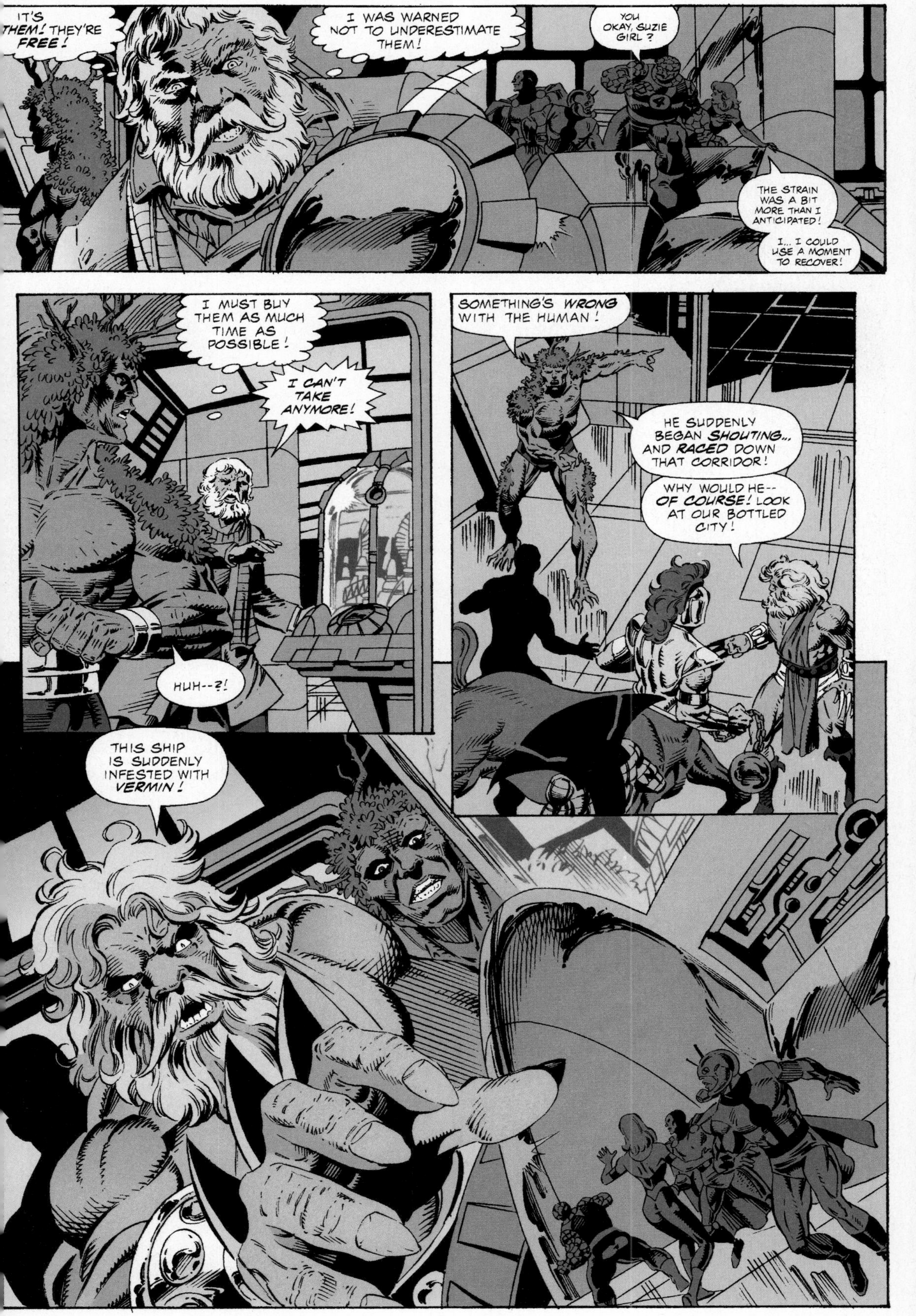

IT'S THEM! THEY'RE FREE!
I WAS WARNED NOT TO UNDERESTIMATE THEM!
YOU OKAY, SUZIE GIRL?
THE STRAIN WAS A BIT MORE THAN I ANTICIPATED!
I... I COULD USE A MOMENT TO RECOVER!
I MUST BUY THEM AS MUCH TIME AS POSSIBLE!
I CAN'T TAKE ANYMORE!
HUH--?!
SOMETHING'S WRONG WITH THE HUMAN!
HE SUDDENLY BEGAN SHOUTING... AND RACED DOWN THAT CORRIDOR!
WHY WOULD HE-- OF COURSE! LOOK AT OUR BOTTLED CITY!
THIS SHIP IS SUDDENLY INFESTED WITH VERMIN!

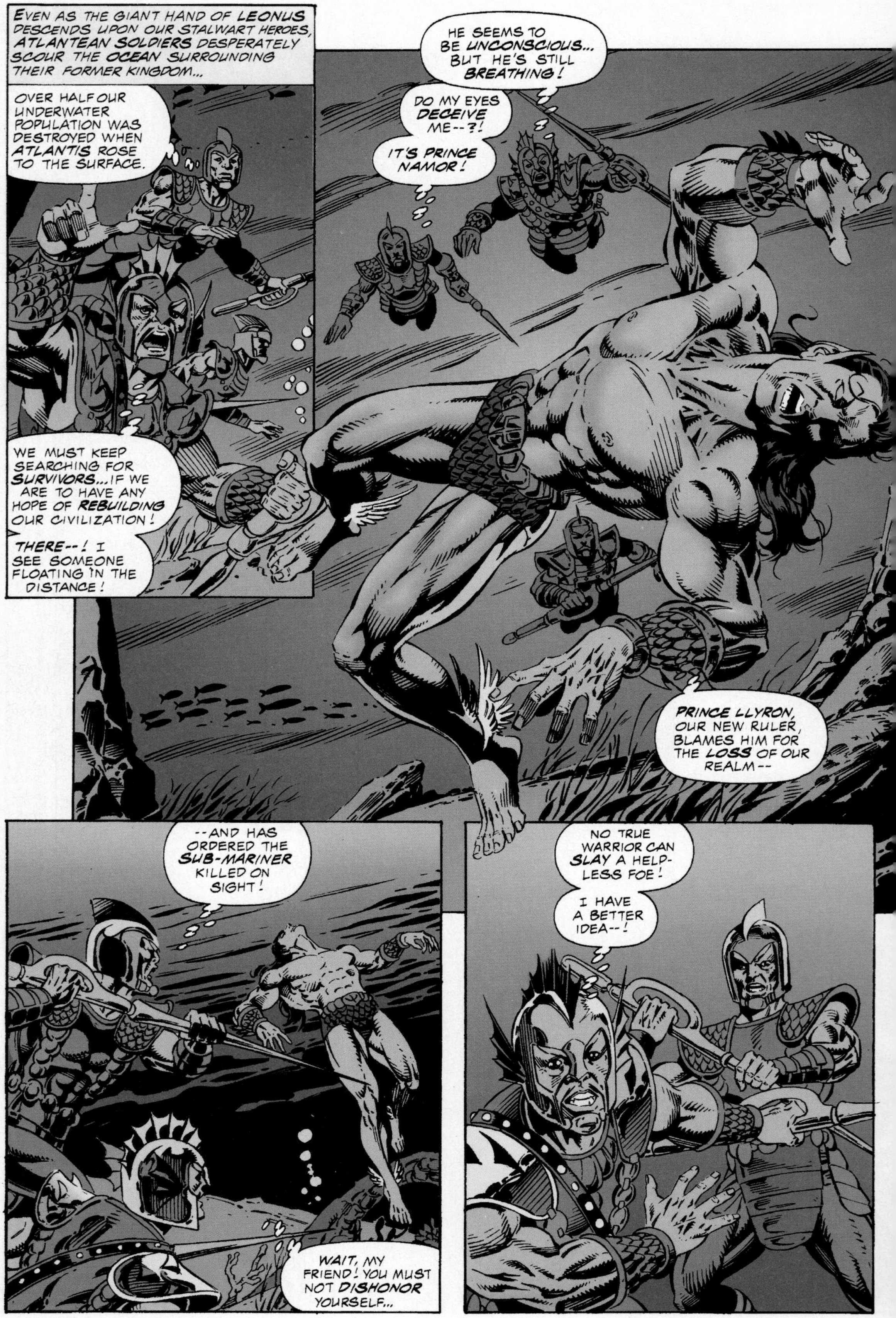
EVEN AS THE GIANT HAND OF LEONUS DESCENDS UPON OUR STALWART HEROES, ATLANTEAN SOLDIERS DESPERATELY SCOUR THE OCEAN SURROUNDING THEIR FORMER KINGDOM...
OVER HALF OUR UNDERWATER POPULATION WAS DESTROYED WHEN ATLANTIS ROSE TO THE SURFACE.
WE MUST KEEP SEARCHING FOR SURVIVORS...IF WE ARE TO HAVE ANY HOPE OF REBUILDING OUR CIVILIZATION!
THERE--! I SEE SOMEONE FLOATING IN THE DISTANCE!
HE SEEMS TO BE UNCONSCIOUS... BUT HE'S STILL BREATHING!
DO MY EYES DECEIVE ME--?!
IT'S PRINCE NAMOR!
PRINCE LLYRON, OUR NEW RULER, BLAMES HIM FOR THE LOSS OF OUR REALM--
--AND HAS ORDERED THE SUB-MARINER KILLED ON SIGHT!
WAIT, MY FRIEND! YOU MUST NOT DISHONOR YOURSELF...
NO TRUE WARRIOR CAN SLAY A HELPLESS FOE!
I HAVE A BETTER IDEA--!

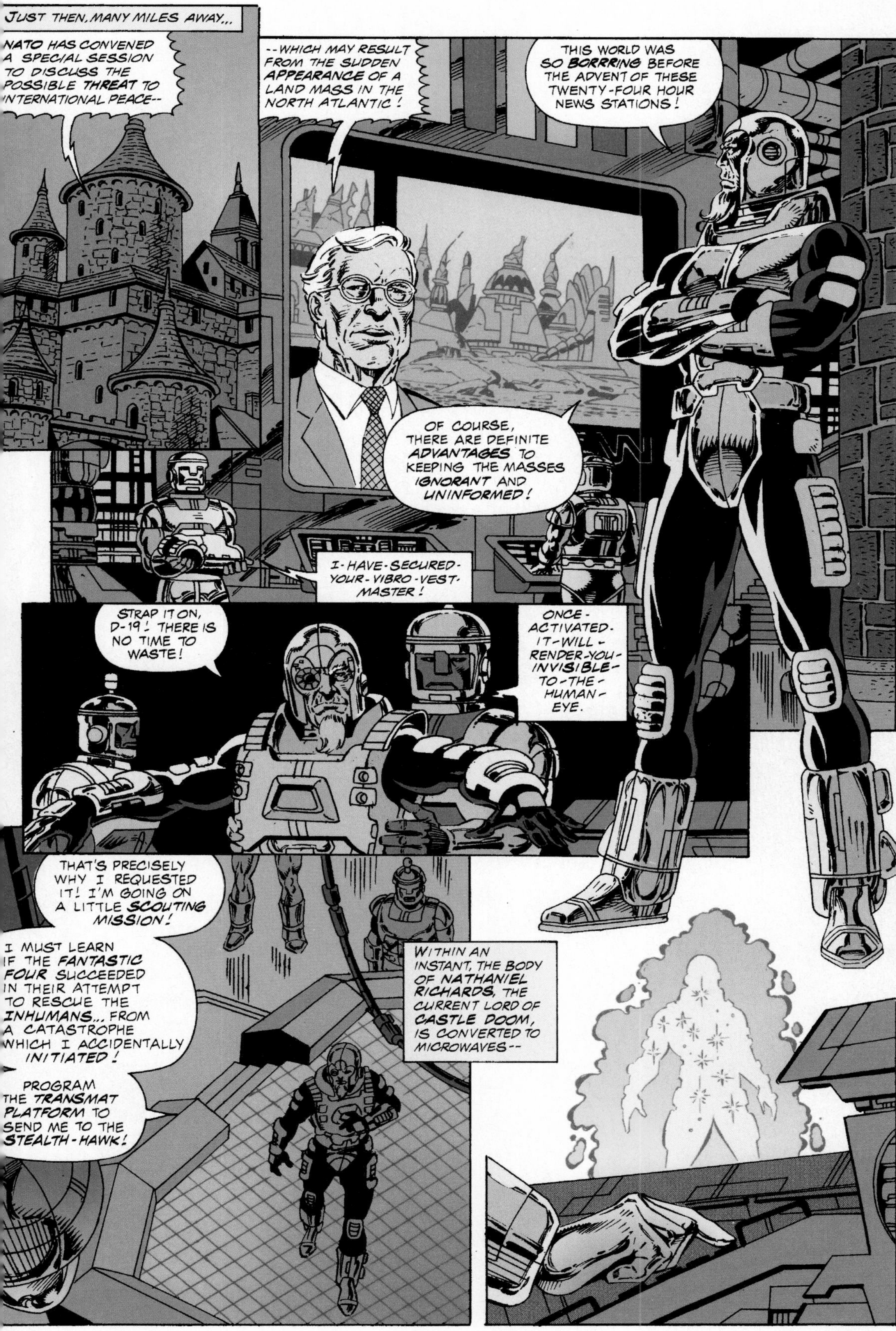
JUST THEN, MANY MILES AWAY...
NATO HAS CONVENED A SPECIAL SESSION TO DISCUSS THE POSSIBLE THREAT TO INTERNATIONAL PEACE--
--WHICH MAY RESULT FROM THE SUDDEN APPEARANCE OF A LAND MASS IN THE NORTH ATLANTIC!
THIS WORLD WAS SO BORRRING BEFORE THE ADVENT OF THESE TWENTY-FOUR HOUR NEWS STATIONS!
OF COURSE, THERE ARE DEFINITE ADVANTAGES TO KEEPING THE MASSES IGNORANT AND UNINFORMED!
I-HAVE-SECURED-YOUR-VIBRO-VEST-MASTER!
STRAP IT ON, D-19! THERE IS NO TIME TO WASTE!
ONCE-ACTIVATED-IT-WILL-RENDER-YOU-INVISIBLE-TO-THE-HUMAN-EYE.
THAT'S PRECISELY WHY I REQUESTED IT! I'M GOING ON A LITTLE SCOUTING MISSION!
I MUST LEARN IF THE FANTASTIC FOUR SUCCEEDED IN THEIR ATTEMPT TO RESCUE THE INHUMANS... FROM A CATASTROPHE WHICH I ACCIDENTALLY INITIATED!
PROGRAM THE TRANSMAT PLATFORM TO SEND ME TO THE STEALTH-HAWK!
WITHIN AN INSTANT, THE BODY OF NATHANIEL RICHARDS, THE CURRENT LORD OF CASTLE DOOM, IS CONVERTED TO MICROWAVES--

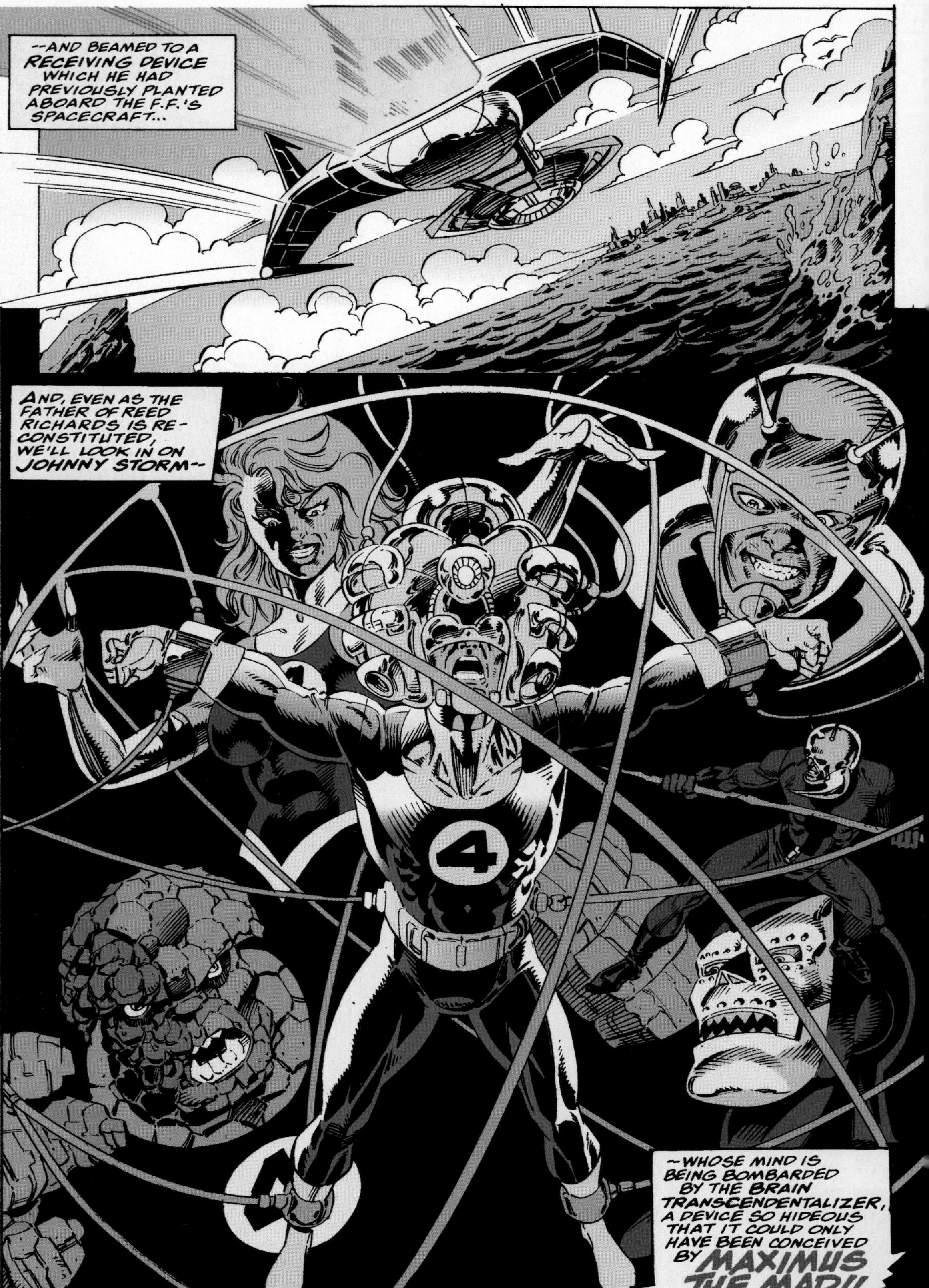
--AND BEAMED TO A RECEIVING DEVICE WHICH HE HAD PREVIOUSLY PLANTED ABOARD THE F.F.'S SPACECRAFT...
AND, EVEN AS THE FATHER OF REED RICHARDS IS RE-CONSTITUTED, WE'LL LOOK IN ON JOHNNY STORM--
--WHOSE MIND IS BEING BOMBARDED BY THE BRAIN TRANSCENDENTALIZER, A DEVICE SO HIDEOUS THAT IT COULD ONLY HAVE BEEN CONCEIVED BY MAXIMUS THE MAD!!

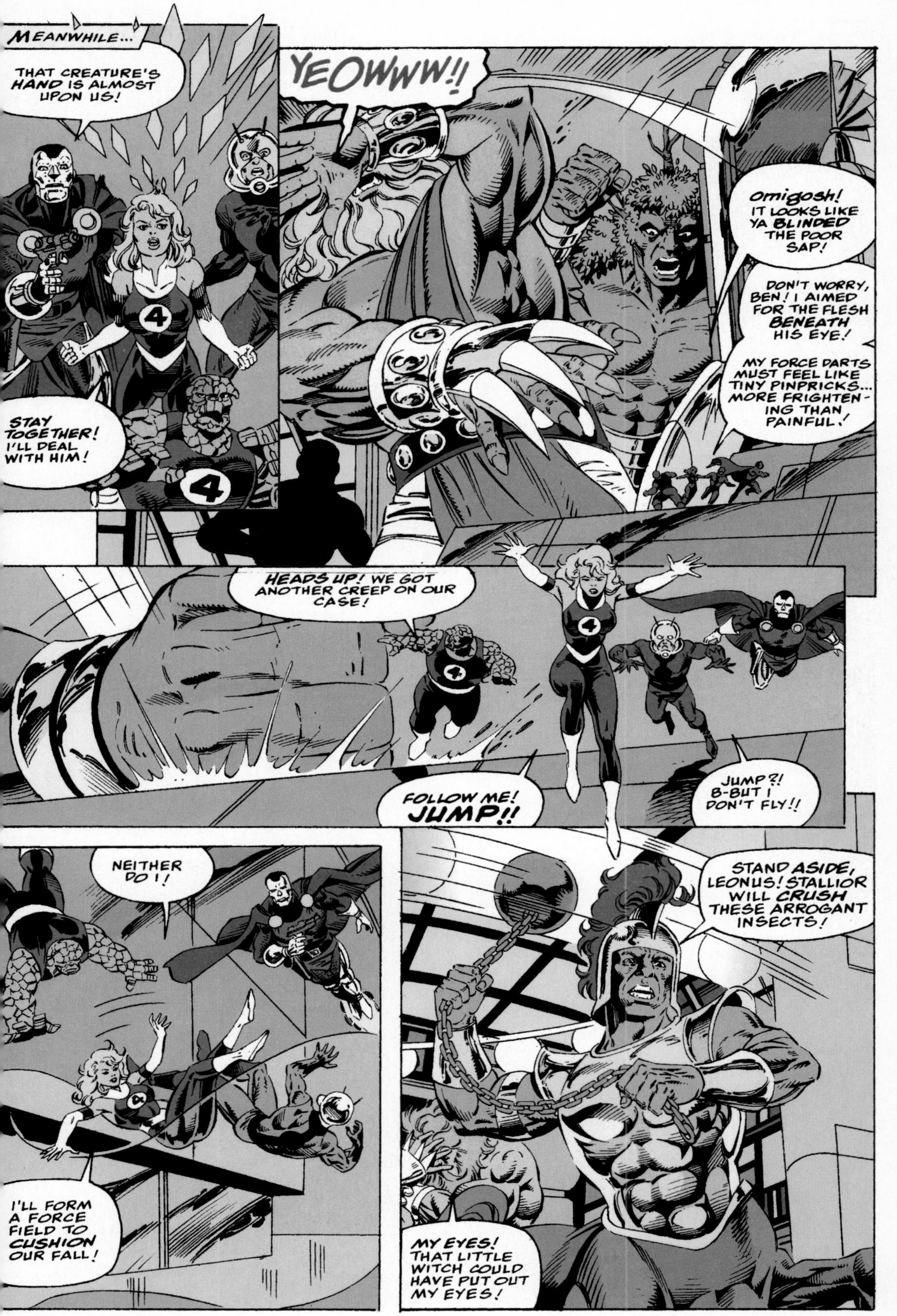
MEANWHILE...
THAT CREATURE'S HAND IS ALMOST UPON US!
YEOWWW!!
STAY TOGETHER! I'LL DEAL WITH HIM!
Omigosh! IT LOOKS LIKE YA BLINDED THE POOR SAP!
DON'T WORRY, BEN! I AIMED FOR THE FLESH BENEATH HIS EYE!
MY FORCE DARTS MUST FEEL LIKE TINY PINPRICKS... MORE FRIGHTENING THAN PAINFUL!
HEADS UP! WE GOT ANOTHER CREEP ON OUR CASE!
FOLLOW ME! JUMP!!
JUMP?! B-BUT I DON'T FLY!!
NEITHER DO I!
I'LL FORM A FORCE FIELD TO CUSHION OUR FALL!
STAND ASIDE, LEONUS! STALLIOR WILL CRUSH THESE ARROGANT INSECTS!
MY EYES! THAT LITTLE WITCH COULD HAVE PUT OUT MY EYES!

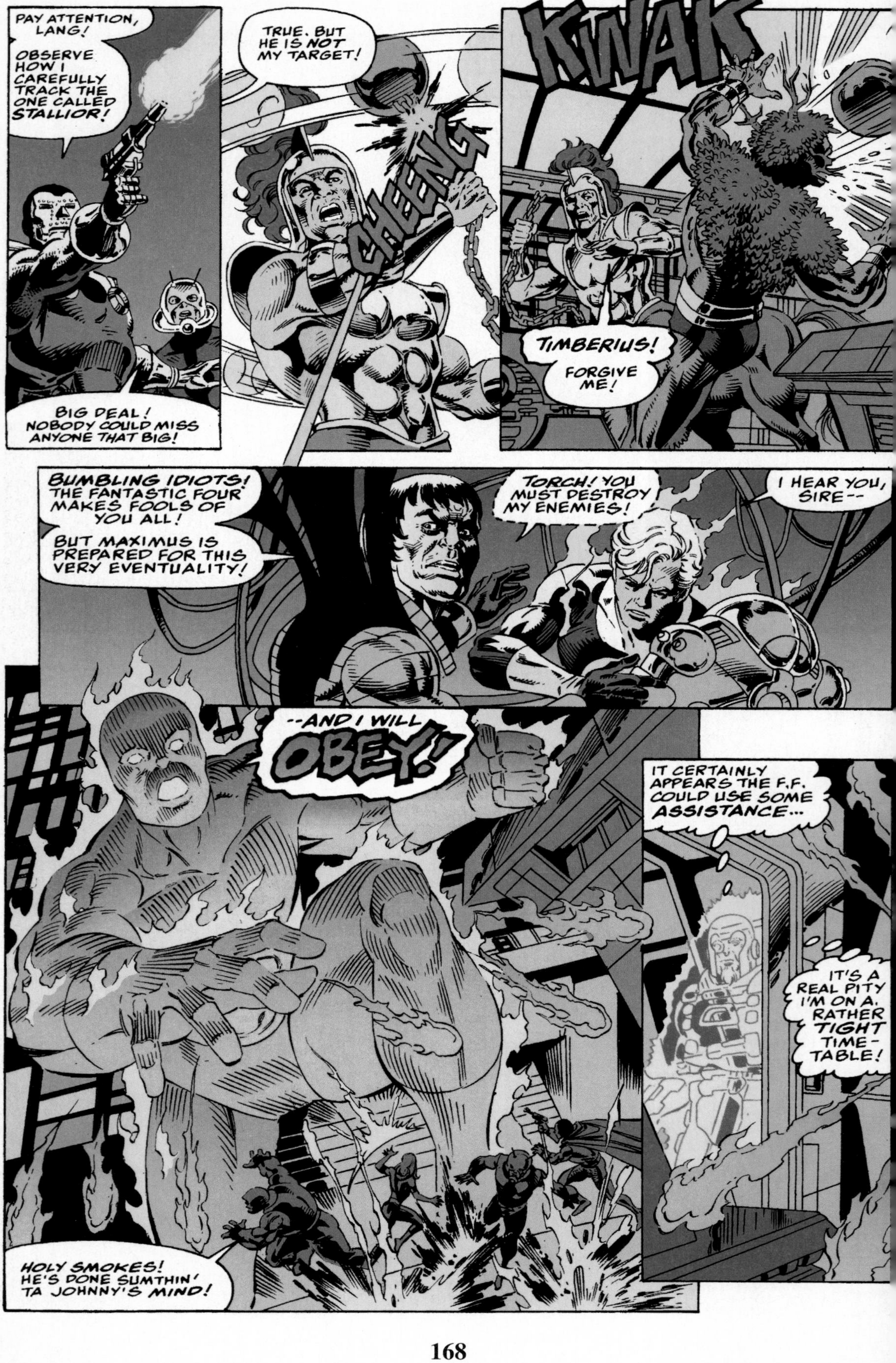
PAY ATTENTION, LANG!
OBSERVE HOW I CAREFULLY TRACK THE ONE CALLED STALLIOR!
BIG DEAL! NOBODY COULD MISS ANYONE THAT BIG!
TRUE. BUT HE IS NOT MY TARGET!
CHEENG
KWAK
TIMBERIUS!
FORGIVE ME!
BUMBLING IDIOTS! THE FANTASTIC FOUR MAKES FOOLS OF YOU ALL!
BUT MAXIMUS IS PREPARED FOR THIS VERY EVENTUALITY!
TORCH! YOU MUST DESTROY MY ENEMIES!
I HEAR YOU, SIRE--
--AND I WILL OBEY!
HOLY SMOKES! HE'S DONE SUMTHIN' TA JOHNNY'S MIND!
IT CERTAINLY APPEARS THE F.F. COULD USE SOME ASSISTANCE...
IT'S A REAL PITY I'M ON A RATHER TIGHT TIME-TABLE!

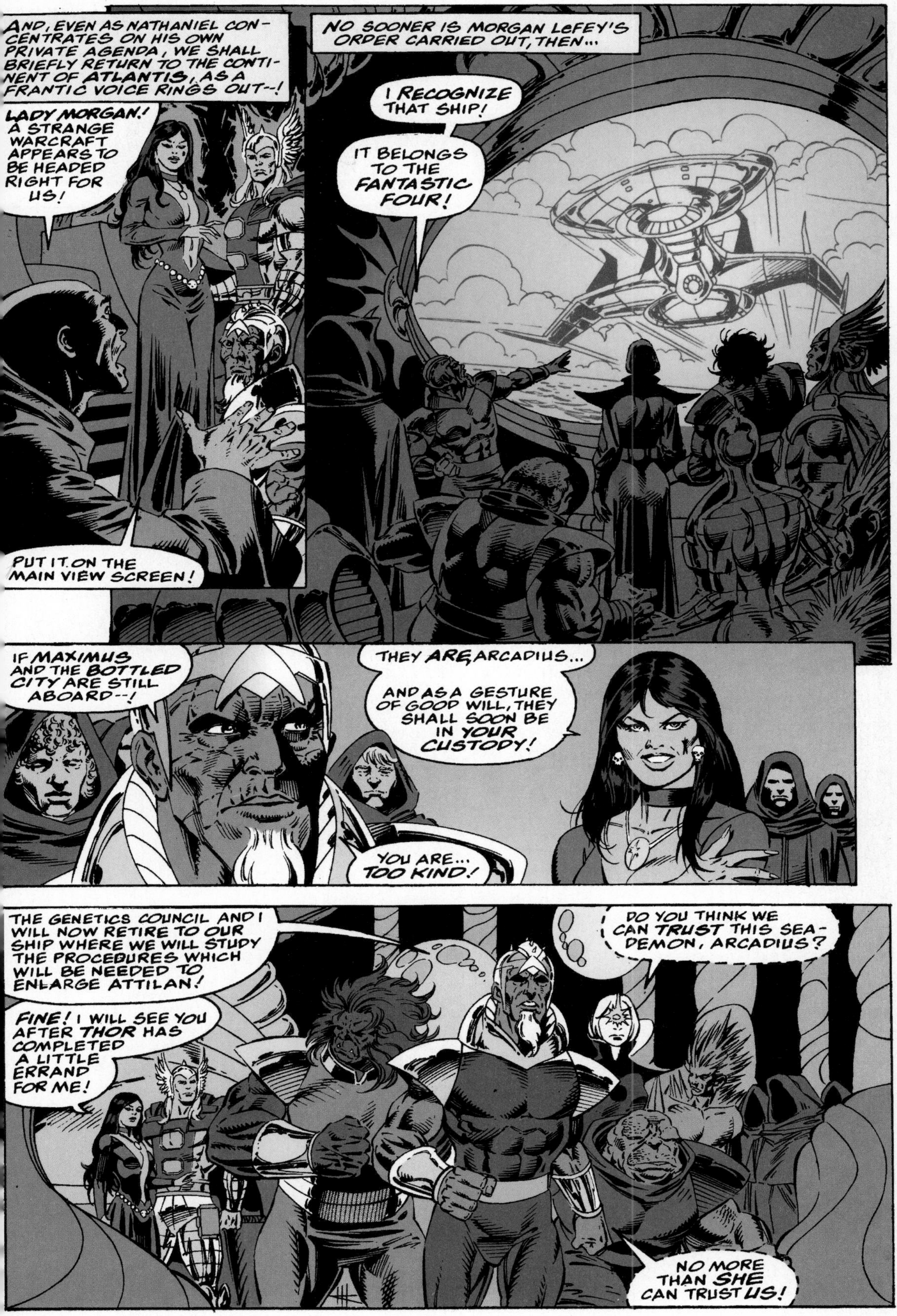
AND, EVEN AS NATHANIEL CONCENTRATES ON HIS OWN PRIVATE AGENDA, WE SHALL BRIEFLY RETURN TO THE CONTINENT OF ATLANTIS, AS A FRANTIC VOICE RINGS OUT--!
LADY MORGAN! A STRANGE WARCRAFT APPEARS TO BE HEADED RIGHT FOR US!
PUT IT ON THE MAIN VIEW SCREEN!
NO SOONER IS MORGAN LeFEY'S ORDER CARRIED OUT, THEN...
I RECOGNIZE THAT SHIP!
IT BELONGS TO THE FANTASTIC FOUR!
IF MAXIMUS AND THE BOTTLED CITY ARE STILL ABOARD--!
THEY ARE, ARCADIUS...
AND AS A GESTURE OF GOOD WILL, THEY SHALL SOON BE IN YOUR CUSTODY!
YOU ARE... TOO KIND!
THE GENETICS COUNCIL AND I WILL NOW RETIRE TO OUR SHIP WHERE WE WILL STUDY THE PROCEDURES WHICH WILL BE NEEDED TO ENLARGE ATTILAN!
FINE! I WILL SEE YOU AFTER THOR HAS COMPLETED A LITTLE ERRAND FOR ME!
DO YOU THINK WE CAN TRUST THIS SEA-DEMON, ARCADIUS?
NO MORE THAN SHE CAN TRUST US!

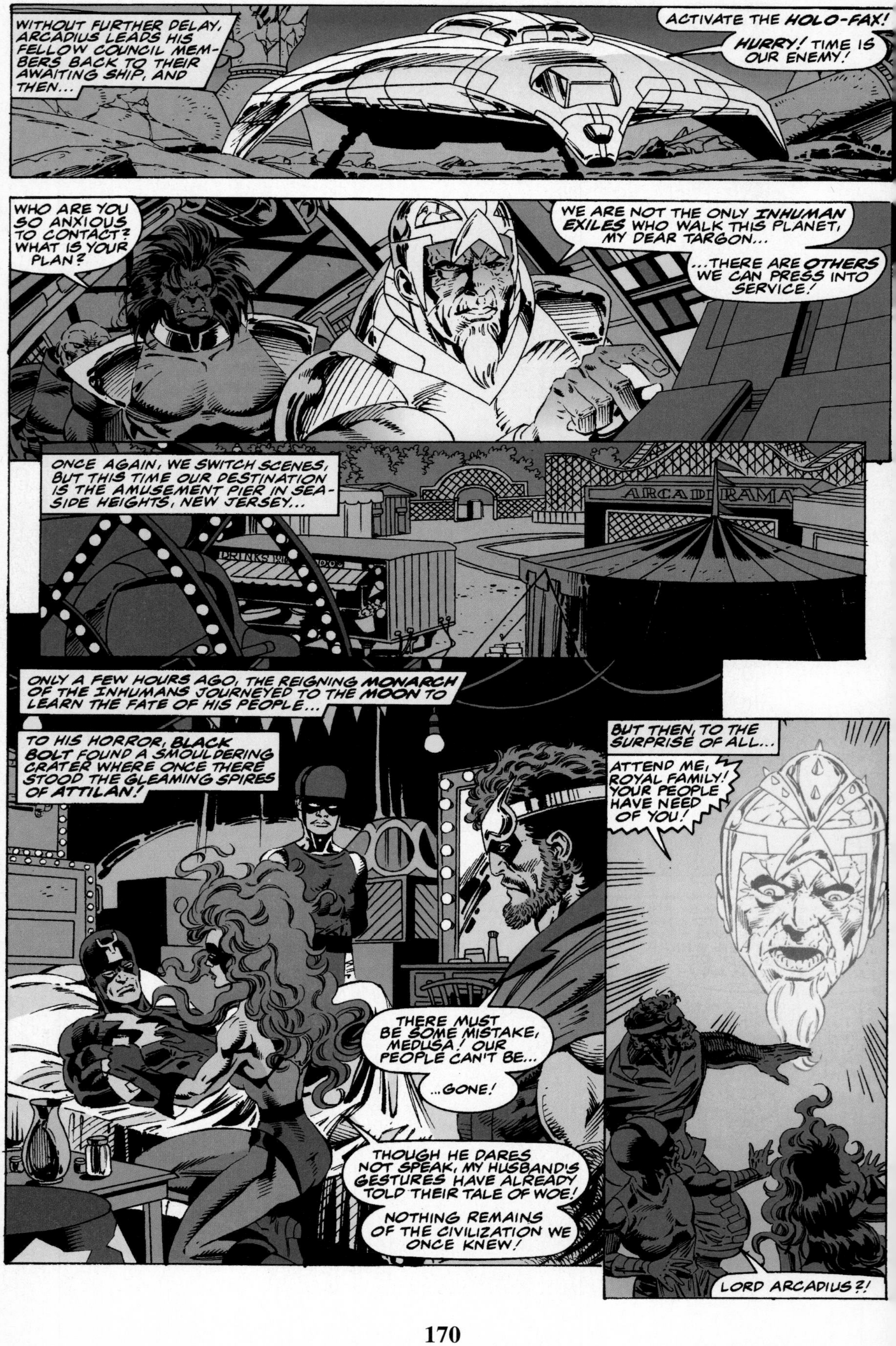

WITHOUT FURTHER DELAY, ARCADIUS LEADS HIS FELLOW COUNCIL MEMBERS BACK TO THEIR AWAITING SHIP, AND THEN...
ACTIVATE THE HOLO-FAX!
HURRY! TIME IS OUR ENEMY!
WHO ARE YOU SO ANXIOUS TO CONTACT? WHAT IS YOUR PLAN?
WE ARE NOT THE ONLY INHUMAN EXILES WHO WALK THIS PLANET, MY DEAR TARGON...
...THERE ARE OTHERS WE CAN PRESS INTO SERVICE!
ONCE AGAIN, WE SWITCH SCENES, BUT THIS TIME OUR DESTINATION IS THE AMUSEMENT PIER IN SEASIDE HEIGHTS, NEW JERSEY...
ARCADIRAMA
ONLY A FEW HOURS AGO, THE REIGNING MONARCH OF THE INHUMANS JOURNEYED TO THE MOON TO LEARN THE FATE OF HIS PEOPLE...
TO HIS HORROR, BLACK BOLT FOUND A SMOULDERING CRATER WHERE ONCE THERE STOOD THE GLEAMING SPIRES OF ATTILAN!
THERE MUST BE SOME MISTAKE, MEDUSA! OUR PEOPLE CAN'T BE...
...GONE!
THOUGH HE DARES NOT SPEAK, MY HUSBAND'S GESTURES HAVE ALREADY TOLD THEIR TALE OF WOE!
NOTHING REMAINS OF THE CIVILIZATION WE ONCE KNEW!
BUT THEN, TO THE SURPRISE OF ALL...
ATTEND ME, ROYAL FAMILY! YOUR PEOPLE HAVE NEED OF YOU!
LORD ARCADIUS?!

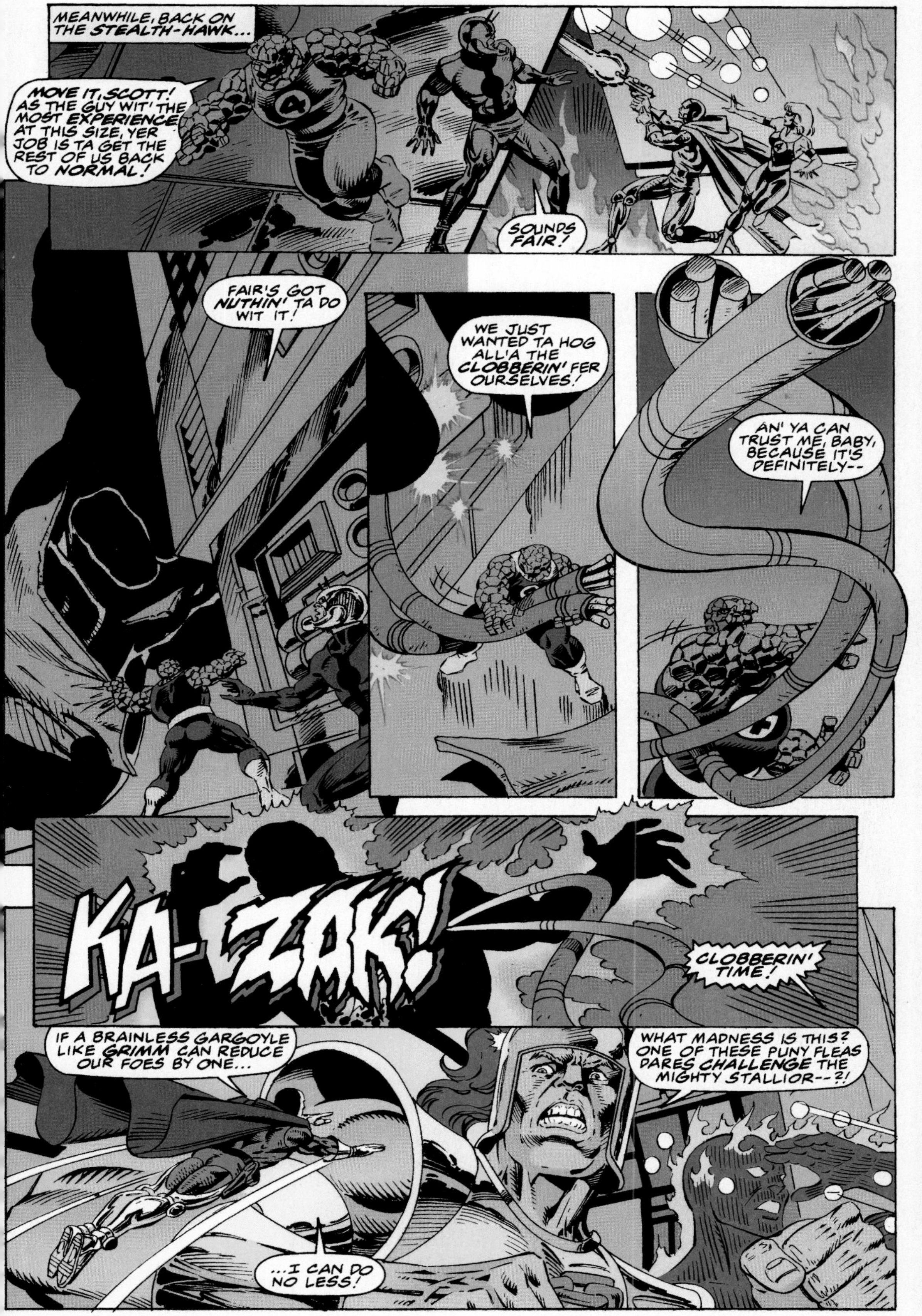
MEANWHILE, BACK ON THE STEALTH-HAWK...
MOVE IT, SCOTT! AS THE GUY WIT' THE MOST EXPERIENCE AT THIS SIZE, YER JOB IS TA GET THE REST OF US BACK TO NORMAL!
SOUNDS FAIR!
FAIR'S GOT NUTHIN' TA DO WIT IT!
WE JUST WANTED TA HOG ALL'A THE CLOBBERIN' FER OURSELVES!
AN' YA CAN TRUST ME, BABY, BECAUSE IT'S DEFINITELY--
KA-ZAK!
CLOBBERIN' TIME!
IF A BRAINLESS GARGOYLE LIKE GRIMM CAN REDUCE OUR FOES BY ONE...
...I CAN DO NO LESS!
WHAT MADNESS IS THIS? ONE OF THESE PUNY FLEAS DARES CHALLENGE THE MIGHTY STALLIOR--?!

DO NOT FLATTER YOURSELF, YOU BARBAROUS BUFFOON!

I AM THE ADOPTED SON OF DOCTOR DOOM!

I POSSESS HIS MEMORIES, HIS PEERLESS GENIUS AND HIS UNEQUALLED MASTERY OF PHYSICAL COMBAT!

I STRIKE FOR HIS HONOR! HIS GLORY!

ZAKAKK

WHILE THE FIGHT RIVETS EVERYONE'S ATTENTION...

ALL THE SECRETS AND HIDDEN SCIENCES OF THE INHUMANS ARE MINE FOR THE TAKING!

I HAVE ONLY TO GRASP YONDER BOTTLE WHEN I RETURN TO LATVERIA!

BUT, EVEN AS THE ELDEST RICHARDS MAKES HIS MOVE...

THE BOTTLED CITY IS SLOWLY RISING IN THE AIR--?!

I'LL FORCE HER TO REVEAL HERSELF BY BLANKETING THE ENTIRE AREA WITH INTENSE HEAT WAVES!

TORCH! I SUSPECT YOUR SISTER IS EMPLOYING HER INVISIBILITY TO STEAL ATTILAN!

NO SWEAT, MAXI, MY MAN!

LOOK! THE OUTLINE OF A FIGURE IS ALREADY BEGINNING TO FORM--

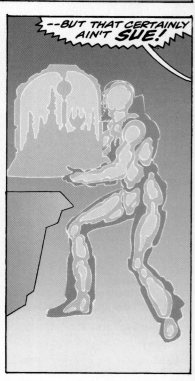

--BUT THAT CERTAINLY AIN'T SUE!

YOU MUSTN'T INTERFERE, JOHNNY! KEEP BACK! I WARN YOU!

NATHAN! I'D RECOGNIZE YOUR SLIMY, TWO-TIMING VOICE ANYWHERE!

HANG ON, OLD MAN! YOU'RE GOING NOWHERE WITHOUT ME!

BOTH ATTILAN AND THE TORCH... GONE! WHISKED AWAY BY SOME UNSEEN FOE!

LEONUS! BEHIND YOU--!

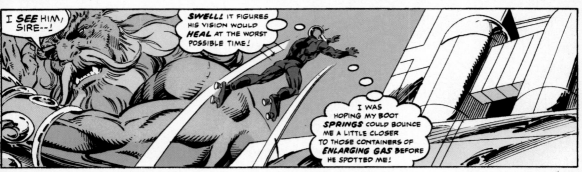

I SEE HIM, SIRE--!

SWELL! IT FIGURES HIS VISION WOULD HEAL AT THE WORST POSSIBLE TIME!

I WAS HOPING MY BOOT SPRINGS COULD BOUNCE ME A LITTLE CLOSER TO THOSE CONTAINERS OF ENLARGING GAS BEFORE HE SPOTTED ME!

YOU AND YOUR COMRADES HUMILIATED ME BEFORE MY LORD AND MASTER--

--AND I WILL HAVE VENGEANCE!

SO NEAR... BUT I WON'T MAKE IT WITHOUT A LITTLE LUCK!

BUT, EVEN AS ANT-MAN SCRAMBLES FORWARD--

BZZAKK

--LUCK ARRIVES FROM AN UNEXPECTED QUARTER!

HIDDEN IN THE SHADOWS, A FLICKER OF A SMILE DARTS ACROSS THE LIPS OF THE MAN KNOWN SIMPLY AS BORIS...

LANG HAS REACHED THE GAS CANISTERS! HE IS ALREADY SIGNALING THE OTHERS--!

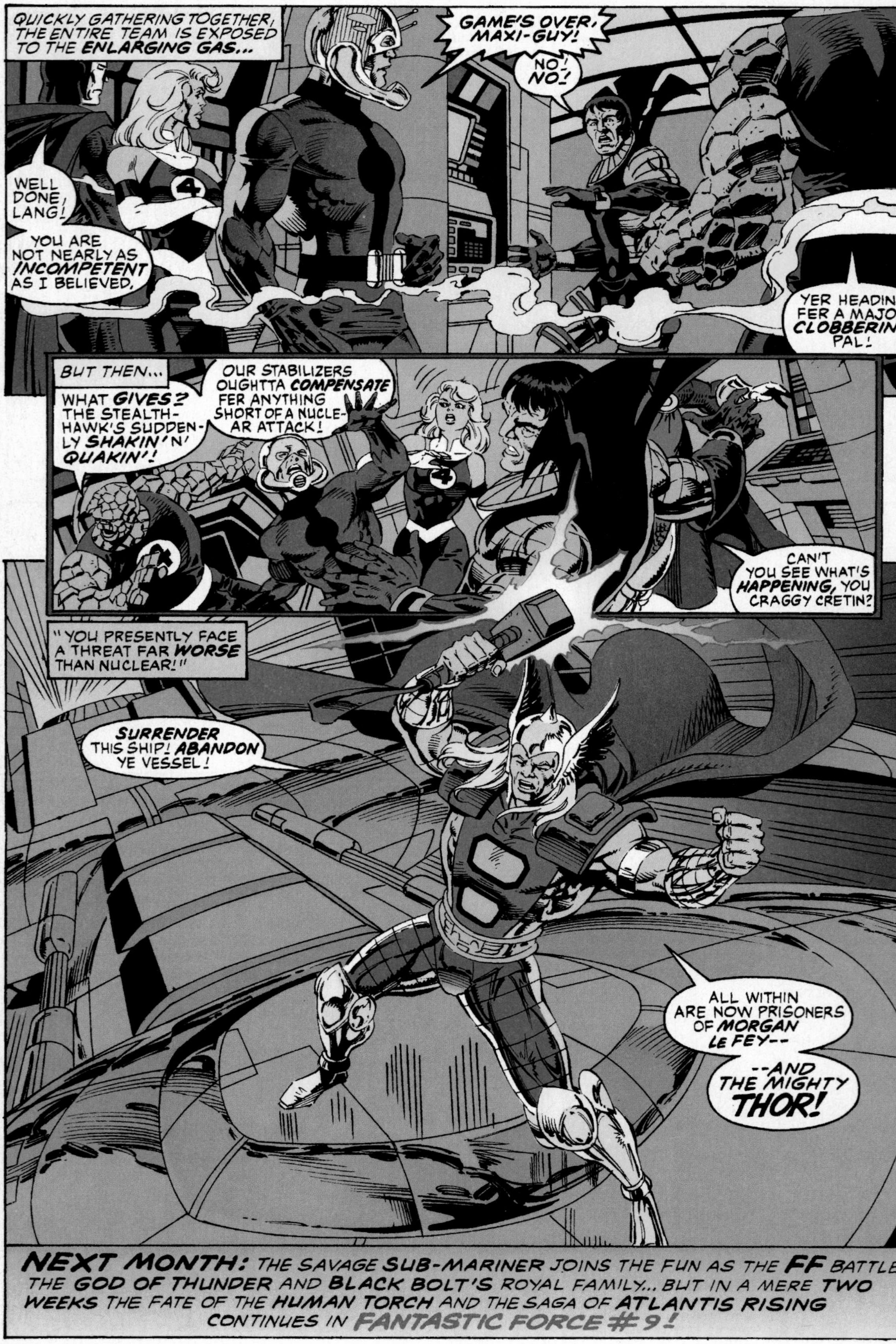
QUICKLY GATHERING TOGETHER, THE ENTIRE TEAM IS EXPOSED TO THE ENLARGING GAS...
GAME'S OVER, MAXI-GUY!
NO! NO!
WELL DONE, LANG!
YOU ARE NOT NEARLY AS INCOMPETENT AS I BELIEVED.
YER HEADIN' FER A MAJOR CLOBBERIN', PAL!
BUT THEN...
WHAT GIVES? THE STEALTH-HAWK'S SUDDEN-LY SHAKIN' N' QUAKIN'!
OUR STABILIZERS OUGHTTA COMPENSATE FER ANYTHING SHORT OF A NUCLE-AR ATTACK!
CAN'T YOU SEE WHAT'S HAPPENING, YOU CRAGGY CRETIN?
"YOU PRESENTLY FACE A THREAT FAR WORSE THAN NUCLEAR!"
SURRENDER THIS SHIP! ABANDON YE VESSEL!
ALL WITHIN ARE NOW PRISONERS OF MORGAN LE FEY--
--AND THE MIGHTY THOR!
NEXT MONTH: THE SAVAGE SUB-MARINER JOINS THE FUN AS THE FF BATTLE THE GOD OF THUNDER AND BLACK BOLT'S ROYAL FAMILY... BUT IN A MERE TWO WEEKS THE FATE OF THE HUMAN TORCH AND THE SAGA OF ATLANTIS RISING CONTINUES IN FANTASTIC FORCE #9!

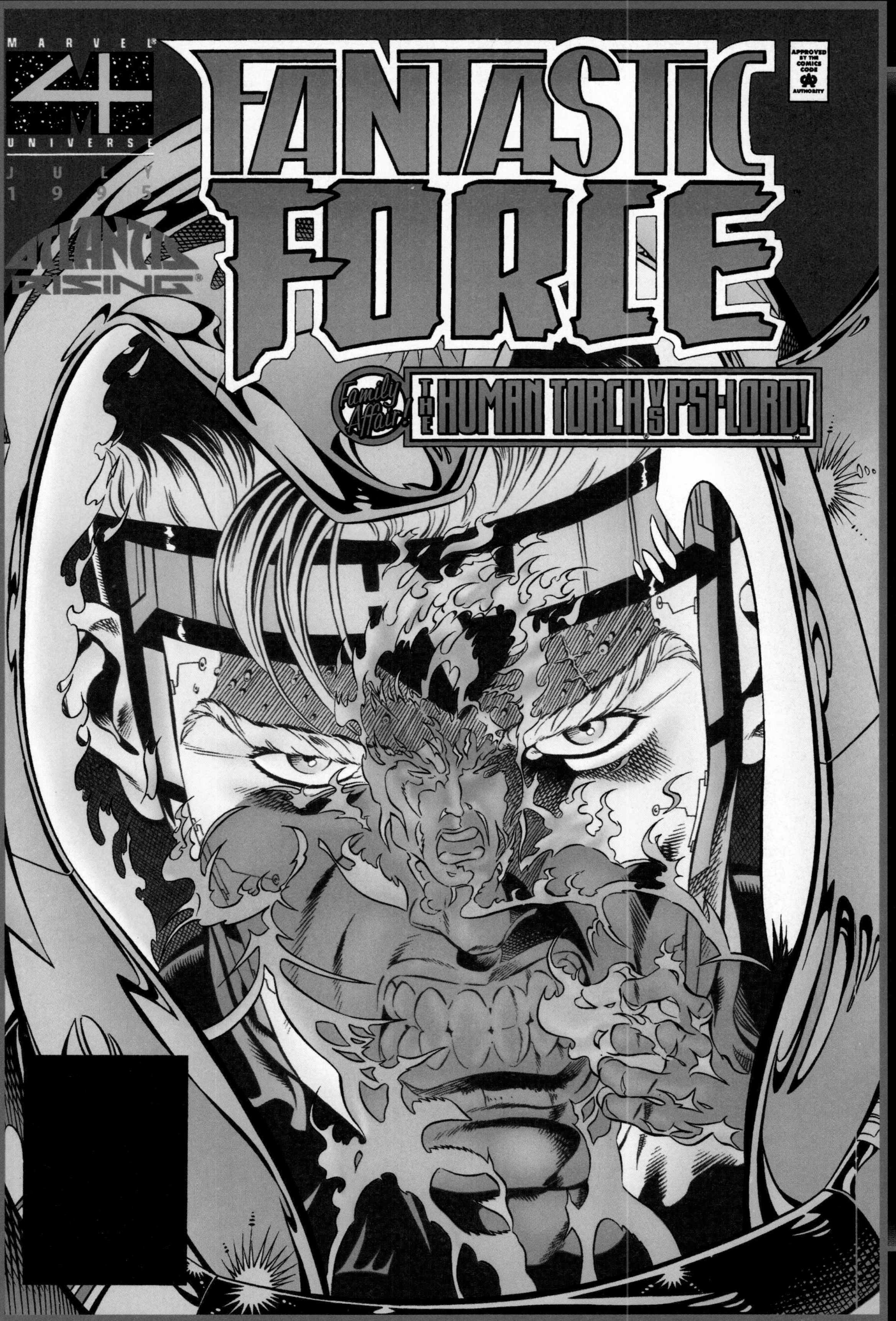
MARVEL
4
UNIVERSE
JULY
1995
APPROVED BY THE COMICS CODE AUTHORITY
FANTASTIC FORCE
ATLANTIS RISING
Family Affair!
THE HUMAN TORCH VS PSI-LORD!

PSI-LORD PSIONIC SUPREME! HUNTARA — WARRIOR PRINCESS OF ELSEWHEN! VIBRAXAS — WAKANDAN MASTER OF VIBRATIONAL FORCE! DEVLOR — INHUMAN POWERHOUSE! YOUNG OUTCASTS TRYING TO DEFINE THEIR ROLE IN A STRANGE AND HOSTILE SOCIETY, WHILE LIVING UP TO THE LEGEND OF THE WORLD'S GREATEST FIGHTING TEAM! STAN LEE PRESENTS ...

FANTASTIC FORCE!

THE TORCH IS PASSED!

Tom Brevoort and Mike Kanterovich
WRITERS
Geoff Isherwood
GUEST PENCILER
Ralph Cabrera and Sam DeLaRosa
INKERS
John Workman
LETTERER
John Kalisz
COLORIST
Nel Yomtov
EDITOR
Mark Gruenwald
EDITOR IN CHIEF

"SOUTH CENTRAL TEXAS. FIFTEEN YEARS AGO.

"THE BETTER PART OF A LIFETIME.

"BUT I WON'T FORGET— COULD NEVER FORGET...

"...WHAT HAPPENED ON THAT FATEFUL NIGHT!"

LIZ'BETH?

WHERE'RE YOU GOIN'?

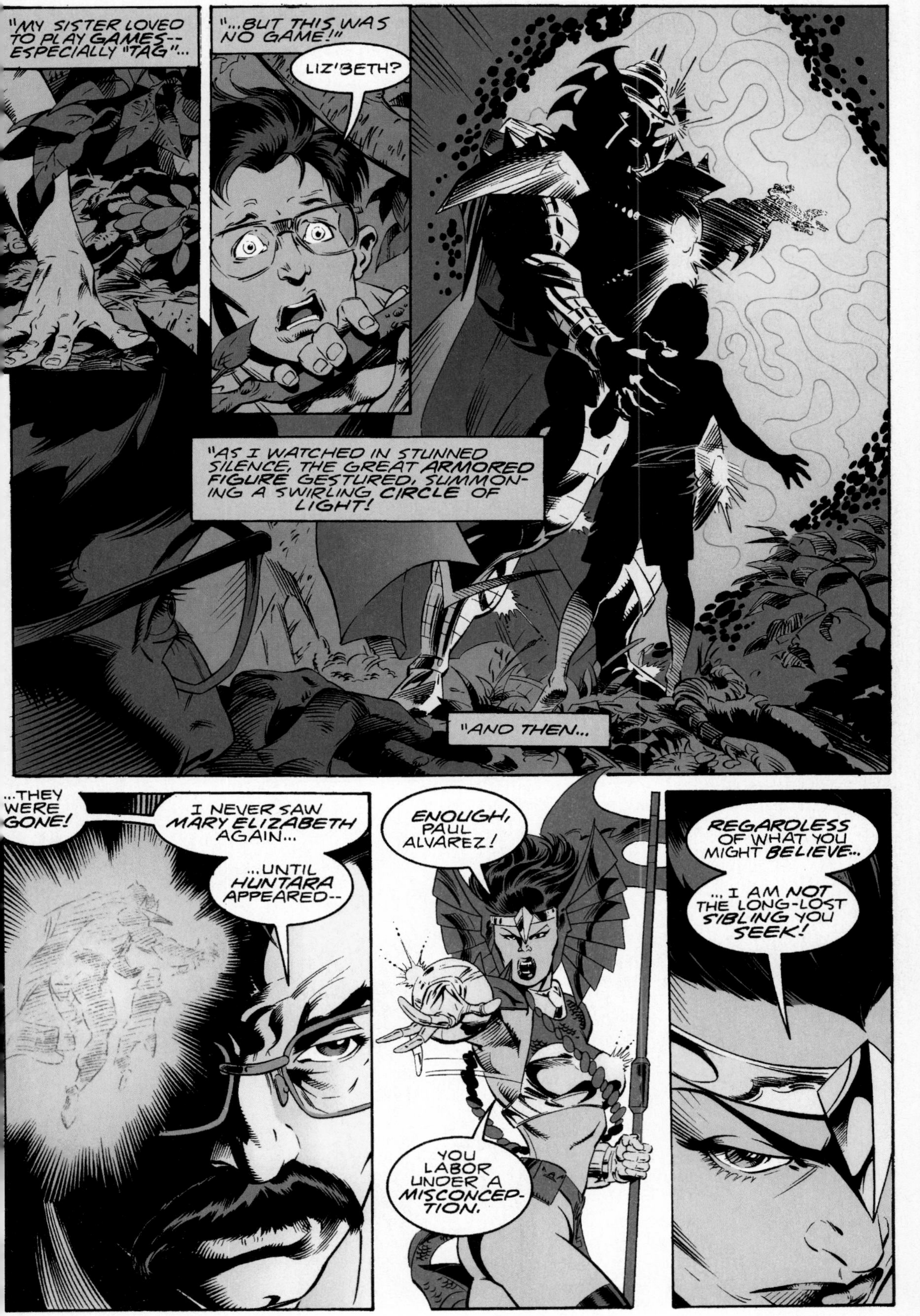
"MY SISTER LOVED TO PLAY GAMES--ESPECIALLY "TAG"...
"...BUT THIS WAS NO GAME!"
LIZ'BETH?
"AS I WATCHED IN STUNNED SILENCE, THE GREAT ARMORED FIGURE GESTURED, SUMMONING A SWIRLING CIRCLE OF LIGHT!
"AND THEN...
...THEY WERE GONE!
I NEVER SAW MARY ELIZABETH AGAIN...
...UNTIL HUNTARA APPEARED--
ENOUGH, PAUL ALVAREZ!
YOU LABOR UNDER A MISCONCEPTION.
REGARDLESS OF WHAT YOU MIGHT BELIEVE...
...I AM NOT THE LONG-LOST SIBLING YOU SEEK!

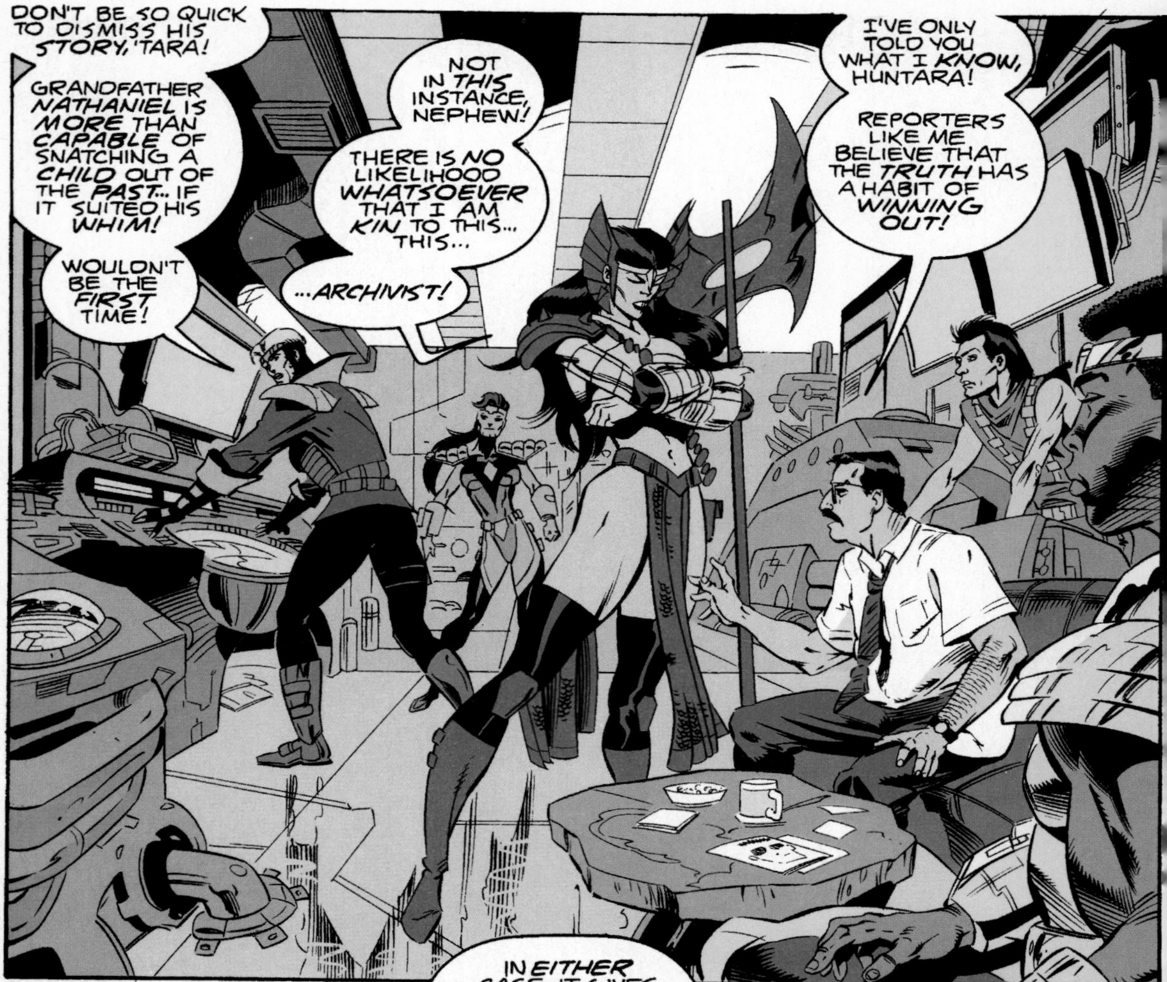
DON'T BE SO QUICK TO DISMISS HIS STORY, 'TARA!
GRANDFATHER NATHANIEL IS MORE THAN CAPABLE OF SNATCHING A CHILD OUT OF THE PAST... IF IT SUITED HIS WHIM!
WOULDN'T BE THE FIRST TIME!
NOT IN THIS INSTANCE, NEPHEW!
THERE IS NO LIKELIHOOD WHATSOEVER THAT I AM KIN TO THIS... THIS...
...ARCHIVIST!
I'VE ONLY TOLD YOU WHAT I KNOW, HUNTARA!
REPORTERS LIKE ME BELIEVE THAT THE TRUTH HAS A HABIT OF WINNING OUT!

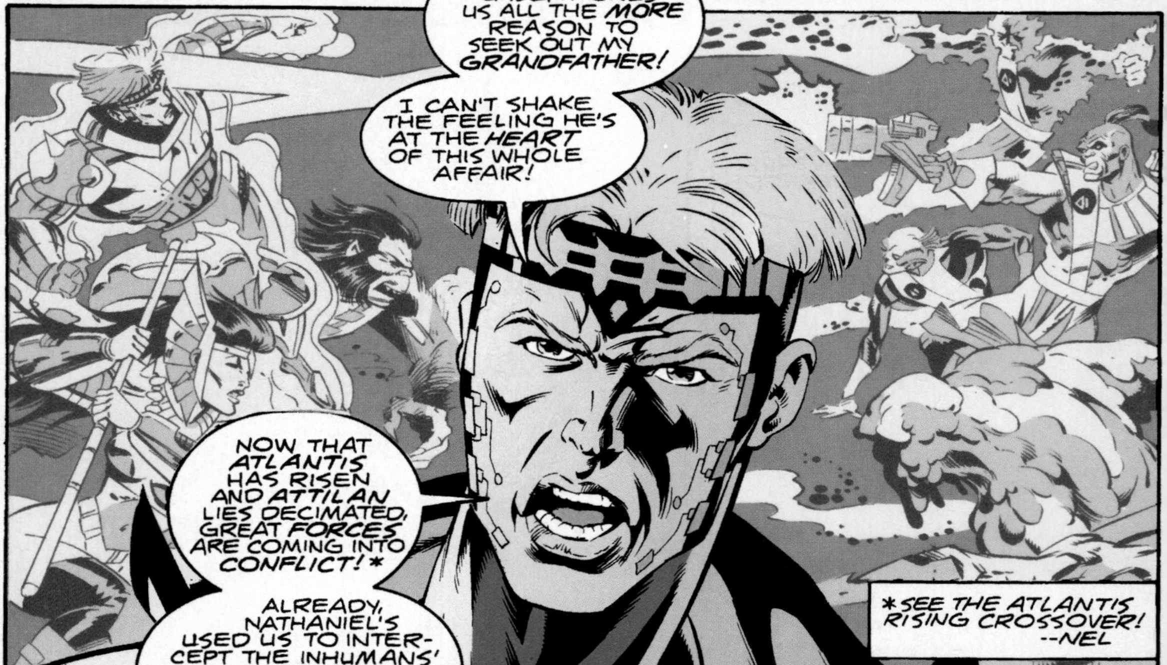
IN EITHER CASE, IT GIVES US ALL THE MORE REASON TO SEEK OUT MY GRANDFATHER!
I CAN'T SHAKE THE FEELING HE'S AT THE HEART OF THIS WHOLE AFFAIR!
NOW THAT ATLANTIS HAS RISEN AND ATTILAN LIES DECIMATED, GREAT FORCES ARE COMING INTO CONFLICT! *
ALREADY, NATHANIEL'S USED US TO INTERCEPT THE INHUMANS' ELITE CRIMSON CADRE AND DESTROY THEIR ATMO-GUN! **
* SEE THE ATLANTIS RISING CROSSOVER! --NEL
** LAST ISH. --NEL

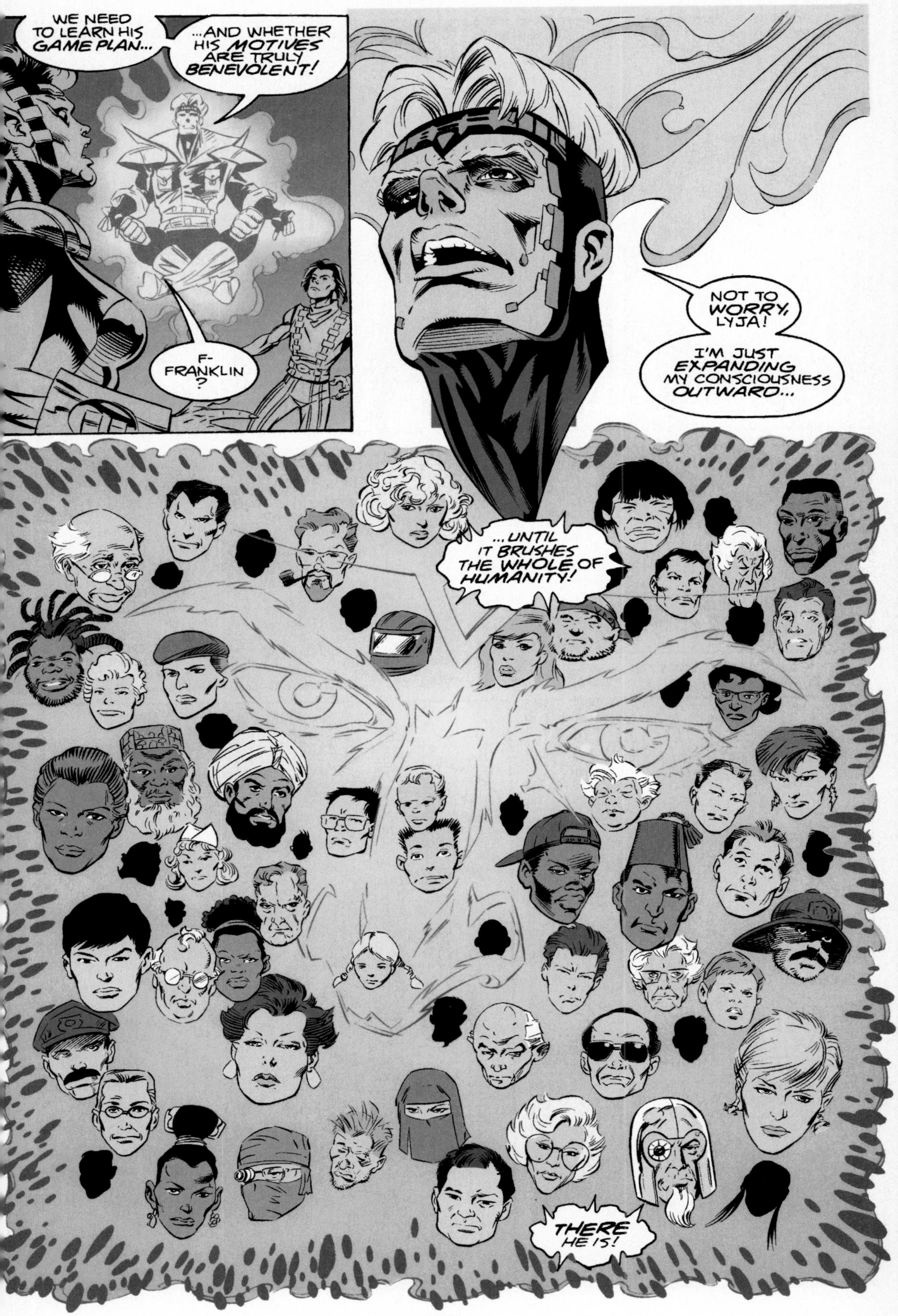

WE NEED TO LEARN HIS GAME PLAN...
...AND WHETHER HIS MOTIVES ARE TRULY BENEVOLENT!
F-FRANKLIN?
NOT TO WORRY, LYJA!
I'M JUST EXPANDING MY CONSCIOUSNESS OUTWARD...
...UNTIL IT BRUSHES THE WHOLE OF HUMANITY!
THERE HE IS!

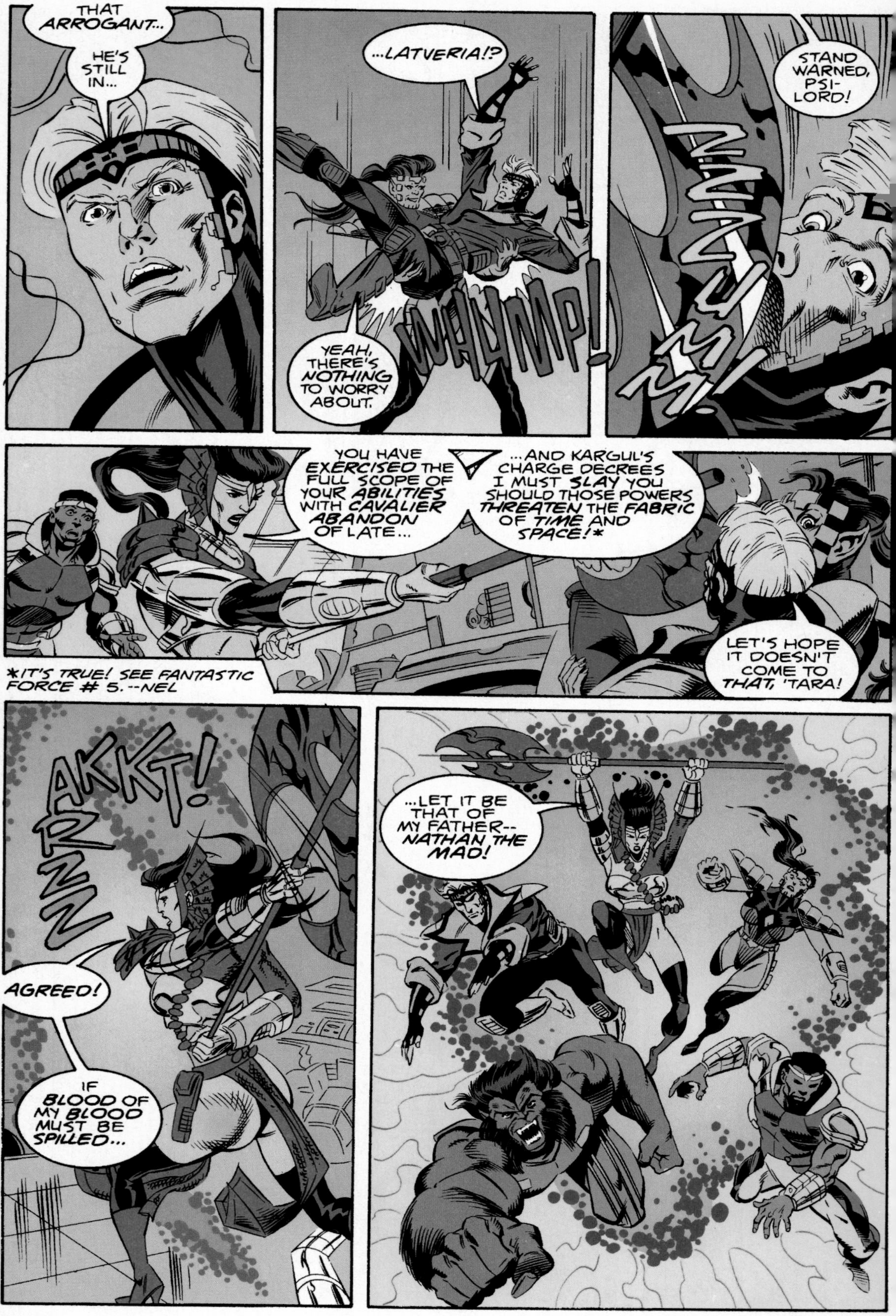
THAT ARROGANT...
HE'S STILL IN...
...LATVERIA!?
YEAH, THERE'S NOTHING TO WORRY ABOUT.
WHUMP!
STAND WARNED, PSI-LORD!
MMMM!
YOU HAVE EXERCISED THE FULL SCOPE OF YOUR ABILITIES WITH CAVALIER ABANDON OF LATE...
...AND KARGUL'S CHARGE DECREES I MUST SLAY YOU SHOULD THOSE POWERS THREATEN THE FABRIC OF TIME AND SPACE!*
LET'S HOPE IT DOESN'T COME TO THAT, 'TARA!
*IT'S TRUE! SEE FANTASTIC FORCE # 5.--NEL
AKKT!
RRZZ
AGREED!
IF BLOOD OF MY BLOOD MUST BE SPILLED...
...LET IT BE THAT OF MY FATHER-- NATHAN THE MAD!

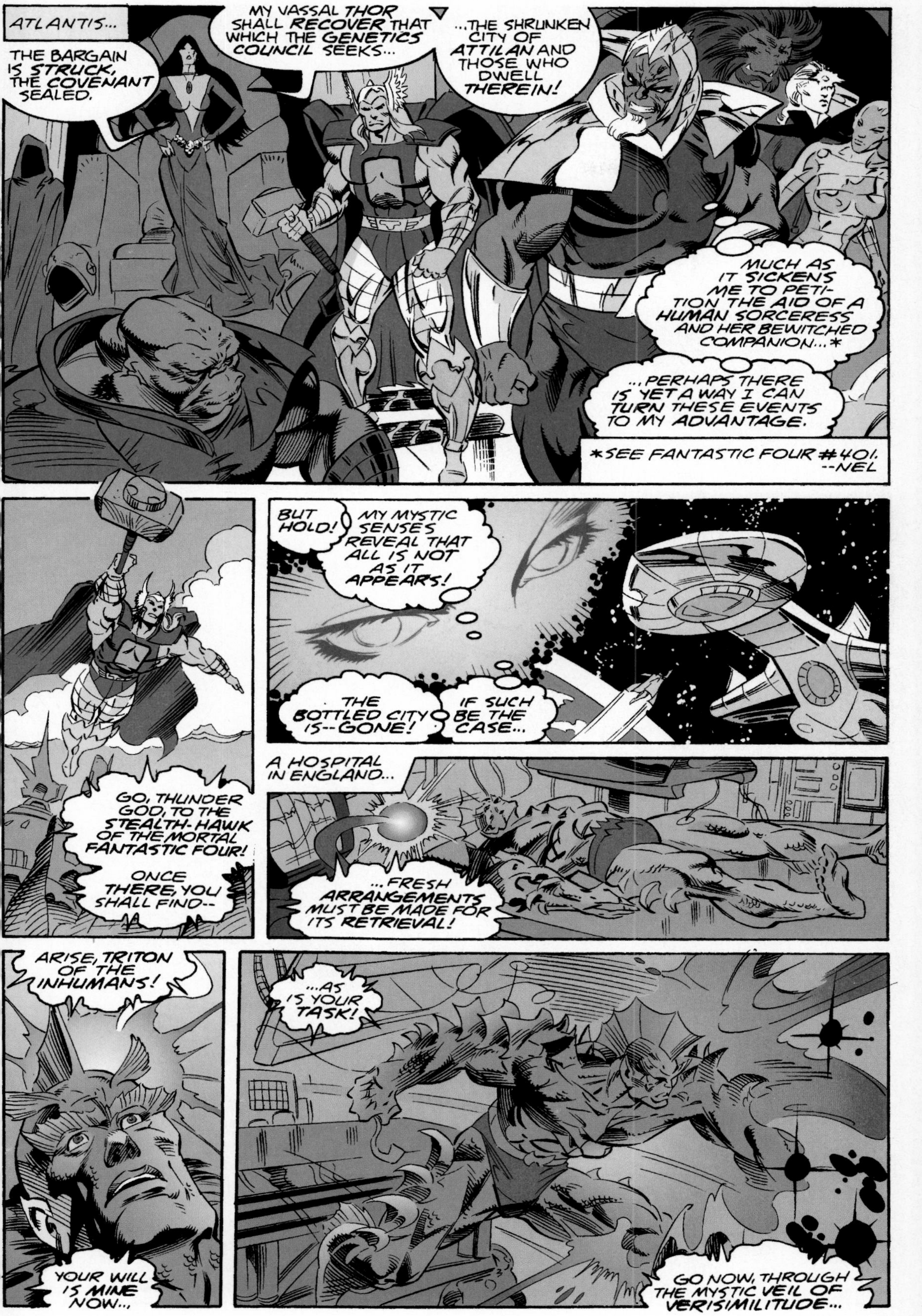

ATLANTIS...
THE BARGAIN IS STRUCK, THE COVENANT SEALED.
MY VASSAL THOR SHALL RECOVER THAT WHICH THE GENETICS COUNCIL SEEKS...
...THE SHRUNKEN CITY OF ATTILAN AND THOSE WHO DWELL THEREIN!
MUCH AS IT SICKENS ME TO PETITION THE AID OF A HUMAN SORCERESS AND HER BEWITCHED COMPANION...*
...PERHAPS THERE IS YET A WAY I CAN TURN THESE EVENTS TO MY ADVANTAGE.
*SEE FANTASTIC FOUR #401. --NEL
GO, THUNDER GOD, TO THE STEALTH-HAWK OF THE MORTAL FANTASTIC FOUR!
ONCE THERE, YOU SHALL FIND--
BUT HOLD!
MY MYSTIC SENSES REVEAL THAT ALL IS NOT AS IT APPEARS!
THE BOTTLED CITY IS--GONE!
IF SUCH BE THE CASE...
A HOSPITAL IN ENGLAND...
...FRESH ARRANGEMENTS MUST BE MADE FOR ITS RETRIEVAL!
ARISE, TRITON OF THE INHUMANS!
YOUR WILL IS MINE NOW...
...AS IS YOUR TASK!
GO NOW, THROUGH THE MYSTIC VEIL OF VERISIMILITUDE...

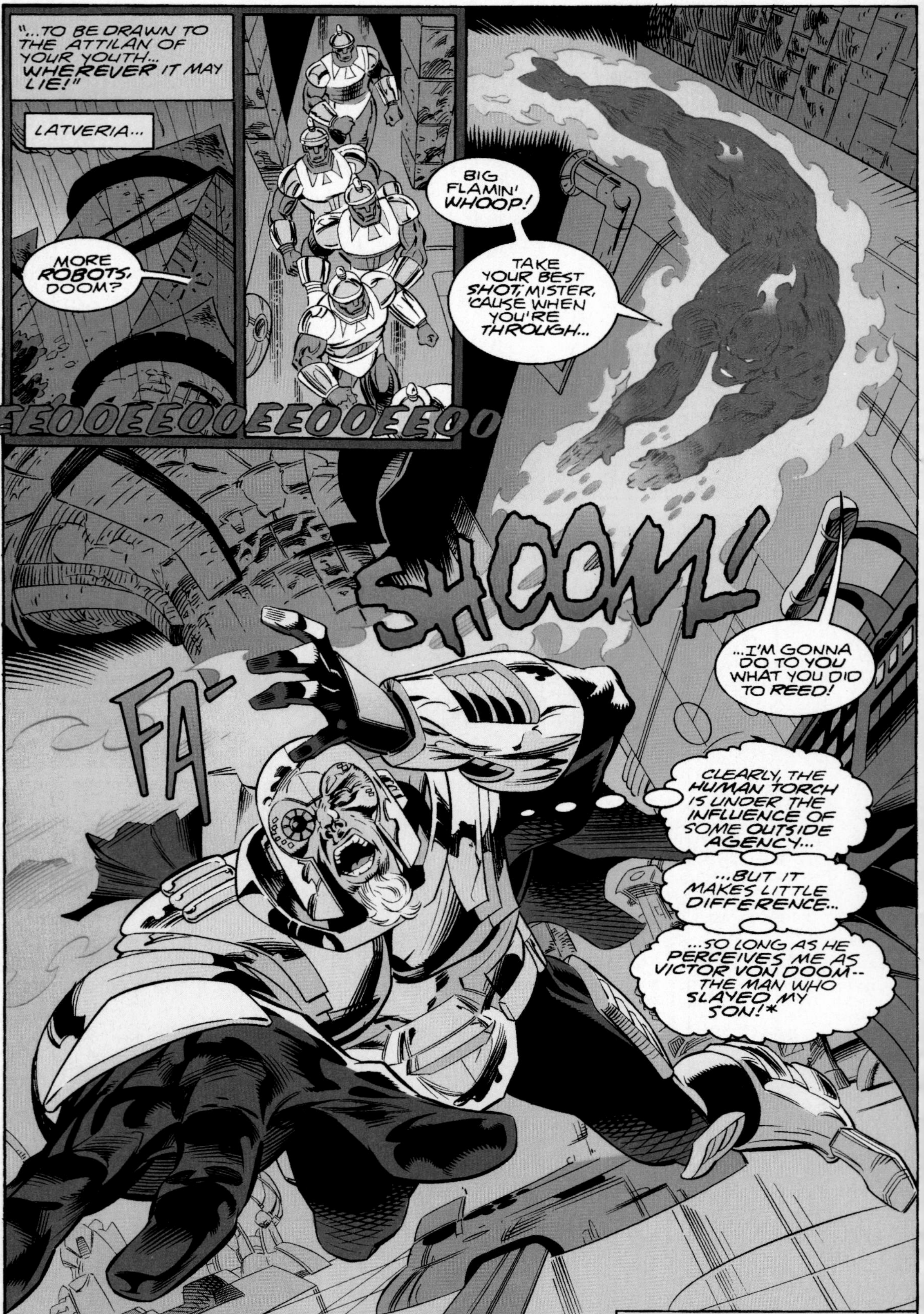
"...TO BE DRAWN TO THE ATTILAN OF YOUR YOUTH... WHEREVER IT MAY LIE!"
LATVERIA...
MORE ROBOTS, DOOM?
EEOOEEEOOEEEOOEEEOO
BIG FLAMIN' WHOOP!
TAKE YOUR BEST SHOT, MISTER, 'CAUSE WHEN YOU'RE THROUGH...
SHOOM!
FA-
...I'M GONNA DO TO YOU WHAT YOU DID TO REED!
CLEARLY, THE HUMAN TORCH IS UNDER THE INFLUENCE OF SOME OUTSIDE AGENCY...
...BUT IT MAKES LITTLE DIFFERENCE...
...SO LONG AS HE PERCEIVES ME AS VICTOR VON DOOM-- THE MAN WHO SLAYED MY SON!*
*FANTASTIC FOUR #381.--NEL

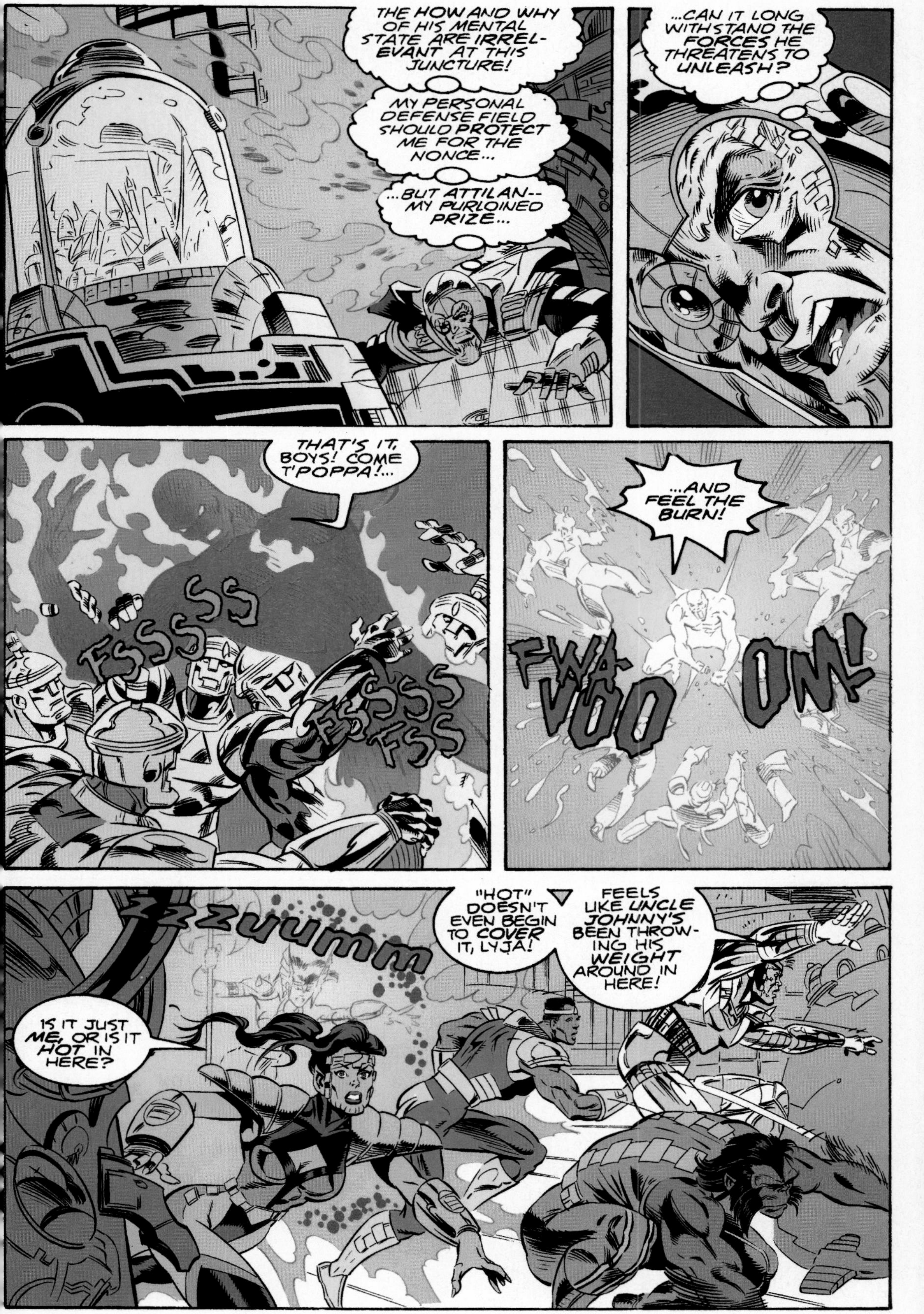
THE HOW AND WHY OF HIS MENTAL STATE ARE IRREL-EVANT AT THIS JUNCTURE!
MY PERSONAL DEFENSE FIELD SHOULD PROTECT ME FOR THE NONCE...
...BUT ATTILAN-- MY PURLOINED PRIZE...
...CAN IT LONG WITHSTAND THE FORCES HE THREATENS TO UNLEASH?
THAT'S IT, BOYS! COME T'POPPA!...
FSSSSS
FSSSSS
FSS
...AND FEEL THE BURN!
FWA VOOOM!
ZZZUUUMM
IS IT JUST ME, OR IS IT HOT IN HERE?
"HOT" DOESN'T EVEN BEGIN TO COVER IT, LYJA!
FEELS LIKE UNCLE JOHNNY'S BEEN THROW-ING HIS WEIGHT AROUND IN HERE!

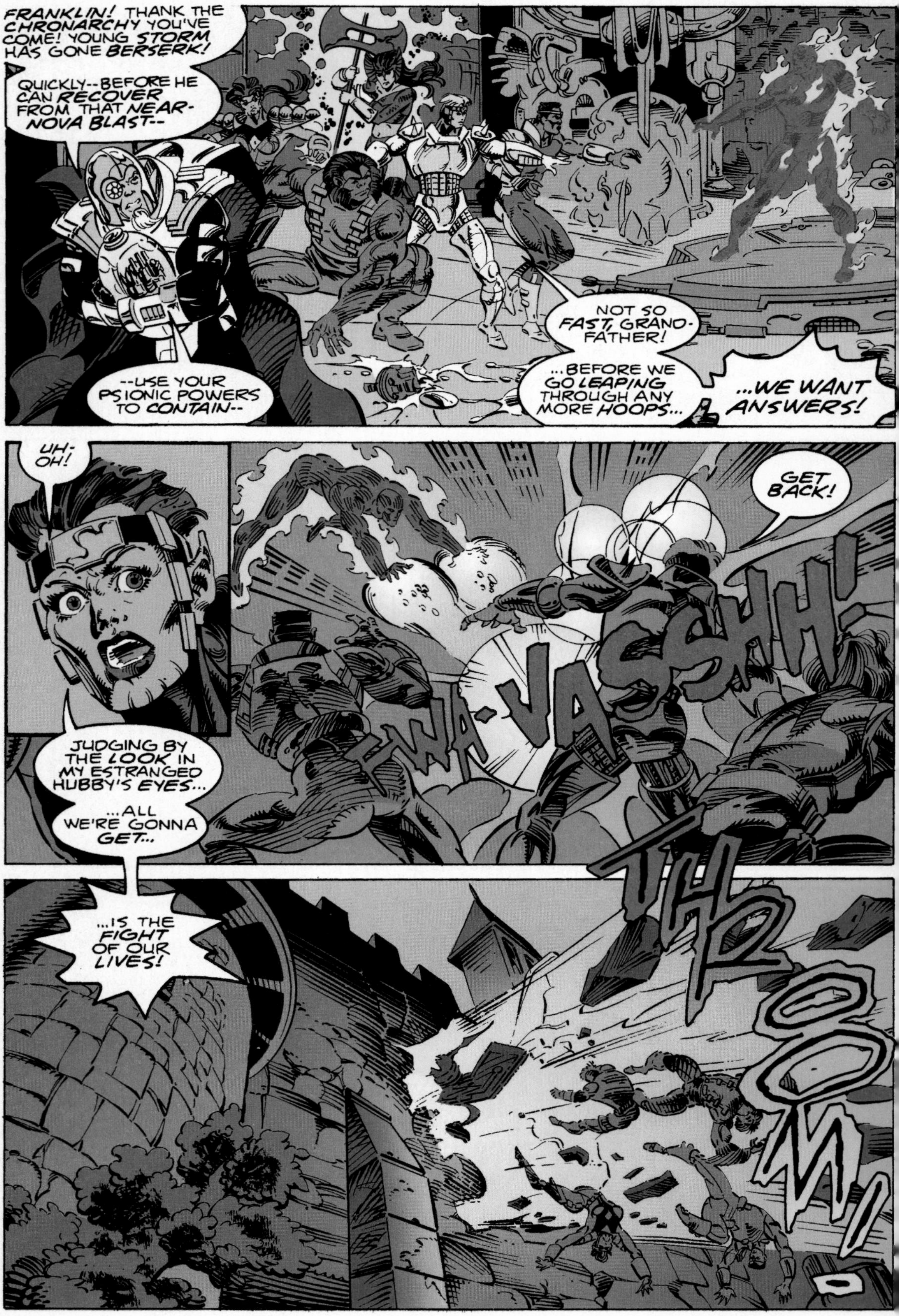

FRANKLIN! THANK THE CHRONARCHY YOU'VE COME! YOUNG STORM HAS GONE BERSERK!
QUICKLY--BEFORE HE CAN RECOVER FROM THAT NEAR-NOVA BLAST--
--USE YOUR PSIONIC POWERS TO CONTAIN--
NOT SO FAST, GRANDFATHER!
...BEFORE WE GO LEAPING THROUGH ANY MORE HOOPS...
...WE WANT ANSWERS!
UH-OH!
GET BACK!
FWA-VASSHH!
JUDGING BY THE LOOK IN MY ESTRANGED HUBBY'S EYES...
...ALL WE'RE GONNA GET...
...IS THE FIGHT OF OUR LIVES!
THROOM!

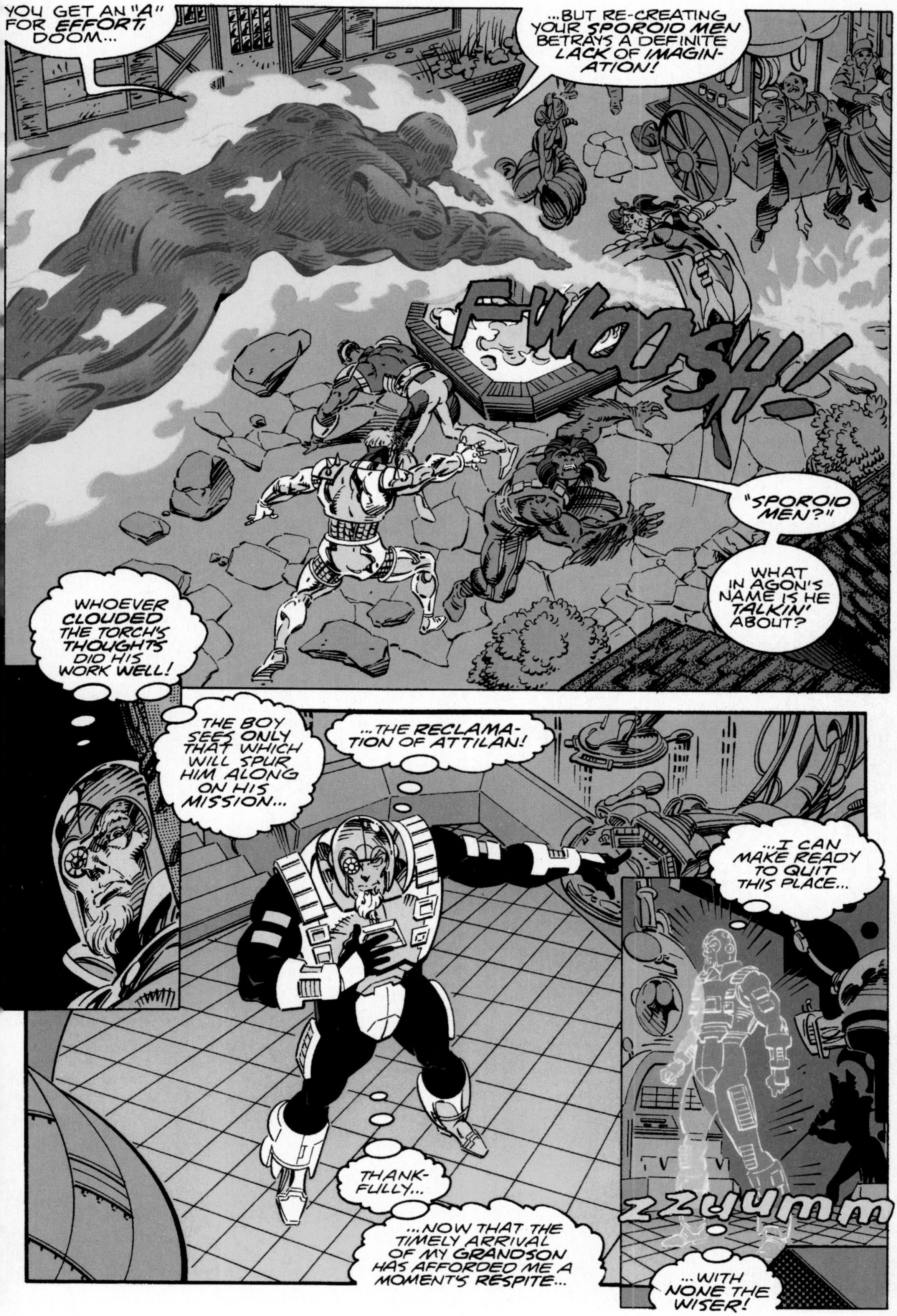
YOU GET AN "A" FOR EFFORT, DOOM...
...BUT RE-CREATING YOUR SPOROID MEN BETRAYS A DEFINITE LACK OF IMAGINATION!
F-WOOSH!
"SPOROID MEN?"
WHAT IN AGON'S NAME IS HE TALKIN' ABOUT?
WHOEVER CLOUDED THE TORCH'S THOUGHTS DID HIS WORK WELL!
THE BOY SEES ONLY THAT WHICH WILL SPUR HIM ALONG ON HIS MISSION...
...THE RECLAMATION OF ATTILAN!
THANKFULLY...
...NOW THAT THE TIMELY ARRIVAL OF MY GRANDSON HAS AFFORDED ME A MOMENT'S RESPITE...
...I CAN MAKE READY TO QUIT THIS PLACE...
ZZUUMM
...WITH NONE THE WISER!

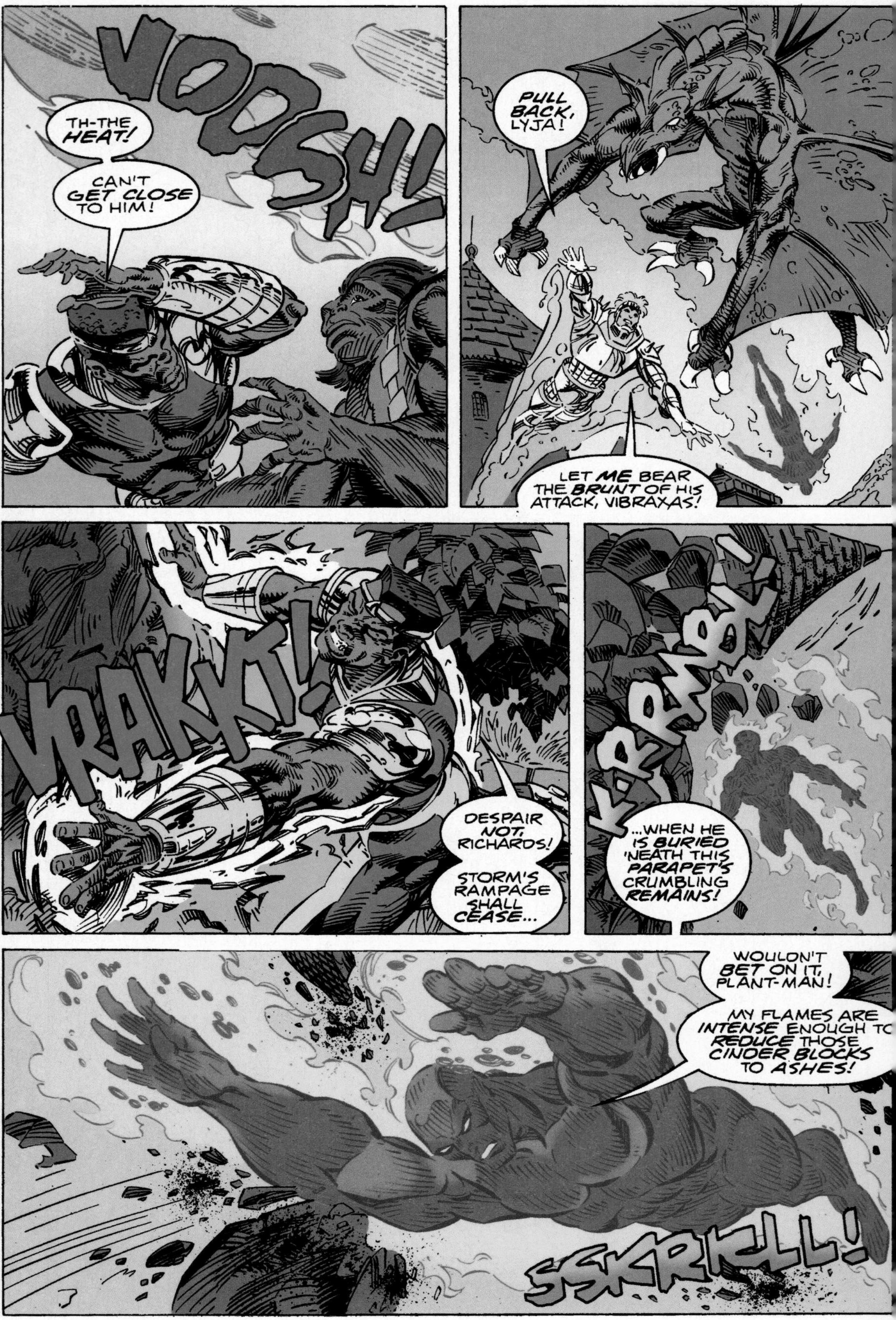
VOOSH!!
TH-THE HEAT!
CAN'T GET CLOSE TO HIM!
PULL BACK, LYJA!
LET ME BEAR THE BRUNT OF HIS ATTACK, VIBRAXAS!
VRAKKT!!
DESPAIR NOT, RICHARDS!
STORM'S RAMPAGE SHALL CEASE...
K-RRMBL!
...WHEN HE IS BURIED 'NEATH THIS PARAPET'S CRUMBLING REMAINS!
WOULDN'T BET ON IT, PLANT-MAN!
MY FLAMES ARE INTENSE ENOUGH TO REDUCE THOSE CINDER BLOCKS TO ASHES!
SSKRKLL!

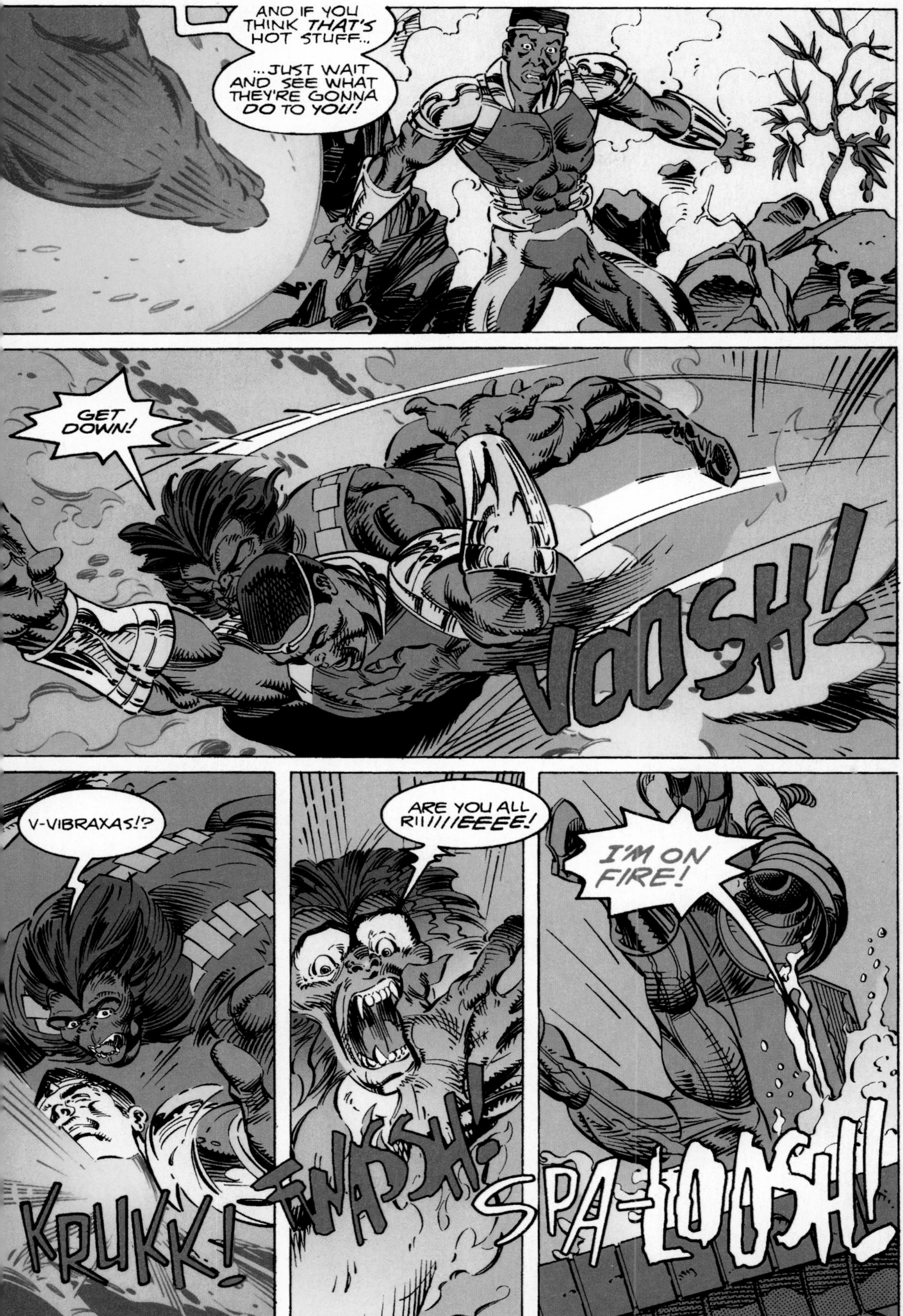
AND IF YOU THINK THAT'S HOT STUFF...
...JUST WAIT AND SEE WHAT THEY'RE GONNA DO TO YOU!
GET DOWN!
VOOSH!
V-VIBRAXAS!?
ARE YOU ALL RIIIIIIEEEEE!
I'M ON FIRE!
KRUKK!
FWASH!
SPA-LOOSH!

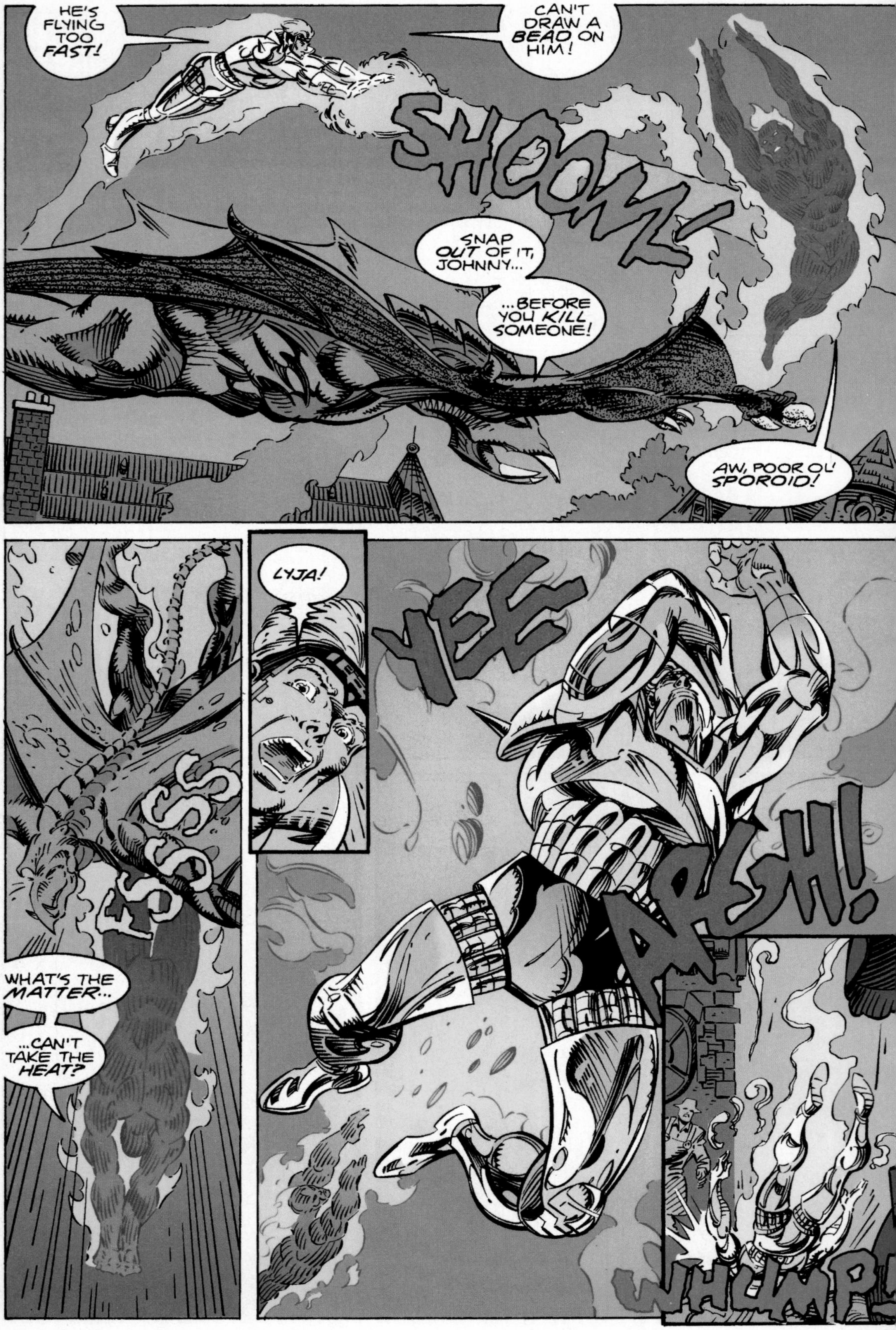
HE'S FLYING TOO FAST!
CAN'T DRAW A BEAD ON HIM!
SHOOM!
SNAP OUT OF IT, JOHNNY...
...BEFORE YOU KILL SOMEONE!
AW, POOR OL' SPOROID!
LYJA!
YEE ARGH!
WHAT'S THE MATTER...
...CAN'T TAKE THE HEAT?
WHUMP!

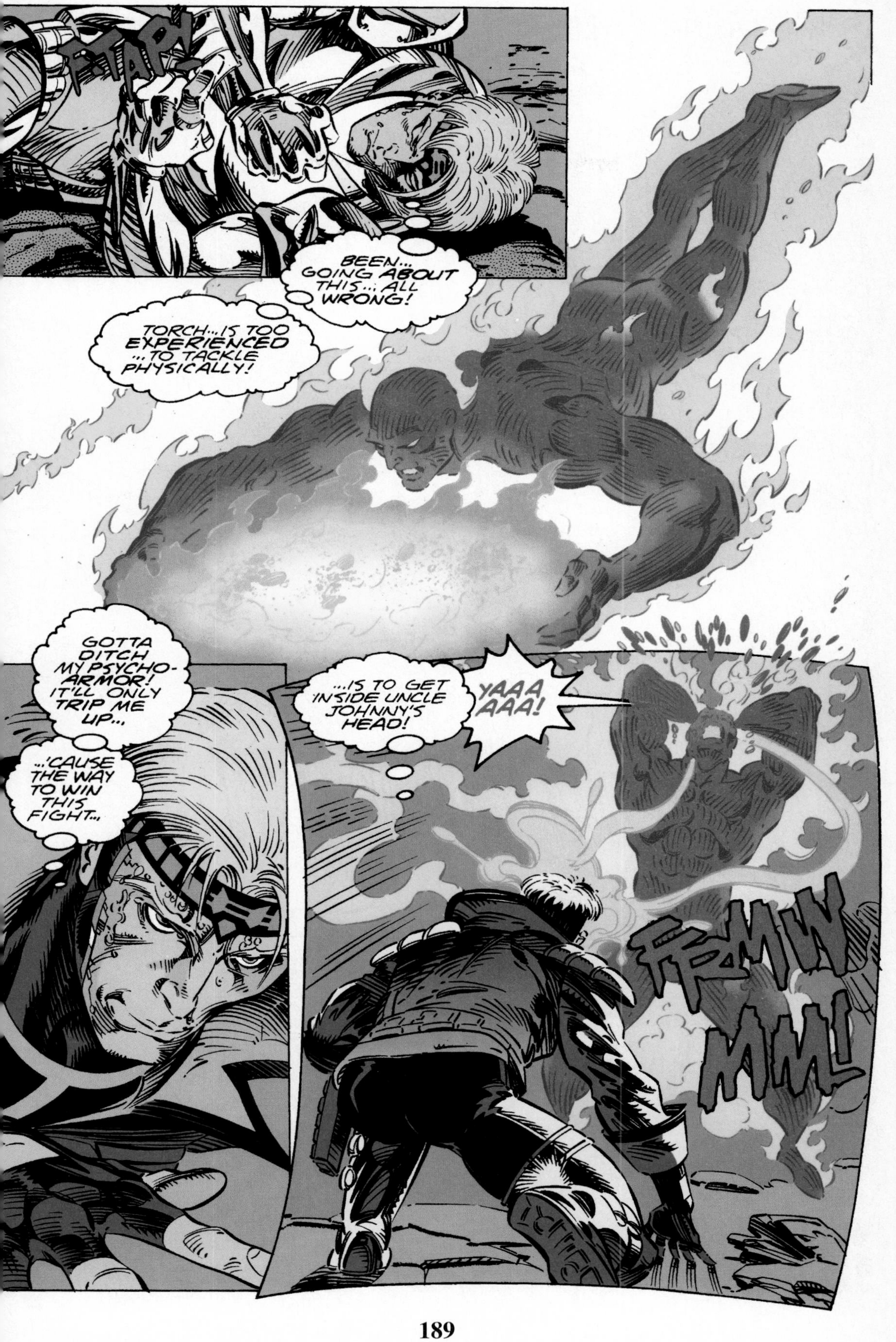
FTAP!
BEEN... GOING ABOUT THIS... ALL WRONG!
TORCH...IS TOO EXPERIENCED ...TO TACKLE PHYSICALLY!
GOTTA DITCH MY PSYCHO-ARMOR! IT'LL ONLY TRIP ME UP...
...'CAUSE THE WAY TO WIN THIS FIGHT...
...IS TO GET INSIDE UNCLE JOHNNY'S HEAD!
YAAAAAA!
FRMMMMM!

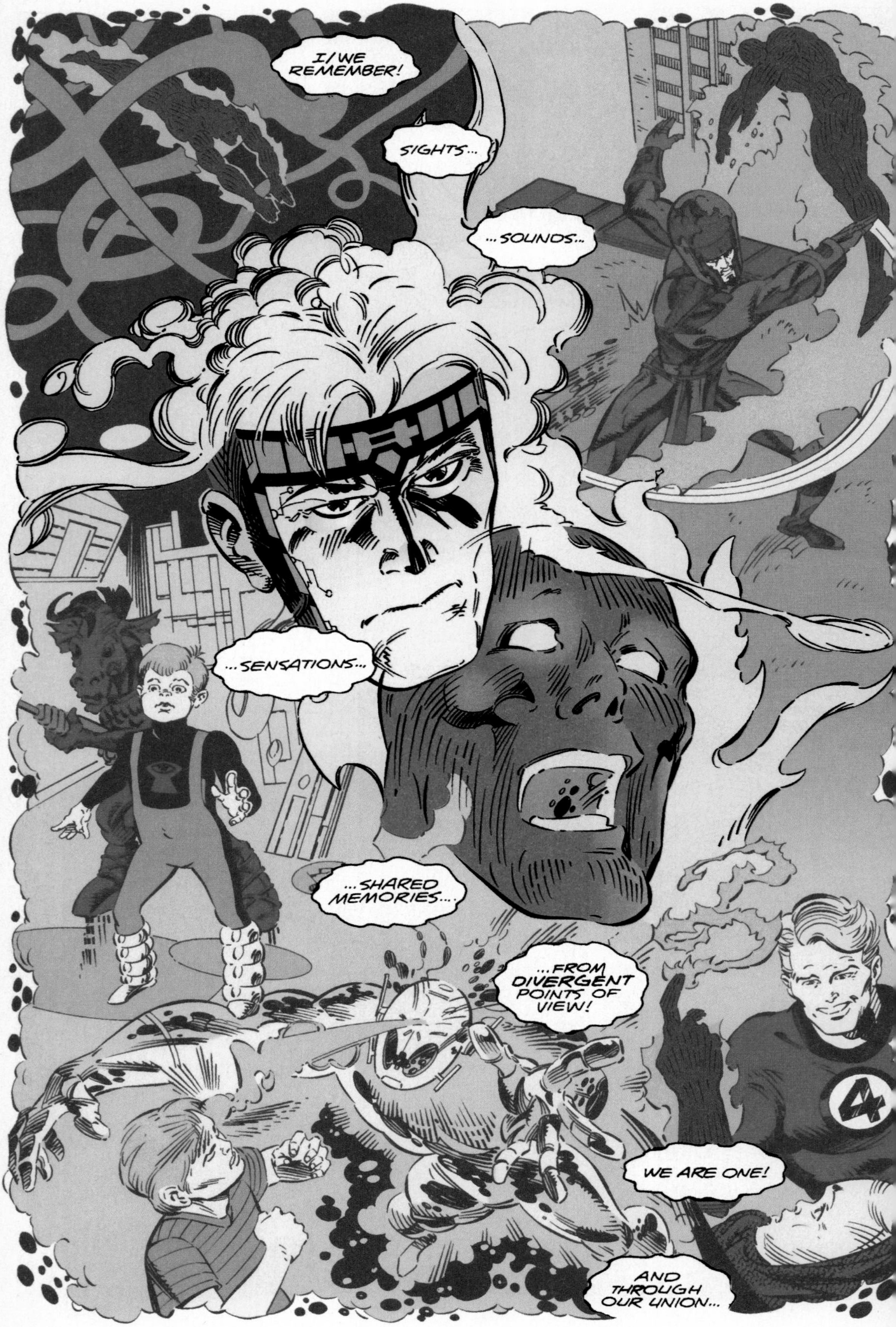
I/WE REMEMBER!
SIGHTS...
...SOUNDS...
...SENSATIONS...
...SHARED MEMORIES....
...FROM DIVERGENT POINTS OF VIEW!
WE ARE ONE!
AND THROUGH OUR UNION...

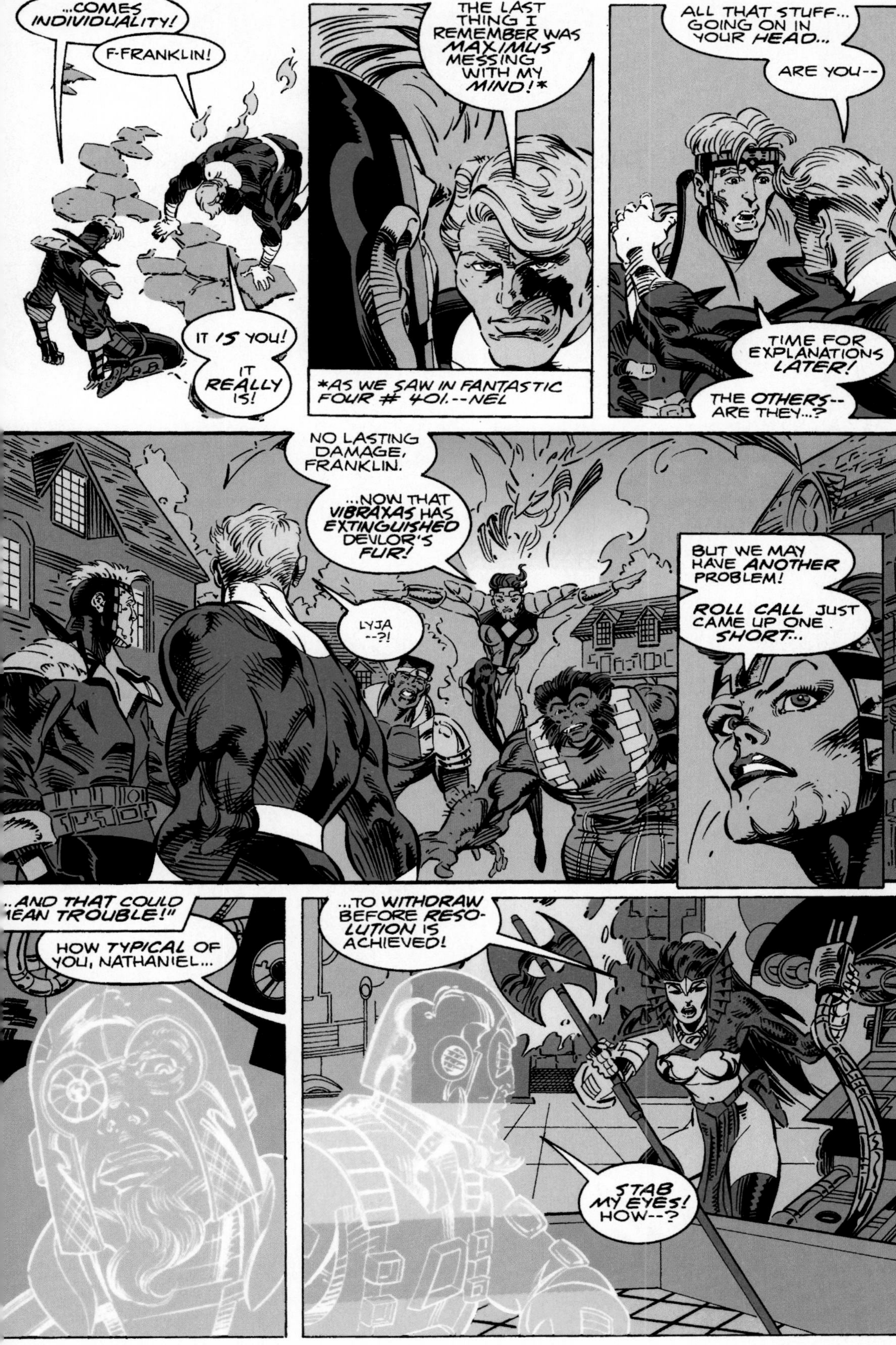
...COMES INDIVIDUALITY!
F-FRANKLIN!
IT IS YOU!
IT REALLY IS!
THE LAST THING I REMEMBER WAS MAXIMUS MESSING WITH MY MIND!*
*AS WE SAW IN FANTASTIC FOUR # 401.--NEL
ALL THAT STUFF... GOING ON IN YOUR HEAD...
ARE YOU--
TIME FOR EXPLANATIONS LATER!
THE OTHERS-- ARE THEY...?
NO LASTING DAMAGE, FRANKLIN.
...NOW THAT VIBRAXAS HAS EXTINGUISHED DEVLOR'S FUR!
LYJA --?!
BUT WE MAY HAVE ANOTHER PROBLEM!
ROLL CALL JUST CAME UP ONE SHORT...
"...AND THAT COULD MEAN TROUBLE!"
HOW TYPICAL OF YOU, NATHANIEL...
...TO WITHDRAW BEFORE RESOLUTION IS ACHIEVED!
STAB MY EYES! HOW--?

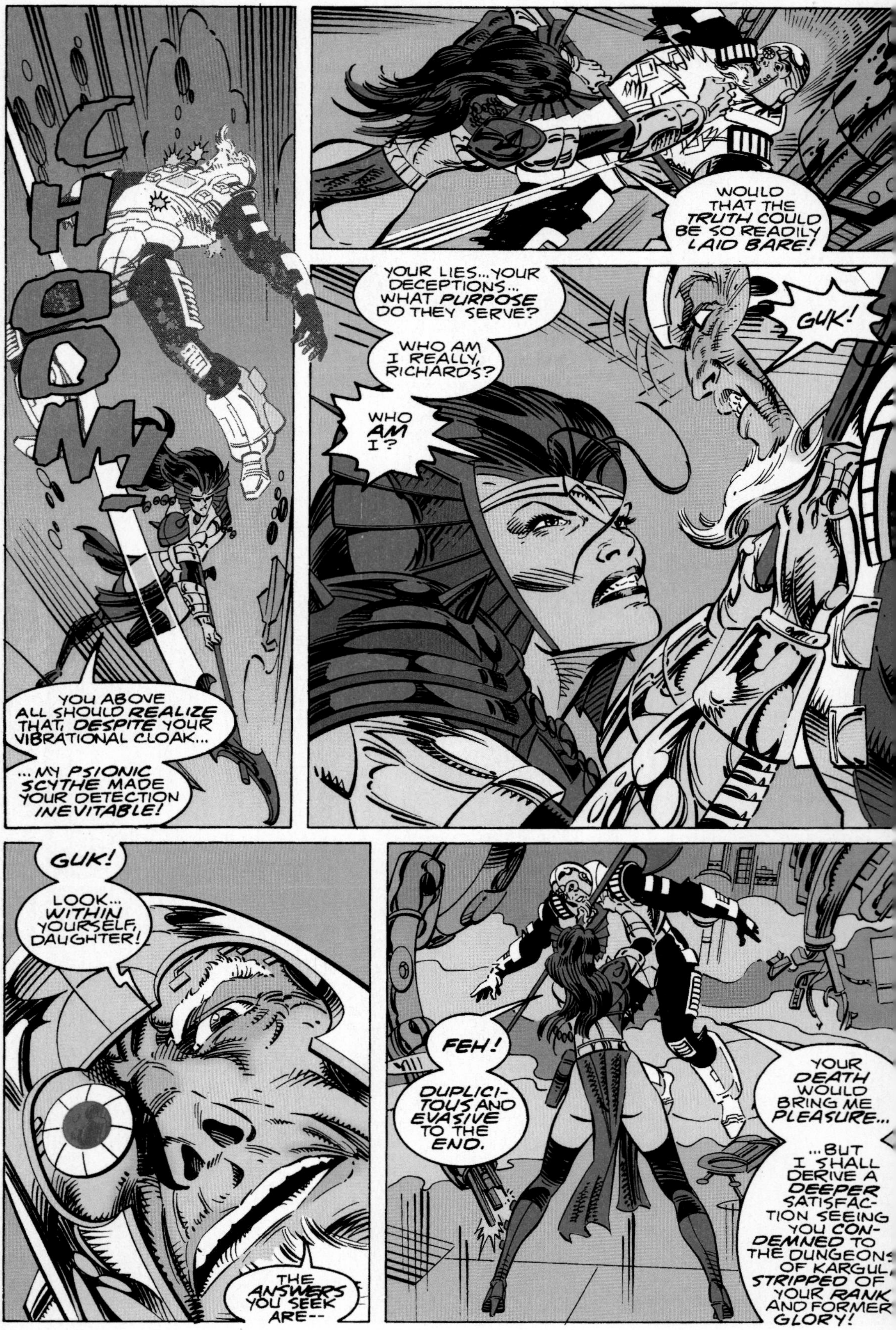
CHOOM
YOU ABOVE ALL SHOULD REALIZE THAT, DESPITE YOUR VIBRATIONAL CLOAK...
...MY PSIONIC SCYTHE MADE YOUR DETECTION INEVITABLE!
WOULD THAT THE TRUTH COULD BE SO READILY LAID BARE!
YOUR LIES... YOUR DECEPTIONS... WHAT PURPOSE DO THEY SERVE?
WHO AM I REALLY, RICHARDS?
WHO AM I?
GUK!
GUK!
LOOK... WITHIN YOURSELF, DAUGHTER!
THE ANSWERS YOU SEEK ARE--
FEH!
DUPLICITOUS AND EVASIVE TO THE END.
YOUR DEATH WOULD BRING ME PLEASURE...
...BUT I SHALL DERIVE A DEEPER SATISFACTION SEEING YOU CONDEMNED TO THE DUNGEONS OF KARGUL, STRIPPED OF YOUR RANK AND FORMER GLORY!

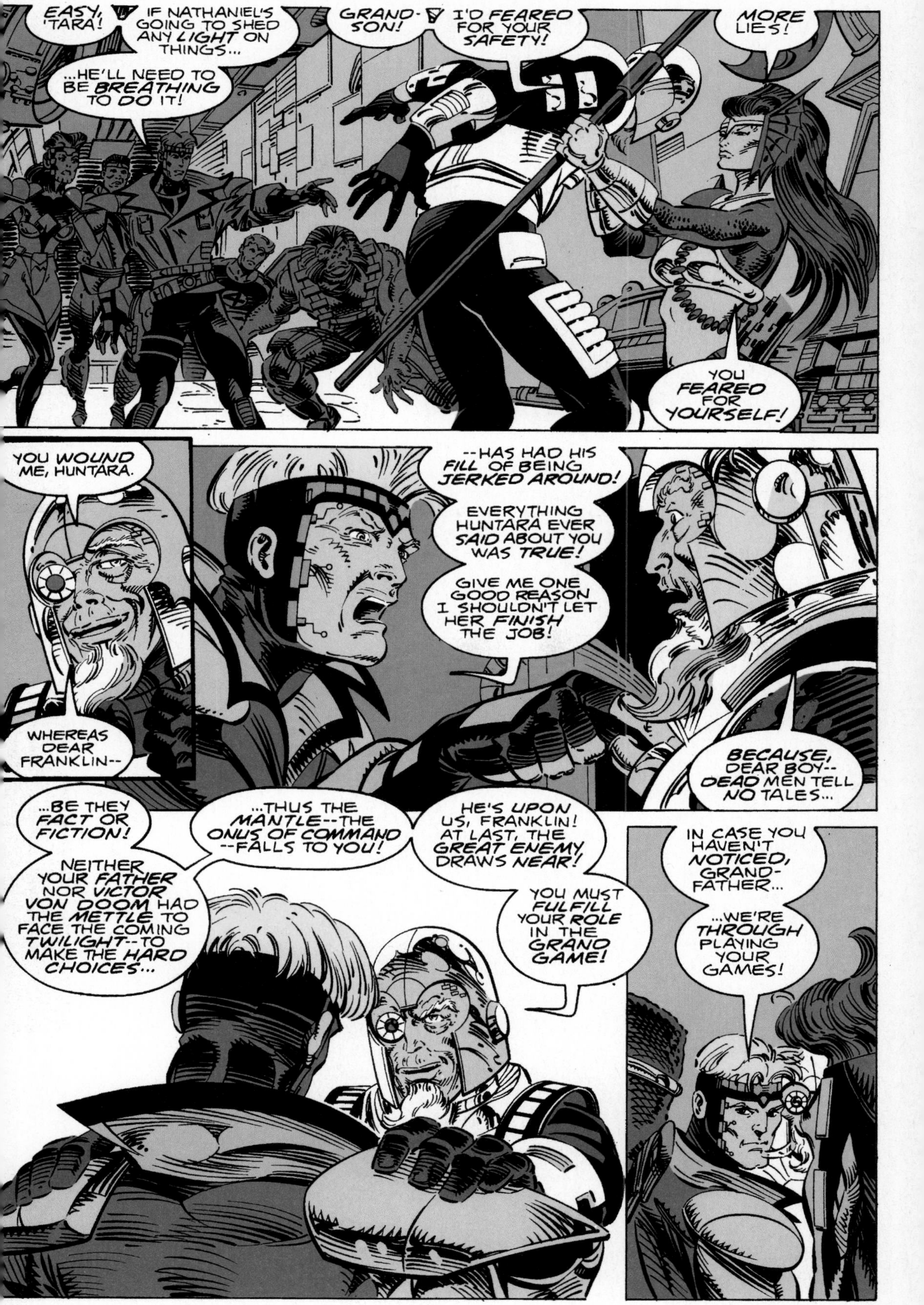
EASY, 'TARA! IF NATHANIEL'S GOING TO SHED ANY LIGHT ON THINGS...
...HE'LL NEED TO BE BREATHING TO DO IT!
GRAND-SON! I'D FEARED FOR YOUR SAFETY!
MORE LIES!
YOU FEARED FOR YOURSELF!
YOU WOUND ME, HUNTARA.
WHEREAS DEAR FRANKLIN--
--HAS HAD HIS FILL OF BEING JERKED AROUND!
EVERYTHING HUNTARA EVER SAID ABOUT YOU WAS TRUE!
GIVE ME ONE GOOD REASON I SHOULDN'T LET HER FINISH THE JOB!
BECAUSE, DEAR BOY-- DEAD MEN TELL NO TALES...
...BE THEY FACT OR FICTION!
NEITHER YOUR FATHER NOR VICTOR VON DOOM HAD THE METTLE TO FACE THE COMING TWILIGHT--TO MAKE THE HARD CHOICES...
...THUS THE MANTLE--THE ONUS OF COMMAND --FALLS TO YOU!
HE'S UPON US, FRANKLIN! AT LAST, THE GREAT ENEMY DRAWS NEAR!
YOU MUST FULFILL YOUR ROLE IN THE GRAND GAME!
IN CASE YOU HAVEN'T NOTICED, GRAND-FATHER...
...WE'RE THROUGH PLAYING YOUR GAMES!

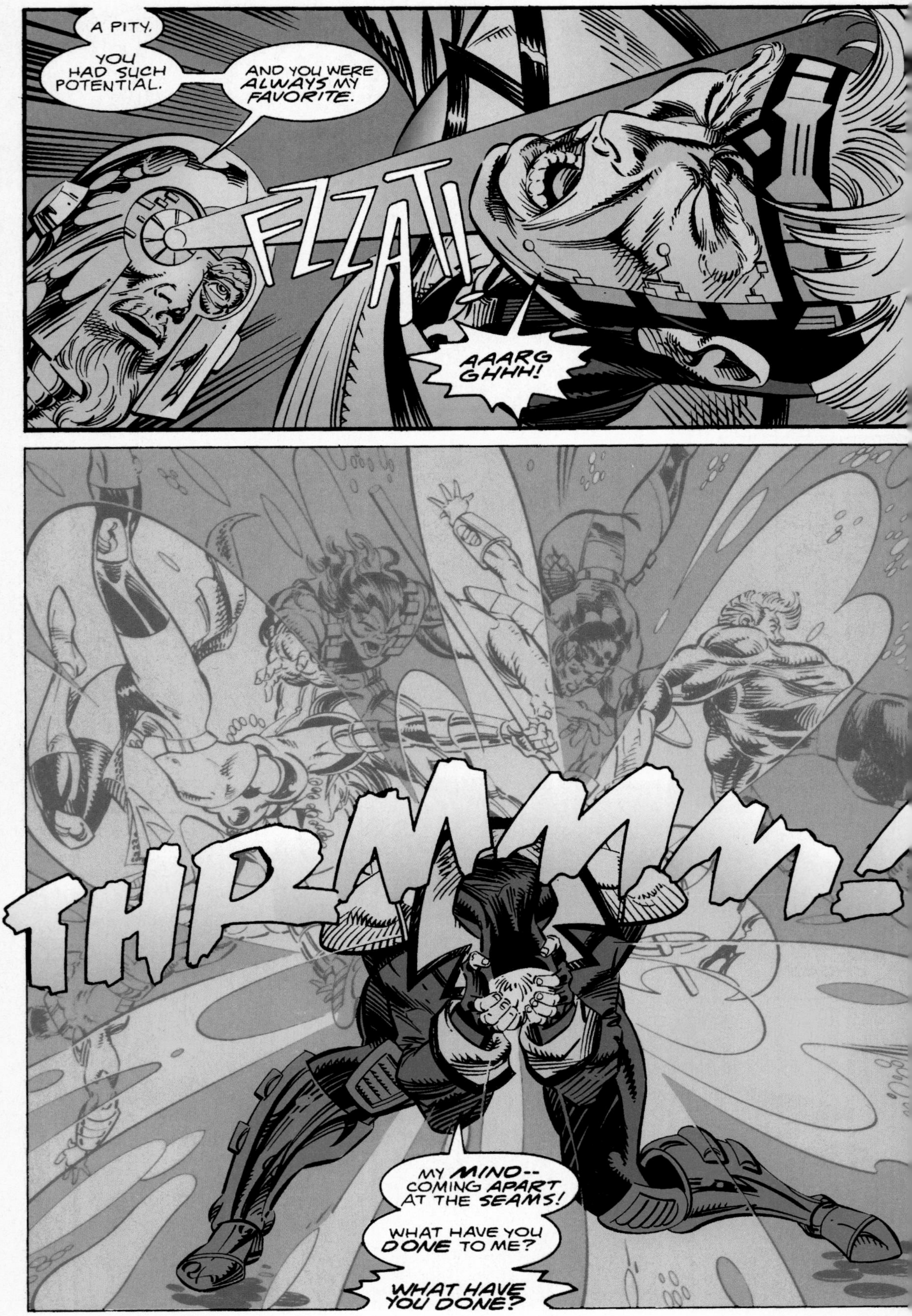
A PITY.
YOU HAD SUCH POTENTIAL.
AND YOU WERE ALWAYS MY FAVORITE.
FZZAT!
AAARGGHHH!
THRMMM!
MY MIND-- COMING APART AT THE SEAMS!
WHAT HAVE YOU DONE TO ME?
WHAT HAVE YOU DONE?

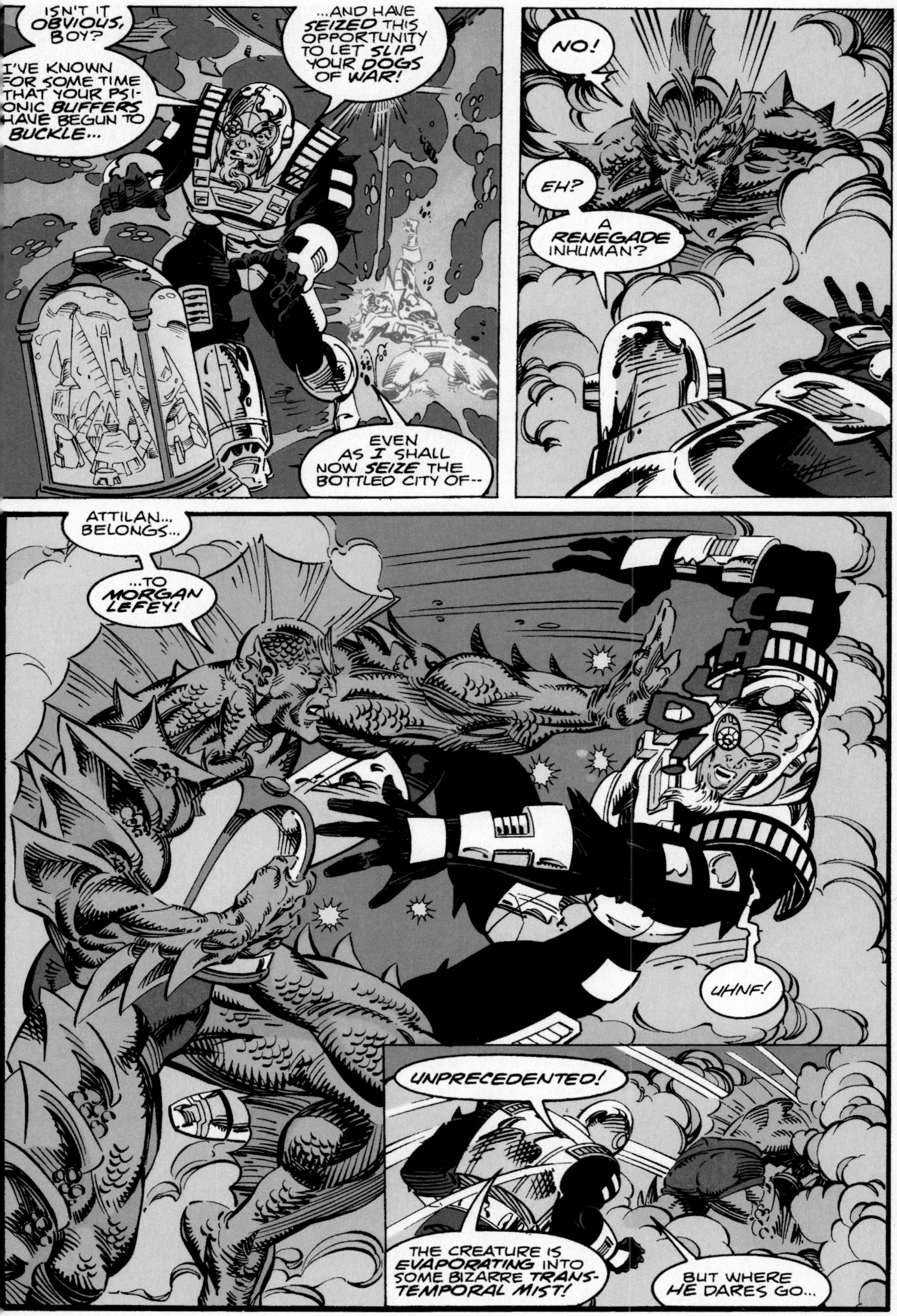
ISN'T IT OBVIOUS, BOY?
I'VE KNOWN FOR SOME TIME THAT YOUR PSI-ONIC BUFFERS HAVE BEGUN TO BUCKLE...
...AND HAVE SEIZED THIS OPPORTUNITY TO LET SLIP YOUR DOGS OF WAR!
EVEN AS I SHALL NOW SEIZE THE BOTTLED CITY OF--
NO!
EH?
A RENEGADE INHUMAN?
ATTILAN... BELONGS...
...TO MORGAN LEFEY!
UHNF!
UNPRECEDENTED!
THE CREATURE IS EVAPORATING INTO SOME BIZARRE TRANS-TEMPORAL MIST!
BUT WHERE HE DARES GO...

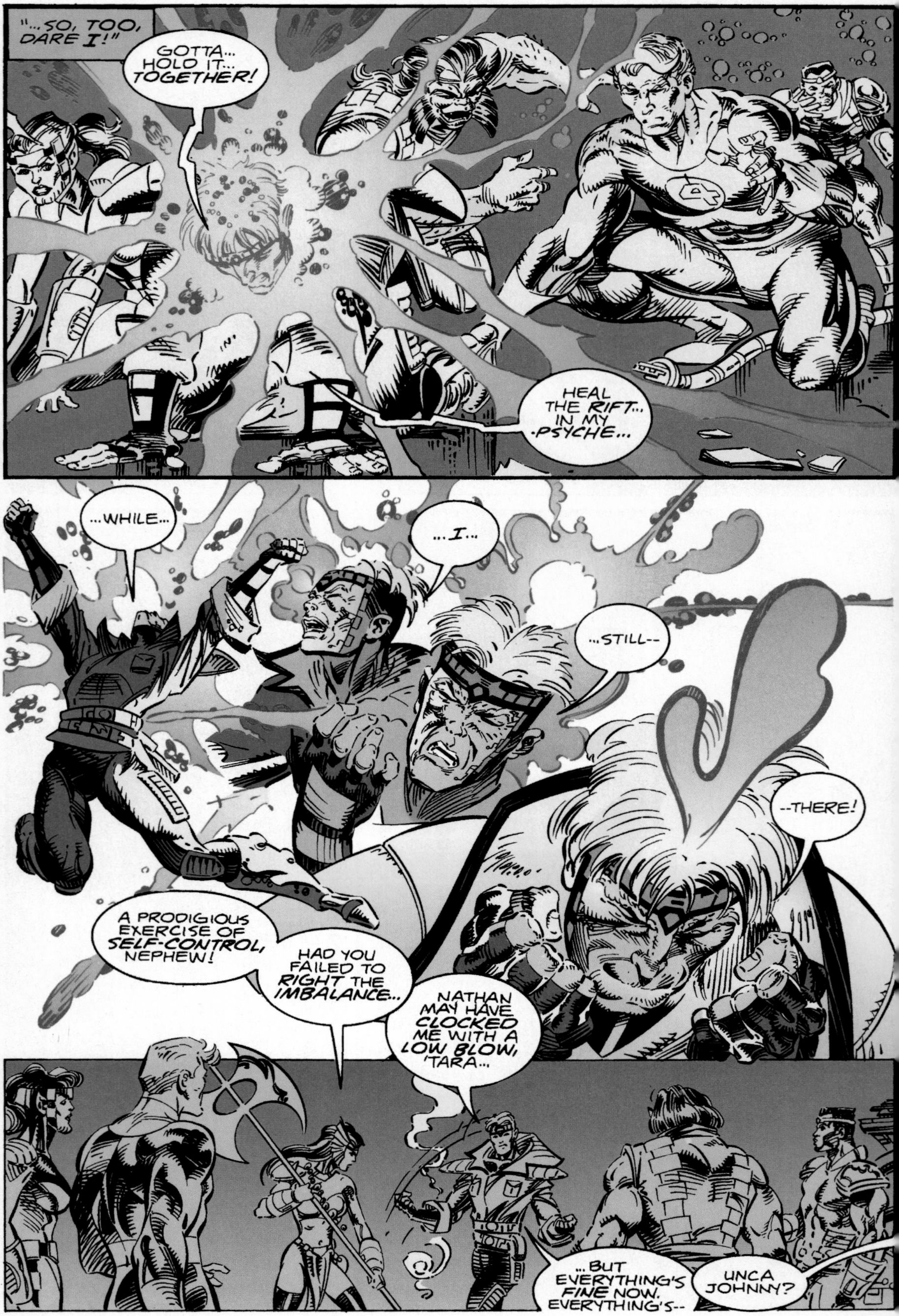
"...SO, TOO, DARE I!"
GOTTA... HOLD IT... TOGETHER!
HEAL THE RIFT... IN MY PSYCHE...
...WHILE...
...I...
...STILL--
--THERE!
A PRODIGIOUS EXERCISE OF SELF-CONTROL, NEPHEW!
HAD YOU FAILED TO RIGHT THE IMBALANCE...
NATHAN MAY HAVE CLOCKED ME WITH A LOW BLOW, 'TARA...
...BUT EVERYTHING'S FINE NOW. EVERYTHING'S--
UNCA JOHNNY?

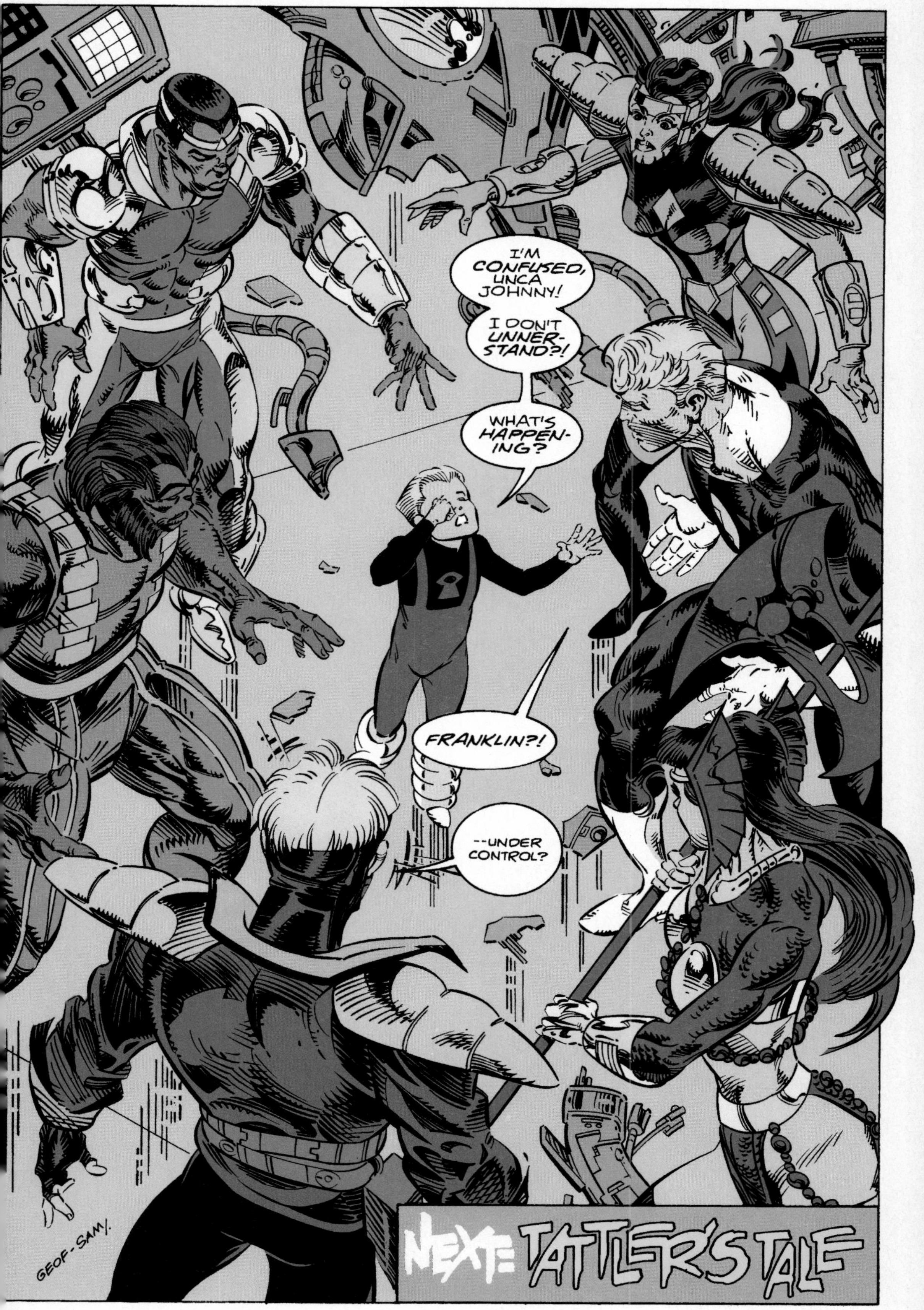
I'M CONFUSED, UNCA JOHNNY!
I DON'T UNNERSTAND?!
WHAT'S HAPPENING?
FRANKLIN?!
--UNDER CONTROL?
GEOF-SAM.
NEXT: TATTLER'S TALE

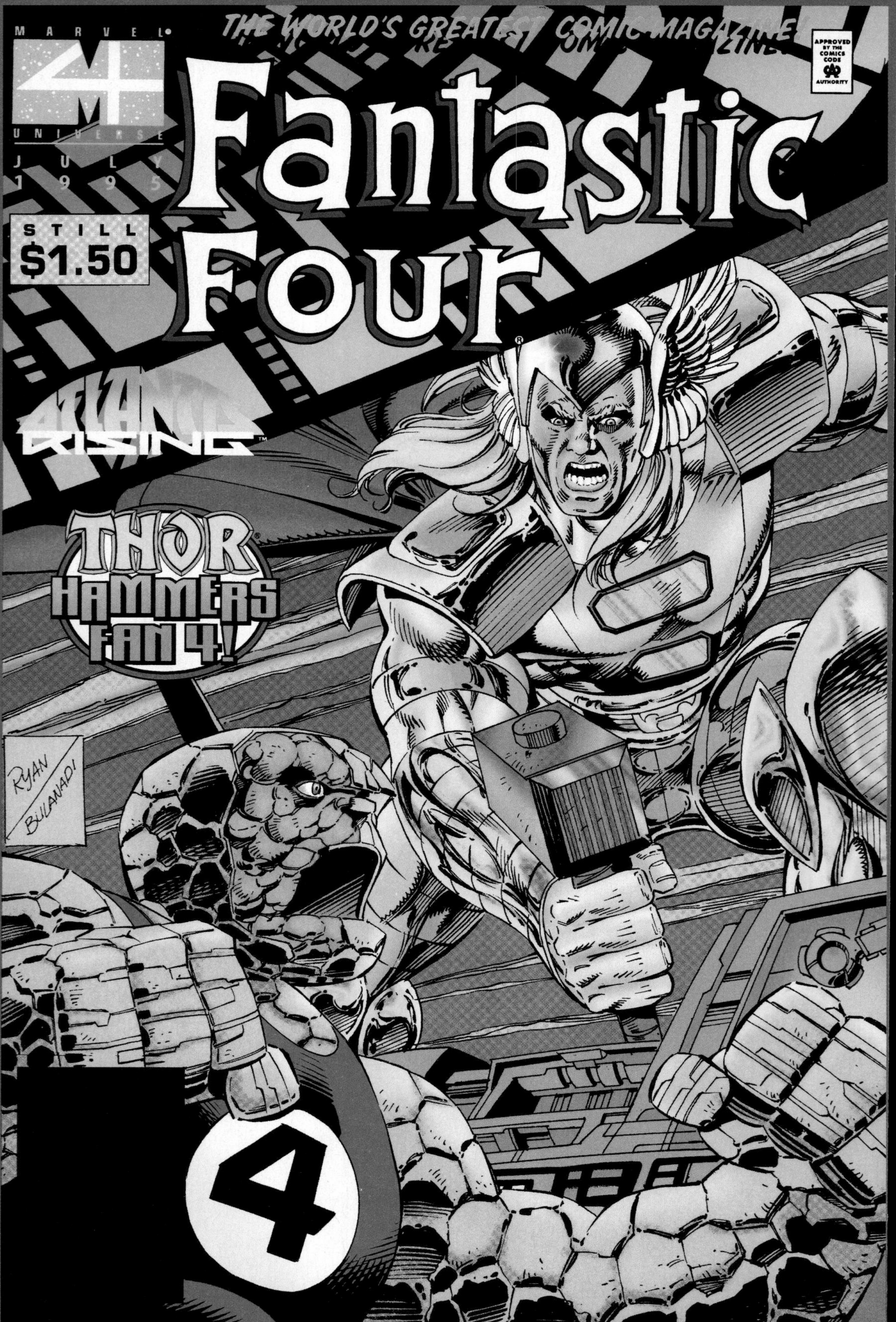
MARVEL
UNIVERSE
JULY 1995
THE WORLD'S GREATEST COMIC MAGAZINE!
APPROVED BY THE COMICS CODE AUTHORITY
Fantastic Four
STILL $1.50
ATLANTIS RISING
THOR HAMMERS FAN 4!
RYAN BULANADI
4

Stan Lee presents

THE FANTASTIC FOUR!

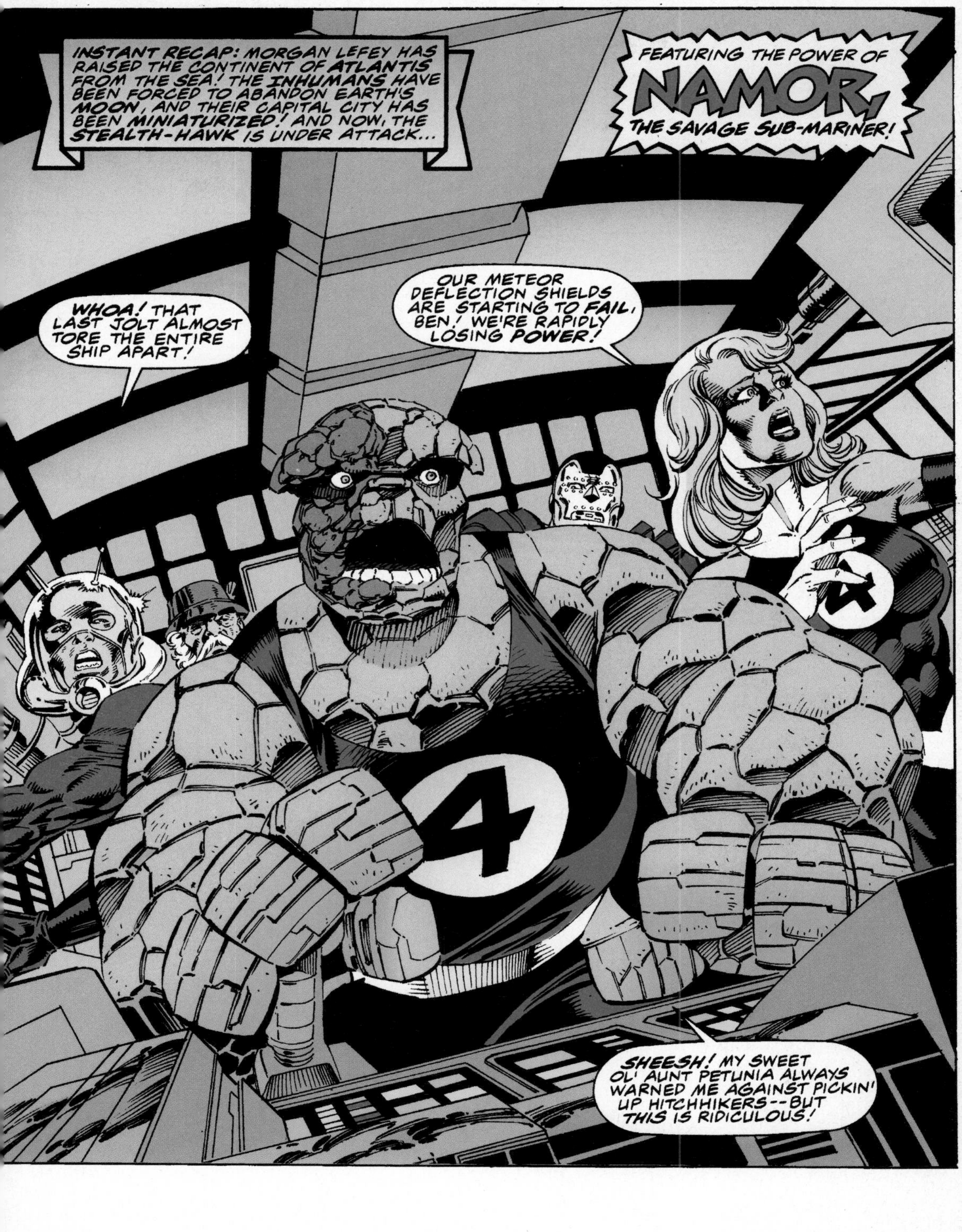
INSTANT RECAP: MORGAN LEFEY HAS RAISED THE CONTINENT OF ATLANTIS FROM THE SEA! THE INHUMANS HAVE BEEN FORCED TO ABANDON EARTH'S MOON, AND THEIR CAPITAL CITY HAS BEEN MINIATURIZED! AND NOW, THE STEALTH-HAWK IS UNDER ATTACK...
FEATURING THE POWER OF NAMOR, THE SAVAGE SUB-MARINER!
WHOA! THAT LAST JOLT ALMOST TORE THE ENTIRE SHIP APART!
OUR METEOR DEFLECTION SHIELDS ARE STARTING TO FAIL, BEN! WE'RE RAPIDLY LOSING POWER!
SHEESH! MY SWEET OL' AUNT PETUNIA ALWAYS WARNED ME AGAINST PICKIN' UP HITCHHIKERS--BUT THIS IS RIDICULOUS!

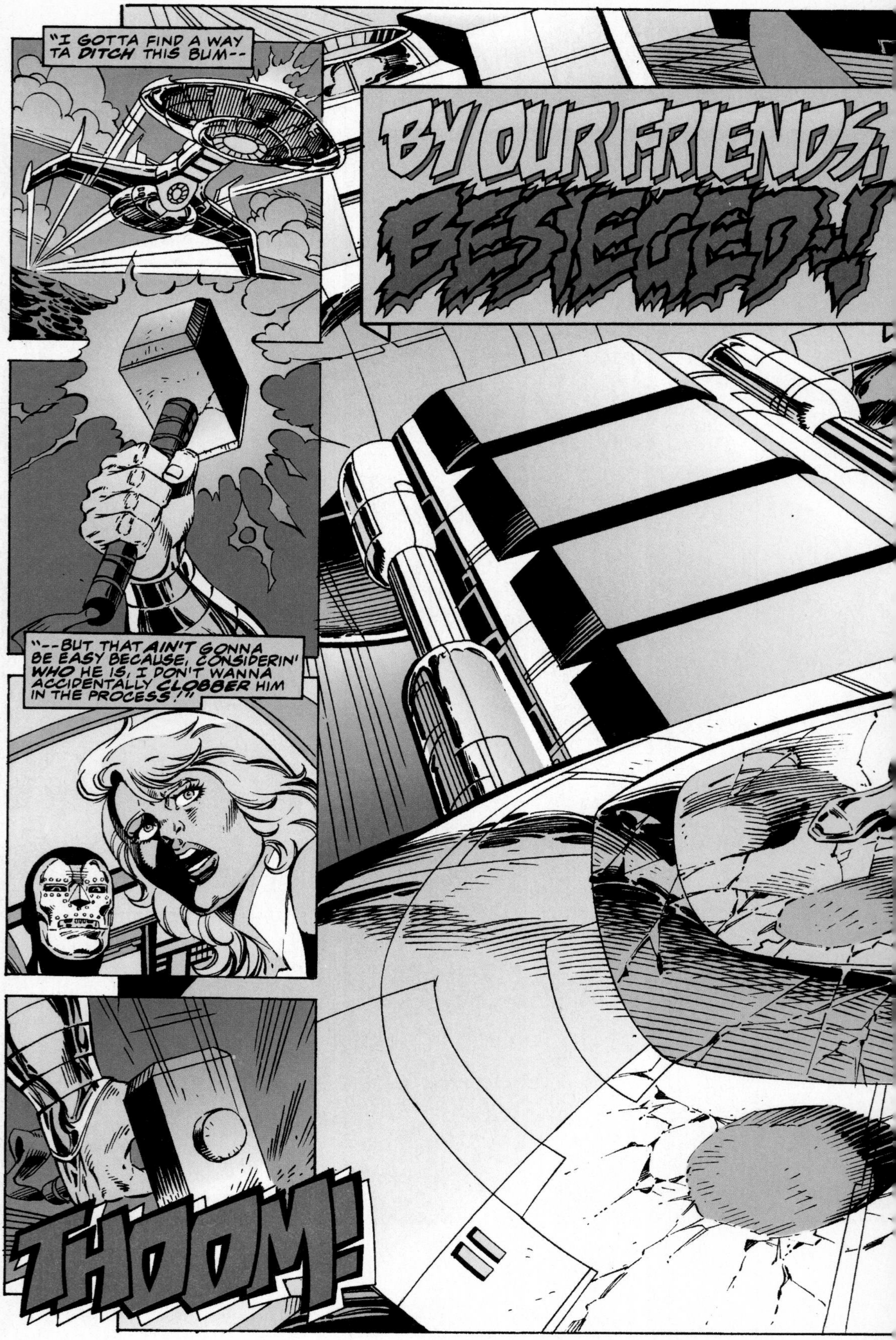
"I GOTTA FIND A WAY TA DITCH THIS BUM--
BY OUR FRIENDS, BESIEGED!
"--BUT THAT AIN'T GONNA BE EASY BECAUSE, CONSIDERIN' WHO HE IS, I DON'T WANNA ACCIDENTALLY CLOBBER HIM IN THE PROCESS!"
THOOM!

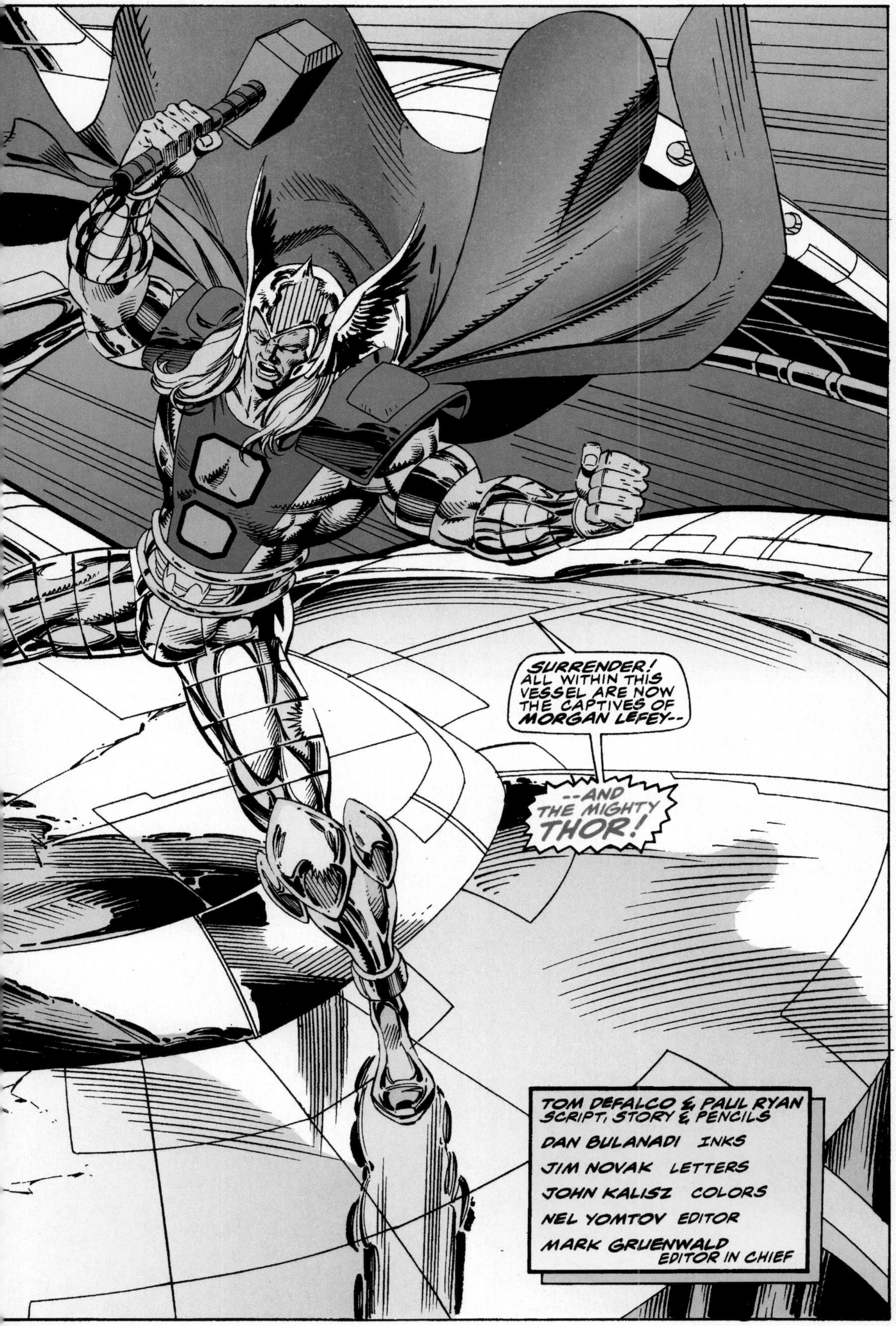
SURRENDER! ALL WITHIN THIS VESSEL ARE NOW THE CAPTIVES OF MORGAN LEFEY--
--AND THE MIGHTY THOR!
TOM DEFALCO & PAUL RYAN SCRIPT, STORY & PENCILS
DAN BULANADI INKS
JIM NOVAK LETTERS
JOHN KALISZ COLORS
NEL YOMTOV EDITOR
MARK GRUENWALD EDITOR IN CHIEF

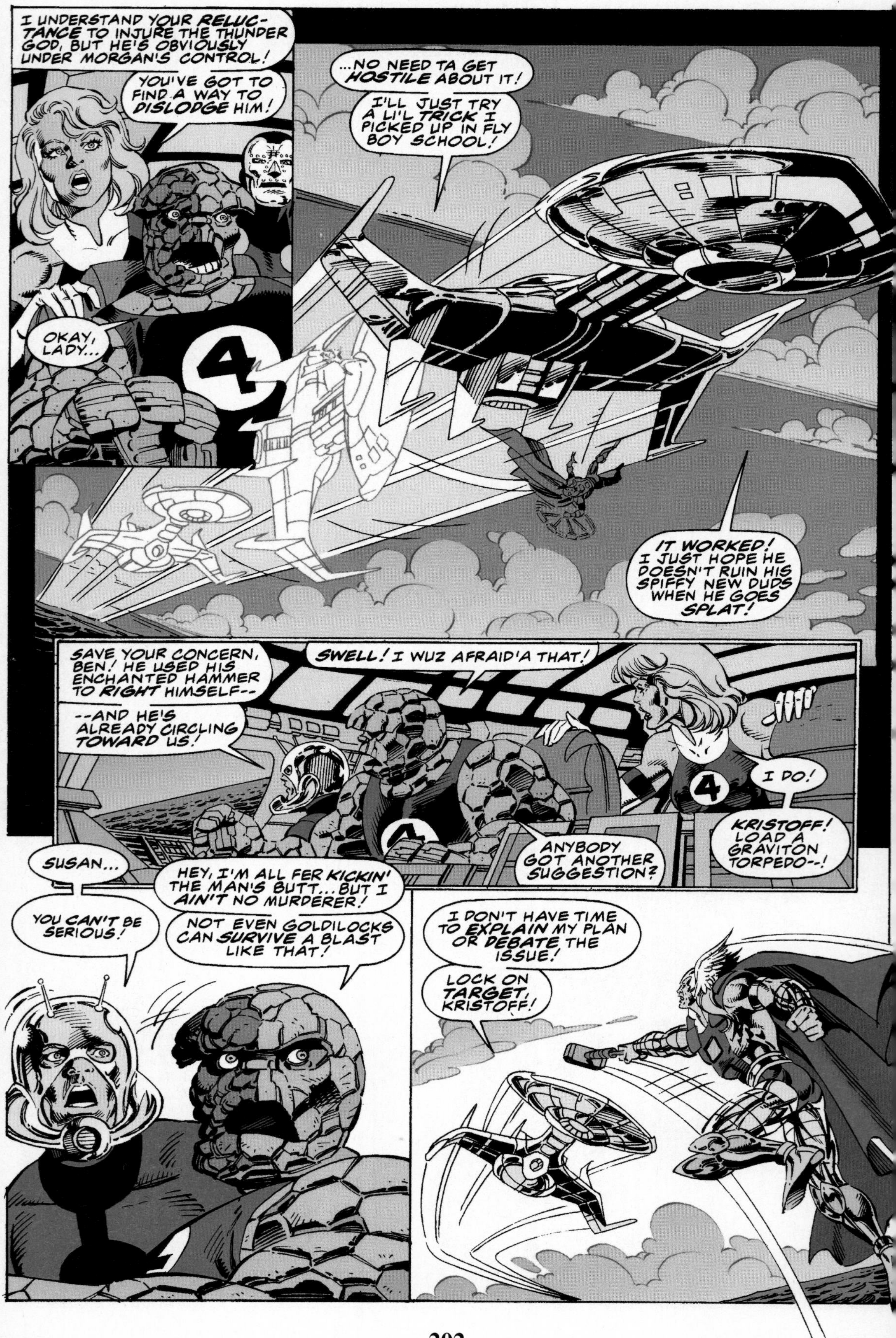

I UNDERSTAND YOUR RELUCTANCE TO INJURE THE THUNDER GOD, BUT HE'S OBVIOUSLY UNDER MORGAN'S CONTROL!
YOU'VE GOT TO FIND A WAY TO DISLODGE HIM!
OKAY, LADY...
...NO NEED TA GET HOSTILE ABOUT IT!
I'LL JUST TRY A LI'L TRICK I PICKED UP IN FLY BOY SCHOOL!
IT WORKED! I JUST HOPE HE DOESN'T RUIN HIS SPIFFY NEW DUDS WHEN HE GOES SPLAT!
SAVE YOUR CONCERN, BEN! HE USED HIS ENCHANTED HAMMER TO RIGHT HIMSELF--
--AND HE'S ALREADY CIRCLING TOWARD US!
SWELL! I WUZ AFRAID'A THAT!
ANYBODY GOT ANOTHER SUGGESTION?
I DO!
KRISTOFF! LOAD A GRAVITON TORPEDO--!
SUSAN...
YOU CAN'T BE SERIOUS!
HEY, I'M ALL FER KICKIN' THE MAN'S BUTT... BUT I AIN'T NO MURDERER!
NOT EVEN GOLDILOCKS CAN SURVIVE A BLAST LIKE THAT!
I DON'T HAVE TIME TO EXPLAIN MY PLAN OR DEBATE THE ISSUE!
LOCK ON TARGET, KRISTOFF!

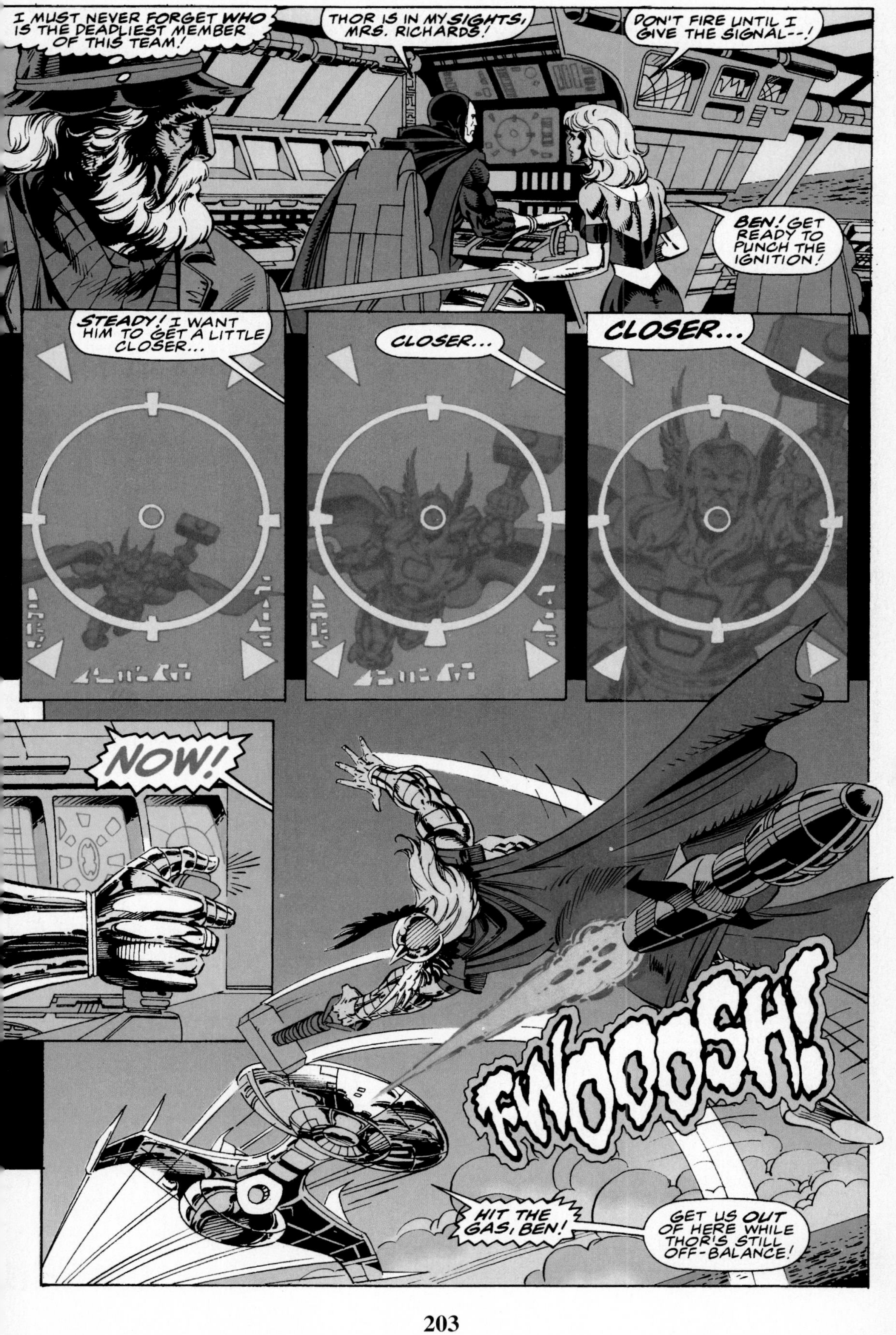
I MUST NEVER FORGET WHO IS THE DEADLIEST MEMBER OF THIS TEAM!
THOR IS IN MY SIGHTS, MRS. RICHARDS!
DON'T FIRE UNTIL I GIVE THE SIGNAL--!
BEN! GET READY TO PUNCH THE IGNITION!
STEADY! I WANT HIM TO GET A LITTLE CLOSER...
CLOSER...
CLOSER...
NOW!
FWOOOSH!
HIT THE GAS, BEN!
GET US OUT OF HERE WHILE THOR'S STILL OFF-BALANCE!

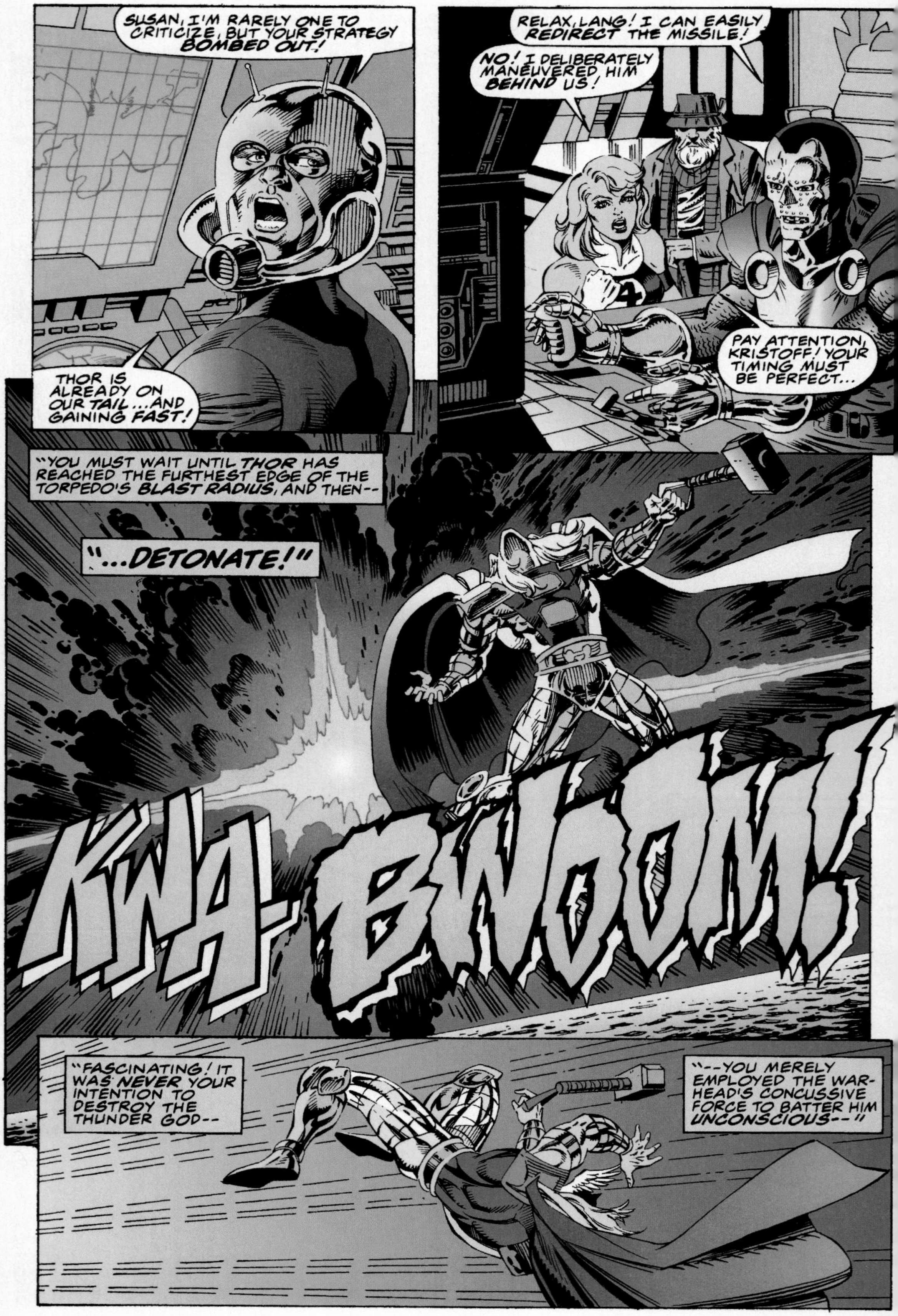

SUSAN, I'M RARELY ONE TO CRITICIZE, BUT YOUR STRATEGY BOMBED OUT!
THOR IS ALREADY ON OUR TAIL... AND GAINING FAST!
RELAX, LANG! I CAN EASILY REDIRECT THE MISSILE!
NO! I DELIBERATELY MANEUVERED HIM BEHIND US!
PAY ATTENTION, KRISTOFF! YOUR TIMING MUST BE PERFECT...
"YOU MUST WAIT UNTIL THOR HAS REACHED THE FURTHEST EDGE OF THE TORPEDO'S BLAST RADIUS, AND THEN--
"...DETONATE!"
KWA-BWOOM!
"FASCINATING! IT WAS NEVER YOUR INTENTION TO DESTROY THE THUNDER GOD--
"--YOU MERELY EMPLOYED THE WAR-HEAD'S CONCUSSIVE FORCE TO BATTER HIM UNCONSCIOUS--"

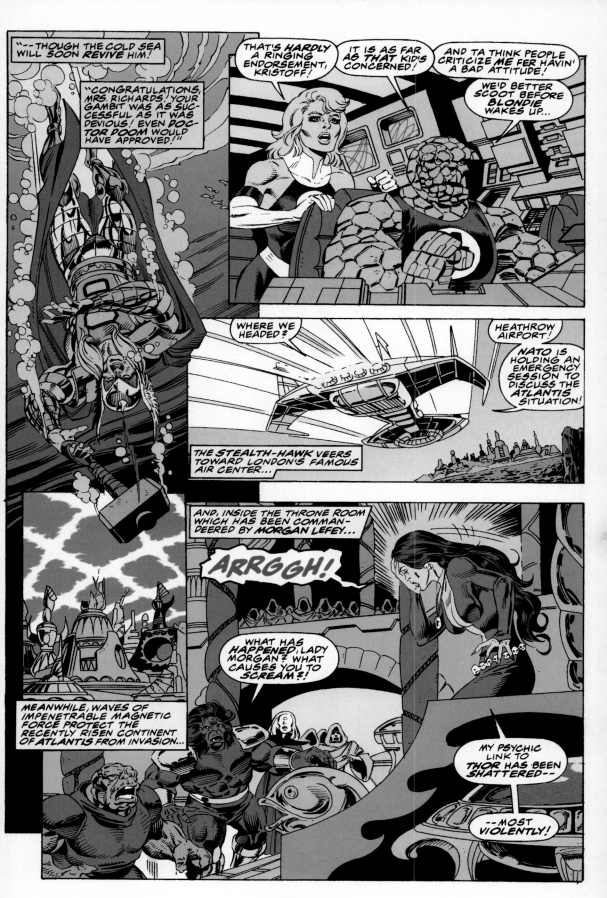

"-- THOUGH THE COLD SEA WILL SOON *REVIVE* HIM!

"CONGRATULATIONS, MRS. *RICHARDS!* YOUR GAMBIT WAS AS SUCCESSFUL AS IT WAS *DEVIOUS!* EVEN *DOCTOR DOOM* WOULD HAVE APPROVED!"

THAT'S *HARDLY* A RINGING ENDORSEMENT, KRISTOFF!

IT IS AS FAR AS *THAT* KID'S CONCERNED!

AND TA THINK PEOPLE CRITICIZE *ME* FER HAVIN' A BAD ATTITUDE!

WE'D BETTER SCOOT BEFORE *BLONDIE* WAKES UP...

WHERE WE HEADED?

HEATHROW AIRPORT! *NATO* IS HOLDING AN *EMERGENCY* SESSION TO DISCUSS THE *ATLANTIS* SITUATION!

THE *STEALTH-HAWK* VEERS TOWARD LONDON'S FAMOUS AIR CENTER...

AND, INSIDE THE THRONE ROOM WHICH HAS BEEN COMMANDEERED BY *MORGAN LEFEY*...

ARRGGH!

MEANWHILE, WAVES OF IMPENETRABLE *MAGNETIC FORCE* PROTECT THE RECENTLY RISEN CONTINENT OF *ATLANTIS* FROM INVASION...

WHAT HAS HAPPENED, LADY MORGAN? WHAT CAUSES YOU TO *SCREAM?!*

MY PSYCHIC LINK TO *THOR* HAS BEEN *SHATTERED* --

-- MOST *VIOLENTLY!*

205

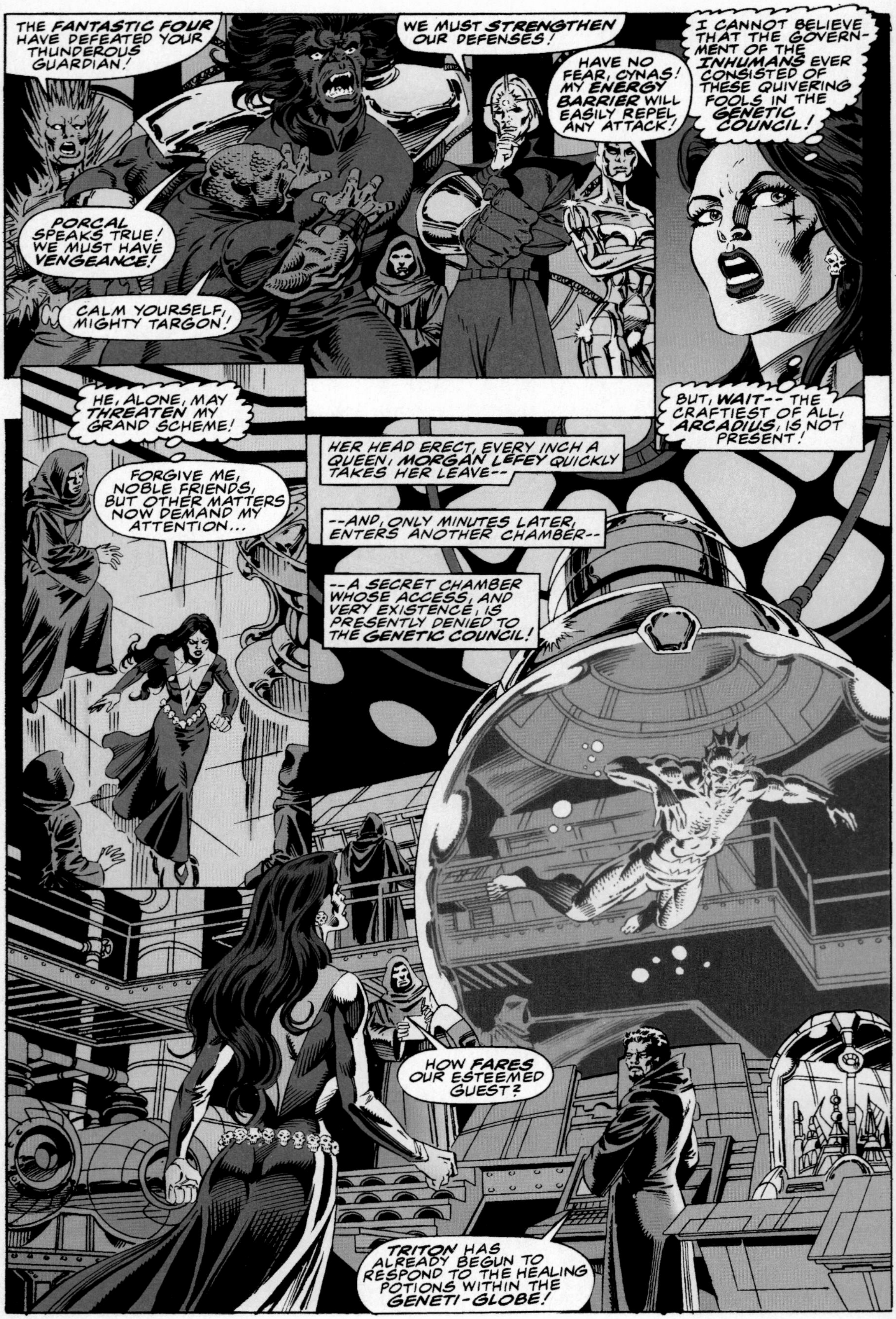
THE FANTASTIC FOUR HAVE DEFEATED YOUR THUNDEROUS GUARDIAN!
WE MUST STRENGTHEN OUR DEFENSES!
HAVE NO FEAR, CYNAS! MY ENERGY BARRIER WILL EASILY REPEL ANY ATTACK!
PORCAL SPEAKS TRUE! WE MUST HAVE VENGEANCE!
CALM YOURSELF, MIGHTY TARGON!
I CANNOT BELIEVE THAT THE GOVERNMENT OF THE INHUMANS EVER CONSISTED OF THESE QUIVERING FOOLS IN THE GENETIC COUNCIL!
BUT, WAIT-- THE CRAFTIEST OF ALL, ARCADIUS, IS NOT PRESENT!
HE, ALONE, MAY THREATEN MY GRAND SCHEME!
FORGIVE ME, NOBLE FRIENDS, BUT OTHER MATTERS NOW DEMAND MY ATTENTION...
HER HEAD ERECT, EVERY INCH A QUEEN, MORGAN LEFEY QUICKLY TAKES HER LEAVE--
--AND, ONLY MINUTES LATER, ENTERS ANOTHER CHAMBER--
--A SECRET CHAMBER WHOSE ACCESS, AND VERY EXISTENCE, IS PRESENTLY DENIED TO THE GENETIC COUNCIL!
HOW FARES OUR ESTEEMED GUEST?
TRITON HAS ALREADY BEGUN TO RESPOND TO THE HEALING POTIONS WITHIN THE GENETI-GLOBE!

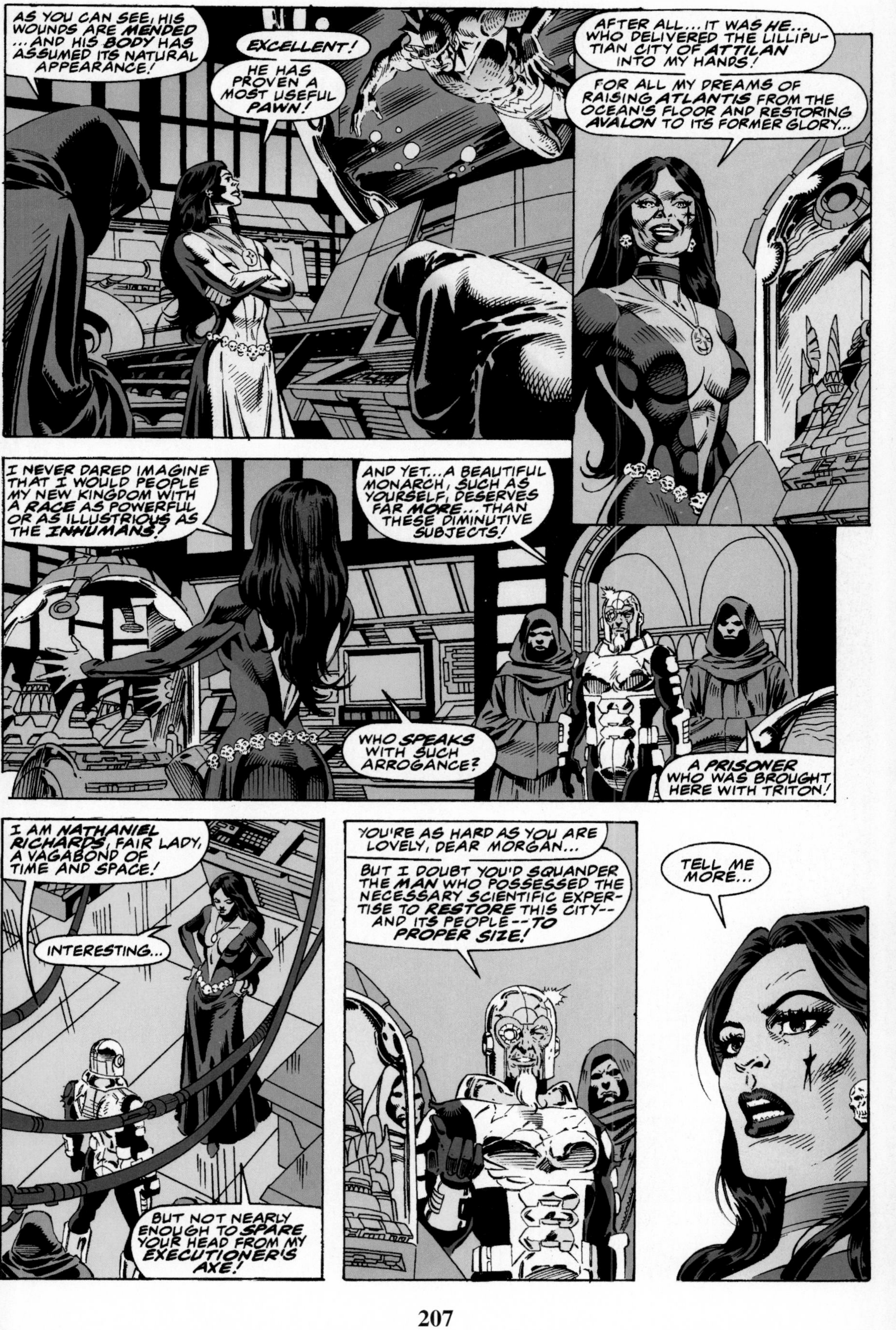
AS YOU CAN SEE, HIS WOUNDS ARE MENDED ...AND HIS BODY HAS ASSUMED ITS NATURAL APPEARANCE!
EXCELLENT!
HE HAS PROVEN A MOST USEFUL PAWN!
AFTER ALL... IT WAS HE... WHO DELIVERED THE LILLIPUTIAN CITY OF ATTILAN INTO MY HANDS!
FOR ALL MY DREAMS OF RAISING ATLANTIS FROM THE OCEAN'S FLOOR AND RESTORING AVALON TO ITS FORMER GLORY...
I NEVER DARED IMAGINE THAT I WOULD PEOPLE MY NEW KINGDOM WITH A RACE AS POWERFUL OR AS ILLUSTRIOUS AS THE INHUMANS!
AND YET... A BEAUTIFUL MONARCH, SUCH AS YOURSELF, DESERVES FAR MORE... THAN THESE DIMINUTIVE SUBJECTS!
WHO SPEAKS WITH SUCH ARROGANCE?
A PRISONER WHO WAS BROUGHT HERE WITH TRITON!
I AM NATHANIEL RICHARDS, FAIR LADY, A VAGABOND OF TIME AND SPACE!
INTERESTING...
BUT NOT NEARLY ENOUGH TO SPARE YOUR HEAD FROM MY EXECUTIONER'S AXE!
YOU'RE AS HARD AS YOU ARE LOVELY, DEAR MORGAN...
BUT I DOUBT YOU'D SQUANDER THE MAN WHO POSSESSED THE NECESSARY SCIENTIFIC EXPERTISE TO RESTORE THIS CITY-- AND ITS PEOPLE--TO PROPER SIZE!
TELL ME MORE...

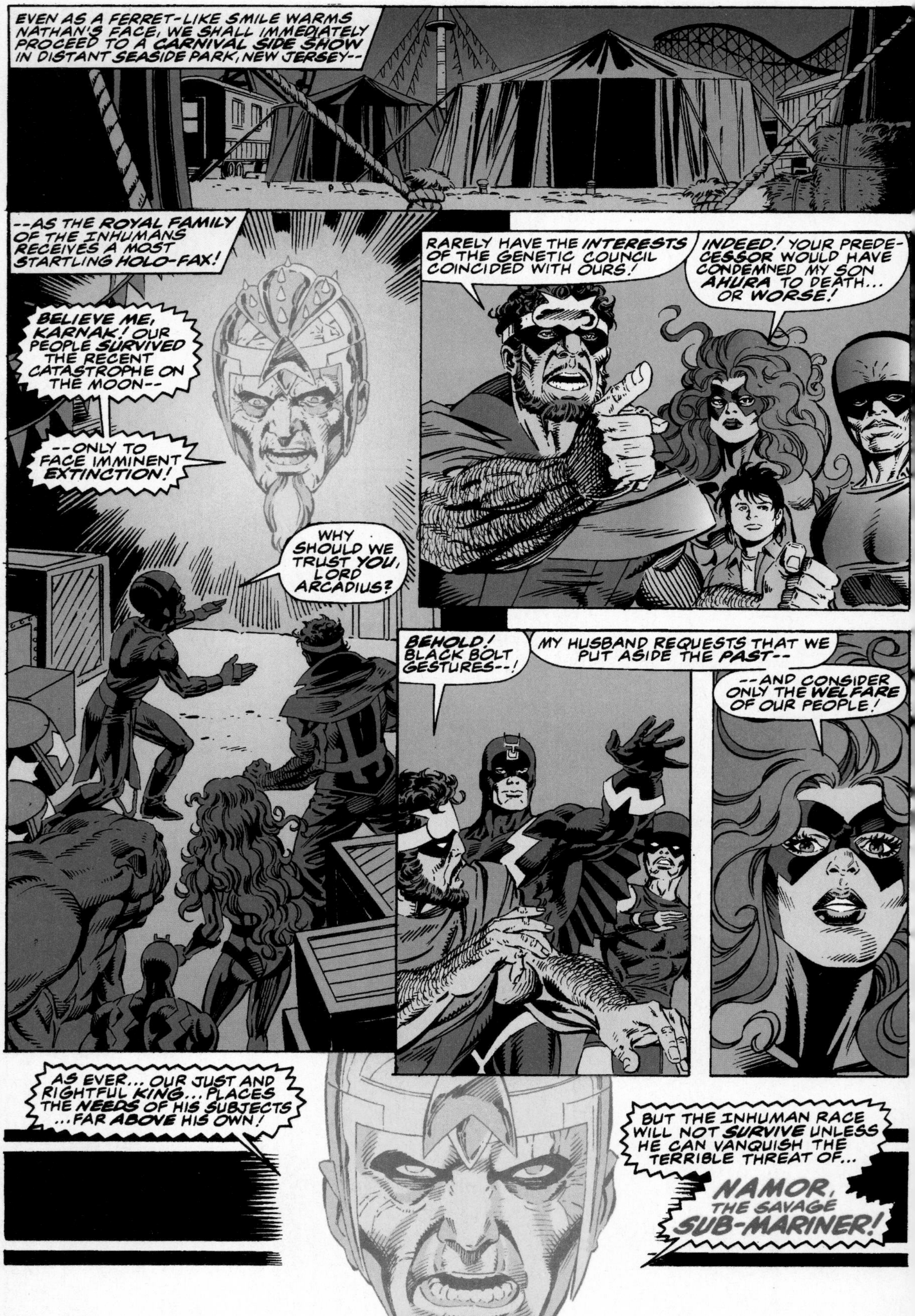
EVEN AS A FERRET-LIKE SMILE WARMS NATHAN'S FACE, WE SHALL IMMEDIATELY PROCEED TO A CARNIVAL SIDE SHOW IN DISTANT SEASIDE PARK, NEW JERSEY--
--AS THE ROYAL FAMILY OF THE INHUMANS RECEIVES A MOST STARTLING HOLO-FAX!
BELIEVE ME, KARNAK! OUR PEOPLE SURVIVED THE RECENT CATASTROPHE ON THE MOON--
--ONLY TO FACE IMMINENT EXTINCTION!
WHY SHOULD WE TRUST YOU, LORD ARCADIUS?
RARELY HAVE THE INTERESTS OF THE GENETIC COUNCIL COINCIDED WITH OURS!
INDEED! YOUR PREDECESSOR WOULD HAVE CONDEMNED MY SON AHURA TO DEATH... OR WORSE!
BEHOLD! BLACK BOLT GESTURES--!
MY HUSBAND REQUESTS THAT WE PUT ASIDE THE PAST--
--AND CONSIDER ONLY THE WELFARE OF OUR PEOPLE!
AS EVER... OUR JUST AND RIGHTFUL KING... PLACES THE NEEDS OF HIS SUBJECTS ...FAR ABOVE HIS OWN!
BUT THE INHUMAN RACE WILL NOT SURVIVE UNLESS HE CAN VANQUISH THE TERRIBLE THREAT OF...
NAMOR, THE SAVAGE SUB-MARINER!

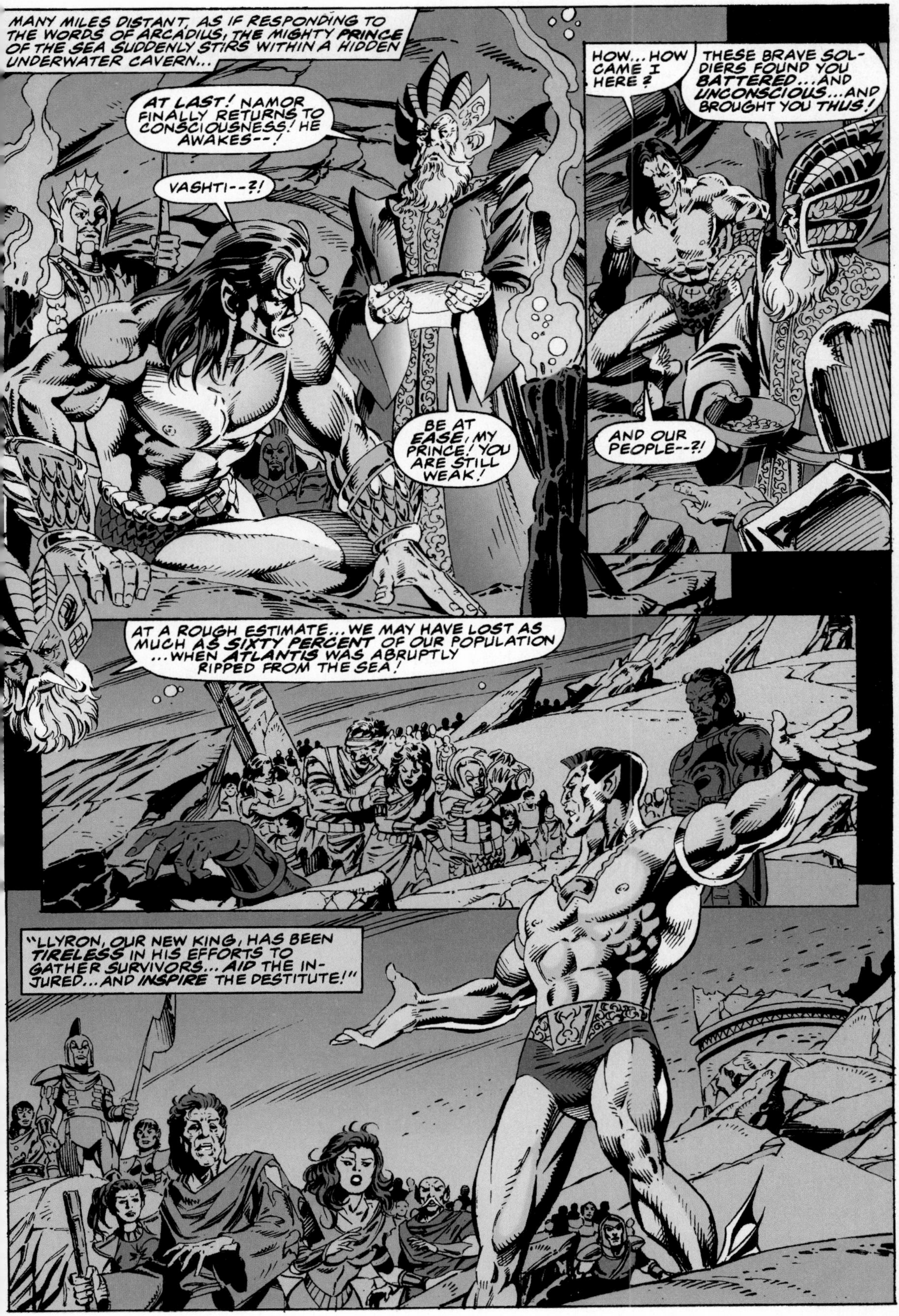
MANY MILES DISTANT, AS IF RESPONDING TO THE WORDS OF ARCADIUS, THE MIGHTY PRINCE OF THE SEA SUDDENLY STIRS WITHIN A HIDDEN UNDERWATER CAVERN...
AT LAST! NAMOR FINALLY RETURNS TO CONSCIOUSNESS! HE AWAKES--!
VASHTI--?!
BE AT EASE, MY PRINCE! YOU ARE STILL WEAK!
HOW... HOW CAME I HERE?
THESE BRAVE SOLDIERS FOUND YOU BATTERED... AND UNCONSCIOUS... AND BROUGHT YOU THUS!
AND OUR PEOPLE--?!
AT A ROUGH ESTIMATE... WE MAY HAVE LOST AS MUCH AS SIXTY PERCENT OF OUR POPULATION ...WHEN ATLANTIS WAS ABRUPTLY RIPPED FROM THE SEA!
"LLYRON, OUR NEW KING, HAS BEEN TIRELESS IN HIS EFFORTS TO GATHER SURVIVORS... AID THE INJURED... AND INSPIRE THE DESTITUTE!"

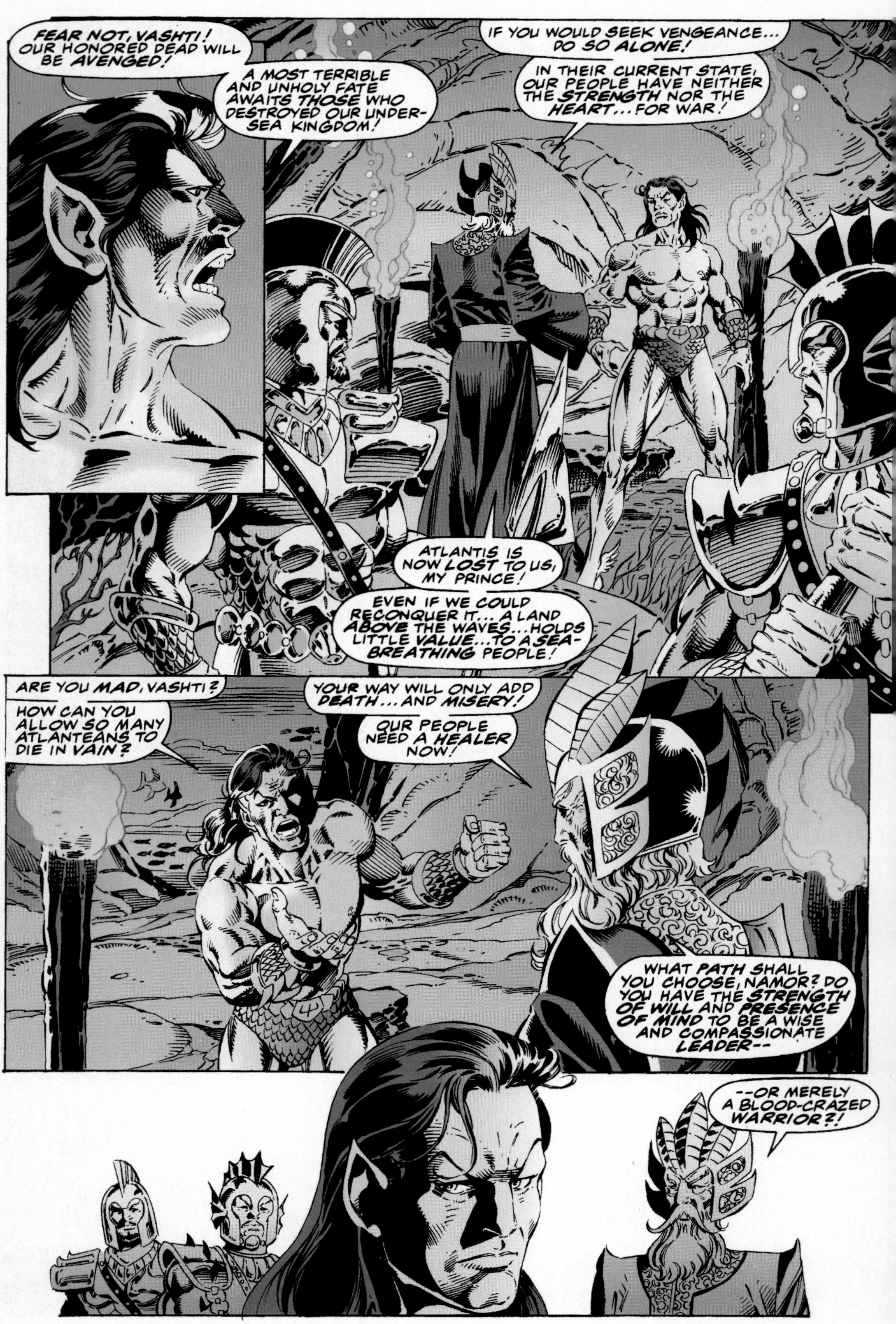
FEAR NOT, VASHTI! OUR HONORED DEAD WILL BE AVENGED!
A MOST TERRIBLE AND UNHOLY FATE AWAITS THOSE WHO DESTROYED OUR UNDER-SEA KINGDOM!
IF YOU WOULD SEEK VENGEANCE... DO SO ALONE!
IN THEIR CURRENT STATE, OUR PEOPLE HAVE NEITHER THE STRENGTH NOR THE HEART... FOR WAR!
ATLANTIS IS NOW LOST TO US, MY PRINCE!
EVEN IF WE COULD RECONQUER IT... A LAND ABOVE THE WAVES... HOLDS LITTLE VALUE... TO A SEA-BREATHING PEOPLE!
ARE YOU MAD, VASHTI?
HOW CAN YOU ALLOW SO MANY ATLANTEANS TO DIE IN VAIN?
YOUR WAY WILL ONLY ADD DEATH... AND MISERY!
OUR PEOPLE NEED A HEALER NOW!
WHAT PATH SHALL YOU CHOOSE, NAMOR? DO YOU HAVE THE STRENGTH OF WILL AND PRESENCE OF MIND TO BE A WISE AND COMPASSIONATE LEADER--
--OR MERELY A BLOOD-CRAZED WARRIOR?!

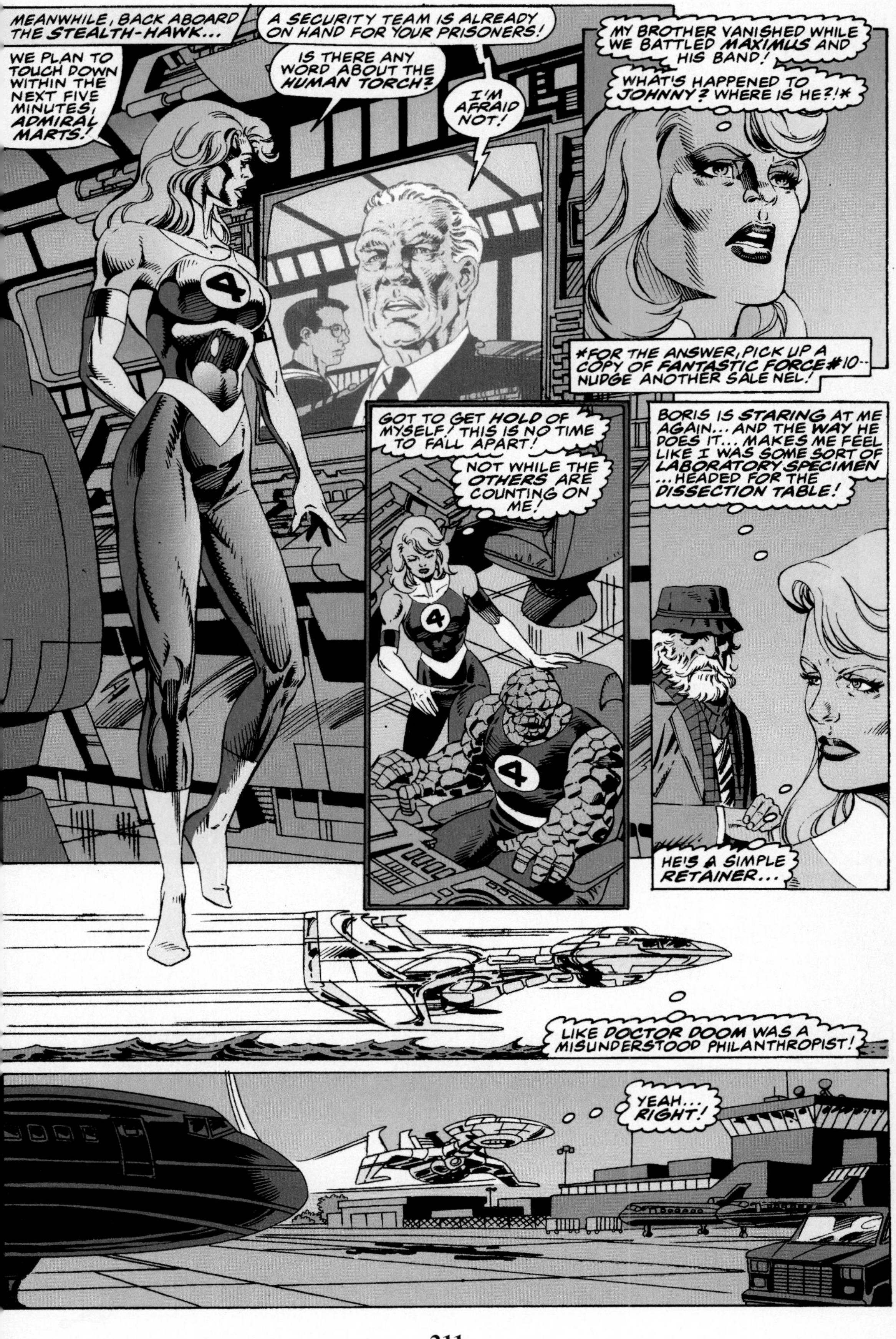
MEANWHILE, BACK ABOARD THE STEALTH-HAWK...
WE PLAN TO TOUCH DOWN WITHIN THE NEXT FIVE MINUTES, ADMIRAL MARTS!
A SECURITY TEAM IS ALREADY ON HAND FOR YOUR PRISONERS!
IS THERE ANY WORD ABOUT THE HUMAN TORCH?
I'M AFRAID NOT!
MY BROTHER VANISHED WHILE WE BATTLED MAXIMUS AND HIS BAND!
WHAT'S HAPPENED TO JOHNNY? WHERE IS HE?!*
*FOR THE ANSWER, PICK UP A COPY OF FANTASTIC FORCE #10-- NUDGE ANOTHER SALE NEL!
GOT TO GET HOLD OF MYSELF! THIS IS NO TIME TO FALL APART!
NOT WHILE THE OTHERS ARE COUNTING ON ME!
BORIS IS STARING AT ME AGAIN... AND THE WAY HE DOES IT... MAKES ME FEEL LIKE I WAS SOME SORT OF LABORATORY SPECIMEN ...HEADED FOR THE DISSECTION TABLE!
HE'S A SIMPLE RETAINER...
LIKE DOCTOR DOOM WAS A MISUNDERSTOOD PHILANTHROPIST!
YEAH... RIGHT!

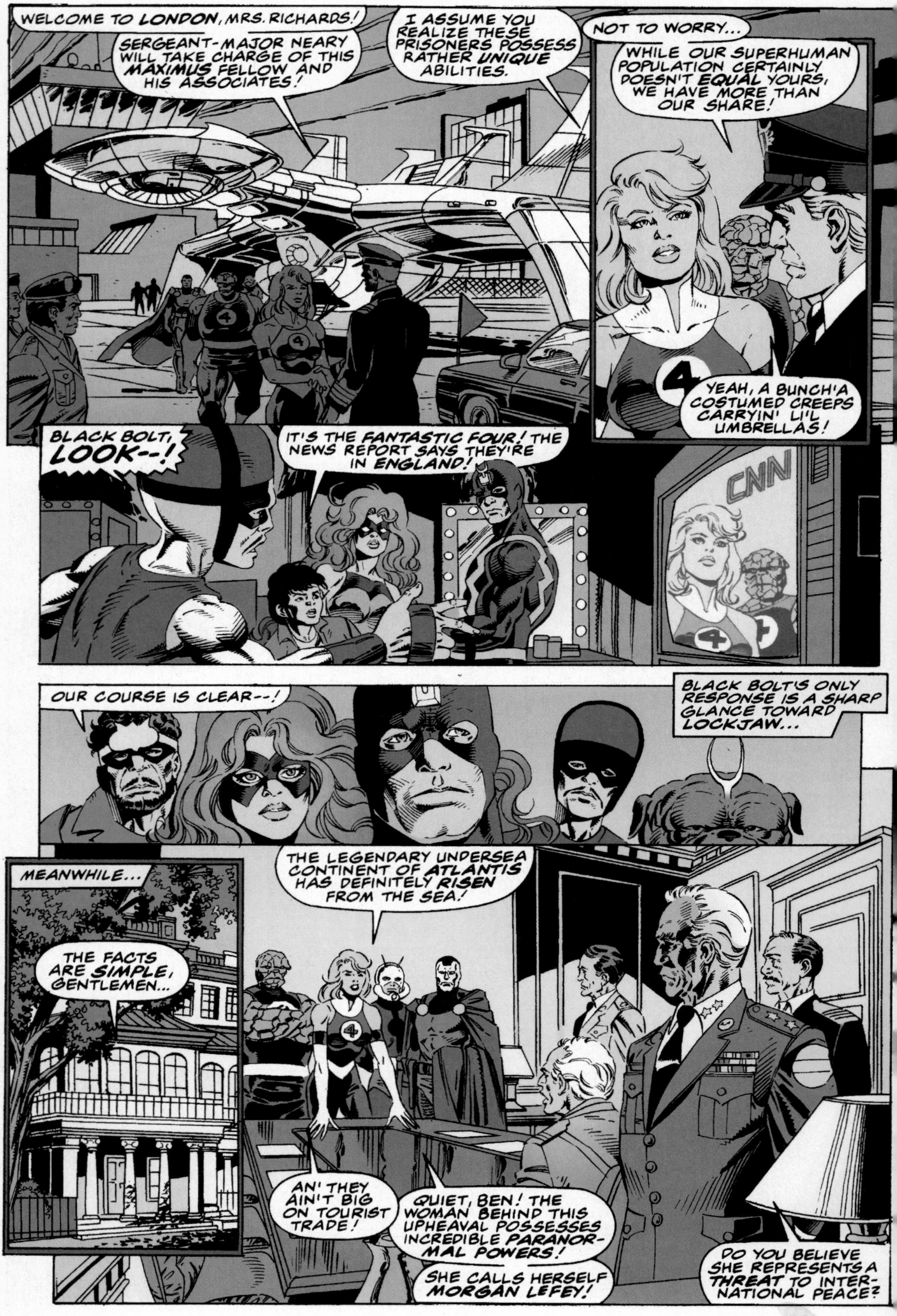
WELCOME TO LONDON, MRS. RICHARDS!
SERGEANT-MAJOR NEARY WILL TAKE CHARGE OF THIS MAXIMUS FELLOW AND HIS ASSOCIATES!
I ASSUME YOU REALIZE THESE PRISONERS POSSESS RATHER UNIQUE ABILITIES.
NOT TO WORRY...
WHILE OUR SUPERHUMAN POPULATION CERTAINLY DOESN'T EQUAL YOURS, WE HAVE MORE THAN OUR SHARE!
YEAH, A BUNCH'A COSTUMED CREEPS CARRYIN' LI'L UMBRELLAS!
BLACK BOLT, LOOK--!
IT'S THE FANTASTIC FOUR! THE NEWS REPORT SAYS THEY'RE IN ENGLAND!
CNN
OUR COURSE IS CLEAR--!
BLACK BOLT'S ONLY RESPONSE IS A SHARP GLANCE TOWARD LOCKJAW...
MEANWHILE...
THE FACTS ARE SIMPLE, GENTLEMEN...
THE LEGENDARY UNDERSEA CONTINENT OF ATLANTIS HAS DEFINITELY RISEN FROM THE SEA!
AN' THEY AIN'T BIG ON TOURIST TRADE!
QUIET, BEN! THE WOMAN BEHIND THIS UPHEAVAL POSSESSES INCREDIBLE PARANORMAL POWERS!
SHE CALLS HERSELF MORGAN LEFEY!
DO YOU BELIEVE SHE REPRESENTS A THREAT TO INTERNATIONAL PEACE?

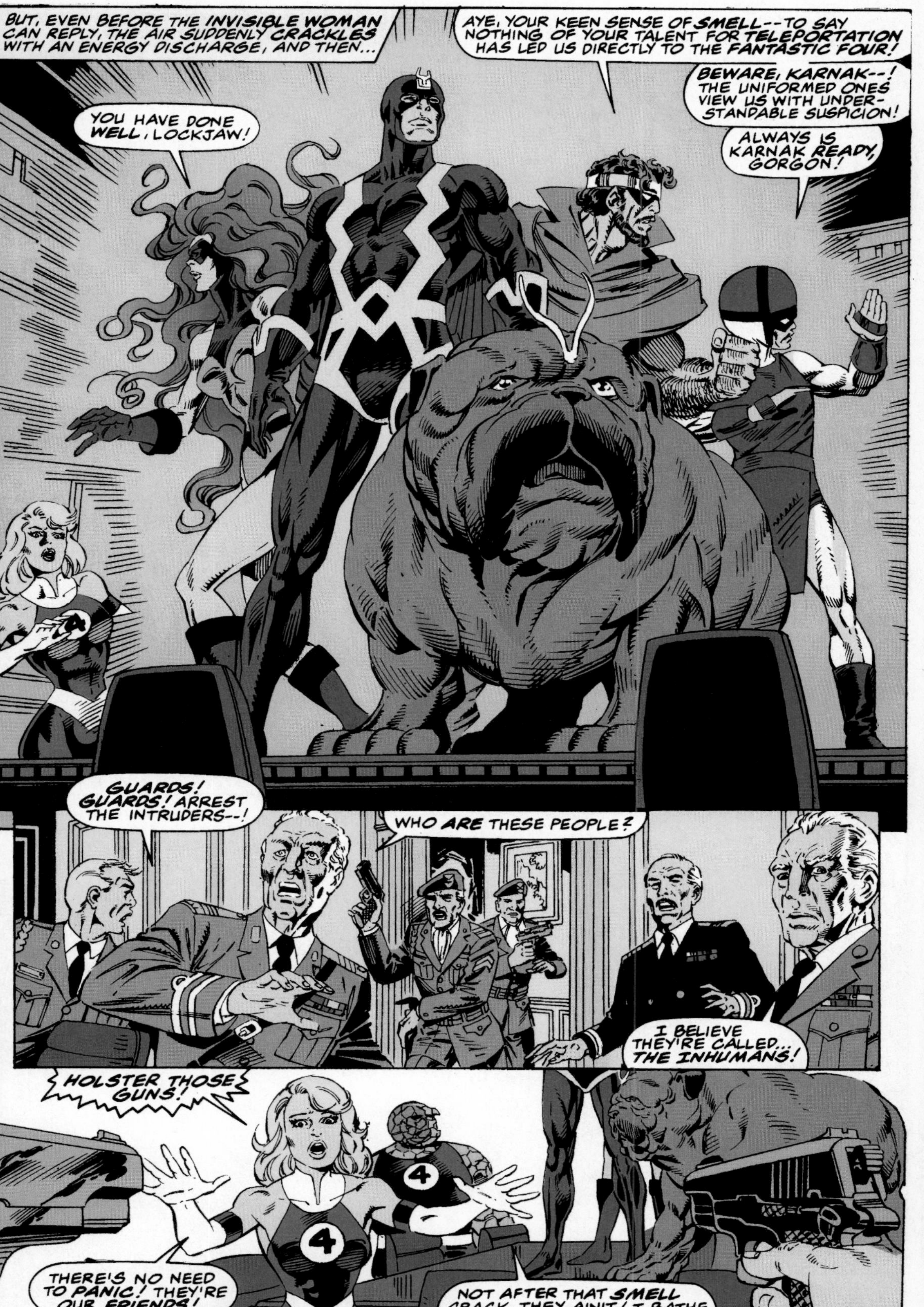
BUT, EVEN BEFORE THE INVISIBLE WOMAN CAN REPLY, THE AIR SUDDENLY CRACKLES WITH AN ENERGY DISCHARGE, AND THEN...
AYE, YOUR KEEN SENSE OF SMELL--TO SAY NOTHING OF YOUR TALENT FOR TELEPORTATION HAS LED US DIRECTLY TO THE FANTASTIC FOUR!
YOU HAVE DONE WELL, LOCKJAW!
BEWARE, KARNAK--! THE UNIFORMED ONES VIEW US WITH UNDERSTANDABLE SUSPICION!
ALWAYS IS KARNAK READY, GORGON!
GUARDS! GUARDS! ARREST THE INTRUDERS--!
WHO ARE THESE PEOPLE?
I BELIEVE THEY'RE CALLED... THE INHUMANS!
HOLSTER THOSE GUNS!
THERE'S NO NEED TO PANIC! THEY'RE OUR FRIENDS!
NOT AFTER THAT SMELL CRACK, THEY AIN'T! I BATHE EVERY SATURDAY NIGHT... WHETHER I NEED IT OR NOT!

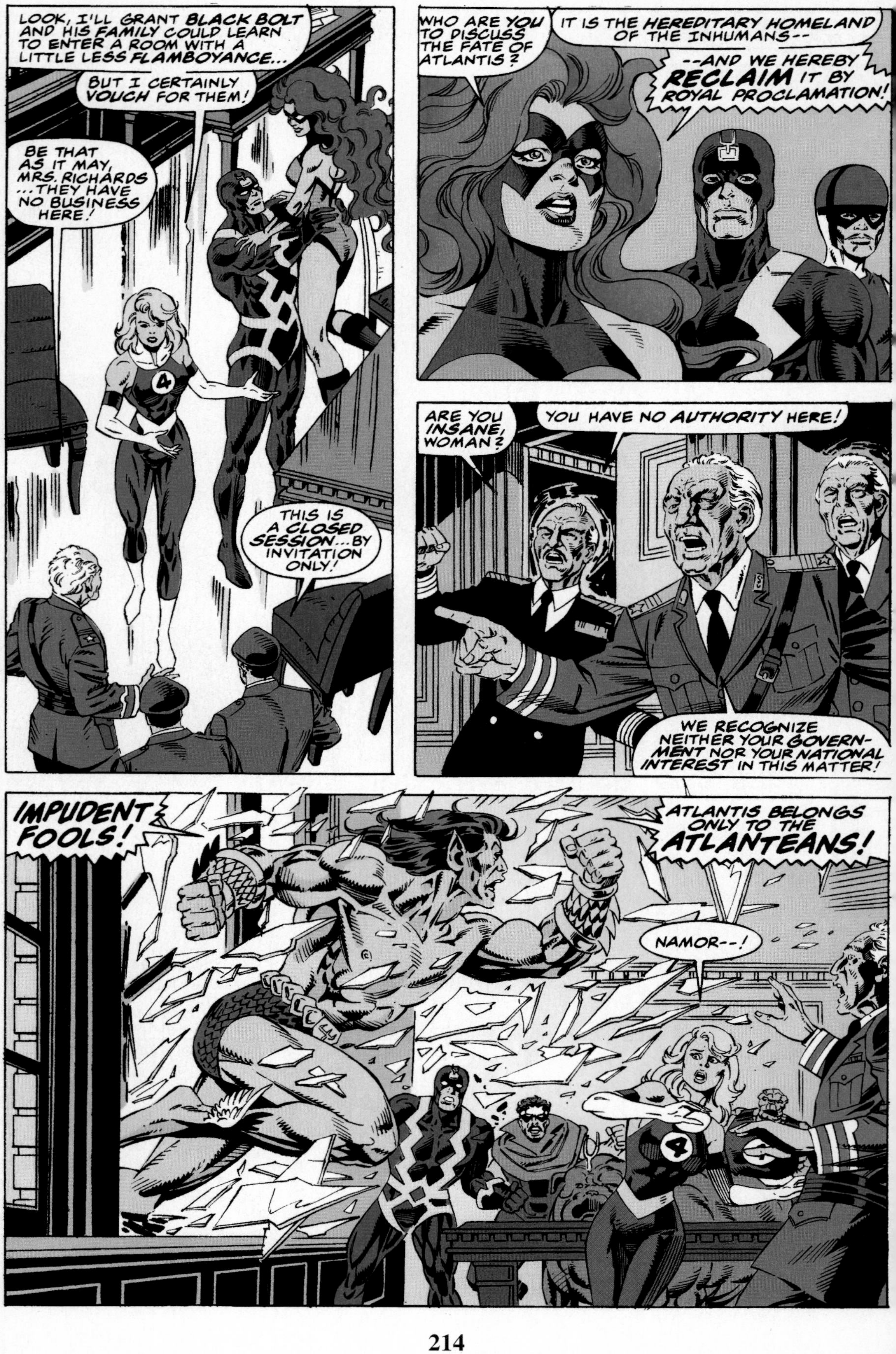
LOOK, I'LL GRANT BLACK BOLT AND HIS FAMILY COULD LEARN TO ENTER A ROOM WITH A LITTLE LESS FLAMBOYANCE...
BUT I CERTAINLY VOUCH FOR THEM!
BE THAT AS IT MAY, MRS. RICHARDS ...THEY HAVE NO BUSINESS HERE!
THIS IS A CLOSED SESSION...BY INVITATION ONLY!
WHO ARE YOU TO DISCUSS THE FATE OF ATLANTIS?
IT IS THE HEREDITARY HOMELAND OF THE INHUMANS--
--AND WE HEREBY RECLAIM IT BY ROYAL PROCLAMATION!
ARE YOU INSANE, WOMAN?
YOU HAVE NO AUTHORITY HERE!
WE RECOGNIZE NEITHER YOUR GOVERNMENT NOR YOUR NATIONAL INTEREST IN THIS MATTER!
IMPUDENT FOOLS!
ATLANTIS BELONGS ONLY TO THE ATLANTEANS!
NAMOR--!

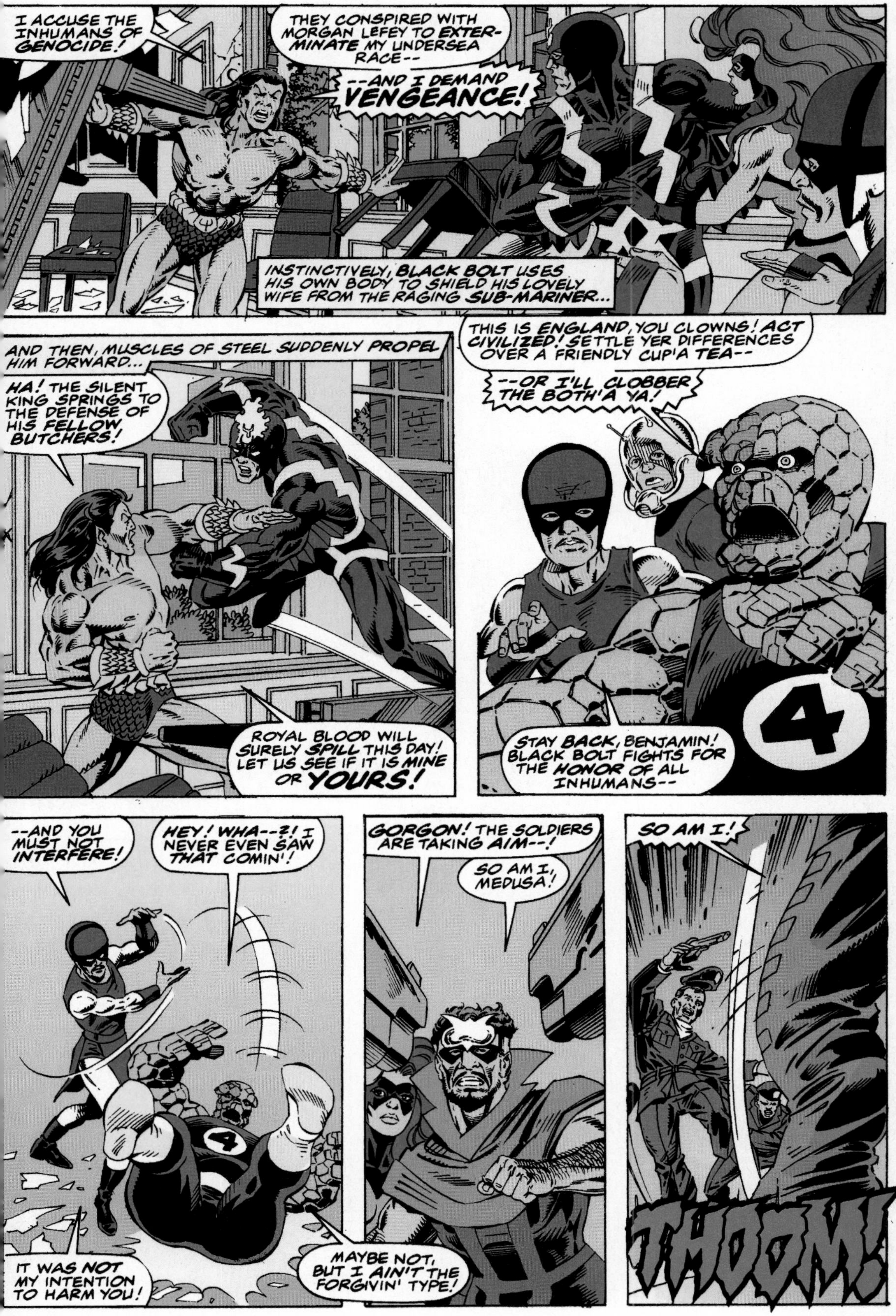
I ACCUSE THE INHUMANS OF GENOCIDE!
THEY CONSPIRED WITH MORGAN LEFEY TO EXTERMINATE MY UNDERSEA RACE--
--AND I DEMAND VENGEANCE!
INSTINCTIVELY, BLACK BOLT USES HIS OWN BODY TO SHIELD HIS LOVELY WIFE FROM THE RAGING SUB-MARINER...
AND THEN, MUSCLES OF STEEL SUDDENLY PROPEL HIM FORWARD...
HA! THE SILENT KING SPRINGS TO THE DEFENSE OF HIS FELLOW BUTCHERS!
ROYAL BLOOD WILL SURELY SPILL THIS DAY! LET US SEE IF IT IS MINE OR YOURS!
THIS IS ENGLAND, YOU CLOWNS! ACT CIVILIZED! SETTLE YER DIFFERENCES OVER A FRIENDLY CUP'A TEA--
--OR I'LL CLOBBER THE BOTH'A YA!
4
STAY BACK, BENJAMIN! BLACK BOLT FIGHTS FOR THE HONOR OF ALL INHUMANS--
--AND YOU MUST NOT INTERFERE!
HEY! WHA--?! I NEVER EVEN SAW THAT COMIN'!
4
IT WAS NOT MY INTENTION TO HARM YOU!
MAYBE NOT, BUT I AIN'T THE FORGIVIN' TYPE!
GORGON! THE SOLDIERS ARE TAKING AIM--!
SO AM I, MEDUSA!
SO AM I!
THOOM!

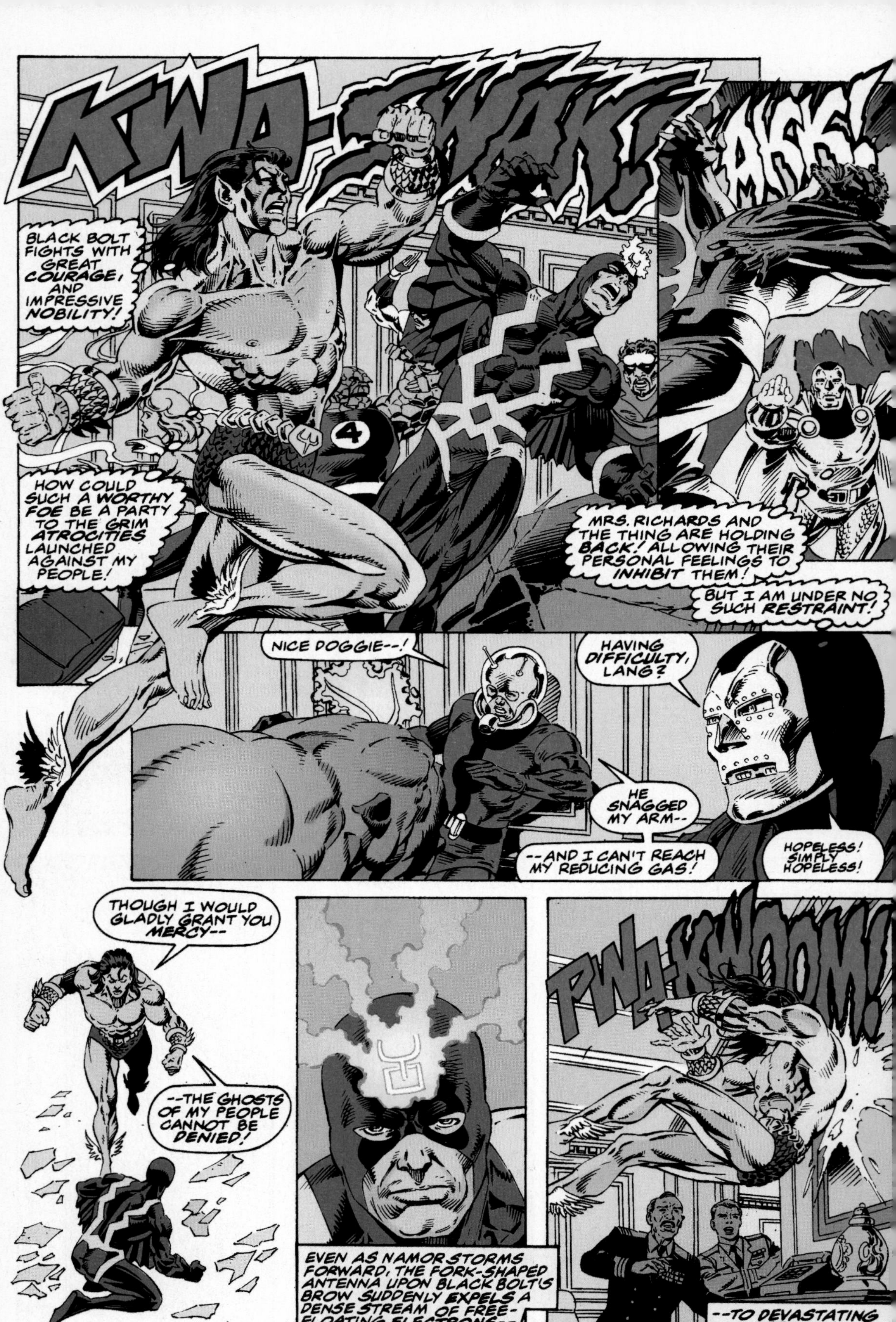
KWA-SWAK!
BLACK BOLT FIGHTS WITH GREAT COURAGE, AND IMPRESSIVE NOBILITY!
HOW COULD SUCH A WORTHY FOE BE A PARTY TO THE GRIM ATROCITIES LAUNCHED AGAINST MY PEOPLE!
MRS. RICHARDS AND THE THING ARE HOLDING BACK! ALLOWING THEIR PERSONAL FEELINGS TO INHIBIT THEM!
BUT I AM UNDER NO SUCH RESTRAINT!
NICE DOGGIE--!
HAVING DIFFICULTY, LANG?
HE SNAGGED MY ARM--
--AND I CAN'T REACH MY REDUCING GAS!
HOPELESS! SIMPLY HOPELESS!
THOUGH I WOULD GLADLY GRANT YOU MERCY--
--THE GHOSTS OF MY PEOPLE CANNOT BE DENIED!
EVEN AS NAMOR STORMS FORWARD, THE FORK-SHAPED ANTENNA UPON BLACK BOLT'S BROW SUDDENLY EXPELS A DENSE STREAM OF FREE-FLOATING ELECTRONS--
PWA-KWOOM!
--TO DEVASTATING EFFECT!

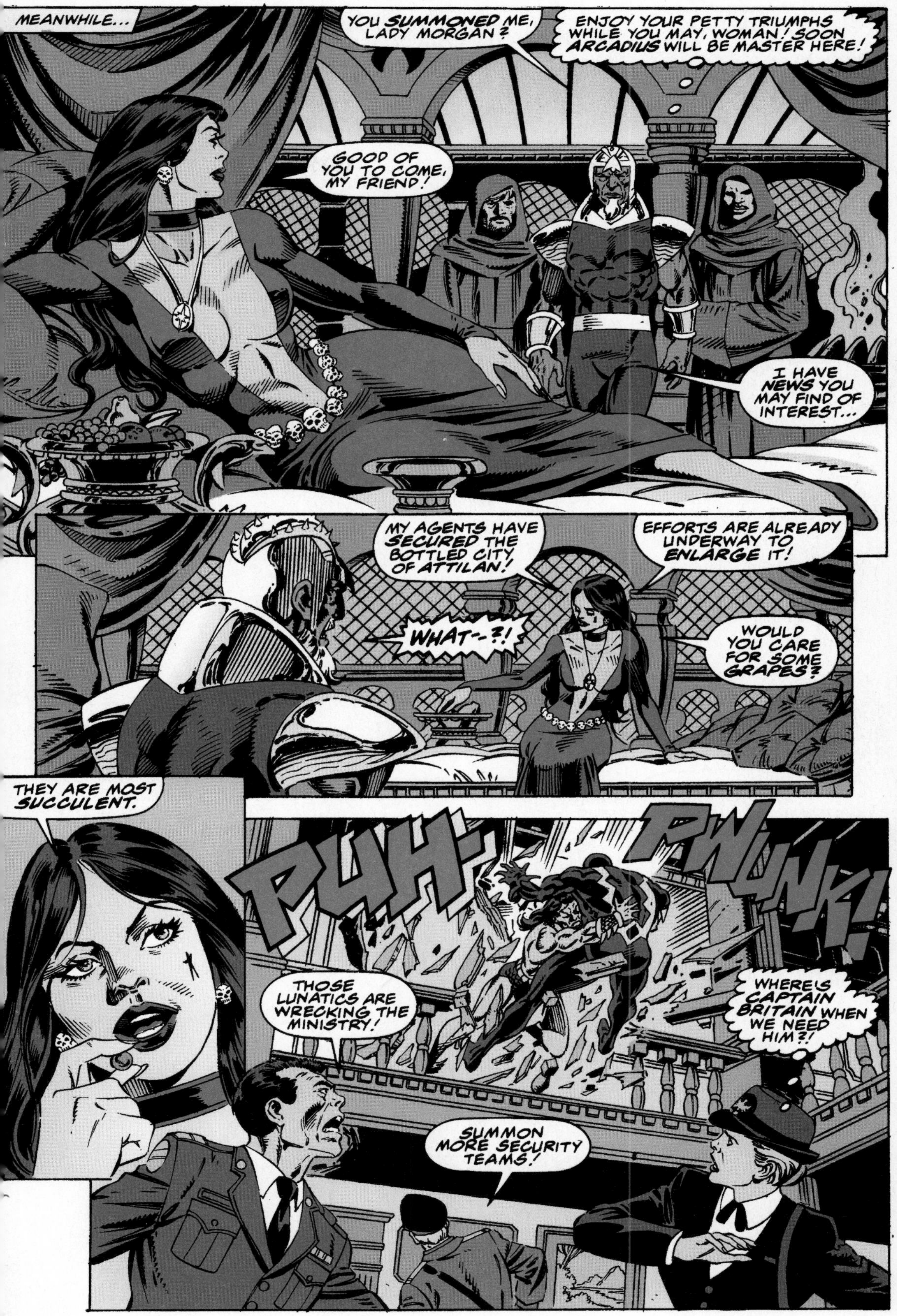
MEANWHILE...
YOU SUMMONED ME, LADY MORGAN?
ENJOY YOUR PETTY TRIUMPHS WHILE YOU MAY, WOMAN! SOON ARCADIUS WILL BE MASTER HERE!
GOOD OF YOU TO COME, MY FRIEND!
I HAVE NEWS YOU MAY FIND OF INTEREST...
MY AGENTS HAVE SECURED THE BOTTLED CITY OF ATTILAN!
EFFORTS ARE ALREADY UNDERWAY TO ENLARGE IT!
WHAT--?!
WOULD YOU CARE FOR SOME GRAPES?
THEY ARE MOST SUCCULENT.
PUH-PWUNK!
THOSE LUNATICS ARE WRECKING THE MINISTRY!
WHERE'S CAPTAIN BRITAIN WHEN WE NEED HIM?!
SUMMON MORE SECURITY TEAMS!

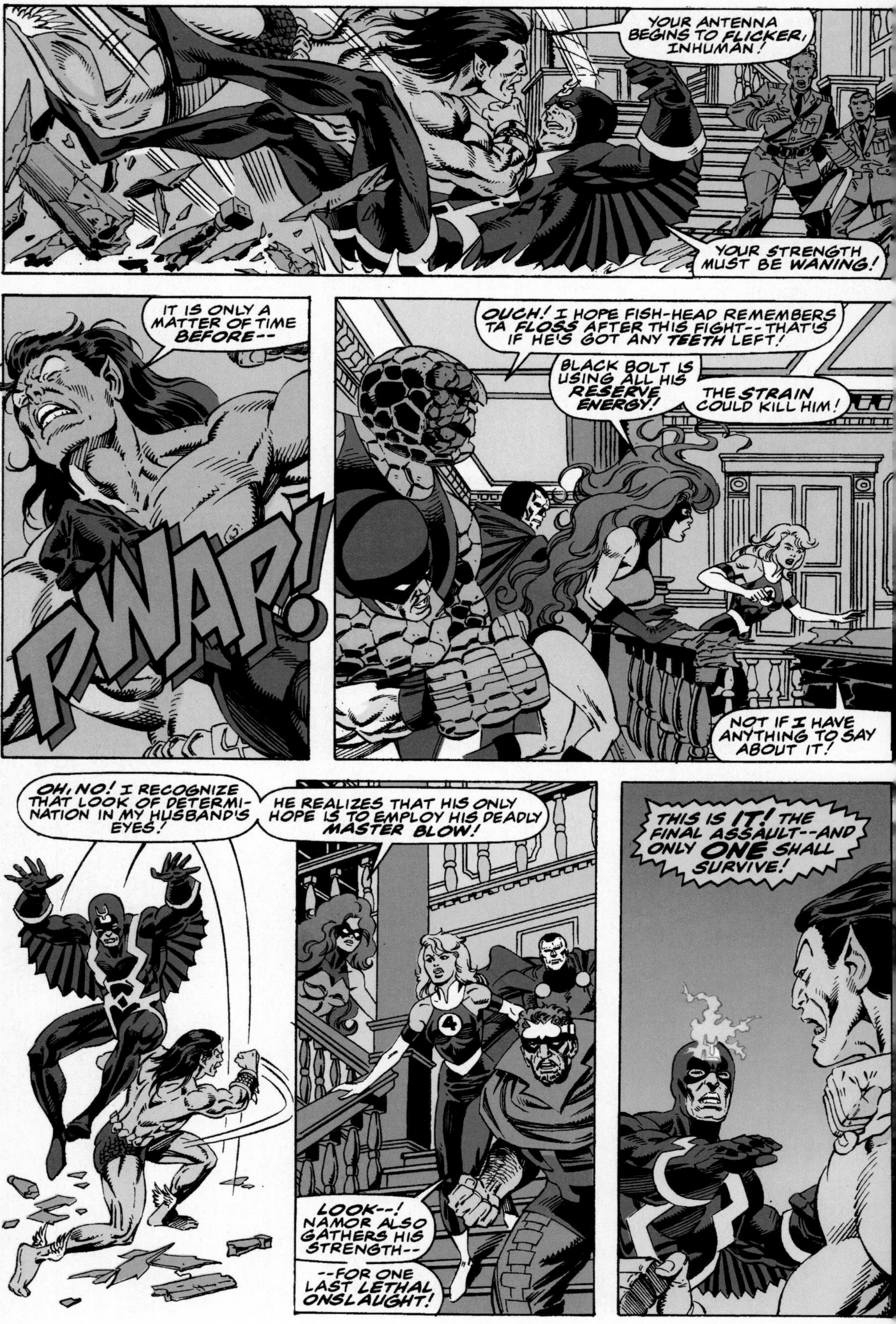
YOUR ANTENNA BEGINS TO FLICKER, INHUMAN!
YOUR STRENGTH MUST BE WANING!
IT IS ONLY A MATTER OF TIME BEFORE--
PWAP!
OUCH! I HOPE FISH-HEAD REMEMBERS TA FLOSS AFTER THIS FIGHT-- THAT'S IF HE'S GOT ANY TEETH LEFT!
BLACK BOLT IS USING ALL HIS RESERVE ENERGY!
THE STRAIN COULD KILL HIM!
NOT IF I HAVE ANYTHING TO SAY ABOUT IT!
OH, NO! I RECOGNIZE THAT LOOK OF DETERMINATION IN MY HUSBAND'S EYES!
HE REALIZES THAT HIS ONLY HOPE IS TO EMPLOY HIS DEADLY MASTER BLOW!
LOOK--! NAMOR ALSO GATHERS HIS STRENGTH--
--FOR ONE LAST LETHAL ONSLAUGHT!
THIS IS IT! THE FINAL ASSAULT--AND ONLY ONE SHALL SURVIVE!

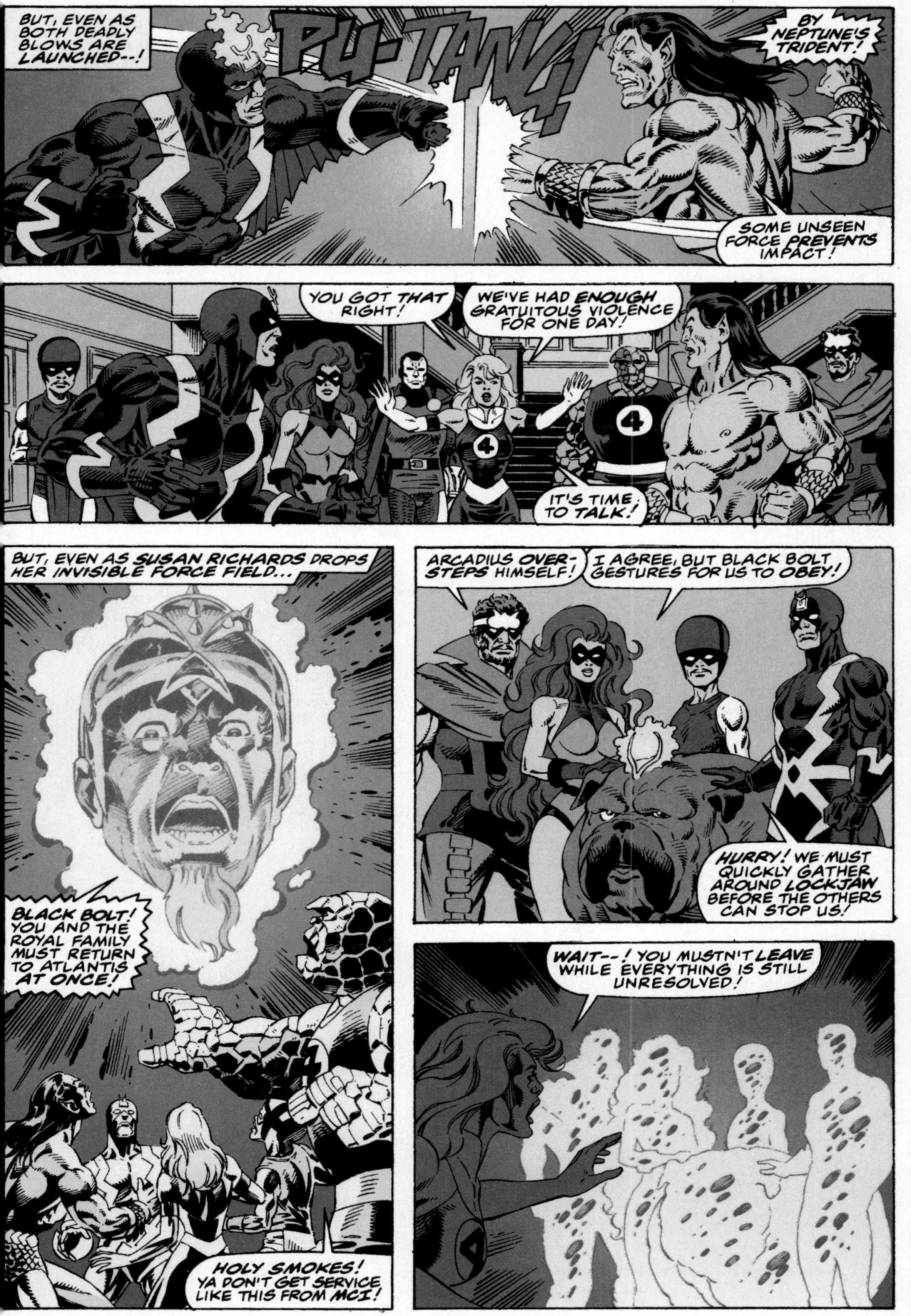
BUT, EVEN AS BOTH DEADLY BLOWS ARE LAUNCHED--!
PU-TANG!
BY NEPTUNE'S TRIDENT!
SOME UNSEEN FORCE PREVENTS IMPACT!
YOU GOT THAT RIGHT!
WE'VE HAD ENOUGH GRATUITOUS VIOLENCE FOR ONE DAY!
IT'S TIME TO TALK!
BUT, EVEN AS SUSAN RICHARDS DROPS HER INVISIBLE FORCE FIELD...
BLACK BOLT! YOU AND THE ROYAL FAMILY MUST RETURN TO ATLANTIS AT ONCE!
HOLY SMOKES! YA DON'T GET SERVICE LIKE THIS FROM MCI!
ARCADIUS OVER-STEPS HIMSELF!
I AGREE, BUT BLACK BOLT GESTURES FOR US TO OBEY!
HURRY! WE MUST QUICKLY GATHER AROUND LOCKJAW BEFORE THE OTHERS CAN STOP US!
WAIT--! YOU MUSTN'T LEAVE WHILE EVERYTHING IS STILL UNRESOLVED!

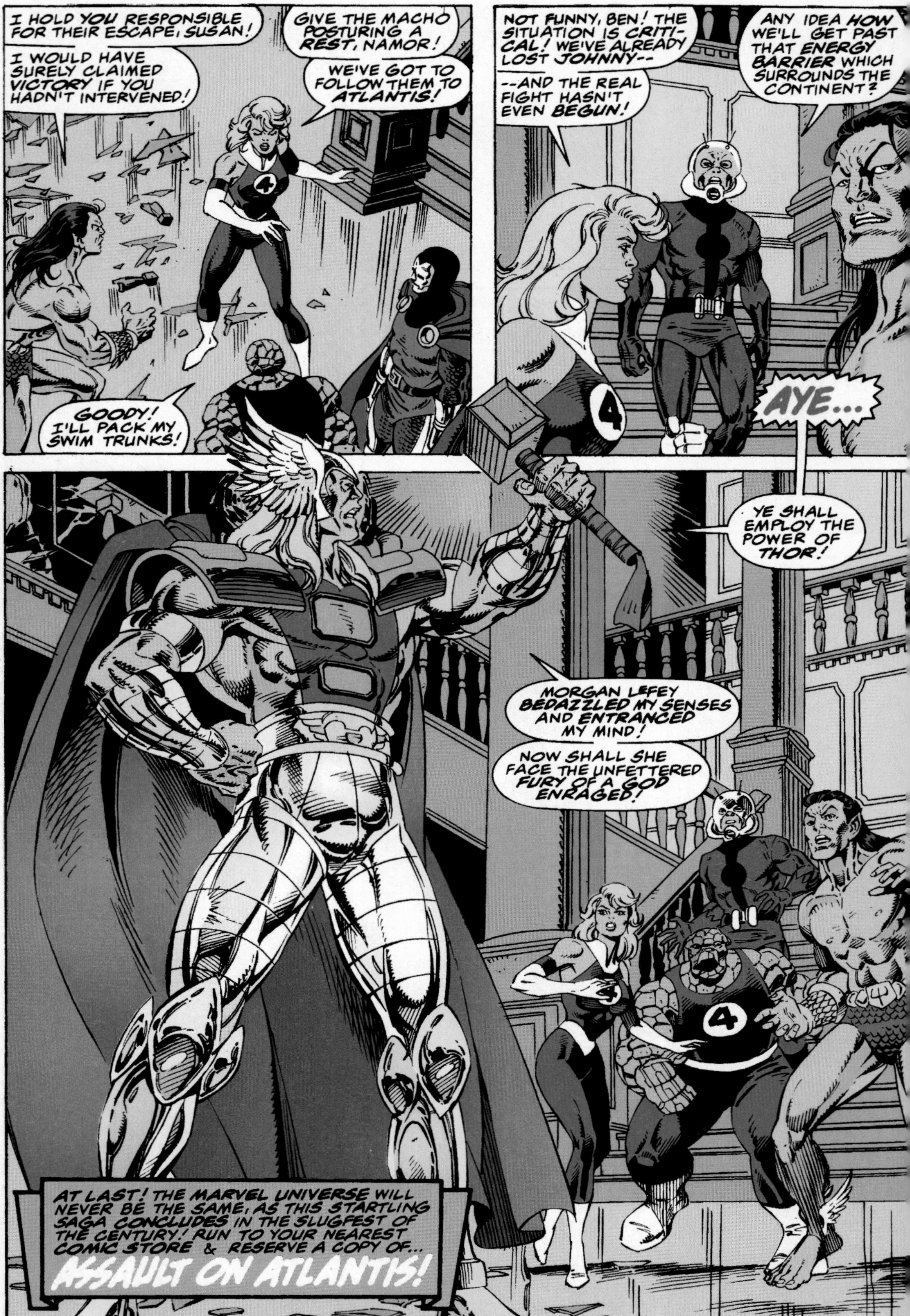
I HOLD YOU RESPONSIBLE FOR THEIR ESCAPE, SUSAN!
I WOULD HAVE SURELY CLAIMED VICTORY IF YOU HADN'T INTERVENED!
GIVE THE MACHO POSTURING A REST, NAMOR!
WE'VE GOT TO FOLLOW THEM TO ATLANTIS!
GOODY! I'LL PACK MY SWIM TRUNKS!
NOT FUNNY, BEN! THE SITUATION IS CRITI-CAL! WE'VE ALREADY LOST JOHNNY--
--AND THE REAL FIGHT HASN'T EVEN BEGUN!
ANY IDEA HOW WE'LL GET PAST THAT ENERGY BARRIER WHICH SURROUNDS THE CONTINENT?
AYE...
YE SHALL EMPLOY THE POWER OF THOR!
MORGAN LEFEY BEDAZZLED MY SENSES AND ENTRANCED MY MIND!
NOW SHALL SHE FACE THE UNFETTERED FURY OF A GOD ENRAGED!
AT LAST! THE MARVEL UNIVERSE WILL NEVER BE THE SAME, AS THIS STARTLING SAGA CONCLUDES IN THE SLUGFEST OF THE CENTURY! RUN TO YOUR NEAREST COMIC STORE & RESERVE A COPY OF...
ASSAULT ON ATLANTIS!

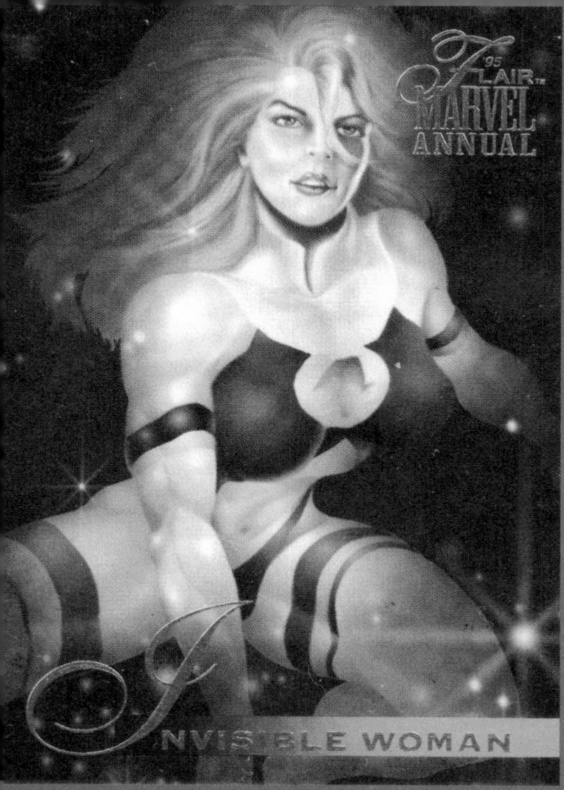
'95 FLAIR MARVEL ANNUAL
INVISIBLE WOMAN

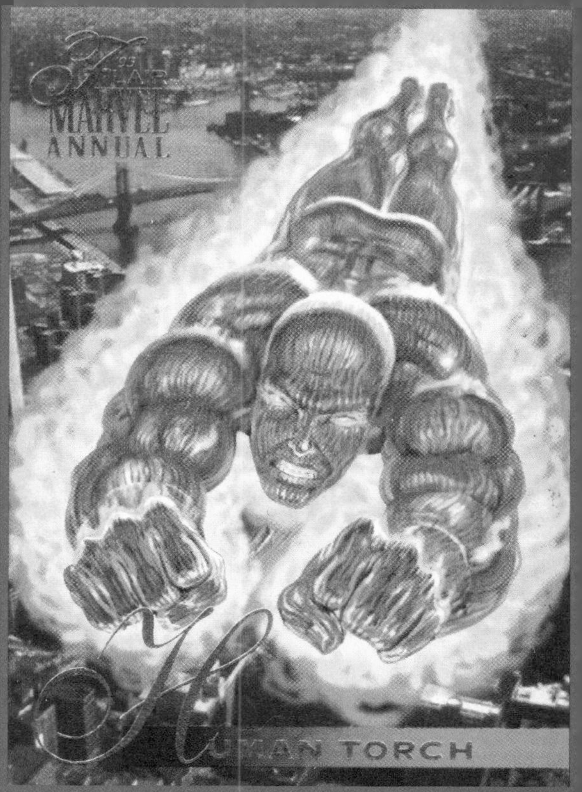
'95 FLAIR MARVEL ANNUAL
HUMAN TORCH

'95 FLAIR MARVEL ANNUAL
TRADING CARDS

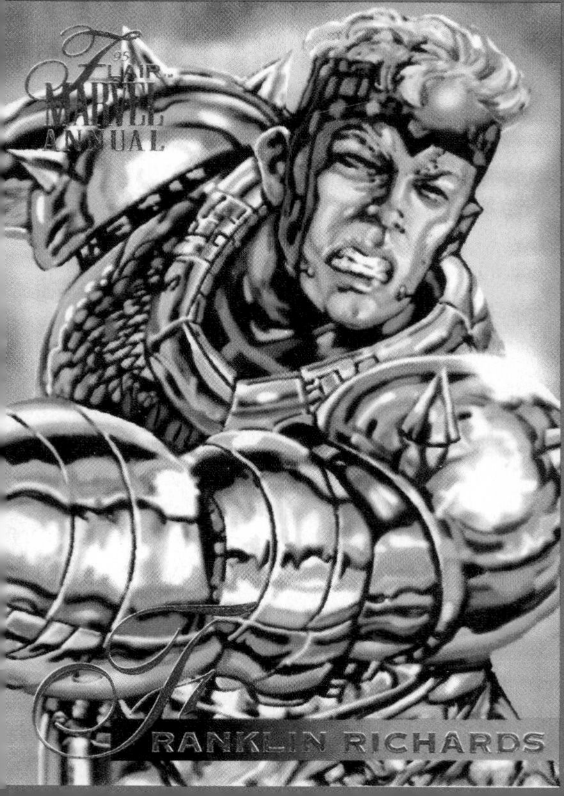
'95 FLAIR MARVEL ANNUAL
FRANKLIN RICHARDS

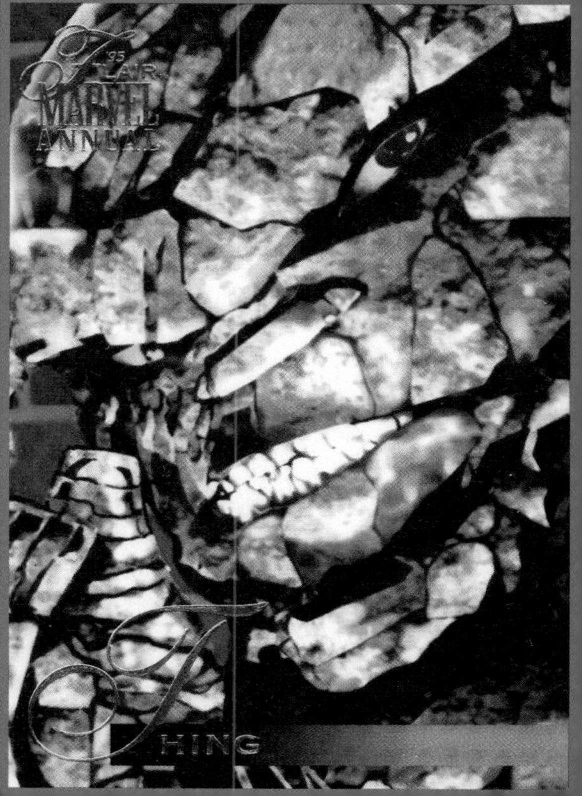
'95 FLAIR MARVEL ANNUAL
THING

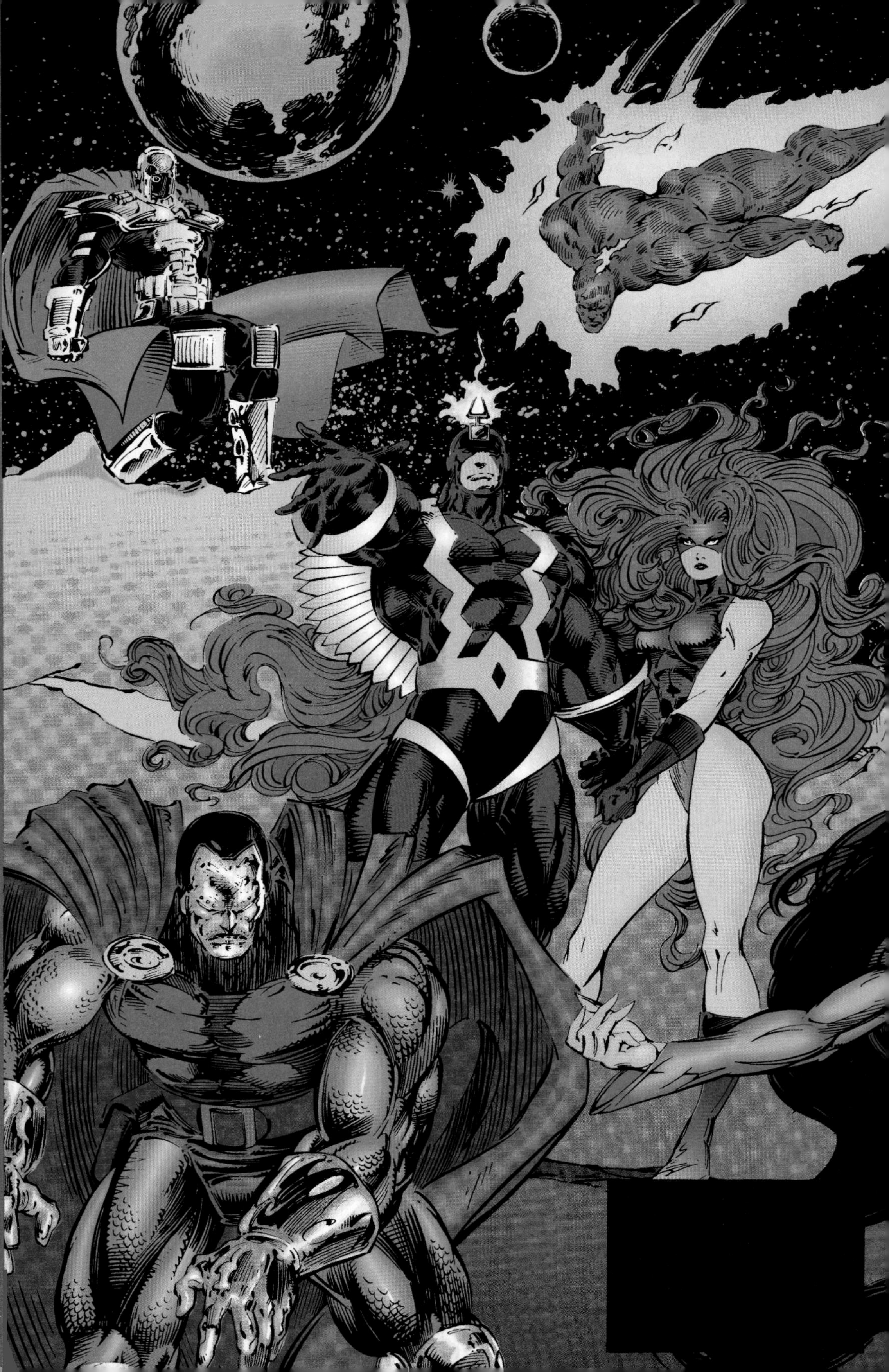

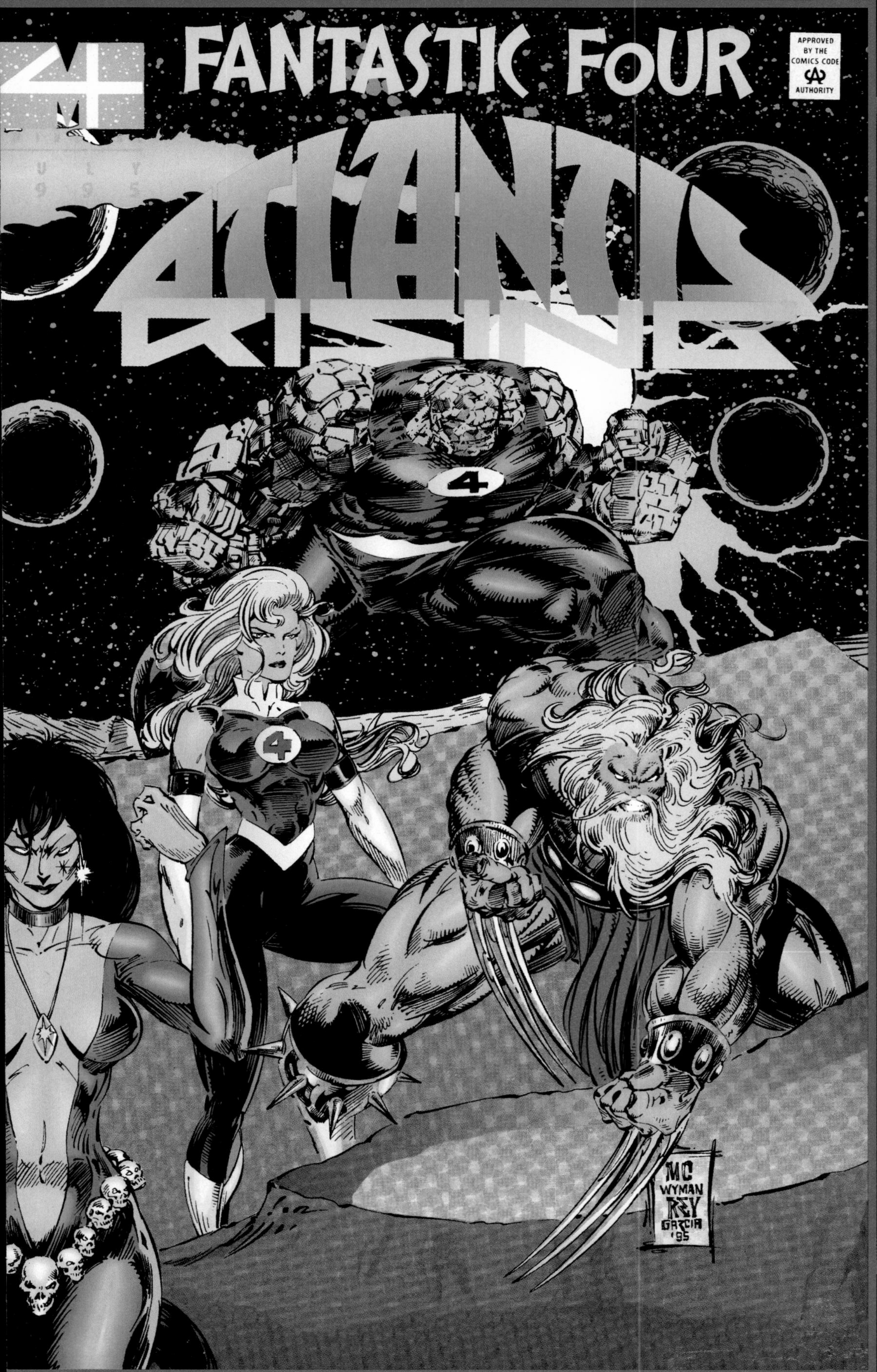
FANTASTIC FOUR
APPROVED BY THE COMICS CODE AUTHORITY
ATLANTIS RISING
MC WYMAN REY GARCIA '95

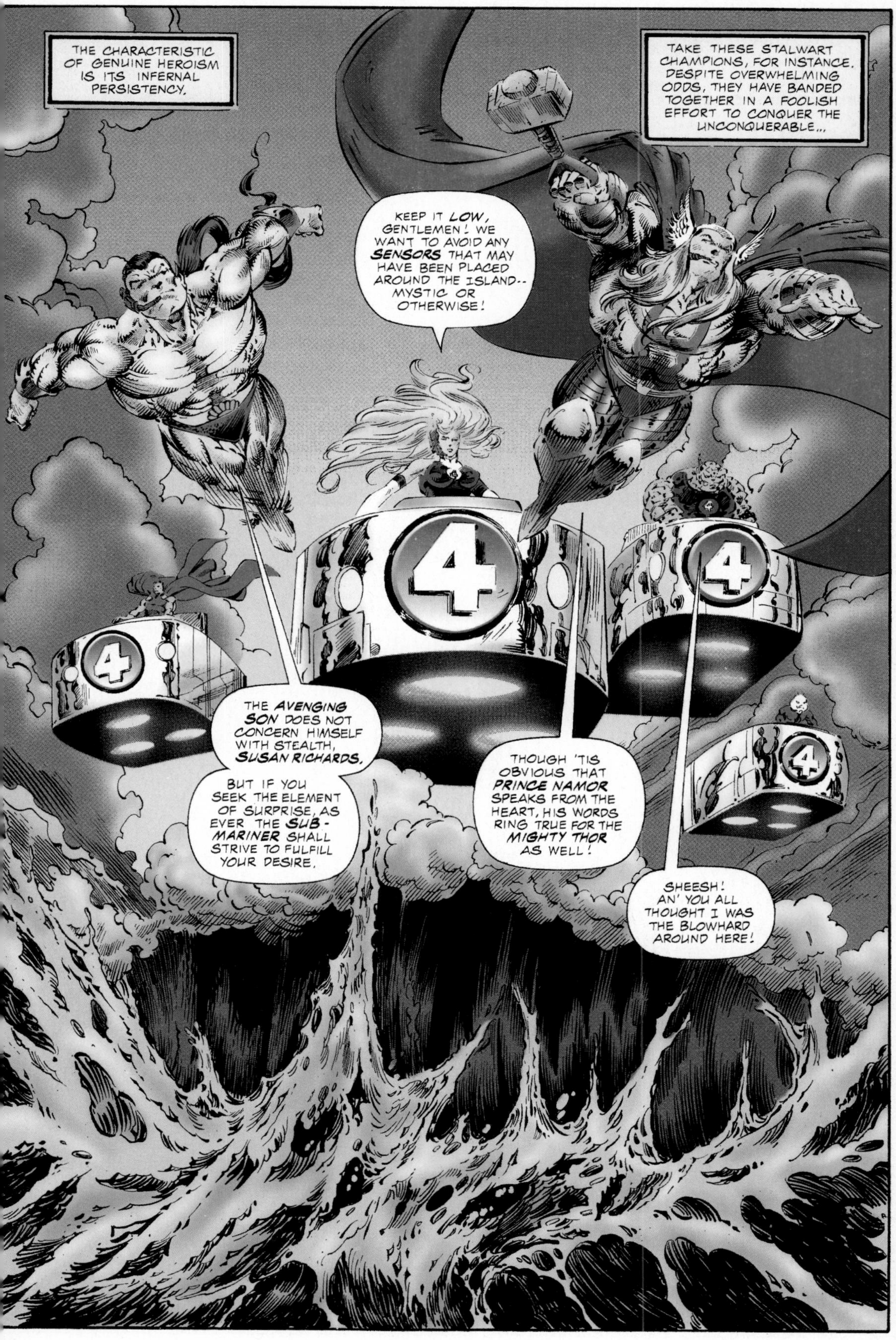
THE CHARACTERISTIC OF GENUINE HEROISM IS ITS INFERNAL PERSISTENCY.
TAKE THESE STALWART CHAMPIONS, FOR INSTANCE. DESPITE OVERWHELMING ODDS, THEY HAVE BANDED TOGETHER IN A FOOLISH EFFORT TO CONQUER THE UNCONQUERABLE...
KEEP IT LOW, GENTLEMEN! WE WANT TO AVOID ANY SENSORS THAT MAY HAVE BEEN PLACED AROUND THE ISLAND-- MYSTIC OR OTHERWISE!
THE AVENGING SON DOES NOT CONCERN HIMSELF WITH STEALTH, SUSAN RICHARDS.
BUT IF YOU SEEK THE ELEMENT OF SURPRISE, AS EVER THE SUB-MARINER SHALL STRIVE TO FULFILL YOUR DESIRE.
THOUGH 'TIS OBVIOUS THAT PRINCE NAMOR SPEAKS FROM THE HEART, HIS WORDS RING TRUE FOR THE MIGHTY THOR AS WELL!
SHEESH! AN' YOU ALL THOUGHT I WAS THE BLOWHARD AROUND HERE!

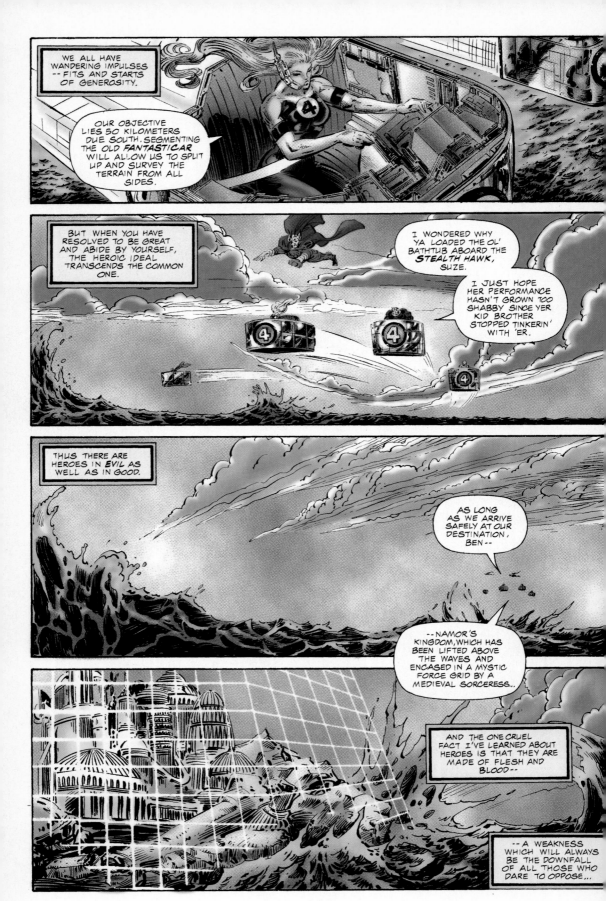

WE ALL HAVE WANDERING IMPULSES -- FITS AND STARTS OF GENEROSITY.

OUR OBJECTIVE LIES 50 KILOMETERS DUE SOUTH. SEGMENTING THE OLD *FANTASTICAR* WILL ALLOW US TO SPLIT UP AND SURVEY THE TERRAIN FROM ALL SIDES.

BUT WHEN YOU HAVE RESOLVED TO BE GREAT AND ABIDE BY YOURSELF, THE HEROIC IDEAL TRANSCEND THE COMMON ONE.

I WONDERED WHY YA LOADED THE OL' BATHTUB ABOARD THE *STEALTH HAWK*, SUZE.

I JUST HOPE HER PERFORMANCE HASN'T GROWN TOO SHABBY SINCE YER KID BROTHER STOPPED TINKERIN' WITH 'ER.

THUS THERE ARE HEROES IN *EVIL* AS WELL AS IN GOOD.

AS LONG AS WE ARRIVE SAFELY AT OUR DESTINATION, BEN --

-- NAMOR'S KINGDOM, WHICH HAS BEEN LIFTED ABOVE THE WAVES AND ENCASED IN A MYSTIC FORCE GRID BY A MEDIEVAL SORCERESS...

AND THE ONE CRUEL FACT I'VE LEARNED ABOUT HEROES IS THAT THEY ARE MADE OF FLESH AND BLOOD --

-- A WEAKNESS WHICH WILL ALWAYS BE THE DOWNFALL OF ALL THOSE WHO DARE TO OPPOSE...

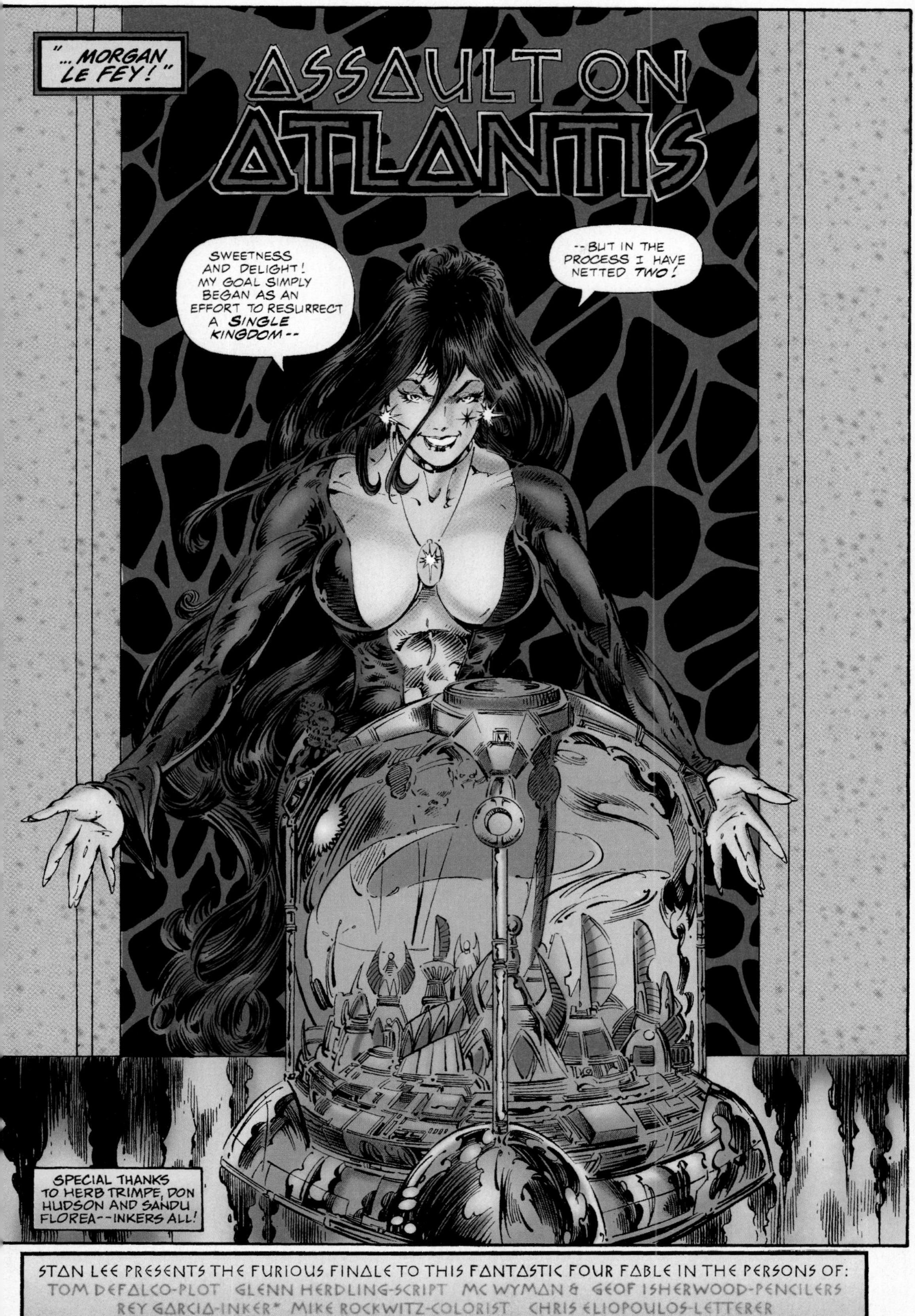
"...MORGAN LE FEY!"
ASSAULT ON ATLANTIS
SWEETNESS AND DELIGHT! MY GOAL SIMPLY BEGAN AS AN EFFORT TO RESURRECT A SINGLE KINGDOM--
--BUT IN THE PROCESS I HAVE NETTED TWO!
SPECIAL THANKS TO HERB TRIMPE, DON HUDSON AND SANDU FLOREA--INKERS ALL!
STAN LEE PRESENTS THE FURIOUS FINALE TO THIS FANTASTIC FOUR FABLE IN THE PERSONS OF:
TOM DEFALCO-PLOT GLENN HERDLING-SCRIPT MC WYMAN & GEOF ISHERWOOD-PENCILERS
REY GARCIA-INKER* MIKE ROCKWITZ-COLORIST CHRIS ELIOPOULOS-LETTERER
NEL YOMTOV-EDITOR MARK GRUENWALD-ONE MAN WHO IS AN ISLAND

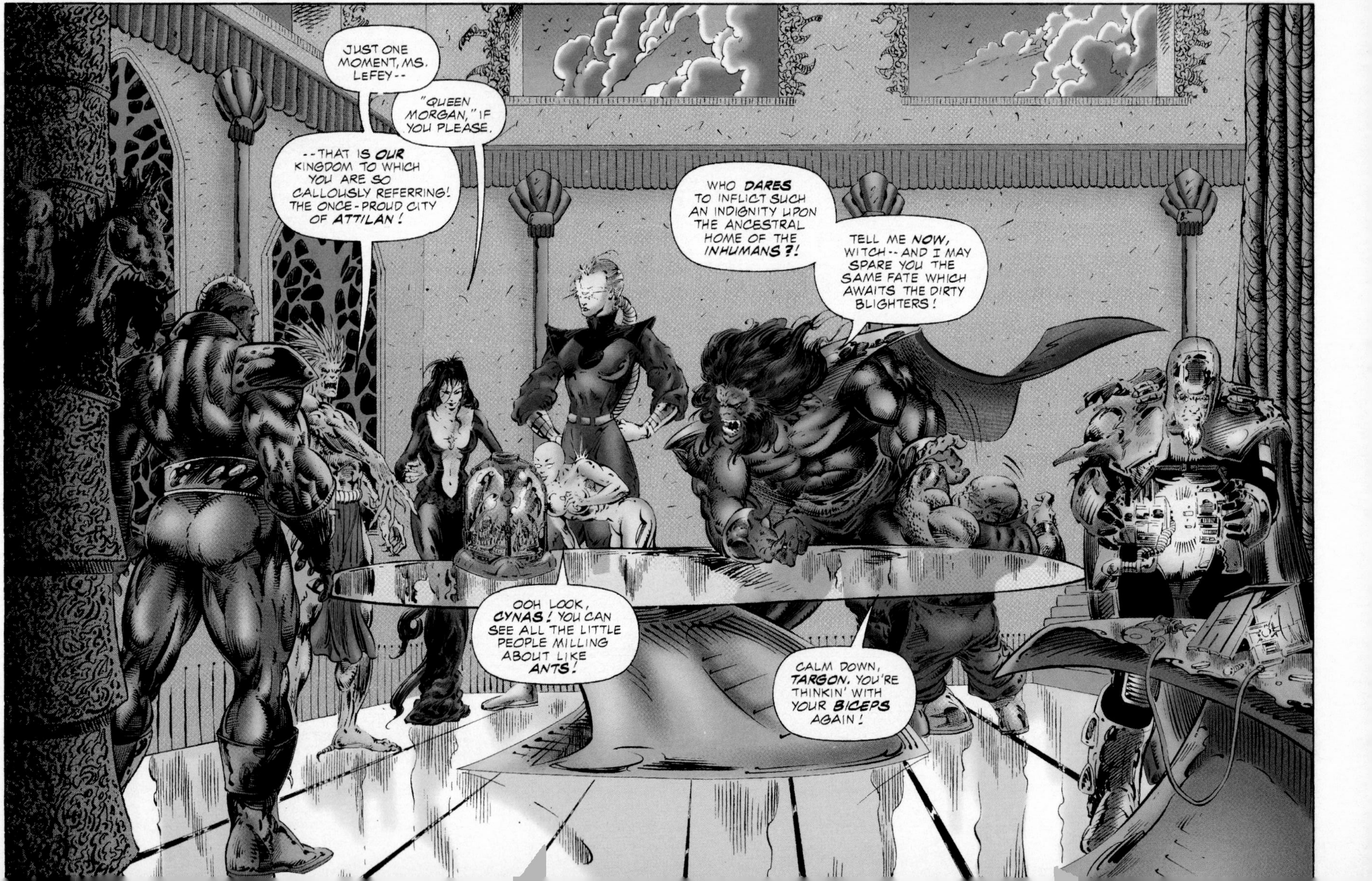
JUST ONE MOMENT, MS. LEFEY--
"QUEEN MORGAN," IF YOU PLEASE.
--THAT IS OUR KINGDOM TO WHICH YOU ARE SO CALLOUSLY REFERRING! THE ONCE-PROUD CITY OF ATTILAN!
WHO DARES TO INFLICT SUCH AN INDIGNITY UPON THE ANCESTRAL HOME OF THE INHUMANS?!
TELL ME NOW, WITCH--AND I MAY SPARE YOU THE SAME FATE WHICH AWAITS THE DIRTY BLIGHTERS!
OOH LOOK, CYNAS! YOU CAN SEE ALL THE LITTLE PEOPLE MILLING ABOUT LIKE ANTS!
CALM DOWN, TARGON. YOU'RE THINKIN' WITH YOUR BICEPS AGAIN!

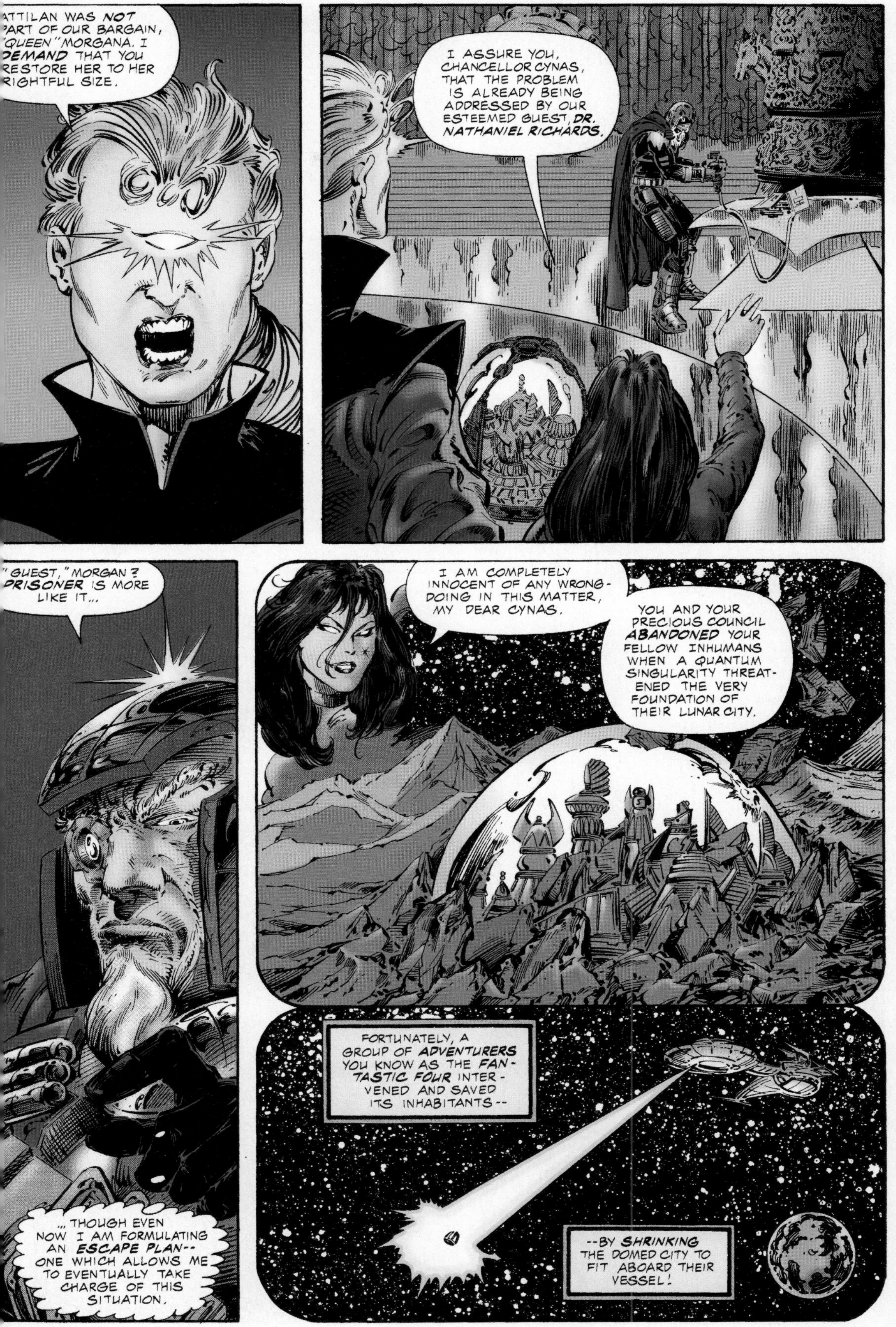
ATTILAN WAS NOT PART OF OUR BARGAIN, "QUEEN" MORGANA. I DEMAND THAT YOU RESTORE HER TO HER RIGHTFUL SIZE.
I ASSURE YOU, CHANCELLOR CYNAS, THAT THE PROBLEM IS ALREADY BEING ADDRESSED BY OUR ESTEEMED GUEST, DR. NATHANIEL RICHARDS.
"GUEST," MORGAN? PRISONER IS MORE LIKE IT...
... THOUGH EVEN NOW I AM FORMULATING AN ESCAPE PLAN-- ONE WHICH ALLOWS ME TO EVENTUALLY TAKE CHARGE OF THIS SITUATION.
I AM COMPLETELY INNOCENT OF ANY WRONG-DOING IN THIS MATTER, MY DEAR CYNAS.
YOU AND YOUR PRECIOUS COUNCIL ABANDONED YOUR FELLOW INHUMANS WHEN A QUANTUM SINGULARITY THREATENED THE VERY FOUNDATION OF THEIR LUNAR CITY.
FORTUNATELY, A GROUP OF ADVENTURERS YOU KNOW AS THE FANTASTIC FOUR INTERVENED AND SAVED ITS INHABITANTS--
--BY SHRINKING THE DOMED CITY TO FIT ABOARD THEIR VESSEL!

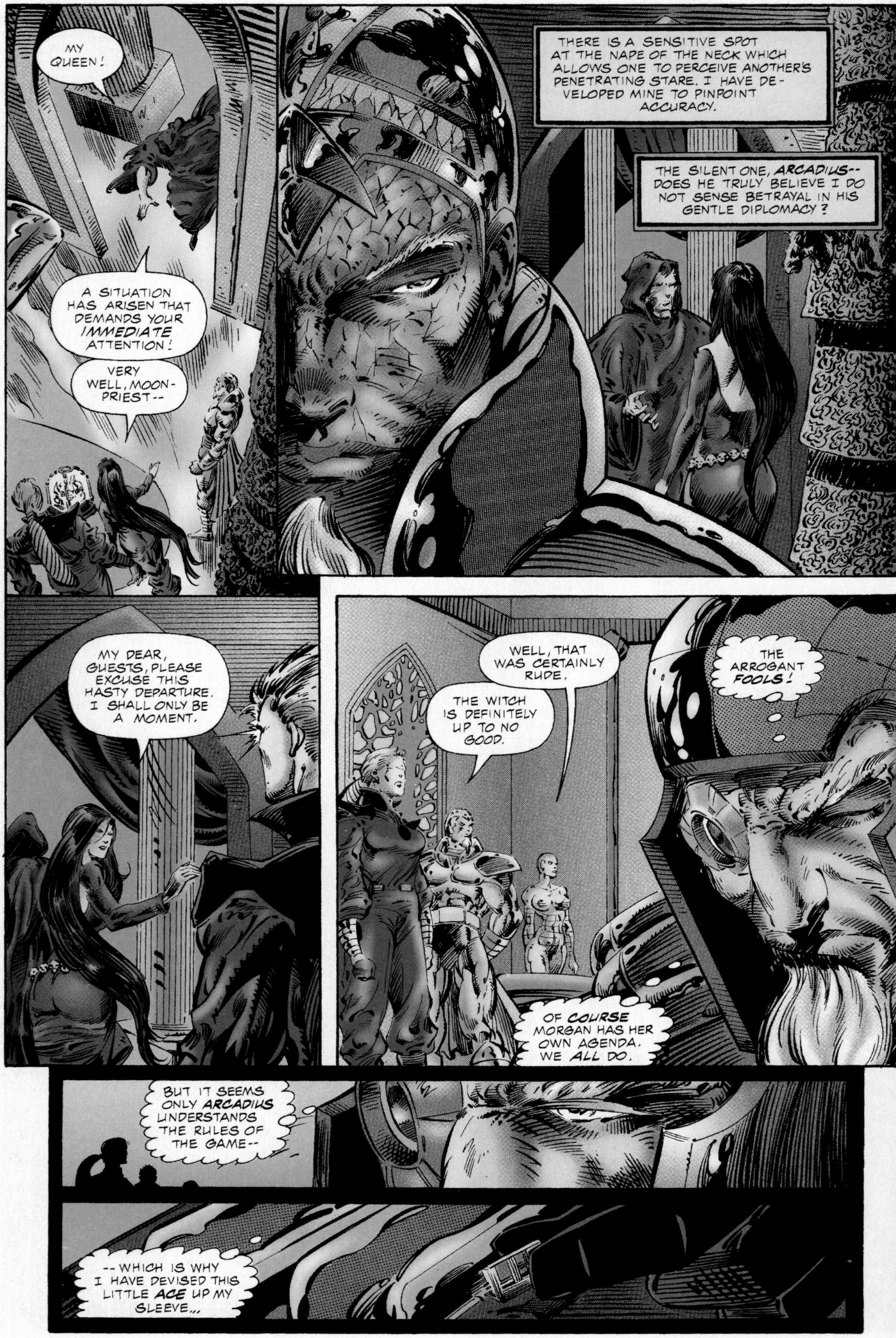
MY QUEEN!
THERE IS A SENSITIVE SPOT AT THE NAPE OF THE NECK WHICH ALLOWS ONE TO PERCEIVE ANOTHER'S PENETRATING STARE. I HAVE DEVELOPED MINE TO PINPOINT ACCURACY.
THE SILENT ONE, ARCADIUS-- DOES HE TRULY BELIEVE I DO NOT SENSE BETRAYAL IN HIS GENTLE DIPLOMACY?
A SITUATION HAS ARISEN THAT DEMANDS YOUR IMMEDIATE ATTENTION!
VERY WELL, MOON-PRIEST--
MY DEAR, GUESTS, PLEASE EXCUSE THIS HASTY DEPARTURE. I SHALL ONLY BE A MOMENT.
WELL, THAT WAS CERTAINLY RUDE.
THE WITCH IS DEFINITELY UP TO NO GOOD.
THE ARROGANT FOOLS!
OF COURSE MORGAN HAS HER OWN AGENDA. WE ALL DO.
BUT IT SEEMS ONLY ARCADIUS UNDERSTANDS THE RULES OF THE GAME--
--WHICH IS WHY I HAVE DEVISED THIS LITTLE ACE UP MY SLEEVE...

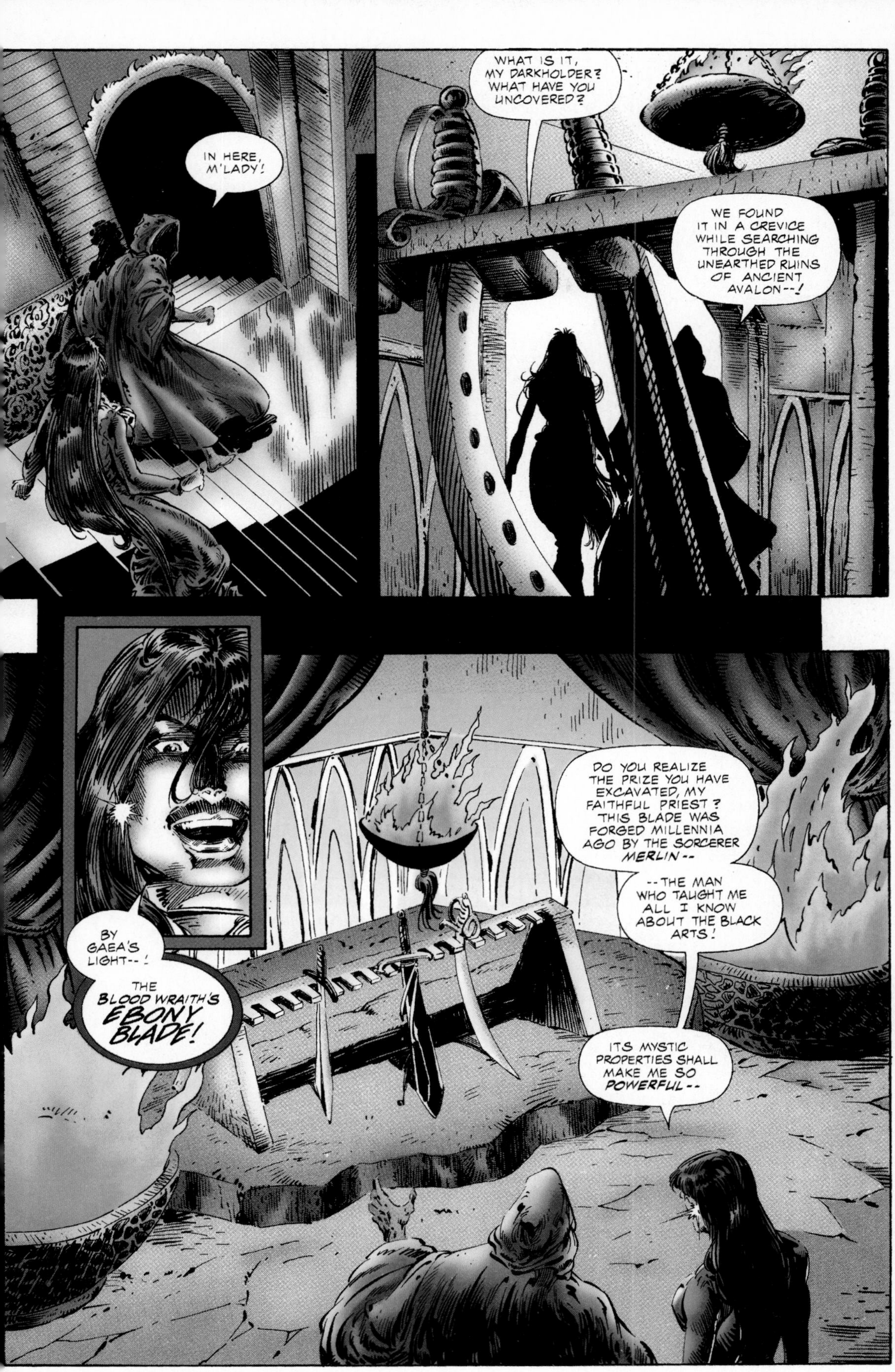

IN HERE, M'LADY!
WHAT IS IT, MY DARKHOLDER? WHAT HAVE YOU UNCOVERED?
WE FOUND IT IN A CREVICE WHILE SEARCHING THROUGH THE UNEARTHED RUINS OF ANCIENT AVALON--!
BY GAEA'S LIGHT--!
THE BLOOD WRAITH'S EBONY BLADE!
DO YOU REALIZE THE PRIZE YOU HAVE EXCAVATED, MY FAITHFUL PRIEST? THIS BLADE WAS FORGED MILLENNIA AGO BY THE SORCERER MERLIN--
--THE MAN WHO TAUGHT ME ALL I KNOW ABOUT THE BLACK ARTS!
ITS MYSTIC PROPERTIES SHALL MAKE ME SO POWERFUL--

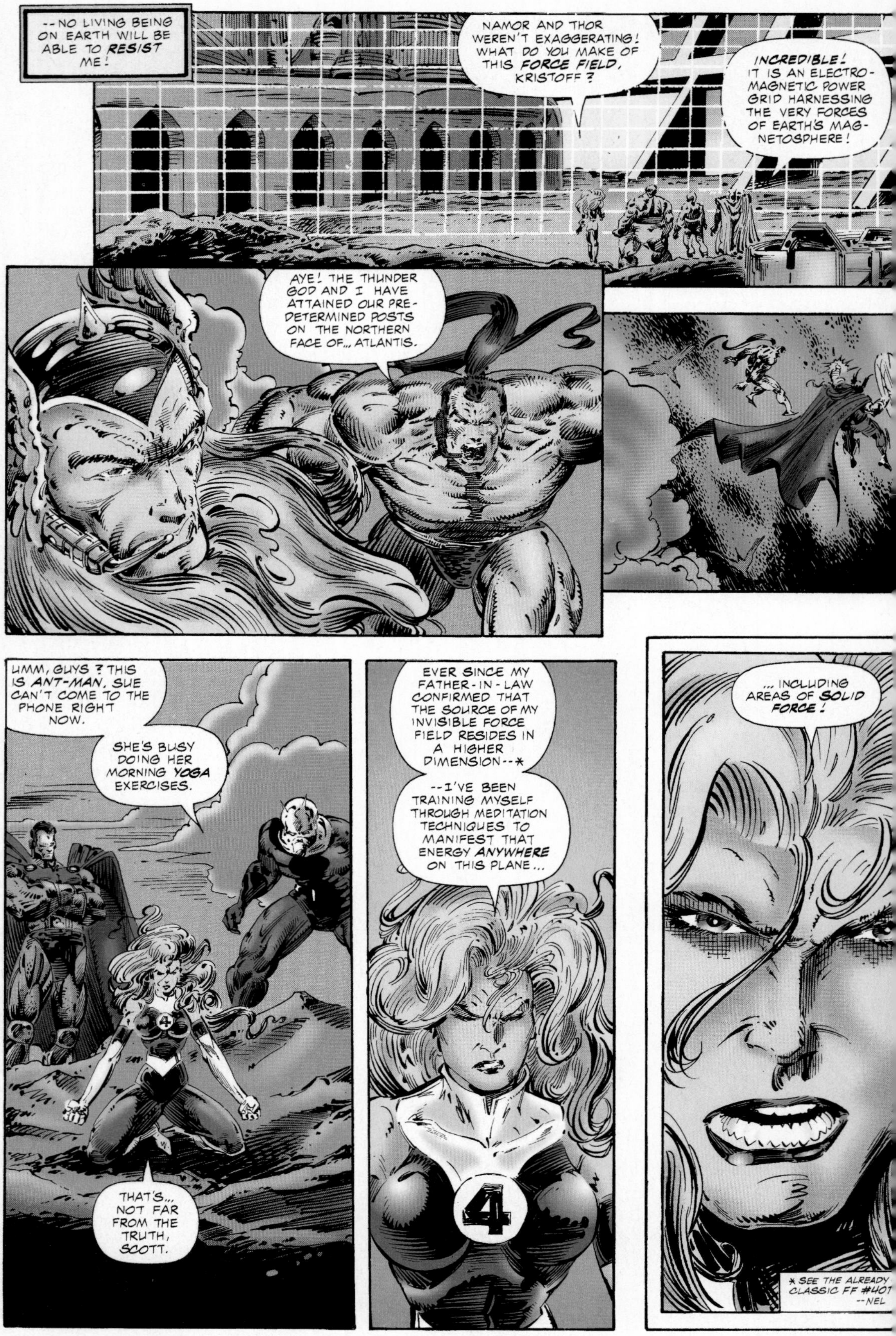
--NO LIVING BEING ON EARTH WILL BE ABLE TO RESIST ME!
NAMOR AND THOR WEREN'T EXAGGERATING! WHAT DO YOU MAKE OF THIS FORCE FIELD, KRISTOFF?
INCREDIBLE! IT IS AN ELECTRO-MAGNETIC POWER GRID HARNESSING THE VERY FORCES OF EARTH'S MAG-NETOSPHERE!
AYE! THE THUNDER GOD AND I HAVE ATTAINED OUR PRE-DETERMINED POSTS ON THE NORTHERN FACE OF... ATLANTIS.
UMM, GUYS? THIS IS ANT-MAN. SUE CAN'T COME TO THE PHONE RIGHT NOW.
SHE'S BUSY DOING HER MORNING YOGA EXERCISES.
THAT'S... NOT FAR FROM THE TRUTH, SCOTT.
EVER SINCE MY FATHER-IN-LAW CONFIRMED THAT THE SOURCE OF MY INVISIBLE FORCE FIELD RESIDES IN A HIGHER DIMENSION--*
--I'VE BEEN TRAINING MYSELF THROUGH MEDITATION TECHNIQUES TO MANIFEST THAT ENERGY ANYWHERE ON THIS PLANE...
...INCLUDING AREAS OF SOLID FORCE!
* SEE THE ALREADY CLASSIC FF #401 --NEL

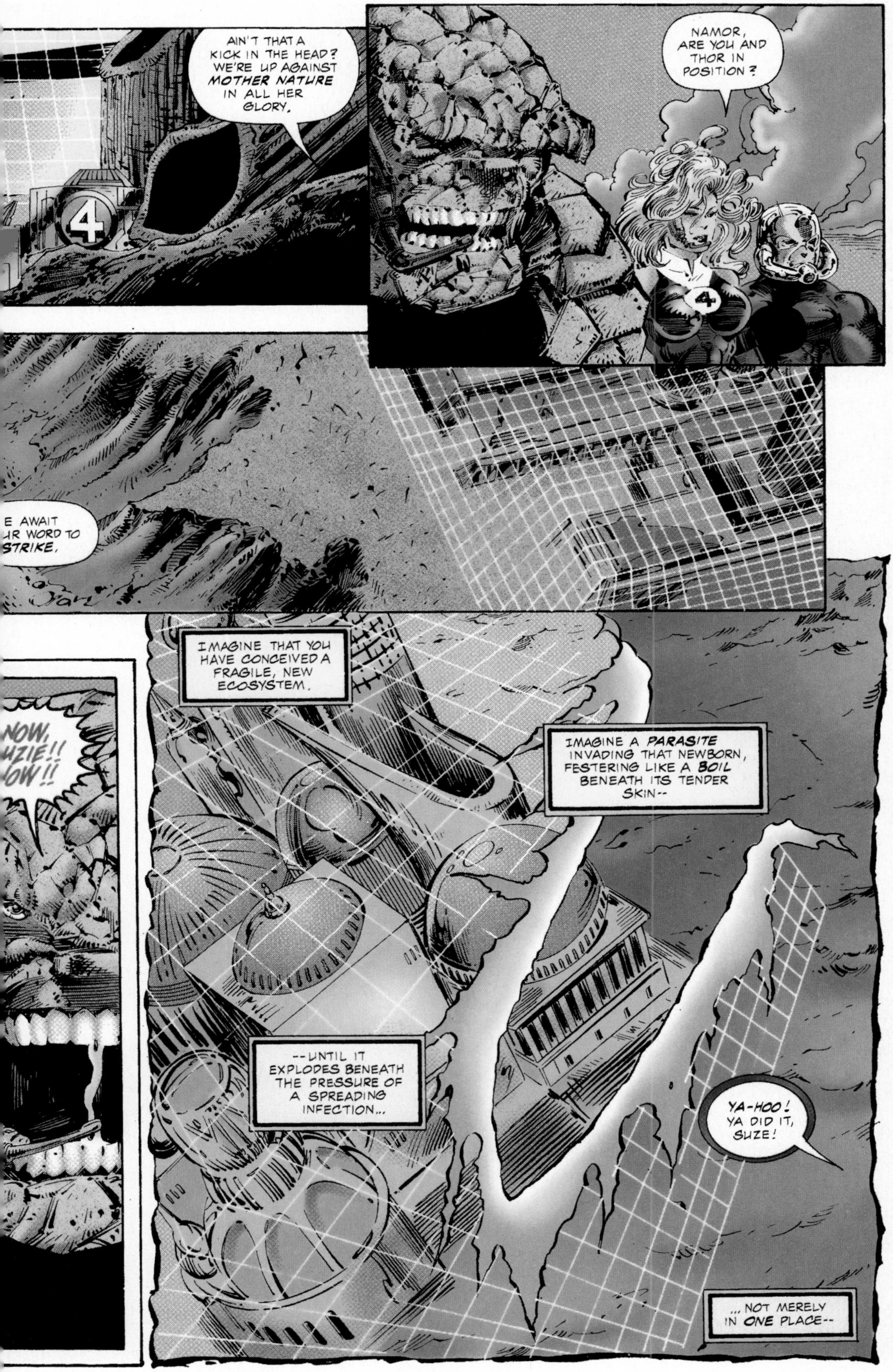
AIN'T THAT A KICK IN THE HEAD? WE'RE UP AGAINST MOTHER NATURE IN ALL HER GLORY.
NAMOR, ARE YOU AND THOR IN POSITION?
E AWAIT UR WORD TO STRIKE.
IMAGINE THAT YOU HAVE CONCEIVED A FRAGILE, NEW ECOSYSTEM.
IMAGINE A PARASITE INVADING THAT NEWBORN, FESTERING LIKE A BOIL BENEATH ITS TENDER SKIN--
NOW, UZIE!! OW!!
--UNTIL IT EXPLODES BENEATH THE PRESSURE OF A SPREADING INFECTION...
YA-HOO! YA DID IT, SUZE!
...NOT MERELY IN ONE PLACE--

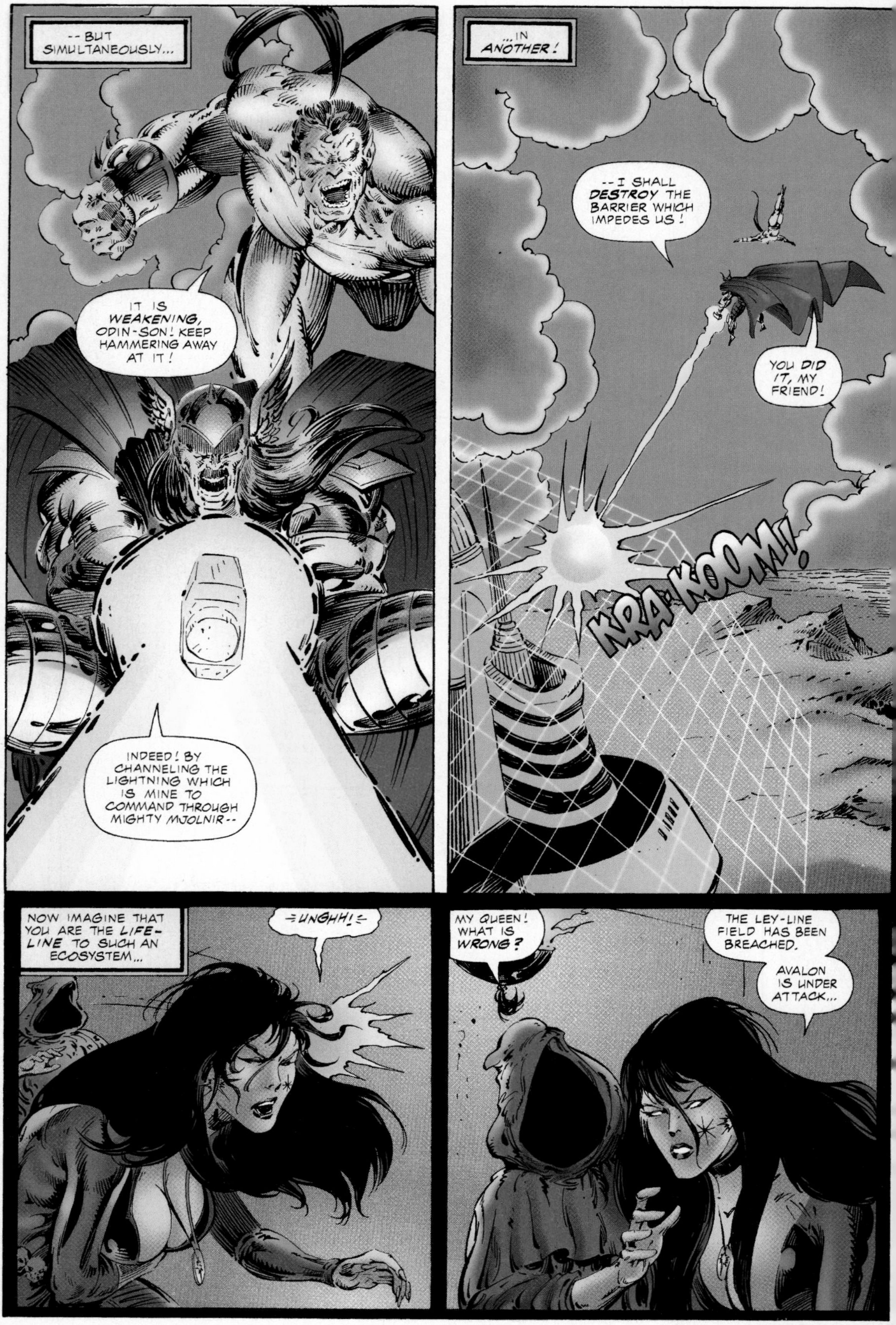

-- BUT SIMULTANEOUSLY...
IT IS *WEAKENING*, ODIN-SON! KEEP HAMMERING AWAY AT IT!
INDEED! BY CHANNELING THE LIGHTNING WHICH IS MINE TO COMMAND THROUGH MIGHTY MJOLNIR--
...IN *ANOTHER*!
--I SHALL *DESTROY* THE BARRIER WHICH IMPEDES US!
YOU *DID IT*, MY FRIEND!
KRA-KOOM!!
NOW IMAGINE THAT YOU ARE THE *LIFE-LINE* TO SUCH AN ECOSYSTEM...
-UNGHH!-
MY QUEEN! WHAT IS *WRONG*?
THE LEY-LINE FIELD HAS BEEN BREACHED.
AVALON IS UNDER ATTACK...

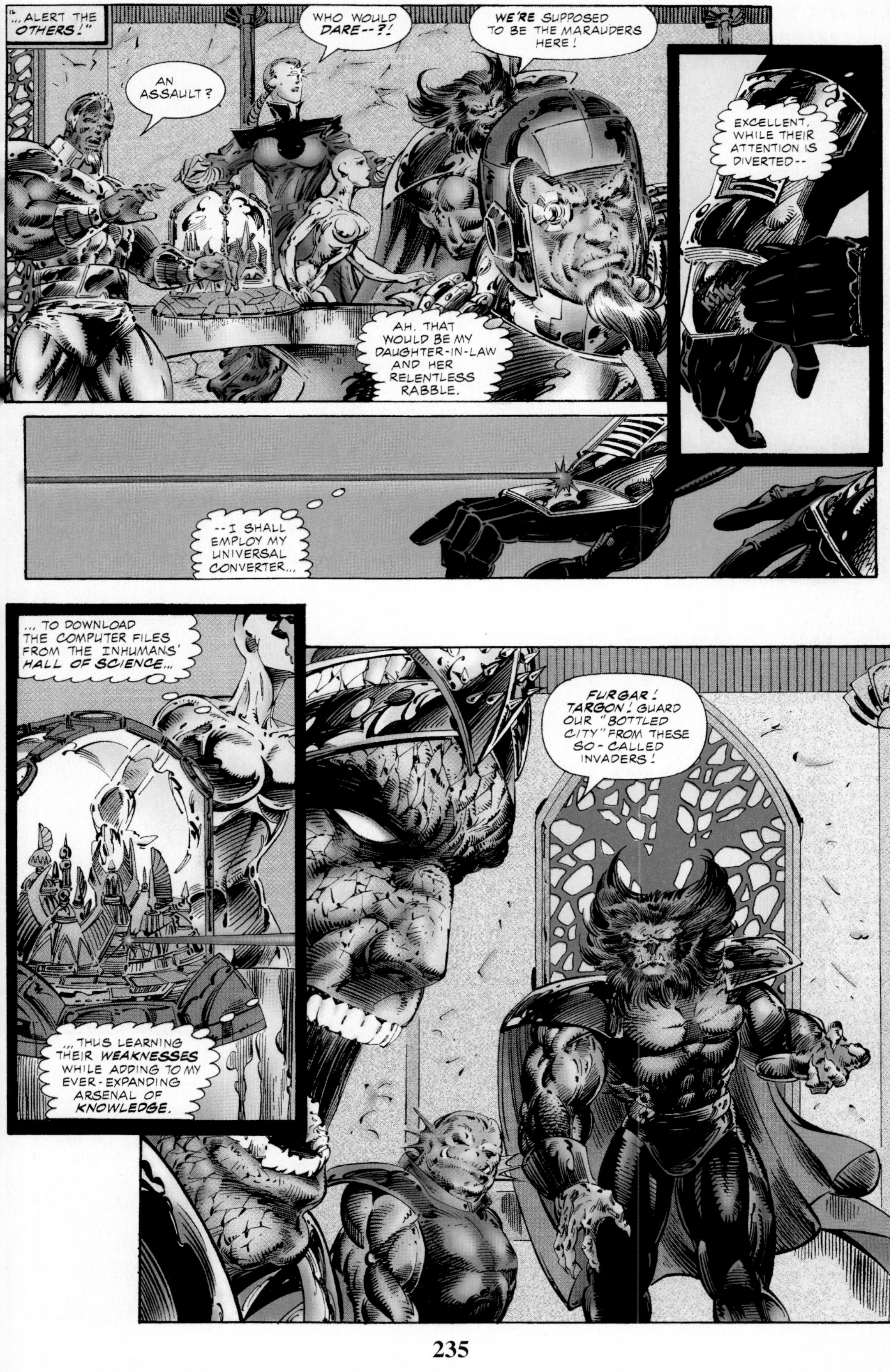
"...ALERT THE OTHERS!"
AN ASSAULT?
WHO WOULD DARE--?!
WE'RE SUPPOSED TO BE THE MARAUDERS HERE!
AH. THAT WOULD BE MY DAUGHTER-IN-LAW AND HER RELENTLESS RABBLE.
EXCELLENT. WHILE THEIR ATTENTION IS DIVERTED--
--I SHALL EMPLOY MY UNIVERSAL CONVERTER...
...TO DOWNLOAD THE COMPUTER FILES FROM THE INHUMANS' HALL OF SCIENCE...
...THUS LEARNING THEIR WEAKNESSES WHILE ADDING TO MY EVER-EXPANDING ARSENAL OF KNOWLEDGE.
FURGAR! TARGON! GUARD OUR "BOTTLED CITY" FROM THESE SO-CALLED INVADERS!

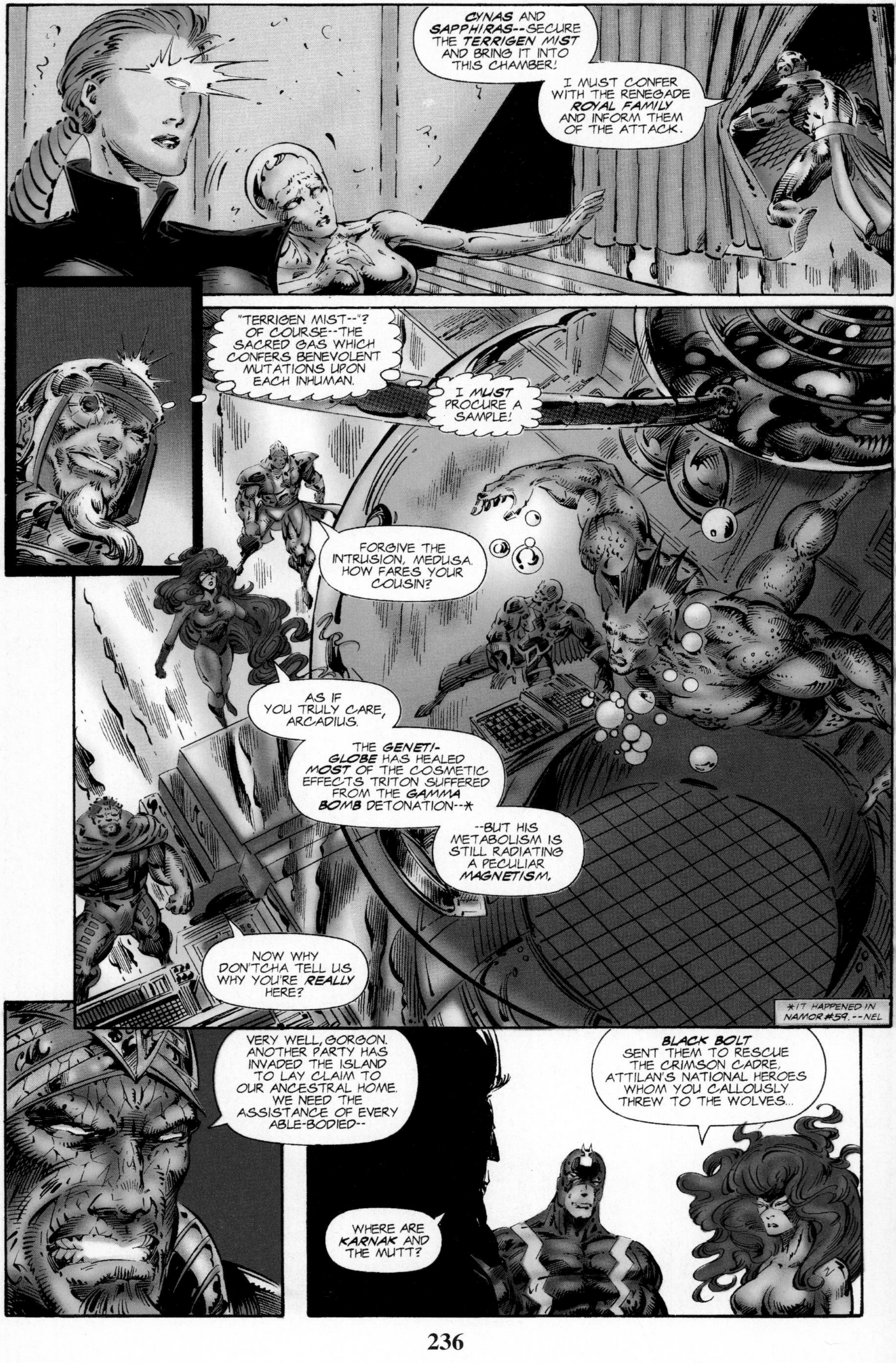
CYNAS AND SAPPHIRAS--SECURE THE TERRIGEN MIST AND BRING IT INTO THIS CHAMBER!
I MUST CONFER WITH THE RENEGADE ROYAL FAMILY AND INFORM THEM OF THE ATTACK.
"TERRIGEN MIST--"? OF COURSE--THE SACRED GAS WHICH CONFERS BENEVOLENT MUTATIONS UPON EACH INHUMAN.
I MUST PROCURE A SAMPLE!
FORGIVE THE INTRUSION, MEDUSA. HOW FARES YOUR COUSIN?
AS IF YOU TRULY CARE, ARCADIUS.
THE GENETI-GLOBE HAS HEALED MOST OF THE COSMETIC EFFECTS TRITON SUFFERED FROM THE GAMMA BOMB DETONATION--*
--BUT HIS METABOLISM IS STILL RADIATING A PECULIAR MAGNETISM.
NOW WHY DON'TCHA TELL US WHY YOU'RE REALLY HERE?
*IT HAPPENED IN NAMOR #59.--NEL
VERY WELL, GORGON. ANOTHER PARTY HAS INVADED THE ISLAND TO LAY CLAIM TO OUR ANCESTRAL HOME. WE NEED THE ASSISTANCE OF EVERY ABLE-BODIED--
WHERE ARE KARNAK AND THE MUTT?
BLACK BOLT SENT THEM TO RESCUE THE CRIMSON CADRE, ATTILAN'S NATIONAL HEROES WHOM YOU CALLOUSLY THREW TO THE WOLVES...

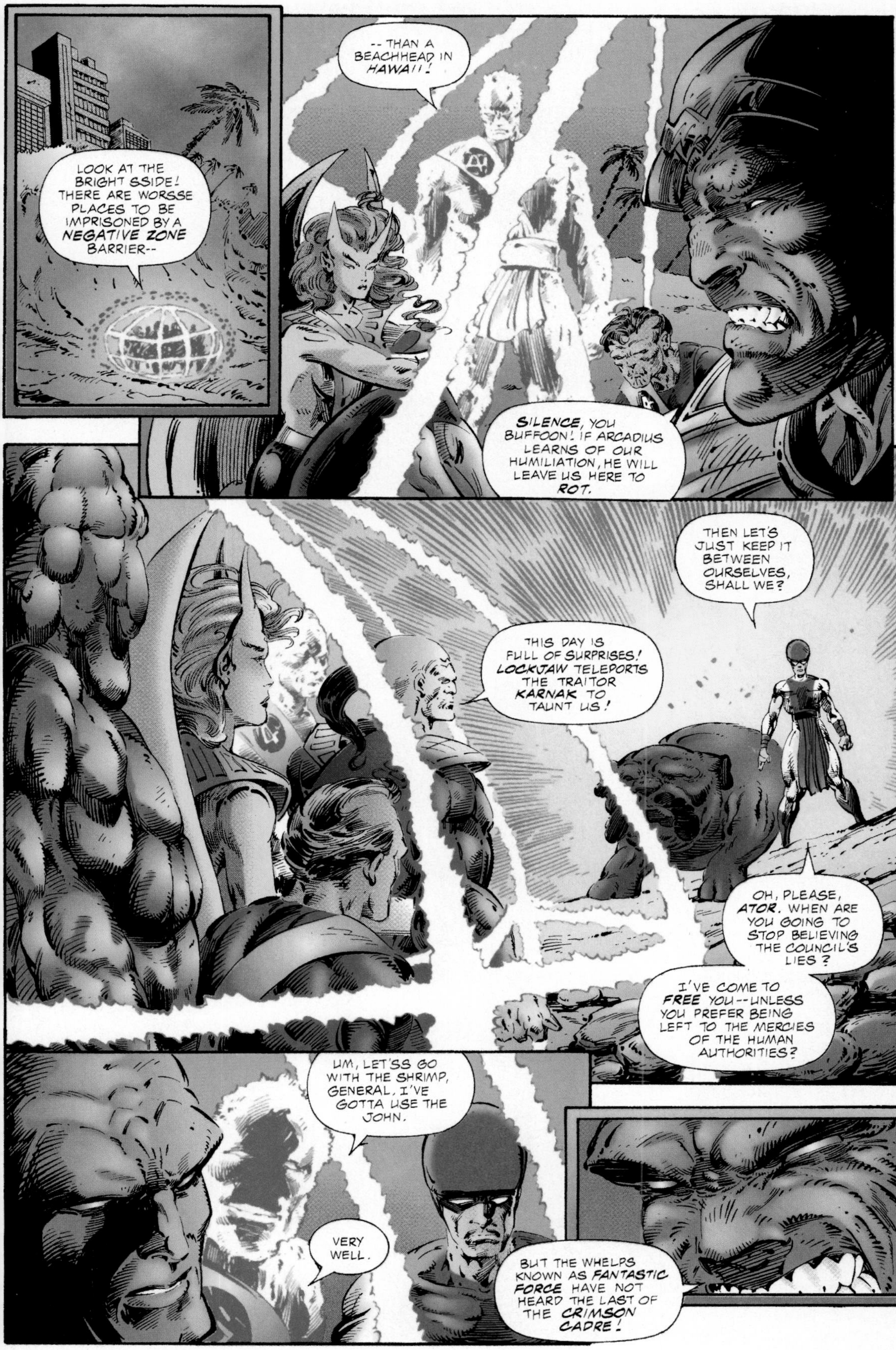
LOOK AT THE BRIGHT SSIDE! THERE ARE WORSSE PLACES TO BE IMPRISONED BY A NEGATIVE ZONE BARRIER--
-- THAN A BEACHHEAD IN HAWAII!
SILENCE, YOU BUFFOON! IF ARCADIUS LEARNS OF OUR HUMILIATION, HE WILL LEAVE US HERE TO ROT.
THEN LET'S JUST KEEP IT BETWEEN OURSELVES, SHALL WE?
THIS DAY IS FULL OF SURPRISES! LOCKJAW TELEPORTS THE TRAITOR KARNAK TO TAUNT US!
OH, PLEASE, ATOR. WHEN ARE YOU GOING TO STOP BELIEVING THE COUNCIL'S LIES?
I'VE COME TO FREE YOU--UNLESS YOU PREFER BEING LEFT TO THE MERCIES OF THE HUMAN AUTHORITIES?
UM, LET'SS GO WITH THE SHRIMP, GENERAL. I'VE GOTTA USE THE JOHN.
VERY WELL.
BUT THE WHELPS KNOWN AS FANTASTIC FORCE HAVE NOT HEARD THE LAST OF THE CRIMSON CADRE!

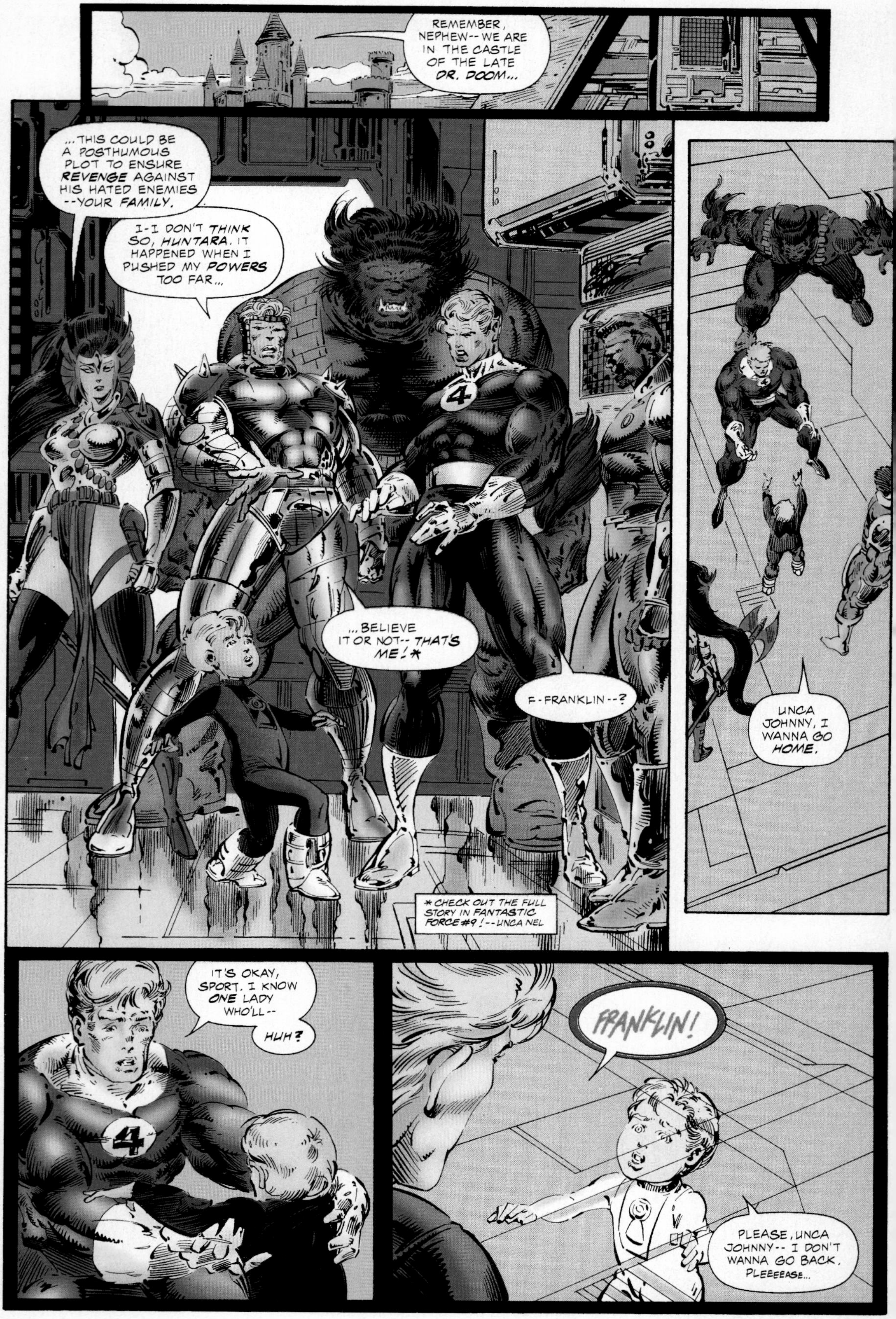
REMEMBER, NEPHEW-- WE ARE IN THE CASTLE OF THE LATE DR. DOOM...
...THIS COULD BE A POSTHUMOUS PLOT TO ENSURE REVENGE AGAINST HIS HATED ENEMIES --YOUR FAMILY.
I-I DON'T THINK SO, HUNTARA. IT HAPPENED WHEN I PUSHED MY POWERS TOO FAR...
...BELIEVE IT OR NOT-- THAT'S ME! *
F-FRANKLIN--?
*CHECK OUT THE FULL STORY IN FANTASTIC FORCE #9! --UNCA NEL
UNCA JOHNNY, I WANNA GO HOME.
IT'S OKAY, SPORT. I KNOW ONE LADY WHO'LL--
HUH?
FRANKLIN!
PLEASE, UNCA JOHNNY-- I DON'T WANNA GO BACK. PLEEEEASE...

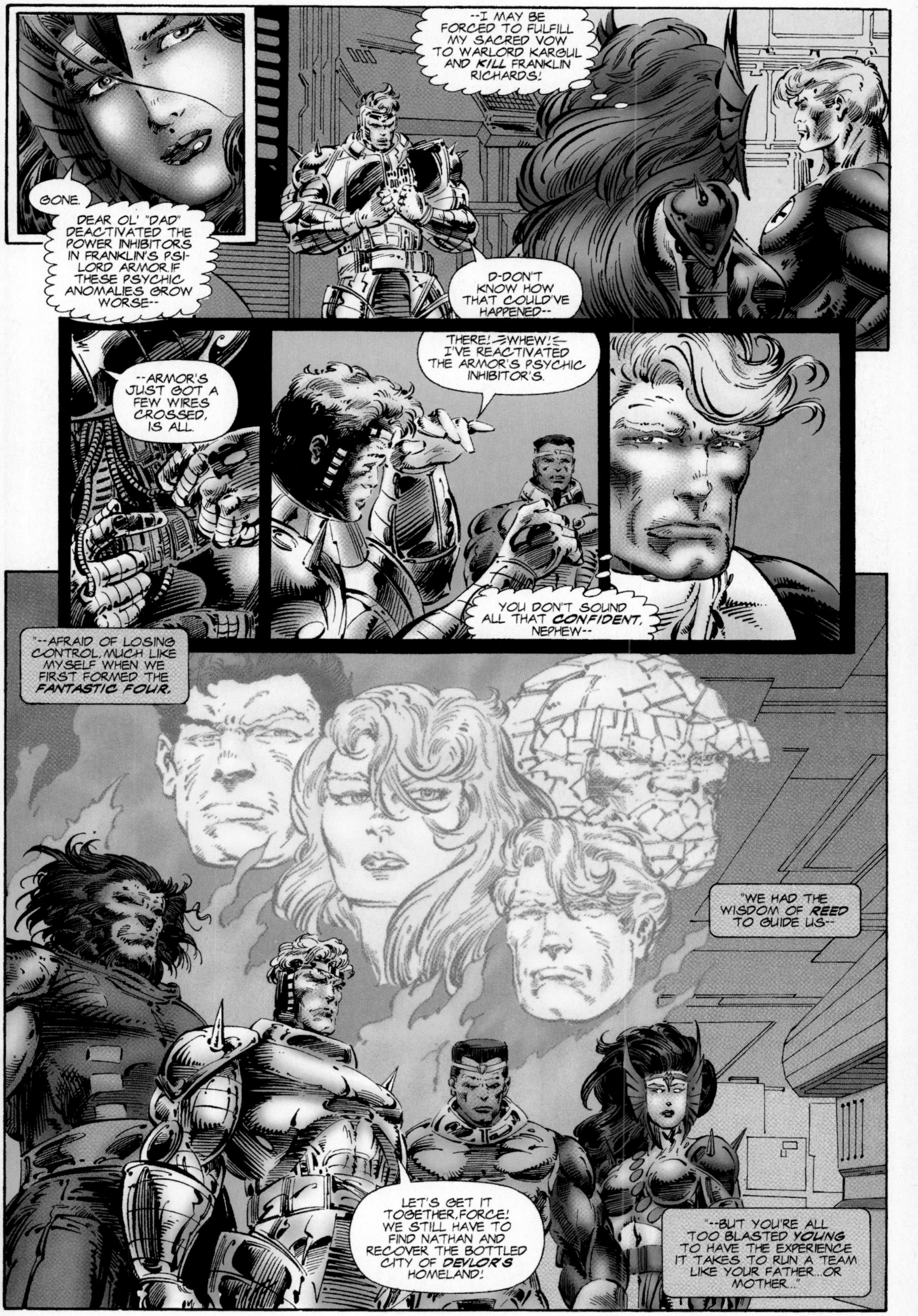
--I MAY BE FORCED TO FULFILL MY SACRED VOW TO WARLORD KARGUL AND KILL FRANKLIN RICHARDS!
GONE.
DEAR OL' "DAD" DEACTIVATED THE POWER INHIBITORS IN FRANKLIN'S PSI-LORD ARMOR. IF THESE PSYCHIC ANOMALIES GROW WORSE--
D-DON'T KNOW HOW THAT COULD'VE HAPPENED--
--ARMOR'S JUST GOT A FEW WIRES CROSSED, IS ALL.
THERE! =WHEW!= I'VE REACTIVATED THE ARMOR'S PSYCHIC INHIBITOR'S.
YOU DON'T SOUND ALL THAT CONFIDENT, NEPHEW--
"--AFRAID OF LOSING CONTROL, MUCH LIKE MYSELF WHEN WE FIRST FORMED THE FANTASTIC FOUR.
"WE HAD THE WISDOM OF REED TO GUIDE US--
LET'S GET IT TOGETHER, FORCE! WE STILL HAVE TO FIND NATHAN AND RECOVER THE BOTTLED CITY OF DEVLOR'S HOMELAND!
"--BUT YOU'RE ALL TOO BLASTED YOUNG TO HAVE THE EXPERIENCE IT TAKES TO RUN A TEAM LIKE YOUR FATHER...OR MOTHER...

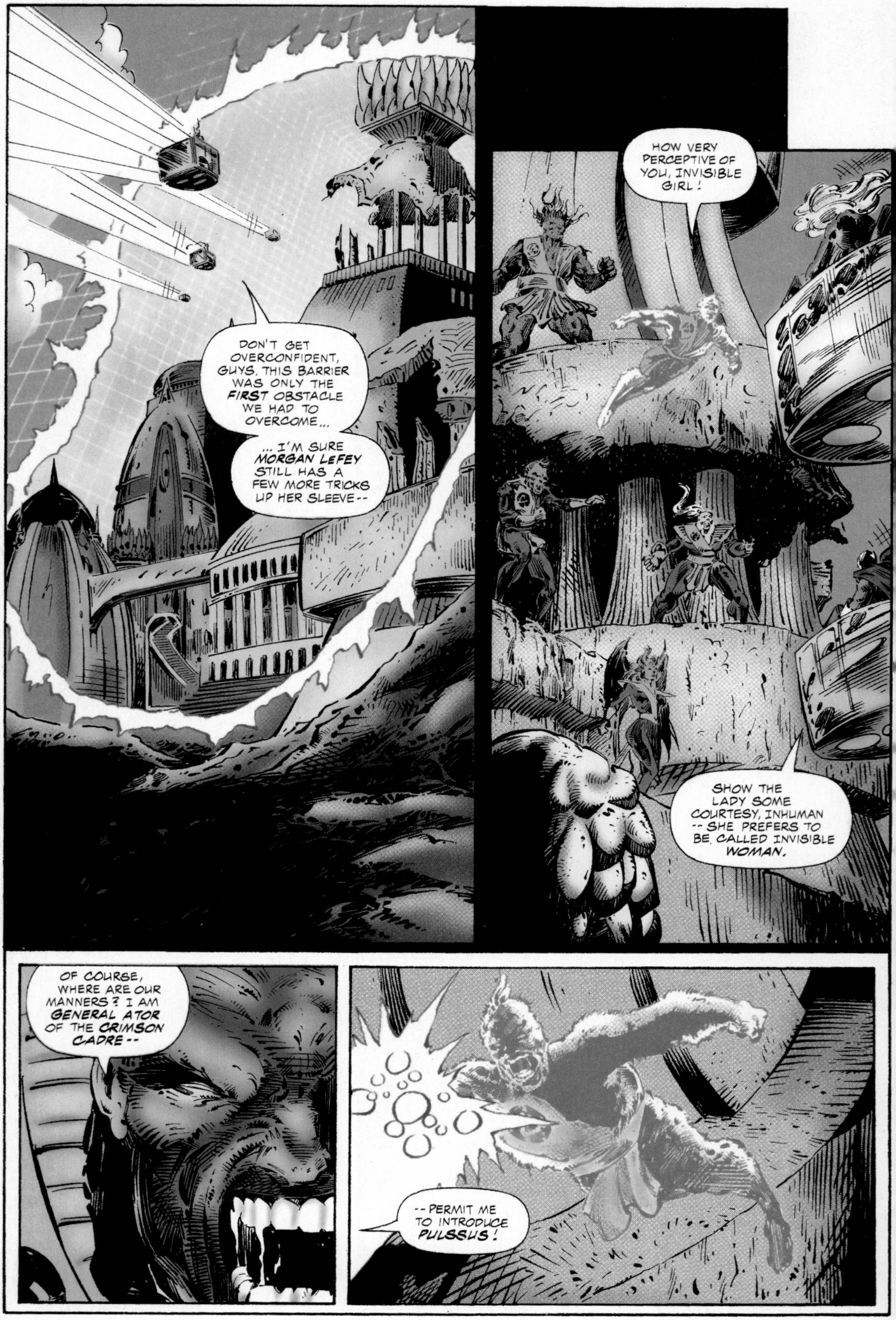
DON'T GET OVERCONFIDENT, GUYS. THIS BARRIER WAS ONLY THE FIRST OBSTACLE WE HAD TO OVERCOME...
... I'M SURE MORGAN LEFEY STILL HAS A FEW MORE TRICKS UP HER SLEEVE--
HOW VERY PERCEPTIVE OF YOU, INVISIBLE GIRL!
SHOW THE LADY SOME COURTESY, INHUMAN -- SHE PREFERS TO BE CALLED INVISIBLE WOMAN.
OF COURSE, WHERE ARE OUR MANNERS? I AM GENERAL ATOR OF THE CRIMSON CADRE--
--PERMIT ME TO INTRODUCE PULSSUS!

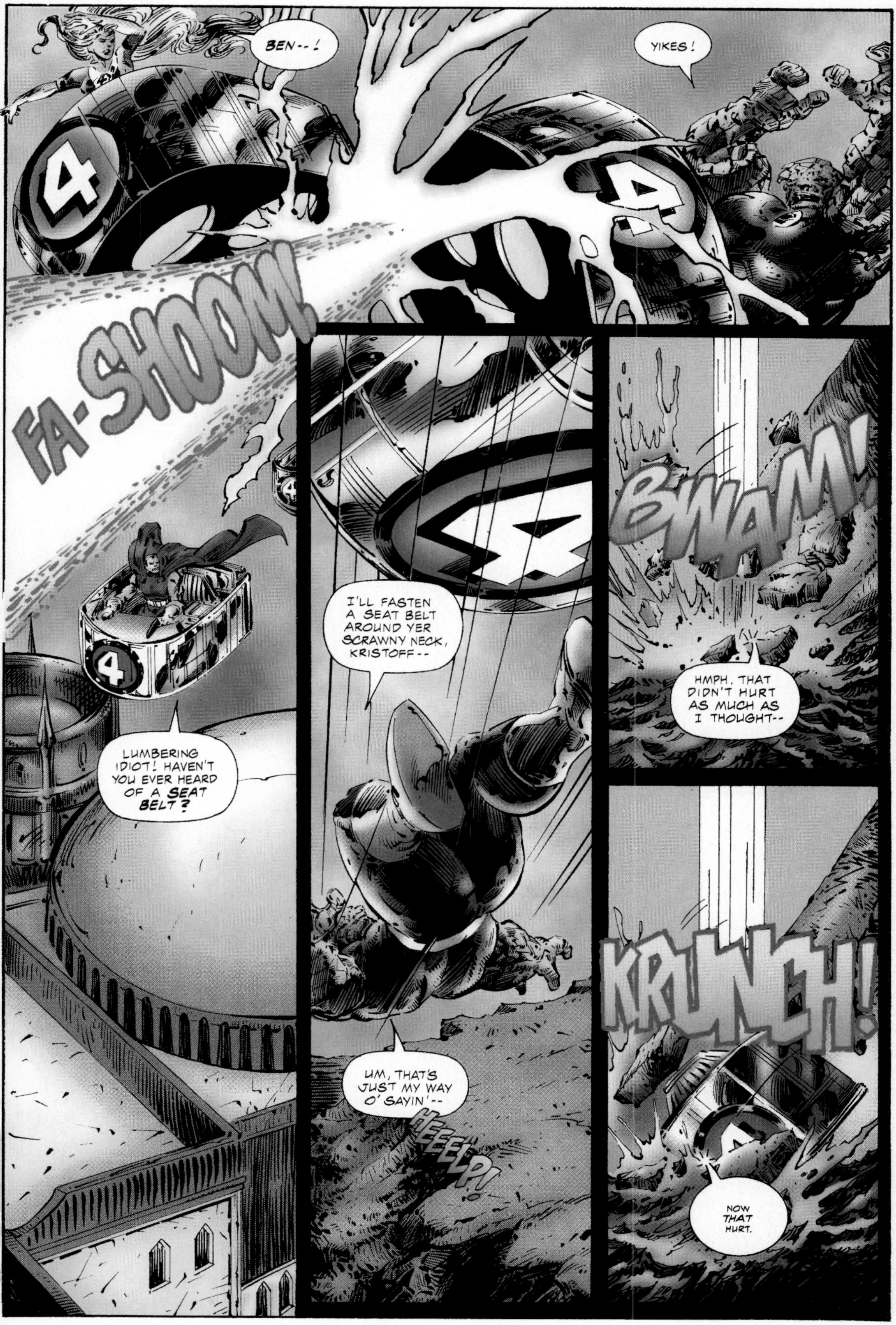
BEN--!
YIKES!
FA-SHOOM!
LUMBERING IDIOT! HAVEN'T YOU EVER HEARD OF A SEAT BELT?
I'LL FASTEN A SEAT BELT AROUND YER SCRAWNY NECK, KRISTOFF--
UM, THAT'S JUST MY WAY O' SAYIN'--
HEEELP!
BWAM!
HMPH. THAT DIDN'T HURT AS MUCH AS I THOUGHT--
KRUNCH!
NOW THAT HURT.

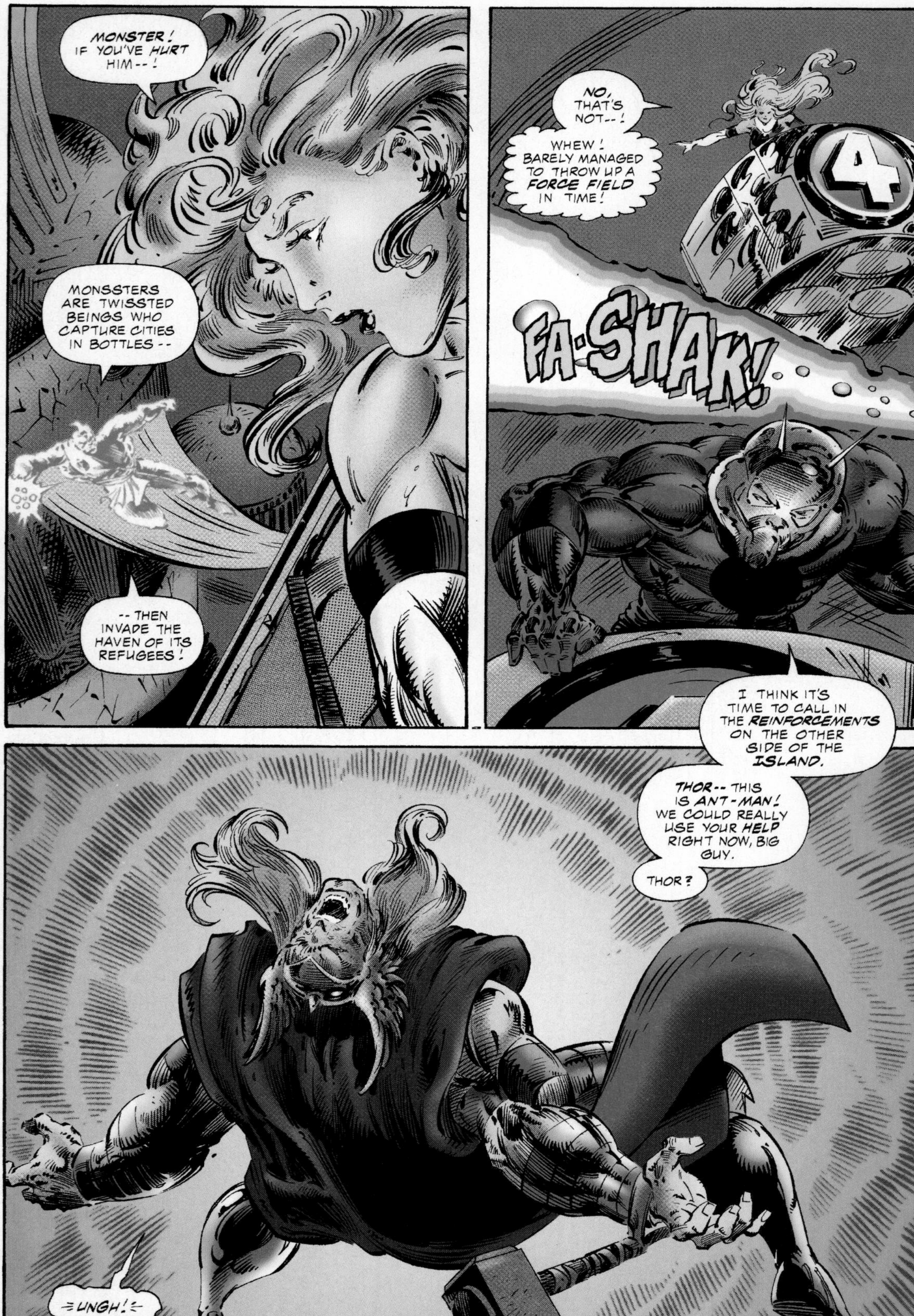
MONSTER! IF YOU'VE HURT HIM--!
MONSSTERS ARE TWISSTED BEINGS WHO CAPTURE CITIES IN BOTTLES--
--THEN INVADE THE HAVEN OF ITS REFUGEES!
NO, THAT'S NOT--!
WHEW! BARELY MANAGED TO THROW UP A FORCE FIELD IN TIME!
FA-SHAK!
I THINK IT'S TIME TO CALL IN THE REINFORCEMENTS ON THE OTHER SIDE OF THE ISLAND.
THOR-- THIS IS ANT-MAN! WE COULD REALLY USE YOUR HELP RIGHT NOW, BIG GUY.
THOR?
UNGH!

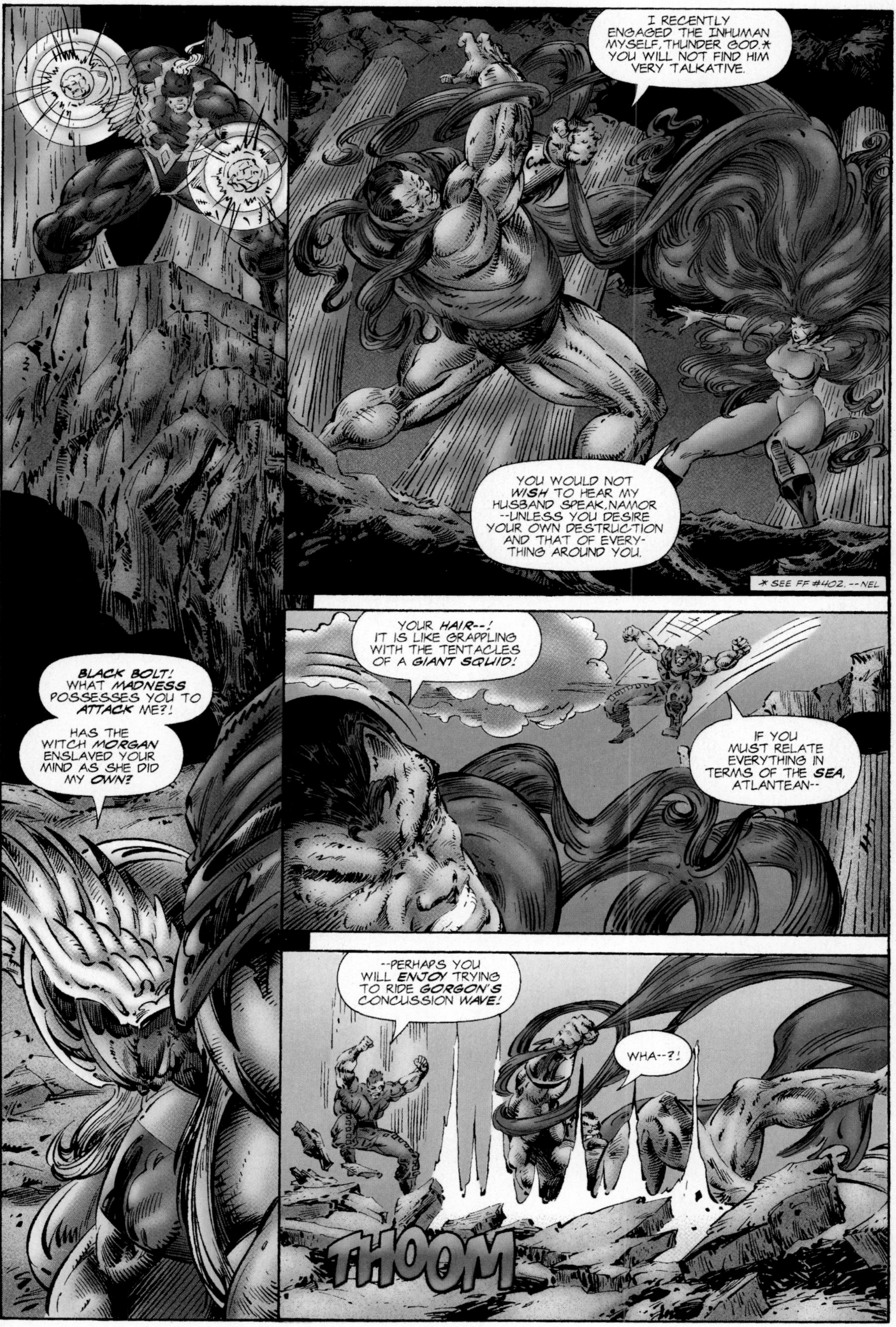
I RECENTLY ENGAGED THE INHUMAN MYSELF, THUNDER GOD.* YOU WILL NOT FIND HIM VERY TALKATIVE.
YOU WOULD NOT WISH TO HEAR MY HUSBAND SPEAK, NAMOR --UNLESS YOU DESIRE YOUR OWN DESTRUCTION AND THAT OF EVERYTHING AROUND YOU.
* SEE FF #402. --NEL
BLACK BOLT! WHAT MADNESS POSSESSES YOU TO ATTACK ME?!
HAS THE WITCH MORGAN ENSLAVED YOUR MIND AS SHE DID MY OWN?
YOUR HAIR--! IT IS LIKE GRAPPLING WITH THE TENTACLES OF A GIANT SQUID!
IF YOU MUST RELATE EVERYTHING IN TERMS OF THE SEA, ATLANTEAN--
--PERHAPS YOU WILL ENJOY TRYING TO RIDE GORGON'S CONCUSSION WAVE!
WHA--?!
THOOM

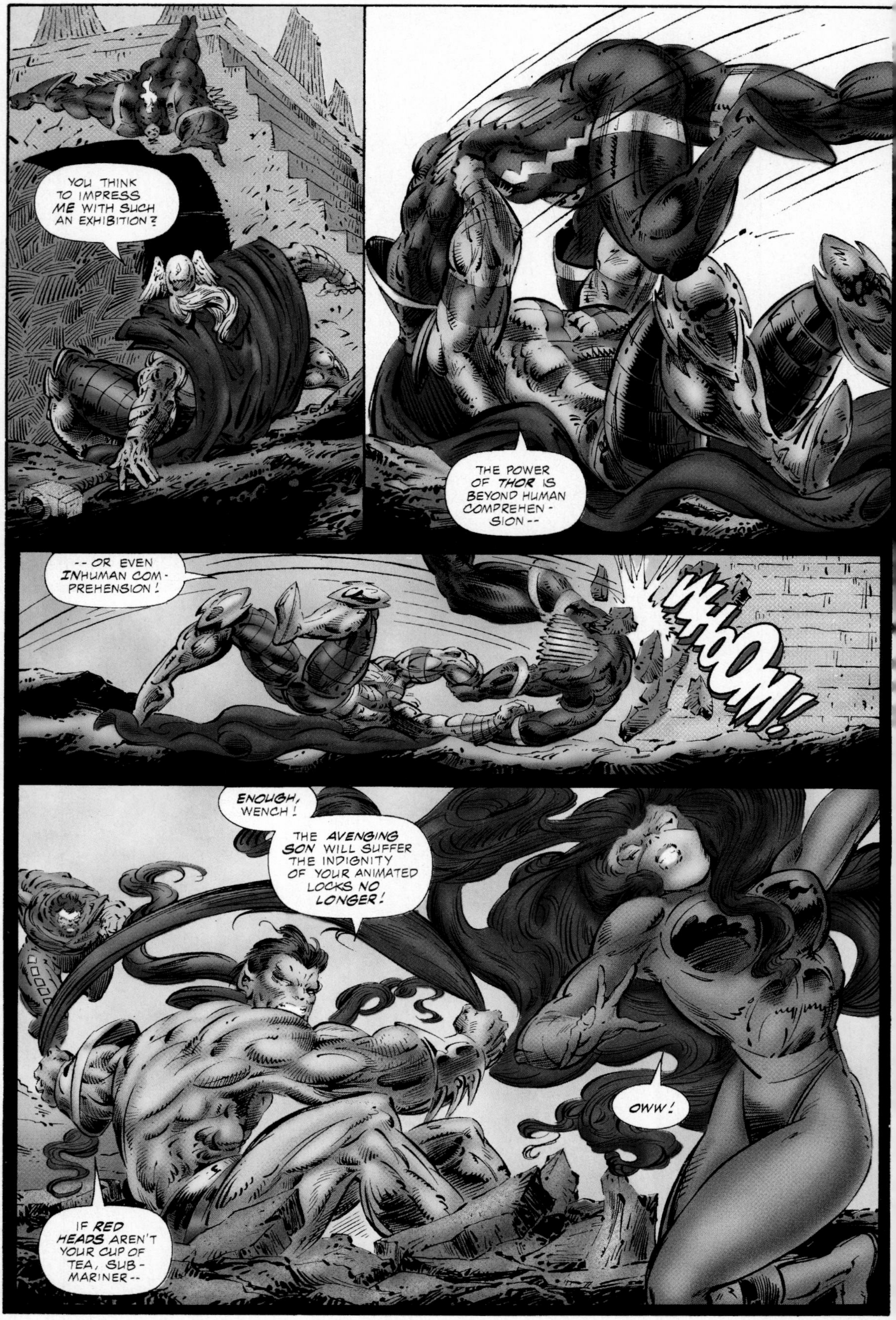
YOU THINK TO IMPRESS ME WITH SUCH AN EXHIBITION?
THE POWER OF THOR IS BEYOND HUMAN COMPREHEN-SION--
--OR EVEN INHUMAN COM-PREHENSION!
WHOOM!
ENOUGH, WENCH!
THE AVENGING SON WILL SUFFER THE INDIGNITY OF YOUR ANIMATED LOCKS NO LONGER!
OWW!
IF RED HEADS AREN'T YOUR CUP OF TEA, SUB-MARINER--

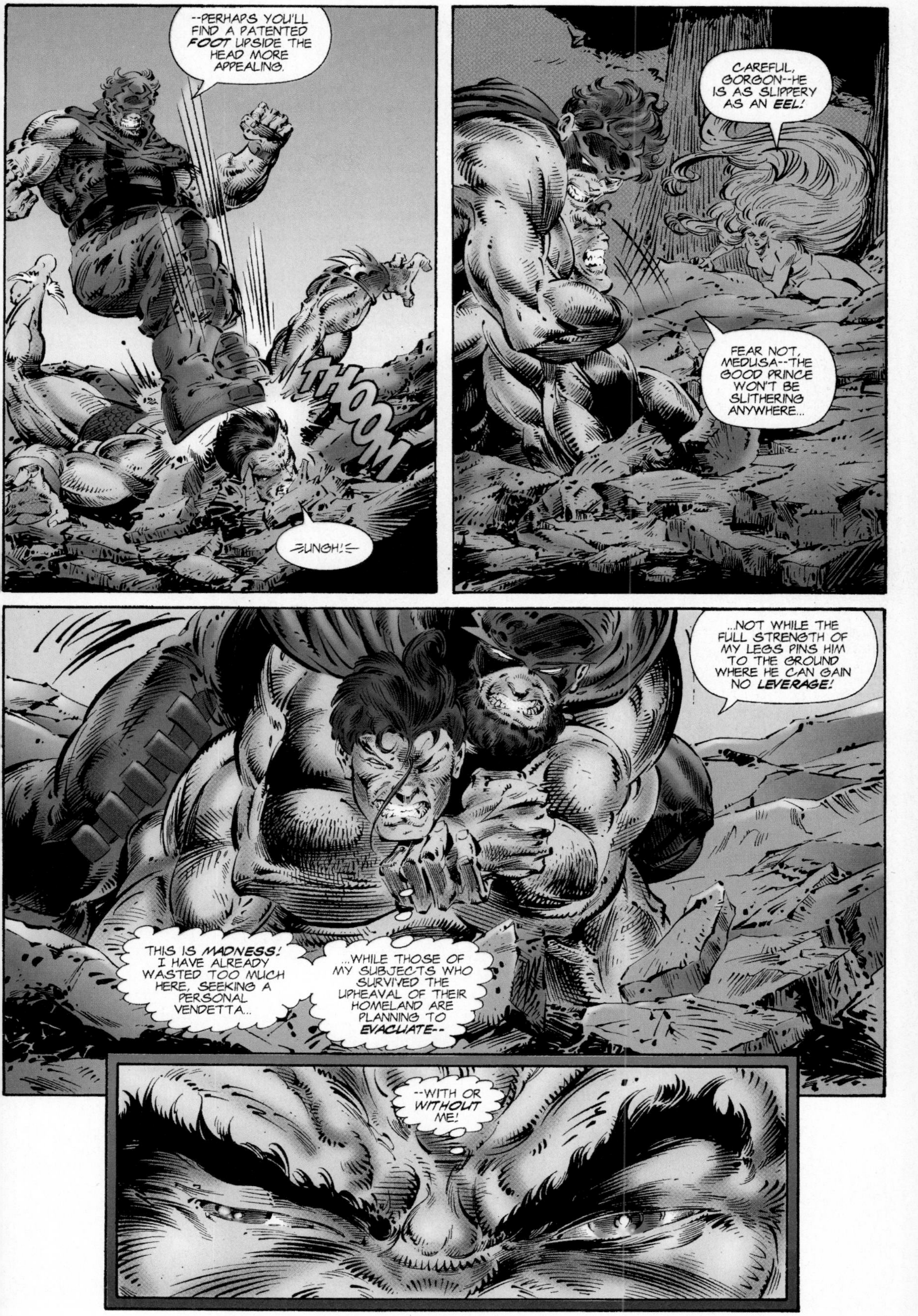
--PERHAPS YOU'LL FIND A PATENTED FOOT UPSIDE THE HEAD MORE APPEALING.
THOOM
UNGH!
CAREFUL, GORGON--HE IS AS SLIPPERY AS AN EEL!
FEAR NOT, MEDUSA--THE GOOD PRINCE WON'T BE SLITHERING ANYWHERE...
...NOT WHILE THE FULL STRENGTH OF MY LEGS PINS HIM TO THE GROUND WHERE HE CAN GAIN NO LEVERAGE!
THIS IS MADNESS! I HAVE ALREADY WASTED TOO MUCH HERE, SEEKING A PERSONAL VENDETTA...
...WHILE THOSE OF MY SUBJECTS WHO SURVIVED THE UPHEAVAL OF THEIR HOMELAND ARE PLANNING TO EVACUATE--
--WITH OR WITHOUT ME!

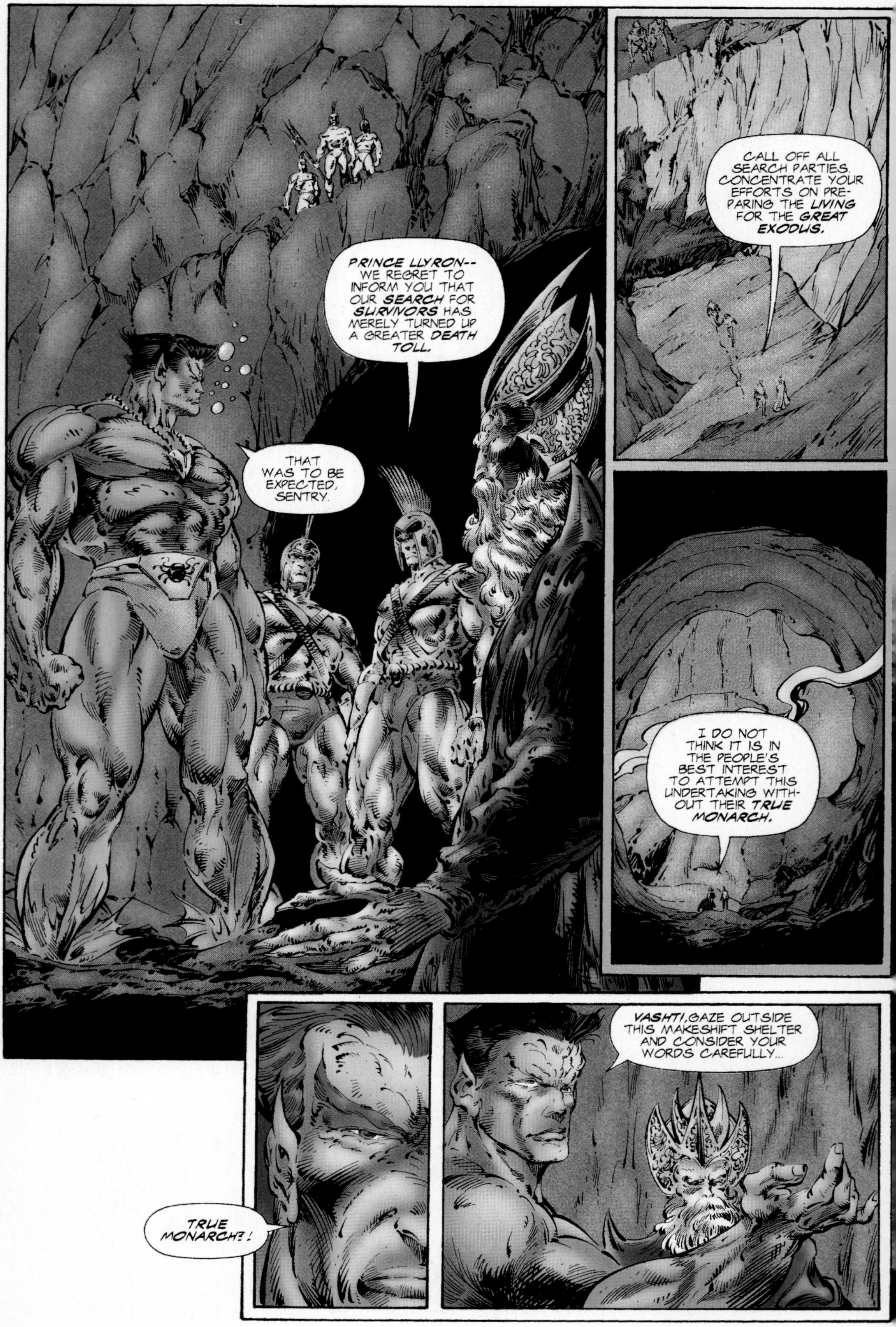
PRINCE LLYRON-- WE REGRET TO INFORM YOU THAT OUR SEARCH FOR SURVIVORS HAS MERELY TURNED UP A GREATER DEATH TOLL.
THAT WAS TO BE EXPECTED, SENTRY.
CALL OFF ALL SEARCH PARTIES. CONCENTRATE YOUR EFFORTS ON PRE-PARING THE LIVING FOR THE GREAT EXODUS.
I DO NOT THINK IT IS IN THE PEOPLE'S BEST INTEREST TO ATTEMPT THIS UNDERTAKING WITH-OUT THEIR TRUE MONARCH.
TRUE MONARCH?!
VASHTI, GAZE OUTSIDE THIS MAKESHIFT SHELTER AND CONSIDER YOUR WORDS CAREFULLY...

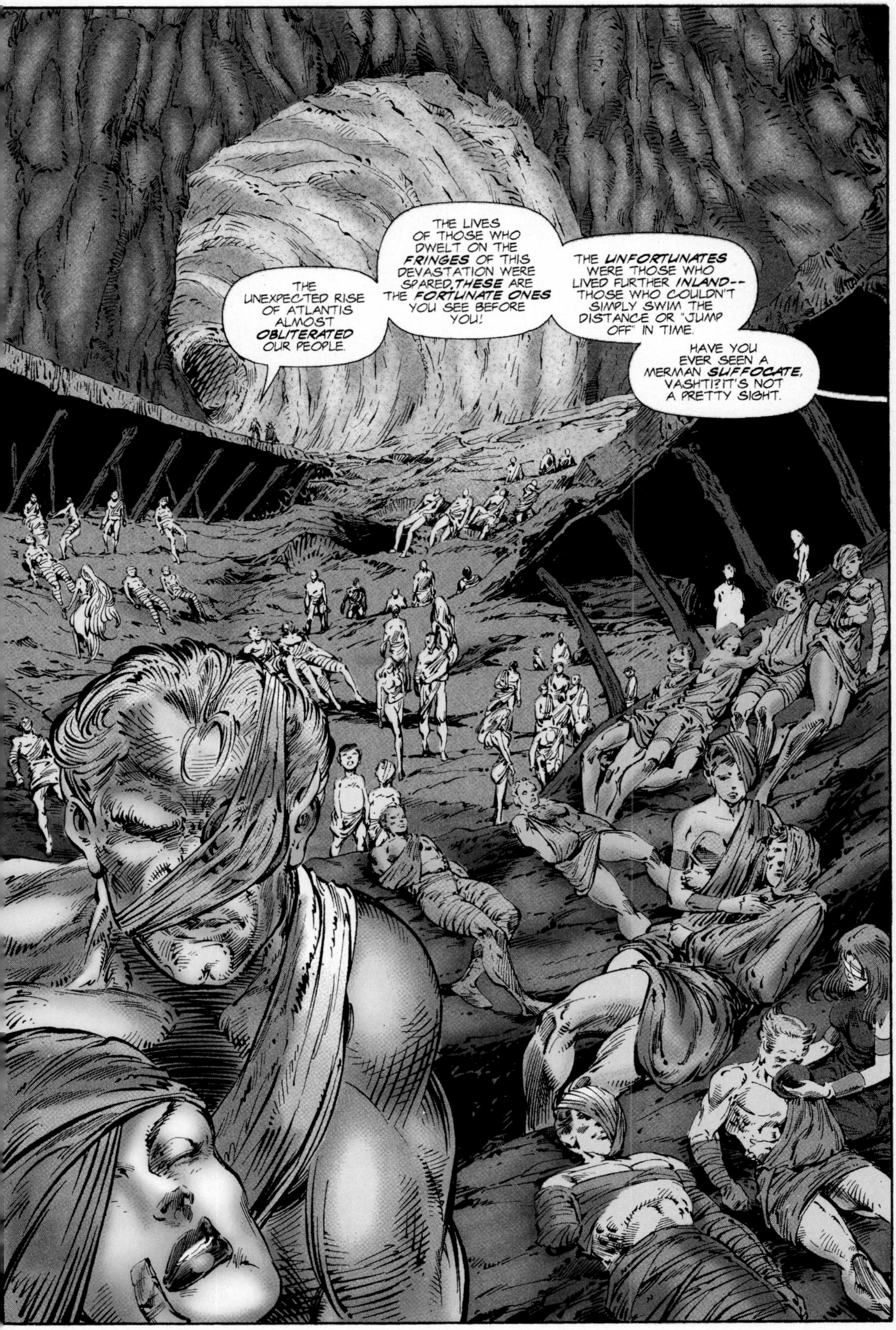
THE UNEXPECTED RISE OF ATLANTIS ALMOST OBLITERATED OUR PEOPLE.
THE LIVES OF THOSE WHO DWELT ON THE FRINGES OF THIS DEVASTATION WERE SPARED. THESE ARE THE FORTUNATE ONES YOU SEE BEFORE YOU!
THE UNFORTUNATES WERE THOSE WHO LIVED FURTHER INLAND-- THOSE WHO COULDN'T SIMPLY SWIM THE DISTANCE OR "JUMP OFF" IN TIME.
HAVE YOU EVER SEEN A MERMAN SUFFOCATE, VASHTI? IT'S NOT A PRETTY SIGHT.

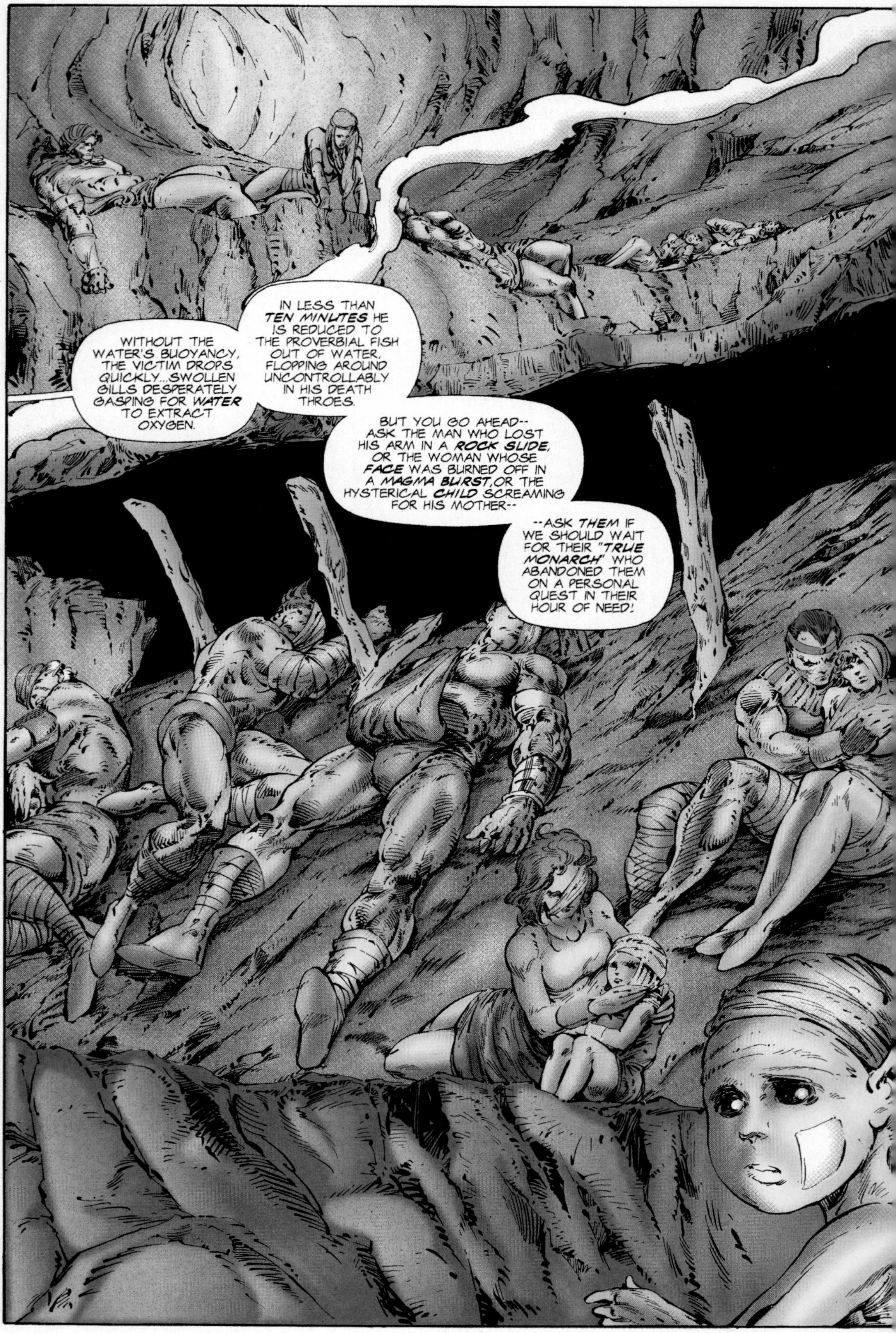
WITHOUT THE WATER'S BUOYANCY, THE VICTIM DROPS QUICKLY...SWOLLEN GILLS DESPERATELY GASPING FOR WATER TO EXTRACT OXYGEN.
IN LESS THAN TEN MINUTES HE IS REDUCED TO THE PROVERBIAL FISH OUT OF WATER, FLOPPING AROUND UNCONTROLLABLY IN HIS DEATH THROES.
BUT YOU GO AHEAD-- ASK THE MAN WHO LOST HIS ARM IN A ROCK SLIDE, OR THE WOMAN WHOSE FACE WAS BURNED OFF IN A MAGMA BURST, OR THE HYSTERICAL CHILD SCREAMING FOR HIS MOTHER--
--ASK THEM IF WE SHOULD WAIT FOR THEIR "TRUE MONARCH" WHO ABANDONED THEM ON A PERSONAL QUEST IN THEIR HOUR OF NEED!

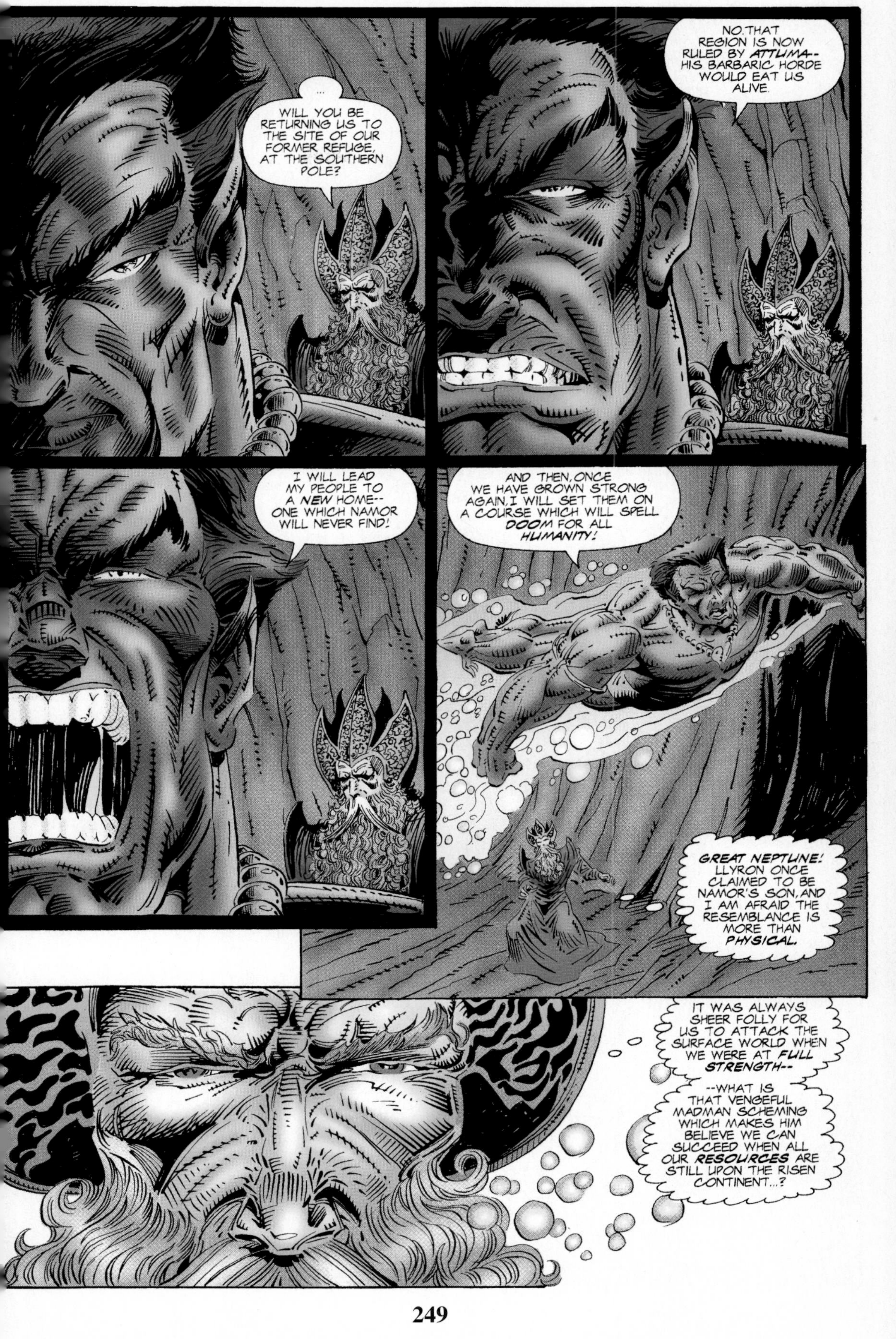
...
WILL YOU BE RETURNING US TO THE SITE OF OUR FORMER REFUGE, AT THE SOUTHERN POLE?
NO. THAT REGION IS NOW RULED BY ATTUMA-- HIS BARBARIC HORDE WOULD EAT US ALIVE.
I WILL LEAD MY PEOPLE TO A NEW HOME-- ONE WHICH NAMOR WILL NEVER FIND!
AND THEN, ONCE WE HAVE GROWN STRONG AGAIN, I WILL SET THEM ON A COURSE WHICH WILL SPELL DOOM FOR ALL HUMANITY!
GREAT NEPTUNE! LLYRON ONCE CLAIMED TO BE NAMOR'S SON, AND I AM AFRAID THE RESEMBLANCE IS MORE THAN PHYSICAL.
IT WAS ALWAYS SHEER FOLLY FOR US TO ATTACK THE SURFACE WORLD WHEN WE WERE AT FULL STRENGTH--
--WHAT IS THAT VENGEFUL MADMAN SCHEMING WHICH MAKES HIM BELIEVE WE CAN SUCCEED WHEN ALL OUR RESOURCES ARE STILL UPON THE RISEN CONTINENT...?

GRRR
IT'LL TAKE MORE THAN A BLASTED CAR WRECK TA KEEP BASHFUL BENJI DOWN, YA CADRE CREEPS!
OH, SURELY YOU DON'T MEAN TO CALL MARGOYLE A CREEP, DO YOU?
RROWF
HUH?? LOCKJAW-- YA BLOCKED MY BEST SUNDAY PUNCH!
AN' MARGOYLE'S COMIN' AT ME! ONLY ONE THING TA DO--
BWAM
AIEAIE
HERE'S MUTT IN YER EYE, SISTER!
WONDER WHY STEINBRENNER DIDN'T SIGN ME UP AS A REPLACEMENT PLAYER DURIN' THE BASEBALL STRIKE?

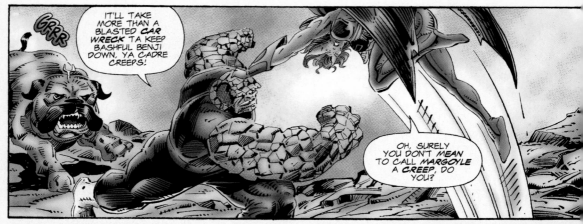

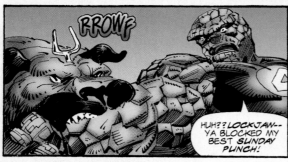

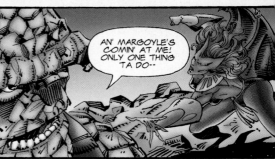

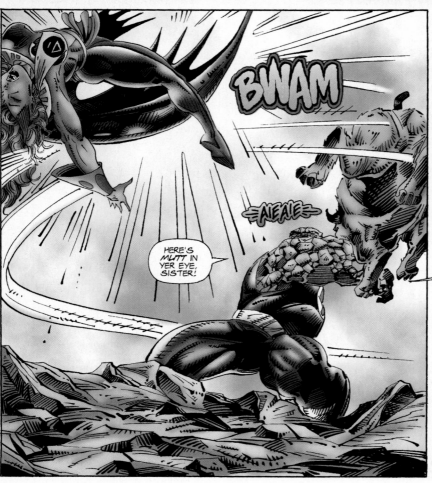

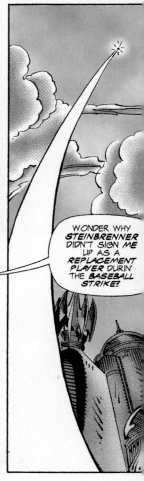

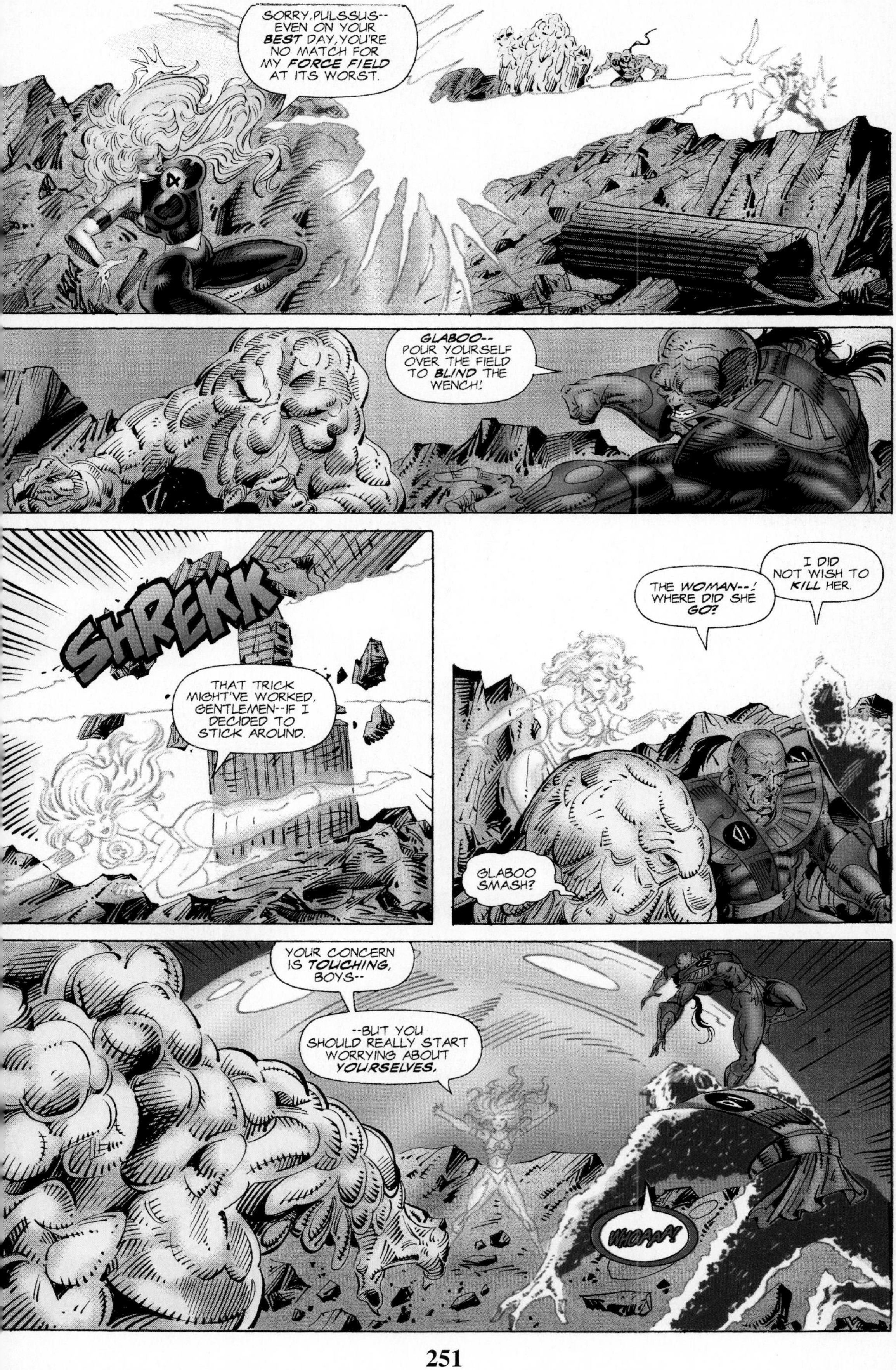
SORRY, PULSSUS-- EVEN ON YOUR BEST DAY, YOU'RE NO MATCH FOR MY FORCE FIELD AT ITS WORST.
GLABOO-- POUR YOURSELF OVER THE FIELD TO BLIND THE WENCH!
SHREKK
THAT TRICK MIGHT'VE WORKED, GENTLEMEN--IF I DECIDED TO STICK AROUND.
THE WOMAN--! WHERE DID SHE GO?
I DID NOT WISH TO KILL HER.
GLABOO SMASH?
YOUR CONCERN IS TOUCHING, BOYS--
--BUT YOU SHOULD REALLY START WORRYING ABOUT YOURSELVES.
WHOAAA!

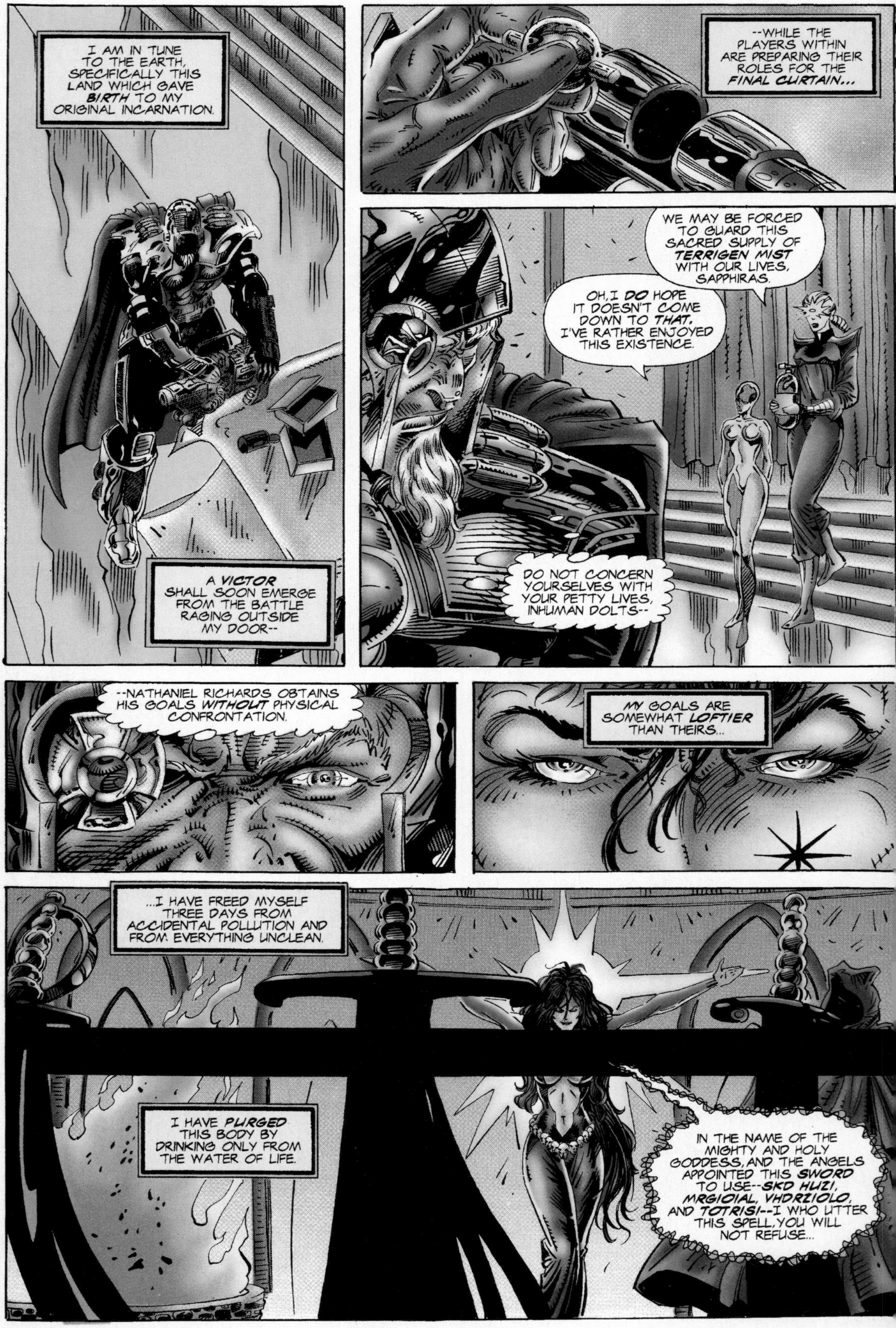

I AM IN TUNE TO THE EARTH, SPECIFICALLY THIS LAND WHICH GAVE BIRTH TO MY ORIGINAL INCARNATION.
A VICTOR SHALL SOON EMERGE FROM THE BATTLE RAGING OUTSIDE MY DOOR--
--WHILE THE PLAYERS WITHIN ARE PREPARING THEIR ROLES FOR THE FINAL CURTAIN...
WE MAY BE FORCED TO GUARD THIS SACRED SUPPLY OF TERRIGEN MIST WITH OUR LIVES, SAPPHIRAS.
OH, I DO HOPE IT DOESN'T COME DOWN TO THAT. I'VE RATHER ENJOYED THIS EXISTENCE.
DO NOT CONCERN YOURSELVES WITH YOUR PETTY LIVES, INHUMAN DOLTS--
--NATHANIEL RICHARDS OBTAINS HIS GOALS WITHOUT PHYSICAL CONFRONTATION.
MY GOALS ARE SOMEWHAT LOFTIER THAN THEIRS...
...I HAVE FREED MYSELF THREE DAYS FROM ACCIDENTAL POLLUTION AND FROM EVERYTHING UNCLEAN.
I HAVE PURGED THIS BODY BY DRINKING ONLY FROM THE WATER OF LIFE.
IN THE NAME OF THE MIGHTY AND HOLY GODDESS, AND THE ANGELS APPOINTED THIS SWORD TO USE--SKD HUZI, MRGIOIAL, VHDRZIOLO, AND TOTRISI--I WHO UTTER THIS SPELL, YOU WILL NOT REFUSE...

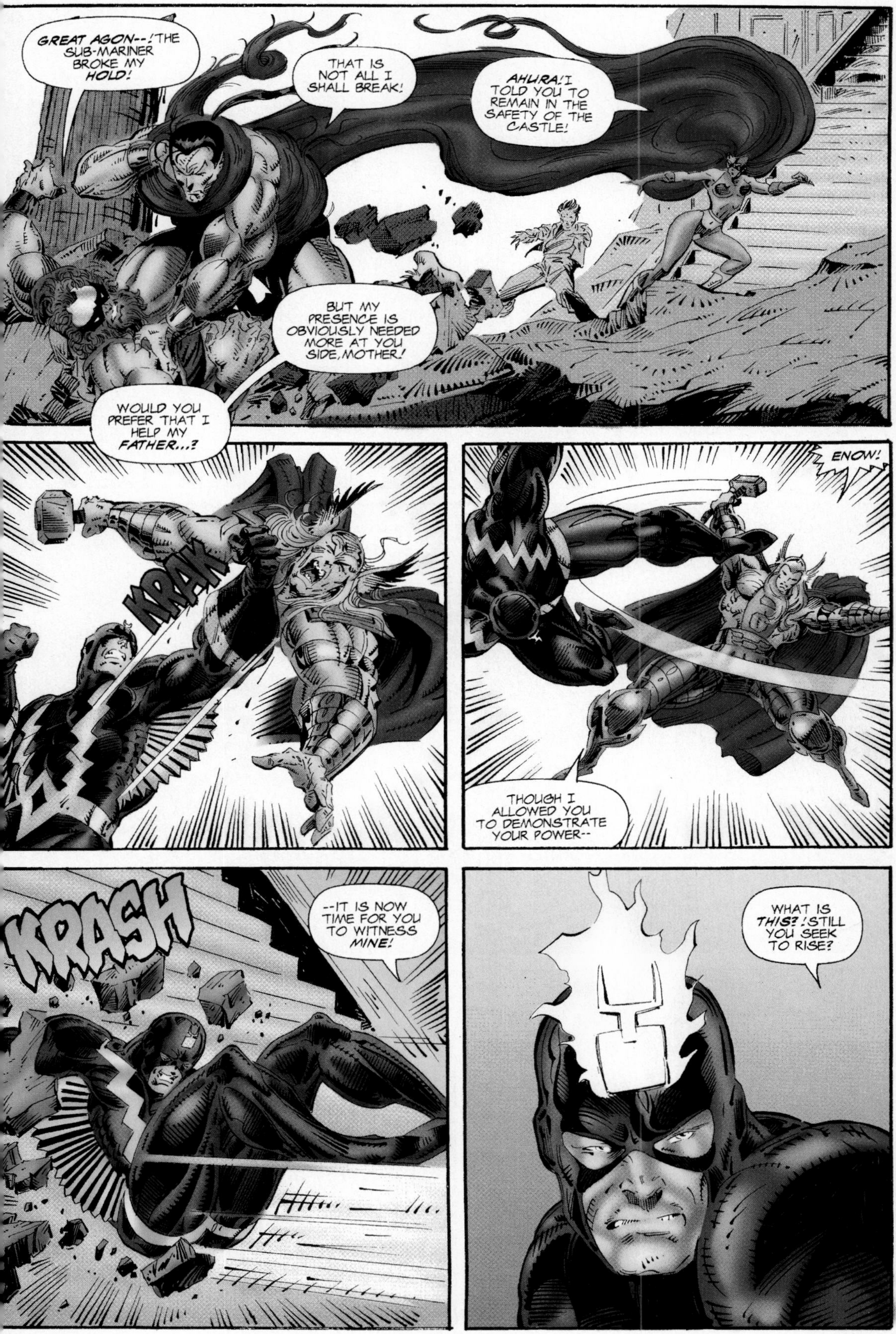
GREAT AGON--! THE SUB-MARINER BROKE MY HOLD!
THAT IS NOT ALL I SHALL BREAK!
AHURA! I TOLD YOU TO REMAIN IN THE SAFETY OF THE CASTLE!
BUT MY PRESENCE IS OBVIOUSLY NEEDED MORE AT YOU SIDE, MOTHER!
WOULD YOU PREFER THAT I HELP MY FATHER...?
KRAK
ENOW!
THOUGH I ALLOWED YOU TO DEMONSTRATE YOUR POWER--
KRASH
--IT IS NOW TIME FOR YOU TO WITNESS MINE!
WHAT IS THIS?! STILL YOU SEEK TO RISE?

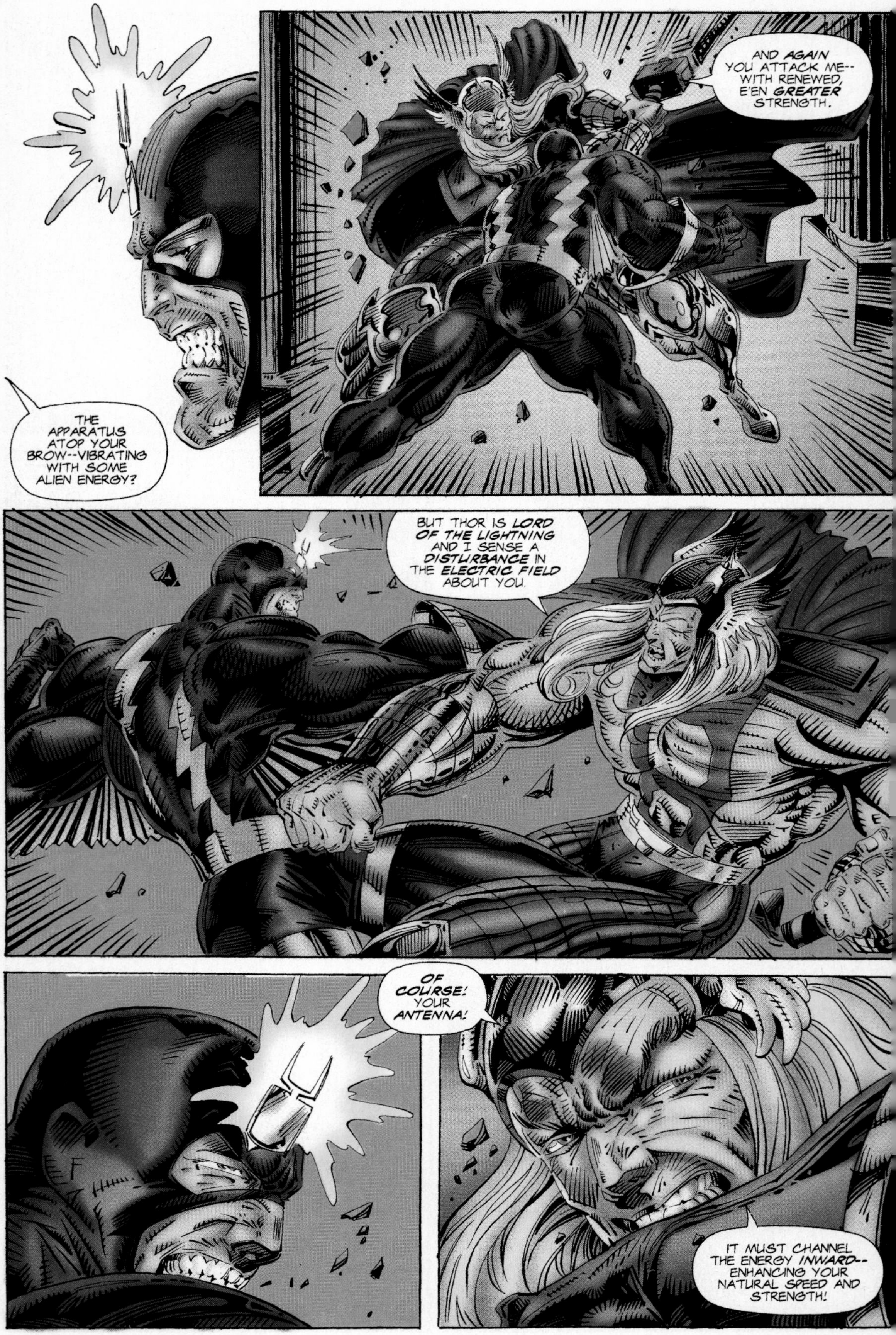
THE APPARATUS ATOP YOUR BROW--VIBRATING WITH SOME ALIEN ENERGY?
AND AGAIN YOU ATTACK ME--WITH RENEWED, E'EN GREATER STRENGTH.
BUT THOR IS LORD OF THE LIGHTNING AND I SENSE A DISTURBANCE IN THE ELECTRIC FIELD ABOUT YOU.
OF COURSE! YOUR ANTENNA!
IT MUST CHANNEL THE ENERGY INWARD--ENHANCING YOUR NATURAL SPEED AND STRENGTH!

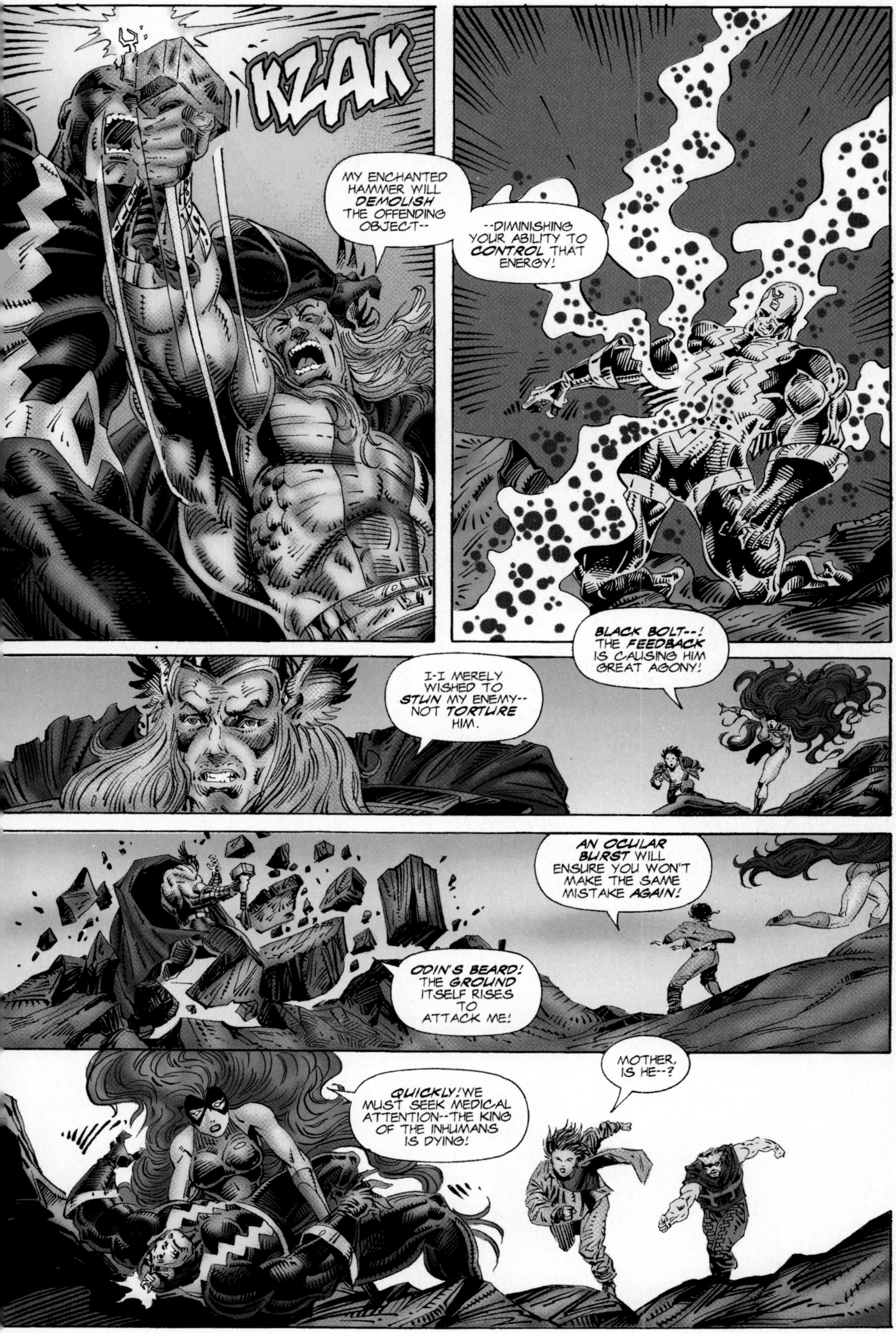
KZAK
MY ENCHANTED HAMMER WILL DEMOLISH THE OFFENDING OBJECT--
--DIMINISHING YOUR ABILITY TO CONTROL THAT ENERGY!
BLACK BOLT--! THE FEEDBACK IS CAUSING HIM GREAT AGONY!
I-I MERELY WISHED TO STUN MY ENEMY--NOT TORTURE HIM.
AN OCULAR BURST WILL ENSURE YOU WON'T MAKE THE SAME MISTAKE AGAIN!
ODIN'S BEARD! THE GROUND ITSELF RISES TO ATTACK ME!
MOTHER, IS HE--?
QUICKLY! WE MUST SEEK MEDICAL ATTENTION--THE KING OF THE INHUMANS IS DYING!

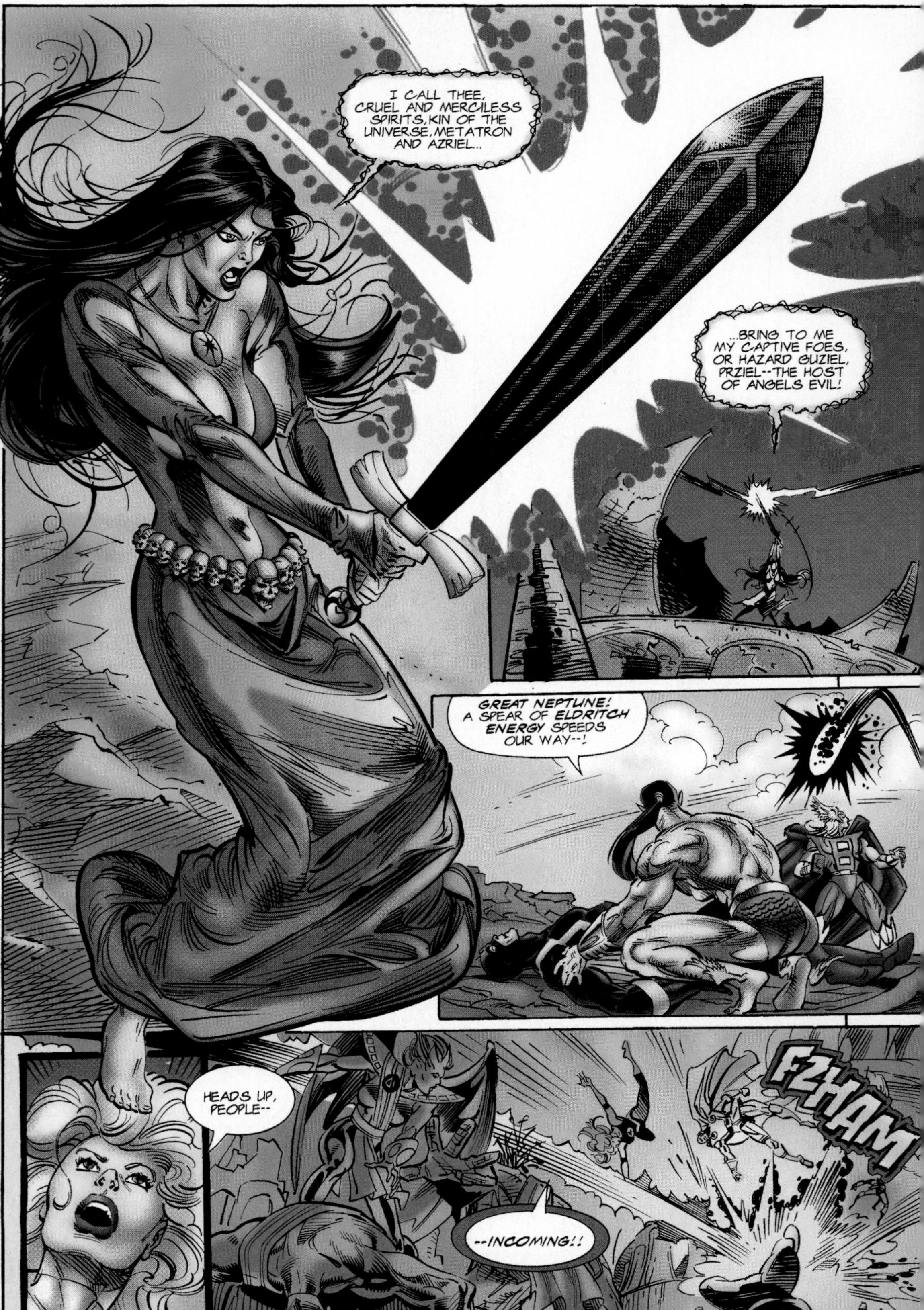
I CALL THEE, CRUEL AND MERCILESS SPIRITS, KIN OF THE UNIVERSE, METATRON AND AZRIEL...
...BRING TO ME MY CAPTIVE FOES, OR HAZARD GUZIEL, PRZIEL--THE HOST OF ANGELS EVIL!
GREAT NEPTUNE! A SPEAR OF ELDRITCH ENERGY SPEEDS OUR WAY--!
HEADS UP, PEOPLE--
--INCOMING!!
FZHAM

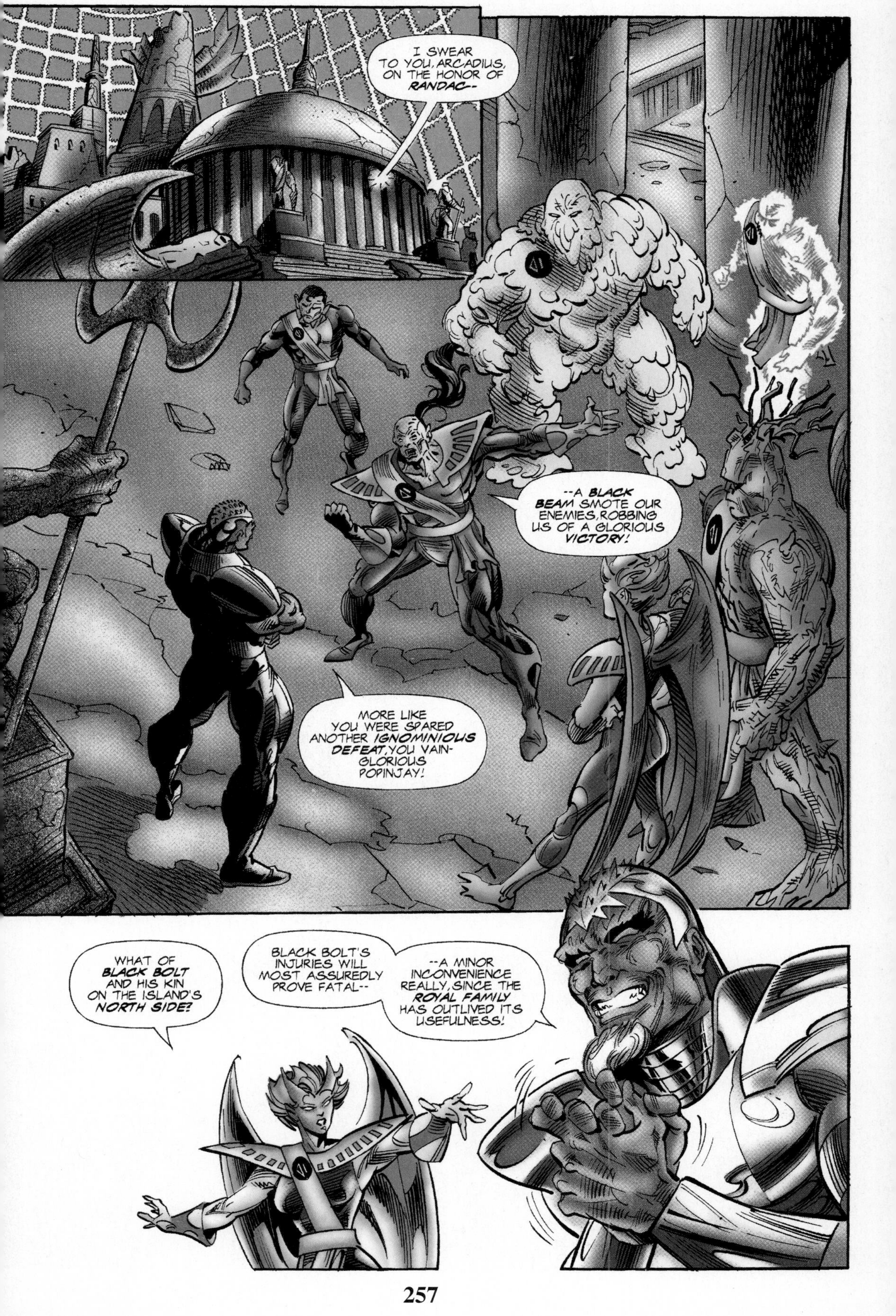
I SWEAR TO YOU, ARCADIUS, ON THE HONOR OF RANDAC--
--A BLACK BEAM SMOTE OUR ENEMIES, ROBBING US OF A GLORIOUS VICTORY!
MORE LIKE YOU WERE SPARED ANOTHER IGNOMINIOUS DEFEAT, YOU VAIN-GLORIOUS POPINJAY!
WHAT OF BLACK BOLT AND HIS KIN ON THE ISLAND'S NORTH SIDE?
BLACK BOLT'S INJURIES WILL MOST ASSUREDLY PROVE FATAL--
--A MINOR INCONVENIENCE REALLY, SINCE THE ROYAL FAMILY HAS OUTLIVED ITS USEFULNESS!

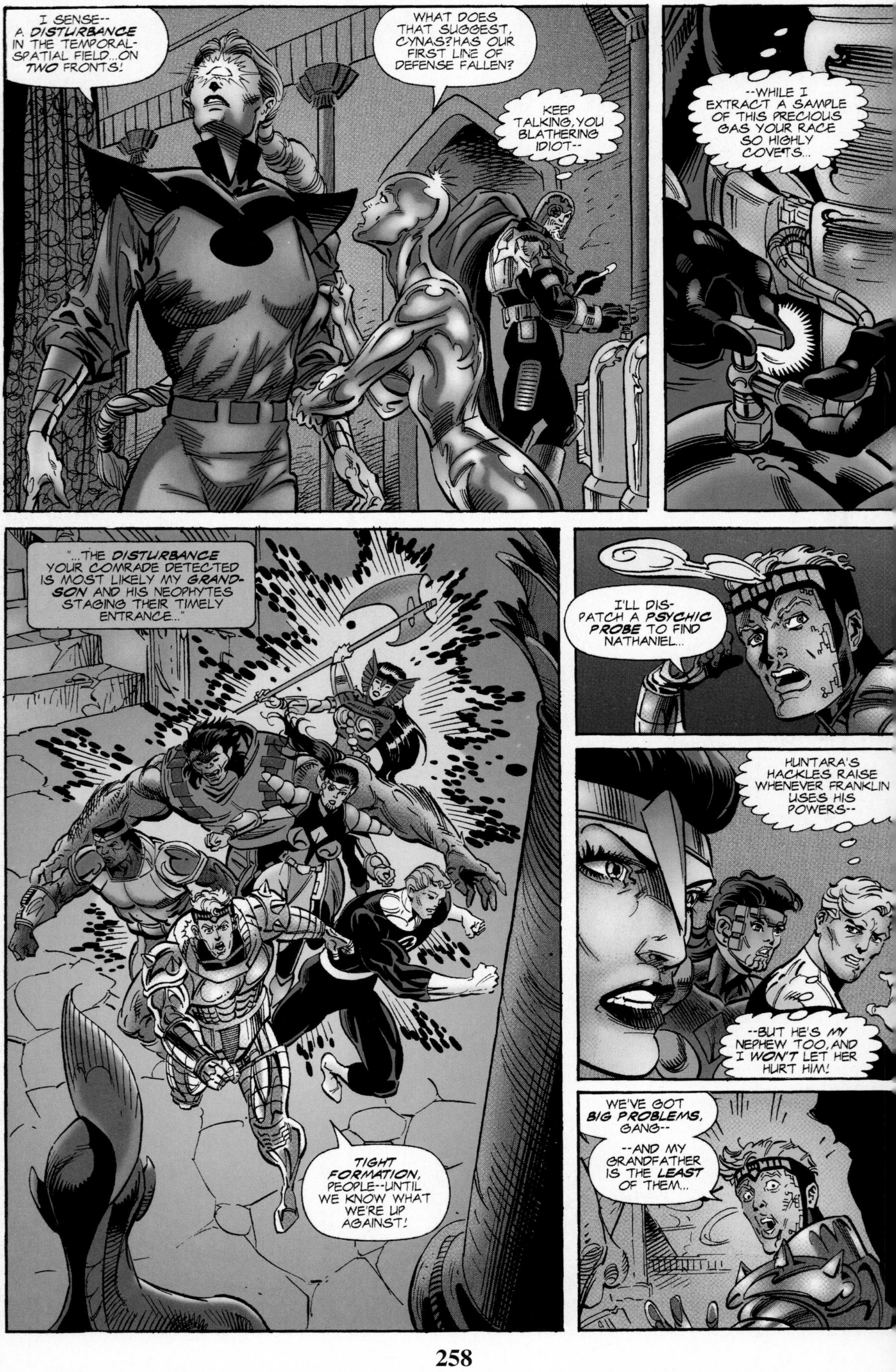
I SENSE-- A DISTURBANCE IN THE TEMPORAL-SPATIAL FIELD...ON TWO FRONTS!
WHAT DOES THAT SUGGEST, CYNAS? HAS OUR FIRST LINE OF DEFENSE FALLEN?
KEEP TALKING, YOU BLATHERING IDIOT--
--WHILE I EXTRACT A SAMPLE OF THIS PRECIOUS GAS YOUR RACE SO HIGHLY COVETS...
"...THE DISTURBANCE YOUR COMRADE DETECTED IS MOST LIKELY MY GRANDSON AND HIS NEOPHYTES STAGING THEIR TIMELY ENTRANCE..."
TIGHT FORMATION, PEOPLE--UNTIL WE KNOW WHAT WE'RE UP AGAINST!
I'LL DISPATCH A PSYCHIC PROBE TO FIND NATHANIEL...
HUNTARA'S HACKLES RAISE WHENEVER FRANKLIN USES HIS POWERS--
--BUT HE'S MY NEPHEW TOO, AND I WON'T LET HER HURT HIM!
WE'VE GOT BIG PROBLEMS, GANG--
--AND MY GRANDFATHER IS THE LEAST OF THEM...

THE INVADERS MYSTERIOUSLY VANISHED ON EACH END OF THE ISLAND!

MORGAN IS OBVIOUSLY TRYING TO PLAY ALL SIDES AGAINST THE MIDDLE.

GO, FIND THE WITCH-- AND *KEEP AN EYE* ON HER!

WE'RE GETTING A LITTLE TIRED OF YOU BOSSING US AROUND, ARCADIUS.

WOULD YOU RATHER STAY AND FACE THE PEOPLE WE *ABANDONED* WHEN I MAKE CONTACT WITH THEM??

UM, WE'LL CATCH YOU LATER.

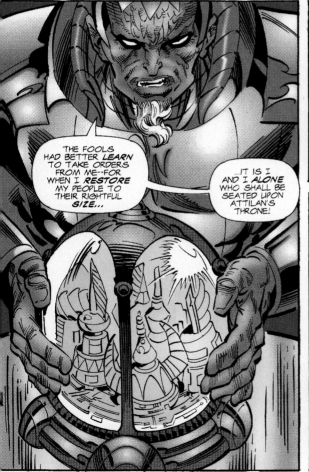

THE FOOLS HAD BETTER *LEARN* TO TAKE ORDERS FROM ME--FOR WHEN I *RESTORE* MY PEOPLE TO THEIR RIGHTFUL *SIZE*...

...IT IS I AND I *ALONE* WHO SHALL BE SEATED UPON ATTILAN'S THRONE!

MY LIEGE--THE *CLOAKED ONE*, HE LOOKS SOMEHOW FAMIL--

YOU!!

UH-OH.

THE ONE WHO SINGLE-HANDEDLY CAUSED THE DESTRUCTION OF THE MOON'S *BLUE AREA!* VENGEANCE SHALL BE *MINE*--

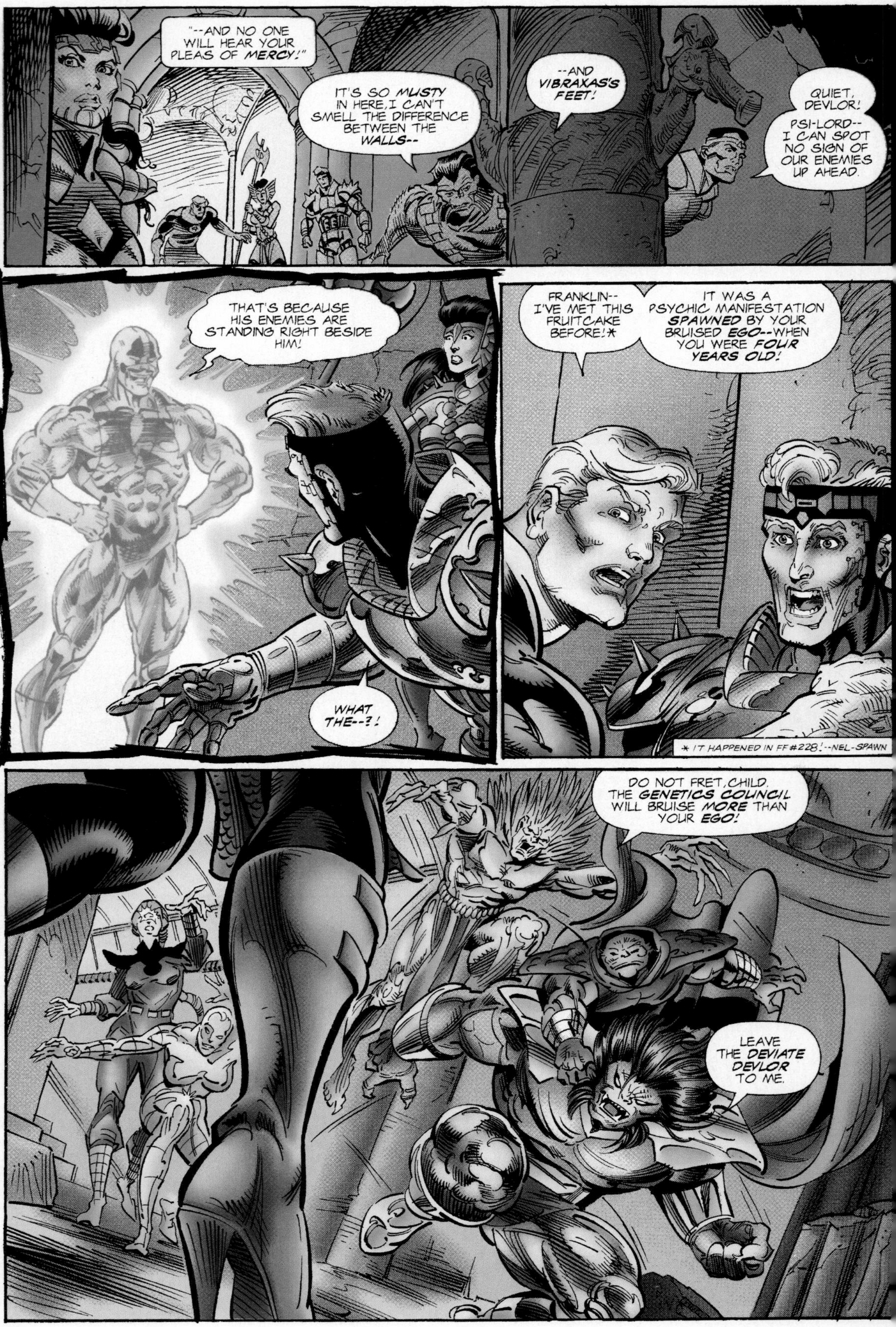
"--AND NO ONE WILL HEAR YOUR PLEAS OF MERCY!"
IT'S SO MUSTY IN HERE, I CAN'T SMELL THE DIFFERENCE BETWEEN THE WALLS--
--AND VIBRAXAS'S FEET!
QUIET, DEVLOR! PSI-LORD-- I CAN SPOT NO SIGN OF OUR ENEMIES UP AHEAD.
THAT'S BECAUSE HIS ENEMIES ARE STANDING RIGHT BESIDE HIM!
WHAT THE--?!
FRANKLIN-- I'VE MET THIS FRUITCAKE BEFORE!*
IT WAS A PSYCHIC MANIFESTATION SPAWNED BY YOUR BRUISED EGO--WHEN YOU WERE FOUR YEARS OLD!
* IT HAPPENED IN FF #228! --NEL-SPAWN
DO NOT FRET, CHILD. THE GENETICS COUNCIL WILL BRUISE MORE THAN YOUR EGO!
LEAVE THE DEVIATE DEVLOR TO ME.

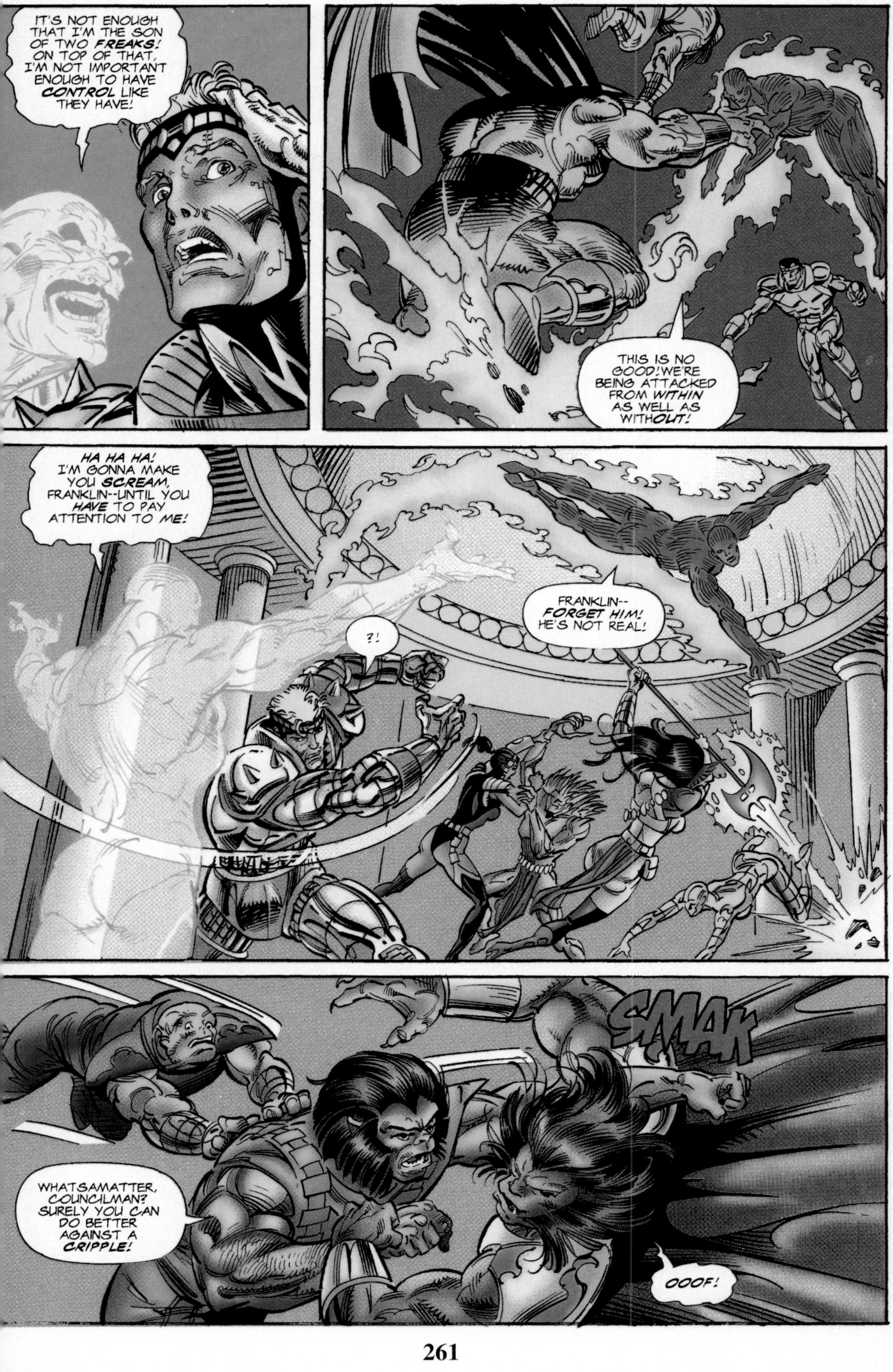
IT'S NOT ENOUGH THAT I'M THE SON OF TWO FREAKS! ON TOP OF THAT, I'M NOT IMPORTANT ENOUGH TO HAVE CONTROL LIKE THEY HAVE!
THIS IS NO GOOD! WE'RE BEING ATTACKED FROM WITHIN AS WELL AS WITHOUT!
HA HA HA! I'M GONNA MAKE YOU SCREAM, FRANKLIN--UNTIL YOU HAVE TO PAY ATTENTION TO ME!
FRANKLIN-- FORGET HIM! HE'S NOT REAL!
?!
SMAK
WHATSAMATTER, COUNCILMAN? SURELY YOU CAN DO BETTER AGAINST A CRIPPLE!
OOOF!

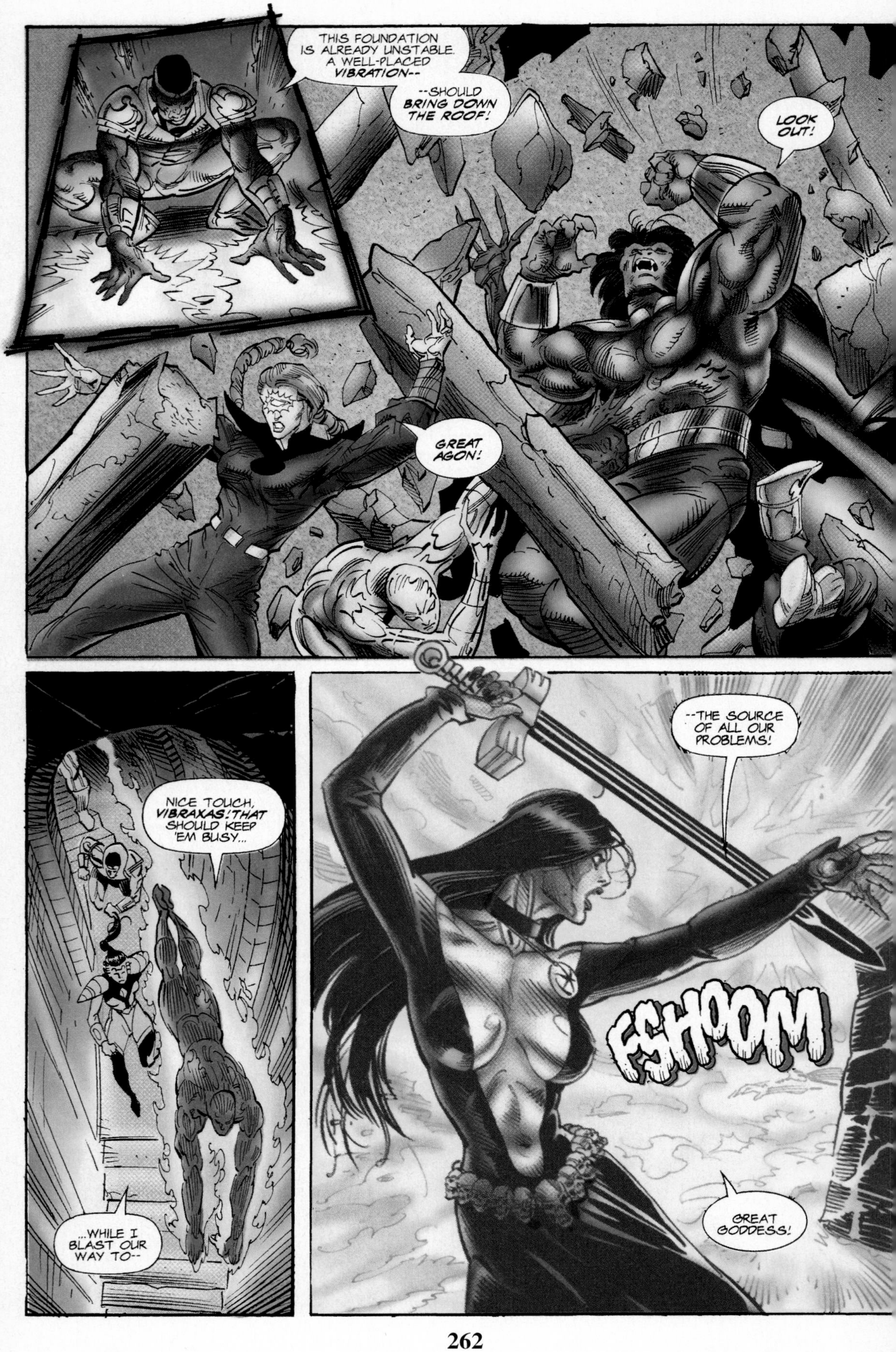
THIS FOUNDATION IS ALREADY UNSTABLE. A WELL-PLACED VIBRATION--
--SHOULD BRING DOWN THE ROOF!
LOOK OUT!
GREAT AGON!
NICE TOUCH, VIBRAXAS! THAT SHOULD KEEP 'EM BUSY...
...WHILE I BLAST OUR WAY TO--
--THE SOURCE OF ALL OUR PROBLEMS!
FSHOOM
GREAT GODDESS!

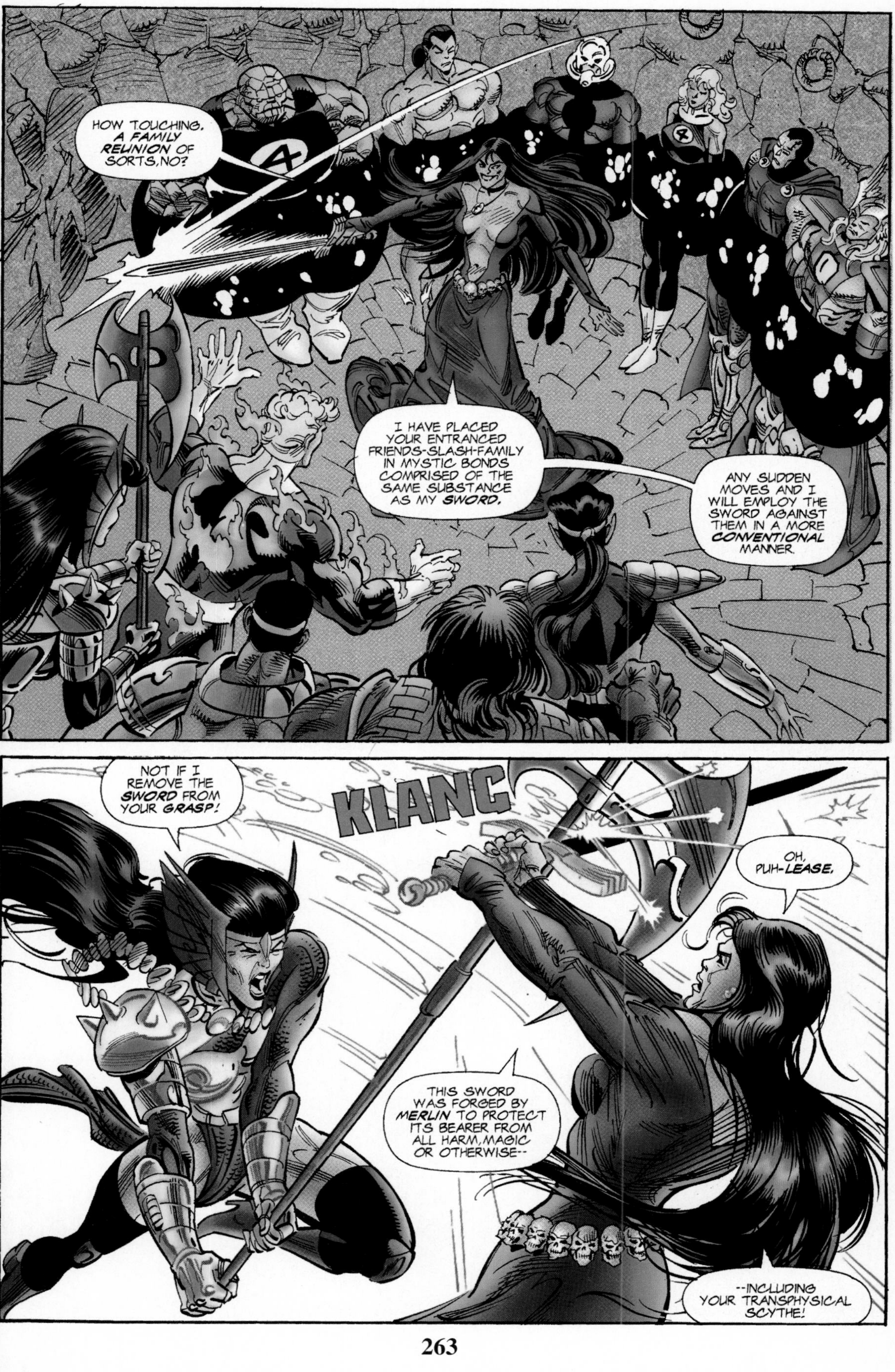
HOW TOUCHING. A FAMILY REUNION OF SORTS, NO?
I HAVE PLACED YOUR ENTRANCED FRIENDS-SLASH-FAMILY IN MYSTIC BONDS COMPRISED OF THE SAME SUBSTANCE AS MY SWORD.
ANY SUDDEN MOVES AND I WILL EMPLOY THE SWORD AGAINST THEM IN A MORE CONVENTIONAL MANNER.
NOT IF I REMOVE THE SWORD FROM YOUR GRASP!
KLANG
OH, PUH-LEASE.
THIS SWORD WAS FORGED BY MERLIN TO PROTECT ITS BEARER FROM ALL HARM, MAGIC OR OTHERWISE--
--INCLUDING YOUR TRANSPHYSICAL SCYTHE!

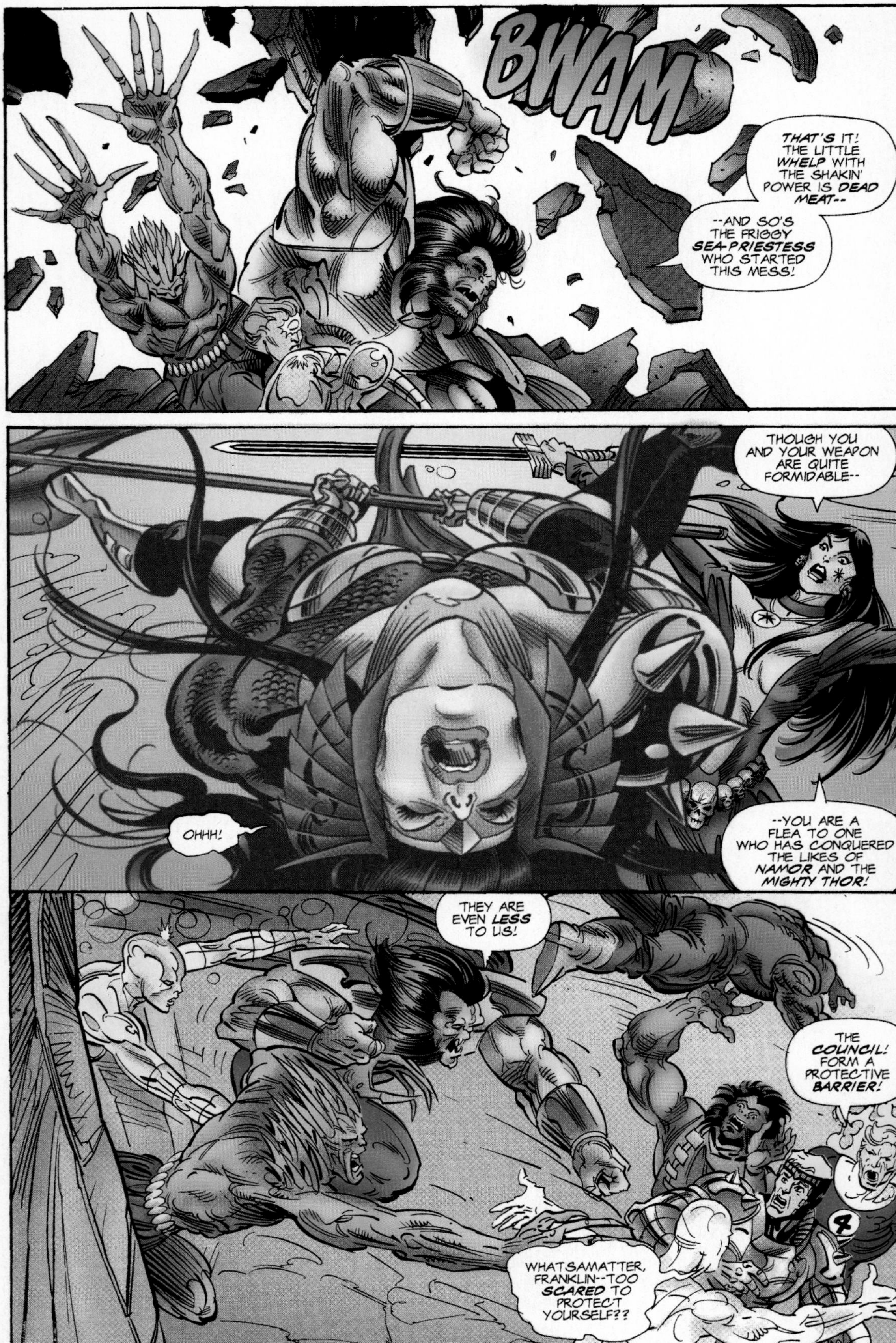
BWAM
THAT'S IT! THE LITTLE WHELP WITH THE SHAKIN' POWER IS DEAD MEAT--
--AND SO'S THE FRIGGY SEA-PRIESTESS WHO STARTED THIS MESS!
THOUGH YOU AND YOUR WEAPON ARE QUITE FORMIDABLE--
OHHH!
--YOU ARE A FLEA TO ONE WHO HAS CONQUERED THE LIKES OF NAMOR AND THE MIGHTY THOR!
THEY ARE EVEN LESS TO US!
THE COUNCIL! FORM A PROTECTIVE BARRIER!
WHATSAMATTER, FRANKLIN--TOO SCARED TO PROTECT YOURSELF??

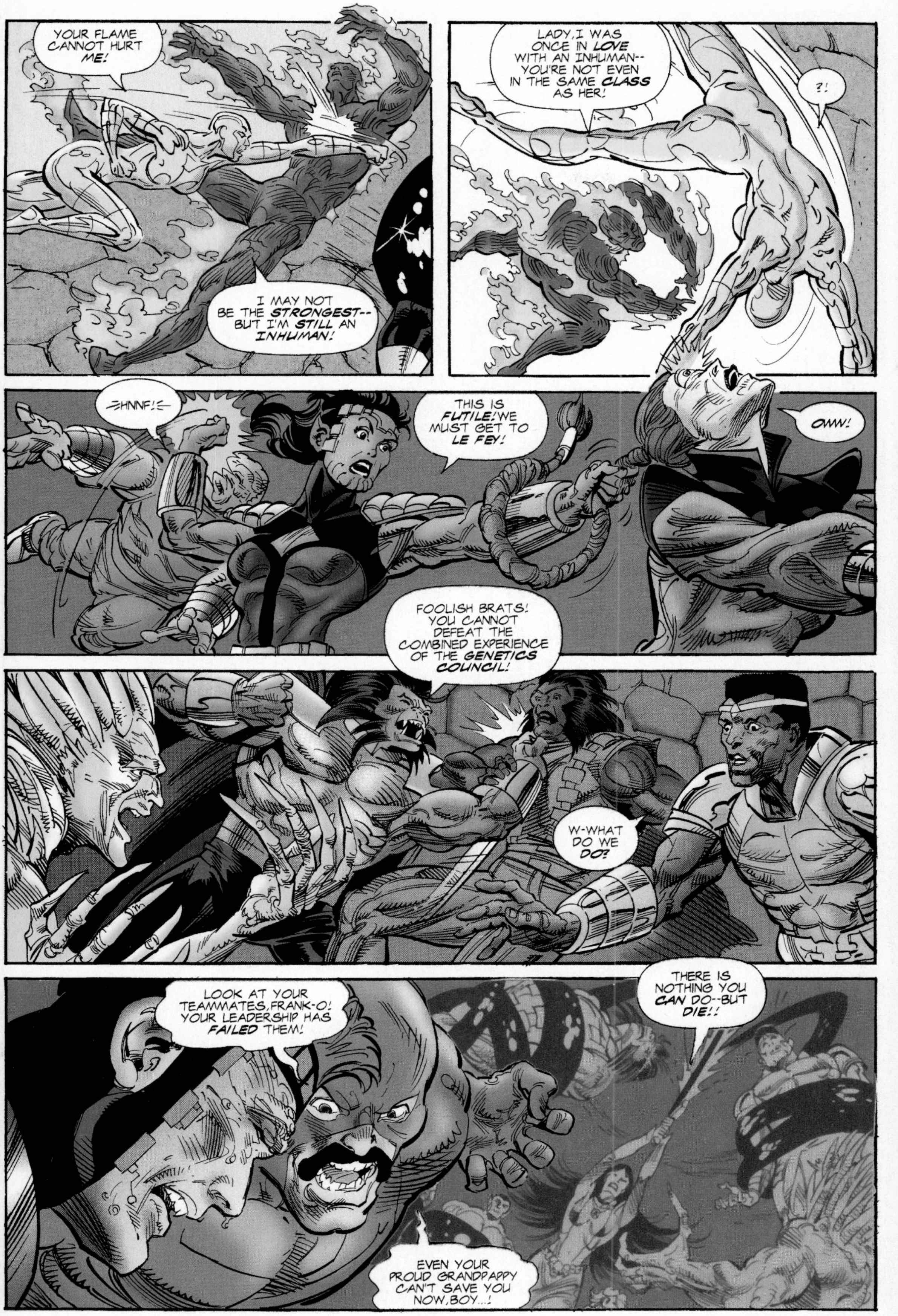
YOUR FLAME CANNOT HURT ME!
I MAY NOT BE THE STRONGEST-- BUT I'M STILL AN INHUMAN!
LADY, I WAS ONCE IN LOVE WITH AN INHUMAN-- YOU'RE NOT EVEN IN THE SAME CLASS AS HER!
?!
HNNF!
THIS IS FUTILE! WE MUST GET TO LE FEY!
OWW!
FOOLISH BRATS! YOU CANNOT DEFEAT THE COMBINED EXPERIENCE OF THE GENETICS COUNCIL!
W-WHAT DO WE DO?
LOOK AT YOUR TEAMMATES, FRANK-O! YOUR LEADERSHIP HAS FAILED THEM!
THERE IS NOTHING YOU CAN DO--BUT DIE!!
EVEN YOUR PROUD GRANDPAPPY CAN'T SAVE YOU NOW, BOY...!

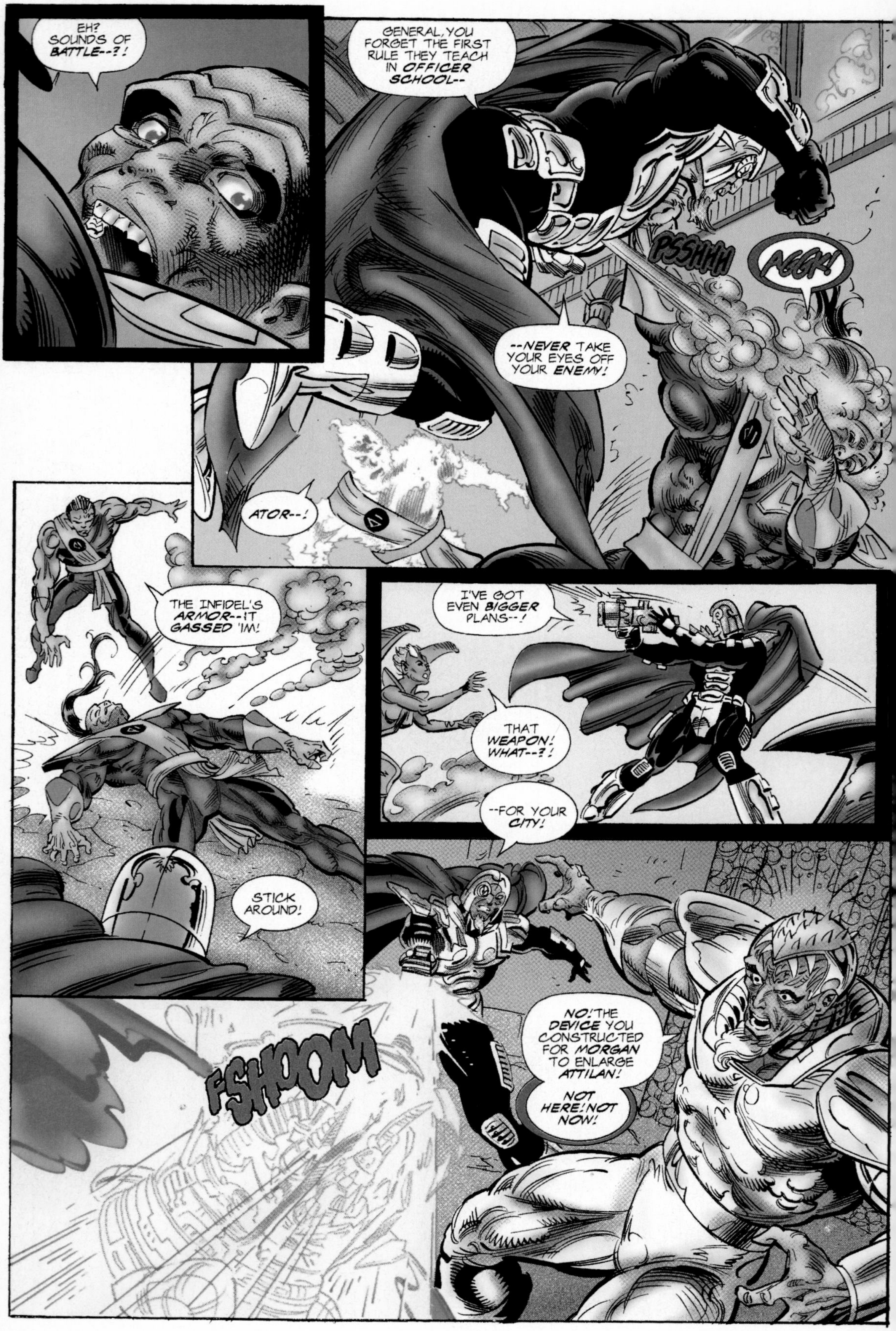
EH? SOUNDS OF BATTLE--?!
GENERAL, YOU FORGET THE FIRST RULE THEY TEACH IN OFFICER SCHOOL--
PSSHHH
AGGK!
--NEVER TAKE YOUR EYES OFF YOUR ENEMY!
ATOR--!
THE INFIDEL'S ARMOR--IT GASSED 'IM!
I'VE GOT EVEN BIGGER PLANS--!
THAT WEAPON! WHAT--?!
--FOR YOUR CITY!
STICK AROUND!
FSHOOM
NO! THE DEVICE YOU CONSTRUCTED FOR MORGAN TO ENLARGE ATTILAN!
NOT HERE! NOT NOW!

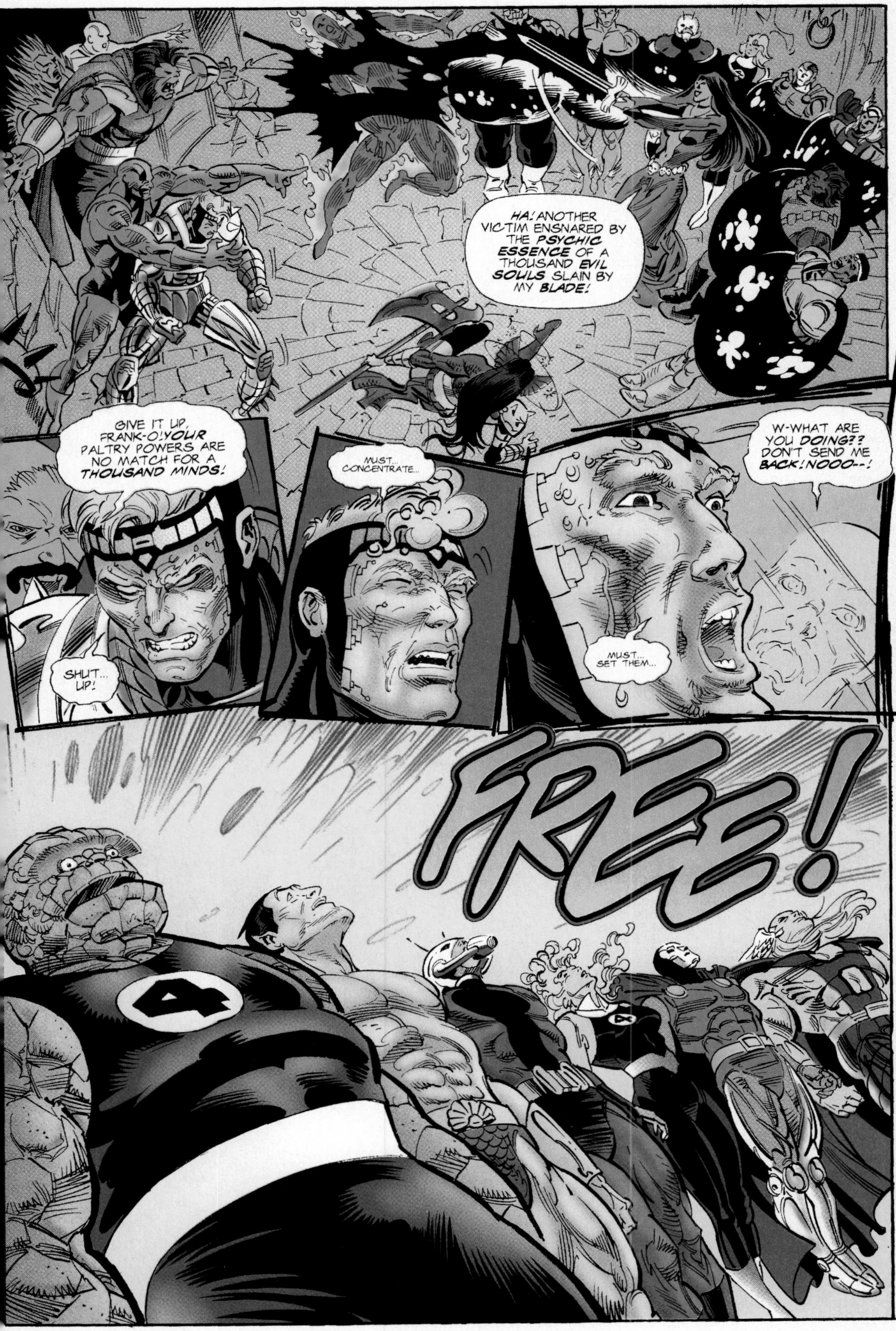
HA! ANOTHER VICTIM ENSNARED BY THE PSYCHIC ESSENCE OF A THOUSAND EVIL SOULS SLAIN BY MY BLADE!
GIVE IT UP, FRANK-O! YOUR PALTRY POWERS ARE NO MATCH FOR A THOUSAND MINDS!
SHUT... UP!
MUST... CONCENTRATE...
W-WHAT ARE YOU DOING?? DON'T SEND ME BACK! NOOO--!
MUST... SET THEM...
FREE!

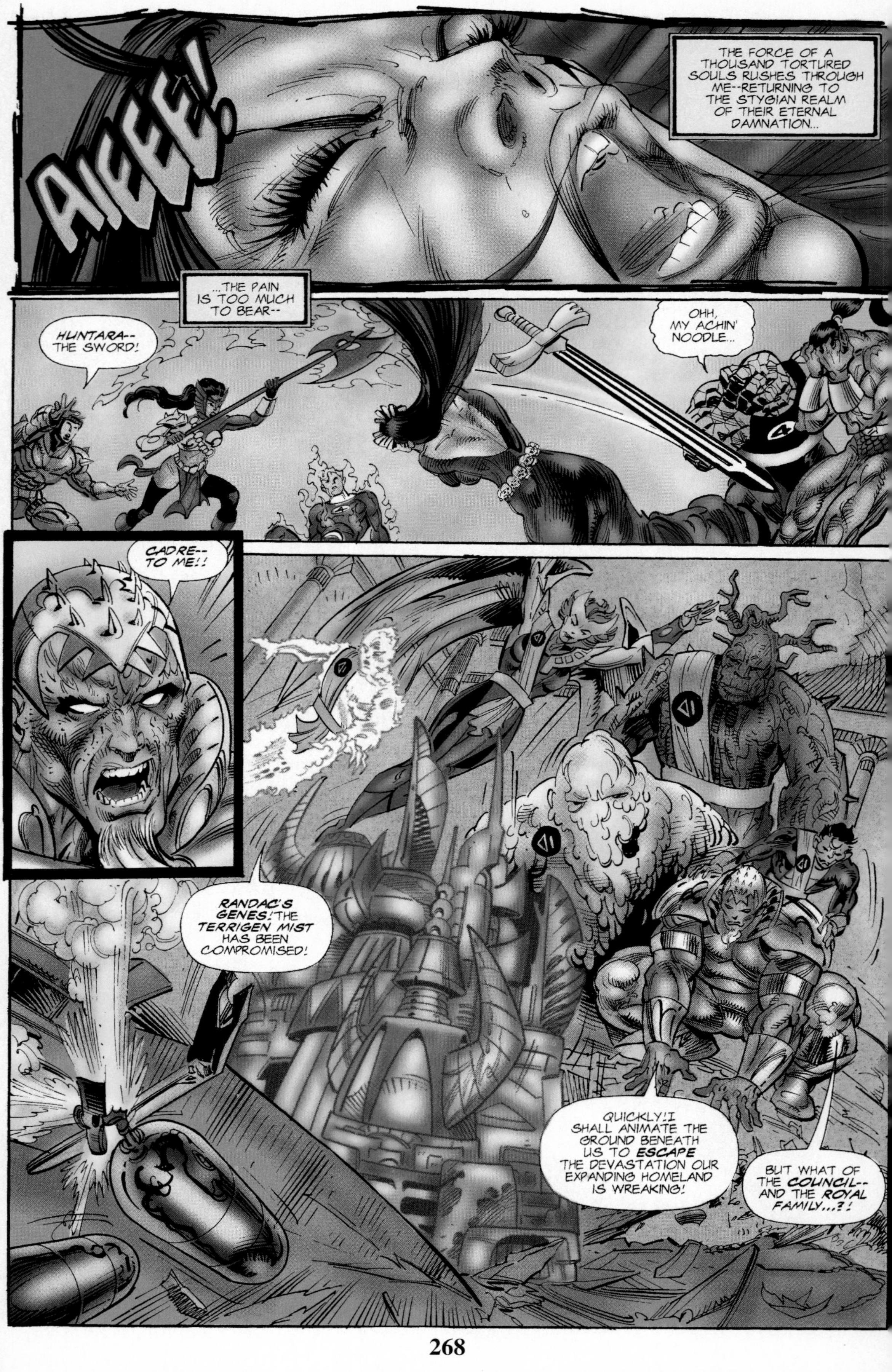
AIEEE!
THE FORCE OF A THOUSAND TORTURED SOULS RUSHES THROUGH ME--RETURNING TO THE STYGIAN REALM OF THEIR ETERNAL DAMNATION...
...THE PAIN IS TOO MUCH TO BEAR--
HUNTARA-- THE SWORD!
OHH, MY ACHIN' NOODLE...
CADRE-- TO ME!!
RANDAC'S GENES! THE TERRIGEN MIST HAS BEEN COMPROMISED!
QUICKLY! I SHALL ANIMATE THE GROUND BENEATH US TO ESCAPE THE DEVASTATION OUR EXPANDING HOMELAND IS WREAKING!
BUT WHAT OF THE COUNCIL-- AND THE ROYAL FAMILY...?!

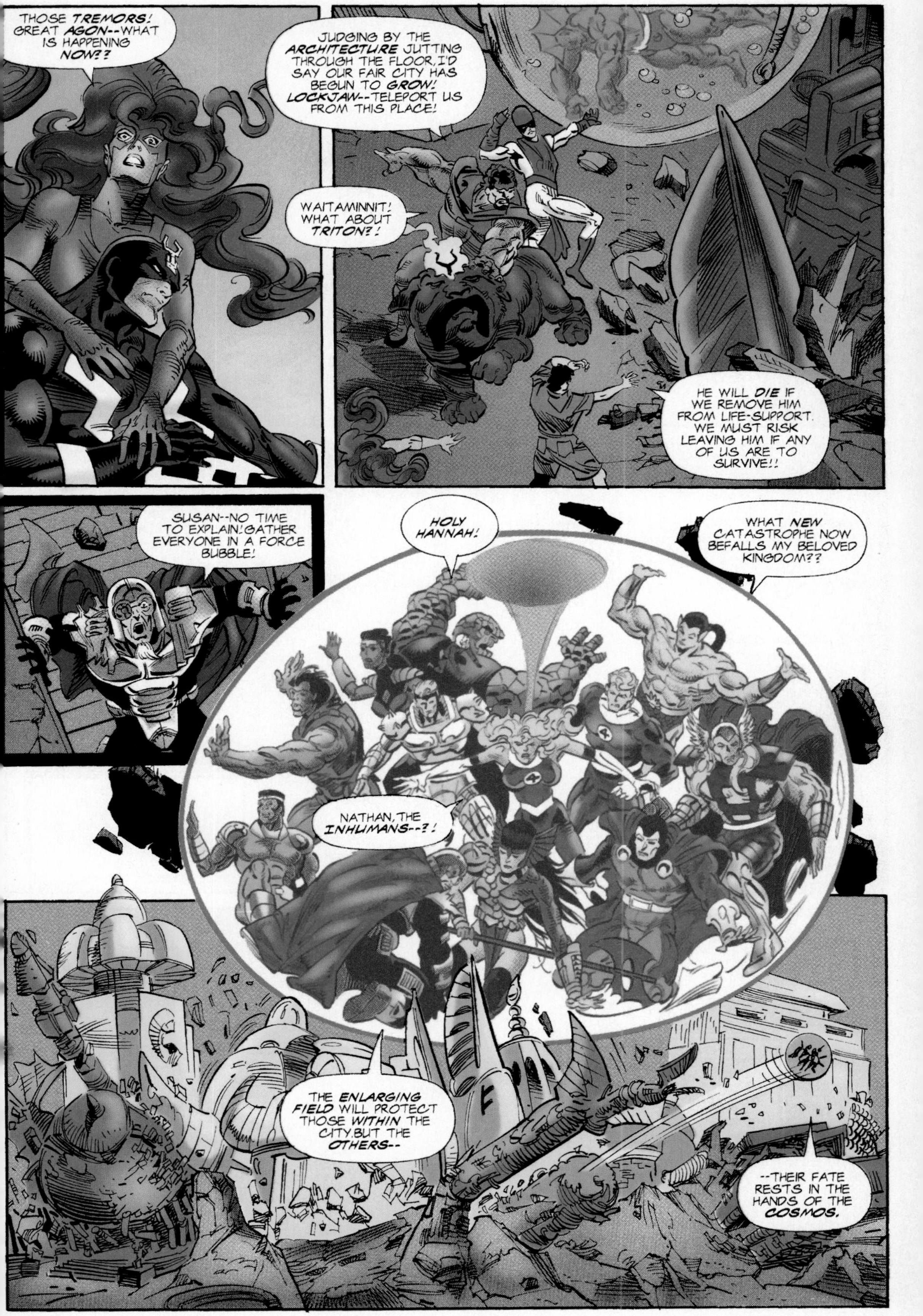
THOSE TREMORS! GREAT AGON--WHAT IS HAPPENING NOW??
JUDGING BY THE ARCHITECTURE JUTTING THROUGH THE FLOOR, I'D SAY OUR FAIR CITY HAS BEGUN TO GROW! LOCKJAW--TELEPORT US FROM THIS PLACE!
WAITAMINNIT! WHAT ABOUT TRITON?!
HE WILL DIE IF WE REMOVE HIM FROM LIFE-SUPPORT. WE MUST RISK LEAVING HIM IF ANY OF US ARE TO SURVIVE!!
SUSAN--NO TIME TO EXPLAIN! GATHER EVERYONE IN A FORCE BUBBLE!
HOLY HANNAH!
WHAT NEW CATASTROPHE NOW BEFALLS MY BELOVED KINGDOM??
NATHAN, THE INHUMANS--?!
THE ENLARGING FIELD WILL PROTECT THOSE WITHIN THE CITY. BUT THE OTHERS--
--THEIR FATE RESTS IN THE HANDS OF THE COSMOS.

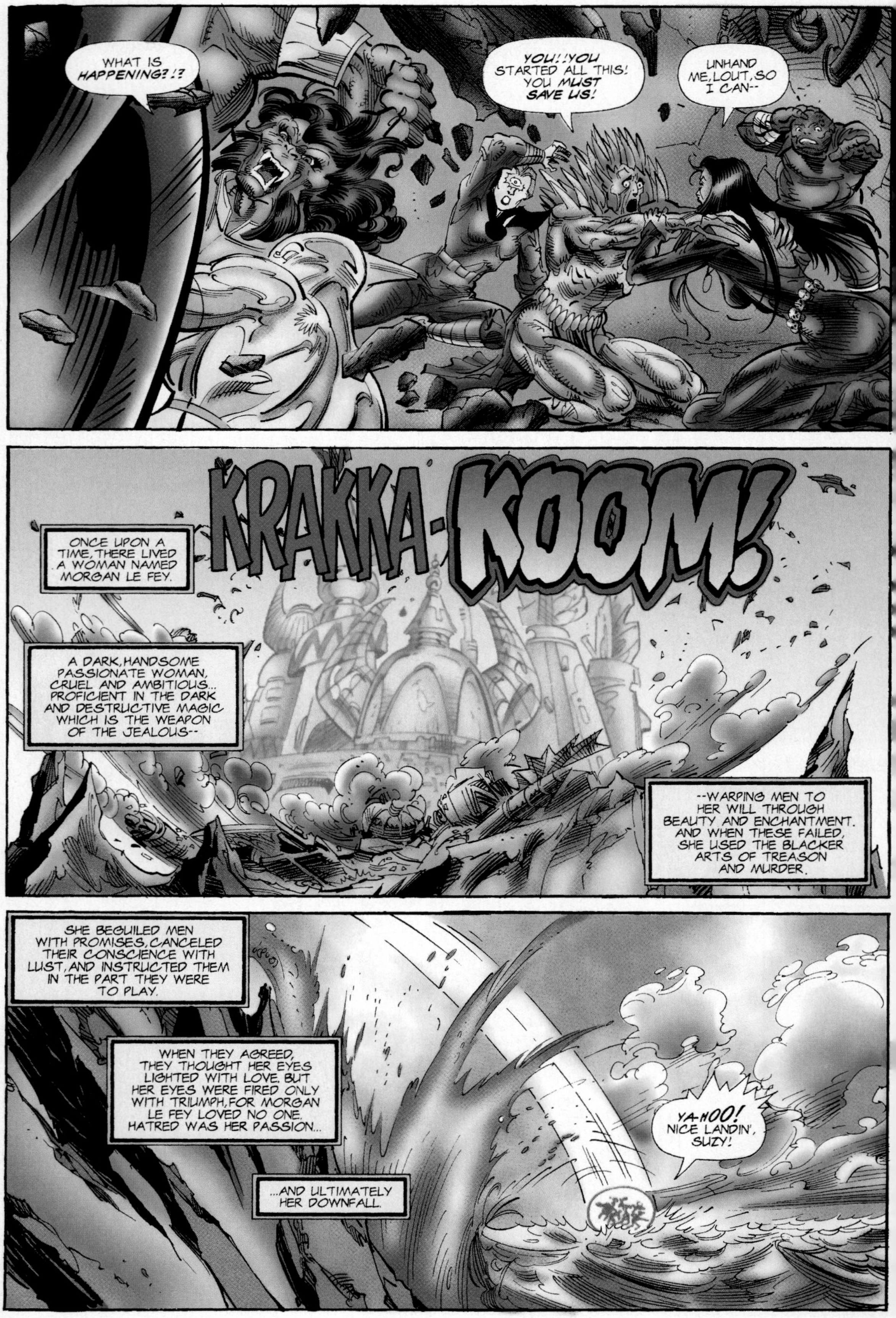
WHAT IS HAPPENING?!?
YOU!!YOU STARTED ALL THIS! YOU MUST SAVE US!
UNHAND ME, LOUT, SO I CAN--
KRAKKA-KOOM!
ONCE UPON A TIME, THERE LIVED A WOMAN NAMED MORGAN LE FEY.
A DARK, HANDSOME PASSIONATE WOMAN, CRUEL AND AMBITIOUS... PROFICIENT IN THE DARK AND DESTRUCTIVE MAGIC WHICH IS THE WEAPON OF THE JEALOUS--
--WARPING MEN TO HER WILL THROUGH BEAUTY AND ENCHANTMENT. AND WHEN THESE FAILED, SHE USED THE BLACKER ARTS OF TREASON AND MURDER.
SHE BEGUILED MEN WITH PROMISES, CANCELED THEIR CONSCIENCE WITH LUST, AND INSTRUCTED THEM IN THE PART THEY WERE TO PLAY.
WHEN THEY AGREED, THEY THOUGHT HER EYES LIGHTED WITH LOVE. BUT HER EYES WERE FIRED ONLY WITH TRIUMPH, FOR MORGAN LE FEY LOVED NO ONE. HATRED WAS HER PASSION...
...AND ULTIMATELY HER DOWNFALL.
YA-HOO! NICE LANDIN', SUZY!

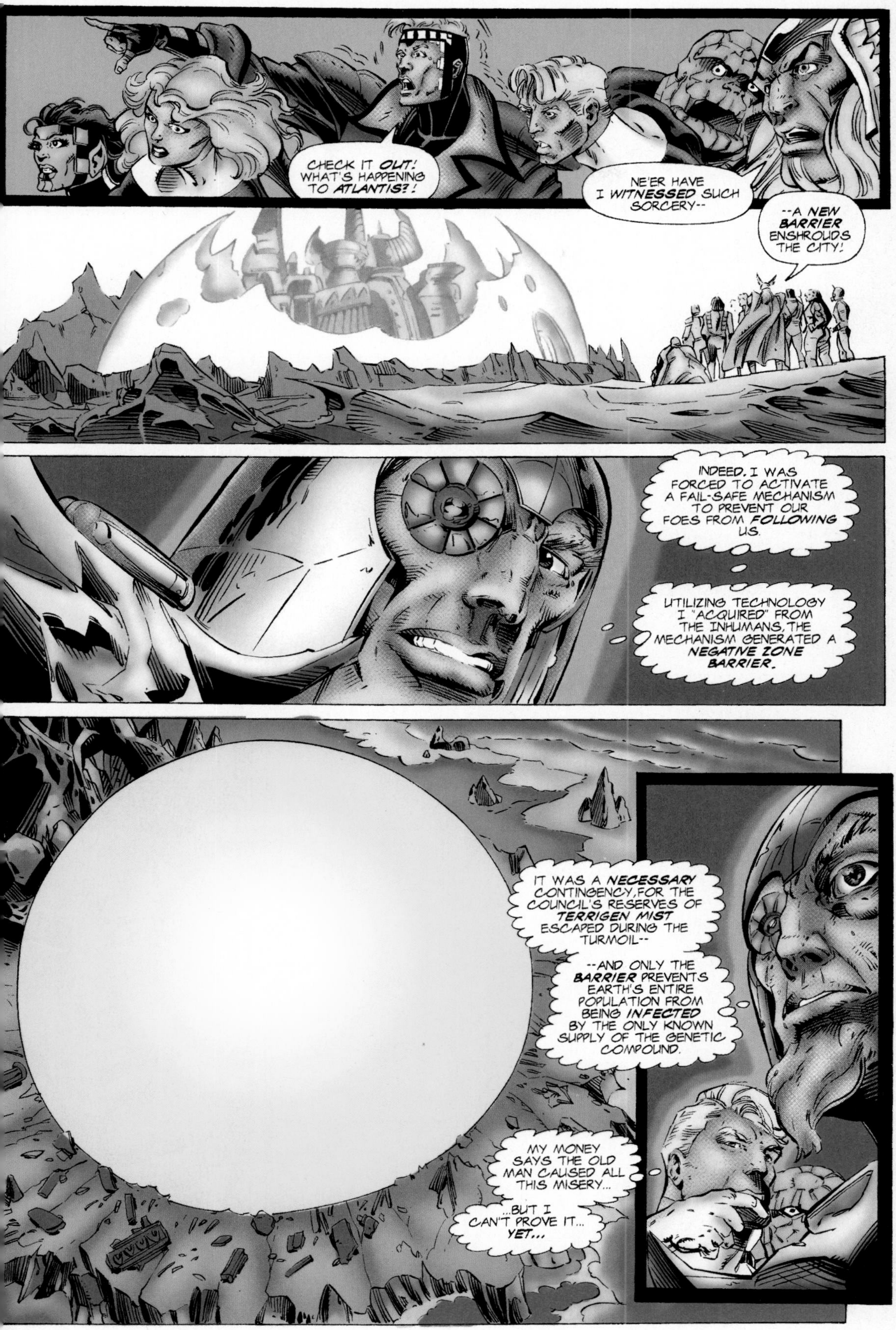
CHECK IT OUT! WHAT'S HAPPENING TO ATLANTIS?!
NE'ER HAVE I WITNESSED SUCH SORCERY--
--A NEW BARRIER ENSHROUDS THE CITY!
INDEED. I WAS FORCED TO ACTIVATE A FAIL-SAFE MECHANISM TO PREVENT OUR FOES FROM FOLLOWING US.
UTILIZING TECHNOLOGY I "ACQUIRED" FROM THE INHUMANS, THE MECHANISM GENERATED A NEGATIVE ZONE BARRIER.
IT WAS A NECESSARY CONTINGENCY, FOR THE COUNCIL'S RESERVES OF TERRIGEN MIST ESCAPED DURING THE TURMOIL--
--AND ONLY THE BARRIER PREVENTS EARTH'S ENTIRE POPULATION FROM BEING INFECTED BY THE ONLY KNOWN SUPPLY OF THE GENETIC COMPOUND.
MY MONEY SAYS THE OLD MAN CAUSED ALL THIS MISERY...
...BUT I CAN'T PROVE IT... YET...

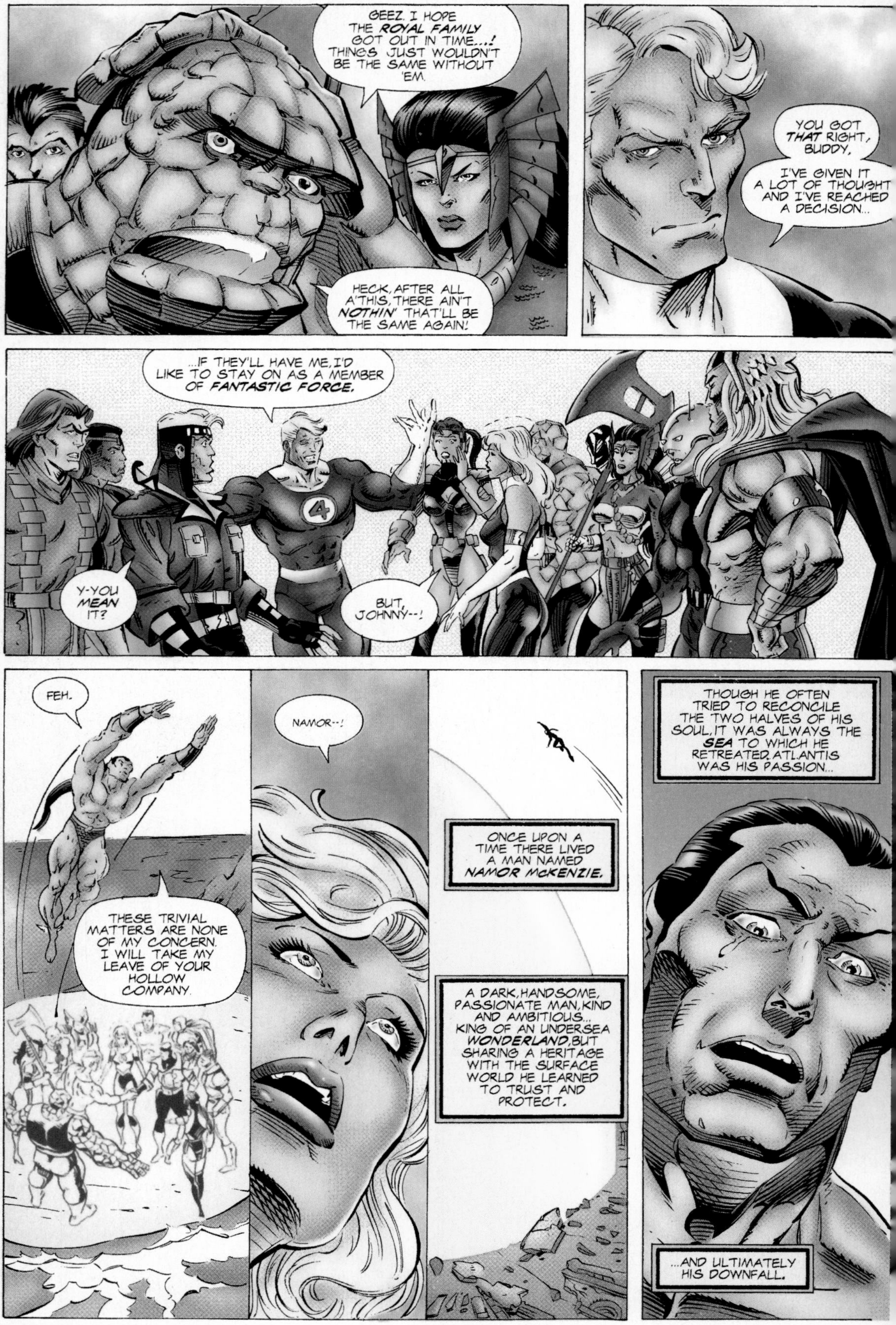
GEEZ. I HOPE THE ROYAL FAMILY GOT OUT IN TIME...! THINGS JUST WOULDN'T BE THE SAME WITHOUT 'EM.
HECK, AFTER ALL A'THIS, THERE AIN'T NOTHIN' THAT'LL BE THE SAME AGAIN!
YOU GOT THAT RIGHT, BUDDY.
I'VE GIVEN IT A LOT OF THOUGHT AND I'VE REACHED A DECISION...
...IF THEY'LL HAVE ME, I'D LIKE TO STAY ON AS A MEMBER OF FANTASTIC FORCE.
Y-YOU MEAN IT?
BUT, JOHNNY--!
FEH.
THESE TRIVIAL MATTERS ARE NONE OF MY CONCERN. I WILL TAKE MY LEAVE OF YOUR HOLLOW COMPANY.
NAMOR--!
ONCE UPON A TIME THERE LIVED A MAN NAMED NAMOR McKENZIE.
A DARK, HANDSOME, PASSIONATE MAN, KIND AND AMBITIOUS... KING OF AN UNDERSEA WONDERLAND, BUT SHARING A HERITAGE WITH THE SURFACE WORLD HE LEARNED TO TRUST AND PROTECT.
THOUGH HE OFTEN TRIED TO RECONCILE THE TWO HALVES OF HIS SOUL, IT WAS ALWAYS THE SEA TO WHICH HE RETREATED. ATLANTIS WAS HIS PASSION...
...AND ULTIMATELY HIS DOWNFALL.

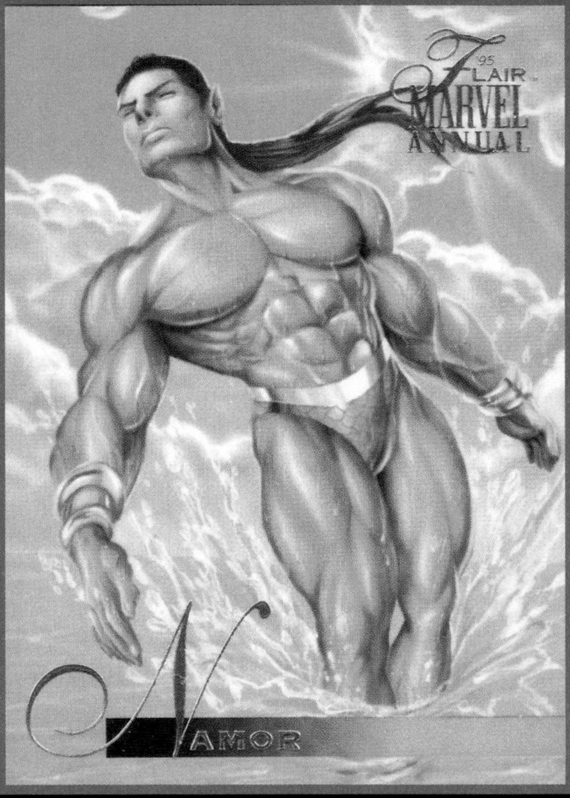
'95 FLAIR MARVEL ANNUAL
NAMOR

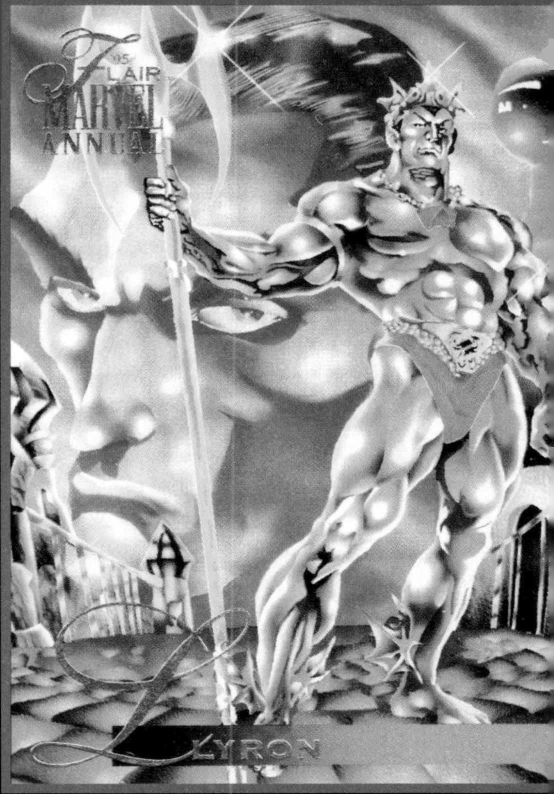
'95 FLAIR MARVEL ANNUAL
LYRON

'95 FLAIR MARVEL ANNUAL TRADING CARDS

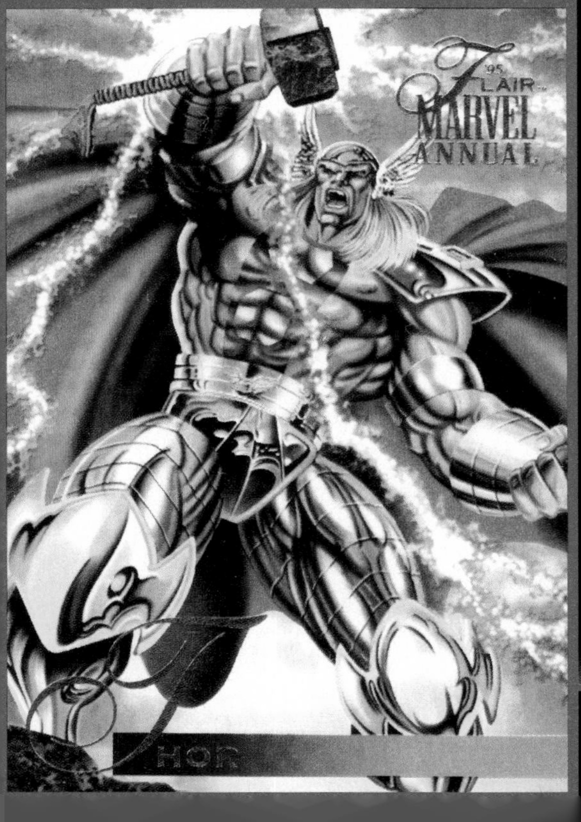
'95 FLAIR MARVEL ANNUAL
THOR

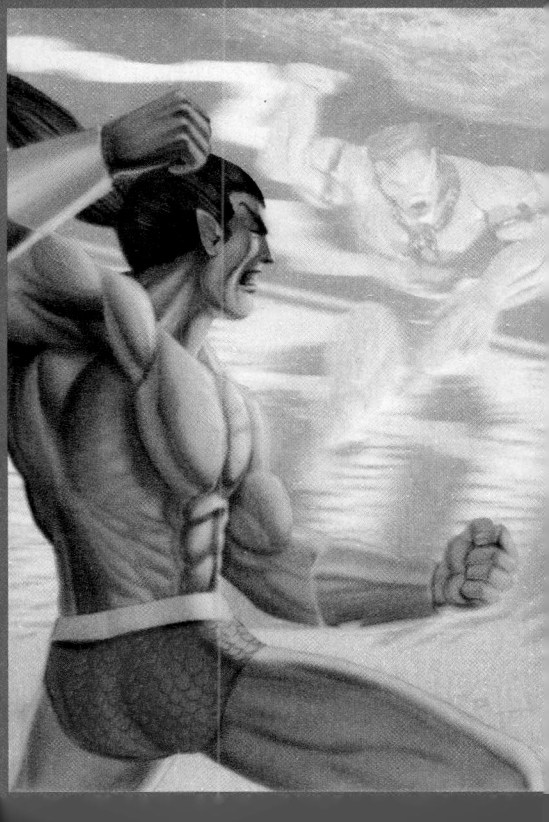

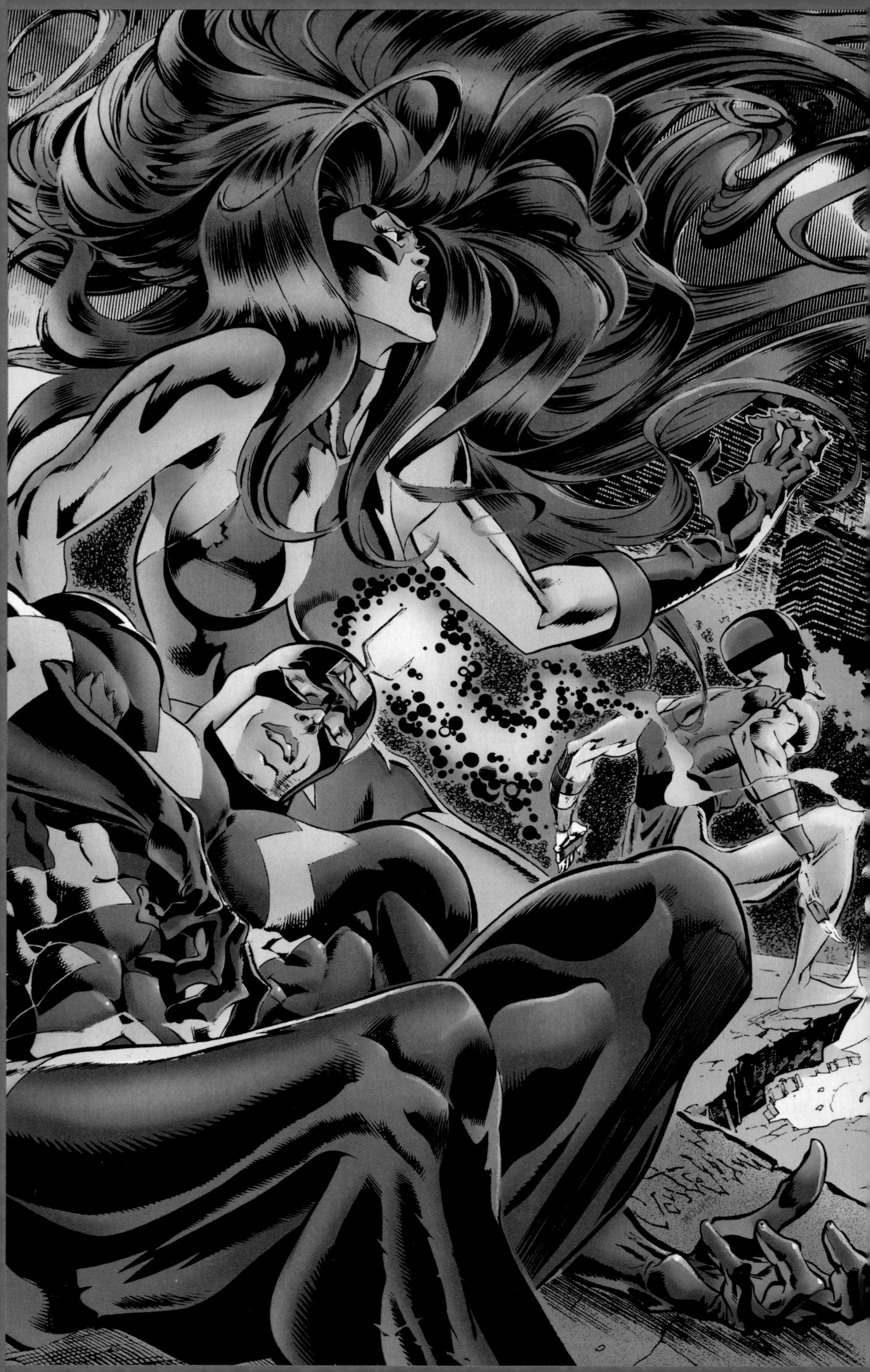

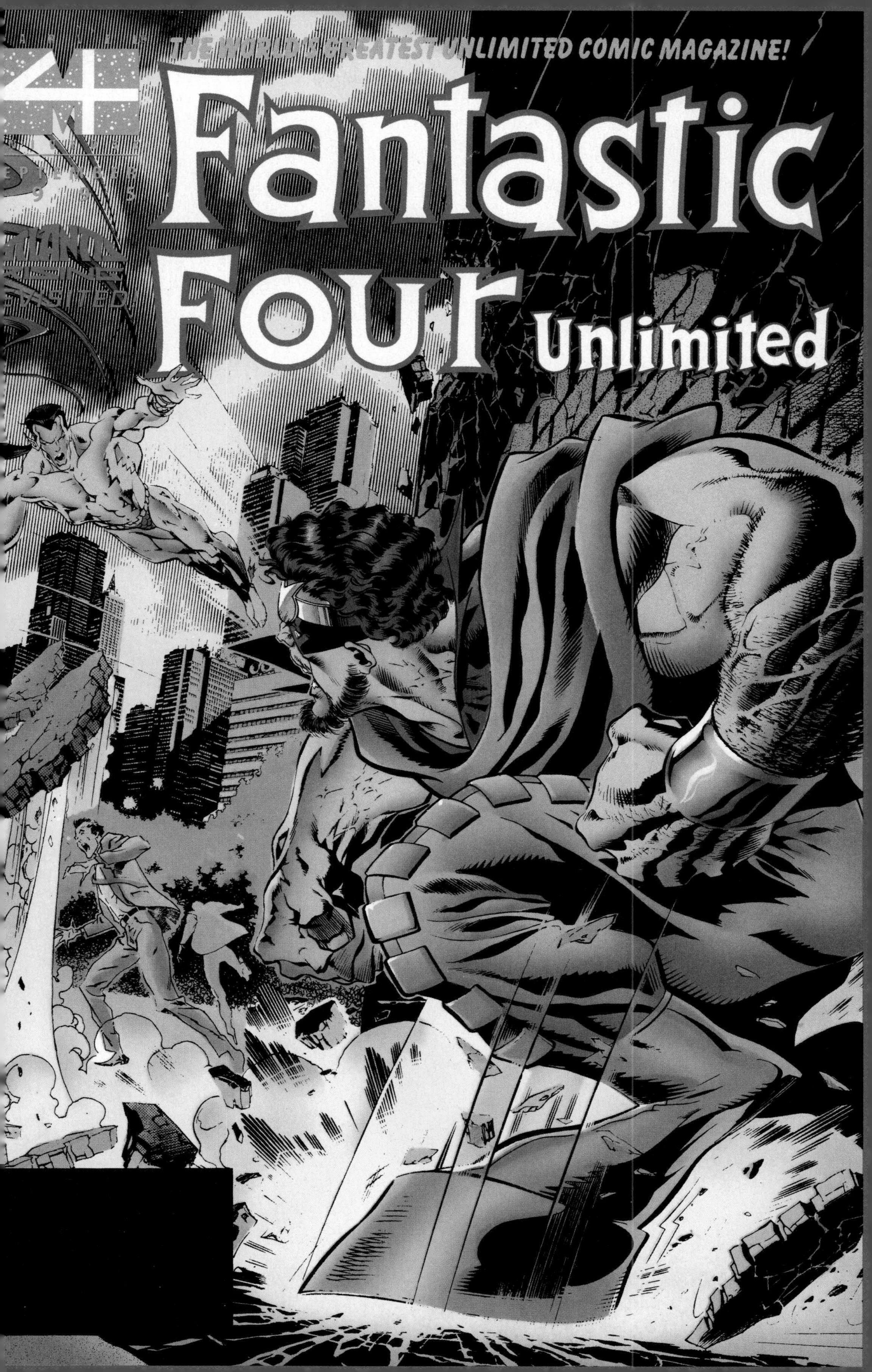
THE WORLD'S GREATEST UNLIMITED COMIC MAGAZINE!
Fantastic Four Unlimited

ATLANTIS RISING

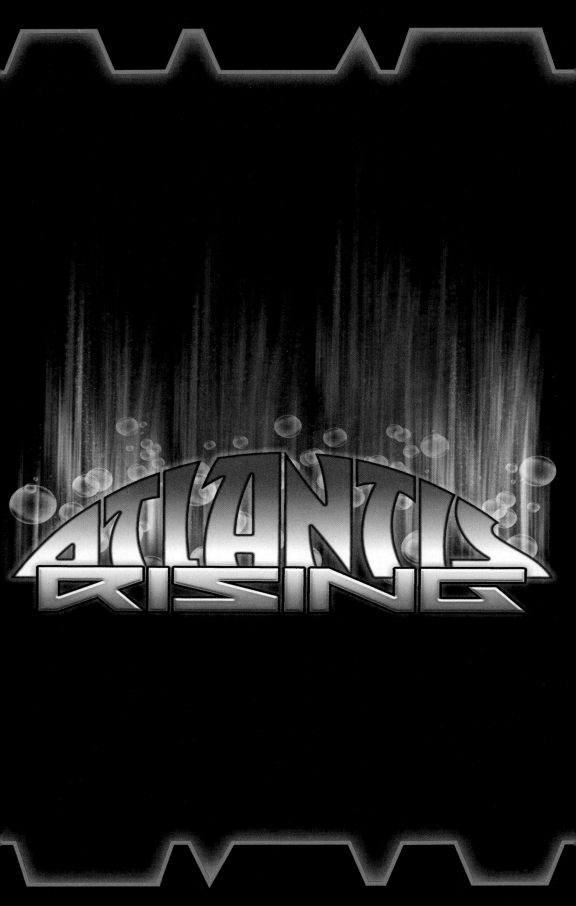

A very special edition of

Fantastic Four Unlimited

featuring the Inhumans
and Prince Namor, the Sub-Mariner!

Stan Lee proudly presents

ATLANTIS RISING

REVISITED!

EDITORIAL STAFF

MARK GRUENWALD
Editor in Chief

NEL YOMTOV
Editor

MICHAEL MARTS
Assistant Editor

MICHAEL COLLINS
Intern

Original FANTASTIC FOUR: ATLANTIS RISING plot
by Tom DeFalco and script by Glen Herdling

Special thanks to THE CHIEF for his creative
guidance and emotional support

TABLE OF CONTENTS

THE STORY OF

ATLANTIS RISING

The raising of the underwater kingdom of Atlantis by the medieval sorceress Morgan Le Fey has destroyed over half the population — the race of homo mermani, whose exiled prince was the legendary Prince Namor, the Sub-Mariner.

Seeking a new homeland themselves — when their lunar home of Attilan is shrunk and encased in a bottle — the Inhumans lay claim to the newly risen continent. The Genetics Council, with the aid of Attilan's national heroes, the Crimson Cadre, journey to Earth to invade Morgan's kingdom.

However, an alliance which includes the Fantastic Four and the Sub-Mariner go to the island to quell the disturbances. Once there, they are attacked by the Royal Family of the Inhumans who have been summoned by the Genetics Council to aid in their conquest of the island.

Before a victor could emerge victorious, the bottled city — now on the risen island — begins to grow causing catastrophic damage. To contain the carnage, Nathaniel Richards, an ally of the Fantastic Four erects a barrier around the island.

The FF and their allies escape the ensuing havoc, but for the Inhumans and Prince Namor, things are just beginning to get interesting ...

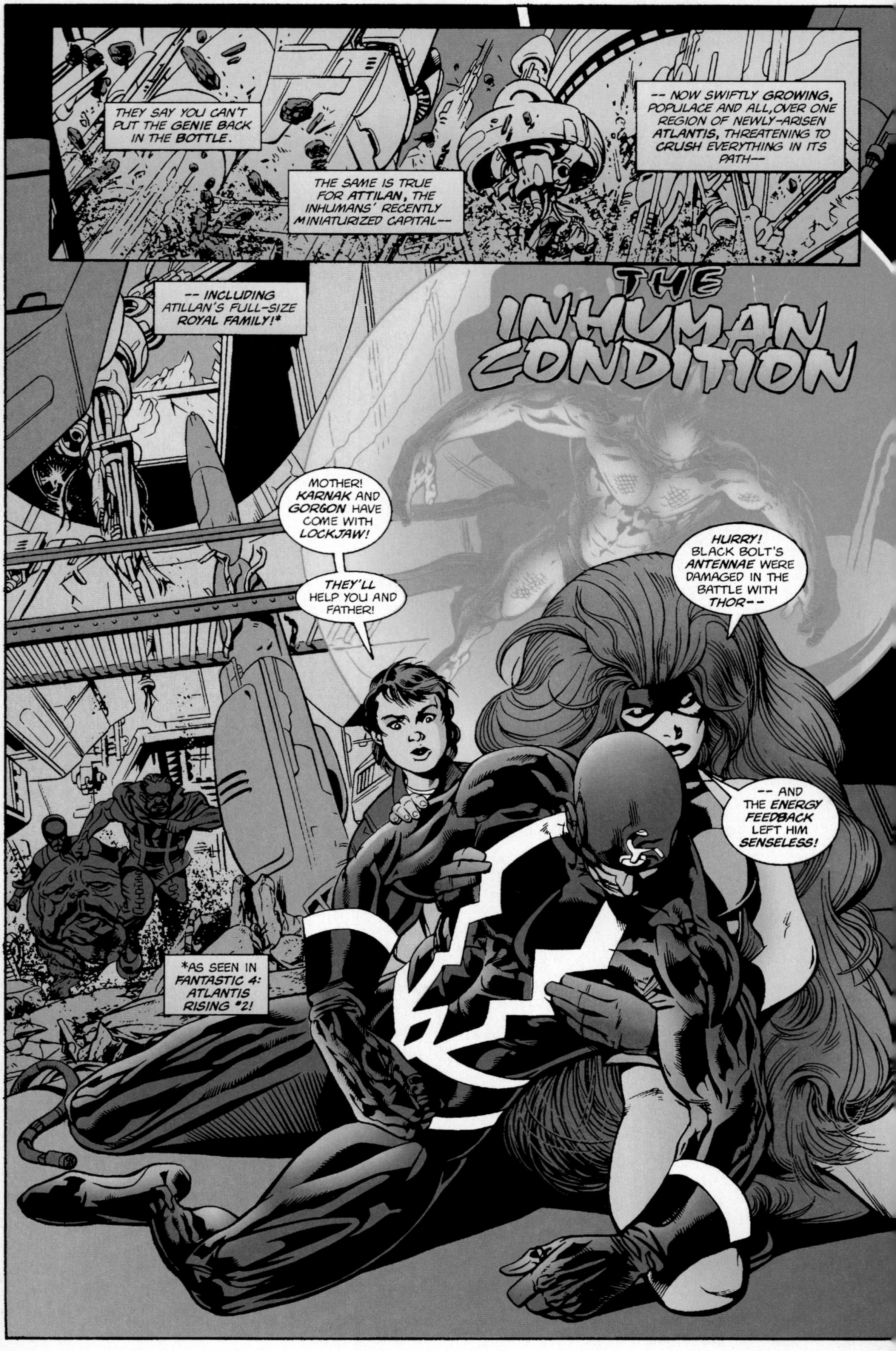

THEY SAY YOU CAN'T PUT THE GENIE BACK IN THE BOTTLE.
THE SAME IS TRUE FOR ATTILAN, THE INHUMANS' RECENTLY MINIATURIZED CAPITAL--
-- NOW SWIFTLY GROWING, POPULACE AND ALL, OVER ONE REGION OF NEWLY-ARISEN ATLANTIS, THREATENING TO CRUSH EVERYTHING IN ITS PATH--
-- INCLUDING ATILLAN'S FULL-SIZE ROYAL FAMILY!*
THE INHUMAN CONDITION
MOTHER! KARNAK AND GORGON HAVE COME WITH LOCKJAW!
THEY'LL HELP YOU AND FATHER!
HURRY! BLACK BOLT'S ANTENNAE WERE DAMAGED IN THE BATTLE WITH THOR--
-- AND THE ENERGY FEEDBACK LEFT HIM SENSELESS!
*AS SEEN IN FANTASTIC 4: ATLANTIS RISING #2!

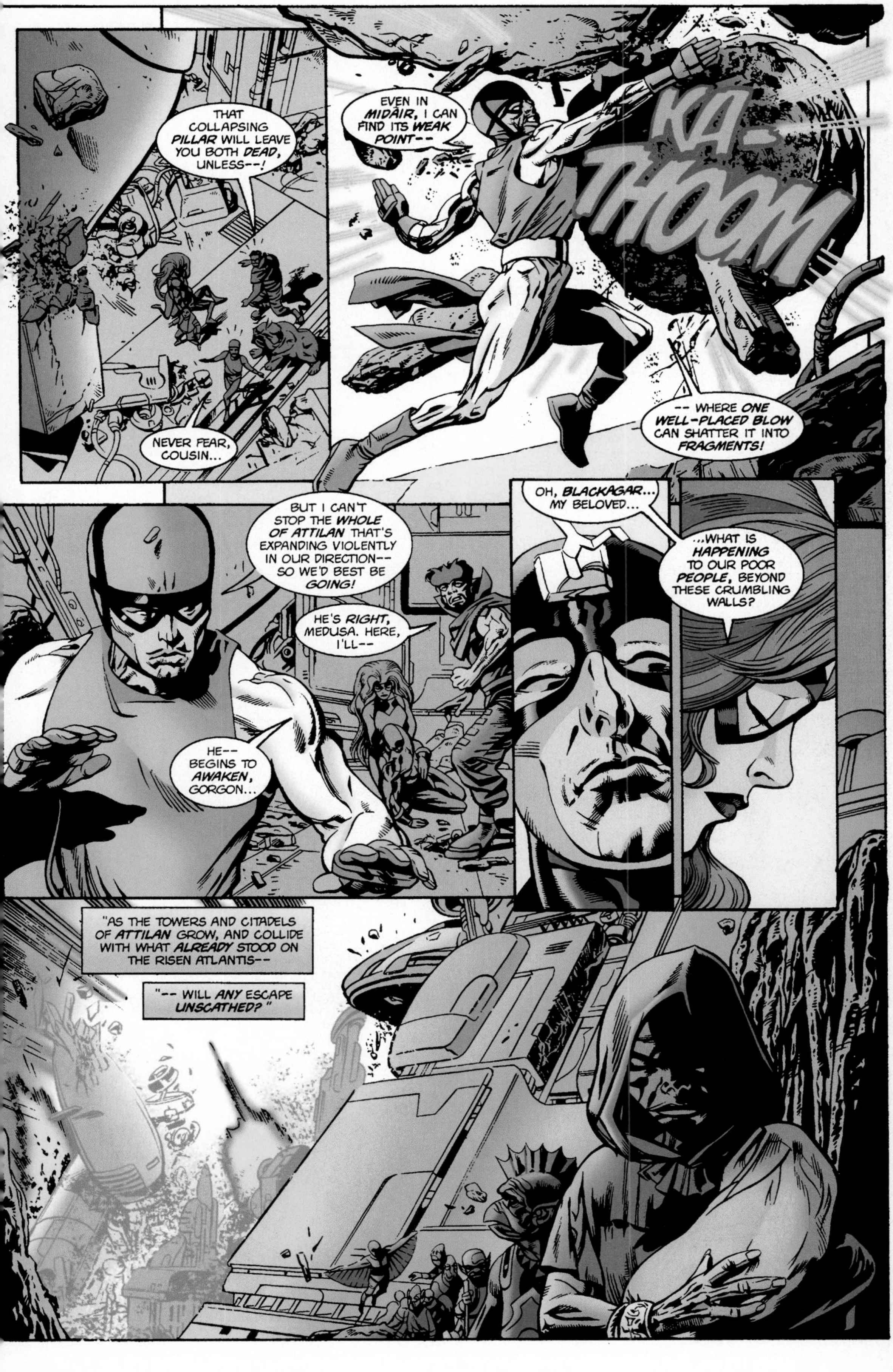
THAT COLLAPSING PILLAR WILL LEAVE YOU BOTH DEAD, UNLESS--!
NEVER FEAR, COUSIN...
EVEN IN MIDAIR, I CAN FIND ITS WEAK POINT--
KA-THOOM
-- WHERE ONE WELL-PLACED BLOW CAN SHATTER IT INTO FRAGMENTS!
BUT I CAN'T STOP THE WHOLE OF ATTILAN THAT'S EXPANDING VIOLENTLY IN OUR DIRECTION-- SO WE'D BEST BE GOING!
HE'S RIGHT, MEDUSA. HERE, I'LL--
HE-- BEGINS TO AWAKEN, GORGON...
OH, BLACKAGAR... MY BELOVED...
...WHAT IS HAPPENING TO OUR POOR PEOPLE, BEYOND THESE CRUMBLING WALLS?
"AS THE TOWERS AND CITADELS OF ATTILAN GROW, AND COLLIDE WITH WHAT ALREADY STOOD ON THE RISEN ATLANTIS--
"-- WILL ANY ESCAPE UNSCATHED?"

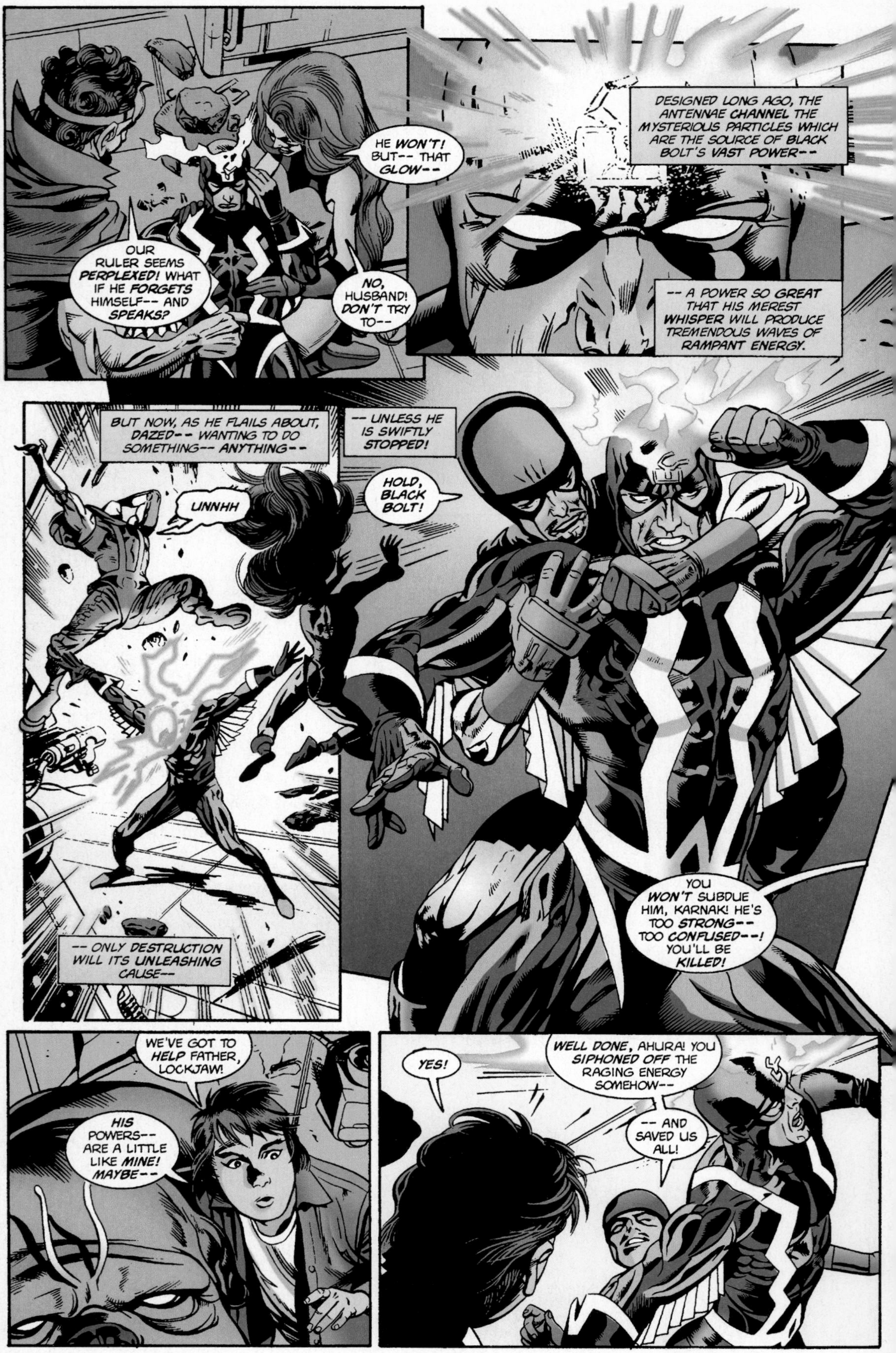
HE WON'T! BUT-- THAT GLOW--
OUR RULER SEEMS PERPLEXED! WHAT IF HE FORGETS HIMSELF-- AND SPEAKS?
NO, HUSBAND! DON'T TRY TO--
DESIGNED LONG AGO, THE ANTENNAE CHANNEL THE MYSTERIOUS PARTICLES WHICH ARE THE SOURCE OF BLACK BOLT'S VAST POWER--
-- A POWER SO GREAT THAT HIS MEREST WHISPER WILL PRODUCE TREMENDOUS WAVES OF RAMPANT ENERGY.
BUT NOW, AS HE FLAILS ABOUT, DAZED-- WANTING TO DO SOMETHING-- ANYTHING--
UNNHH
-- ONLY DESTRUCTION WILL ITS UNLEASHING CAUSE--
-- UNLESS HE IS SWIFTLY STOPPED!
HOLD, BLACK BOLT!
YOU WON'T SUBDUE HIM, KARNAK! HE'S TOO STRONG-- TOO CONFUSED--! YOU'LL BE KILLED!
WE'VE GOT TO HELP FATHER, LOCKJAW!
HIS POWERS-- ARE A LITTLE LIKE MINE! MAYBE--
YES!
WELL DONE, AHURA! YOU SIPHONED OFF THE RAGING ENERGY SOMEHOW--
-- AND SAVED US ALL!

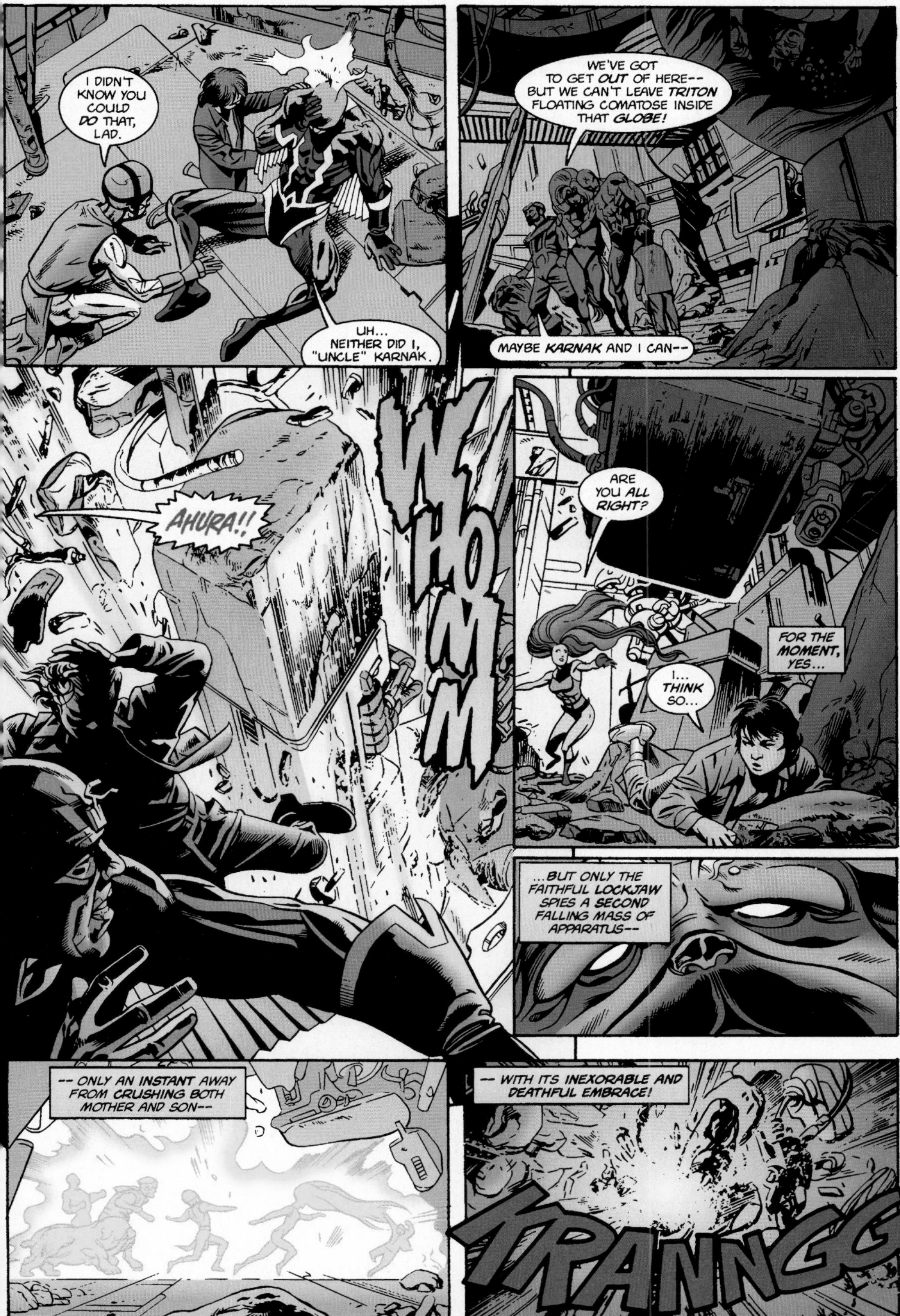
I DIDN'T KNOW YOU COULD DO THAT, LAD.
UH... NEITHER DID I, "UNCLE" KARNAK.
WE'VE GOT TO GET OUT OF HERE-- BUT WE CAN'T LEAVE TRITON FLOATING COMATOSE INSIDE THAT GLOBE!
MAYBE KARNAK AND I CAN--
AHURA!!
WHOM
ARE YOU ALL RIGHT?
FOR THE MOMENT, YES...
I... THINK SO...
...BUT ONLY THE FAITHFUL LOCKJAW SPIES A SECOND FALLING MASS OF APPARATUS--
-- ONLY AN INSTANT AWAY FROM CRUSHING BOTH MOTHER AND SON--
-- WITH ITS INEXORABLE AND DEATHFUL EMBRACE!
KRANNGG

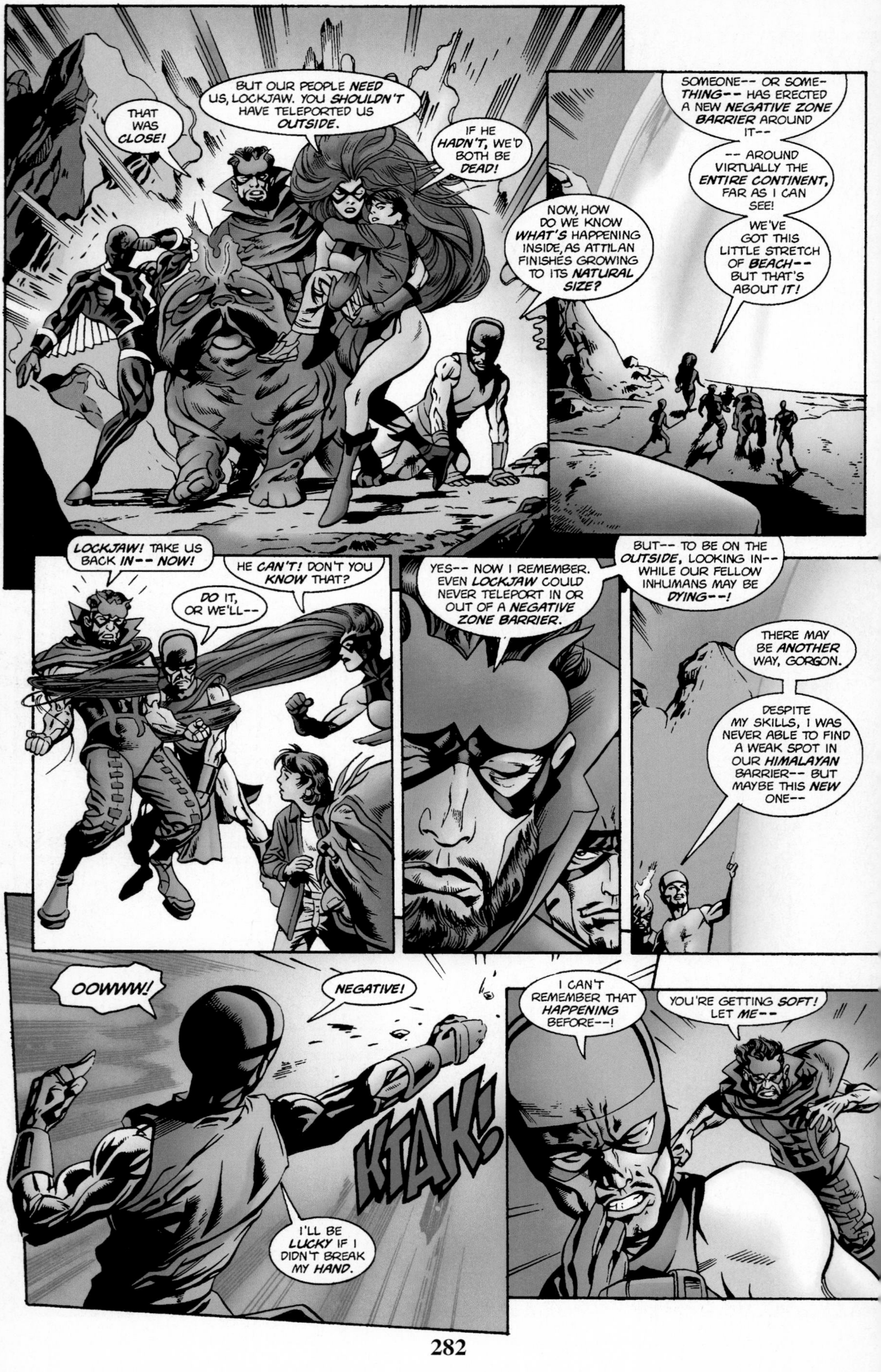

THAT WAS CLOSE!
BUT OUR PEOPLE NEED US, LOCKJAW. YOU SHOULDN'T HAVE TELEPORTED US OUTSIDE.
IF HE HADN'T, WE'D BOTH BE DEAD!
NOW, HOW DO WE KNOW WHAT'S HAPPENING INSIDE, AS ATTILAN FINISHES GROWING TO ITS NATURAL SIZE?
SOMEONE-- OR SOMETHING-- HAS ERECTED A NEW NEGATIVE ZONE BARRIER AROUND IT--
-- AROUND VIRTUALLY THE ENTIRE CONTINENT, FAR AS I CAN SEE!
WE'VE GOT THIS LITTLE STRETCH OF BEACH-- BUT THAT'S ABOUT IT!
LOCKJAW! TAKE US BACK IN-- NOW!
HE CAN'T! DON'T YOU KNOW THAT?
DO IT, OR WE'LL--
YES-- NOW I REMEMBER. EVEN LOCKJAW COULD NEVER TELEPORT IN OR OUT OF A NEGATIVE ZONE BARRIER.
BUT-- TO BE ON THE OUTSIDE, LOOKING IN-- WHILE OUR FELLOW INHUMANS MAY BE DYING--!
THERE MAY BE ANOTHER WAY, GORGON.
DESPITE MY SKILLS, I WAS NEVER ABLE TO FIND A WEAK SPOT IN OUR HIMALAYAN BARRIER-- BUT MAYBE THIS NEW ONE--
OOWWW!
NEGATIVE!
KTAK!
I'LL BE LUCKY IF I DIDN'T BREAK MY HAND.
I CAN'T REMEMBER THAT HAPPENING BEFORE--!
YOU'RE GETTING SOFT! LET ME--

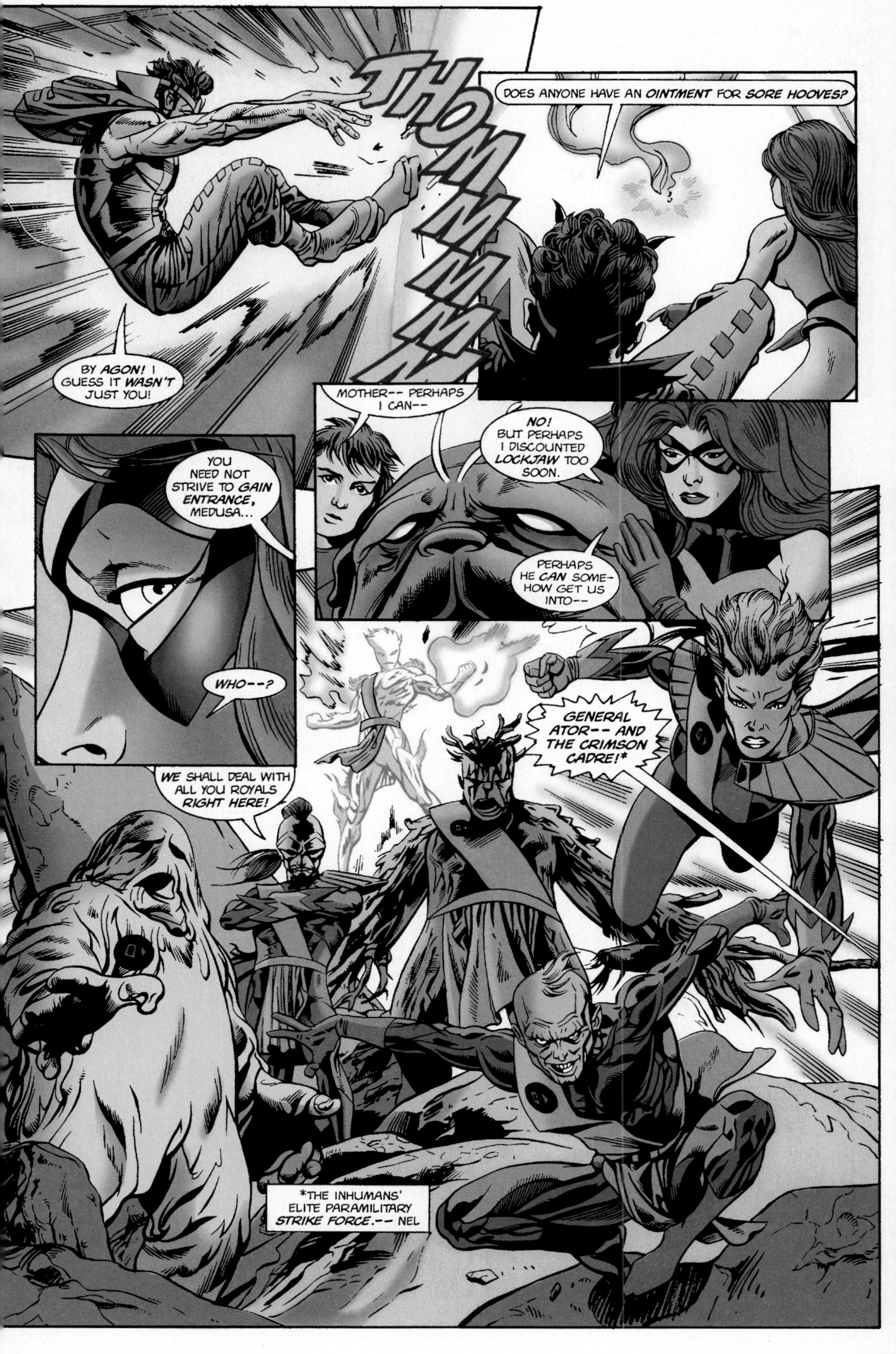
THOMMMMM
DOES ANYONE HAVE AN OINTMENT FOR SORE HOOVES?
BY AGON! I GUESS IT WASN'T JUST YOU!
MOTHER-- PERHAPS I CAN--
NO! BUT PERHAPS I DISCOUNTED LOCKJAW TOO SOON.
PERHAPS HE CAN SOMEHOW GET US INTO--
YOU NEED NOT STRIVE TO GAIN ENTRANCE, MEDUSA...
WHO--?
GENERAL ATOR-- AND THE CRIMSON CADRE!*
WE SHALL DEAL WITH ALL YOU ROYALS RIGHT HERE!
*THE INHUMANS' ELITE PARAMILITARY STRIKE FORCE.-- NEL

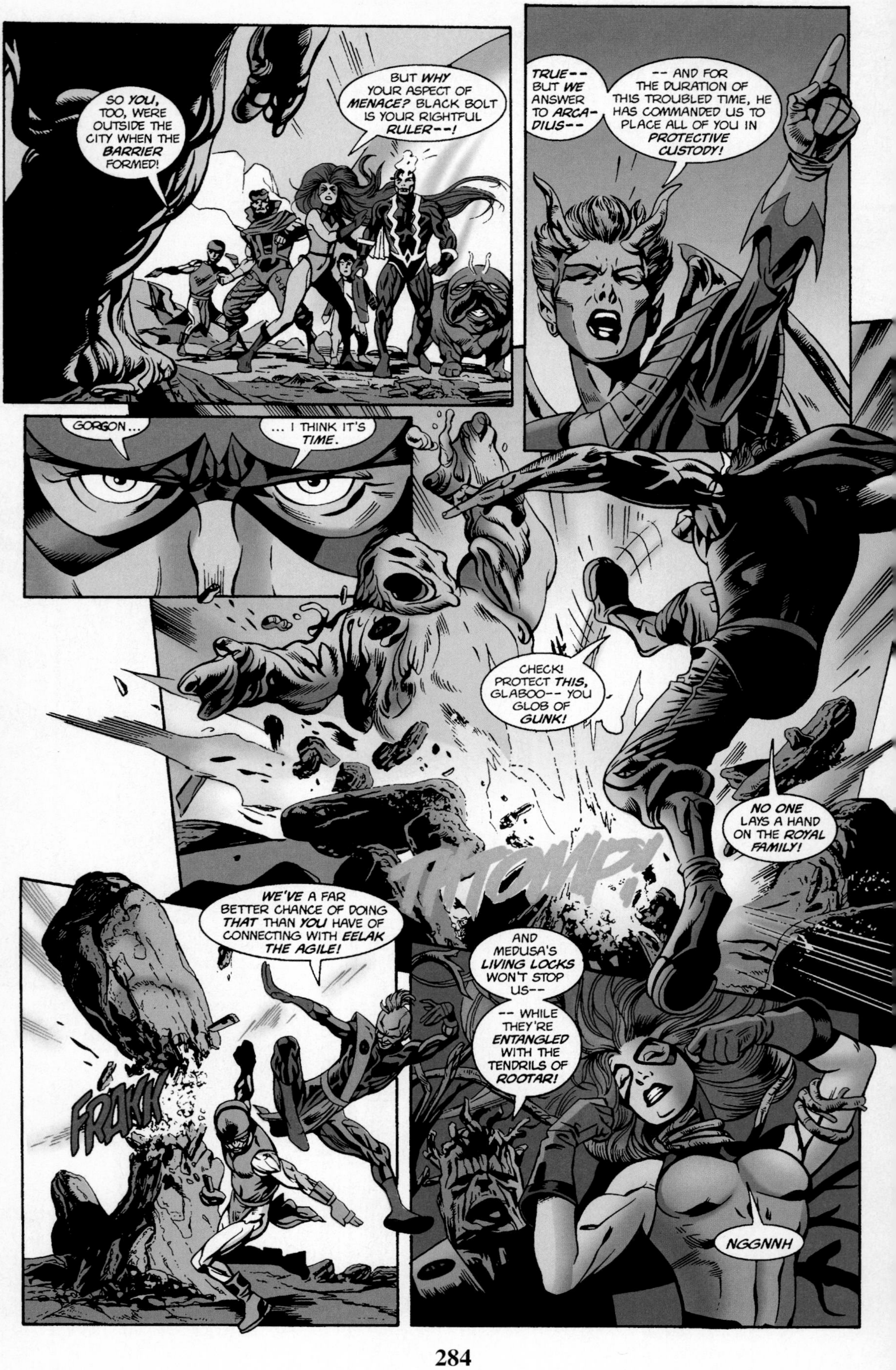

SO YOU, TOO, WERE OUTSIDE THE CITY WHEN THE BARRIER FORMED!
BUT WHY YOUR ASPECT OF MENACE? BLACK BOLT IS YOUR RIGHTFUL RULER--!
TRUE-- BUT WE ANSWER TO ARCADIUS--
-- AND FOR THE DURATION OF THIS TROUBLED TIME, HE HAS COMMANDED US TO PLACE ALL OF YOU IN PROTECTIVE CUSTODY!
GORGON...
... I THINK IT'S TIME.
CHECK! PROTECT THIS, GLABOO-- YOU GLOB OF GUNK!
NO ONE LAYS A HAND ON THE ROYAL FAMILY!
WE'VE A FAR BETTER CHANCE OF DOING THAT THAN YOU HAVE OF CONNECTING WITH EELAK THE AGILE!
FRAKK
AND MEDUSA'S LIVING LOCKS WON'T STOP US--
-- WHILE THEY'RE ENTANGLED WITH THE TENDRILS OF ROOTAR!
NGGNNH

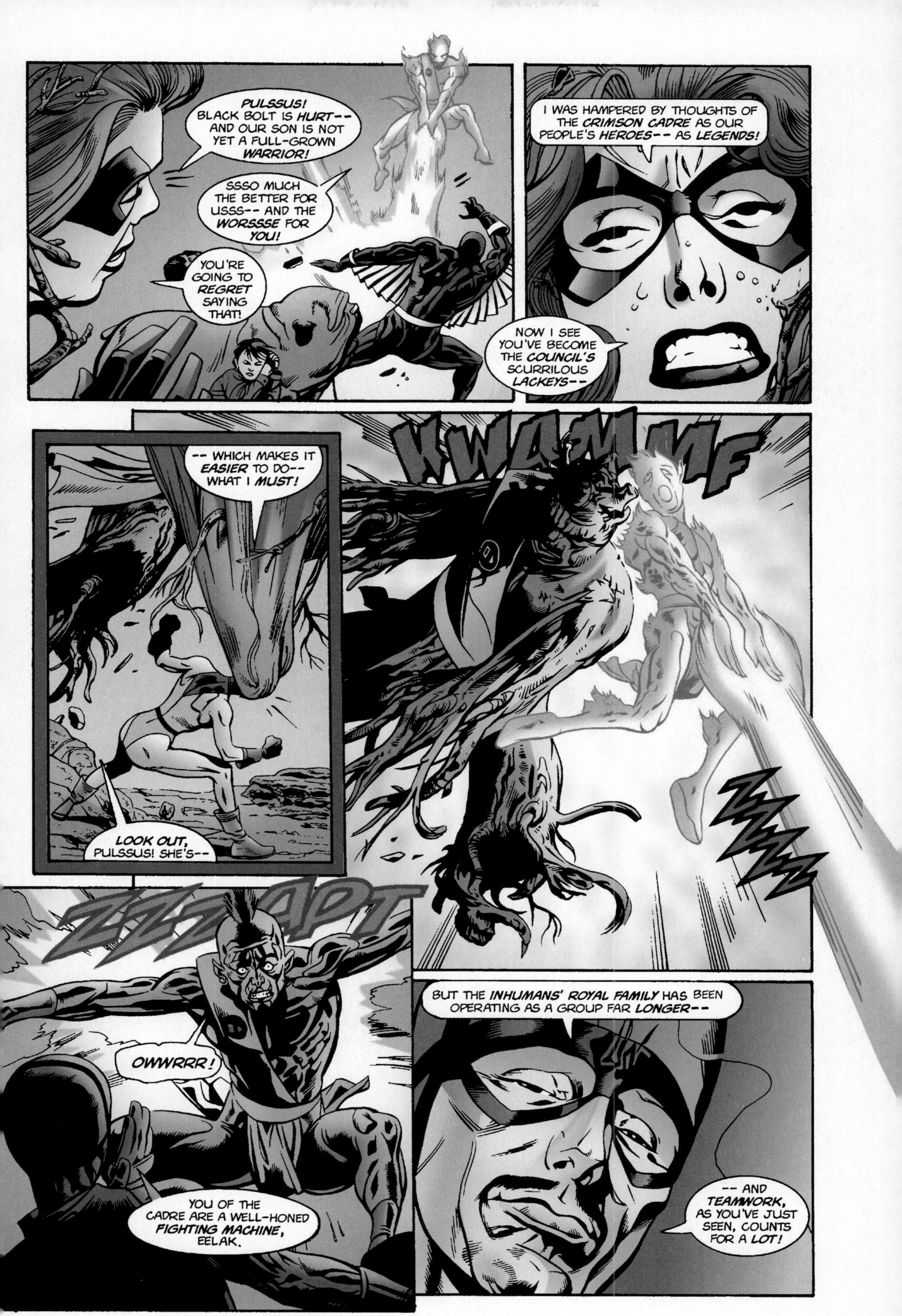
PULSSUS! BLACK BOLT IS HURT-- AND OUR SON IS NOT YET A FULL-GROWN WARRIOR!
SSSO MUCH THE BETTER FOR USSS-- AND THE WORSSSE FOR YOU!
YOU'RE GOING TO REGRET SAYING THAT!
I WAS HAMPERED BY THOUGHTS OF THE CRIMSON CADRE AS OUR PEOPLE'S HEROES-- AS LEGENDS!
NOW I SEE YOU'VE BECOME THE COUNCIL'S SCURRILOUS LACKEYS--
-- WHICH MAKES IT EASIER TO DO-- WHAT I MUST!
LOOK OUT, PULSSUS! SHE'S--
KWAMMF
ZZZAPT
OWWRRR!
YOU OF THE CADRE ARE A WELL-HONED FIGHTING MACHINE, EELAK.
BUT THE INHUMANS' ROYAL FAMILY HAS BEEN OPERATING AS A GROUP FAR LONGER--
-- AND TEAMWORK, AS YOU'VE JUST SEEN, COUNTS FOR A LOT!

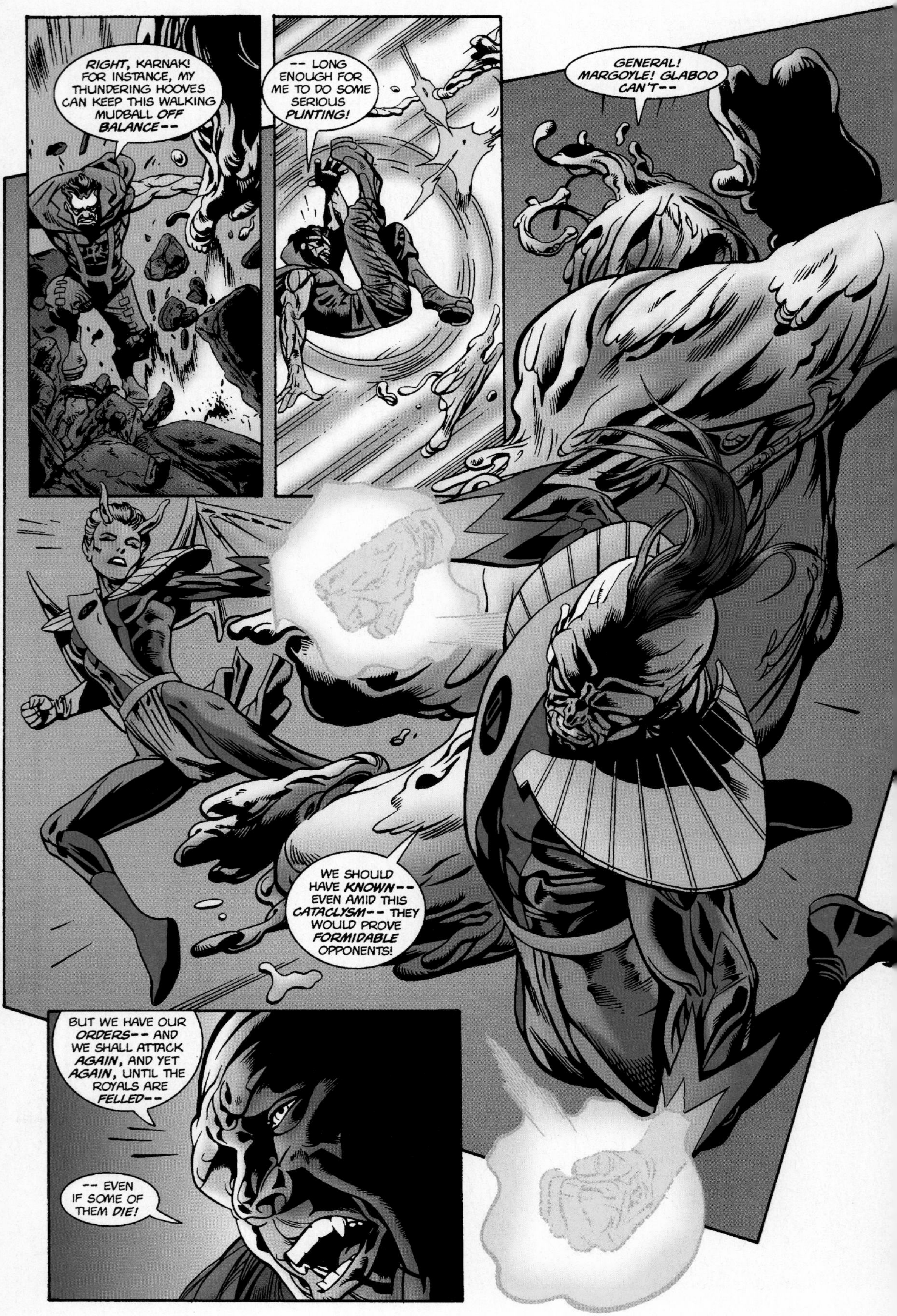
RIGHT, KARNAK! FOR INSTANCE, MY THUNDERING HOOVES CAN KEEP THIS WALKING MUDBALL OFF BALANCE--
-- LONG ENOUGH FOR ME TO DO SOME SERIOUS PUNTING!
GENERAL! MARGOYLE! GLABOO CAN'T--
WE SHOULD HAVE KNOWN-- EVEN AMID THIS CATACLYSM-- THEY WOULD PROVE FORMIDABLE OPPONENTS!
BUT WE HAVE OUR ORDERS-- AND WE SHALL ATTACK AGAIN, AND YET AGAIN, UNTIL THE ROYALS ARE FELLED--
-- EVEN IF SOME OF THEM DIE!

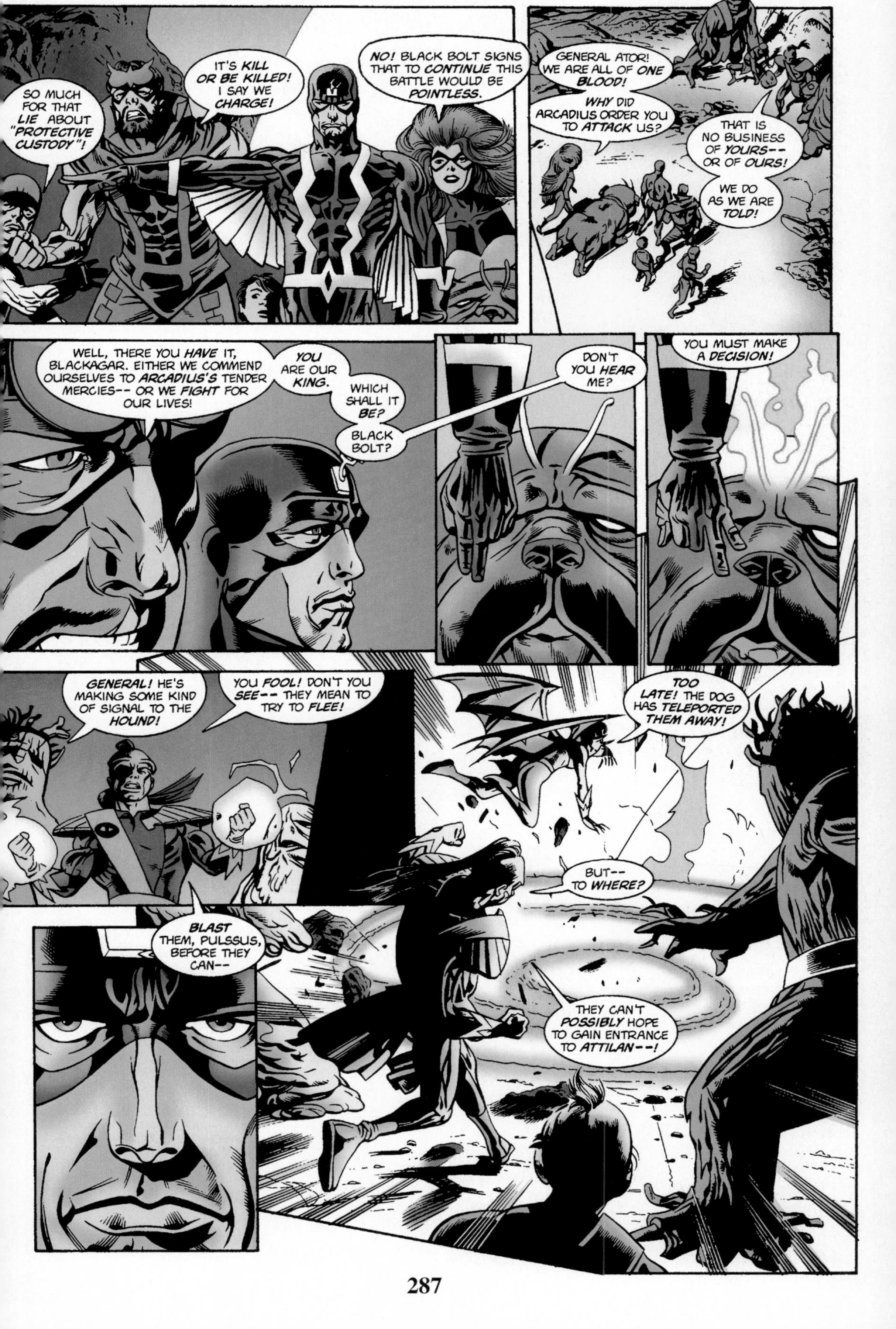
SO MUCH FOR THAT LIE ABOUT "PROTECTIVE CUSTODY"!
IT'S KILL OR BE KILLED! I SAY WE CHARGE!
NO! BLACK BOLT SIGNS THAT TO CONTINUE THIS BATTLE WOULD BE POINTLESS.
GENERAL ATOR! WE ARE ALL OF ONE BLOOD!
WHY DID ARCADIUS ORDER YOU TO ATTACK US?
THAT IS NO BUSINESS OF YOURS-- OR OF OURS!
WE DO AS WE ARE TOLD!
WELL, THERE YOU HAVE IT, BLACKAGAR. EITHER WE COMMEND OURSELVES TO ARCADIUS'S TENDER MERCIES-- OR WE FIGHT FOR OUR LIVES!
YOU ARE OUR KING.
WHICH SHALL IT BE?
BLACK BOLT?
DON'T YOU HEAR ME?
YOU MUST MAKE A DECISION!
GENERAL! HE'S MAKING SOME KIND OF SIGNAL TO THE HOUND!
YOU FOOL! DON'T YOU SEE-- THEY MEAN TO TRY TO FLEE!
TOO LATE! THE DOG HAS TELEPORTED THEM AWAY!
BUT-- TO WHERE?
BLAST THEM, PULSSUS, BEFORE THEY CAN--
THEY CAN'T POSSIBLY HOPE TO GAIN ENTRANCE TO ATTILAN--!

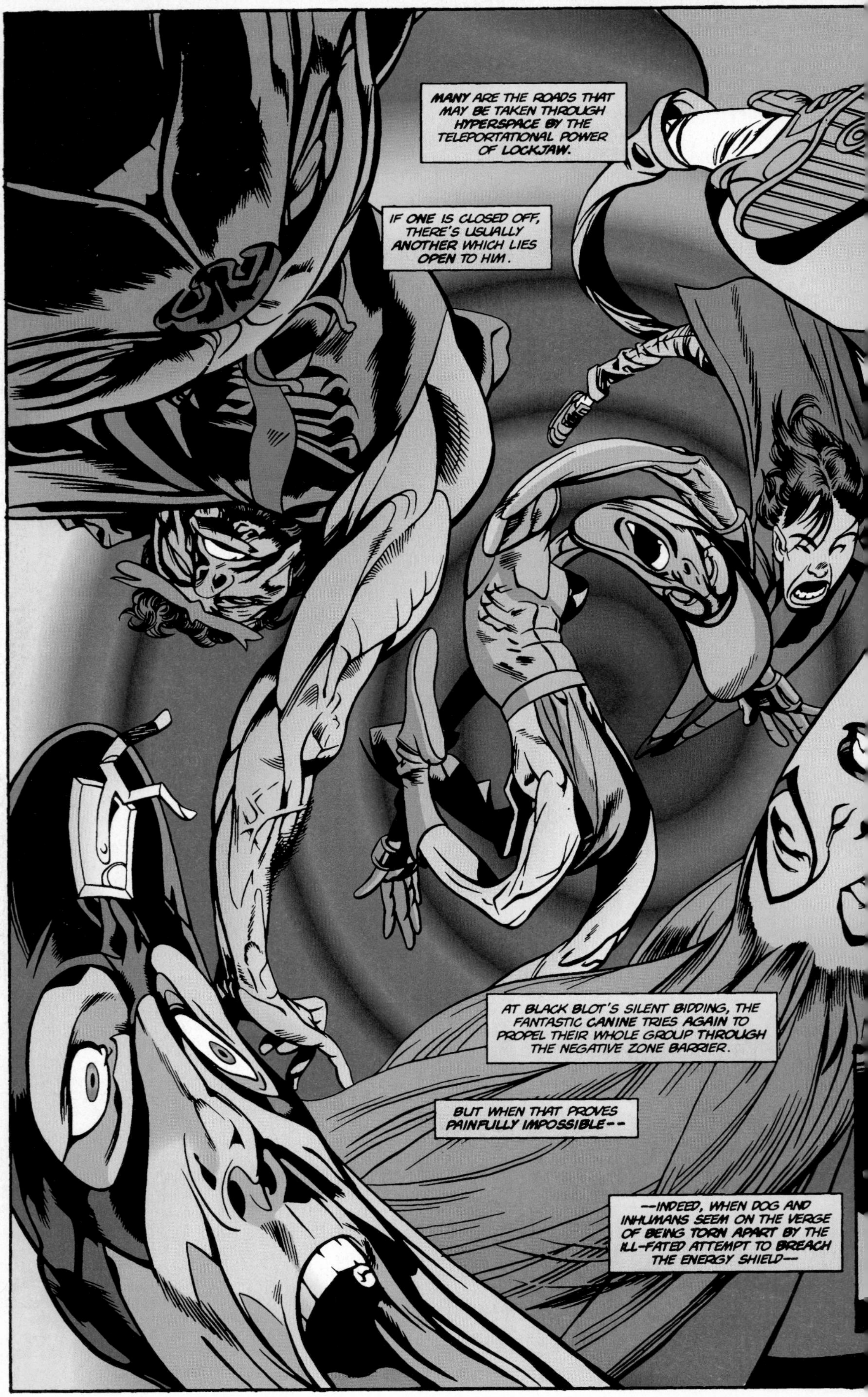
MANY ARE THE ROADS THAT MAY BE TAKEN THROUGH HYPERSPACE BY THE TELEPORTATIONAL POWER OF LOCKJAW.
IF ONE IS CLOSED OFF, THERE'S USUALLY ANOTHER WHICH LIES OPEN TO HIM.
AT BLACK BLOT'S SILENT BIDDING, THE FANTASTIC CANINE TRIES AGAIN TO PROPEL THEIR WHOLE GROUP THROUGH THE NEGATIVE ZONE BARRIER.
BUT WHEN THAT PROVES PAINFULLY IMPOSSIBLE--
--INDEED, WHEN DOG AND INHUMANS SEEM ON THE VERGE OF BEING TORN APART BY THE ILL-FATED ATTEMPT TO BREACH THE ENERGY SHIELD--

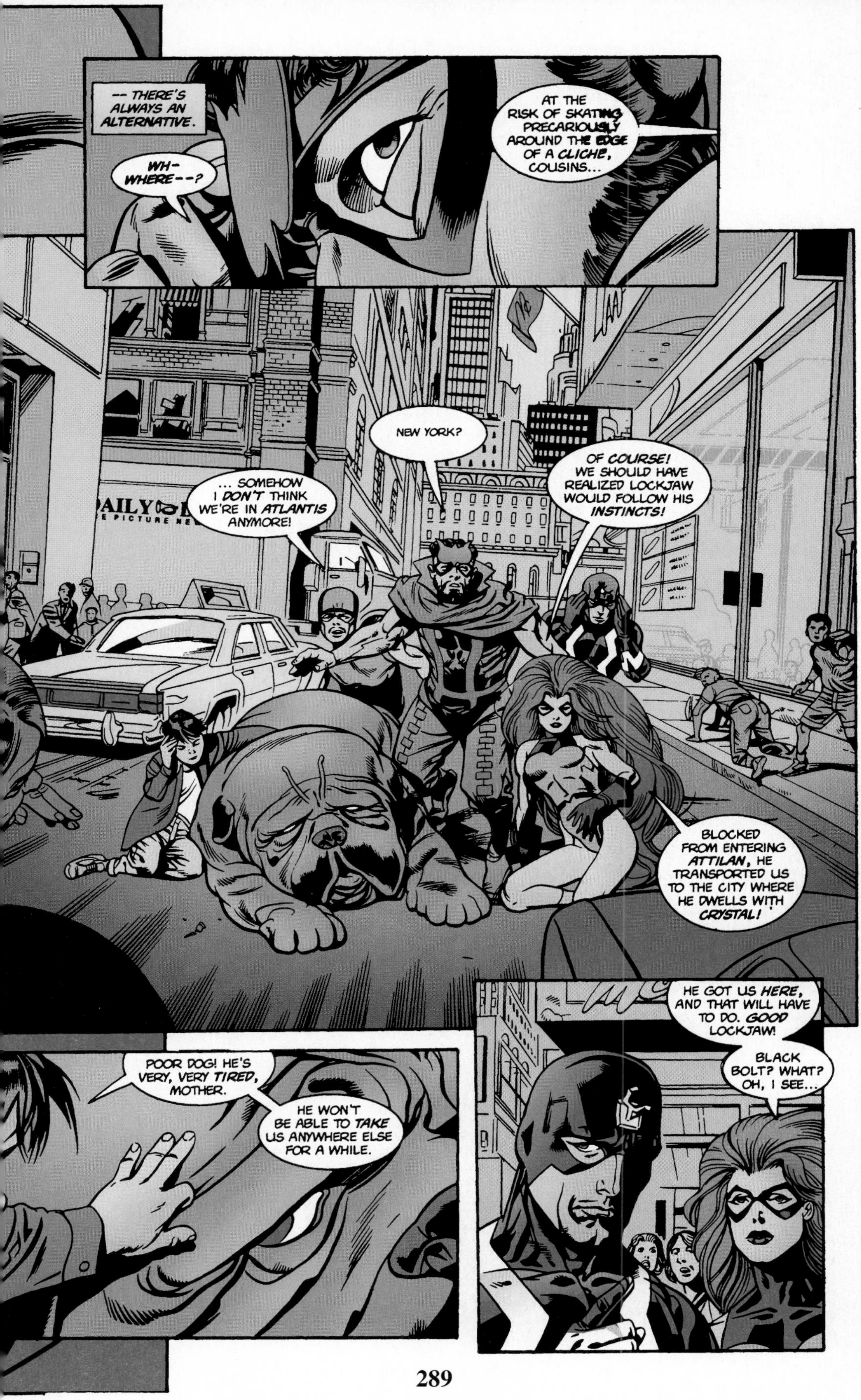
-- THERE'S ALWAYS AN ALTERNATIVE.
AT THE RISK OF SKATING PRECARIOUSLY AROUND THE EDGE OF A CLICHE, COUSINS...
WH- WHERE--?
NEW YORK?
... SOMEHOW I DON'T THINK WE'RE IN ATLANTIS ANYMORE!
OF COURSE! WE SHOULD HAVE REALIZED LOCKJAW WOULD FOLLOW HIS INSTINCTS!
BLOCKED FROM ENTERING ATTILAN, HE TRANSPORTED US TO THE CITY WHERE HE DWELLS WITH CRYSTAL!
POOR DOG! HE'S VERY, VERY TIRED, MOTHER.
HE WON'T BE ABLE TO TAKE US ANYWHERE ELSE FOR A WHILE.
HE GOT US HERE, AND THAT WILL HAVE TO DO. GOOD LOCKJAW!
BLACK BOLT? WHAT? OH, I SEE...

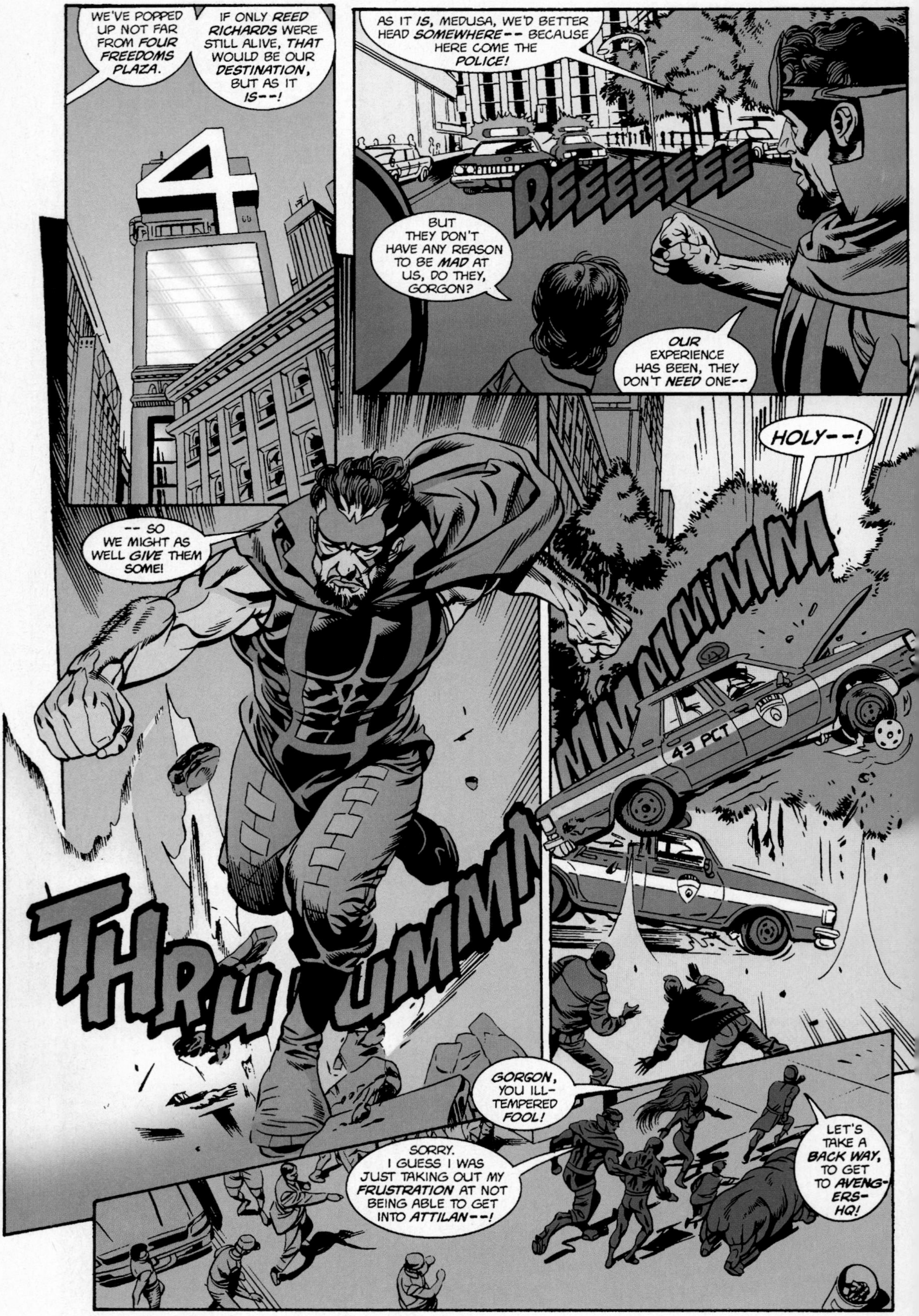

WE'VE POPPED UP NOT FAR FROM FOUR FREEDOMS PLAZA.
IF ONLY REED RICHARDS WERE STILL ALIVE, THAT WOULD BE OUR DESTINATION, BUT AS IT IS--!
AS IT IS, MEDUSA, WE'D BETTER HEAD SOMEWHERE-- BECAUSE HERE COME THE POLICE!
REEEEEEE
BUT THEY DON'T HAVE ANY REASON TO BE MAD AT US, DO THEY, GORGON?
OUR EXPERIENCE HAS BEEN, THEY DON'T NEED ONE--
-- SO WE MIGHT AS WELL GIVE THEM SOME!
HOLY--!
MMMMMMMMM
THRUMMM
43 PCT
GORGON, YOU ILL-TEMPERED FOOL!
SORRY. I GUESS I WAS JUST TAKING OUT MY FRUSTRATION AT NOT BEING ABLE TO GET INTO ATTILAN--!
LET'S TAKE A BACK WAY, TO GET TO AVENGERS-HQ!

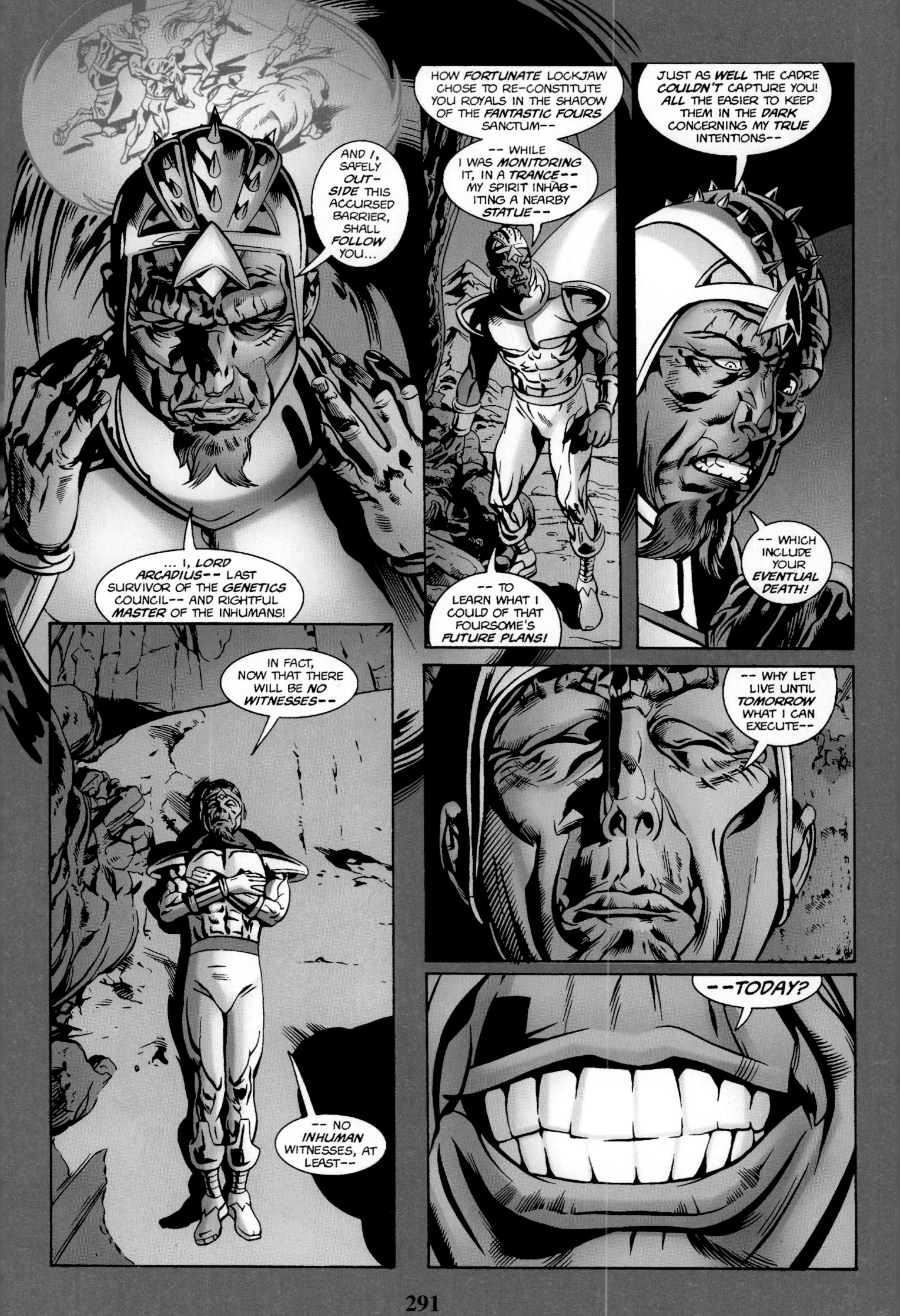
AND I, SAFELY OUT-SIDE THIS ACCURSED BARRIER, SHALL FOLLOW YOU...
... I, LORD ARCADIUS-- LAST SURVIVOR OF THE GENETICS COUNCIL-- AND RIGHTFUL MASTER OF THE INHUMANS!
HOW FORTUNATE LOCKJAW CHOSE TO RE-CONSTITUTE YOU ROYALS IN THE SHADOW OF THE FANTASTIC FOURS SANCTUM--
-- WHILE I WAS MONITORING IT, IN A TRANCE-- MY SPIRIT INHAB-ITING A NEARBY STATUE--
-- TO LEARN WHAT I COULD OF THAT FOURSOME'S FUTURE PLANS!
JUST AS WELL THE CADRE COULDN'T CAPTURE YOU! ALL THE EASIER TO KEEP THEM IN THE DARK CONCERNING MY TRUE INTENTIONS--
-- WHICH INCLUDE YOUR EVENTUAL DEATH!
IN FACT, NOW THAT THERE WILL BE NO WITNESSES--
-- NO INHUMAN WITNESSES, AT LEAST--
-- WHY LET LIVE UNTIL TOMORROW WHAT I CAN EXECUTE--
--TODAY?

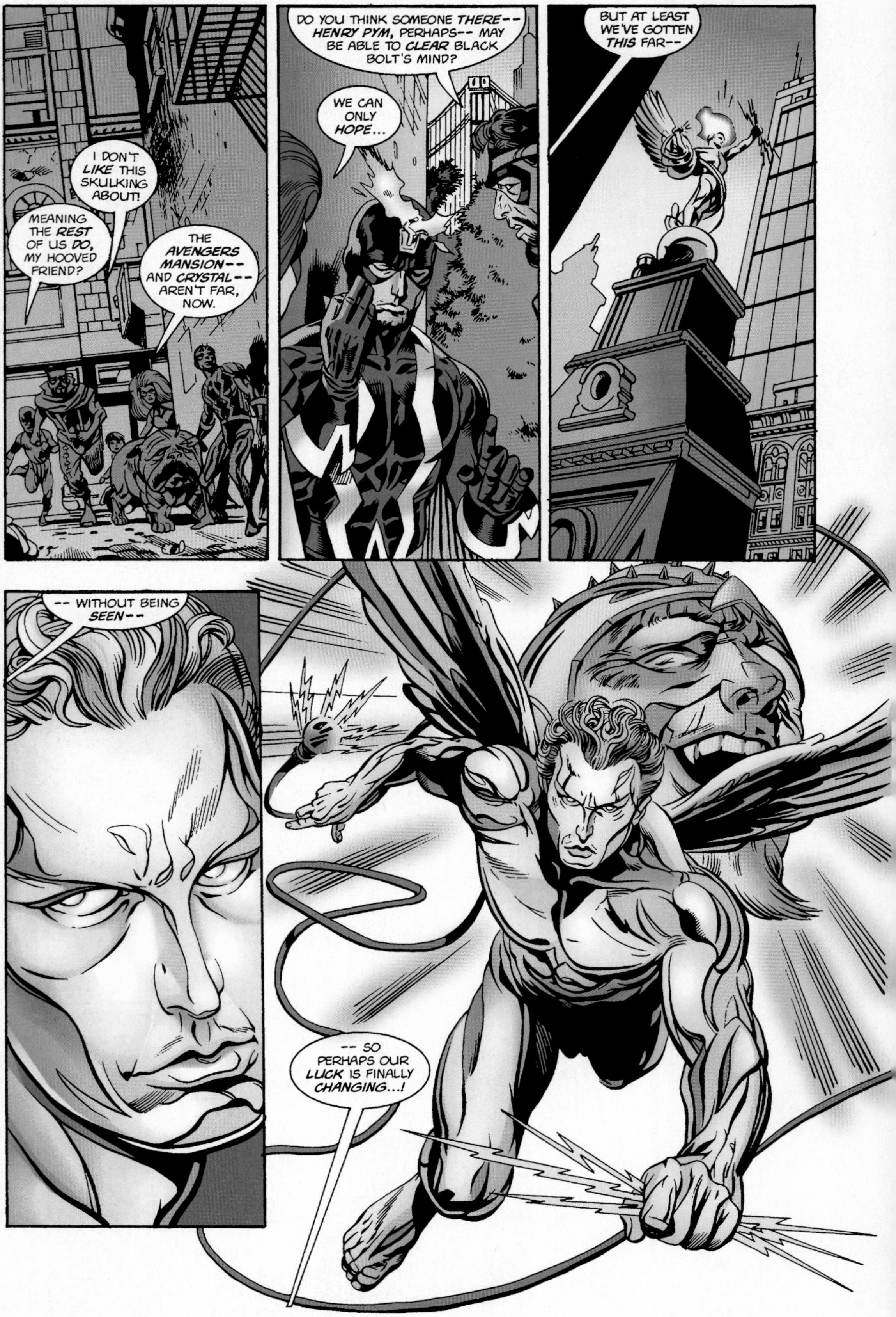
I DON'T LIKE THIS SKULKING ABOUT!
MEANING THE REST OF US DO, MY HOOVED FRIEND?
THE AVENGERS MANSION-- AND CRYSTAL-- AREN'T FAR, NOW.
DO YOU THINK SOMEONE THERE-- HENRY PYM, PERHAPS-- MAY BE ABLE TO CLEAR BLACK BOLT'S MIND?
WE CAN ONLY HOPE...
BUT AT LEAST WE'VE GOTTEN THIS FAR--
-- WITHOUT BEING SEEN--
-- SO PERHAPS OUR LUCK IS FINALLY CHANGING...!

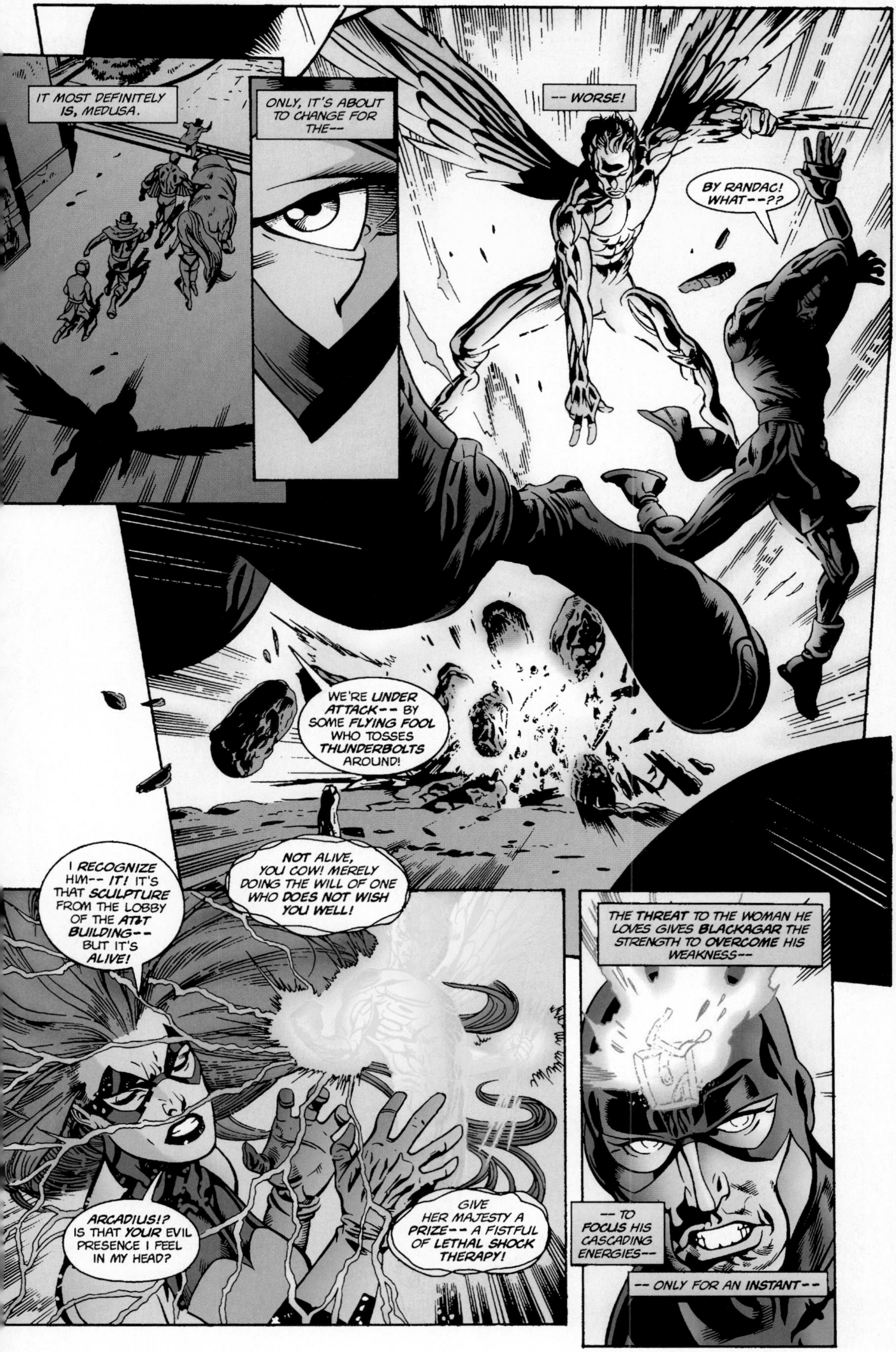
IT MOST DEFINITELY IS, MEDUSA.
ONLY, IT'S ABOUT TO CHANGE FOR THE--
-- WORSE!
BY RANDAC! WHAT--??
WE'RE UNDER ATTACK-- BY SOME FLYING FOOL WHO TOSSES THUNDERBOLTS AROUND!
I RECOGNIZE HIM-- IT! IT'S THAT SCULPTURE FROM THE LOBBY OF THE AT&T BUILDING-- BUT IT'S ALIVE!
NOT ALIVE, YOU COW! MERELY DOING THE WILL OF ONE WHO DOES NOT WISH YOU WELL!
ARCADIUS!? IS THAT YOUR EVIL PRESENCE I FEEL IN MY HEAD?
GIVE HER MAJESTY A PRIZE-- A FISTFUL OF LETHAL SHOCK THERAPY!
THE THREAT TO THE WOMAN HE LOVES GIVES BLACKAGAR THE STRENGTH TO OVERCOME HIS WEAKNESS--
-- TO FOCUS HIS CASCADING ENERGIES--
-- ONLY FOR AN INSTANT--

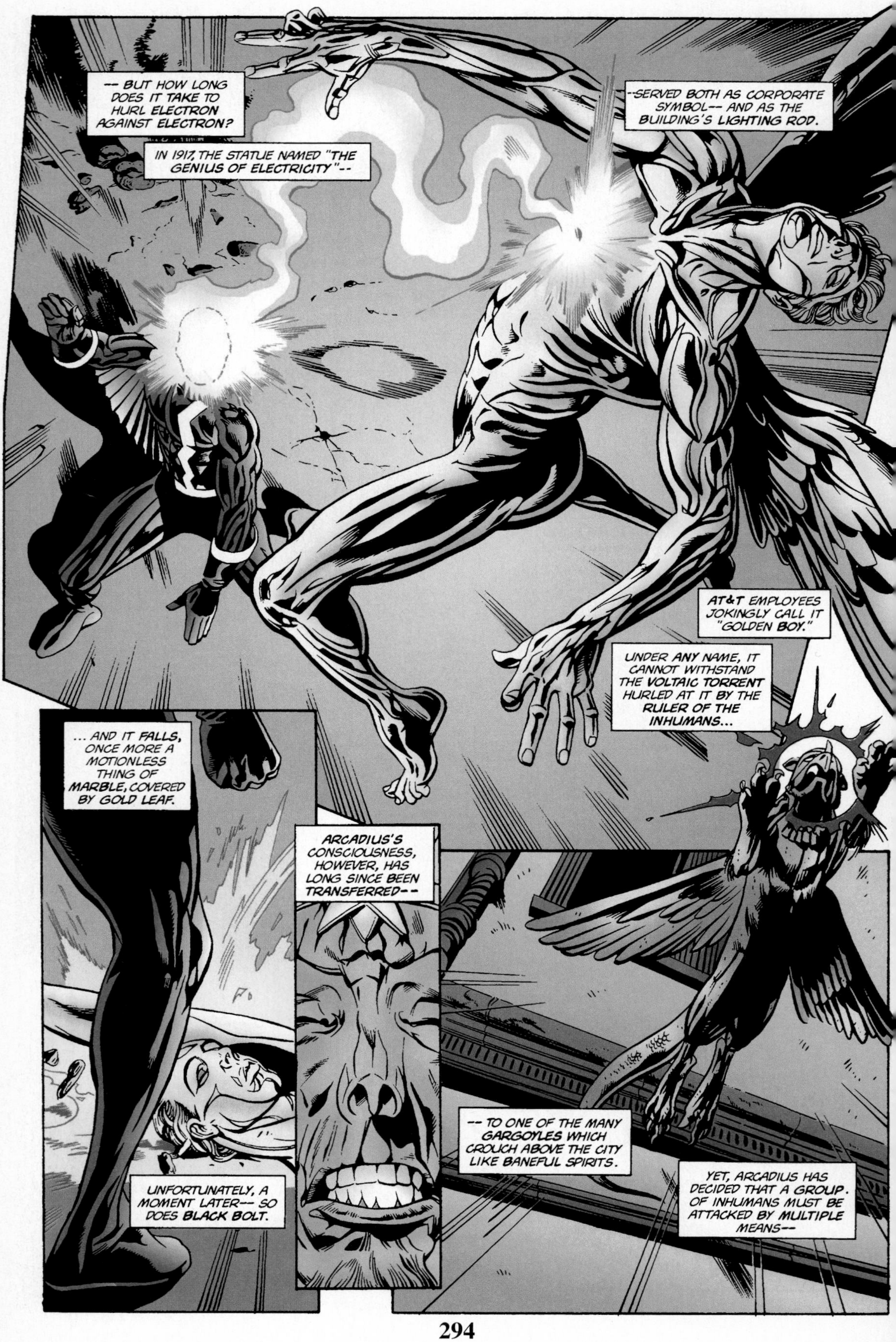
-- BUT HOW LONG DOES IT TAKE TO HURL ELECTRON AGAINST ELECTRON?
IN 1917, THE STATUE NAMED "THE GENIUS OF ELECTRICITY"--
--SERVED BOTH AS CORPORATE SYMBOL-- AND AS THE BUILDING'S LIGHTING ROD.
AT&T EMPLOYEES JOKINGLY CALL IT "GOLDEN BOY."
UNDER ANY NAME, IT CANNOT WITHSTAND THE VOLTAIC TORRENT HURLED AT IT BY THE RULER OF THE INHUMANS...
... AND IT FALLS, ONCE MORE A MOTIONLESS THING OF MARBLE, COVERED BY GOLD LEAF.
UNFORTUNATELY, A MOMENT LATER-- SO DOES BLACK BOLT.
ARCADIUS'S CONSCIOUSNESS, HOWEVER, HAS LONG SINCE BEEN TRANSFERRED--
-- TO ONE OF THE MANY GARGOYLES WHICH CROUCH ABOVE THE CITY LIKE BANEFUL SPIRITS.
YET, ARCADIUS HAS DECIDED THAT A GROUP OF INHUMANS MUST BE ATTACKED BY MULTIPLE MEANS--

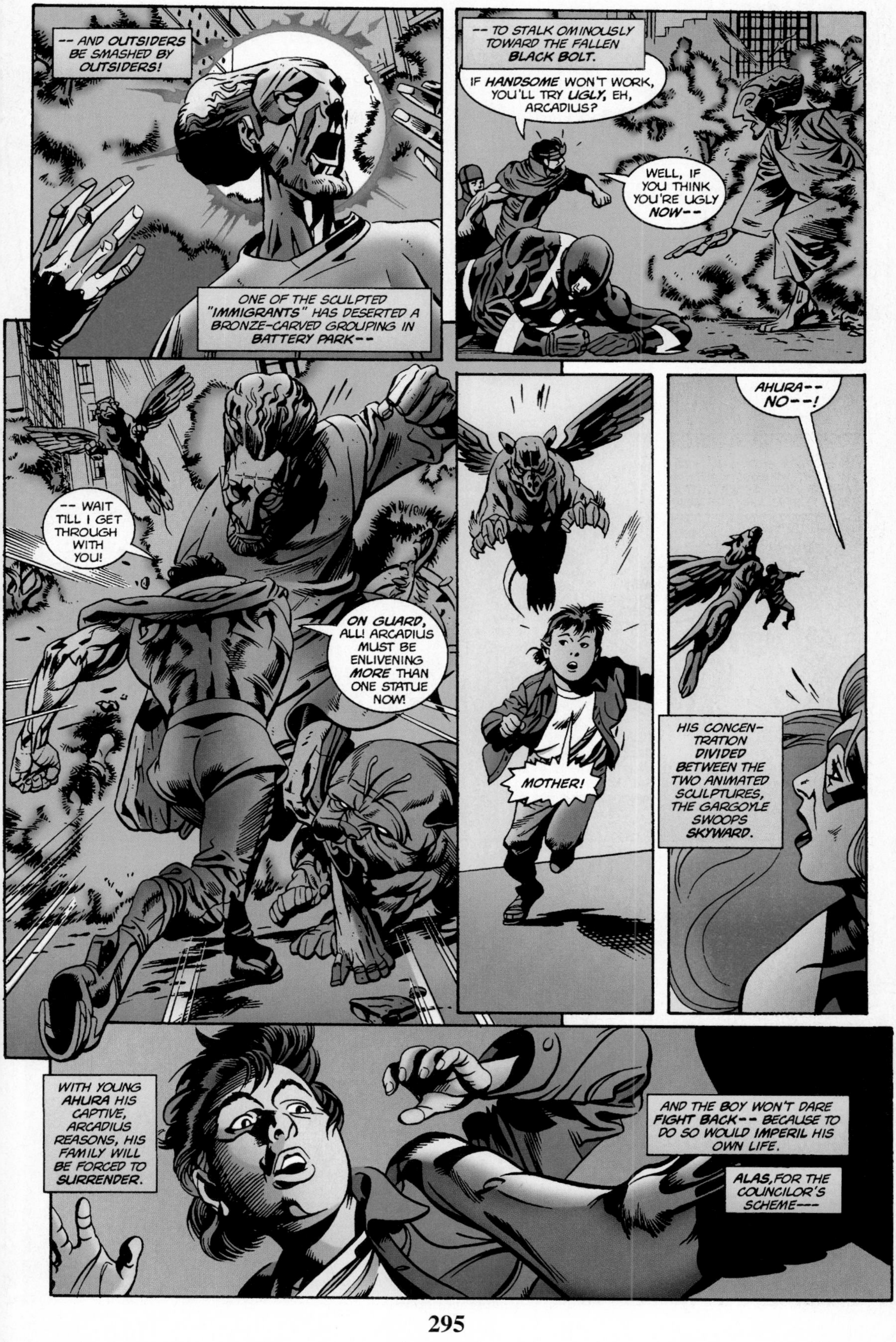
-- AND OUTSIDERS BE SMASHED BY OUTSIDERS!
ONE OF THE SCULPTED "IMMIGRANTS" HAS DESERTED A BRONZE-CARVED GROUPING IN BATTERY PARK--
-- TO STALK OMINOUSLY TOWARD THE FALLEN BLACK BOLT.
IF HANDSOME WON'T WORK, YOU'LL TRY UGLY, EH, ARCADIUS?
WELL, IF YOU THINK YOU'RE UGLY NOW--
-- WAIT TILL I GET THROUGH WITH YOU!
ON GUARD, ALL! ARCADIUS MUST BE ENLIVENING MORE THAN ONE STATUE NOW!
MOTHER!
AHURA-- NO--!
HIS CONCENTRATION DIVIDED BETWEEN THE TWO ANIMATED SCULPTURES, THE GARGOYLE SWOOPS SKYWARD.
WITH YOUNG AHURA HIS CAPTIVE, ARCADIUS REASONS, HIS FAMILY WILL BE FORCED TO SURRENDER.
AND THE BOY WON'T DARE FIGHT BACK-- BECAUSE TO DO SO WOULD IMPERIL HIS OWN LIFE.
ALAS, FOR THE COUNCILOR'S SCHEME---

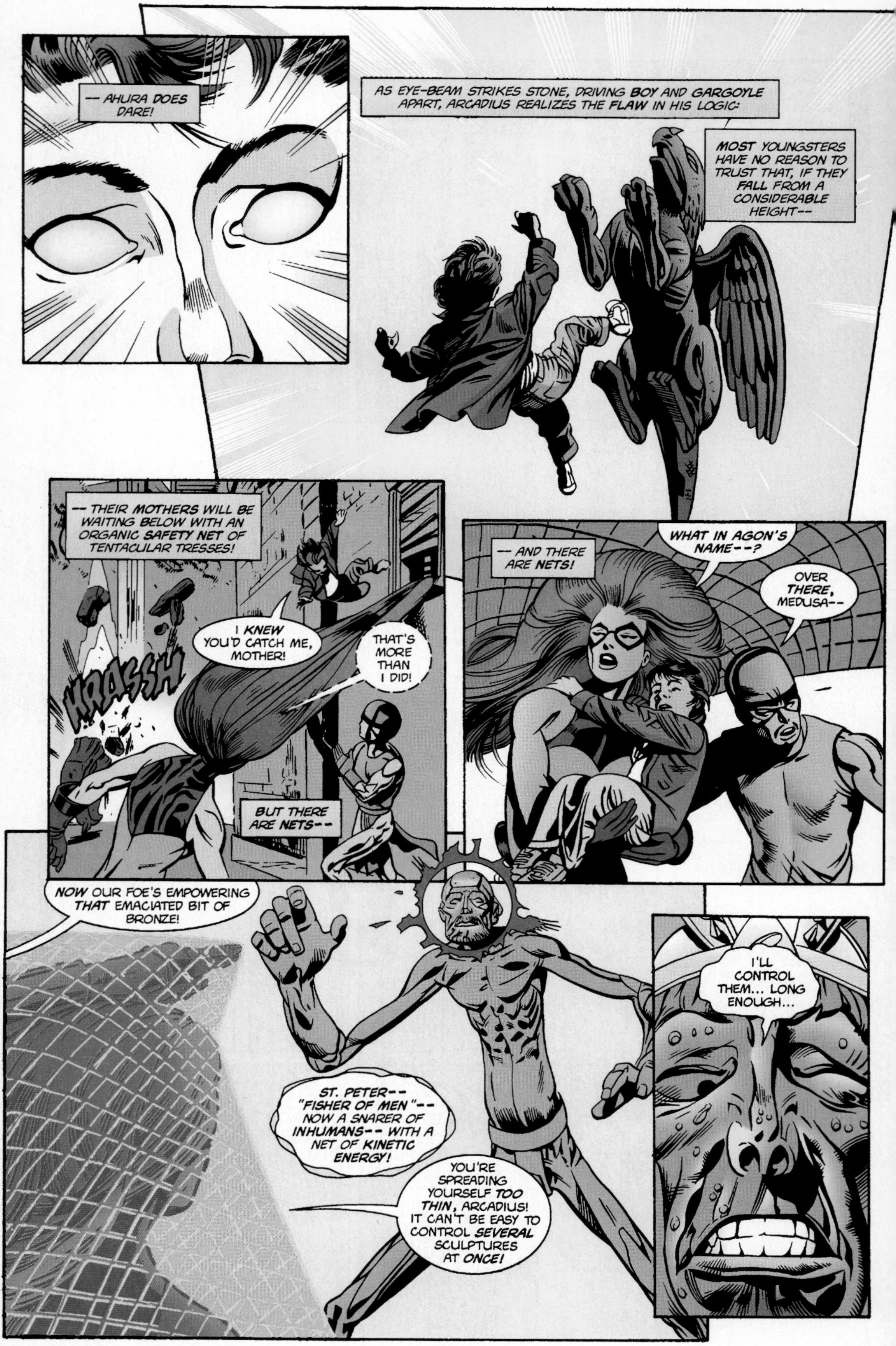
-- AHURA DOES DARE!
AS EYE-BEAM STRIKES STONE, DRIVING BOY AND GARGOYLE APART, ARCADIUS REALIZES THE FLAW IN HIS LOGIC:
MOST YOUNGSTERS HAVE NO REASON TO TRUST THAT, IF THEY FALL FROM A CONSIDERABLE HEIGHT--
-- THEIR MOTHERS WILL BE WAITING BELOW WITH AN ORGANIC SAFETY NET OF TENTACULAR TRESSES!
HRASSH
I KNEW YOU'D CATCH ME, MOTHER!
THAT'S MORE THAN I DID!
BUT THERE ARE NETS--
-- AND THERE ARE NETS!
WHAT IN AGON'S NAME--?
OVER THERE, MEDUSA--
NOW OUR FOE'S EMPOWERING THAT EMACIATED BIT OF BRONZE!
ST. PETER-- "FISHER OF MEN"-- NOW A SNARER OF INHUMANS-- WITH A NET OF KINETIC ENERGY!
YOU'RE SPREADING YOURSELF TOO THIN, ARCADIUS! IT CAN'T BE EASY TO CONTROL SEVERAL SCULPTURES AT ONCE!
I'LL CONTROL THEM... LONG ENOUGH...

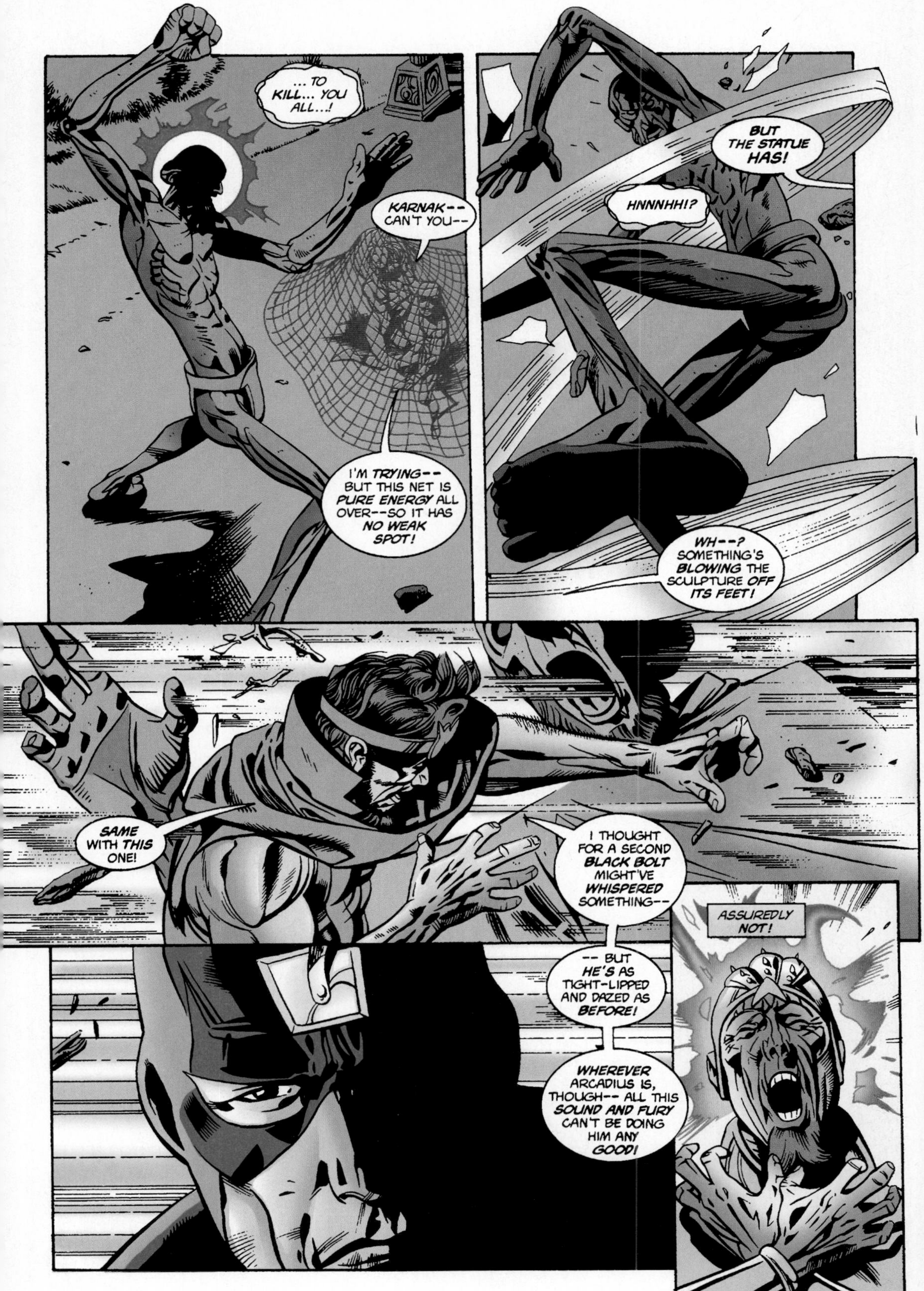
... TO KILL... YOU ALL...!
KARNAK-- CAN'T YOU--
I'M TRYING-- BUT THIS NET IS PURE ENERGY ALL OVER--SO IT HAS NO WEAK SPOT!
BUT THE STATUE HAS!
HNNNHH!?
WH--? SOMETHING'S BLOWING THE SCULPTURE OFF ITS FEET!
SAME WITH THIS ONE!
I THOUGHT FOR A SECOND BLACK BOLT MIGHT'VE WHISPERED SOMETHING--
-- BUT HE'S AS TIGHT-LIPPED AND DAZED AS BEFORE!
WHEREVER ARCADIUS IS, THOUGH-- ALL THIS SOUND AND FURY CAN'T BE DOING HIM ANY GOOD!
ASSURÉDLY NOT!

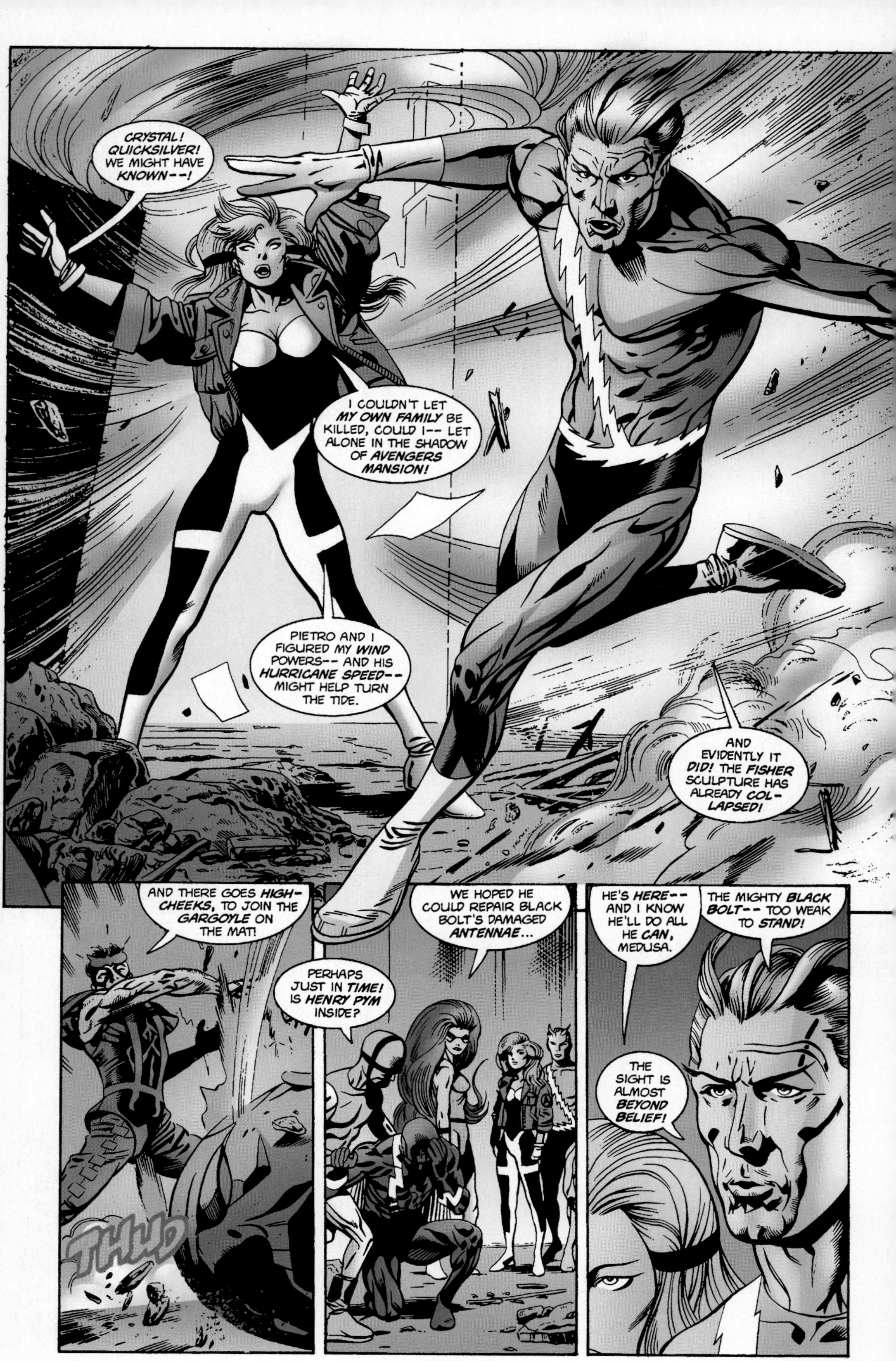

CRYSTAL! QUICKSILVER! WE MIGHT HAVE KNOWN--!
I COULDN'T LET MY OWN FAMILY BE KILLED, COULD I-- LET ALONE IN THE SHADOW OF AVENGERS MANSION!
PIETRO AND I FIGURED MY WIND POWERS-- AND HIS HURRICANE SPEED-- MIGHT HELP TURN THE TIDE.
AND EVIDENTLY IT DID! THE FISHER SCULPTURE HAS ALREADY COL-LAPSED!
AND THERE GOES HIGH-CHEEKS, TO JOIN THE GARGOYLE ON THE MAT!
THUD
WE HOPED HE COULD REPAIR BLACK BOLT'S DAMAGED ANTENNAE...
PERHAPS JUST IN TIME! IS HENRY PYM INSIDE?
HE'S HERE-- AND I KNOW HE'LL DO ALL HE CAN, MEDUSA.
THE MIGHTY BLACK BOLT-- TOO WEAK TO STAND!
THE SIGHT IS ALMOST BEYOND BELIEF!

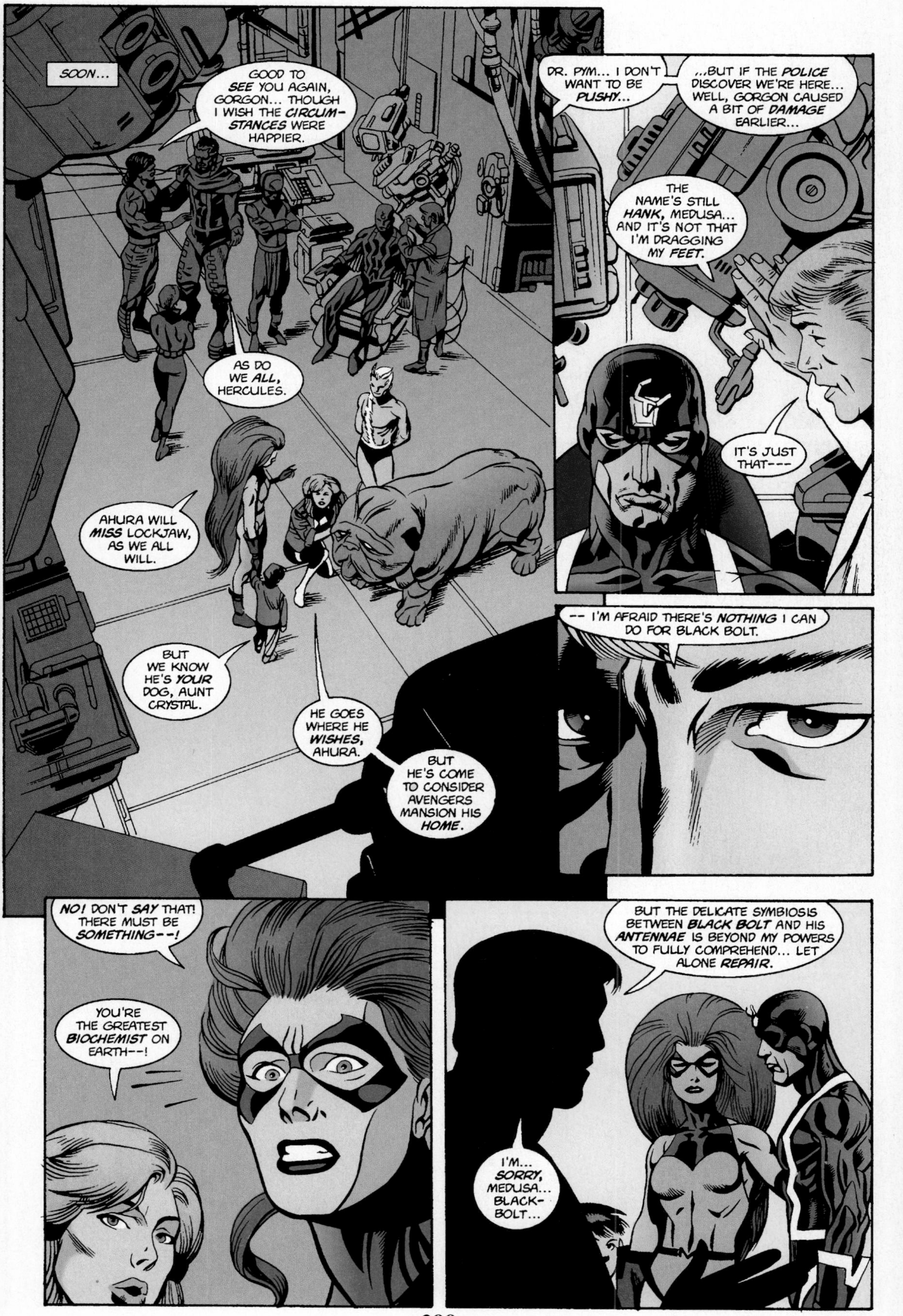
SOON...
GOOD TO SEE YOU AGAIN, GORGON... THOUGH I WISH THE CIRCUMSTANCES WERE HAPPIER.
AS DO WE ALL, HERCULES.
AHURA WILL MISS LOCKJAW, AS WE ALL WILL.
BUT WE KNOW HE'S YOUR DOG, AUNT CRYSTAL.
HE GOES WHERE HE WISHES, AHURA.
BUT HE'S COME TO CONSIDER AVENGERS MANSION HIS HOME.
DR. PYM... I DON'T WANT TO BE PUSHY...
...BUT IF THE POLICE DISCOVER WE'RE HERE... WELL, GORGON CAUSED A BIT OF DAMAGE EARLIER...
THE NAME'S STILL HANK, MEDUSA... AND IT'S NOT THAT I'M DRAGGING MY FEET.
IT'S JUST THAT---
-- I'M AFRAID THERE'S NOTHING I CAN DO FOR BLACK BOLT.
NO! DON'T SAY THAT! THERE MUST BE SOMETHING--!
YOU'RE THE GREATEST BIOCHEMIST ON EARTH--!
BUT THE DELICATE SYMBIOSIS BETWEEN BLACK BOLT AND HIS ANTENNAE IS BEYOND MY POWERS TO FULLY COMPREHEND... LET ALONE REPAIR.
I'M... SORRY, MEDUSA... BLACK-BOLT...

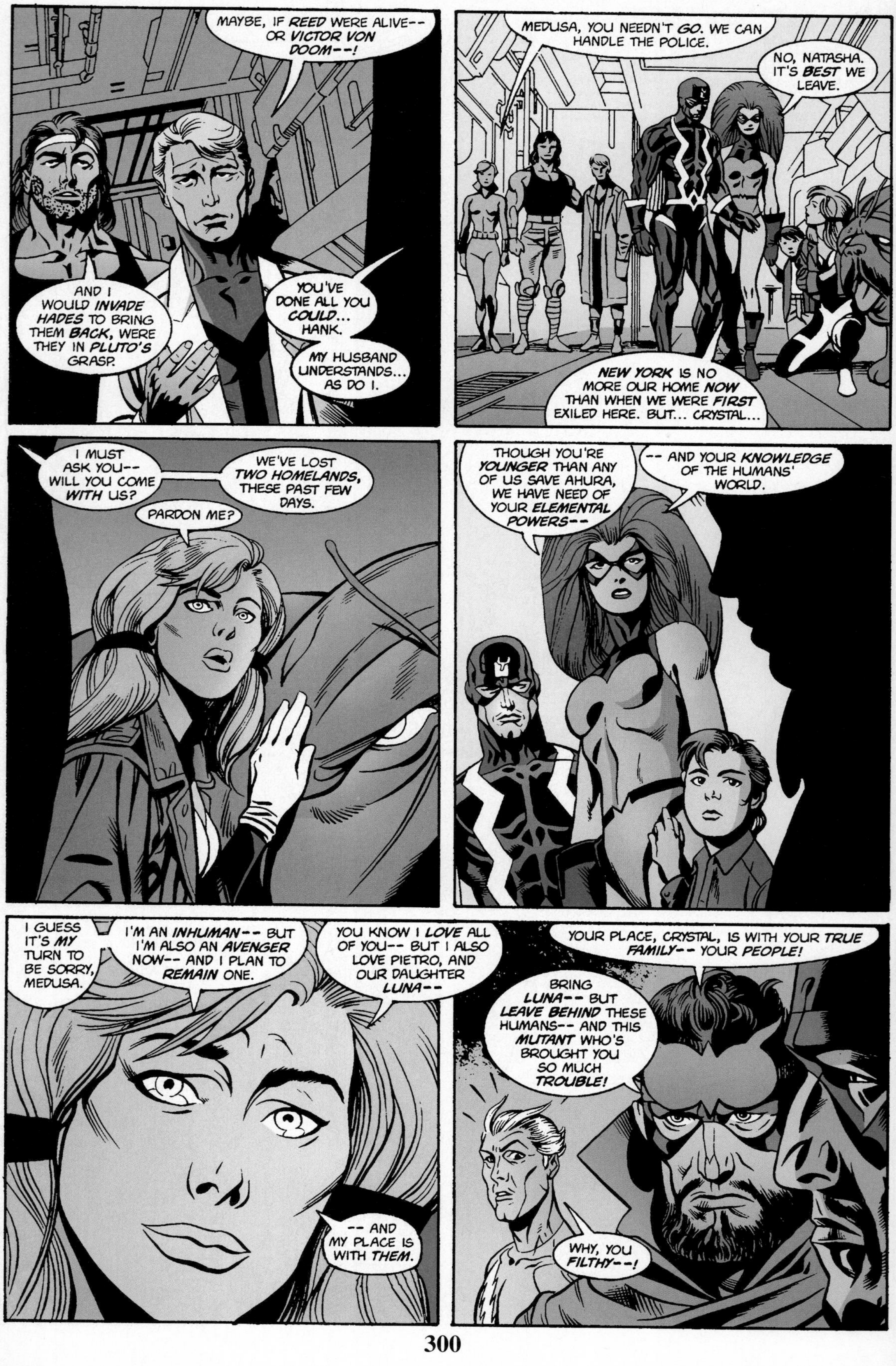
MAYBE, IF REED WERE ALIVE-- OR VICTOR VON DOOM--!
AND I WOULD INVADE HADES TO BRING THEM BACK, WERE THEY IN PLUTO'S GRASP.
YOU'VE DONE ALL YOU COULD... HANK.
MY HUSBAND UNDERSTANDS... AS DO I.
MEDUSA, YOU NEEDN'T GO. WE CAN HANDLE THE POLICE.
NO, NATASHA. IT'S BEST WE LEAVE.
NEW YORK IS NO MORE OUR HOME NOW THAN WHEN WE WERE FIRST EXILED HERE. BUT... CRYSTAL...
I MUST ASK YOU-- WILL YOU COME WITH US?
WE'VE LOST TWO HOMELANDS, THESE PAST FEW DAYS.
PARDON ME?
THOUGH YOU'RE YOUNGER THAN ANY OF US SAVE AHURA, WE HAVE NEED OF YOUR ELEMENTAL POWERS--
-- AND YOUR KNOWLEDGE OF THE HUMANS' WORLD.
I GUESS IT'S MY TURN TO BE SORRY, MEDUSA.
I'M AN INHUMAN-- BUT I'M ALSO AN AVENGER NOW-- AND I PLAN TO REMAIN ONE.
YOU KNOW I LOVE ALL OF YOU-- BUT I ALSO LOVE PIETRO, AND OUR DAUGHTER LUNA--
-- AND MY PLACE IS WITH THEM.
YOUR PLACE, CRYSTAL, IS WITH YOUR TRUE FAMILY-- YOUR PEOPLE!
BRING LUNA-- BUT LEAVE BEHIND THESE HUMANS-- AND THIS MUTANT WHO'S BROUGHT YOU SO MUCH TROUBLE!
WHY, YOU FILTHY--!

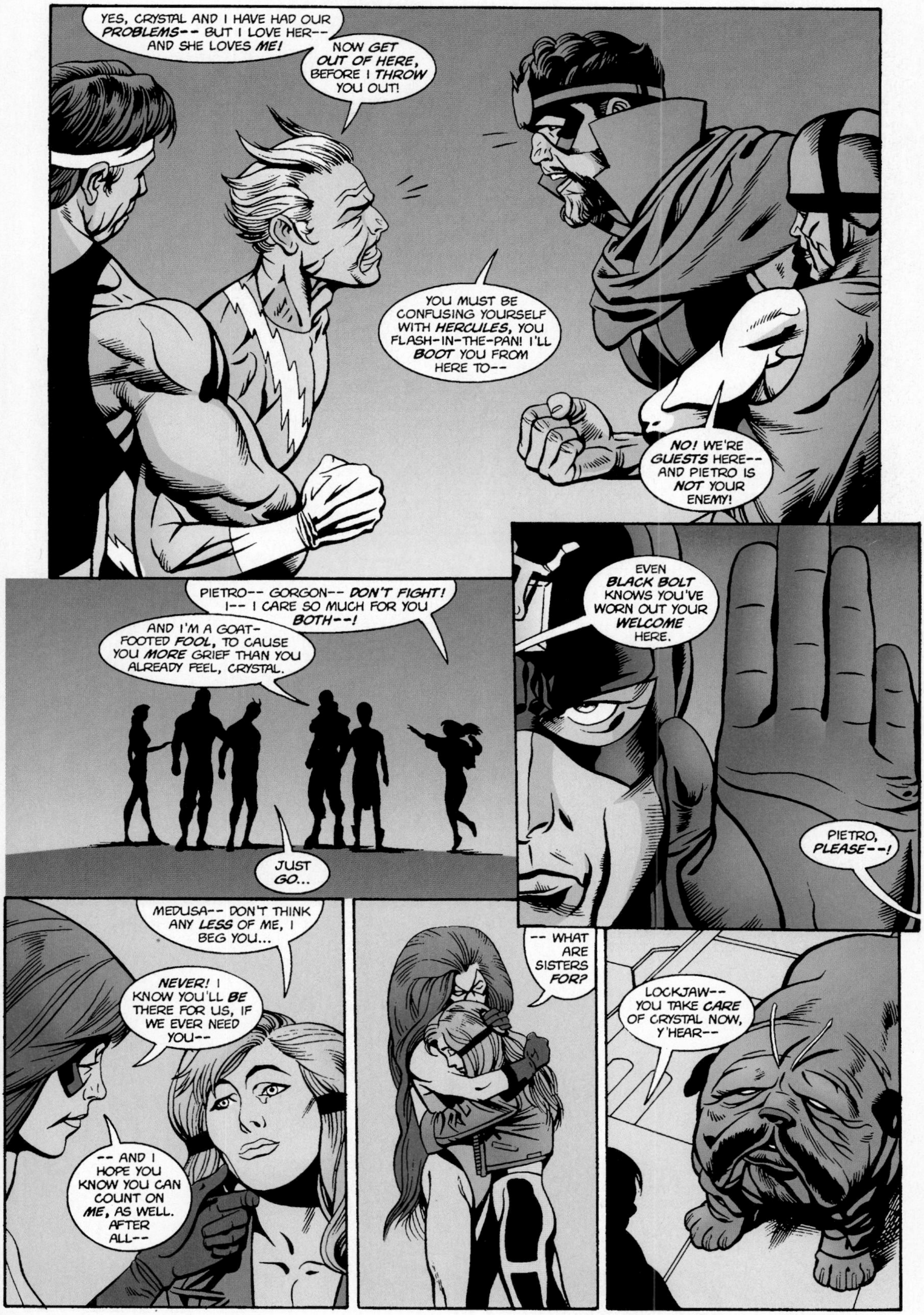
YES, CRYSTAL AND I HAVE HAD OUR PROBLEMS-- BUT I LOVE HER-- AND SHE LOVES ME!
NOW GET OUT OF HERE, BEFORE I THROW YOU OUT!
YOU MUST BE CONFUSING YOURSELF WITH HERCULES, YOU FLASH-IN-THE-PAN! I'LL BOOT YOU FROM HERE TO--
NO! WE'RE GUESTS HERE-- AND PIETRO IS NOT YOUR ENEMY!
EVEN BLACK BOLT KNOWS YOU'VE WORN OUT YOUR WELCOME HERE.
PIETRO, PLEASE--!
PIETRO-- GORGON-- DON'T FIGHT! I-- I CARE SO MUCH FOR YOU BOTH--!
AND I'M A GOAT-FOOTED FOOL, TO CAUSE YOU MORE GRIEF THAN YOU ALREADY FEEL, CRYSTAL.
JUST GO...
MEDUSA-- DON'T THINK ANY LESS OF ME, I BEG YOU...
NEVER! I KNOW YOU'LL BE THERE FOR US, IF WE EVER NEED YOU--
-- AND I HOPE YOU KNOW YOU CAN COUNT ON ME, AS WELL. AFTER ALL--
-- WHAT ARE SISTERS FOR?
LOCKJAW-- YOU TAKE CARE OF CRYSTAL NOW, Y'HEAR--

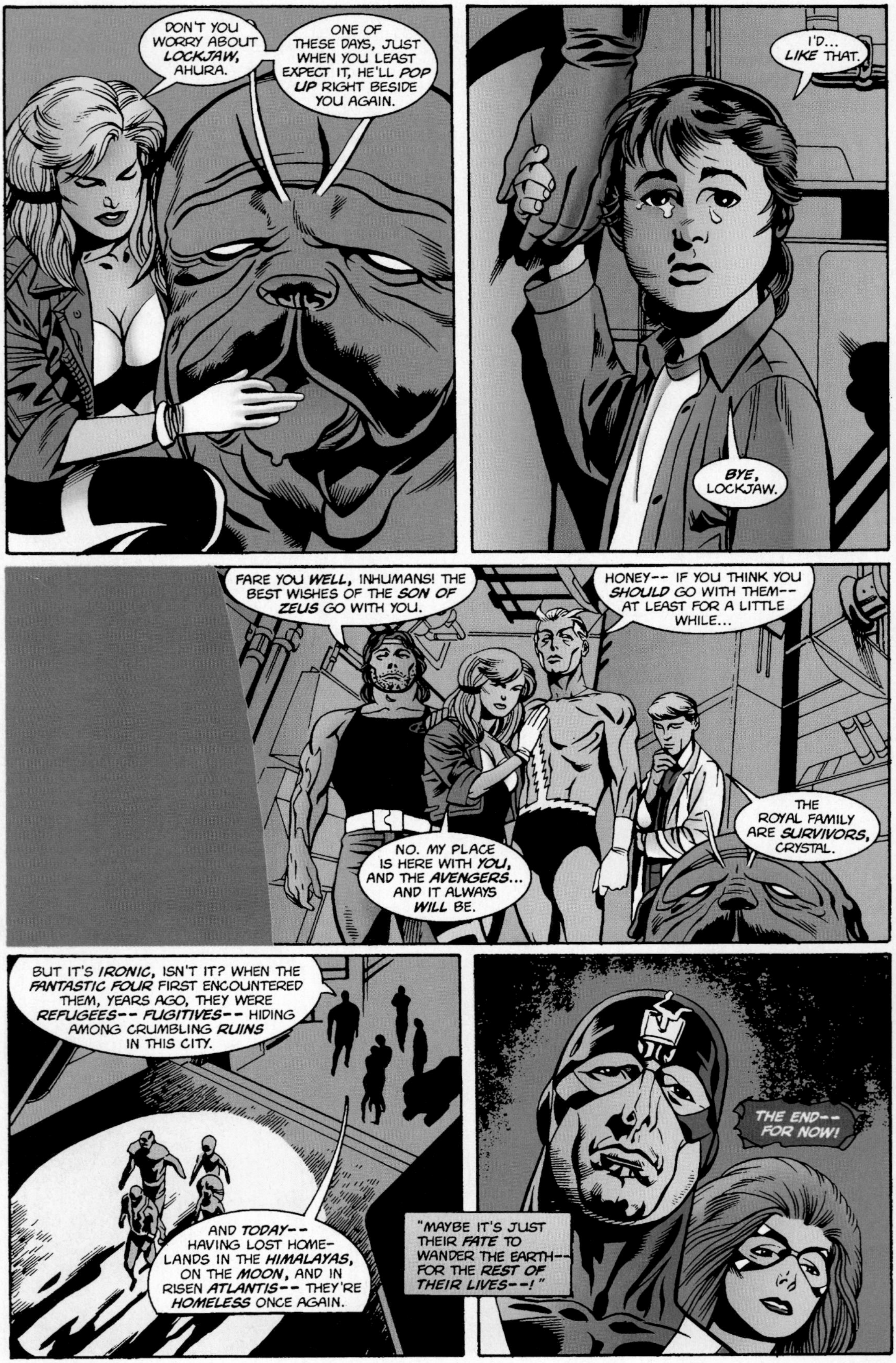
DON'T YOU WORRY ABOUT LOCKJAW, AHURA.
ONE OF THESE DAYS, JUST WHEN YOU LEAST EXPECT IT, HE'LL POP UP RIGHT BESIDE YOU AGAIN.
I'D... LIKE THAT.
BYE, LOCKJAW.
FARE YOU WELL, INHUMANS! THE BEST WISHES OF THE SON OF ZEUS GO WITH YOU.
HONEY-- IF YOU THINK YOU SHOULD GO WITH THEM-- AT LEAST FOR A LITTLE WHILE...
NO. MY PLACE IS HERE WITH YOU, AND THE AVENGERS... AND IT ALWAYS WILL BE.
THE ROYAL FAMILY ARE SURVIVORS, CRYSTAL.
BUT IT'S IRONIC, ISN'T IT? WHEN THE FANTASTIC FOUR FIRST ENCOUNTERED THEM, YEARS AGO, THEY WERE REFUGEES-- FUGITIVES-- HIDING AMONG CRUMBLING RUINS IN THIS CITY.
AND TODAY-- HAVING LOST HOME-LANDS IN THE HIMALAYAS, ON THE MOON, AND IN RISEN ATLANTIS-- THEY'RE HOMELESS ONCE AGAIN.
"MAYBE IT'S JUST THEIR FATE TO WANDER THE EARTH-- FOR THE REST OF THEIR LIVES--!"
THE END-- FOR NOW!

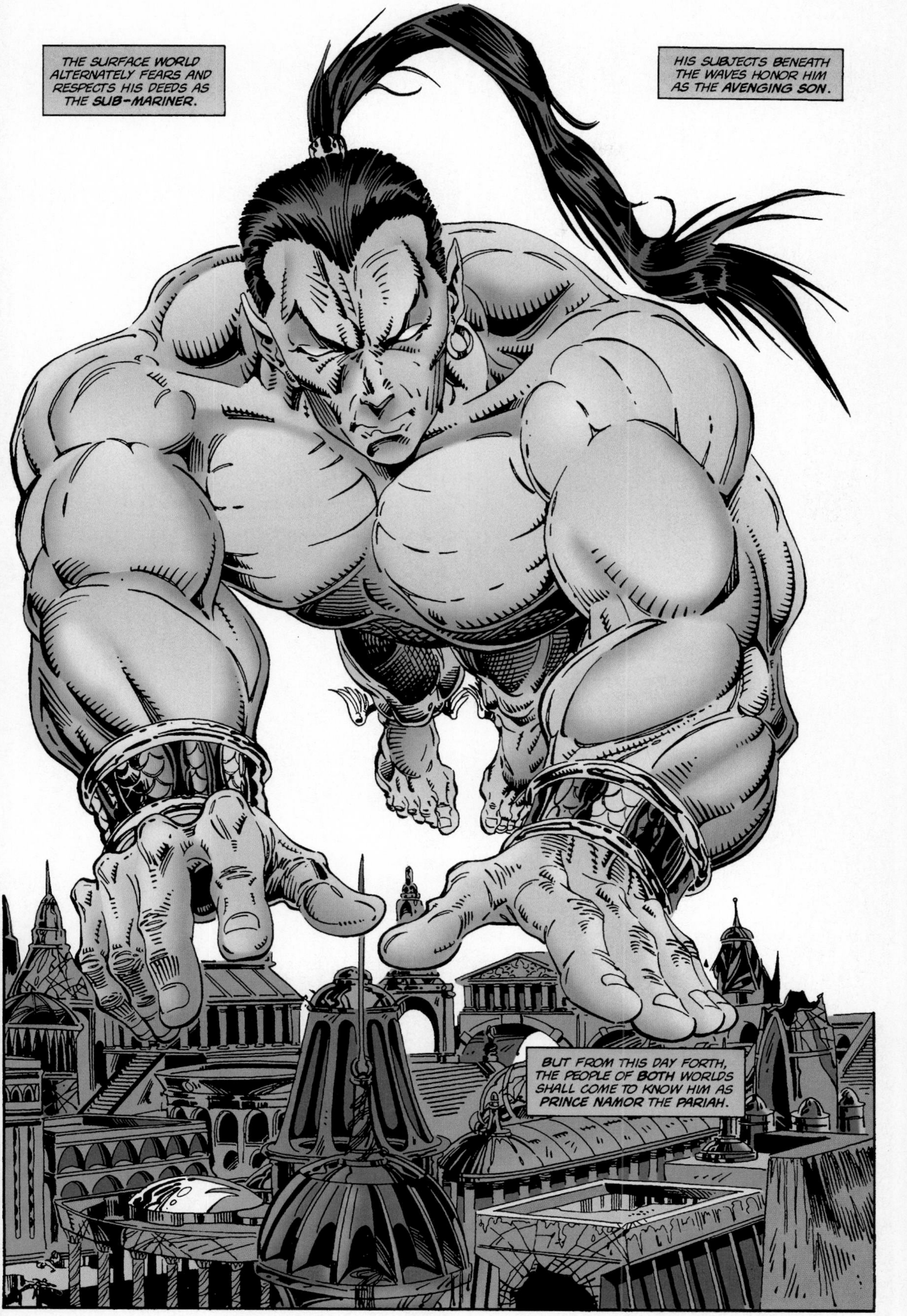
THE SURFACE WORLD ALTERNATELY FEARS AND RESPECTS HIS DEEDS AS THE SUB-MARINER.
HIS SUBJECTS BENEATH THE WAVES HONOR HIM AS THE AVENGING SON.
BUT FROM THIS DAY FORTH, THE PEOPLE OF BOTH WORLDS SHALL COME TO KNOW HIM AS PRINCE NAMOR THE PARIAH.

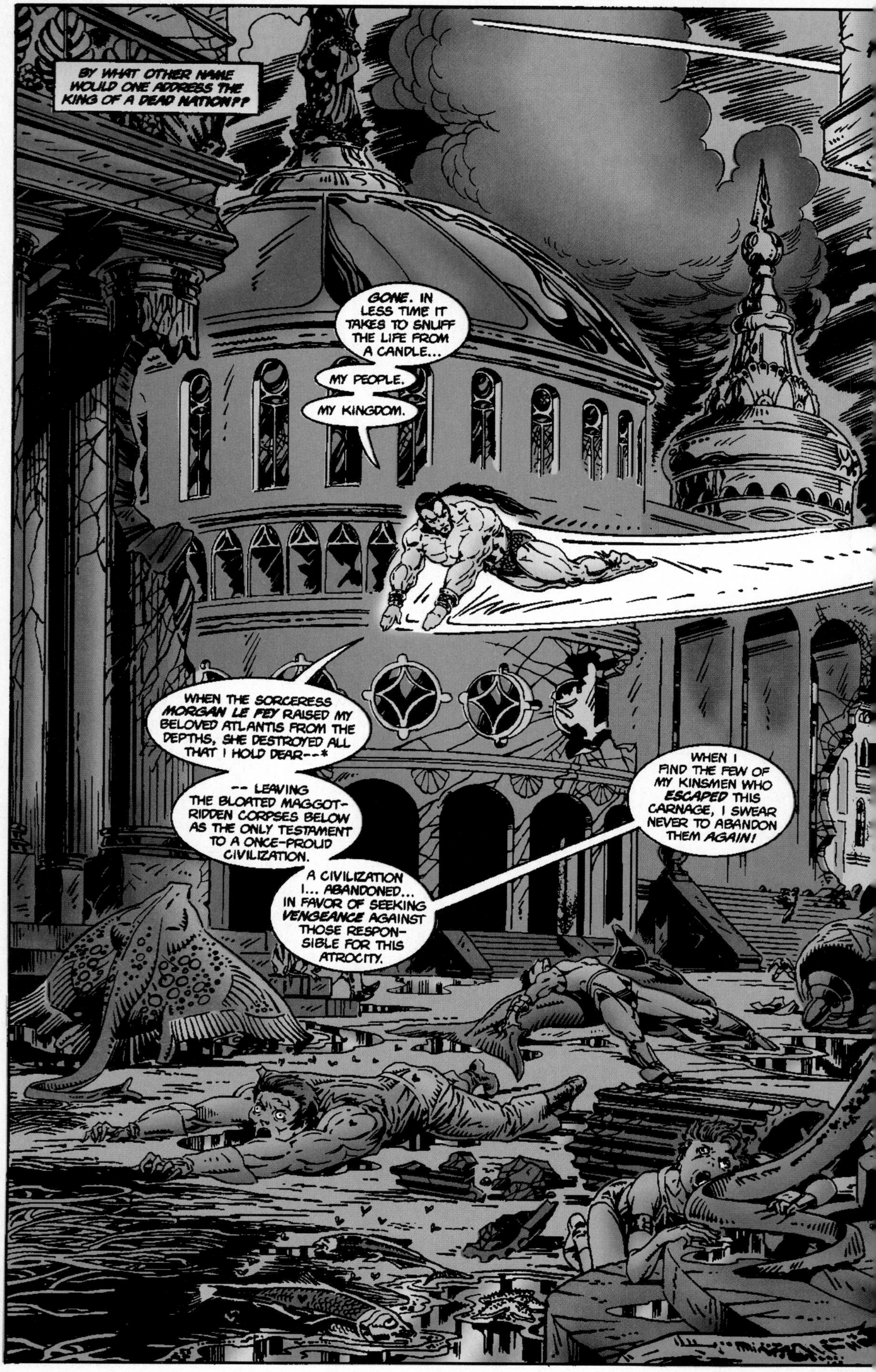
BY WHAT OTHER NAME WOULD ONE ADDRESS THE KING OF A DEAD NATION??
GONE. IN LESS TIME IT TAKES TO SNUFF THE LIFE FROM A CANDLE...
MY PEOPLE.
MY KINGDOM.
WHEN THE SORCERESS MORGAN LE FEY RAISED MY BELOVED ATLANTIS FROM THE DEPTHS, SHE DESTROYED ALL THAT I HOLD DEAR--*
-- LEAVING THE BLOATED MAGGOT-RIDDEN CORPSES BELOW AS THE ONLY TESTAMENT TO A ONCE-PROUD CIVILIZATION.
A CIVILIZATION I... ABANDONED... IN FAVOR OF SEEKING VENGEANCE AGAINST THOSE RESPONSIBLE FOR THIS ATROCITY.
WHEN I FIND THE FEW OF MY KINSMEN WHO ESCAPED THIS CARNAGE, I SWEAR NEVER TO ABANDON THEM AGAIN!

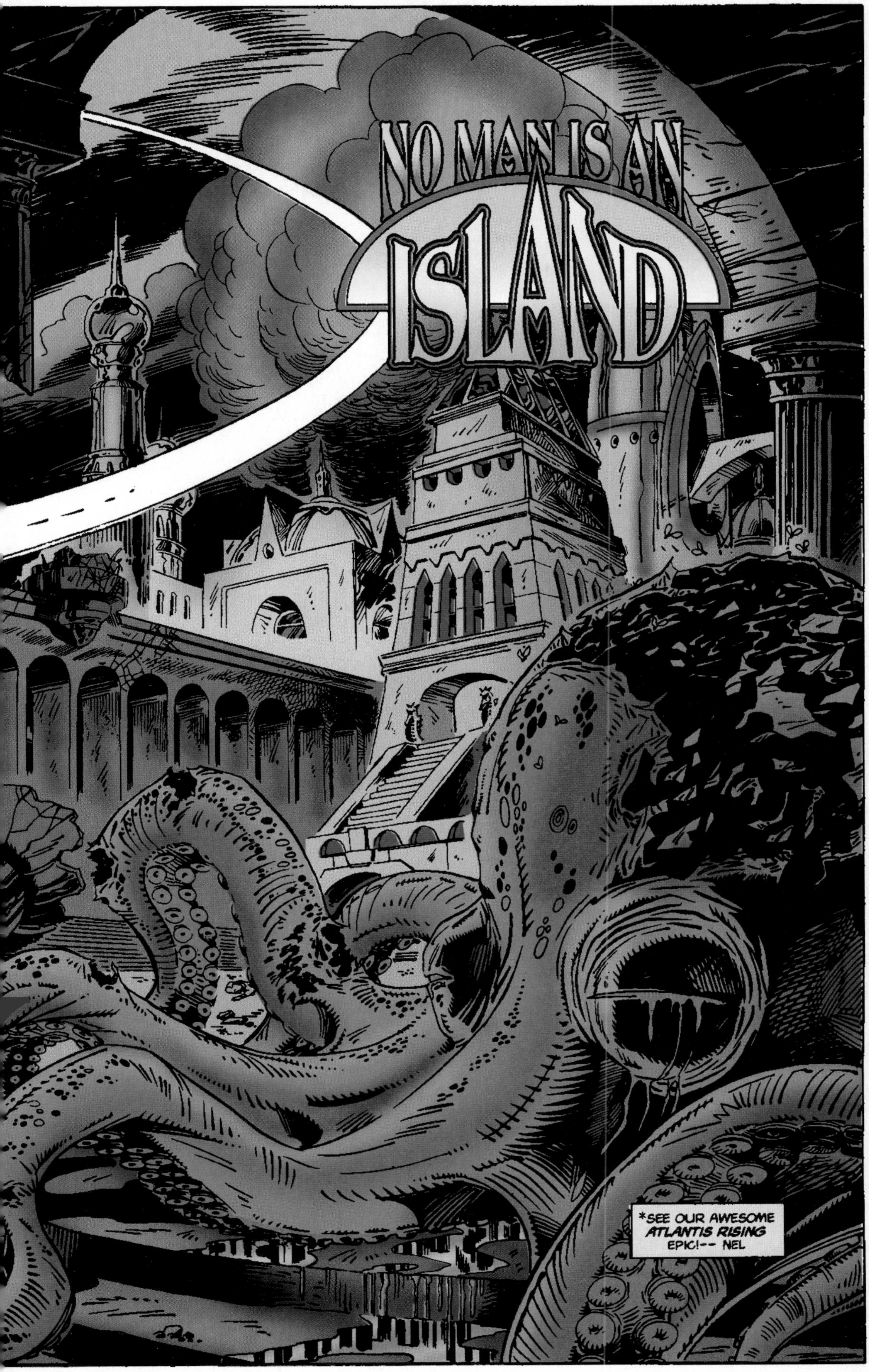
NO MAN IS AN ISLAND
*SEE OUR AWESOME ATLANTIS RISING EPIC!-- NEL

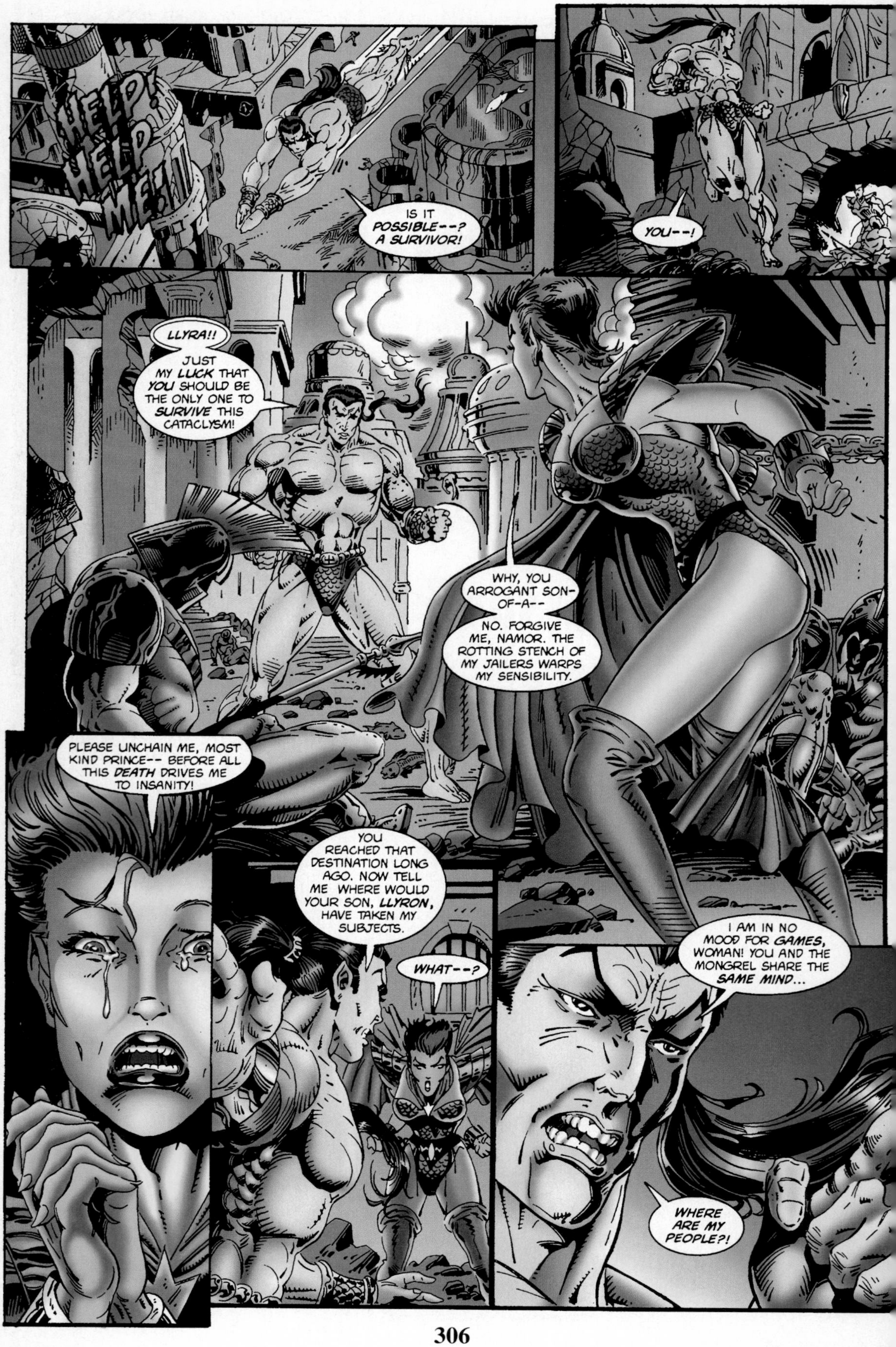

HELP! HELP ME!!
IS IT POSSIBLE--? A SURVIVOR!
YOU--!
LLYRA!!
JUST MY LUCK THAT YOU SHOULD BE THE ONLY ONE TO SURVIVE THIS CATACLYSM!
WHY, YOU ARROGANT SON-OF-A--
NO. FORGIVE ME, NAMOR. THE ROTTING STENCH OF MY JAILERS WARPS MY SENSIBILITY.
PLEASE UNCHAIN ME, MOST KIND PRINCE-- BEFORE ALL THIS DEATH DRIVES ME TO INSANITY!
YOU REACHED THAT DESTINATION LONG AGO. NOW TELL ME WHERE WOULD YOUR SON, LLYRON, HAVE TAKEN MY SUBJECTS.
WHAT--?
I AM IN NO MOOD FOR GAMES, WOMAN! YOU AND THE MONGREL SHARE THE SAME MIND...
WHERE ARE MY PEOPLE?!

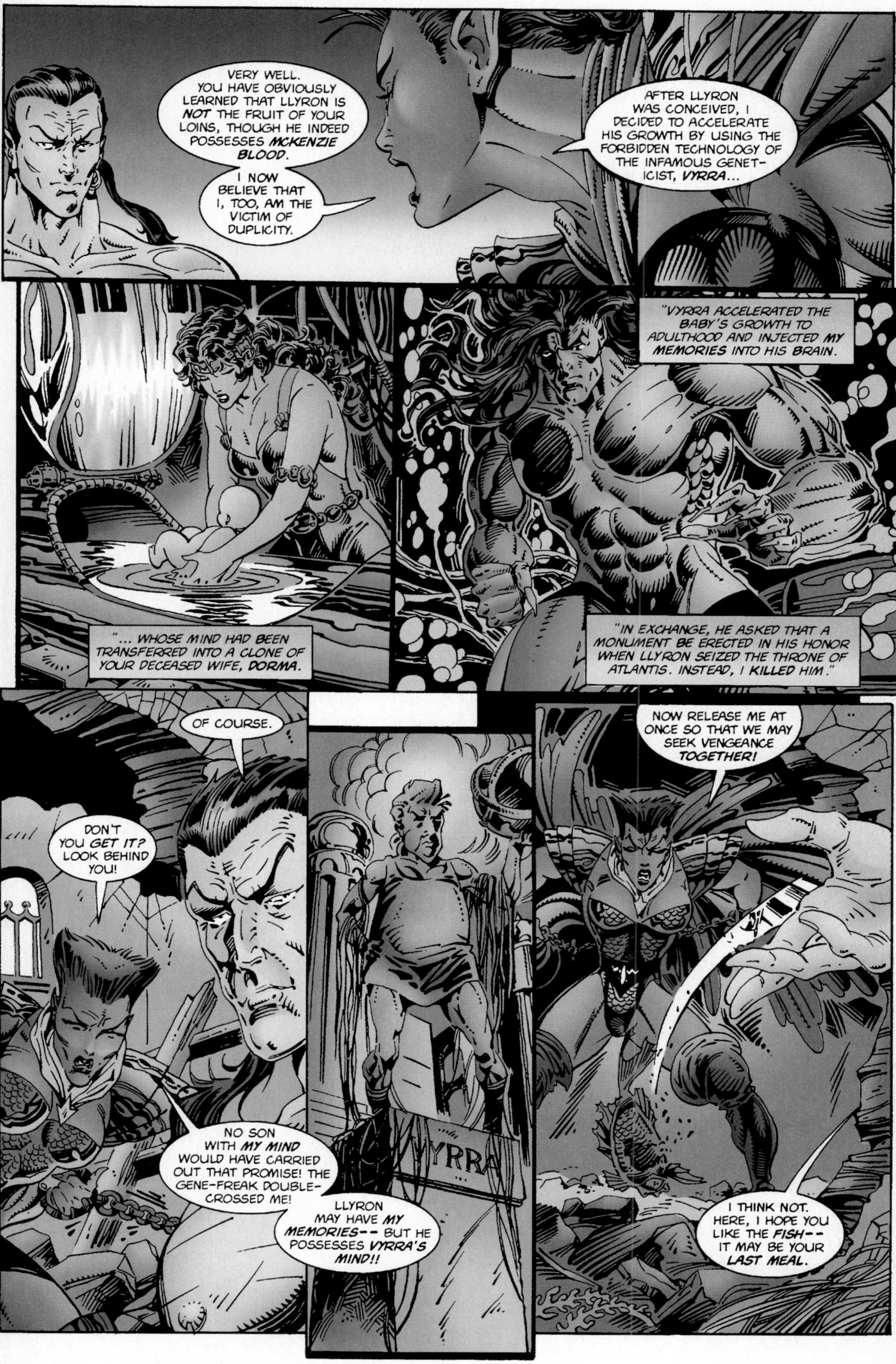
VERY WELL. YOU HAVE OBVIOUSLY LEARNED THAT LLYRON IS NOT THE FRUIT OF YOUR LOINS, THOUGH HE INDEED POSSESSES MCKENZIE BLOOD.
I NOW BELIEVE THAT I, TOO, AM THE VICTIM OF DUPLICITY.
AFTER LLYRON WAS CONCEIVED, I DECIDED TO ACCELERATE HIS GROWTH BY USING THE FORBIDDEN TECHNOLOGY OF THE INFAMOUS GENET-ICIST, VYRRA...
"... WHOSE MIND HAD BEEN TRANSFERRED INTO A CLONE OF YOUR DECEASED WIFE, DORMA.
"VYRRA ACCELERATED THE BABY'S GROWTH TO ADULTHOOD AND INJECTED MY MEMORIES INTO HIS BRAIN.
"IN EXCHANGE, HE ASKED THAT A MONUMENT BE ERECTED IN HIS HONOR WHEN LLYRON SEIZED THE THRONE OF ATLANTIS. INSTEAD, I KILLED HIM."
OF COURSE.
DON'T YOU GET IT? LOOK BEHIND YOU!
NO SON WITH MY MIND WOULD HAVE CARRIED OUT THAT PROMISE! THE GENE-FREAK DOUBLE-CROSSED ME!
LLYRON MAY HAVE MY MEMORIES-- BUT HE POSSESSES VYRRA'S MIND!!
VYRRA
NOW RELEASE ME AT ONCE SO THAT WE MAY SEEK VENGEANCE TOGETHER!
I THINK NOT. HERE, I HOPE YOU LIKE THE FISH-- IT MAY BE YOUR LAST MEAL.

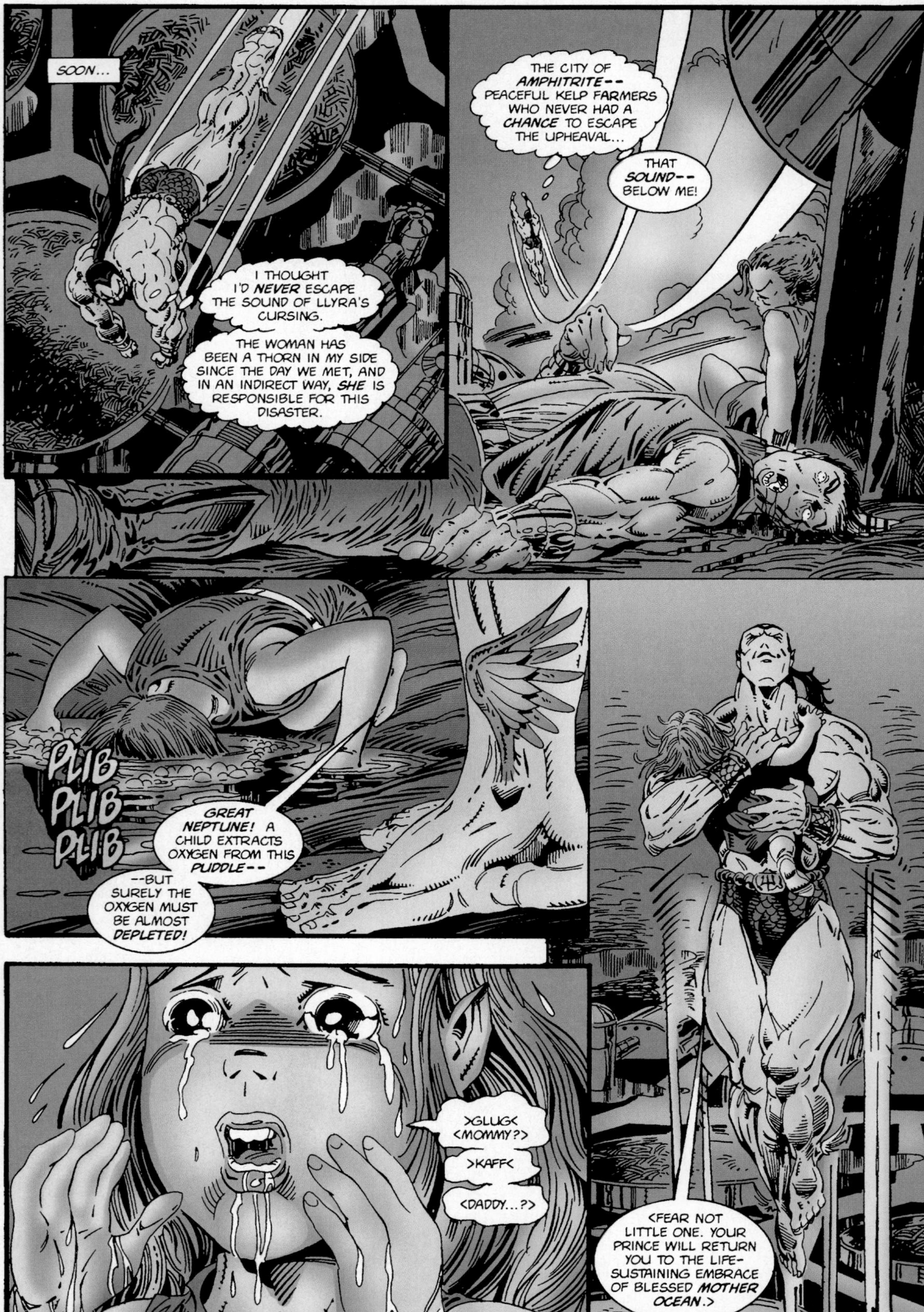
SOON...
I THOUGHT I'D NEVER ESCAPE THE SOUND OF LLYRA'S CURSING.
THE WOMAN HAS BEEN A THORN IN MY SIDE SINCE THE DAY WE MET, AND IN AN INDIRECT WAY, SHE IS RESPONSIBLE FOR THIS DISASTER.
THE CITY OF AMPHITRITE-- PEACEFUL KELP FARMERS WHO NEVER HAD A CHANCE TO ESCAPE THE UPHEAVAL...
THAT SOUND-- BELOW ME!
PLIB PLIB PLIB
GREAT NEPTUNE! A CHILD EXTRACTS OXYGEN FROM THIS PUDDLE--
--BUT SURELY THE OXYGEN MUST BE ALMOST DEPLETED!
>GLUG< <MOMMY?>
>KAFF<
<DADDY...?>
<FEAR NOT LITTLE ONE. YOUR PRINCE WILL RETURN YOU TO THE LIFE-SUSTAINING EMBRACE OF BLESSED MOTHER OCEAN.>

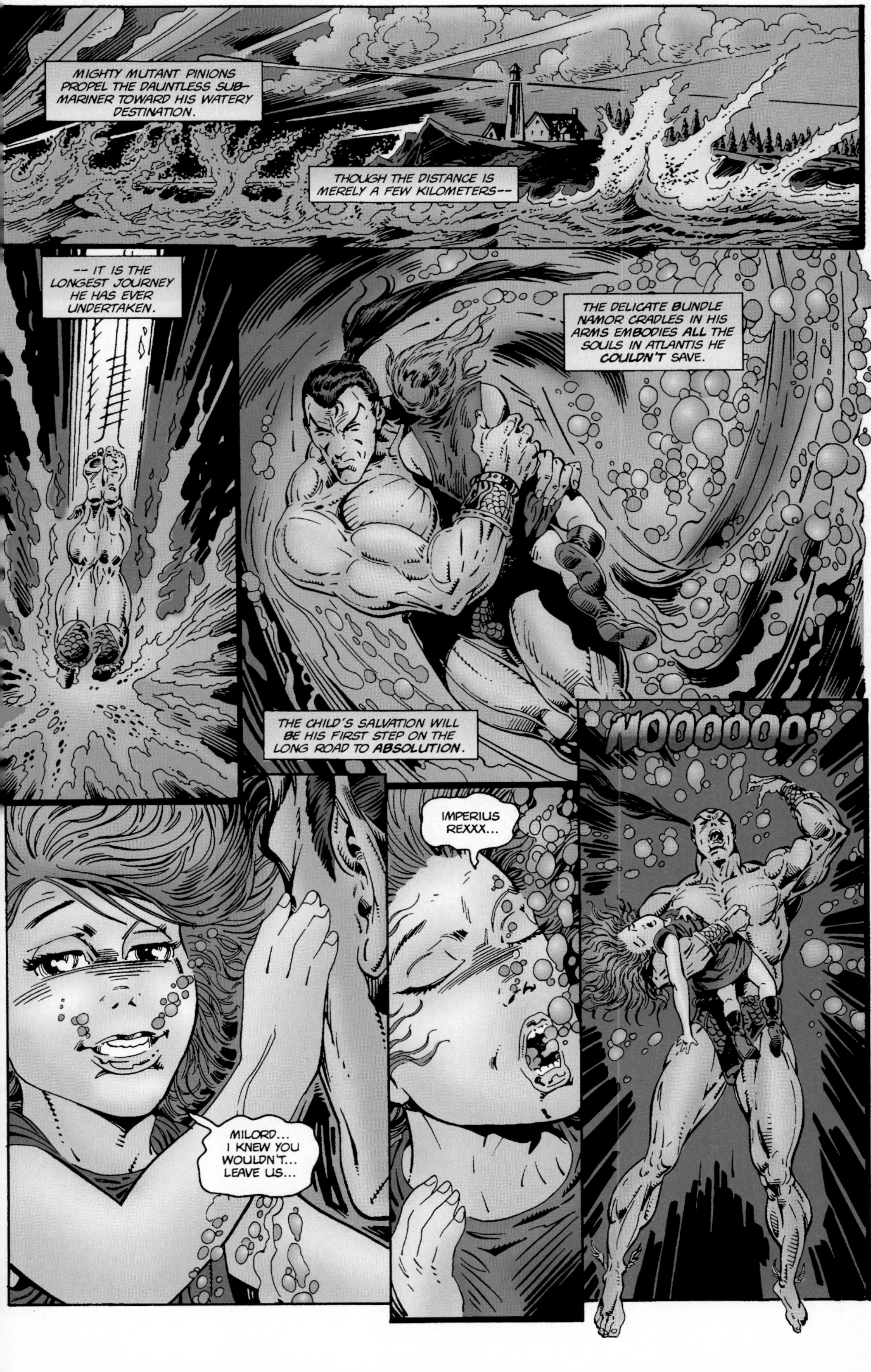

MIGHTY MUTANT PINIONS PROPEL THE DAUNTLESS SUB-MARINER TOWARD HIS WATERY DESTINATION.
THOUGH THE DISTANCE IS MERELY A FEW KILOMETERS--
-- IT IS THE LONGEST JOURNEY HE HAS EVER UNDERTAKEN.
THE DELICATE BUNDLE NAMOR CRADLES IN HIS ARMS EMBODIES ALL THE SOULS IN ATLANTIS HE COULDN'T SAVE.
THE CHILD'S SALVATION WILL BE HIS FIRST STEP ON THE LONG ROAD TO ABSOLUTION.
MILORD... I KNEW YOU WOULDN'T... LEAVE US...
IMPERIUS REXXX...
NOOOOOOO!

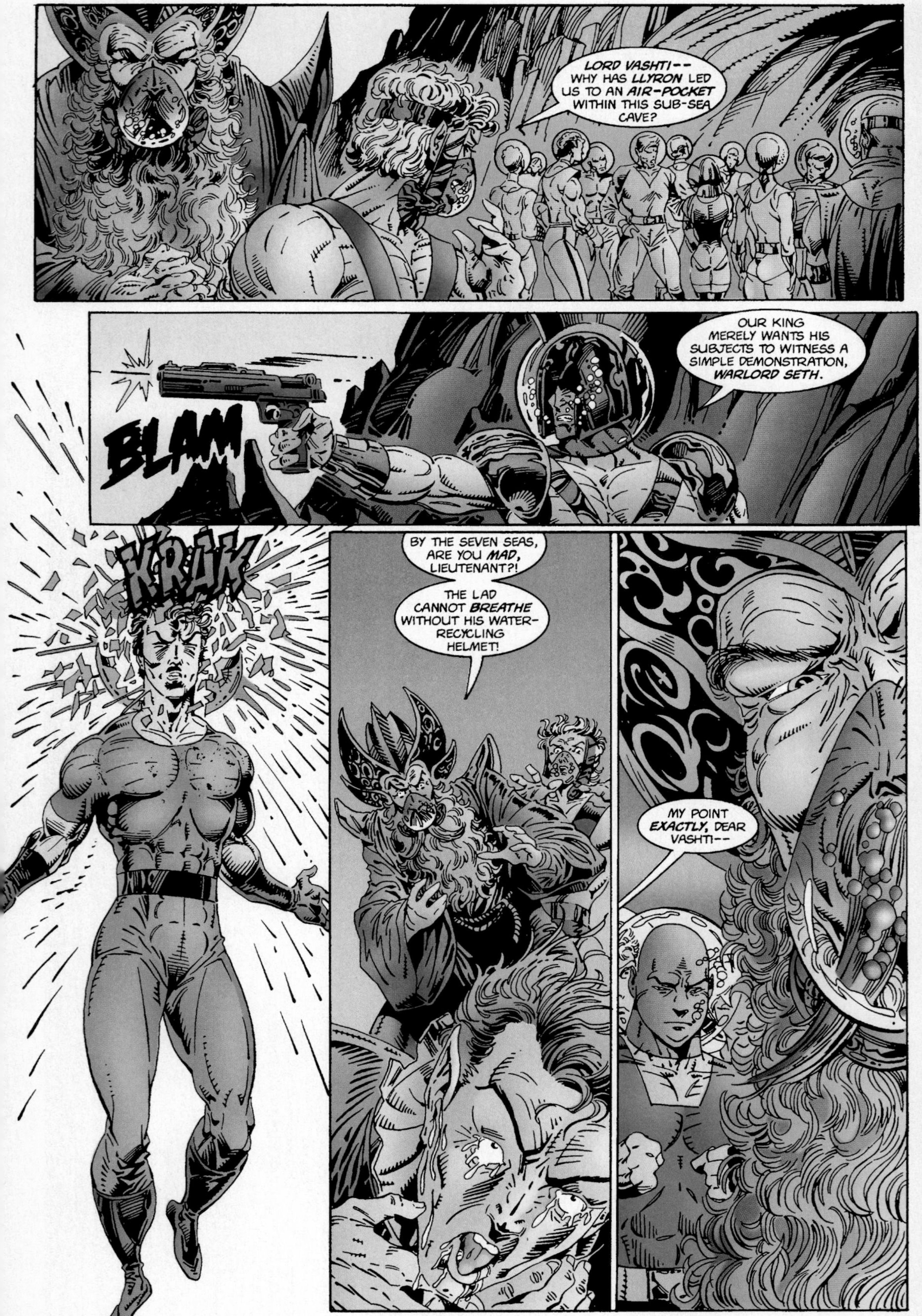
LORD VASHTI-- WHY HAS LLYRON LED US TO AN AIR-POCKET WITHIN THIS SUB-SEA CAVE?
OUR KING MERELY WANTS HIS SUBJECTS TO WITNESS A SIMPLE DEMONSTRATION, WARLORD SETH.
BLAM
KRAK
BY THE SEVEN SEAS, ARE YOU MAD, LIEUTENANT?!
THE LAD CANNOT BREATHE WITHOUT HIS WATER-RECYCLING HELMET!
MY POINT EXACTLY, DEAR VASHTI--

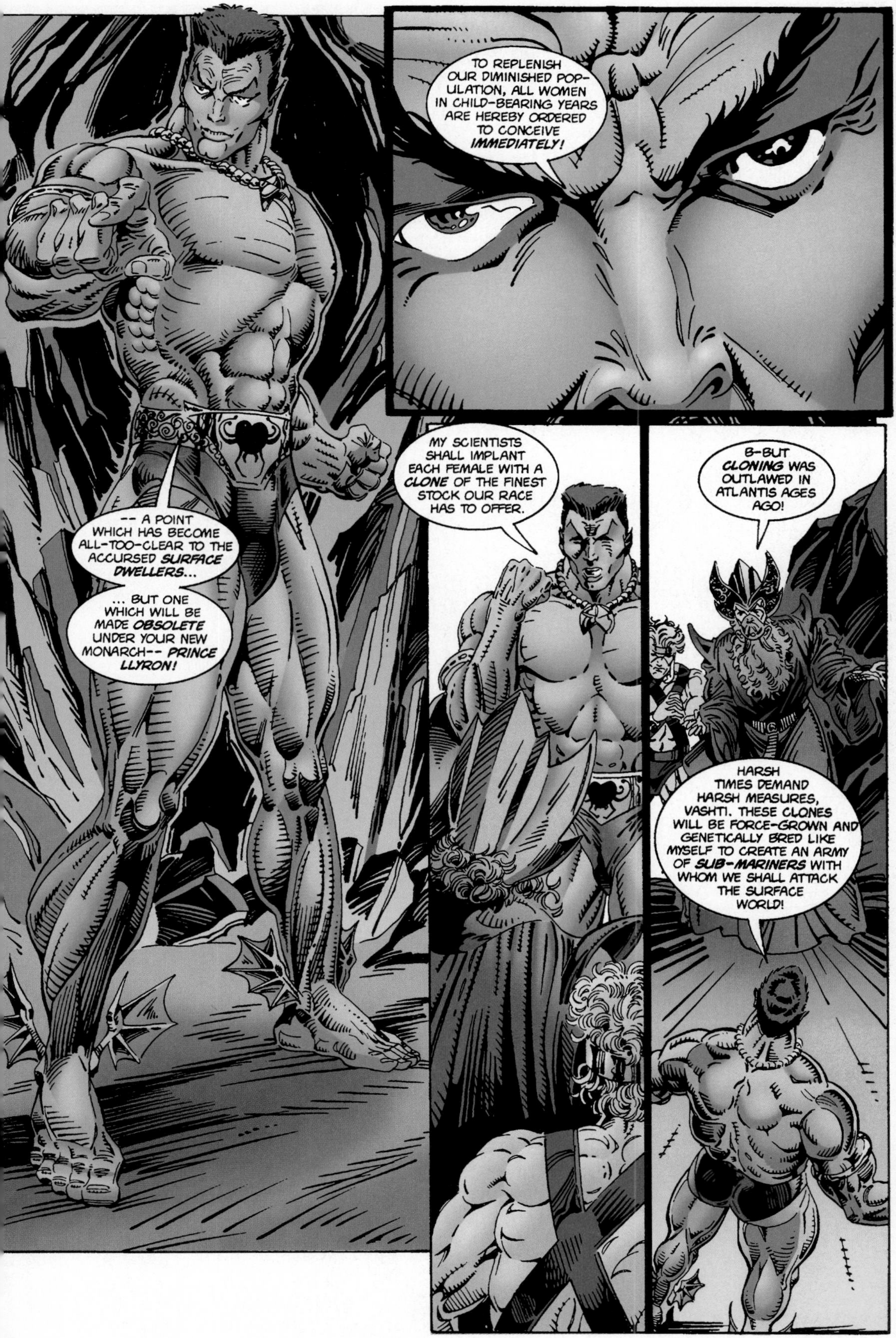

-- A POINT WHICH HAS BECOME ALL-TOO-CLEAR TO THE ACCURSED SURFACE DWELLERS...
... BUT ONE WHICH WILL BE MADE OBSOLETE UNDER YOUR NEW MONARCH-- PRINCE LLYRON!
TO REPLENISH OUR DIMINISHED POPULATION, ALL WOMEN IN CHILD-BEARING YEARS ARE HEREBY ORDERED TO CONCEIVE IMMEDIATELY!
MY SCIENTISTS SHALL IMPLANT EACH FEMALE WITH A CLONE OF THE FINEST STOCK OUR RACE HAS TO OFFER.
B-BUT CLONING WAS OUTLAWED IN ATLANTIS AGES AGO!
HARSH TIMES DEMAND HARSH MEASURES, VASHTI. THESE CLONES WILL BE FORCE-GROWN AND GENETICALLY BRED LIKE MYSELF TO CREATE AN ARMY OF SUB-MARINERS WITH WHOM WE SHALL ATTACK THE SURFACE WORLD!

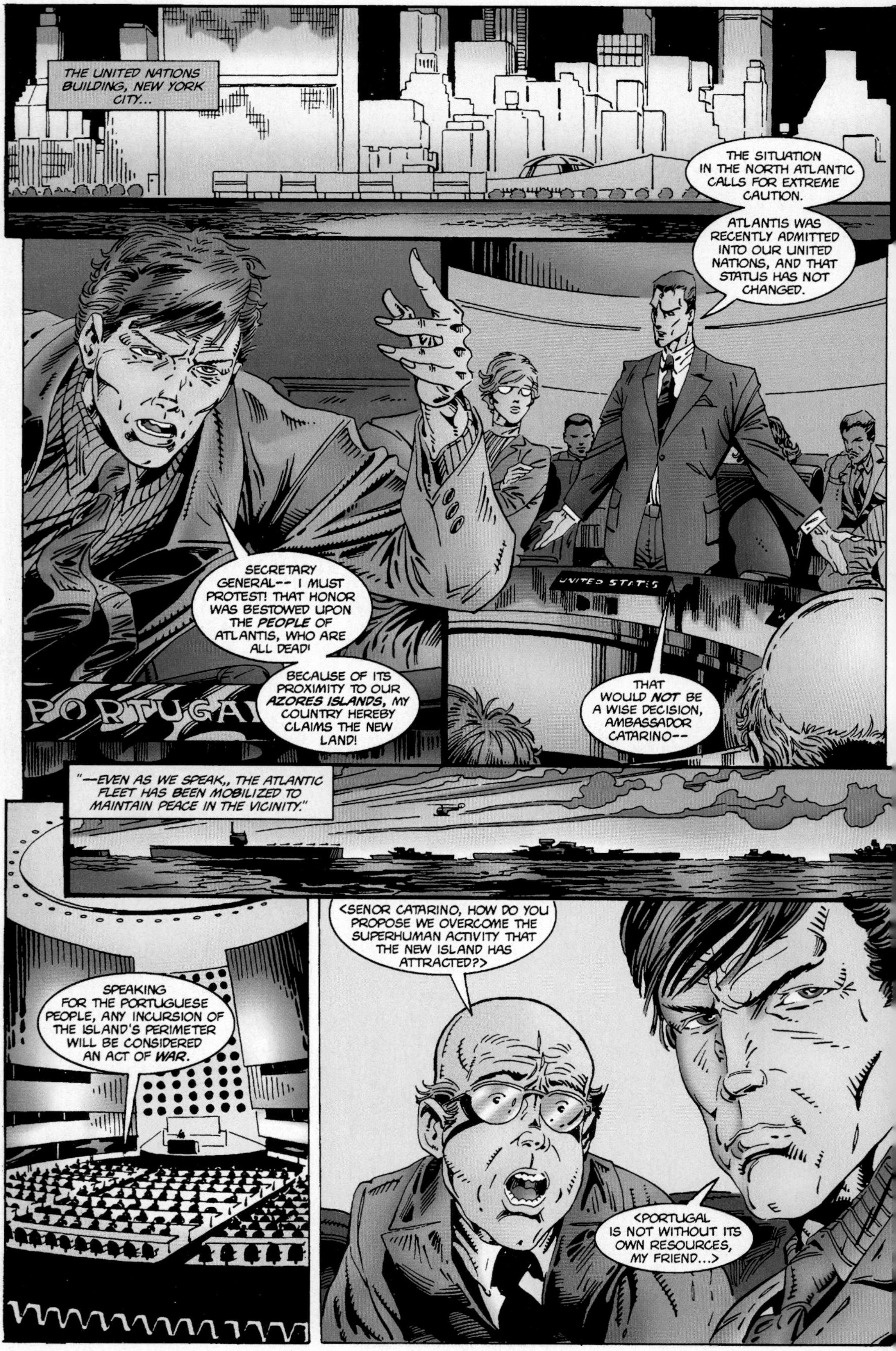
THE UNITED NATIONS BUILDING, NEW YORK CITY...
THE SITUATION IN THE NORTH ATLANTIC CALLS FOR EXTREME CAUTION.
ATLANTIS WAS RECENTLY ADMITTED INTO OUR UNITED NATIONS, AND THAT STATUS HAS NOT CHANGED.
SECRETARY GENERAL-- I MUST PROTEST! THAT HONOR WAS BESTOWED UPON THE *PEOPLE* OF ATLANTIS, WHO ARE ALL DEAD!
BECAUSE OF ITS PROXIMITY TO OUR ***AZORES ISLANDS,*** MY COUNTRY HEREBY CLAIMS THE NEW LAND!
UNITED STATES
THAT WOULD ***NOT*** BE A WISE DECISION, AMBASSADOR CATARINO--
"--EVEN AS WE SPEAK,, THE ATLANTIC FLEET HAS BEEN MOBILIZED TO MAINTAIN PEACE IN THE VICINITY."
SPEAKING FOR THE PORTUGUESE PEOPLE, ANY INCURSION OF THE ISLAND'S PERIMETER WILL BE CONSIDERED AN ACT OF ***WAR.***
<SENOR CATARINO, HOW DO YOU PROPOSE WE OVERCOME THE SUPERHUMAN ACTIVITY THAT THE NEW ISLAND HAS ATTRACTED?>
<PORTUGAL IS NOT WITHOUT ITS OWN RESOURCES, MY FRIEND...>

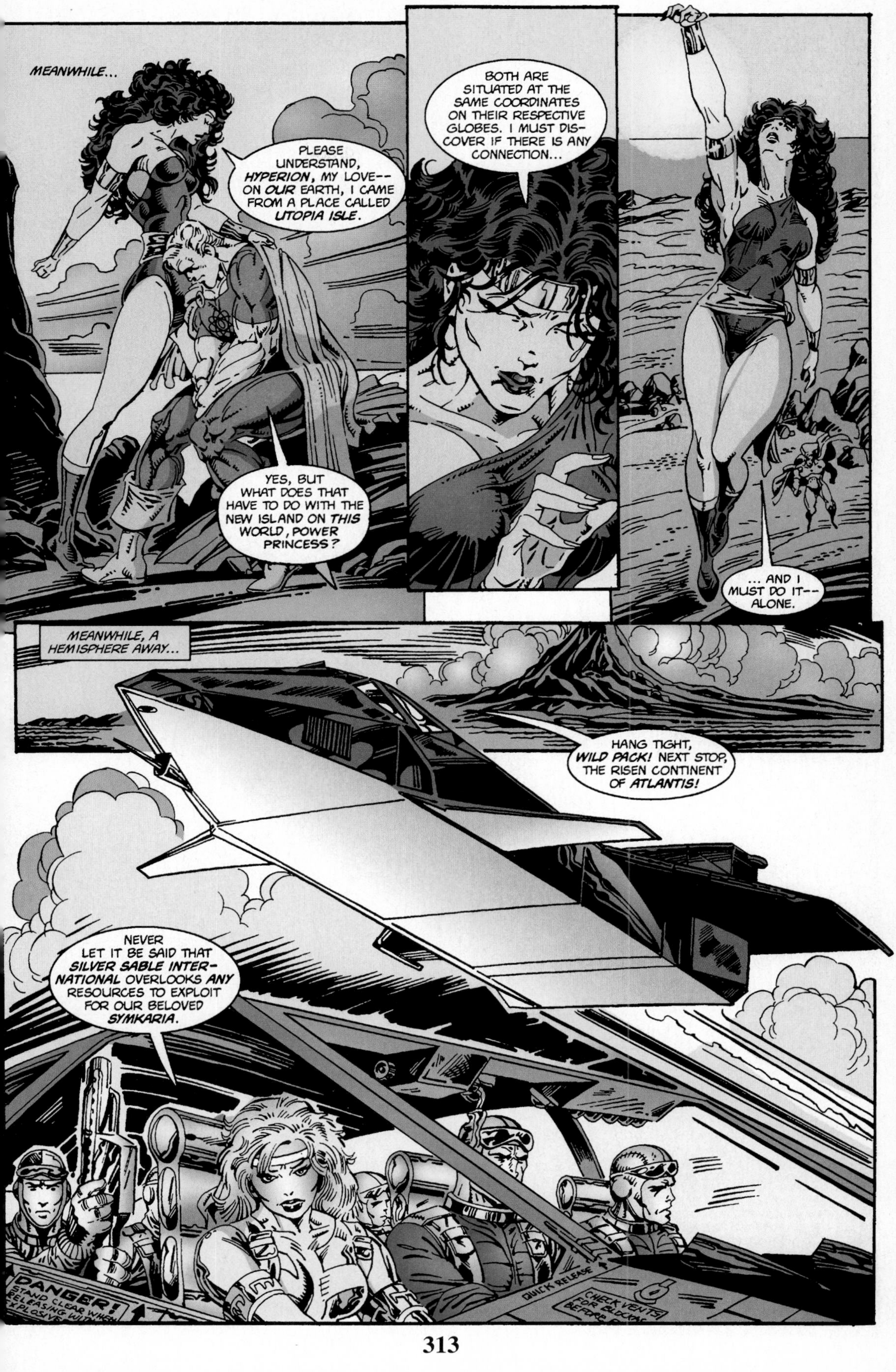
MEANWHILE...
PLEASE UNDERSTAND, HYPERION, MY LOVE-- ON OUR EARTH, I CAME FROM A PLACE CALLED UTOPIA ISLE.
YES, BUT WHAT DOES THAT HAVE TO DO WITH THE NEW ISLAND ON THIS WORLD, POWER PRINCESS?
BOTH ARE SITUATED AT THE SAME COORDINATES ON THEIR RESPECTIVE GLOBES. I MUST DISCOVER IF THERE IS ANY CONNECTION...
... AND I MUST DO IT-- ALONE.
MEANWHILE, A HEMISPHERE AWAY...
HANG TIGHT, WILD PACK! NEXT STOP, THE RISEN CONTINENT OF ATLANTIS!
NEVER LET IT BE SAID THAT SILVER SABLE INTERNATIONAL OVERLOOKS ANY RESOURCES TO EXPLOIT FOR OUR BELOVED SYMKARIA.
DANGER!
STAND CLEAR WHEN RELEASING
QUICK RELEASE
CHECK VENTS

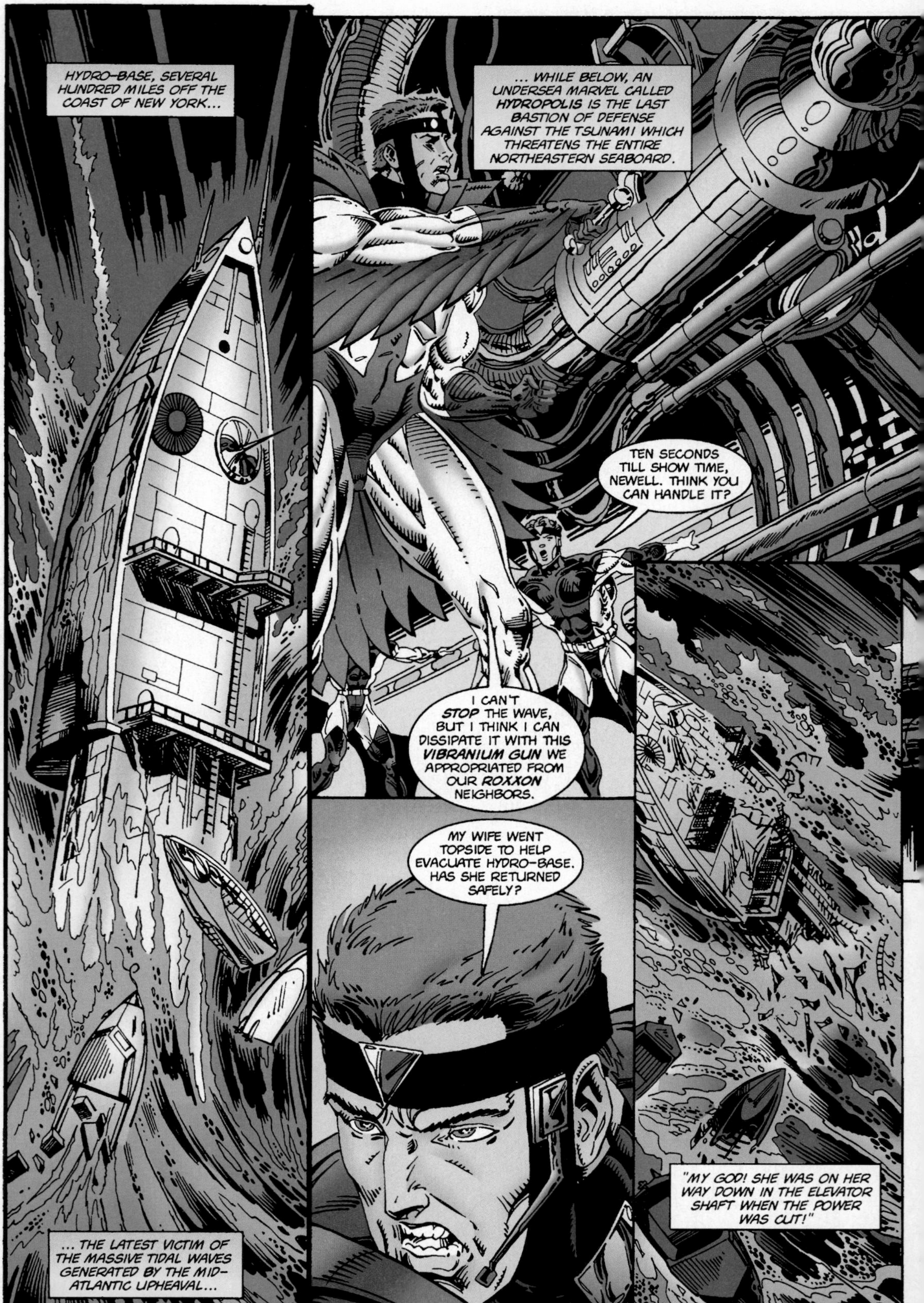
HYDRO-BASE, SEVERAL HUNDRED MILES OFF THE COAST OF NEW YORK...
...THE LATEST VICTIM OF THE MASSIVE TIDAL WAVES GENERATED BY THE MID-ATLANTIC UPHEAVAL...
...WHILE BELOW, AN UNDERSEA MARVEL CALLED HYDROPOLIS IS THE LAST BASTION OF DEFENSE AGAINST THE TSUNAMI WHICH THREATENS THE ENTIRE NORTHEASTERN SEABOARD.
TEN SECONDS TILL SHOW TIME, NEWELL. THINK YOU CAN HANDLE IT?
I CAN'T STOP THE WAVE, BUT I THINK I CAN DISSIPATE IT WITH THIS VIBRANIUM GUN WE APPROPRIATED FROM OUR ROXXON NEIGHBORS.
MY WIFE WENT TOPSIDE TO HELP EVACUATE HYDRO-BASE. HAS SHE RETURNED SAFELY?
"MY GOD! SHE WAS ON HER WAY DOWN IN THE ELEVATOR SHAFT WHEN THE POWER WAS CUT!"

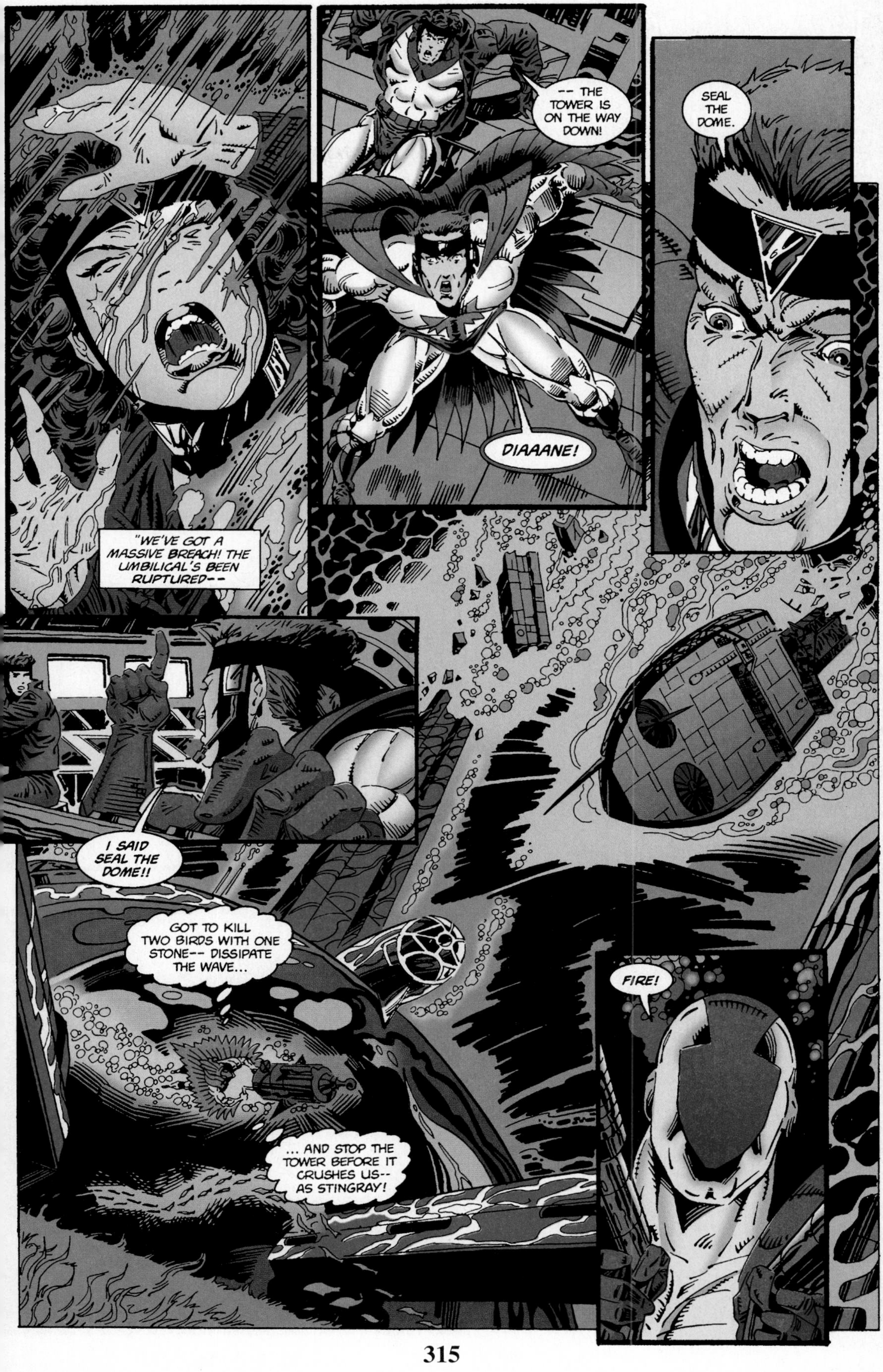

-- THE TOWER IS ON THE WAY DOWN!
DIAAANE!
SEAL THE DOME.
"WE'VE GOT A MASSIVE BREACH! THE UMBILICAL'S BEEN RUPTURED--
I SAID SEAL THE DOME!!
GOT TO KILL TWO BIRDS WITH ONE STONE-- DISSIPATE THE WAVE...
... AND STOP THE TOWER BEFORE IT CRUSHES US-- AS STINGRAY!
FIRE!

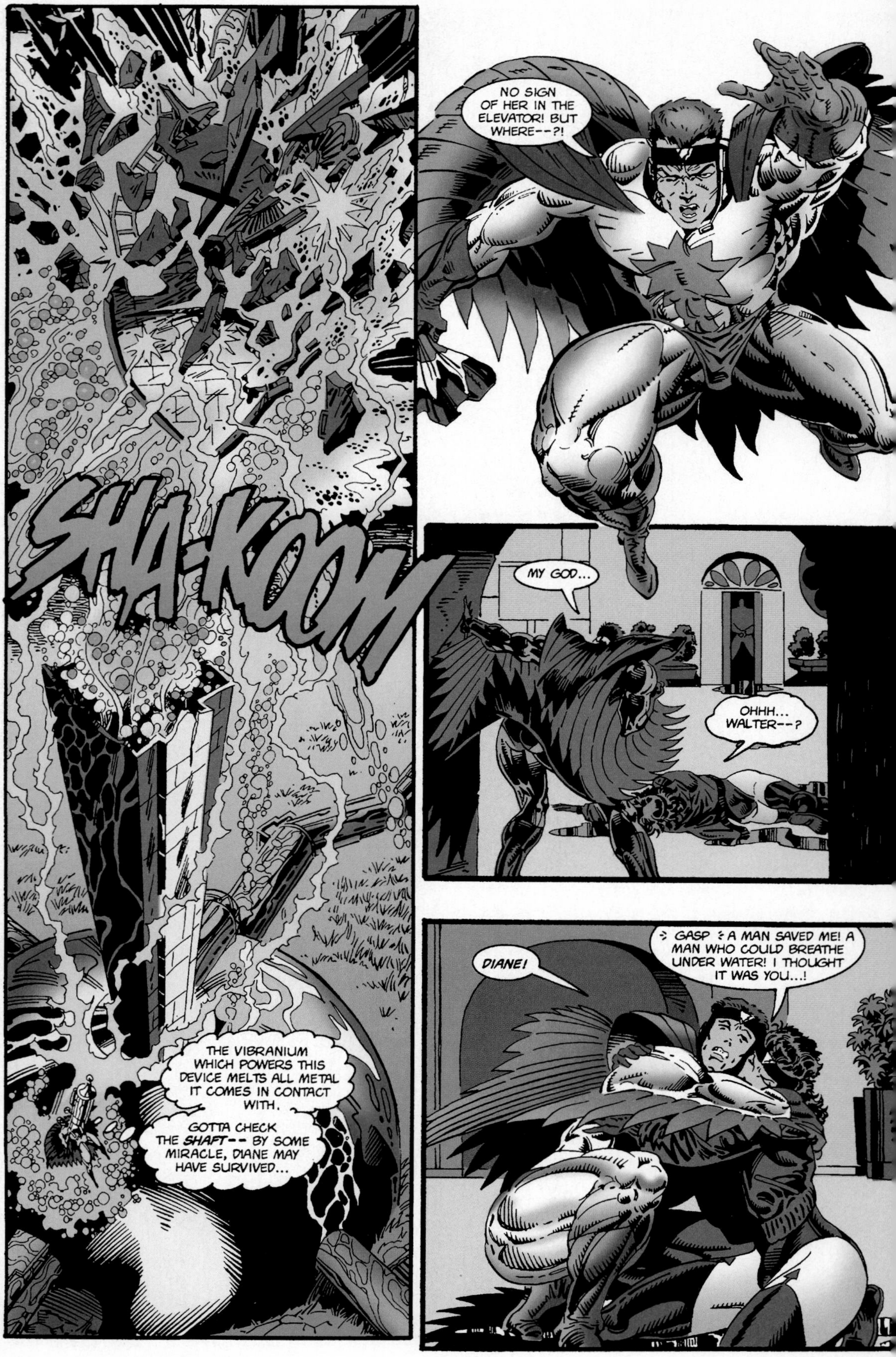
SHA-KOOM
NO SIGN OF HER IN THE ELEVATOR! BUT WHERE--?!
THE VIBRANIUM WHICH POWERS THIS DEVICE MELTS ALL METAL IT COMES IN CONTACT WITH.
GOTTA CHECK THE SHAFT-- BY SOME MIRACLE, DIANE MAY HAVE SURVIVED...
MY GOD...
OHHH... WALTER--?
DIANE!
GASP A MAN SAVED ME! A MAN WHO COULD BREATHE UNDER WATER! I THOUGHT IT WAS YOU...!

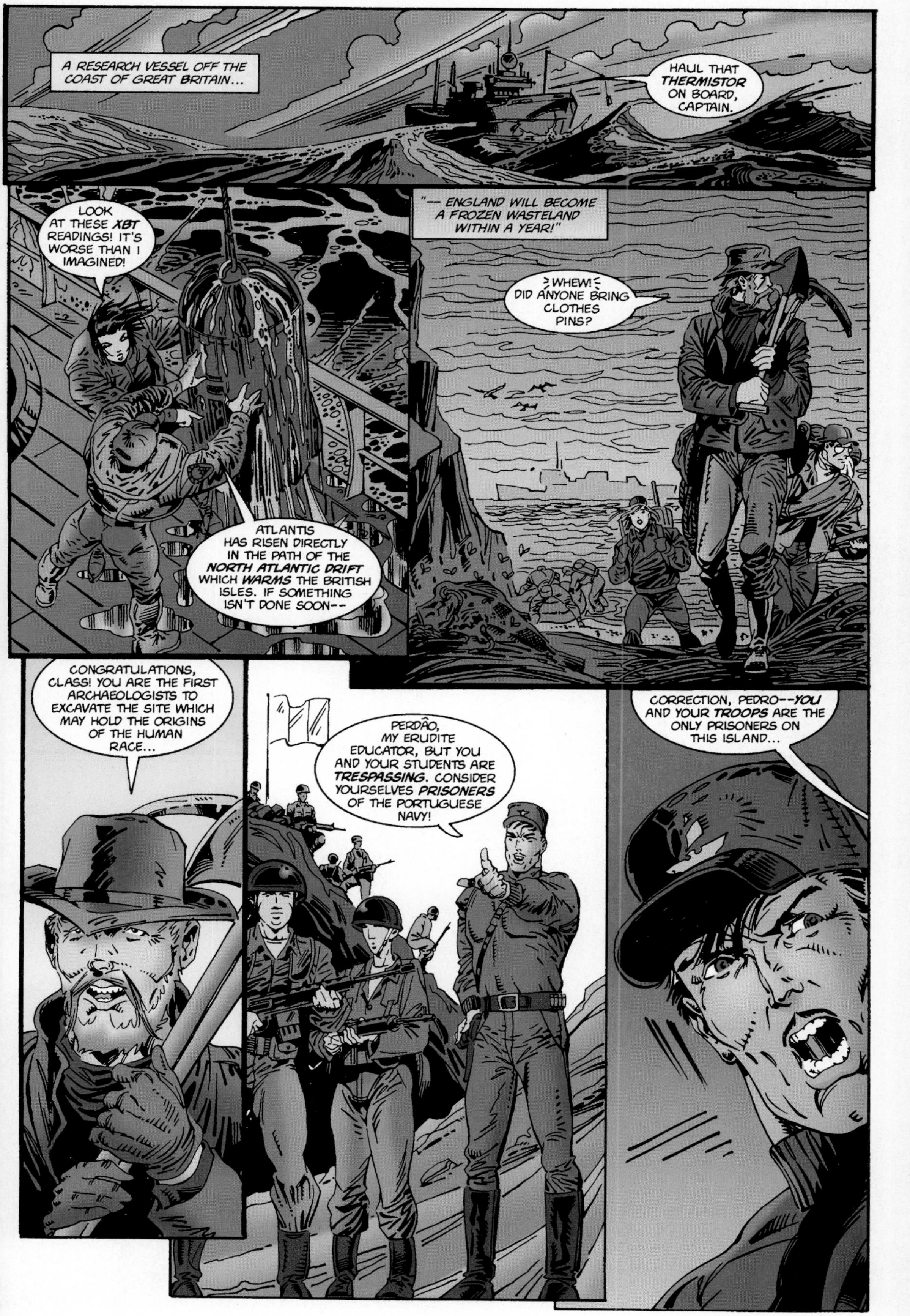

A RESEARCH VESSEL OFF THE COAST OF GREAT BRITAIN...
HAUL THAT THERMISTOR ON BOARD, CAPTAIN.
LOOK AT THESE XBT READINGS! IT'S WORSE THAN I IMAGINED!
ATLANTIS HAS RISEN DIRECTLY IN THE PATH OF THE NORTH ATLANTIC DRIFT WHICH WARMS THE BRITISH ISLES. IF SOMETHING ISN'T DONE SOON--
"-- ENGLAND WILL BECOME A FROZEN WASTELAND WITHIN A YEAR!"
WHEW! DID ANYONE BRING CLOTHES PINS?
CONGRATULATIONS, CLASS! YOU ARE THE FIRST ARCHAEOLOGISTS TO EXCAVATE THE SITE WHICH MAY HOLD THE ORIGINS OF THE HUMAN RACE...
PERDÃO, MY ERUDITE EDUCATOR, BUT YOU AND YOUR STUDENTS ARE TRESPASSING. CONSIDER YOURSELVES PRISONERS OF THE PORTUGUESE NAVY!
CORRECTION, PEDRO--YOU AND YOUR TROOPS ARE THE ONLY PRISONERS ON THIS ISLAND...

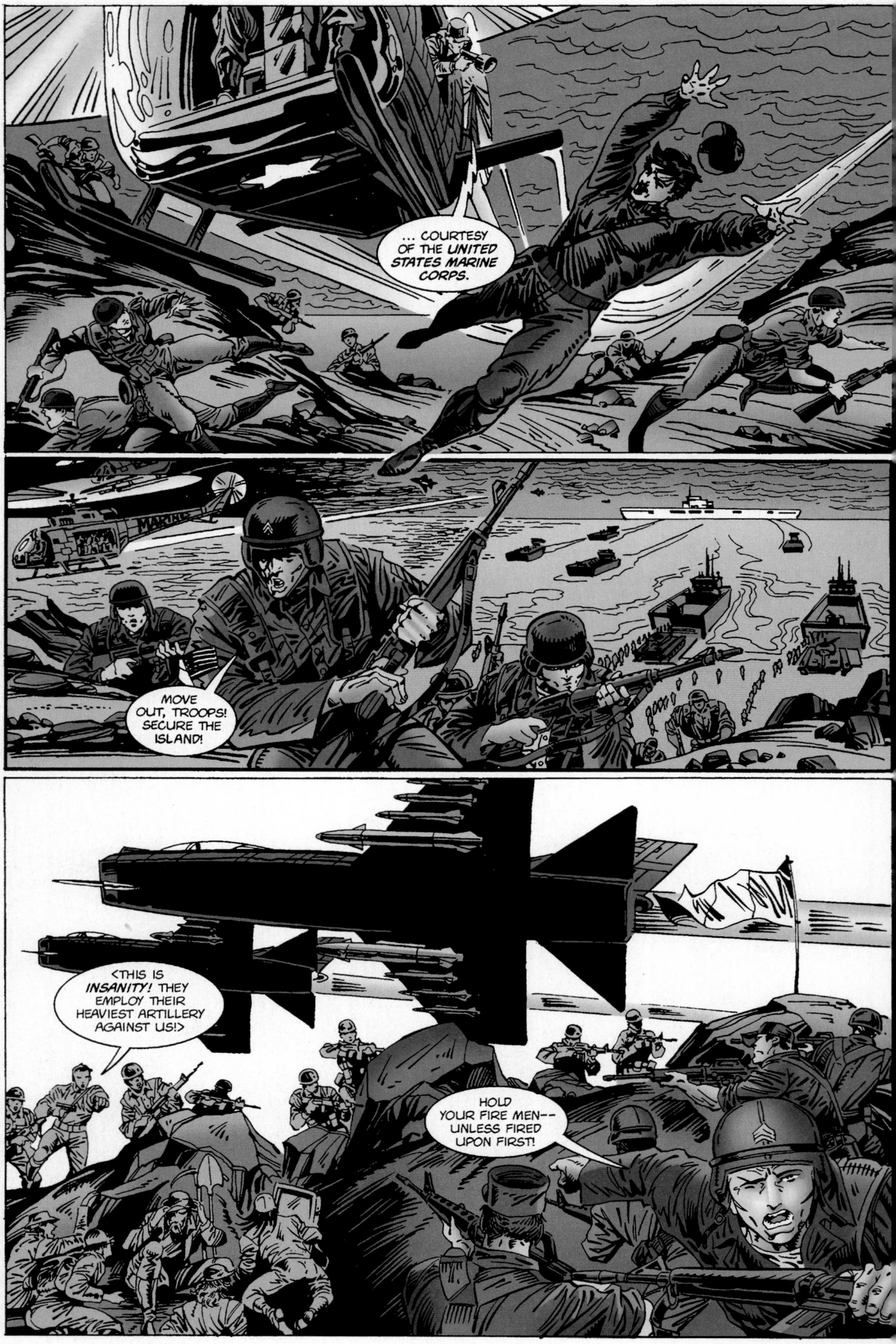
... COURTESY OF THE UNITED STATES MARINE CORPS.
MOVE OUT, TROOPS! SECURE THE ISLAND!
<THIS IS INSANITY! THEY EMPLOY THEIR HEAVIEST ARTILLERY AGAINST US!>
HOLD YOUR FIRE MEN-- UNLESS FIRED UPON FIRST!

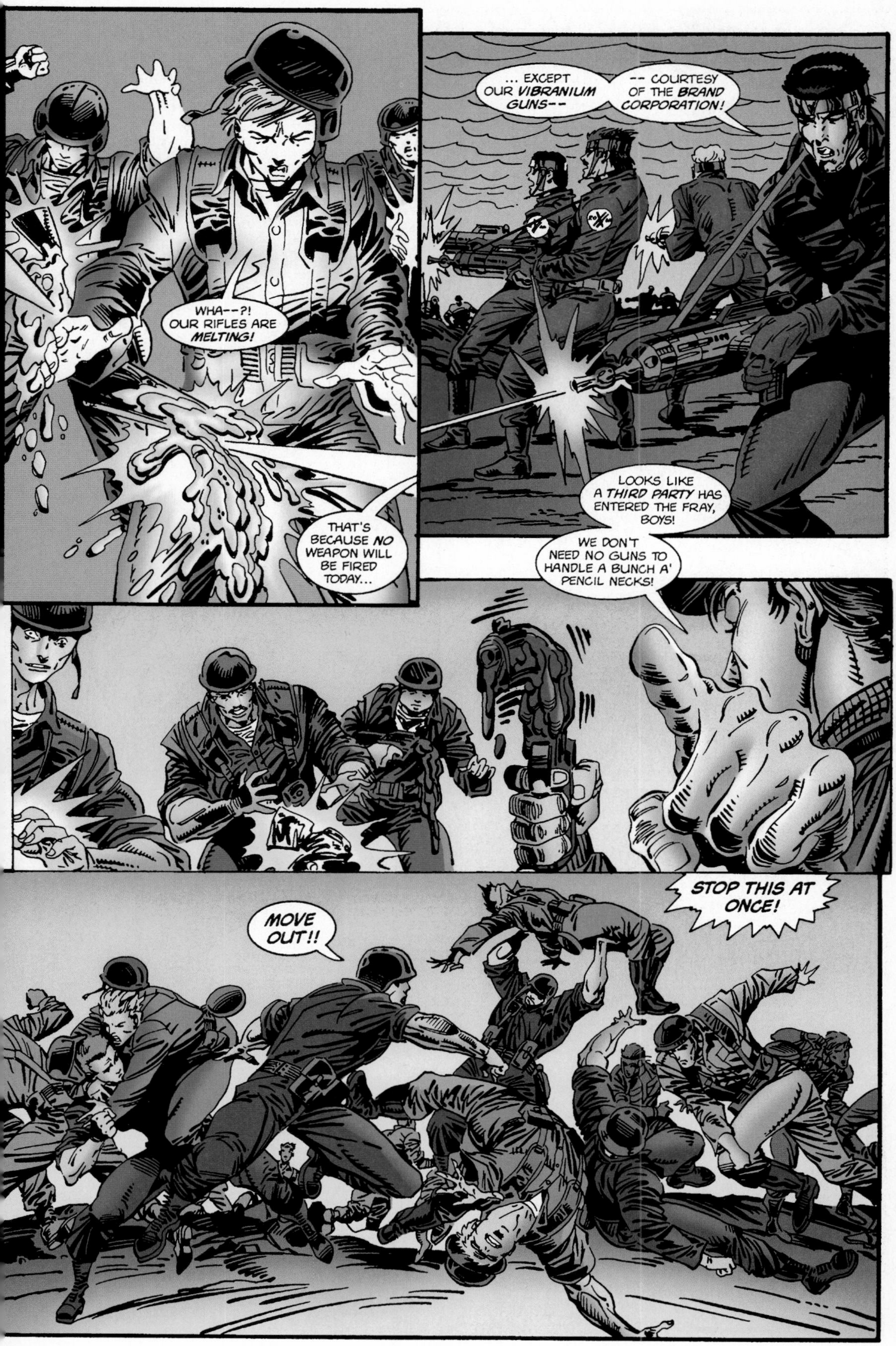
WHA--?! OUR RIFLES ARE MELTING!
THAT'S BECAUSE NO WEAPON WILL BE FIRED TODAY...
... EXCEPT OUR VIBRANIUM GUNS--
-- COURTESY OF THE BRAND CORPORATION!
LOOKS LIKE A THIRD PARTY HAS ENTERED THE FRAY, BOYS!
WE DON'T NEED NO GUNS TO HANDLE A BUNCH A' PENCIL NECKS!
MOVE OUT!!
STOP THIS AT ONCE!

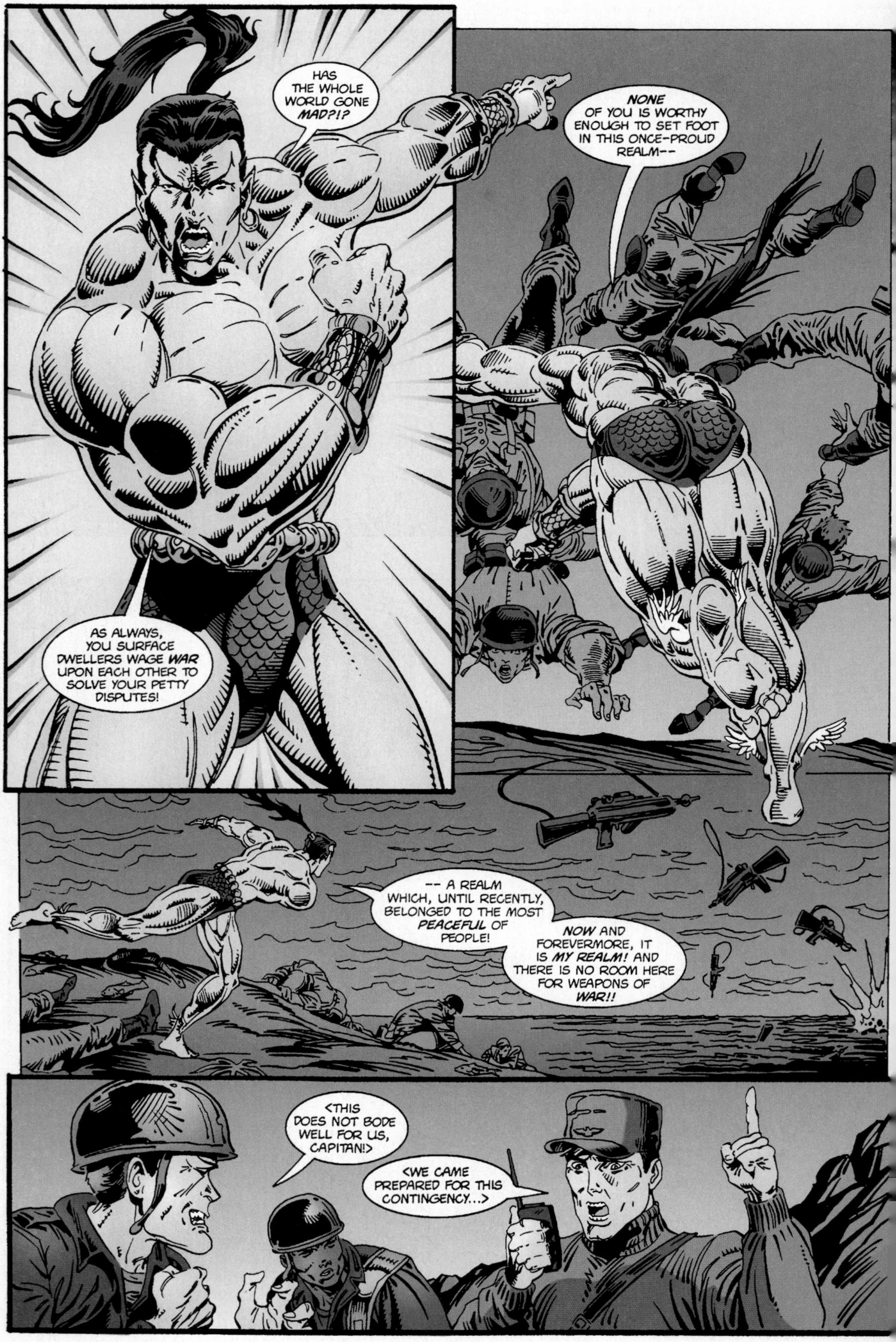
HAS THE WHOLE WORLD GONE *MAD?!?*
AS ALWAYS, YOU SURFACE DWELLERS WAGE *WAR* UPON EACH OTHER TO SOLVE YOUR PETTY DISPUTES!
NONE OF YOU IS WORTHY ENOUGH TO SET FOOT IN THIS ONCE-PROUD REALM--
-- A REALM WHICH, UNTIL RECENTLY, BELONGED TO THE MOST *PEACEFUL* OF PEOPLE!
NOW AND FOREVERMORE, IT IS *MY REALM!* AND THERE IS NO ROOM HERE FOR WEAPONS OF *WAR!!*
<THIS DOES NOT BODE WELL FOR US, CAPITAN!>
<WE CAME PREPARED FOR THIS CONTINGENCY...>

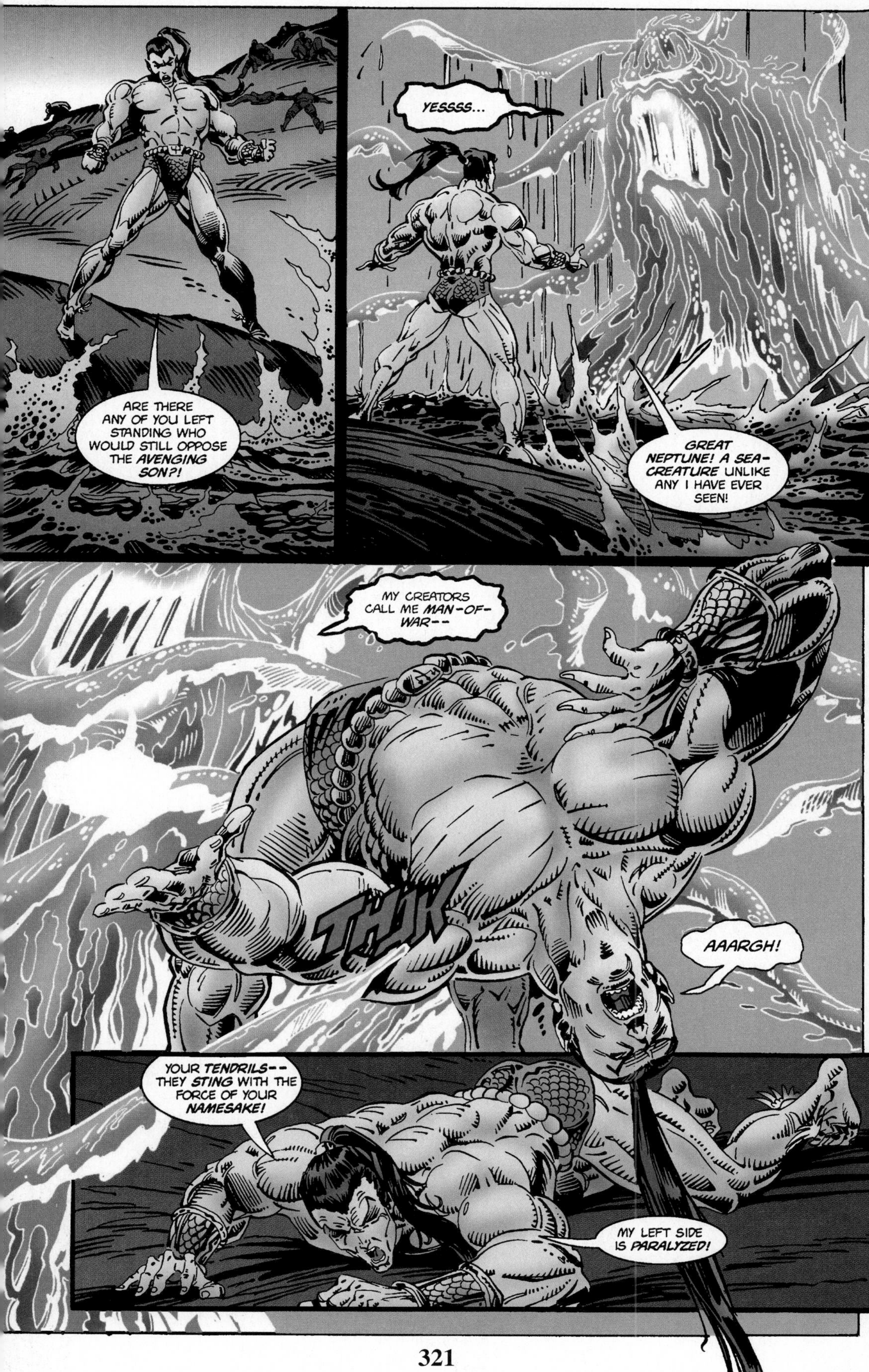
ARE THERE ANY OF YOU LEFT STANDING WHO WOULD STILL OPPOSE THE AVENGING SON?!
YESSSS...
GREAT NEPTUNE! A SEA-CREATURE UNLIKE ANY I HAVE EVER SEEN!
MY CREATORS CALL ME MAN-OF-WAR--
THUK
AAARGH!
YOUR TENDRILS--THEY STING WITH THE FORCE OF YOUR NAMESAKE!
MY LEFT SIDE IS PARALYZED!

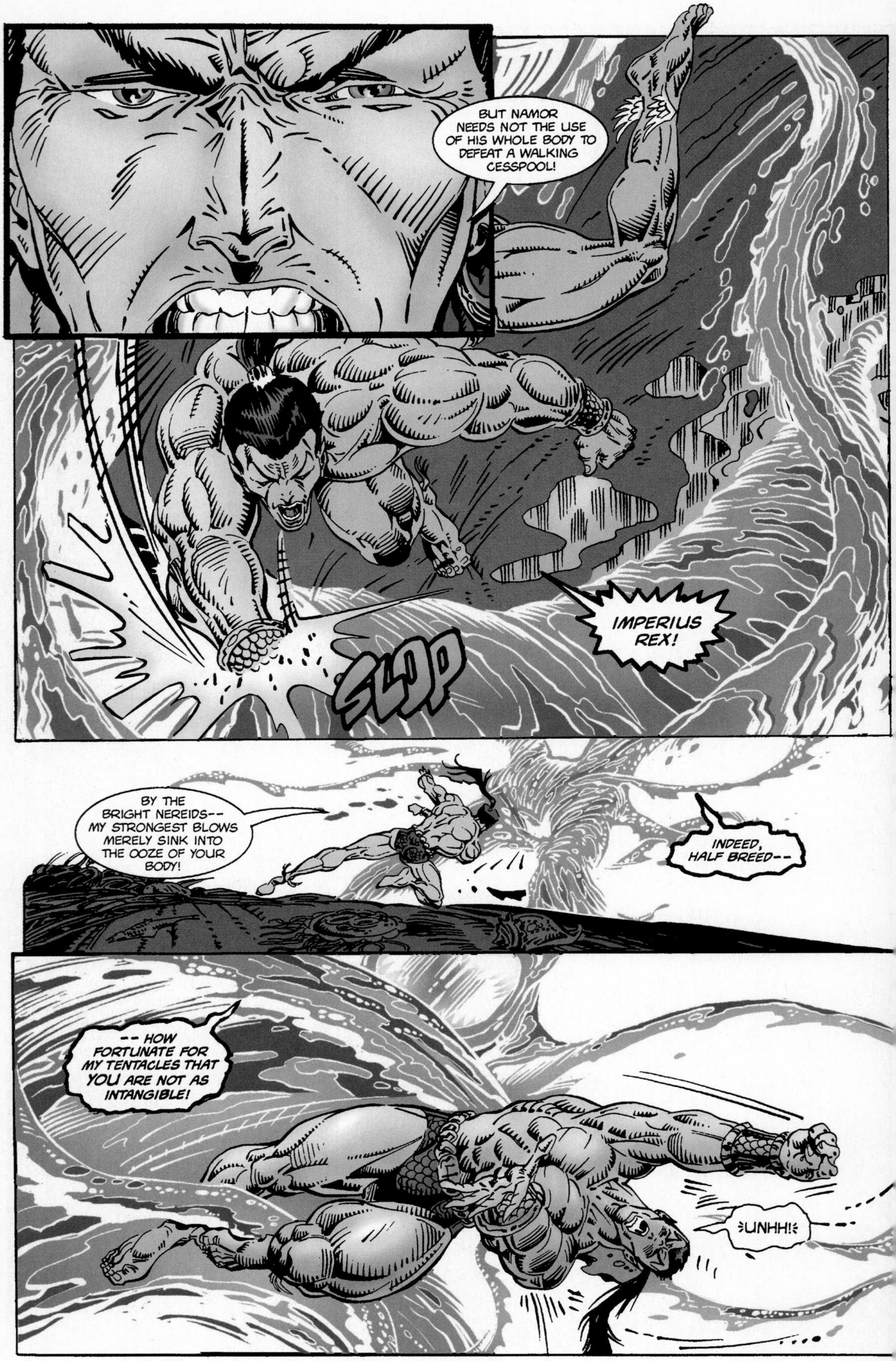
BUT NAMOR NEEDS NOT THE USE OF HIS WHOLE BODY TO DEFEAT A WALKING CESSPOOL!
IMPERIUS REX!
SLOP
BY THE BRIGHT NEREIDS-- MY STRONGEST BLOWS MERELY SINK INTO THE OOZE OF YOUR BODY!
INDEED, HALF BREED--
-- HOW FORTUNATE FOR MY TENTACLES THAT YOU ARE NOT AS INTANGIBLE!
UNHH!

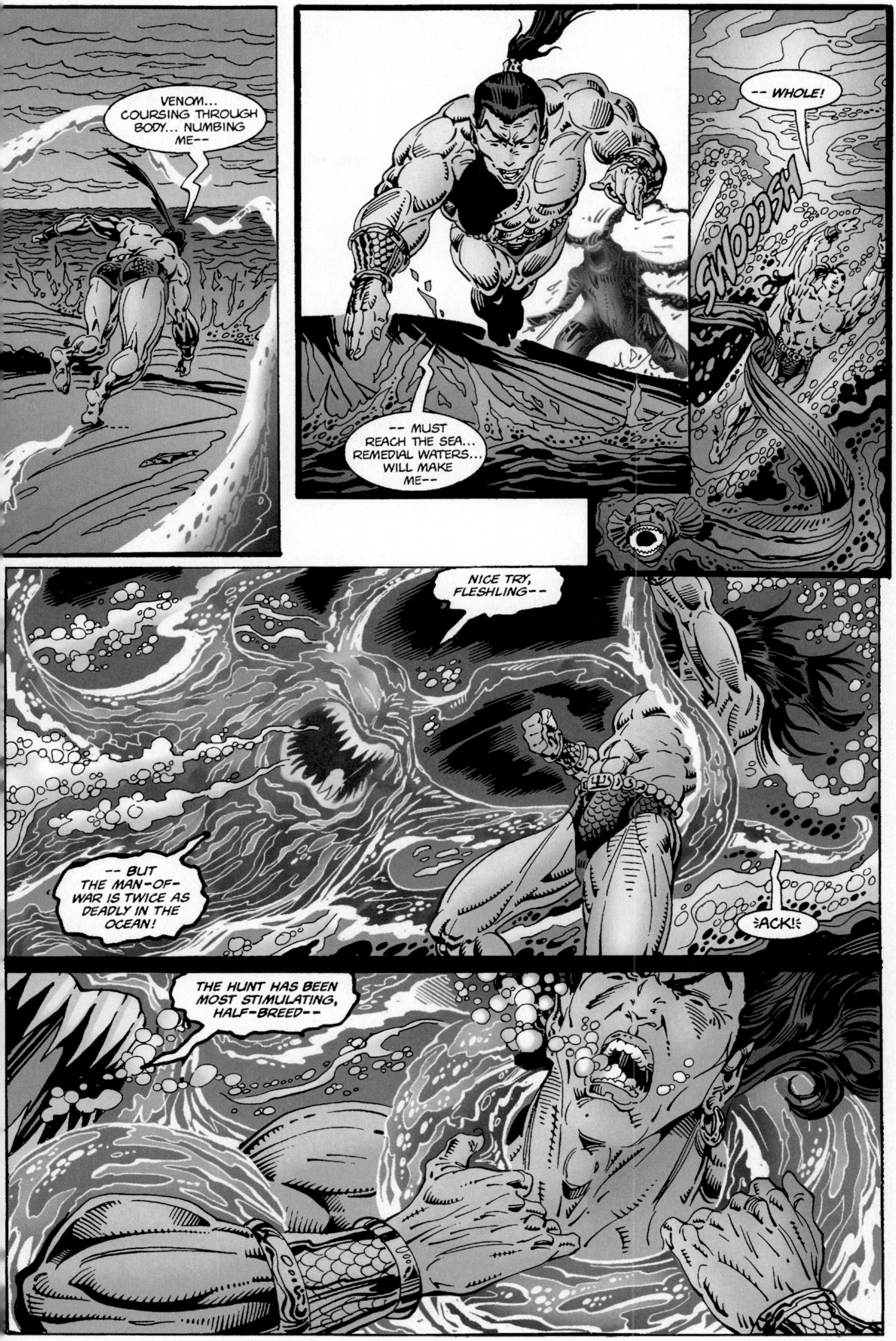
VENOM... COURSING THROUGH BODY... NUMBING ME--
-- MUST REACH THE SEA... REMEDIAL WATERS... WILL MAKE ME--
-- WHOLE!
SWOOOSH
NICE TRY, FLESHLING--
-- BUT THE MAN-OF-WAR IS TWICE AS DEADLY IN THE OCEAN!
ACK!
THE HUNT HAS BEEN MOST STIMULATING, HALF-BREED--

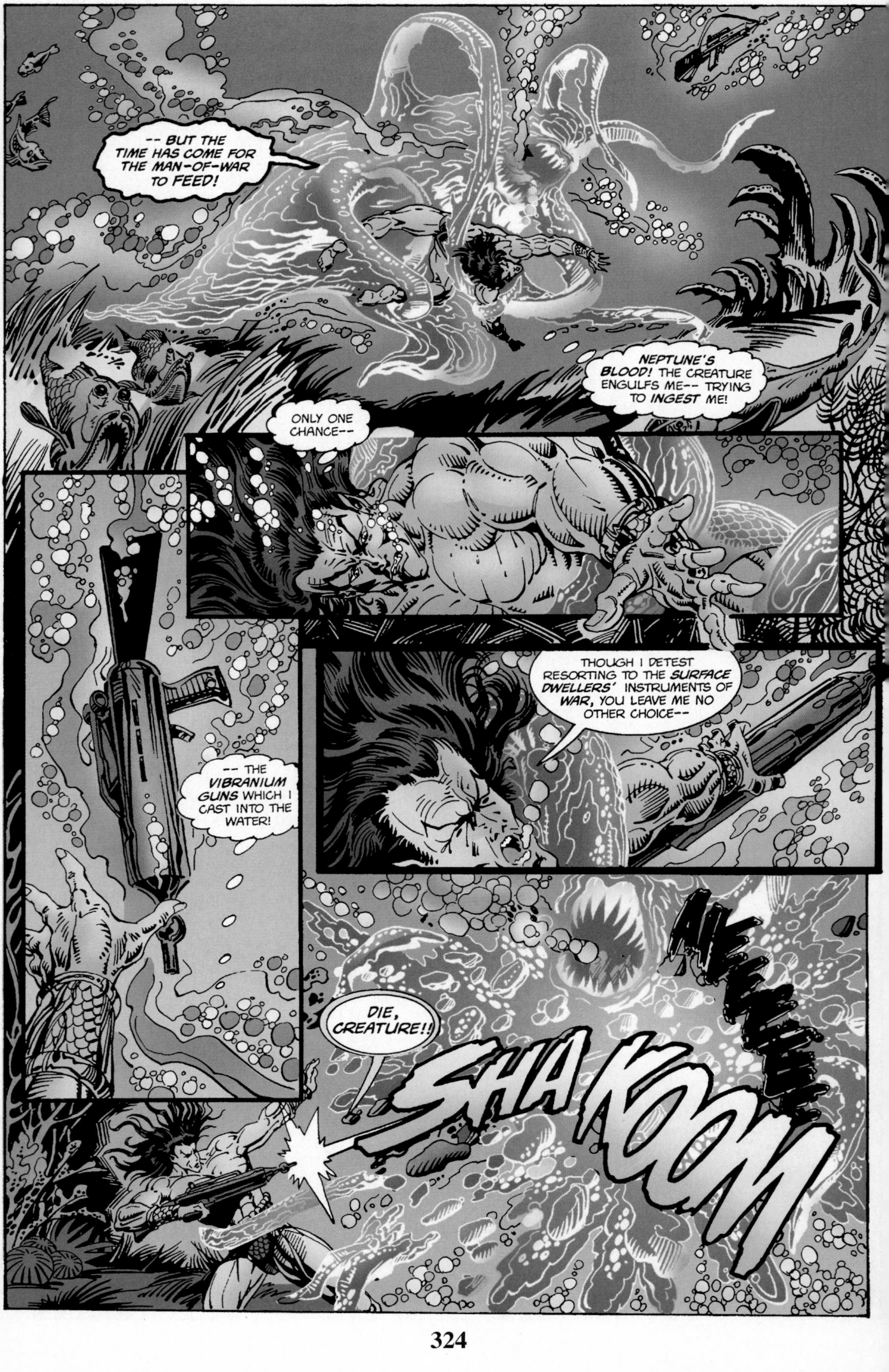
-- BUT THE TIME HAS COME FOR THE MAN-OF-WAR TO FEED!
NEPTUNE'S BLOOD! THE CREATURE ENGULFS ME-- TRYING TO INGEST ME!
ONLY ONE CHANCE--
-- THE VIBRANIUM GUNS WHICH I CAST INTO THE WATER!
THOUGH I DETEST RESORTING TO THE SURFACE DWELLERS' INSTRUMENTS OF WAR, YOU LEAVE ME NO OTHER CHOICE--
DIE, CREATURE!!
SHA KOOM

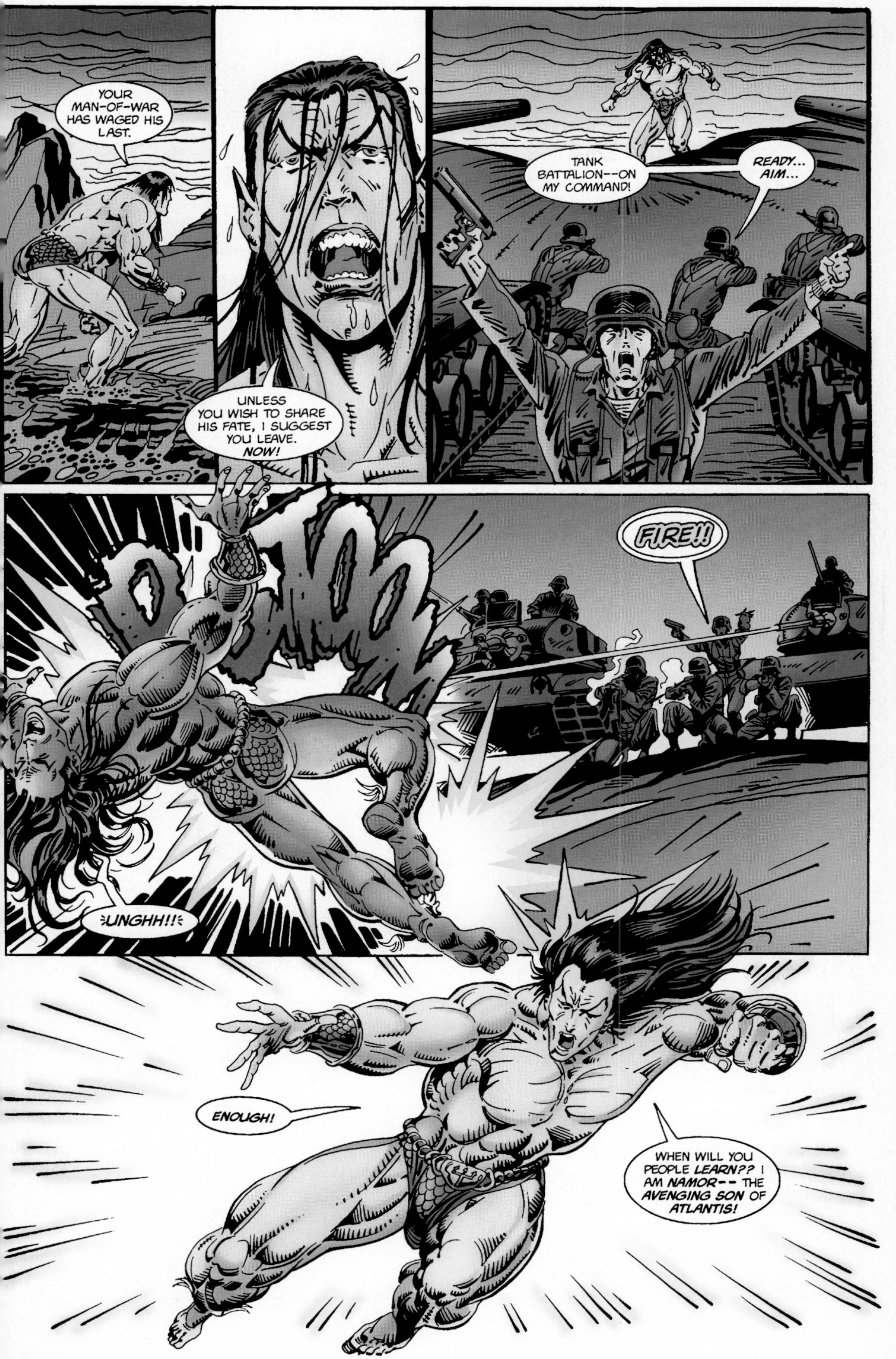
YOUR MAN-OF-WAR HAS WAGED HIS LAST.
UNLESS YOU WISH TO SHARE HIS FATE, I SUGGEST YOU LEAVE. NOW!
TANK BATTALION--ON MY COMMAND!
READY... AIM...
FIRE!!
UNGHH!!
ENOUGH!
WHEN WILL YOU PEOPLE LEARN?? I AM NAMOR-- THE AVENGING SON OF ATLANTIS!

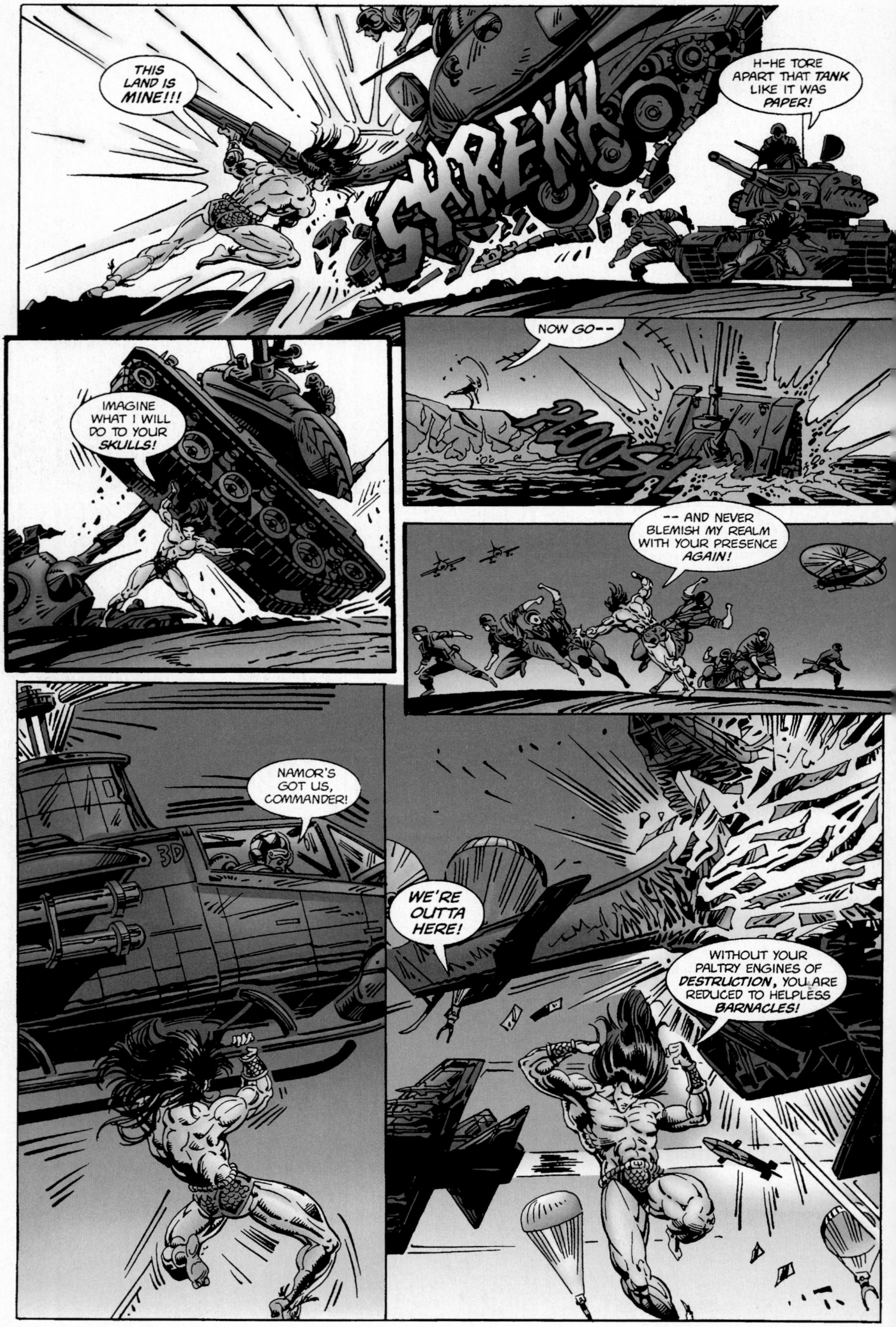

THIS LAND IS MINE!!!
SKREKK
H-HE TORE APART THAT TANK LIKE IT WAS PAPER!
IMAGINE WHAT I WILL DO TO YOUR SKULLS!
NOW GO--
PLOOSH
-- AND NEVER BLEMISH MY REALM WITH YOUR PRESENCE AGAIN!
NAMOR'S GOT US, COMMANDER!
3D
WE'RE OUTTA HERE!
WITHOUT YOUR PALTRY ENGINES OF DESTRUCTION, YOU ARE REDUCED TO HELPLESS BARNACLES!

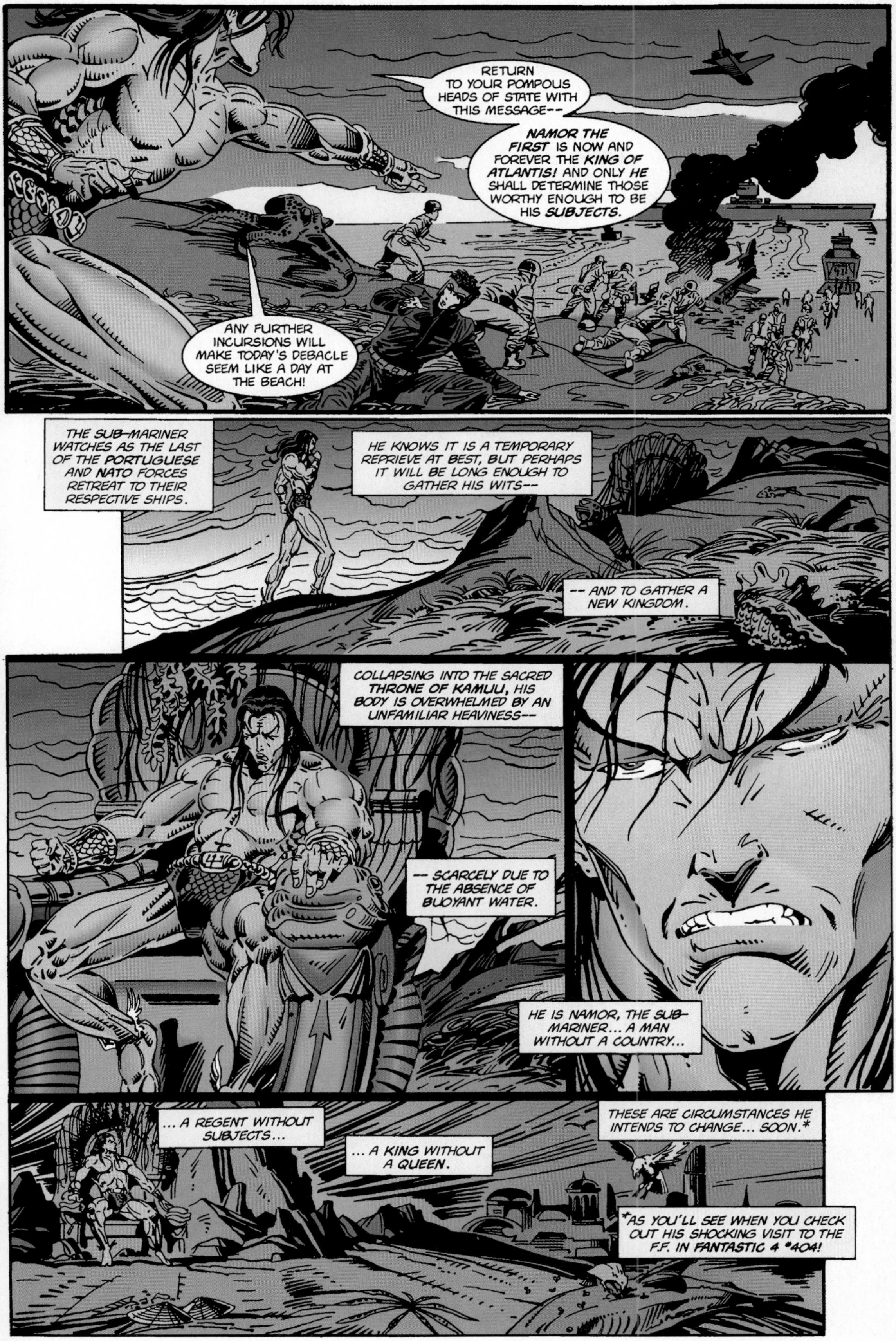
RETURN TO YOUR POMPOUS HEADS OF STATE WITH THIS MESSAGE--
NAMOR THE FIRST IS NOW AND FOREVER THE KING OF ATLANTIS! AND ONLY HE SHALL DETERMINE THOSE WORTHY ENOUGH TO BE HIS SUBJECTS.
ANY FURTHER INCURSIONS WILL MAKE TODAY'S DEBACLE SEEM LIKE A DAY AT THE BEACH!
THE SUB-MARINER WATCHES AS THE LAST OF THE PORTUGUESE AND NATO FORCES RETREAT TO THEIR RESPECTIVE SHIPS.
HE KNOWS IT IS A TEMPORARY REPRIEVE AT BEST, BUT PERHAPS IT WILL BE LONG ENOUGH TO GATHER HIS WITS--
-- AND TO GATHER A NEW KINGDOM.
COLLAPSING INTO THE SACRED THRONE OF KAMUU, HIS BODY IS OVERWHELMED BY AN UNFAMILIAR HEAVINESS--
-- SCARCELY DUE TO THE ABSENCE OF BUOYANT WATER.
HE IS NAMOR, THE SUB-MARINER... A MAN WITHOUT A COUNTRY...
... A REGENT WITHOUT SUBJECTS...
... A KING WITHOUT A QUEEN.
THESE ARE CIRCUMSTANCES HE INTENDS TO CHANGE... SOON.*
*AS YOU'LL SEE WHEN YOU CHECK OUT HIS SHOCKING VISIT TO THE F.F. IN FANTASTIC 4 #404!

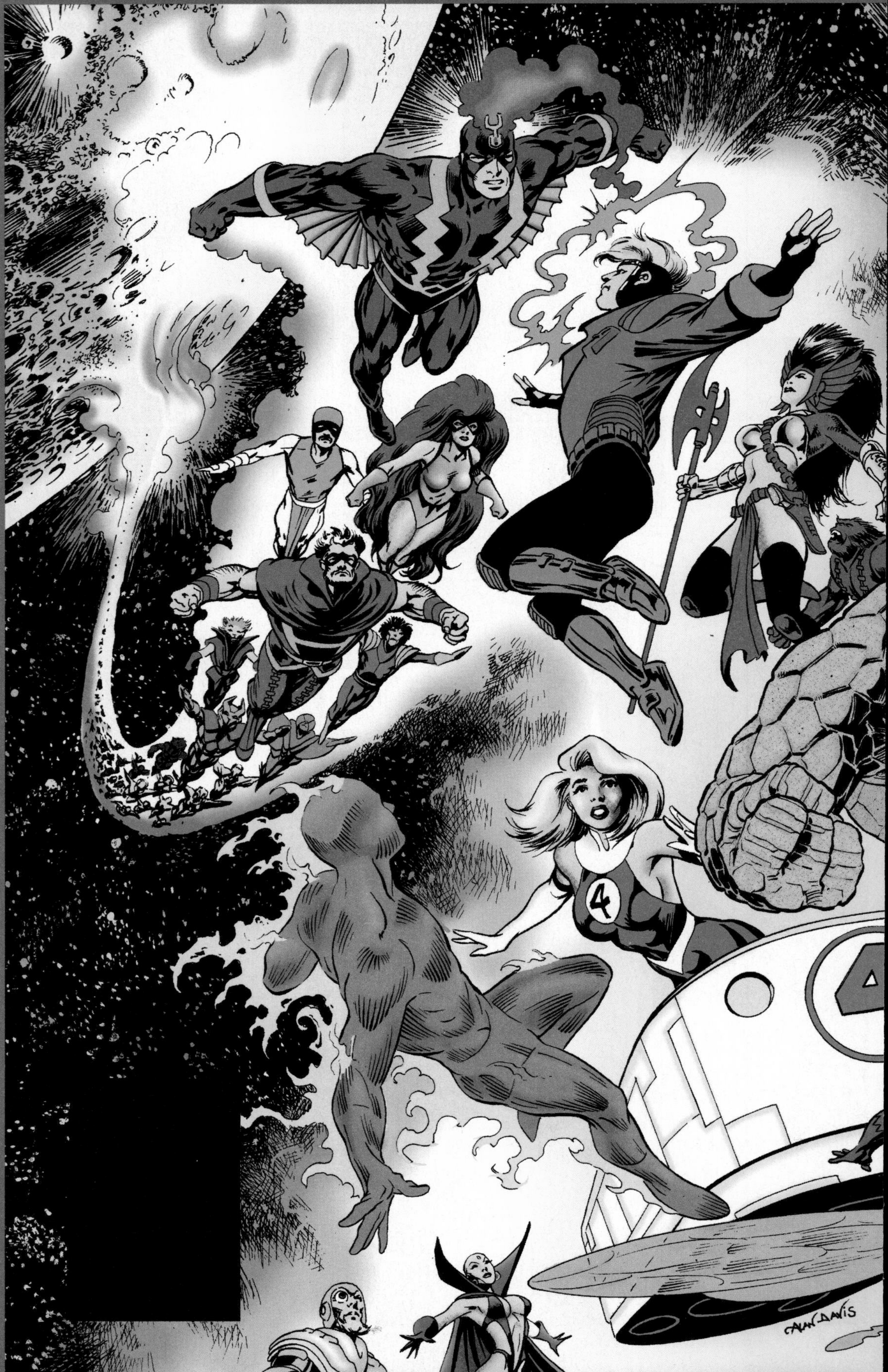
ALAN DAVIS

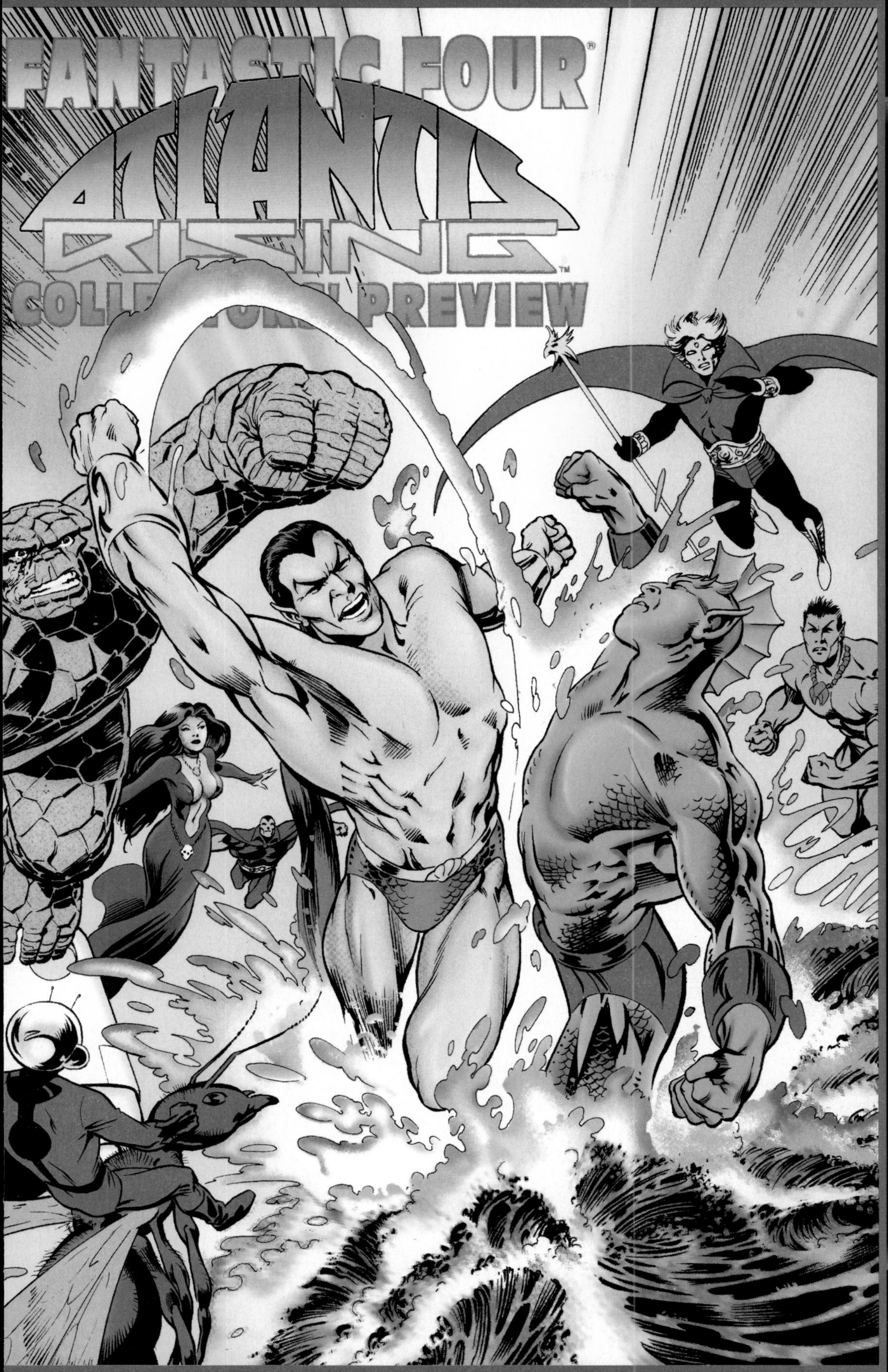
FANTASTIC FOUR®
ATLANTIS
RISING™
PREVIEW

THE ATLANTIS CROSSING

Atlantis is rising. Namor takes some pretty drastic actions, alienating people as usual. The concept could have been that simple and straightforward.

Under the helm of FANTASTIC FOUR writer Tom DeFalco and Mark Gruenwald, Marvel Editor-in-Chief of Super Heroes and Cosmic Powers, however, what could have just been a tale centering on angry, dislocated ocean-dwellers is slated to involve Reed Richards' sinister father Nathaniel Richards, classic Marvel villainess Morgan Le Fey, a giant tidal wave heading straight for Monster Island, the disappearance of the Infinity Gems, just about all of Marvel's entire pack of Inhumans, and plenty of new faces. Of course, the Fantastic Four, Fantastic Force, and Warlock and the Infinity Watch are caught right smack in the middle of the mess.

Marvel Universe crossovers have a reputation for being all-encompassing patchworks disrupting the status quo and linking old and new characters and continuities. This spring's "Atlantis Rising" is no exception. According to DeFalco, Gruenwald, and former FANTASTIC FOUR editor Ralph Macchio, "Atlantis Rising" represents the ordinary crossover formula multiplied times 10. Atlantis actually rises as the ultimate cliffhanger/climax of NAMOR's final issue, #62, shipping in March. The epic storyline then runs through two special one-shots called ATLANTIS RISING ALPHA and OMEGA, FANTASTIC FOUR #401-402, FANTASTIC FORCE #8-9, and is calculated to take WARLOCK AND THE INFINITY WATCH out with a bang in its final two issues, #41-42. The plot is jam-packed with world-disrupting crises, competing villains, and more than a passing link to the action-packed, classic Jack Kirby/Stan Lee era of the FANTASTIC FOUR's first 100 issues.

"We approached Tom DeFalco and asked, 'what sorts of things could we do if we played around with the whole FANTASTIC FOUR mythos and threw all the pieces in different and interesting ways?'" Gruenwald said. "'Atlantis Rising' definitely stems from FANTASTIC FOUR continuity, but it will *not* be like the same things we've seen before."

While a popular shelf topic at new age bookstores, raising Atlantis in the Marvel Universe was a completely new idea. Originally conceived by NAMOR writer Glenn Herdling, its purpose was to cause tidal waves just in that title. Green-skinned and blue-skinned Atlanteans had attacked the surface world multiple times, but Herdling intended "Atlantis Rising" to have nothing to do in terms of action or tone with the "Atlantis Attacks" scenario that ran through 1989's summer annuals.

"We needed something to hype up NAMOR a little bit," Herdling offered. "We'd destroyed Atlantis so many times in the

past that
it's just get-
ing routine;
you know, new
writer comes on
board, gotta
destroy Atlantis. It's
getting boring. So I said,
well, what would be some-
thing different we could do with Atlantis?
Well, we've never *raised* Atlantis before.'"

The intent to keep the story far from
the same old Atlantis routine continues
into Gruenwald's vision of the series.
Other than the fact that they involve
Atlantis, 'Atlantis Attacks' and 'Atlantis
Rising' are *nothing* like each other," he
stressed. "For one thing, Atlanteans don't
like Atlantis rising because they don't
want a piece of their real estate to be in
the air. It's not going to be Atlantis con-
quers the surface world; this is a turf war
or a piece of real estate."

Competing for Atlantis will be various
factions of the Inhumans, the alien
Deviant Tantalus, and Morgan Le Fey, who
actually raises Atlantis in the first place.
Morgan, a sorceress who has wreaked
havoc for Spider-Woman, among others,
while trapped on the astral plane for centuries, has now been physically reincarnated. "When her memories from her previous life come through, she wants to raise
Avalon, the kingdom she once ruled. We
learn that Avalon was once a province of

Atlantis,
so by
doing so,
she raises
Atlantis."

Ironically, the one
group that will have
the *least* interest in the
risen land is the Atlanteans
themselves. The implications of such an
event actually would be devastating for
the Atlanteans who suffocate in the open
air. "All the Atlanteans who are now living
there have to try to get off quick," said
Herdling. "Of course, many don't make it."

According to Gruenwald, it will not
be the entire massive continent of Atlantis
that will rise, only sections that will simply
appear like a new chain of large islands
—very rugged, arid, empty islands. "They
won't have a lot of vegetation because
(the land) has been at the bottom of the
sea. It will, however, include the capital
city of Atlantis, but no other architecture.
It's basically going to be a barren hunk of
rock that will be claimed by factions who
want to grab it to accomplish their various
goals."

Then-FANTASTIC FOUR editor Ralph
Macchio felt the idea had too many
exciting implications to be used just in
NAMOR. He pitched the idea first at an
Avengers summit. At this time, though, the
story just involved Atlantis, with the
Inhumans yet to be added to the sce-

nario. Members of the Avengers creative teams, however, felt it was too NAMOR-specific. Then, about eight months ago, Mark Gruenwald, now Editor-in-Chief of Marvel Super Heroes and Cosmic Powers, was looking for the perfect plotline for a momentous event in the FANTASTIC FOUR line of books—some really great crossover material. Simultaneously, FANTASTIC FOUR writer Tom DeFalco was planning a set of exciting plot twists to lead up to and culminate in FANTASTIC FOUR #400 and had no interest in anything to do with Atlantis. Then over one of those Marvel crossover power lunches, Ralph Macchio came up with a new dimension to the story, one that involved Nathaniel Richards and the Inhumans, and DeFalco became *very* interested.

"Originally, it seemed boring to me because it was such a real world story," DeFalco recalled, with a chuckle. "In the real world, civilizations and countries will go to war over 10 yards of land, but in the comic book world, the stakes aren't high enough. Then, as we discussed it more and more, I realized how it could play into something that I wanted to do. As a result of the events in FANTASTIC FOUR #400, the Watcher is no longer at his Citadel, and Reed Richards' father, Nathaniel Richards—a sweet, loving person—decides to sneak into the Watcher's headquarters and steal all the scientific stuff going on there. (This) sets off some fail-safes which cause the Blue Area of the Moon basically to cease to exist, which really wouldn't be a problem except the Inhumans live there.

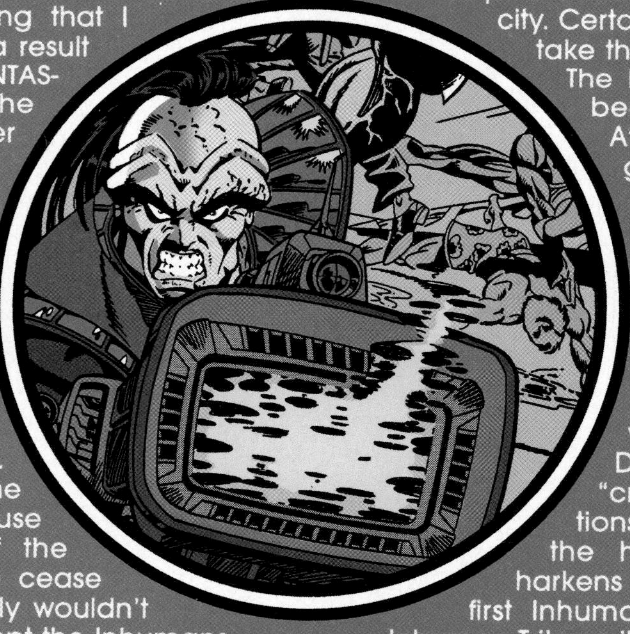

"So we now have this established civilization that really needs a place to go and live. Once I got to that point, I thought, 'Oh, and they're going to bring up Atlantis.' I suddenly saw a connection between the two, and I said, 'Oh, man, I can't believe it. I'm doing the same goofy story that I didn't like (at first). I suckered myself into it."

Tossing in the Inhumans and current FANTASTIC FOUR nemesis Nathaniel Richards suddenly transformed an idea that could have seemed too NAMOR-specific into a full-fledged FANTASTIC FOUR storyline. "It's ironic that the guy who originally opposed this is the one who's going to carry it out and make it great," Gruenwald noted, adding that because DeFalco is such a good writer, it makes his editorial job all the more easier and enjoyable. In fact, because of Gruenwald's confidence in DeFalco, he asked him to pen the initial outline of what events will happen in each episode of the crossover.

According to DeFalco, the Fantastic Four will set off on a mission to rescue the Inhumans, who, similarly to the Atlanteans, find themselves without a suitable atmosphere. The only catch, he said, will be a major one—"Unfortunately, the Fantastic Four and the Inhumans are not getting along these days. They solve the problem in a very unique manner; they drop a shrinking bomb on the city. Certain of the Inhumans take this as an act of war. The Fantastic Four only become aware of Atlantis when they get back to Earth on the run."

Back to create mayhem will be mad geneticist Maximus, developer of the super-weapon, the Atmo-Gun, a weapon, which in DeFalco's words, "creates sonic vibrations that could destroy the human race and harkens back to the very first Inhumans story." Aquatic Inhuman Triton will also play a major role, which will assure "he will lose a lot of friends." He has also thrown in new Inhuman characters, such as Ator, who leads a strike force called the Crimson Cadre, introduced a few issues before the crossover in FANTASTIC FOUR. "When we think of the Inhumans, we think based on the royal family (Black Bolt, Medusa, Crystal, etc.), but these are just other fighters; we can have familiar faces doing nasty things."

In terms of character development among the actual Fantastic Four, DeFalco offered just four sentences: "Johnny will be dealing with some new heartaches that have been dropped on him as a result of #400. Sue is also going to be dealing with coming to terms with some information she has learned in #400. Kristoff will be getting used to his new duties as a member of the Fantastic Four. And nothing bad happens to Ben in these two issues."

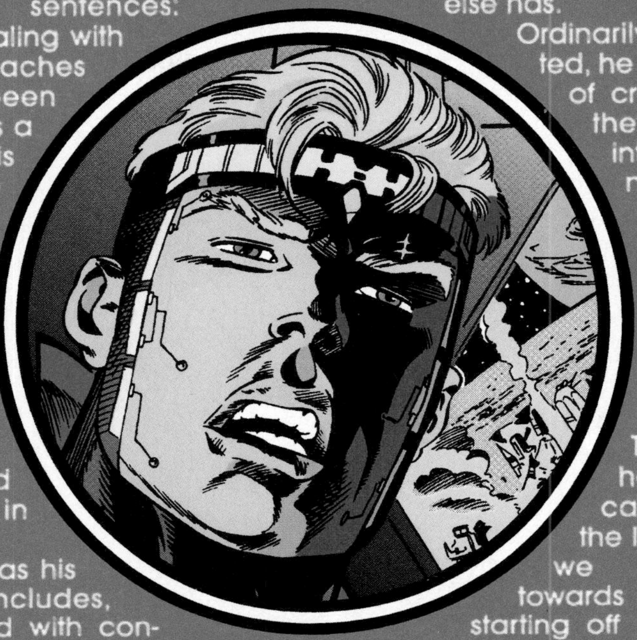

As for Namor, as his own title concludes, Herdling was faced with condensing a three-part storyline and tying up any loose ends in one issue. NAMOR #62 is not officially part of the crossover but launches the whole shebang which includes the actual first motions of the continent's raising by Morgan Le Fey. As the crossover continues, Namor himself will continue to play a key role, but, as DeFalco described him, "He's going to end up essentially a man without a country. He's going to become Namor, the avenging son again. He's going to be going through major angst. A great part of his people will be destroyed in the upheaval and the rest have lost their land. He's going to do some very foolish things and just endear himself to everyone," says DeFalco with affectionate sarcasm.

Both DeFalco and Gruenwald stated that they wanted to bring back more of an anti-hero edge to the character, the shades of gray that could make him a villain more easily than a hero like he once was portrayed. "He's not going to be the sweetheart (he's been in recent times)," DeFalco continued. "The only difference is that he's still going to have a thing for Sue. Their relationship is going to start heating up again as she starts to get on with her life. At least initially, he has the front row seat. But Sue has come into her own in the last couple of years. She's no longer the shy, retiring, sweet thing that she used to be, and Namor's going to have a hard time dealing with that just like everybody else has."

Ordinarily, DeFalco admitted, he is not all that fond of crossovers because they can develop into a coordination nightmare between editors and writers, but for "Atlantis Rising," he makes an exception because, in his view, the timing was perfect. "FANTASTIC FOUR has had a very complicated storyline for the last few years, and we were building towards a conclusion and starting off in new directions. Everything comes to a climax in issue #400, so Mark had come to me and said, 'well, what comes next?' I bounced off a couple of ideas for the next couple of storylines. What I didn't realize is that he was actually soliciting ideas for a crossover."

More than that, he refused to take credit for all the good ideas, stating that one of the pleasurable aspects of this crossover is precisely the cooperative creative spirit that has developed between him and the other writers and editors involved. "As we all started talking, me, Mark Gruenwald, Tom (FANTASTIC FORCE) Brevoort, Glenn Herdling, and John (WARLOCK) Arcudi, everybody started throwing ideas into the pile. It just seemed that we were all going in similar directions, so we're getting to have fun together."

Initially, he had only outlined the first half of the crossover, just enough to help the marketing department pen their solicitations and advertising, and in order to leave other writers plenty of freedom to add their own ideas. "At least Mark Gruenwald and Ralph Macchio, and I, all know what the final goal is and where it all ends. We only did the first part, hoping that in the course of working with it, the other guys could come up with maybe even better directions."

Speaking of that conclusion, i.e. who

wins Atlantis, DeFalco stressed that the intention right now was that all the contenders would lose to some extent, but some would "lose more fatally than others. The question is not how much you're going to win at the end but how much is this going to cost you in the course. Nobody walks away glowing. Well, one person walks away glowing for at least a page, and then," DeFalco laughed heartily, "he gets it. *Boy, does he get it.*"

Finding a link to FANTASTIC FORCE was not difficult since Franklin Richards is also Nathaniel Richards' grandson and Reed and Sue's son, and this new team was conceived as a successor of sorts to the old ideals of the Fantastic Four. According to Gruenwald, adding a fledgling series into a crossover is not any more challenging than working with an older, more established one, such as FANTASTIC FOUR, but the process still has its subtle distinctions.

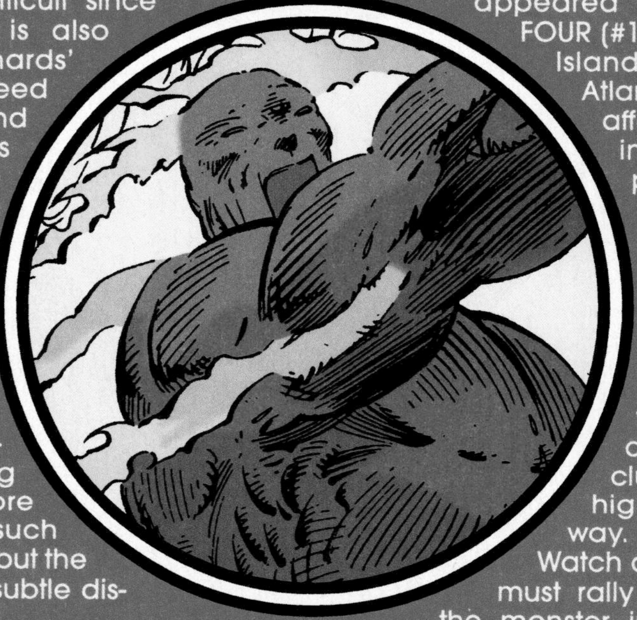

"There is not that much difference once you figure out the logical fit for that book being in the crossover," Gruenwald said. "The only difference between FANTASTIC FORCE and FANTASTIC FOUR, which will be over 400 issues old, is that FANTASTIC FOUR has a whole lot of continuity to play with, along with a status quo that everyone knows can be changed. FANTASTIC FORCE, however, is only nine issues old, it doesn't have that back-story, so if you mess with it, it doesn't mean as much. You have to bear it in mind that it may not be as meaningful to make a major change in a new book."

As for FORCE members, DeFalco said to watch for Franklin Richards to continue down a road he will start in FANTASTIC FOUR #400. "It'll be the kind of change we did with Sue (Richards) where we slowly added to her character. For a while, people said, 'man, what a b-ch.' And then they realized, 'oh, she had to change.'" Devlor, of course, must choose sides between the Fantastic Four and Forc and his people, the Inhumans.

While WARLOCK AND THE INFINIT WATCH has never been closely tied to th FANTASTIC FOUR, Gruenwald defende the series' inclusion in the crossover o grounds of both Marvel history and se mic logic. "To begin with, we decided t get the WARLOCK book involve because Adam Warlock premiered a 'Him' in FANTASTIC FOUR (#66). Also, a sup porting character, the Mole Ma appeared in the FANTASTI FOUR (#1). Besides, Monst Island is also in th Atlantic and would b affected by the sh in the tectoni plate, the tid wave, and all th chaos."

Inclusion i the "Atlant Rising" crossove allowe Gruenwald an the book's cre ative team to co clude the book in high-profile, excitin way. First off, the Infinit Watch and the Mole Ma must rally together to hel the monster inhabitants of th island to higher ground and safety. Th logical conclusion of the series will hav more to do with the impact of events ta gential to the actual disaster, such as th sudden vanishing of the Infinity Gem which provided the whole reason for th teaming of the Infinity Watch.

"Warlock discovers the answer to th mystery of who Maxam is, the big cha acter from the future who's been hangin around for a couple of dozen issues now Gruenwald added. "This results in a co flict between the two characters which resolved in a dramatic way that leave Warlock '*incapacitated*,' shall we say? A the end of the Infinity Watch, the group basically split up, having lost its purpose As far as where the Infinity Gems go, tha will actually be answered in a separat publication called SILVER SURFER/RUNE, tie-in with Malibu (Marvel's sister compa ny). Individuals have various fates. W leave them in various places. Nobod dies permanently, but they have becom scattered as a result of an event which happens concurrent to the first ATLANTIS RISING, which comes out in April."

All of which underlines Gruenwald's contention that "The neat thing about this is that virtually all of it will stem from the FANTASTIC FOUR continuity at some point in its 30-plus year history. *That's the back story.*"

And by the way, at the end of "Atlantis Rising," the continent does not somehow get sent back down again at the end of the crossover. Gruenwald intends to leave the land mass up "for good, indefinitely," hoping it will stimulate even more exciting and provocative plot twists.

"We haven't done any more long-range thinking about the characters themselves and where they are going to end up by the end of the storyline," Gruenwald offered enthusiastically. "The whole point of moving players around on the chessboard in different configurations is to make things interesting. We're hoping that just the fact that they're in different positions will spur ideas and interesting storylines."

When Herdling first suggested the concept of raising Atlantis, he said that he hoped it would become a "new playground for Marvel characters." While other editors have not expressed an intent to pick up on the plotline yet, it will be open to them, Gruenwald noted. Conversely, he also would neither promise nor write off the possibility of an actual INHUMANS limited or ongoing series in the near future. In his words, "We have no concrete plans right now. We're using this event to consolidate many of the concepts in the line rather than to relaunch anything, but it's certainly being considered."

DeFalco noted, though, that plenty of other Marvel super heroes will appear as at least one or two panel guest-stars in ATLANTIS RISING. "We're going to try and stick in as many as we can because (FANTASTIC FOUR penciler) Paul Ryan has been complaining to me that every other issue he's got to create and design new characters and there are so many old ones that he would love to have the opportunity to draw. After this crossover, he's never going to make that comment again. A lot of people are going to show up for a panel or two. Avengers, X-Men, Spider-Man, we're going to have the whole universe. Obviously, Thunderstrike has to have his panel just to make a fool of himself."

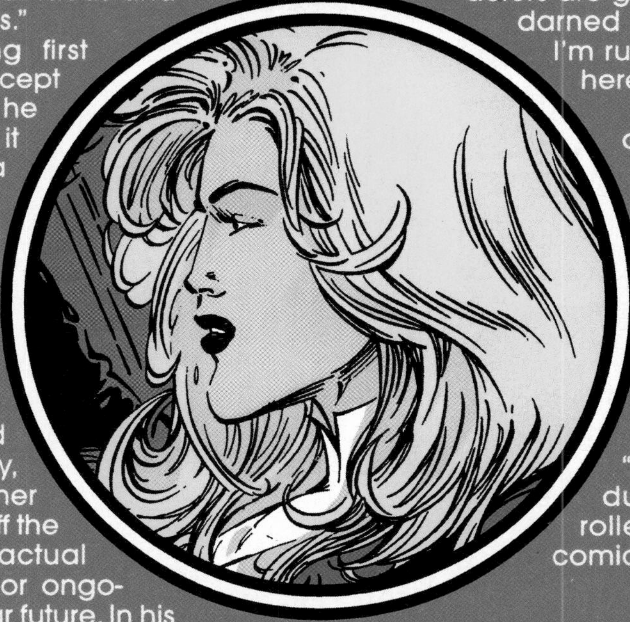

No longer fettered by the daily office grind of being Marvel's Editor-in-Chief, DeFalco is content to sit at his computer terminal in his home office beneath a giant poster-sized flowchart that spreads across an entire wall.

"Yeah, there's a lot of stuff going on in FANTASTIC FOUR, and I keep swearing that we've got to make life easier for ourselves," DeFalco said, the "we" referring to Ryan, whom he considers a complete plotting partner. "My flowchart for where the book is going, where all the characters are going, has gotten so darned complicated that I'm running out of space here."

"What Paul Ryan and myself are trying to do with the FANTASTIC FOUR is to match the spirit of the FANTASTIC FOUR of the '60s as opposed to just really copying the past," he added, summing it all up. "We're trying to produce the wildest rollercoaster ride in comics."

Anya Martin *is a fiction writer and freelance journalist who has written extensively about comics and rock music.*

GEOGRAPHIC ISOLATION

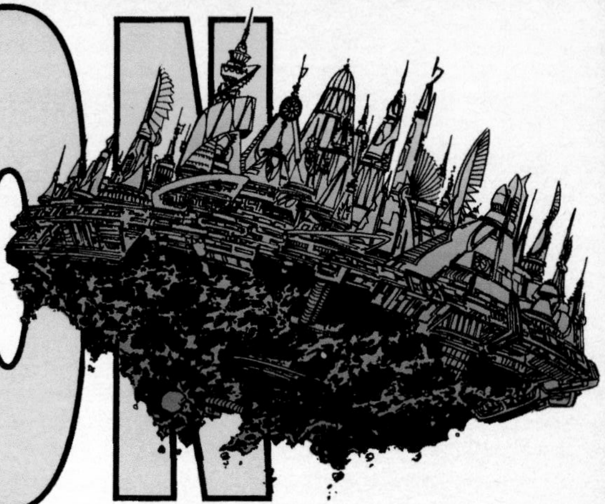

The deep blue waters of the Atlantic Ocean hold many secrets. Over time, the waves have provided a refuge for those who desired an escape from human civilization. For example, the sunken continent of Atlantis, now an underwater haven for the water-breathing Atlanteans, sank beneath the surface thousands of years ago.

But Atlantis isn't the only such pivotal island that exists (or has existed) in the waters of the Atlantic to the east and southeast of the United States. In the region of the Bermuda Triangle stands Monster Island, and other seemingly mythical islands that have appeared in the Atlantic waters at one time or another include Attilan and Avalon. Something drew all these civilizations to settle there, and the answers to their mysteries lie within the deep dark waters.

Atlantis itself was a small continent that sank about twenty thousand years ago. Over the centuries, the ancient race of underwater beings survived and prospered in their undersea city, but always remained enemies to the humans who treated the oceans poorly. (This Atlantis is actually one of *two* such cities, the other of which existed for a time under the icy waters off the Antarctic.) Prince Namor, leader of the Atlanteans, has been allies with — and savagely fought *against* — the many humans and mutants who struggle above the surface. Atlantis has remained somewhat isolated from human contact, at times, and it's future fate will depend upon it's relation to the surface societies.

Monster Island is located in the heart of the Bermuda Triangle, a place plagued with mystery and intrigue. Recently, Adam Warlock and his Infinity Watch have settled there to protect the all-powerful Infinity Gems. The value of Monster Island lies in it's location in the Bermuda Triangle, a location feared by humans and far out in the infamous, remote Atlantic waters. Thus, it is another example of it's residents fear of human discovery, and of isolation to avoid contact.

One island that no longer exists in the Atlantic region, but had a history

Inhumans. Attilan was the ancient safe haven built by the Inhumans in the Northern Atlantic ocean, to separate themselves from the savage humans of centuries past. The Inhumans themselves are a race of advanced humans that have called Earth "home" since the early existence of mankind. In the 20th century, the Inhumans — still advanced beyond human understanding — decided to move their island city to a more remote location tucked away in the Himalayan Mountains. Black Bolt, Ruler of the Inhumans, had them excavate the base of the island and attach anti-gravity generators, thus to move Attilan to the mountains.

A short time later, the Himilayan location proved just as precarious when global governments became aware of the Inhumans hideout. Once again, Black Bolt decided to dig out the city, this time to move it to the Blue City on the Moon. It currently exists there, but is nonetheless intrinsically tied to the catastrophic events taking place in the Atlantic.

which made a *brief* appearance in the Atlantic is the extra-dimensional Avalon, home of the Celtic gods. When Avalon appeared in the region, the gods that inhabit the island were allies to the gods of Asgard, including the Asgardian king, Odin. The sorceress Morgan LeFey wants to restore that island of Avalon, even though the original only existed in the region for a short time.

Humans, with their greedy and destructive ways, drove these odd yet rich cultures out into the sea, where their citizens seeking refuge there to avoid human beings. They journeyed to the blue waters to make their homes because they thought they could excape man. And for a while they succeeded, but as time passes the Earth becomes a smaller and smaller place.

Aside from studying for his degree in English, writer ***Jay Franco*** *is an avid comics reader and collector and plans to create a shrine dedicated to the Galaxy's most notorious bounty*

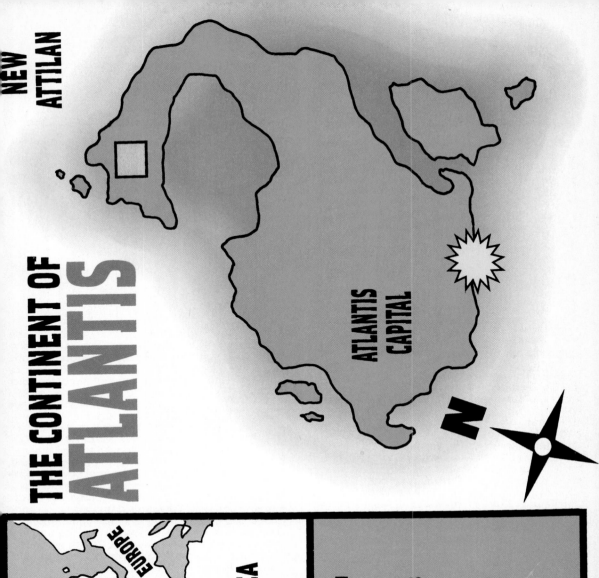

NEW ATTILAN

THE CONTINENT OF ATLANTIS

ATLANTIS CAPITAL

N

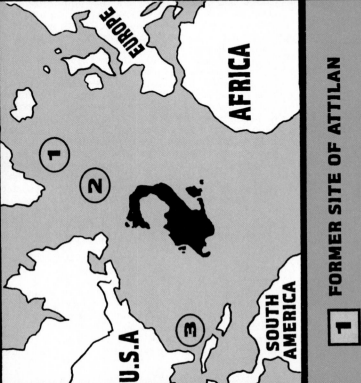

EUROPE

AFRICA

U.S.A

SOUTH AMERICA

1. FORMER SITE OF ATTILAN

2. FORMER SITE OF ATLANTIS

3. BERMUDA TRIANGLE (MONSTER ISLAND)

WHAT A LONG STRANGE TRIP IT'S BEEN

A woman with long, red, psychokinetic hair. A powerful monarch who dare not speak lest his voice destroy all around him. A giant, mustachioed dog with a teleportational talent and a tuning fork on his head.

These are Medusa, Black Bolt, and Lockjaw of the Inhumans.

Monster Island. The Watcher. Namor, and Atlantis. Otherworldly characters and exotic locales, all of which have played bizarre roles in the strange saga of the Fantastic Four.

Since the supposed deaths of Victor Von Doom and Reed Richards in FANTASTIC FOUR #381, the lives of Johnny Storm, Sue Richards, and the ever-cynical Ben Grimm have taken so many twists and turns; recent events in the FF recall the Stan Lee/Jack Kirby heyday when, month to month, the reader never could anticipate what was going to happen next. And events are about to undergo a much *larger* upheaval during the "Atlantis Rising" saga, which will also involve the characters from NAMOR, FANTASTIC FORCE, and WARLOCK.

But the roots of the cataclysmic–potentially apocalyptic–incidents were firmly planted between the original Marvel Age of the early 60s and Jack Kirby's mid-'70s return to The House Of Ideas. And some of those roots even grew from seeds planted in the '40s and '50s.

According to Mark Gruenwald, Editor-in-Chief of the "Marvel Classic Super Heroes" and "Cosmic Powers" titles, the creators behind "Atlantis Rising" are *consciously* attempting to not only use this classic material, but to give it a uniquely contemporary spin. "All this stuff we're dealing with has to do with characters that Stan Lee and Jack Kirby introduced in the first 100 issues of FANTASTIC FOUR," he acknowledged. "The title had one of the longest runs of the same creative team of artist-writer of any comic book." Indeed, Lee and Kirby collaborated on an impressive, uninterrupted 102 issues from FANTASTIC FOUR #1 (November 1961) to "The Strength Of The Sub-Mariner" (issue #102, September 1970)–an unbroken, record partnership. Following Kirby's departure, Lee penned a further 12 issues before bowing out as regular writer with the tale, "The Secret Of The Eternals" (FANTASTIC FOUR #115, October 1971)–one *month* shy of a full decade on "The World's Greatest Comics Magazine."

Lee and Kirby's collaboration on FANTASTIC FOUR yielded the legacy of incredibly weird characters and situations they created–heroes, villains, and situations which continue to resonate throughout the Marvel Universe to this day, as events in "Atlantis Rising" will attest. While Dr. Doom, the Red Ghost, and the Molecule Man were all formidable early opponents, their superhuman powers and unique powerful abilities seem dull beside such Inhuman characters as Gorgon, a super-strong man with hooves instead of feet who can stomp the ground and cause an earthquake; Triton, the scaly aquatic humanoid who, on dry land, must wear special moisture-preserving robes; or Medusa's Avenger sister, Crystal, with her ability to manipulate the four elements as a psionic "weather witch."

When Black Bolt, Karnak, and the rest of The Inhumans turned up in FANTASTIC FOUR #45 searching for Medusa (who had appeared a few issues prior as a member of the Wizard's *Frightful Four*), Stan Lee and Jack Kirby achieved a new level of creativity—bizarre even by standards they'd previously set.

Prior to that issue, in fact in the first three issues of Fantastic Four, Reed, Johnny, Sue, and Ben had faced threats posed by the Mole Man from Monster Island, the Skrulls from Outer Space, and the hypnotic menace of the Miracle Man. In issue #4 Namor, The Sub-Mariner (and Marvel's first mutant) returned, and what set Namor apart from these others was his moral ambiguity, which made him much more of a threat and gave him characteristics which afforded him a significant role in the unfolding destinies of the team.

The Prince of Atlantis, created by artist Bill Everett in 1939, had always been one of Stan Lee's favorite characters. "I loved him because he was many-faceted. It was hard to decide sometimes if he was hero or villain, but to me he was always a hero," Lee explained. "He was three-dimensional; he wasn't just a good guy who was 100 percent good, nor was he a bad guy who was 100 percent bad. He was a villain in the sense he didn't like the human race. He

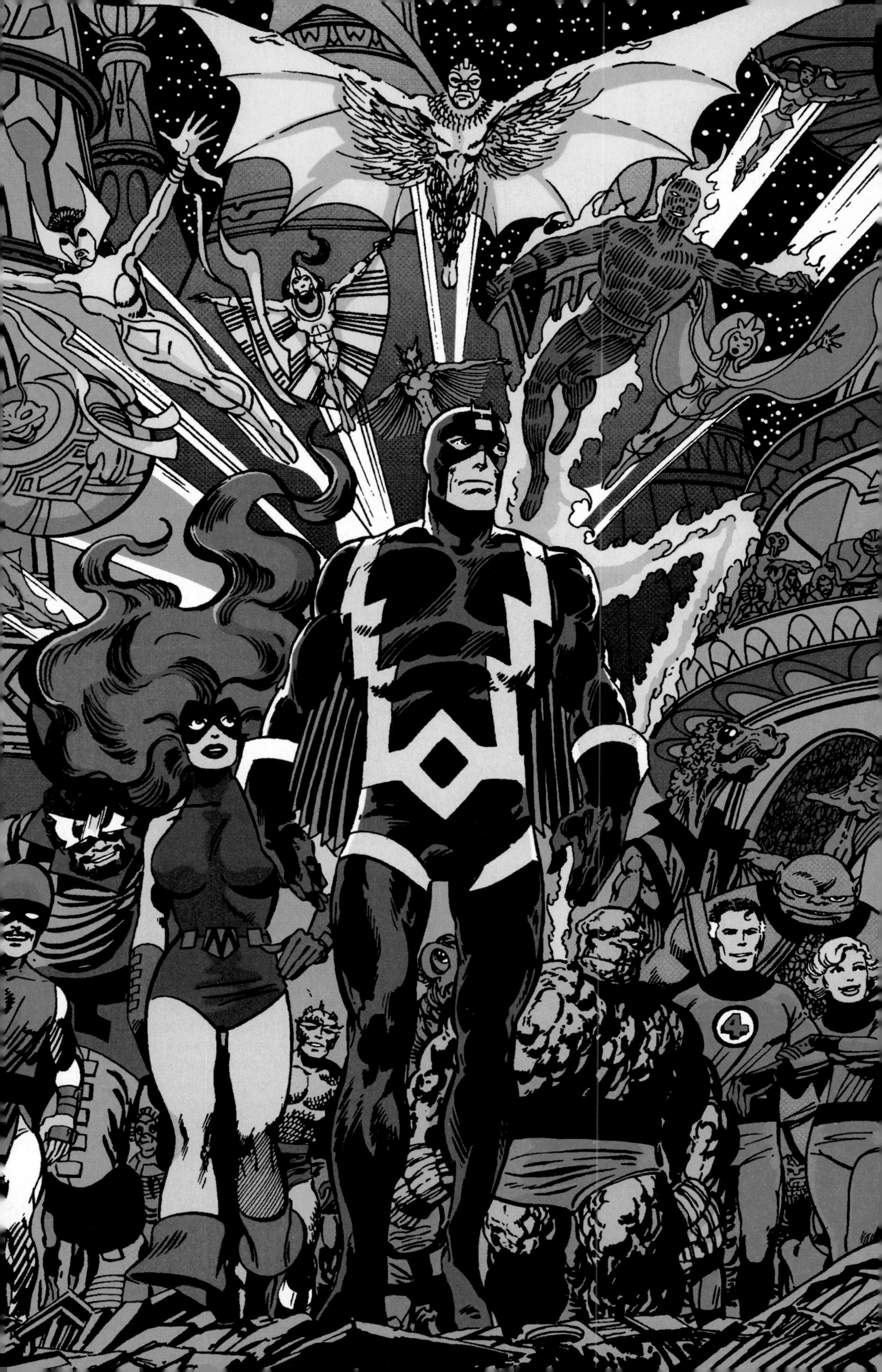

had no time for us because he saw us destroying the planet–I guess he was the first ecologist–but at the same time there was a great *nobility* to him. His word was his bond. Namor had all the attributes of a hero, and what interested me the most was he felt *we* were the villains. It's fun to write a character like that."

According to Lee, *no* idea was too outlandish. "With the Inhumans, I was just looking for a different type of group–mutants who had powers *beyond* those of The X-Men. I thought that if they lived in some strange country, then maybe there was something different about the atmosphere which explained the way they were," said Lee, referring to the unique environmental conditions later described as responsible for the characters' different powers.

"I loved Black Bolt–the fact that he couldn't speak, because if he did he would destroy everything. He could only communicate with imperial gestures. Jack came up with several of the ideas like the dog — Lockjaw, and Gorgon, who could kick the ground and make the earth shake."

But, asked what inspired him and Kirby to create the Inhumans, Lee admitted there was no clear-cut answer. "It's the hardest thing in the world trying to figure out where an idea comes from. You sit down to write a story and gaze off into space and something hits you. Very often, I would start writing one thing, and then I'd get the germ of an idea. As I was typing, the thing would build and grow, and it would turn into something else by the time I got to the bottom of the page. Ideas feed off themselves, and before you know it, you've got a gaggle of ideas."

If Lee's initial ideas seemed strange, then under Jack Kirby's pencil, they took on even more bizarre dimensions which, in turn nourished further ground-breaking concepts. The Inhumans' origins, for example.

As established in early THOR issues, the Inhumans were created 25,000 years ago a part of a genetic experiment performed by the alien race the Kree, in an attempt to create superhuman warriors to serve them. The the Inhumans were abandoned, for reasons which have never been understood. They even predate the Atlanteans, but not the Eternals–who were created via an experiment conducted on primitive man by yet *another* race of mysterious extraterrestrials, the Celestials.

The Inhumans wandered the Eurasian continent for many years until they settled o a small island situated in the North Atlantic, which they named Attilan. Civilization and technology evolved at a rate far faster than for the Eternals; genetics, and eugenics in particular, came to play large role in developing Inhuman civilization and the formation of a "genocracy"–a society ruled by those geneticall superior. It wasn't until 4000 years later that human civilization begar to make its presence felt with the building of its first great city on the island continent Atlantis.

Inhuman society was content to remair isolated from the expanding Atlantean empire, and probably used technology to cloak their existence, although the similarity between the names Atlantis and Attilan is a remarkable coincidence, and may indicate some Inhuman and human interaction.

But within a few short millennia, Atlantean expansion was suddenly shattered in a global cataclysm caused partially by the drastic actions of King Kamuu of Atlantis and the race known as the Deviants.

Like the Eternals, the Deviants were *also* created as a genetic experiment conducted

... MUTANTS WHO HAD POWERS BEYOND THOSE OF THE X-MEN.

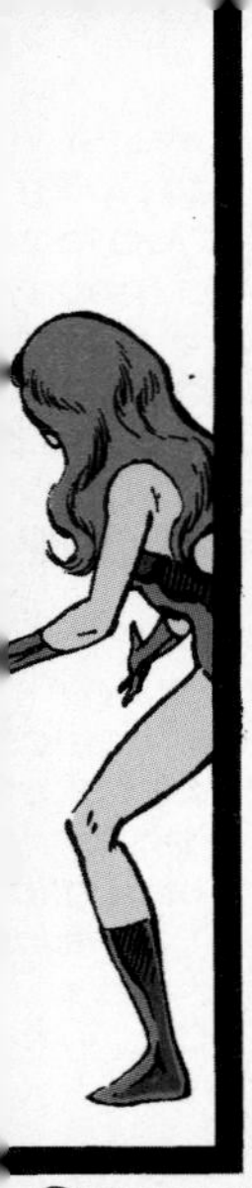

by the Celestials. *Unlike* the Eternals–who remained apart from humankind–the genetically unstable Deviants conquered human nations and chose the island continent of Lemuria (in the Pacific Ocean) as the center of their civilization. Atlantis *alone* remained free of their rule, despite the Deviants' plans to conquer the continent and city. Their final invasion attempt was thwarted when King Kamuu opened the Atlantean magma pits, destroying the army of Deviant-controlled Lemurian barbarians.

This action, unfortunately, triggered a seismological fault which shook the foundations of Atlantis. Concurrently, the Deviants launched an attack on the Celestials, and in retaliation the Celestials detonated a nuclear weapon, which destroyed Lemuria. The resultant shock waves, combined with the geothermal instability around Atlantis, created the Great Cataclysm that devastated most of the Earth.

Both Atlantis and Lemuria sank beneath the seas, but the Inhumans remained unscathed thanks to their technology.

Yet another bizarre Lee/Kirby character has trod a long, complex path to the present. In FANTASTIC FOUR #66-67 the golden-skinned, genetically engineered being known as "Him" emerged, bizarrely enough, from a super-scientific cocoon. Almost immediately, "Him" (he?) departed for the stars. only to be picked up by the likes of Roy Thomas, Gil Kane, and Jim Starlin for a series of the most famous comics of the '70s. "Him" became Adam Warlock.

Journeying full-circle, Warlock (with his Infinity Watch) recently came to live on Monster Island–the site of FANTASTIC FOUR #1–but they, too, will be propelled into action during "Atlantis Rising," when the new continent plunges Monster Island under the rising waves!

If all this historical material appears maddeningly complex, consider the fact that the Marvel Universe did not evolve through some master design. It expanded on a month-to-month basis via Stan Lee's collaborations with Jack Kirby and other talented artists like Steve Ditko, John Buscema, and John Romita, Sr.

"We were lucky," Lee admitted. "We weren't trying to create a universe; we were just trying to tell good stories. And whatever we did in those early years fit nicely into the whole mosaic. We never did what they do today, and I envy the fact the editors of all the books get together and decide what the storylines are going to be for the next six months to a year. I think it's wonderful to be able to do that, but we never had time."

Call it luck, divine intervention, or just uninhibited inspiration–one fact is clear; the creative chemistry between Lee and Kirby resulted in incredibly imaginative and *quirky* concepts. "There's no doubt about it. It was the way Jack portrayed *everything* that gave it the power and the life it all had," Lee said. "Jack had a way of drawing characters who looked incredibly heroic all the time, who were filled with nobility. Even some of the villains, like Doom, had that quality."

All this seems even more remarkable when considering the tough time constraints and punishing publishing schedules Marvel worked under during the '60s. Yet this factor led to the formation of the "Marvel method" whereby a writer (mainly Stan, in those days) wrote a plot, which was then translated into pages by the artist, with the writer scripting dialogue and captions *after* the artwork had been approved. And somewhere between

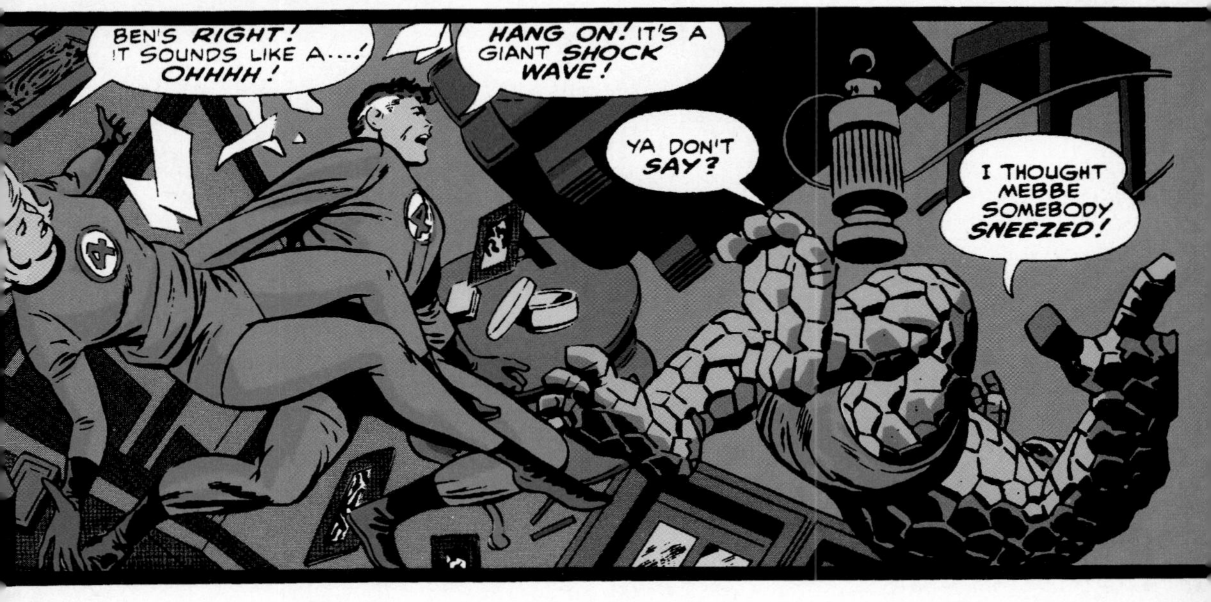
BEN'S RIGHT! IT SOUNDS LIKE A...! OHHHH!
HANG ON! IT'S A GIANT SHOCK WAVE!
YA DON'T SAY?
I THOUGHT MEBBE SOMEBODY SNEEZED!

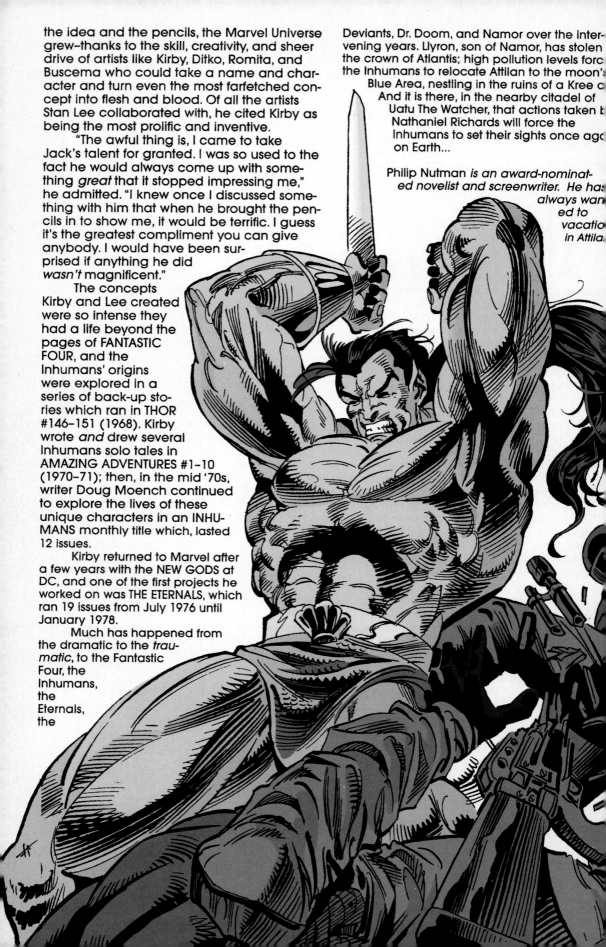

the idea and the pencils, the Marvel Universe grew–thanks to the skill, creativity, and sheer drive of artists like Kirby, Ditko, Romita, and Buscema who could take a name and character and turn even the most farfetched concept into flesh and blood. Of all the artists Stan Lee collaborated with, he cited Kirby as being the most prolific and inventive.

"The awful thing is, I came to take Jack's talent for granted. I was so used to the fact he would always come up with something *great* that it stopped impressing me," he admitted. "I knew once I discussed something with him that when he brought the pencils in to show me, it would be terrific. I guess it's the greatest compliment you can give anybody. I would have been surprised if anything he did *wasn't* magnificent."

The concepts Kirby and Lee created were so intense they had a life beyond the pages of FANTASTIC FOUR, and the Inhumans' origins were explored in a series of back-up stories which ran in THOR #146–151 (1968). Kirby wrote *and* drew several Inhumans solo tales in AMAZING ADVENTURES #1–10 (1970–71); then, in the mid '70s, writer Doug Moench continued to explore the lives of these unique characters in an INHUMANS monthly title which, lasted 12 issues.

Kirby returned to Marvel after a few years with the NEW GODS at DC, and one of the first projects he worked on was THE ETERNALS, which ran 19 issues from July 1976 until January 1978.

Much has happened from the dramatic to the *traumatic*, to the Fantastic Four, the Inhumans, the Eternals, the

Deviants, Dr. Doom, and Namor over the intervening years. Llyron, son of Namor, has stolen the crown of Atlantis; high pollution levels forc the Inhumans to relocate Attilan to the moon' Blue Area, nestling in the ruins of a Kree c And it is there, in the nearby citadel of Uatu The Watcher, that actions taken b Nathaniel Richards will force the Inhumans to set their sights once aga on Earth...

Philip Nutman *is an award-nominat-ed novelist and screenwriter. He ha always wan ed to vacatio in Attila.*

"ATLANTIS RISING" CONTEST-ENTRY PAGE FROM *FANTASTIC FOUR #401*

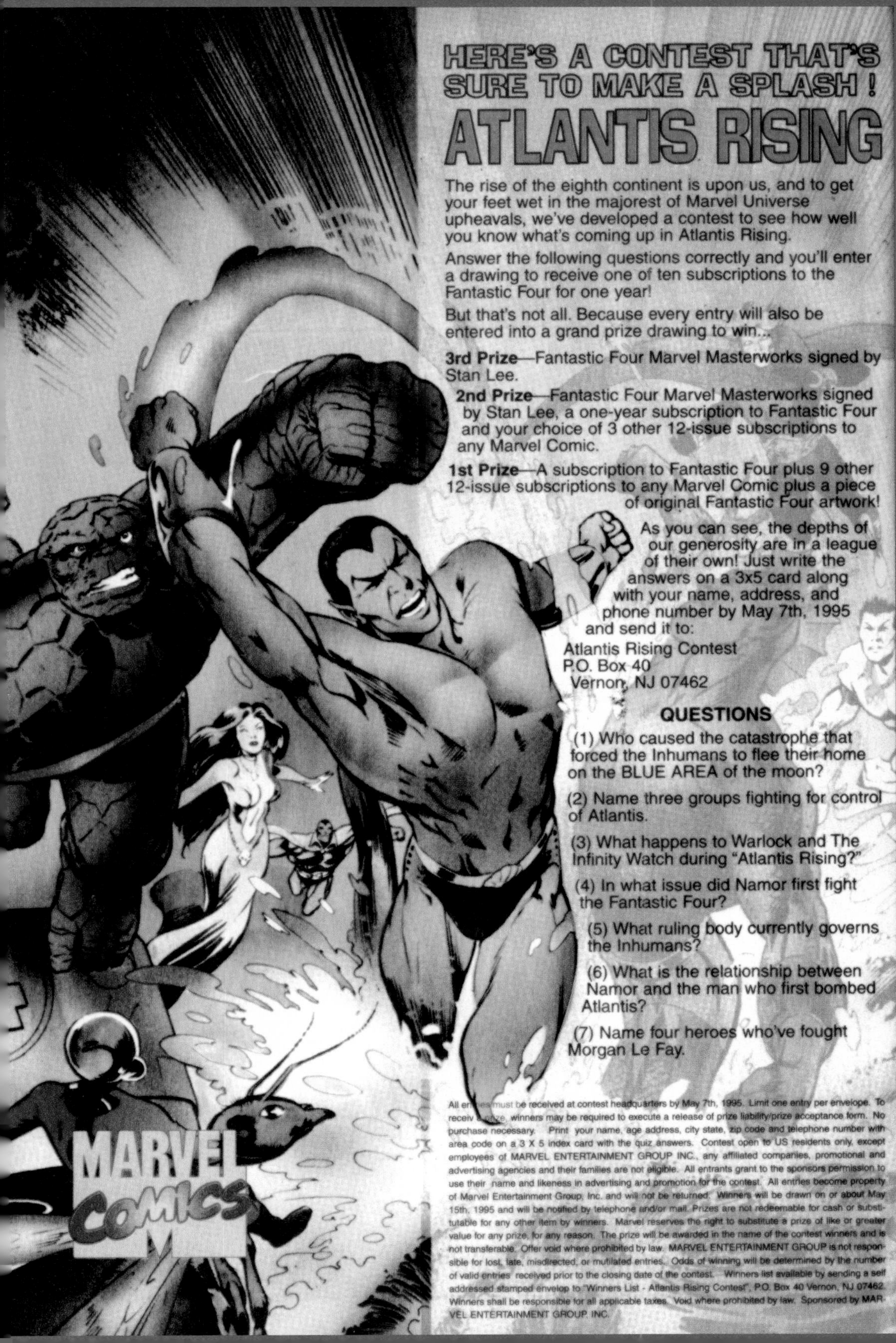
HERE'S A CONTEST THAT'S SURE TO MAKE A SPLASH!
ATLANTIS RISING
The rise of the eighth continent is upon us, and to get your feet wet in the majorest of Marvel Universe upheavals, we've developed a contest to see how well you know what's coming up in Atlantis Rising.
Answer the following questions correctly and you'll enter a drawing to receive one of ten subscriptions to the Fantastic Four for one year!
But that's not all. Because every entry will also be entered into a grand prize drawing to win...
3rd Prize—Fantastic Four Marvel Masterworks signed by Stan Lee.
2nd Prize—Fantastic Four Marvel Masterworks signed by Stan Lee, a one-year subscription to Fantastic Four and your choice of 3 other 12-issue subscriptions to any Marvel Comic.
1st Prize—A subscription to Fantastic Four plus 9 other 12-issue subscriptions to any Marvel Comic plus a piece of original Fantastic Four artwork!
As you can see, the depths of our generosity are in a league of their own! Just write the answers on a 3x5 card along with your name, address, and phone number by May 7th, 1995 and send it to:
Atlantis Rising Contest
P.O. Box 40
Vernon, NJ 07462
QUESTIONS
(1) Who caused the catastrophe that forced the Inhumans to flee their home on the BLUE AREA of the moon?
(2) Name three groups fighting for control of Atlantis.
(3) What happens to Warlock and The Infinity Watch during "Atlantis Rising?"
(4) In what issue did Namor first fight the Fantastic Four?
(5) What ruling body currently governs the Inhumans?
(6) What is the relationship between Namor and the man who first bombed Atlantis?
(7) Name four heroes who've fought Morgan Le Fay.
All en[illegible] must be received at contest headquarters by May 7th, 1995. Limit one entry per envelope. To receiv[illegible], winners may be required to execute a release of prize liability/prize acceptance form. No purchase necessary. Print your name, age address, city state, zip code and telephone number with area code on a 3 X 5 index card with the quiz answers. Contest open to US residents only, except employees of MARVEL ENTERTAINMENT GROUP INC., any affiliated companies, promotional and advertising agencies and their families are not eligible. All entrants grant to the sponsors permission to use their name and likeness in advertising and promotion for the contest. All entries become property of Marvel Entertainment Group, Inc. and will not be returned. Winners will be drawn on or about May 15th, 1995 and will be notified by telephone and/or mail. Prizes are not redeemable for cash or substitutable for any other item by winners. Marvel reserves the right to substitute a prize of like or greater value for any prize, for any reason. The prize will be awarded in the name of the contest winners and is not transferable. Offer void where prohibited by law. MARVEL ENTERTAINMENT GROUP is not responsible for lost, late, misdirected, or mutilated entries. Odds of winning will be determined by the number of valid entries received prior to the closing date of the contest. Winners list available by sending a self addressed stamped envelop to "Winners List - Atlantis Rising Contest", P.O. Box 40 Vernon, NJ 07462. Winners shall be responsible for all applicable taxes. Void where prohibited by law. Sponsored by MARVEL ENTERTAINMENT GROUP, INC.
MARVEL COMICS

AVALON
ARISING

For many readers, the "Atlantis Rising" crossover may be a first introduction to Morgan LeFey. However, Morgan has woven her schemes for more than a millennium, and this is far from her first brush with the heroes of the twentieth century. So, for the sake of those readers who are unfamiliar with Morgan (and those who'd simply like a quick trip down memory lane), let's take a brief look at some of Morgan's past bids for power.

Half human/half faerie and possessed of vast mystic abilities, Morgan's origin lies in the sixth century. She was the half-sister of the legendary King Arthur, the prize student of the archmage Merlin... and also their greatest foe. Morgan wanted nothing more than to rule, clashing numerous times with Arthur and Merlin, with Camelot as the prize. Often, Morgan was driven back by the original Black Knight (ancestor of the Avengers' modern-day Knight), as well as the occasional time traveling hero, such as Iron Man, who'd been thrown back in time during a battle with Doctor Doom in IRON MAN #150.

Morgan's final defeat came in a climactic battle with Arthur and all the knights of the Round Table. As punishment for her deeds, Morgan was imprisoned in her castle; free to enter other dimensions, but she could not physically leave her castle on Earth. Far from humbled, Morgan's punishment merely gave her a second goal. She was determined not only to rule, but also to be free.

We don't know just how many times

Morgan tried to free herself over the centuries. However, she first projected her astral self into our time in SPIDER-WOMAN #2, when she possessed a petty thief and turned him into the magical knight Excaliber! As it turned out, the original Spider-Woma (a predecessor to the current one) was nearby. This Spider-Woman, secretly Jessica Drew, had spent the first thirty years of her life in suspended animation a Wundagore Mountain. She arose with the spider-like ability to stick to walls and hurl bioelectric venom blasts. With the aid of these powers, Spider-Woman soon defeated Excaliber and broke Morgan's spell.

Before long, Spider-Woman would become Morgan's greatest foe in the twentieth century. Still, Morgan's initial battle with Spider-Woman seemed like a chance encounter. And when Morgan struck second time (SPIDER-WOMAN #5-6), confounding Spider-Woman with illusions, and trapping her with uncontrollable Werewolf by Night, it simply seemed like an attempt at revenge for her earlier defeat.

Over time, it became clear that Morgan's inte est in Spider-Woman was not simply due to chance The light began to dawn in SPIDER-WOMAN #41 & 44 when Morgan resumed her campaign for power wi a vengeance. Determined to rule in *any* century, Morgan transformed a modern-day Renaissance fe tival into Camelot, and Spider-Woman herself into Morgan LeFey! Spider-Woman broke Morgan's hold and reversed the situation, gaining her first clue to Morgan's hidden intentions when Morgan referred t her as "Childe of the Darkhold."

The Darkhold was a grimoire, a mystic tome that was the repository of power for the demonic elder god Chthon. Morgan was determined to com mand its power as she had centuries earlier. The Darkhold would provide her with enough power to break the spell that imprisoned her and finally rule the world! Since the Darkhold had been buried beneath Wundagore for centuries, Spider-Woman's years at Wundagore had left her with an unbreakable link to its evil energies. So Morgan planned to control Spider-Woman and, through her, the Darkho itself!

Their ongoing struggle reached its peak in SPI DER-WOMAN #50, when an ancient sorcerer named Magnus brought Spider-Woman's spirit back to Morgan's time, to combat her evil at its root. During the course of the battle, Spider-Woman destroyed Morgan's physical body with her venom blasts. But Morgan returned the favor. When Spider-Woman ed to the twentieth century, she found her own apparently dead; and could not return to it! It later turned out that Spider-Woman's body ot dead, but only comatose, as revealed in GERS #240-241. Once this was discovered, her was soon reanimated.— but by Morgan! By Spider-Woman's body, Morgan had managed e physical form in our time and escape from ng imprisonment! It took the combined power gnus, the Avengers, and Doctor Strange to Morgan out and restore Spider-Woman to her body. However, the victory carried a weighty . Magnus sacrificed his very existence, and Spider-Woman finally returned to her body, iscovered that she had lost the ability to enom blasts. She was Spider-Woman no r–she was now simply Jessica Drew.

Even after Spider-Woman retired from per hero game, Morgan was still up to d tricks. In IRON MAN #209, she once tried to take physical form, this time by ssing a woman named Lissa Russell. But brother Jack (AKA, Werewolf by Night), e help of Iron Man, drove her back to stral form.

Not long after, Morgan made a d attempt at restoring Avalon in rn times, this time in the shadow of on Bridge (even though the bridge ests in Arizona)! As the BLACK HT Limited Series revealed, Morgan earned from her previous defeat, mprisoned Doctor Strange g with the Valkyrie) to pre- him from interfering with lans. Still, Morgan 't reckoned with Whitman, the rn-day Black t and his pected he of nces- e al

t!

her, the two Knights shattered or Strange's mystic s and smashed lans yet again.

Nevertheless, Morgan d be called things, she ever been a As even this history s, she has stently ed from

at

ot- er e- t s

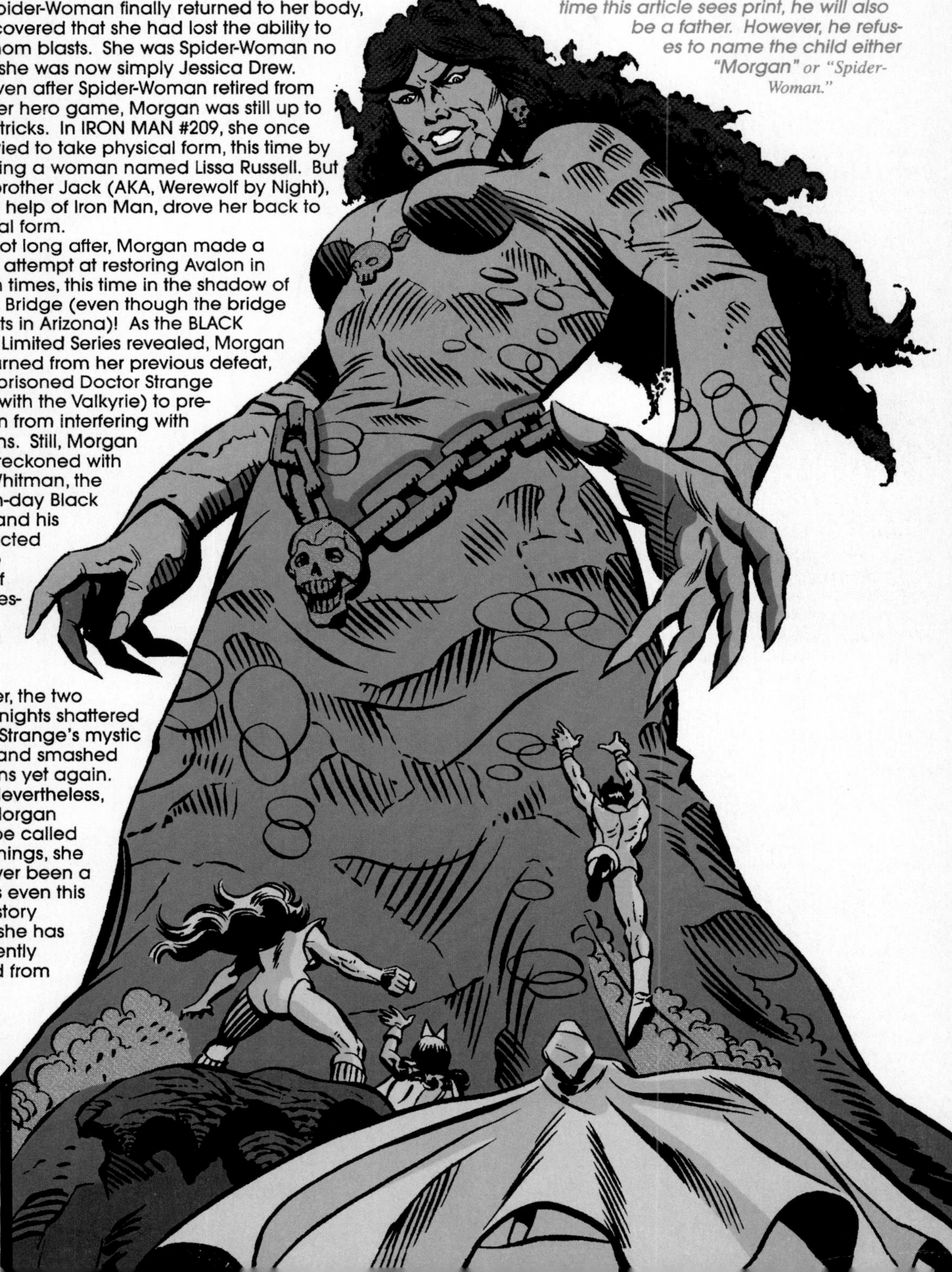

accordingly. In the "Atlantis Rising" crossover, Morgan will once again try to bring the glory of Avalon into modern times, with herself as its ruler. But this time, Morgan won't be transforming a fair or restoring a mere city. This time, she'll be reaching across the centuries to raise an entire lost continent!

What other devilish surprises will Morgan have up her sleeve?

That, only time will tell...

Sholly Fisch *has written freelance for Marvel for the past ten years, and by the time this article sees print, he will also be a father. However, he refuses to name the child either* "Morgan" *or* "Spider-Woman."

A Tale of

They had the best of intentions, they had the worst of intentions. Two men, each of a different generation, each of a different culture, each with a different directive. Yet still, each sharing a common bond and a common mask in the roles they played as pretenders to the throne, pretenders to the Latverian legacy of Victor Von Doom.

The two players, Nathaniel Richards and Kristoff, who have, at different junctures, taken on the mantle of Doom, each play pivotal roles in the impending "Atlantis Rising" crossover, which will be playing itself out through the FANTASTIC FOUR

titles in the coming months. It is here that these two characters will become better defined and have their true destinies fleshed out. FANTASTIC FOUR writer Tom DeFalco said, "If you've never read the FANTASTIC FOUR or have never been exposed to Nathan or Kristoff, it's not going to matter. Their motivations and character identifications will be in these stories." Yet he also noted that, "In order for a reader to follow *any* story, they have to understand who the characters are and what the characters want. Consequently, you have to know who Kristoff is and who Nathaniel is."

So while readers will be updated and briefed on these key characters, it is with accurate understanding in mind that we offer a brief, but more complete, history of the two.

Nathaniel Richards remains the most mysterious of the two, albeit by a very narrow margin. Having burst onto the scene within the last few years, he's claimed to be the patriarch of the Richards clan, an allegation that remains to be proved, and currently masquerades as Doctor Doom, the greatest adversary of the Fantastic Four and his supposed son, Reed. Little is truly known about Nathaniel, and his alliance seems more arbitrary than familial. His motives, thus far, have solely been to further his own ends by whatever means necessary. "He does what *he* feels is right," noted DeFalco, adding, "Even at the cost of his own grandson (Franklin)."

Regardless of his true colors, it is his past

actions that have made him unpopular with the Fantastic Four and his future actions that will make him unpopular with the rest of the Marvel Universe. "He stole away Susan Richards' son Franklin and didn't bring him back until he was ten years older," pointed out editor-in-chief Mark Gruenwald, "He stole away ten years of mother/child bonding." Coupled with possible misgivings about Nathaniel, his future adds to his mystery as well as further complicating things for our heroes. Gruenwald also concurs, as most, that Nathaniel is the most dangerous of the two Doom wannabes, "He's been around longer and has more resources," he said. It is Nathaniel, after all, who sets the events into motion which lead up to the "Atlantis Rising" crossover and the violation of the Inhumans' home on the moon.

It is the Terrigen Mist at the home base the Watcher he seeks to possess and Gruenwald noted he would do so at all cost, even at the cost of human, and Inhuman, life.

So, as lives hang in the balance, as well as the relationship with his family — Nathaniel plots on, serving whatever mysterious purpose that is his agenda. It is in playing the role of Doom that he gets the power base he needs to continue his game plan, and it's a role that he's more than qualified for. While his ultimate goal remains uncertain for the time being, one thing that *is* clear about Nathaniel is that we've only just begun to understand the history of this complex character.

It is somewhat easier to understand the character of Kristoff. While just as complex as Nathaniel, the manchild Kristoff's past is shrouded in less mystery for the reader.

Having made his first appearance in FANTASTIC FOUR #247, his history has been charted and observed. The orphaned boy was taken in by Doom as a ward after a period of turmoil in Latveria during which Doom had witnessed the death of the boy's mother. Doom and Kristoff were since tethered in a bond that

Two Dooms

brought out Doom's "fatherly" instinct and resulted in his naming Kristoff his heir. Shortly after these events, Doom met with one of his many untimely deaths and his robots, acting under his previous instructions, implanted the youth with Doom's early memories.

Having only received Doom's *early* memories created many conflicts for Kristoff and he approached them with an unpreparedness that the real Doom would not have. This resulted in his being captured, and held prisoner by Reed Richards, after blowing up the Baxter Building. Using the technology implanted by Doom's robots, however, he managed to escape in true Doctor Doom fashion and returned to Latveria.

Upon his return home it was revealed that the real Doctor Doom had also returned and attempted to regain his throne. A problem of his own creation now faced the real Doctor: since Kristoff, as well as his own robots, had determined that the younger ruler was the real Doom. His royal lineage now in jeopardy, Doom acted in a most unfatherly fashion, sending forth his minions from another time to kill Kristoff. It seemed they'd succeeded in their mission — at least until recently.

Of late Kristoff has resurfaced, seemingly resurrected — an issue which leaves the Fantastic Four in quite a quandary. This goes beyond the Doogie Howser-esque mentality of Kristoff simply being an ultra-intelligent child. This is, in fact, a man in a child's body. Having spent time with other children, Kristoff, now twelve, is increasingly interested in the youth that was denied him. Also at a loss is Susan Richards, a person who lately has surrounded herself with an exceedingly high number of unlikely allies, because as writer DeFalco explained, "She sees this little boy and treats him like a little boy and lets him do little boy things. She has to keep reminding herself that he is, in fact, one of the most dangerous individuals alive."

It is in this that one must note that if any-

one has the right to be a pretender to the Doom throne, it would be Kristoff. His participation in this story deals less with his involvement in setting the wheels of fate into motion and more with his development as a child. In a rotating exchange of masks, readers must be prepared to face Kristoff as a force to be reckoned with. The primary reason for the involvement of Nathaniel and Kristoff in the "Atlantis Rising" crossover, cites Mark Gruenwald, is the need for new challenges for the Fantastic Four. "They're both interesting variations on a Doom-like character," he said.

"Doom is one of the greatest villains created in comics. Still, there is a limit to the amount of time you can have the Fantastic Four fight Doom before readers say, 'come on, give me a different story.' So we're taking some of the trappings of Doom and giving them different twists. Kristoff is going through young, impulsive things that Doom should be over by now. Nathaniel likes empire building, not unlike Doom. There's a primal connection between Nathaniel and Reed, which makes things even more tense than in Reed's relationship with Doom, because now we're talking father and son. In real life blood bonds are uninteresting. In fiction you want people to be related to each other, so you can relate to the primal forces that motivate them. This story just gives you a whole lot of material that reveals new aspects to old characters and parallel aspects to new characters."

And when the masks have been removed, counterfeits standing revealed, how will they fare? Remember, little escapes the eyes of Doctor Doom and little occurs without his hands guiding the events. Be it Kristoff or Nathaniel or Victor himself, one thing is certain–Doom will likely prevail. It's in the history. It's in the blood.....

Darren Dean, *the artist formerly known as the artist formerly known as Prince, lives on an ant farm in New Jersey where he is plugging away on his first novel.*

NAMOR THE SUB-MARINER #60, PAGE 20 ART BY GEOF ISHERWOOD

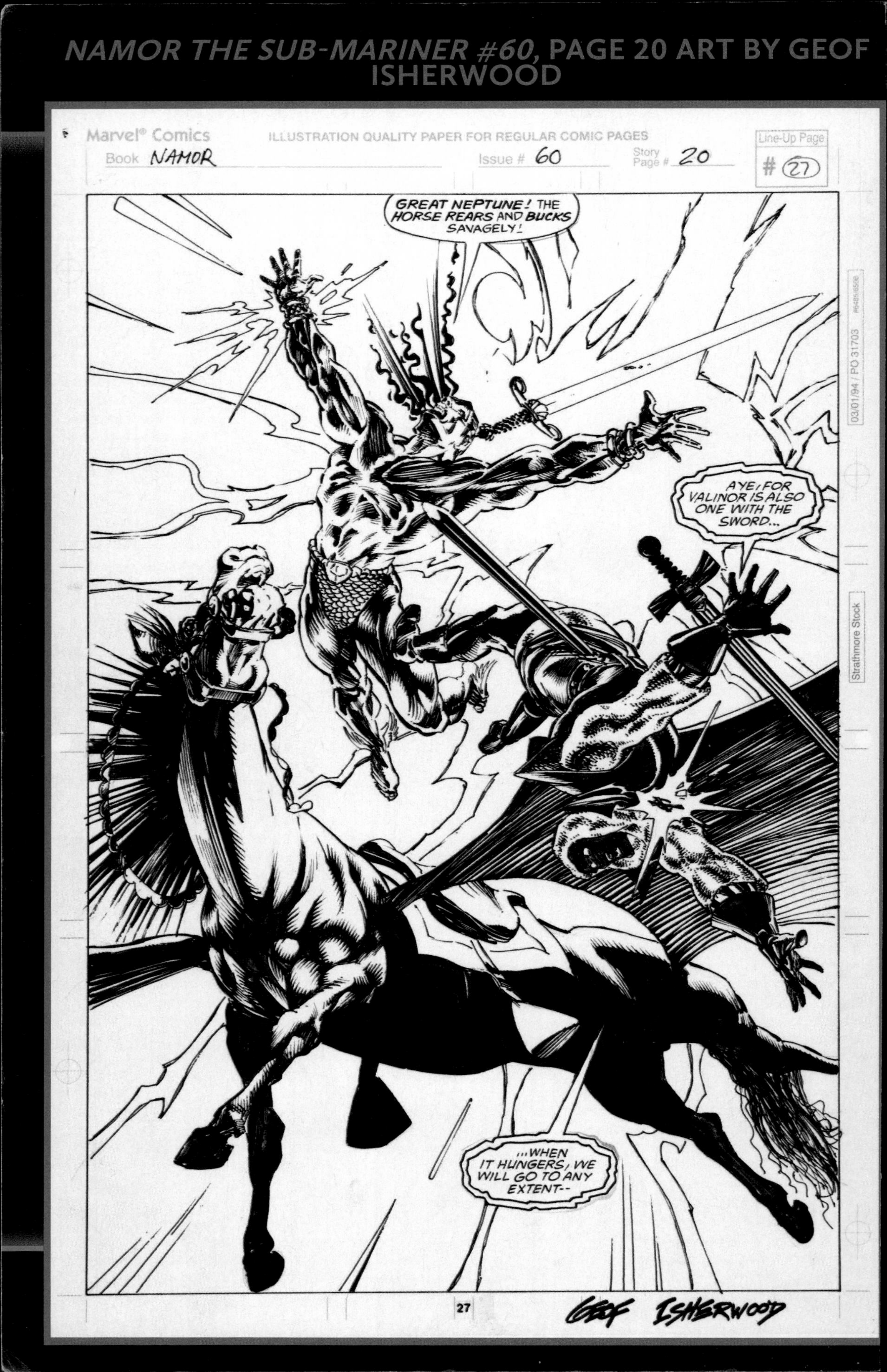
Marvel® Comics
ILLUSTRATION QUALITY PAPER FOR REGULAR COMIC PAGES
Line-Up Page
Book NAMOR
Issue # 60
Story Page # 20
27
GREAT NEPTUNE! THE HORSE REARS AND BUCKS SAVAGELY!
AYE, FOR VALINOR IS ALSO ONE WITH THE SWORD...
...WHEN IT HUNGERS, WE WILL GO TO ANY EXTENT--
27
GEOF ISHERWOOD
03/01/94 / PO 31703
Strathmore Stock

FANTASTIC FOUR #402, PAGE 20 ART BY PAUL RYAN & DANNY BULANADI

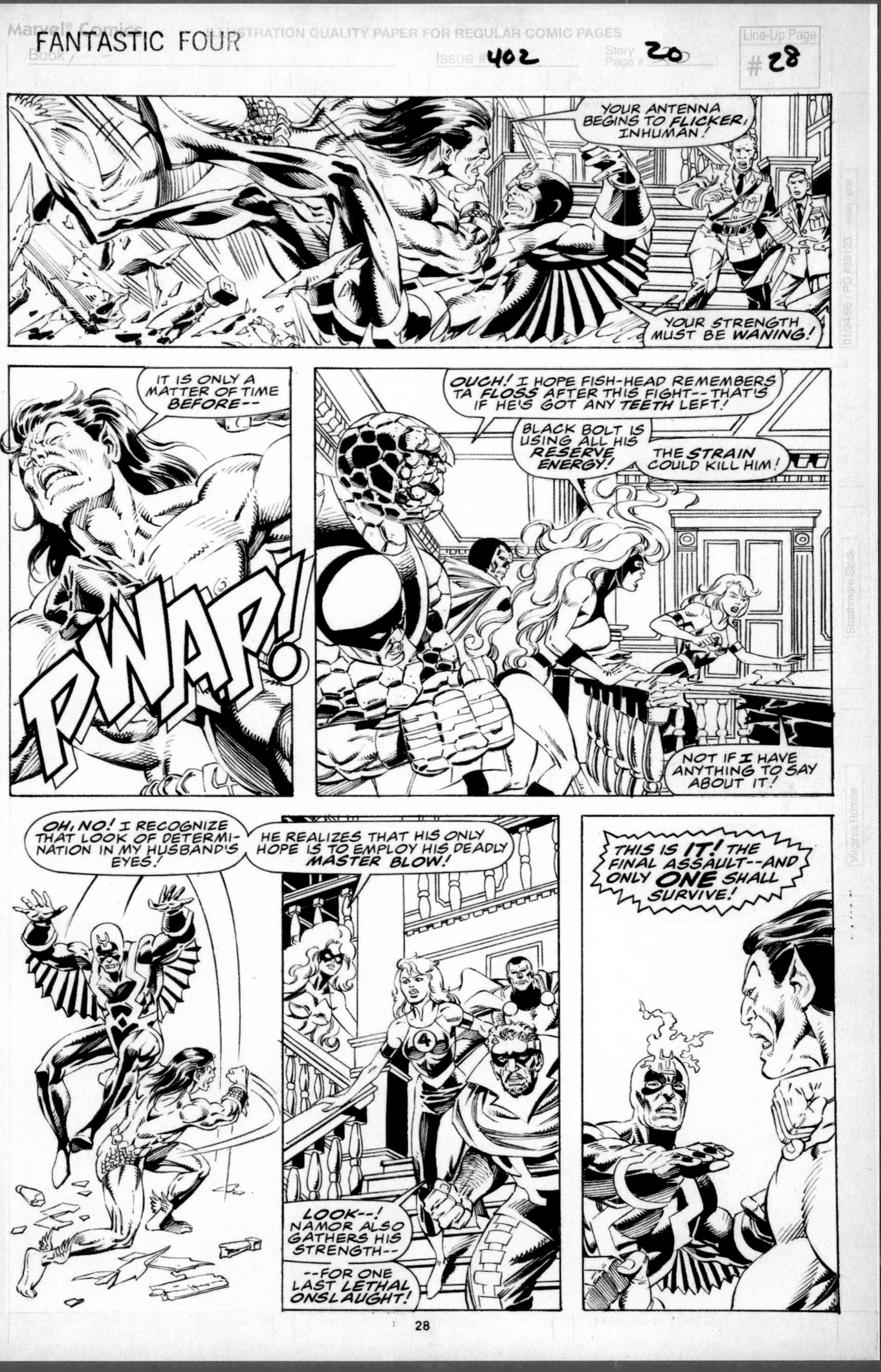
FANTASTIC FOUR
402
20
#28
YOUR ANTENNA BEGINS TO FLICKER, INHUMAN!
YOUR STRENGTH MUST BE WANING!
IT IS ONLY A MATTER OF TIME BEFORE--
PWAP!
OUCH! I HOPE FISH-HEAD REMEMBERS TA FLOSS AFTER THIS FIGHT--THAT'S IF HE'S GOT ANY TEETH LEFT!
BLACK BOLT IS USING ALL HIS RESERVE ENERGY!
THE STRAIN COULD KILL HIM!
NOT IF I HAVE ANYTHING TO SAY ABOUT IT!
OH, NO! I RECOGNIZE THAT LOOK OF DETERMINATION IN MY HUSBAND'S EYES!
HE REALIZES THAT HIS ONLY HOPE IS TO EMPLOY HIS DEADLY MASTER BLOW!
LOOK--! NAMOR ALSO GATHERS HIS STRENGTH--
--FOR ONE LAST LETHAL ONSLAUGHT!
THIS IS IT! THE FINAL ASSAULT--AND ONLY ONE SHALL SURVIVE!
28

LLYRON

REAL NAME: Llyron MacKenzie
ALIASES: Son of Namor
IDENTITY: Publicly known
OCCUPATION: Rebel warrior; former ruler of Atlantis
CITIZENSHIP: Atlantis
PLACE OF BIRTH: Vyrra's Cave, near Atlantis
KNOWN RELATIVES: Llyra Morris (mother), Leon MacKenzie (Black Moray, father), Lawrence MacKenzie (paternal grandfather), Llyron (maternal grandfather, deceased), Rhonda Morris (maternal grandmother), Leonard MacKenzie (paternal great-grandfather, deceased), Namor MacKenzie (Sub-Mariner, paternal great-half-uncle), extended family via Namor
GROUP AFFILIATION: None
EDUCATION: Assimilated through minds of Llyra and Vyrra
FIRST APPEARANCE: Namor, the Sub-Mariner #54 (1994)

HISTORY: Namor MacKenzie, the son of human Leonard MacKenzie and Atlantean Fen, became the superhuman Sub-Mariner in the early 20th Century. Fen seemingly died in a bombing on Atlantis, and Leonard, who was also believed dead, eventually remarried and fathered another son, Lawrence, who in turn fathered Leon. Leonard was eventually killed, while Leon was employed by the rich Marrs Corporation. Meanwhile, Namor developed a long-standing rivalry with the metamorph Llyra, the former empress of another undersea kingdom, Lemuria. Llyra desired to wed Namor to claim Atlantis' throne, but Namor developed a deep hatred of her, partly because she caused the death of Namor's actual bride, Dorma. In an elaborate plot, Llyra posed as Phoebe Marrs, the owner of Marrs Corporation, and seduced Leon MacKenzie, intentionally becoming pregnant. To conceal her true plans, she posed as Namor's old flame Invisible Woman and seduced Namor so that he would believe her

child to be his. Llyra then found the cave of Vyrra, an Atlantean scientist exiled for his illegal cloning experiments, one of which cloned Namor's cousin, Namora, producing a cloned child whom Namora raised as Namorita. Vyrra genetically accelerated Llyra's child's birth and aging. Not wanting the child to be mindless, Vyrra copied Llyra's mind and memories into its brain, but secretly copied his own mind into the brain as well, wanting part of himself to live on in a powerful form. These two minds, merging with the child's own slowly developing mind, produced a brilliant and deadly composite psyche with full access to Llyra's memories and cunning and Vyrra's vast scientific knowledge and ambitions. When the male child awoke, he was genetically developed to age 16, and proved to be a super-powerful amphibian like Namor, though Llyron's skin was green like his mother's. Llyra murdered Vyrra, unwilling to share her secret with anyone else and unaware that Vyrra's mind had been copied into Llyron's as well, then named the child Llyron (likely after her father), and took Llyron to undersea Atlantis. She announced that Llyron was the son of Namor and thus had claim to the throne. Despite Namor's protestations, Llyron won the loyalties of Atlantis' ruling council by defeating Namor's allies, the criminal Tiger Shark and his lover Tamara Rahn.

Seeking to further discredit Namor, Llyron, as Atlantis' ambassador, approached the United Nations with an offer of alliance, which the U.N. later accepted. Llyron successfully repelled a pre-arranged attack of a sea monster assault — including the walking whale Giganto (offspring of its namesake who had died in battle with the Fantastic Four years before) and the parasitic Hagfish, which Llyron slew — framing Namor for attacking the surface world with these monsters as heralds. Llyron was soon hailed as Atlantis' ruler despite his true parentage being revealed, as Atlantean law recognized Llyron and Namor sharing a common ancestry and willingly declared Llyron rightful ruler. Llyron had Llyra imprisoned, at which point she realized that Vyrra's mind inhabited Llyron's form as well; Llyron later constructed a monument to Vyrra on Atlantean soil. When the sorceress Morgan Le Fay raised Atlantis to the surface, much of Atlantis' population was killed, and Llyron used his leadership skills to gather the people together. Llyron ordered that all the fertile women of Atlantis be implanted with clone fetuses so that a powerful army could be raised with which to attack the surface world, a likely plot of Vyrra's. It is unknown what became of this plot or why Llyron was removed from power, but Atlantis soon elected a new ruler. Llyron joined the At'la'tique rebellion against Atlantis. As part of the super-powered rebel team Fathom Five, Llyron attacked several cities on the surface and battled the Thunderbolts until Radioactive Man instilled him with radiation and threw him back to the sea. Captured, Llyron unintentionally afflicted much of Atlantis with this radiation from his cell in Atlantis; feeling remorse over innocents suffering, Radioative Man cured the Atlanteans.

HEIGHT: 6'2"
WEIGHT: 278 lbs.
EYES: Blue-Gray
HAIR: Black

ABILITIES/ACCESSORIES: Llyron possesses the abilities of a sub-mariner, an Atlantean-human hybrid. He has Class 100 superhuman strength, reptilian wings on his ankles that grant him flight, and superhuman durability, reflexes, and speed, capable of swimming up to 60 miles per hour. Llyron can breathe in both air and water and survive in the ocean's crushing depths, where he is able to see as well. It is unknown if Llyron can mentally communicate with sea life.

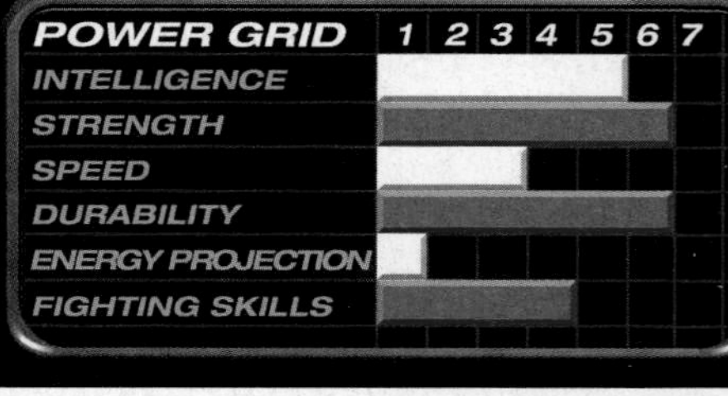

AS INFANT | VYRRA

POWER GRID	1	2	3	4	5	6	7
INTELLIGENCE							
STRENGTH							
SPEED							
DURABILITY							
ENERGY PROJECTION							
FIGHTING SKILLS							

Art by Geof Isherwood with John Byrne (right inset)
Text by Chad Anderson

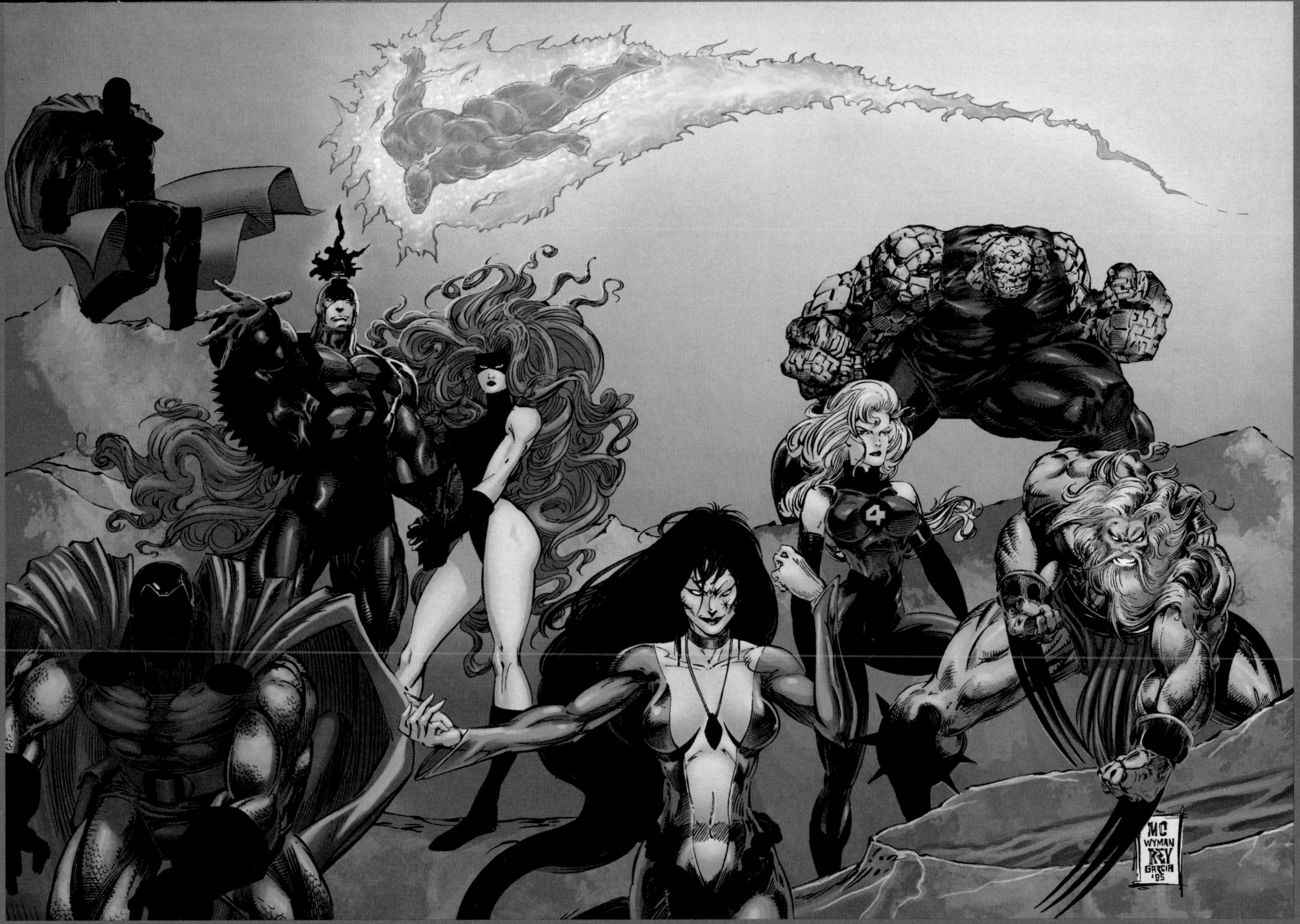
MC
WYMAN
REY
GARCIA
'95

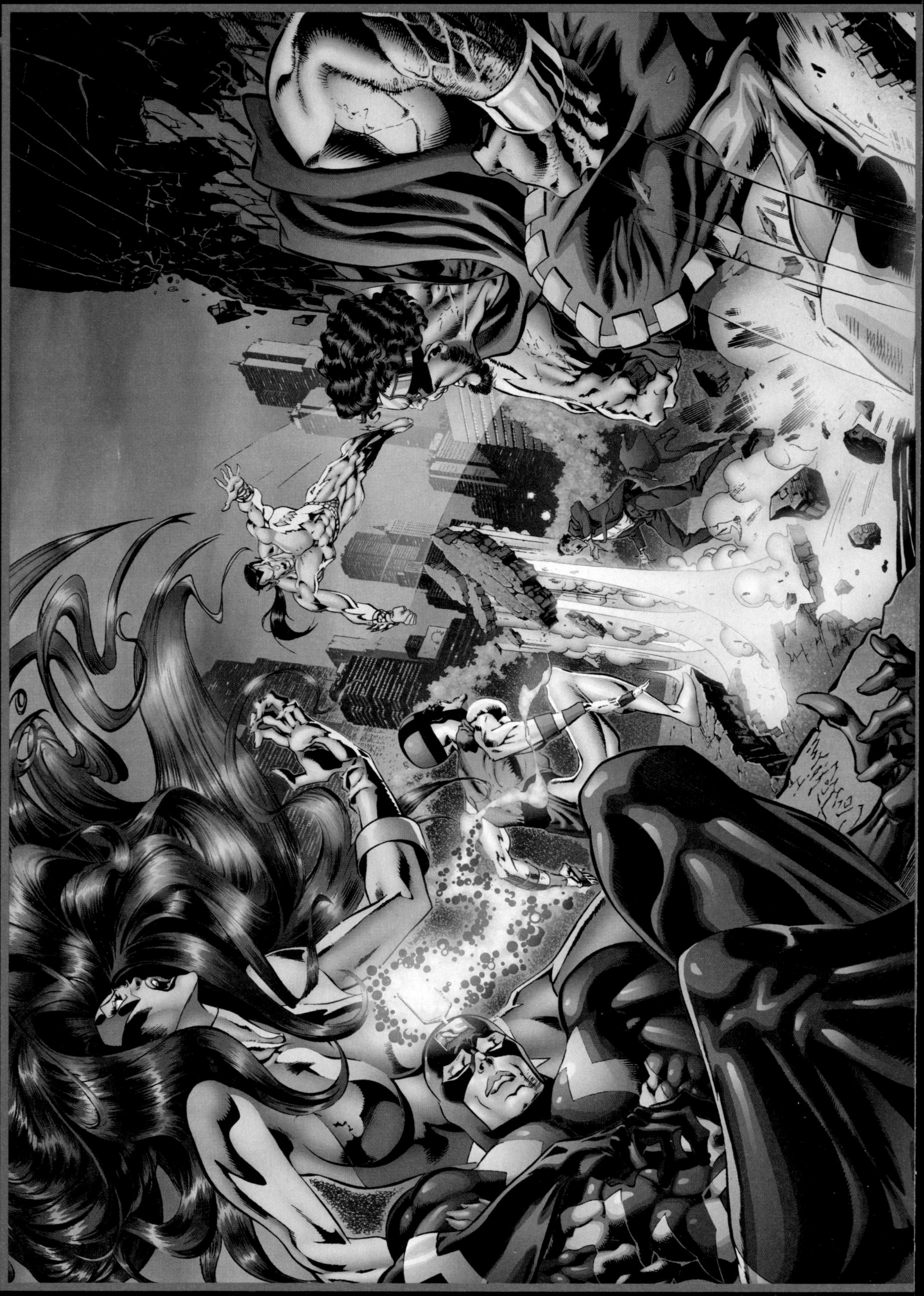